ECONOMICS AND CONSUMER

LAURA L. MARTIN

LAURA L. MARTIN

Economics and consumer behavior

Angus Deaton, William Church Osborne Professor of Public Affairs
and Professor of Economics and International Affairs,
Princeton University
John Muellbauer, Professor of Economics, Nuffield College, Oxford

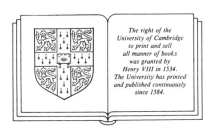

*The right of the
University of Cambridge
to print and sell
all manner of books
was granted by
Henry VIII in 1534.
The University has printed
and published continuously
since 1584.*

Cambridge University Press
Cambridge
London · New York · New Rochelle
Melbourne · Sydney

Published by the Press Syndicate of the University of Cambridge
The Pitt Building, Trumpington Street, Cambridge CB2 1RP
32 East 57th Street, New York, NY 10022, USA
10 Stamford Road, Oakleigh, Melbourne 3166, Australia

First published 1980
Reprinted 1981, 1982
Reprinted with corrections 1983
Reprinted 1984, 1985, 1986, 1987

Printed in the United States of America

Library of Congress Cataloging in Publication Data

Deaton, Angus.

Economics and consumer behavior

Bibliography: p.

Includes index.

1. Consumption (Economics) 2. Consumers.
3. Utility theory. I. Muellbauer, John, joint author.
II. Title.
HB801.D36   658.8′34   79–17090
ISBN 0 521 22850 6   hard covers
ISBN 0 521 29676 5   paperback

CONTENTS

TABLES AND FIGURES

PREFACE

This book is about the economic theory of consumer behavior and its uses in economic analysis. It is about the tools and language of utility theory and their application to a field that ranges from empirical work on commodity demand to abstract questions of social choice. The basic theory is the familiar one, although we have made extensive use of cost functions and related "duality" concepts to present it in a way that simplifies what is often seen as difficult or inaccessible material. This, and the range of subject matter, broader than any previous book on consumer behavior, are the most distinctive features of the book. Our main purpose in writing it is to provide in one place a complete toolbox of utility theory together with a demonstration of the power of these tools in action over a wide front of economics. Although the use of utility theory runs as a common thread throughout the book, only a fraction of the space deals with the standard textbook model of choice subject to a linear budget constraint. In recent years, important work has been done in many areas of economics by applying consumer theory to nonstandard situations, for example, to discrete choice, to rationing, to labor supply, to fertility, to quality choice, to choice with complex nonlinear budget constraints resulting from tax and benefit systems, liquidity constraints, uncertainty, and so on. Most of this work emphasizes careful modeling of the *constraints* that consumers face, including the statistical and econometric consequences. We believe this to be a productive approach and much of the book is concerned with it. There is a further area of economics that uses consumer theory as an essential input and that has progressed rapidly in recent years. This is the field of welfare economics, including index number theory and social choice. Many of the important developments in that field are based on straightforward applications of the theory discussed in this book, and we include these examples as part of our catalog of the usefulness of utility theory in economics.

The book is designed to be used in courses teaching theoretical and applied economics at the level of final year undergraduates (particularly Part One) and of graduate courses leading to M.A. and Ph.D. degrees. It should also be of use to professional economists who have a direct or indirect interest in consumer behavior. The structure of the book is designed to permit maximum flexibility in use. Part One, which covers the basic theory and its applications, including the consumption function, durable goods and labor supply, is a self-contained module. Except where indicated, this material is written to be accessible to final year undergraduates and can be used as an introductory complete course or as a refresher for those who want a straightforward presentation of duality in demand theory. Part One is also a prerequisite for other sections of the book. Part Two is a largely theoretical discussion of aggregation and separability; this will be of greatest interest to specialists in economic theory (e.g., in a graduate theory course), but the main issues are discussed informally in the early sections of both chapters. Part Three is on welfare economics; the chapters on index numbers and household welfare comparisons are straightforward and form a natural extension to Part One for undergraduate use. The chapter on social choice and inequality is inevitably more difficult and is at a similar level to the material on separability. Part Four is more heterogeneous and is designed largely for graduate use. In each of the topics discussed we have attempted to face the subject matter on its own terms, going well beyond traditional confines when the material demands it. If the discussion occasionally becomes difficult, we hope it will be rewarding, because it is in these chapters that many of the most interesting applications of consumer theory are to be found. Given Part One, Chapters from 10 through 14 can be combined in numerous combinations with blocks from Parts Two and Three. We also envisage much of this material, particularly Chapters 11, 12, and 13 on labor supply, the consumption function, and durable goods, as well as Chapter 3 of Part One, being used as parts of applied econometrics courses. Even so, although we frequently discuss the formulation of likelihood functions and present empirical results, we have spent little time on specifically econometric issues, mostly for reasons of space.

There are no mathematical prerequisites for this book other than a good knowledge of calculus, including partial differentiation, and a familiarity with notions of concavity and the basic concepts of mathematical statistics. Unlike many texts on consumer theory, this book makes little use of matrix algebra apart from the largely notational use of vectors and dot products. In Chapters 1 through 8, which contain the material that is generally suitable for undergraduate work, harder sections are starred (*) or double starred (**); the latter can be omitted at first reading even by a reader continuing to Part Four. We have included over three hundred exercises that seek to complete, reinforce, or extend the material in the text. Those which are more difficult than their immediate neighbors are starred; some of these are very difficult indeed. Each chapter ends with a guide to further reading and all works cited are listed together at the end of the book.

Writing this book, we have accumulated debts to many people. Intellectual debts are the most important and the hardest to quantify, but the influence, work, and example of both Richard Stone and Terence Gorman have had great effects over the years on the way we have come to approach the subject. More specifically, we have been heavily dependent on the advice and comments of colleagues who read preliminary drafts of chapters on specialist subjects. In this context we should like to thank David Demery, Peter Hammond, Oliver Hart, Tony Jackson, Richard Layard, Richard Lecomber, and Amartya Sen. General comments, particularly on drafts of the early chapters, were made by Erwin Diewert, Avinash Dixit, Ben Fine, the late Miles Fleming, Arnold Merkies, Jan van Overhagen, and Henri Theil. We are especially grateful to Gerald Kennally who read and commented on it all. Not least, several groups of students at the universities of Amsterdam, Bristol, and Birkbeck, London, suffered through early versions; the protests of John Wrigglesworth, in particular, were most effective in securing remedial action. Finally, Ton Barten, Martin Browning, and Barry Murphy were helpful in ironing out some of the defects surviving into the first impression. The typing was done with great speed, precision, and unfailing pleasantness by Mary Harthan and Gillian Baker in Bristol. Finally, our greatest thanks go to Helge and to Catherine who put up with us while we wrote it.

University of Bristol   Angus Deaton
Birkbeck College   John Muellbauer

PART ONE

Consumer demand analysis

The limits to choice • Preferences and demand • The theory at work • Extensions to the basic model

CHAPTER 1

The limits to choice

Consumer behavior is frequently presented in terms of preferences, on the one hand, and possibilities on the other. The emphasis in the discussion is commonly placed on *preferences,* on the axioms of choice, on utility functions and their properties. The specification of which choices are actually available is given a secondary place and, frequently, only very simple possibilities are considered. In this book, we shall have a great deal to say about preferences, and discussion of them begins in Chapter 2. We begin, however, with the *limits to choice* rather than with the choices themselves. Unlike preferences, the opportunities for choice are often directly observable so that, to the extent that variations in behavior can be traced to variations in opportunities, we have a straightforward and objective explanation of observed phenomena. It is our view that much can be so explained and that the part played by preferences in determining behavior tends to be overestimated. Hence, this first chapter considers what can be said about behavior without detailed consideration of how choices are made. A large part of this book, from Chapters 2 to 9, works with one very special assumption about the opportunity set, namely that choices are constrained by fixed, known prices in such a way that the total value of the objects chosen should not exceed some predetermined total. In this case, we say that the consumer faces a linear budget constraint. A detailed examination of more complex situations is postponed until Chapters 10 to 14 by which stage the basic material will have been covered. Although this later analysis is technically more difficult, nonlinear budget constraints arise frequently in practice and in §1.1 we present a largely diagrammatic survey of both the linear and nonlinear cases. This provides an elementary introduction to the later material as well as providing a preview of the topics to be covered in the rest of the book. For uniformity of usage, the limits to choice will be described through the "constraints" facing consumers even though, for the moment, nothing is being optimized. Indeed, no formal assumptions are made about choice itself; for the most part, the likely implications of the constraints under consideration will be obvious enough.

Section 1.2 focusses on the simple linear budget constraint that underlies much of the subsequent analysis. Again, without specific assumptions about choices, we can make quite far-reaching deductions about behavior and we explore the consequences of these for empirical analysis. Finally, as a preparation for Chapter 2, we use a model of *irrational* choice proposed by Becker (1962) to suggest that the use of preference orderings is only one way in which models of consumer behavior may be completed.

1.1 The nature of opportunity sets

The linear budget constraint

The simplest and single most important type of opportunity set is that which arises when the household has an exogenous budget, outlay or total expenditure x, which is to be spent within a given period on some or all of n commodities. These can be bought in nonnegative quantities q_i at given fixed prices p_i. The constraint can then be written

$$x \geq \sum_{i=1}^{n} p_i q_i \tag{1.1}$$

When $n = 2$, (1.1) is illustrated in Figure 1.1 by the area in the triangle $A0B$ since q_1 and q_2 must be nonnegative. The coordinates of the points A and B are marked; at A all of the budget is spent on good 2 so that $q_2 = x/p_2$ and $q_1 = 0$ and conversely at B. Note an immediate complication which arises if there is a basic survival constraint. An example is illustrated in the diagram.

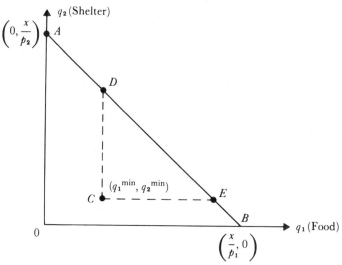

Figure 1.1. A linear budget constraint with a survival constraint.

Here q_1^{min} and q_2^{min} represent the minimum quantities of the two goods necessary for survival within the period. Hence, choice is restricted to the triangle *DCE*, so that for a household with a budget as low as $x = p_1 q_1^{min} + p_2 q_2^{min}$, there is no choice; it must buy at *C* or cease to exist. In general, the survival constraints may take a variety of forms; for example, with very little shelter, more food is needed for survival than with a great deal of shelter.

The formalization of choice within a linear budget constraint is the main topic of Chapter 2. In spite of its limitations, of which more below, reinterpretation of the p's, q's, and x allows a wide field of application for (1.1), given suitable, but often restrictive assumptions. If q_1 is taken to be leisure and q_2 some composite of goods, then Figure 1.1 can be interpreted as the situation facing a consumer with a fixed money wage, no income tax (other than a proportional one) and no unearned income. We shall follow this further in §4.1. Alternatively, q_1 and q_2 may be taken as composites of goods in two different periods with p_1 and p_2 as the two corresponding price levels. If the consumer begins period one with no assets, if he can save or borrow at an interest rate of zero, and if income arising in the two periods, y_1 and y_2, is to be spent, the budget constraint is

$$y_1 + y_2 \geq p_1 q_1 + p_2 q_2 \tag{1.2}$$

which, with x equivalent to $y_1 + y_2$ is simply equation (1.1). As we shall see in §4.2, assets and interest rates can be incorporated into (1.2) without losing the analogy with the basic constraint (1.1). The analogy can even be extended to purchases of durable goods, albeit under restrictive assumptions, again see §4.2. Finally, consider the more radical reinterpretation of (1.1), which takes x not as individual expenditure but as national income or expenditure and which interprets the q_i's as the incomes of each of the individual households. In this analogy, taking each of the p_i's as unity makes (1.1) the problem faced by the government in allocating a fixed total income between its citizens. Further analysis of this problem is in Chapter 9, especially §9.2.

Nonlinear constraints

Implicit in the linear budget constraint is the institutional setting of efficient markets with negligible transactions costs. Therefore, as our first example of nonlinear constraints, it is instructive to take the example of a barter economy. Let *A* in Figure 1.2 be a household's initial endowment of food and clothing. Without a general medium of exchange, information and transactions costs prevent the household which wishes to trade clothing for food along *AB* from being in touch with those willing to trade food for clothing along *AC* so that the rate of exchange differs in the two directions. It is also likely that different households will face different divergent pairs of rates of

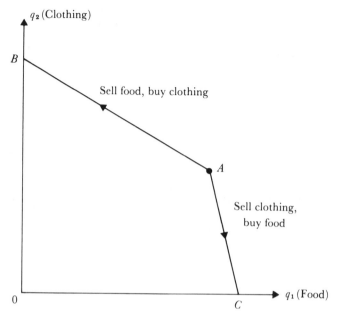

Figure 1.2. Budget constraint in a barter economy.

exchange. The development of trading posts with some centralization of transactions is likely to reduce the divergence between the rates of exchange while, it can be argued, a fully monetized competitive economy will effectively eliminate it altogether. However, we shall later see examples where, even in a developed market economy, informational problems are likely to cause divergences to occur between buying and selling prices faced by a given household.

Even in the simplest case of spending a fixed total on specified goods within a single period, nonlinearities may arise. In many countries, for example, households face a two-part or even three-part tariff in paying for fuel such as gas or electricity. The first few units typically come at a high price with extra units at a reduced rate giving rise to the budget constraint illustrated in Figure 1.3. A similar situation occurs if discounts are given on bulk purchases. An extreme case of nonlinear pricing that works in the opposite direction is when the price becomes infinite above some specified level of purchases. This is precisely equivalent to the imposition of a *ration* in the form of an upper limit on purchases, as occurs, for example, in wartime. Rationing of a different type may occur when a household has no direct control over its consumption of some particular good such as housing, in the short run, or defense expenditure. In this case, the household may be constrained to consume *more* than it wishes. We return to the topic of rationing in §4.3

Figure 1.3. The budget constraint with a two-part tariff.

Nonlinearities become even more pervasive when we move to questions of leisure choice or intertemporal behavior. Take first the case where the consumer can choose the number of hours he can work, faces a fixed wage rate, ω, but has some transfer income, μ, say. Hence if T is the total number of hours available and q_0 is leisure, the budget constraint is

$$\mu + \omega(T - q_0) \geq \Sigma \, p_i q_i \tag{1.3}$$

Figure 1.4 illustrates this for two values of ω, ω^1 and ω^2. Note that this budget constraint, unlike that of Figure 1.1, is kinked outwards at A. Kinks of this type are characteristic of many of the nonlinear budget constraints we shall consider. Points such as A are of considerable practical importance since there turn out to be good theoretical reasons for expecting a fraction of consumers to make that particular choice. We shall take up this point formally later; in the present example, the choice between A and some point between A and B^1 or B^2 is the choice whether or not to participate in the labor force and this question will be discussed in §11.1. In general, we can think of consumers as being continuously distributed along the budget line according to tastes, circumstances, and so on, and if points to the right of A were feasible, we should expect some consumers to choose them. As it is, all such consumers must make do with A so that, in contrast to any other point along AB, a finite proportion of the population will be found at A itself.

In practice, Figure 1.4 is likely to be too simple. In Figure 1.5, beyond a certain number of hours of work (to the left of C), hours are paid at a higher overtime rate, but if hours go to the left of D, the worker becomes liable for income tax. We thus have two outward kinks (at D and B) and an inward kink (at C). When we come to consider specific models of how choices are made, we

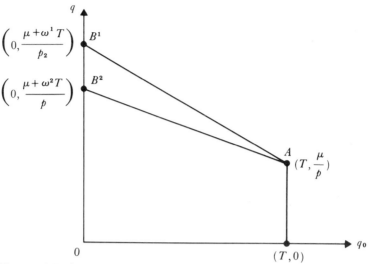

Figure 1.4. Budget constraint between leisure and other goods with transfer income.

shall see that such kinks have important consequences since, under many such models, points with outward kinks are rather frequently chosen with the opposite being true for inward kinks. As a final example in the leisure-goods context, note that budget sets may not be areas as illustrated so far but rather points or lines. Figure 1.6 illustrates the available choices when there are three jobs each with different hours of work and wage rates. Clearly, there is a wide range of possibilities that combine elements of Figures 1.4 to 1.6 and some of these will be discussed in Chapter 11. In that chapter, we shall argue the importance of correctly specifying choice sets for the understanding and interpretation of labor market behavior. In the broader context, the analysis of voluntary and involuntary unemployment and hence of much of macro-economics hinges on the constraints which consumers are assumed to face in the labor market.

Different, but equally important nonlinearities arise when we turn to opportunity sets in which goods or leisure are distinguished according to the periods in which they are consumed. Equation (1.2) illustrated the linear budget constraint for two periods with a zero interest rate and no assets. If the consumer in this model wishes to spend more than his income in period 1, borrowing with repayment in period 2 will be required. However, consumers are not always able to borrow so that, as illustrated in Figure 1.7, the budget constraint is not ABC but rather ABD so that, once again, we have an outward kink. Consumers at B spend all their current income and, for as long as they remain there, have a marginal propensity to consume of unity: If we make

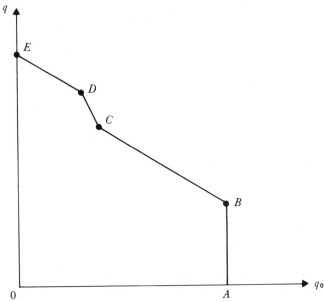

Figure 1.5. The budget constraint for leisure and other goods in the presence of overtime premia and an income tax.

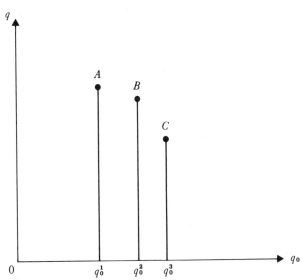

Figure 1.6. The budget constraint with three alternative jobs.

this situation less extreme by allowing for interest rates, but assume that the consumer pays a higher rate for borrowing than for lending, the budget constraint will still be kinked but less severely. The line ABE in Figure 1.7 illustrates a higher rate for borrowing than lending. Situations similar to these are discussed in Chapter 12, while in Chapter 13, on durable goods, additional nonlinearities are considered that arise through imperfect secondhand markets (where buying and selling prices differ) and the discreteness.that is due to the indivisibility of many durable goods. As in the leisure case, the distinction between unfettered choice along a linear intertemporal budget constraint and relatively constrained choice at kinks like B in Figure 1.7 turns out to be crucial for macroeconomic analysis. Indeed, the existence and properties of the Keynesian consumption function cannot be understood without the existence of nonlinearities in both leisure and intertemporal budget constraints.

One of the important postwar developments in consumer theory has been in the construction of models in which the household is viewed as a producer, combining market goods with one another and with leisure through household production functions. The object of this activity is the production of a limited number of basic goods that are regarded as the real object of consumer choice. If there are two such basic goods z_1 and z_2, their output is lim-

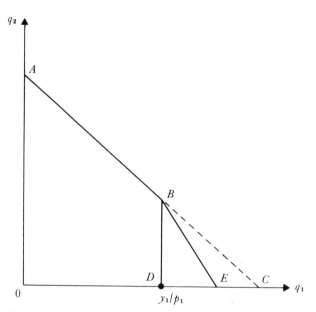

Figure 1.7. Intertemporal choice with "imperfect" capital markets.

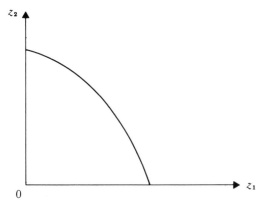

Figure 1.8. The budget constraint for the outputs of household production.

ited by the time available for household production and by the wage rate and the prices of market commodities. If the production functions allow smooth substitution between time and market goods as inputs, a typical budget constraint might be as illustrated in Figure 1.8; the analogy with the cost-minimizing firm is clear. Frequently, the technology is assumed to be of the fixed coefficient type. Figure 1.9 illustrates the famous "diet" problem in which a household requires two outputs z_1 (protein) and z_2 (calories). These are provided by four different market foods which, if total food expenditure is spent on them, lead to points A, B, C, and D. Points along the line segments can be reached by buying mixed bundles, but the constraint stops short of the

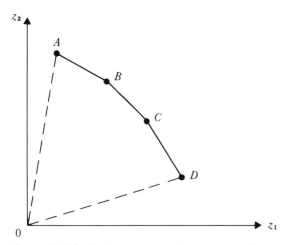

Figure 1.9. The budget constraint for the diet problem with four market goods.

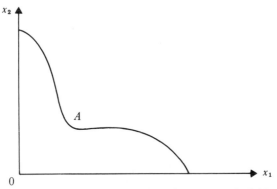

Figure 1.10. The allocation problem between two individuals when output depends on distribution.

axes because there may well be no foods which are 100 percent protein or 100 percent calories. We discuss household production models further in Chapter 10.

As a final example that goes beyond individual choice, consider again the case of a government attempting to allocate total output amongst its citizens. If total output is independent of its allocation, the constraint is the linear one at 45 degrees to the axes. In practice, however, a guaranteed equal allocation is likely to affect the incentives to work and to produce so that egalitarian distributions may well be associated with low total output and vice versa. An extreme case is illustrated in Figure 1.10, where x_1 and x_2 are the allocations to each of two households. Attempts to ensure an egalitarian allocation in the region of A will ensure that both households are relatively badly off. Alternative solutions, however, can only produce a large allocation for one household and not for both. Optimal solutions to such problems are complex and we discuss the issues involved in Chapter 9.

Information and consumer perceptions

To understand consumer behavior, we must recognize that the budget constraint that is relevant is the constraint perceived by the decision maker. In many of the examples already given, full information on the opportunities available may not be easily available to everyone. In the leisure-goods choice, for example, many countries have extremely complicated tax and social security systems and it is clear that many consumers are not perfectly informed. Again, in Figure 1.10, the government is in practice unlikely to have anything but the vaguest information on the possibilities of trading off efficiency for equity in the population at large. However, the invalidity of the perfect information assumption is nowhere more serious than in models of choice over time. The future is inherently uncertain. The consumer-worker may become unexpectedly unemployed, his house may burn down or his financial assets may be eroded by unexpectedly high rates of inflation. A formal analysis of uncertainty is rather difficult and in some ways rather unsatisfactory (see Chapter 14). But, at least under some models, uncertainty in the intertemporal content will add a precautionary element to behavior, particularly as regards saving and the holding of liquid assets. Such behavior is strongly influenced by the constraint facing consumers and, once again, kinks in budget sets are important. In Figure 1.7, the consumer who cannot borrow (*ABD*) is in a much worse position to withstand unexpected financial misfortune than is the consumer who can (*ABE* or *ABC*). Similarly, an individual who knows that durable goods bought this period can only be sold next period at a heavy discount will be cautious in his present purchases and will be particularly keen to avoid buying too much. Chapters 12, 13, and 14 take up these issues in depth.

Interactions between agents

For many problems, it is adequate to model consumers individually, each making his own choices subject to his own budget constraint. Group behavior can then be derived as the sum of its parts. Sometimes, however, the opportunities available to any one consumer depend crucially on what others do, and opportunity sets must then be modeled to reflect this dependence. A classic example is in public goods provision where the impossibility of excluding any individual from the enjoyment of the good once it has been provided renders an individualistic analysis inappropriate. The amount of national defense available to me depends, not on what I am prepared to finance (or only infinitesimally), but on what is already being provided by my fellow citizens. A consumer who takes this into account will always show an unwillingness to buy more of the public good, since he gets such poor value for his money, yet this does not reflect the true worth he attaches to extra units of provision. Recent, highly ingenious work has gone into the problem of how to redesign budget sets (via taxes and subsidies) so that consumers will choose on an individualistic basis those quantities that fulfill their collective needs.

One of the dangers of not recognizing interdependencies between consumers is that we can mistake highly constrained behavior for free choice. If we wish to attach welfare significance to behavior, such a mistake is of the highest importance, since freely chosen positions tend to be regarded as optimal while those adopted under coercion are clearly not so. A classic example of this at the individual level is the assurance game, see Sen (1967), typical data for which are given in Table 1.1. Prisoners A and B are both guilty and are being separately questioned. If both maintain their innocence, both are

Table 1.1. *The assurance game: payoffs (years in jail) for prisoners A and B*

Action of A	Action of B	
	Confess	Not Confess
Confess	5(A), 5(B)	2(A), 20(B)
Not confess	20(A), 2(B)	0(A), 0(B)

discharged and this is clearly the preferred position for both. However if A maintains his innocence but B confesses, A will be jailed for twenty years so that the "not confess" strategy is an extremely risky one. By contrast, confession, although ruling out an absolute discharge, can lead at the worst to five years' imprisonment. Hence, if A has little taste for risk for its own sake, he is likely to choose the safer strategy, especially if he knows that B is making similar calculations and that B knows that he knows, and so on. If these arguments are correct, both prisoners are likely to confess although this outcome makes them both worse off than if they had both refused to do so.

Such examples are not merely philosophical paradoxes. What Keynes called the "fallacy of composition," that the whole is not merely the sum of its parts, is an essentially similar phenomenon. If employers knew that the unemployed workers they do not employ would spend the extra income they do not earn on the goods the employers do not produce because of insufficient demand, collective action would reduce unemployment although individual action cannot. If such constraints are not recognized, we are forced into the patent absurdity of interpreting mass unemployment as voluntarily chosen leisure and hence condemning any policy that attempts to remedy it.

1.2 The implications of a linear budget constraint

Notwithstanding the importance of nonlinearities and of the other issues in §1.1, a great deal of consumer demand analysis is built on the assumption of a simple linear budget constraint. We write this in equality form

$$x = \sum_k p_k q_k \qquad\qquad (2.1)$$

with total expenditure x, prices p_k and quantities q_k. The use of the equality, as opposed to the inequality of (1.1), will be justified if consumers always attain the upper boundary of the opportunity set. This will happen if the consumer cannot completely satisfy all his wants within the budget constraint; there is always some good more of which is desirable. The use of (2.1) rules out the nonlinearities, indivisibilities, uncertainties, and interdependencies of

§1.1 It also assumes that the total amount to be spent x is decided separately from how its details are to be made up. Possible justifications for this will be discussed in Chapter 5. Note carefully that x is total expenditure and not income; we shall maintain a close distinction between these concepts throughout the book.

Properties of demand functions

Assume that demand functions exist; the consumer, by some means or other, has rules for deciding how much of each good to purchase faced with given prices and total outlay. We write these functions as

$$q_i = g_i(x, p) \tag{2.2}$$

These relationships giving quantities as a function of prices and total expenditures we shall refer to as *Marshallian* demand functions; other types of demand functions will be introduced in Chapter 2. We shall assume that the Marshallian demand functions are continuously differentiable and postpone also to Chapter 2 any consideration of why this might be so.

The fact that the demand functions satisfy the budget constraint (2.1) immediately places a constraint on the functions g_i. Specifically,

$$\sum_k p_k g_k(x, p) = x \tag{2.3}$$

and as we shall see below, this can by no means be satisfied by any arbitrary selection of functions g. Equation (2.3), for obvious reasons, is referred to as the *adding-up restriction*. But this does not exhaust the implications of the budget constraint. Consider some vector of purchases q, and assume that it satisfies (2.1) for prices p and outlay x. Then, since the constraint is linear and homogeneous in x and p, the vector q will also satisfy the constraints for any multiple of x and p. If total expenditure and prices are twice as high, the constraint is the same. Formally, for any positive number θ and, for all i from 1 to n,

$$g_i(\theta x, \theta p) = g_i(x, p) \tag{2.4}$$

This restriction implies that the demand functions are homogeneous of degree zero, so that (2.4) is known as the *homogeneity restriction*. It is also known as "absence of money illusion" since the units in which prices and outlay are expressed have no effect on purchases. Note that to get this result we have made a weak but not trivial assumption about behavior. This is that prices and outlay play no role in choice other than in determining the budget constraint, so that the units in which prices and outlay are measured have no effect on the consumer's perception of opportunities. One case that violates this assumption occurs when the quality of a good is judged by its absolute price (although homogeneity survives if quality is judged by the relative price of a good, see Exercise 1.13).

Equations (2.3) and (2.4) are important tools of demand analysis and it is sometimes useful to express them as restrictions on the derivatives of the demand functions, rather than on the functions themselves. The adding-up restriction, see Exercise 1.7, implies that, for $i = 1, \ldots, n$

$$\sum_k p_k \frac{\partial g_k}{\partial x} = 1; \quad \sum_k p_k \frac{\partial g_k}{\partial p_i} + q_i = 0 \qquad (2.5)$$

so that changes in x and in p cause rearrangements in purchases that do not violate the budget constraint. The two parts of (2.5) are sometimes referred to as Engel and Cournot aggregation, respectively. The homogeneity restriction, see Exercise 1.8, implies that, $i = 1, \ldots, n$,

$$\sum_k p_k \frac{\partial g_i}{\partial p_k} + x \frac{\partial g_i}{\partial x} = 0 \qquad (2.6)$$

This says no more than that a proportionate change in p and x will leave purchases of good i unchanged.

These formulas can be expressed somewhat more neatly if we introduce some important new notation. The *budget shares* w_i are defined by

$$w_i = p_i q_i / x \qquad (2.7)$$

and are the fractions of total expenditure going to each good. The logarithmic derivatives of the Marshallian demands are the *total expenditure elasticities* and *price elasticities;* for the former e_i, $i = 1, \ldots, n$,

$$e_i = \partial \log g_i(x, p) / \partial \log x \qquad (2.8)$$

while for the latter, e_{ij}, $i, j = 1, \ldots, n$

$$e_{ij} = \partial \log g_i(x, p) / \partial \log p_j \qquad (2.9)$$

The diagonal elements e_{ii} are the *own-price* elasticities, while off-diagonal e_{ij} terms are *cross-price* elasticities. These Marshallian elasticities are also known as uncompensated or gross elasticities for reasons which will become apparent in Chapter 2.

It is then a simple exercise to show that (2.5) is equivalent to

$$\sum_k w_k e_k = 1; \quad \sum_k w_k e_{ki} + w_i = 0 \qquad (2.10)$$

and that (2.6) is

$$\sum_k e_{ik} + e_i = 0 \qquad (2.11)$$

Empirical specifications

The easy comprehensibility of the elasticity concept and the fact that elasticities are pure numbers has led many economists to see the estimation of elasticities as the primary aim of empirical demand analysis. Hence the equation

$$\log q_i = \alpha_i + e_i \log x + \sum_k e_{ik} \log p_k + u_i \tag{2.12}$$

has frequently been estimated on time series data of expenditures, outlay, and prices. Estimates of e_i and of e_{ik} for some relevant range of k (typically those goods thought to be closely associated with i) can be obtained by ordinary least squares regression applied to (2.12) one good at a time. The homogeneity restriction can then be checked out by seeing whether the estimates satisfy (2.11) or, more precisely, by imposing the restriction a priori and using standard statistical tests to test its validity. By contrast, the adding-up restriction cannot be accommodated within the double logarithmic specification. To see this, write (2.7) as

$$\log w_i = \log q_i + \log p_i - \log x \tag{2.13}$$

so that under the double logarithmic model

$$\log w_i = \alpha_i + (e_i - 1)\log x + (e_{ii} + 1)\log p_i + \sum_{k \neq i} e_{ik} \log p_k \tag{2.14}$$

The adding-up restriction (2.10) tells us that the sum of e_i's weighted by w_i's is unity so that we must *either* have all the e_i's equal to unity *or* at least one of them must be larger than unity. If the former is true, the model is not very interesting since it implies identical expenditure patterns at all levels of total expenditure, and elementary inspection of the data shows this to be false. Consider then the second alternative, that there exists at least one "luxury" good for which $e_i > 1$ and at least one "necessity" for which $e_i < 1$. We then lump all luxuries together and write E_1 for total expenditure on them, while E_2 is defined as outlay less total expenditure on necessities (goods for which $e_i = 1$ can be allocated to either group). Equation (2.12) can then be used to examine the behavior of E_1 and E_2 as x increases and it can be shown, see Exercise 1.14, that the two totals must take the general form illustrated in Figure 1.11, with E_1 equal to E_2 at the three points $0, B$, and C. In the region between B and C, total expenditures add up to less than the budget, and elsewhere, except at the origin, the budget is exceeded. Hence, the double logarithmic model will only satisfy adding up generally if we reverse our original supposition and take $e_i = 1$ for all goods. In this case, demands take the form,

$$p_i q_i = \alpha_i^* x \qquad \text{where } \alpha_i^* = e^{\alpha_i} \tag{2.15}$$

In spite of this implicit rejection of adding up, it is sometimes argued that for the analysis of a single commodity, the use of (2.12) does not commit us to

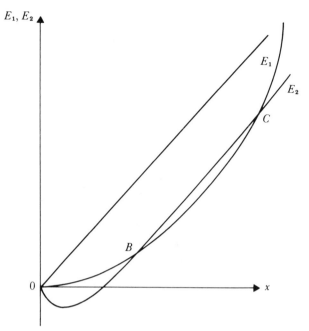

Figure 1.11. The violation of adding-up by constant elasticity demand functions.

logarithmic forms for the equations that remain unspecified. This argument
is satisfactory if the double logarithmic form is used only for restricted ranges
of total outlay. Note that expenditure on even one single luxury will eventually exceed the total budget if x becomes large enough, while for x small
enough, expenditure on a single necessity will exceed x. Well before either of
these occurs, the demand pattern predicted by the model will have become
very distorted. We thus see little virtue in the use of this model, particularly
since there exist models that are equally simple but otherwise more satisfactory.

   Demand analysis is concerned not only with the analysis of time-series data
but also with the explanation of behavioral differences between households in
cross-section studies. In such studies, it is usually assumed that all households
face identical prices so that explanations of behavioral differences are sought
in differences in total expenditure and in household characteristics, particularly those concerned with family composition. The homogeneity of demand
functions can play no part in such an analysis since no price variation is observed, but adding up, which restricts total expenditure elasticities, is still important. Even so, the tradition in studies of family budgets has been to choose
functional forms relating purchases to total expenditure on the basis of
goodness of fit without paying much attention to this requirement.

If for the moment we abstract from family composition effects (see Chapter 8 for a full discussion), and if prices are absorbed into the functional form, (2.2) becomes

$$q_i = g_i^*(x) \qquad q_i \; f\left(\text{Income}\right) \tag{2.16}$$

This relationship is commonly referred to as an *Engel curve*. Equation (2.16) can also be multiplied by p_i to give expenditures $p_i q_i$ as functions of x, and these too can be called Engel curves. Since p_i is the same for all households, the graph of purchases against household outlays is only being scaled by a fixed multiple if we move to the expenditure basis. Engel curves can be used to classify goods into *luxuries, necessities,* and *inferior goods*. Luxuries are goods that take up a larger share of the budget of better-off households and vice versa for necessities. From equation (2.14) we can see that the budget share of a good will increase or decrease with total expenditure as e_i is greater than or less than unity. Hence $e_i > 1$ and $e_i < 1$ are sometimes used to define luxuries and necessities, respectively. Inferior goods are those the purchase of which declines absolutely (not just proportionately) as x increases; in this case $e_i < 0$.

A wide selection of functional forms for Engel curves has been explored in the literature. For example, Prais and Houthakker (1955), in their classic study of Engel curves, experiment with double logarithmic, semilogarithmic ($q_i = \alpha_i + \beta_i \log x$), and log reciprocal ($\log q_i = \alpha_i - \beta_i x^{-1}$) forms, each of which has some claim to superiority, at least for some goods and over part of the expenditure range. More complex forms, such as the cumulative distribution function of the lognormal distribution, have been suggested that combine many of the desirable features of the simpler forms. None of these forms is fully consistent with adding up, and although this may be less serious a problem than in time-series analysis, the theoretical plausibility of these models is not enhanced by their failure to meet this requirement. One extremely useful form which is consistent with adding up was first estimated by Working (1943), was used successfully by Leser (1963), and will be extended in various ways in this book. This relates budget shares linearly to the logarithm of outlay,

$$w_i = \alpha_i + \beta_i \log x \tag{2.17}$$

where α_i and β_i are parameters to be estimated. Adding up requires that $\Sigma w_i = 1$, which is satisfied provided

$$\Sigma \alpha_i = 1, \quad \Sigma \beta_i = 0 \tag{2.18}$$

Indeed, if (2.17) is estimated equation by equation by ordinary least squares, the parameter estimates $\hat{\alpha}_i$ and $\hat{\beta}_i$, say, will satisfy (2.18) automatically, see Exercise 1.12 below. The model allows luxuries ($\beta_i > 0$), necessities ($\beta_i < 0$), and inferior goods. Some possible Engel curves that it implies are shown in Figure 1.12.

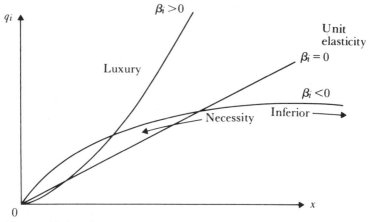

Figure 1.12. Engel curves for model (2.17).

To take a practical example, Table 1.2 lists the ordinary least squares estimates of α and β, which are obtained using expenditures of one man and one woman households with head of household under 65 taken from the British 1974 Family Expenditure Survey. The $\hat{\alpha}$'s add to unity and the $\hat{\beta}$'s to zero, as they must. The R^2-statistics are reasonably high given that the dependent variables are estimated in shares form, and are even higher if the equations are reexpressed in levels. Note, however, that each regression is based on only six observations so that the scope for poor fits is limited. Food, drink, and tobacco (group 1) and housing and fuel (group 2) are classed as necessities ($\beta_i <$ 0) while the remaining two groups are luxuries ($\beta_i > 0$). Hence the Engel curves for clothing and durables and for services, transport, and other are convex from below while those for food, drink, and tobacco and for housing and fuel are concave from below. An extended version of this model is discussed further in Chapter 3.

Table 1.2. *Parameter estimates for four Engel curves (standard errors in parentheses)*

Group	$\hat{\alpha}$	$\hat{\beta}$	R^2
1. Food, drink, and tobacco	0.947	−0.164	0.9591
	(0.063)	(0.017)	
2. Housing and fuel	0.492	−0.077	0.8771
	(0.054)	(0.014)	
3. Clothing and durables	−0.180	0.092	0.8975
	(0.058)	(0.016)	
4. Services, transport and other	−0.259	0.149	0.9658
	(0.052)	(0.014)	

Further restrictions on demand functions

Adding up and homogeneity are as far as a linear budget constraint will take us. To go further, we must say more about the basis of choice. To this end, we introduce the apparatus of preferences and utility functions in Chapter 2, and we shall make great use of it in the rest of the book. But is this the only interesting way of being more precise about the nature of consumer behavior? Are preferences a crucial element in describing behavior? Probably not. As we saw in §1.1, the presence of indivisibilities, kinks, and other nonlinearities may limit choice to the extent that only very mild additional assumptions are required to describe behavior completely. But even with a linear budget constraint, where the scope for choice is at its widest, restrictions similar to those that come from preferences could be derived from other assumptions, and although the results would be different in detail, the important features of demand are likely to remain. In our view, the real importance of preferences and utility is that they provide us with a widely applicable language in which to discuss consumer behavior, and we hope to demonstrate in this book that systematic use of the language is of immense power in aiding and guiding our thought. No doubt other languages could be developed to the same end, but they have not been, at least not to the same extent. However, in order to give an indication of the way in which we might begin if we did not wish to use preferences, it is worth looking at a model of "irrational" choice suggested by Becker (1962).

Becker takes a linear budget constraint and describes "impulsive" behavior as consumers choosing points at random along the budget line with all points equally likely to be chosen. Restriction of behavior to the budget line (rather than inside it) suggests that more is being assumed to be better than less, an assumption that will turn out also to be important in defining preferences. However, impulsive behavior of this type, for the market as a whole, will lead to an average choice at the midpoint of the budget line. Hence, with two goods as an example, average market demands are given by

$$q_1 = \frac{1}{2}\frac{x}{p_1}, \quad q_2 = \frac{1}{2}\frac{x}{p_2} \tag{2.19}$$

Such demand functions are not only specific in functional form, but they slope downwards as well as being homogeneous and adding up. This specific example is not realistic but the general principle behind it is important. If relative prices change, the change in the position of the budget line is alone enough to make it highly likely that demand will move towards the good whose relative price has fallen. In Figure 1.13 with initial situation AB, assume choice is at X. $A'B'$ represents a fall in the price of good 1 accompanied by a fall in total expenditure so that X is on the new budget line. Comparison of the two situations shows that, although the area $0A'XB$ is available in both,

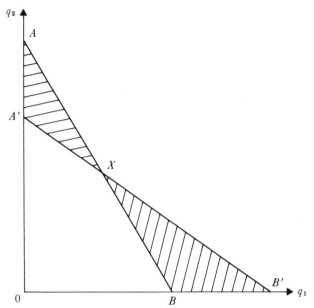

Figure 1.13. The basis for downward-sloping demand curves.

$AA'X$ (with high q_2 and low q_1) is excluded after q_1 has become cheaper and $XB'B$ (with high q_1 and low q_2) is included after the change. Hence, whatever principle of choice is adopted, it is very likely that the relative fall in price of good 1 will lead to an increase in its demand. Becker's example exploits this directly by setting market demand at the midpoint of the budget constraint, and it would not be difficult to think of other principles that give similar results. In general, of course, such ad hoc models of behavior are to be avoided in application; as we shall see, one of the advantages of working with preferences is that the empirical properties of the resulting models are known and understood in advance.

Exercises

Note: In order to illustrate the issues more clearly, Exercises 1.1, 1.4, and 1.13 make use of utility functions or indifference curves. These exercises can be postponed until Chapter 2 has been studied but can be solved from first principles.

1.1. Complete Figure 1.5 by drawing in indifference curves, convex to the origin, such that a consumer trying to reach the highest available curve will choose (1) D, (2) B, (3) a point along CB, (4) E. If the indifference curves of different consumers have different slopes, explain why more consumers are likely to choose D or B than any *single* point along ED or CB. Is it possible to draw an indifference curve such that C is the optimal point?

1.2. Draw a budget constraint for a consumer choosing between "motoring services" and "food," assuming that total expenditure on both is predetermined and that the only way of obtaining motoring services is by owning no cars (zero services), one car (low services), or two cars (high services). (The cost of owning three cars is assumed to more than exhaust the consumer's budget.) How is the budget constraint altered if the consumer can hire in or hire out motoring services at rates that are less favorable than owning?

1.3. Individuals A and B face budget constraints $x^A = p_1^A q_1 + p_2^A q_2$ and $x^B = p_1^B q_1 + p_2^B q_2$ for two goods q_1 and q_2, where $p_1^A/p_2^A \neq p_1^B/p_2^B$. Draw both constraints on a single diagram. Assume that A and B now join to form a single household, pooling x^A and x^B and their consumption but still purchasing separately at the two sets of prices. Draw the "family" budget constraint. Will each individual "specialize" in purchasing?

1.4. All consumers face a budget constraint $q_1 + q_2 \leq x$ with the additional constraint $q_2 \leq a$. Each consumer has a utility function of the form $q_1^\epsilon q_2^{1-\epsilon}$, $0 \leq \epsilon \leq 1$. Show that for $\epsilon > 1 - a/x$, the choice of $q_1 = \epsilon x$, $q_2 = (1 - \epsilon)x$ yields higher utility than $q_2 = a$, $q_1 = x - a$. Show that if ϵ is rectangularly distributed over households between $\epsilon = 0$ and $\epsilon = 1$, and that if $x = 100$ and $a = 40$, 60 percent of households choose the "kink" point $q_2 = a$.

1.5. State conditions under which the following demand functions satisfy "adding up."

(a) $p_i q_i = \alpha_i + \beta_i x + \sum_{j=1}^n \gamma_{ij} p_j$
(b) $w_i = \alpha_i + \beta_i \log x + \sum_{j=1}^n \gamma_{ij} \log p_j$
(c) $p_i q_i = \alpha_i + \beta_i x + \gamma_i x^2$

1.6. State conditions under which the demand functions of the previous exercise are homogeneous.

1.7. Differentiate the budget constraint in equation (2.1) with respect to x and p_j in turn to prove (2.5).

1.8. Write down the total differential of equation (2.2) to obtain dq_i in terms of dx and the dp_j's. Using the fact that $dq_i = 0$ if $dx/x = dp_j/p_j = \alpha$, say, prove (2.6). Use (2.6) to check the results of Exercise 1.6.

1.9. Let w_i as a function of x and p be $f_i(x, p)$. Show that good i is a luxury (i.e., has a total expenditure elasticity greater than one) if and only if $\partial f_i/\partial x > 0$. Alternatively, show that $\partial w_i/\partial \log x > 0$ is an equivalent condition for a luxury good.

1.10. Suppose good 1 has a constant elasticity Engel curve $p_1 q_1 = \lambda_1 x^{\beta_1}$ and that all other goods have Engel curves of the form $p_i q_i = \alpha_i + \gamma_i x + \lambda_i x^{\beta_1}$. What parameter restrictions will allow adding up to be satisfied?

1.11. All Engel curve functions involving only a few parameters are likely to be implausible for some values of total expenditure. Given that expenditures on each good must be nonnegative and have to satisfy adding up, and that (for this example) no good is inferior, what restrictions must be placed on the range of x for the following functional forms?

(a) $w_i = \alpha_i + \beta_i \log x$
(b) $p_i q_i = \gamma_i + \lambda_i x$
(c) $p_i q_i = \gamma_i + \lambda_i x + \mu_i x^2$

1.12.* To estimate the equation (2.17) from T observations on w_i and $\log x$, denote the matrix X by $\mathbf{X} = [\iota \ \log \mathbf{x}]$ where ι is a vector of T ones and $\log \mathbf{x}$ is the vector of observations on $\log x$. The ordinary least squares (OLS) estimator of $\boldsymbol{\beta}_i$, the parameter vector in the ith regression, is then $\hat{\boldsymbol{\beta}}_i = (\mathbf{X}'\mathbf{X})^{-1}\mathbf{X}'\mathbf{w}_i$ for vector $\mathbf{w}_i$. Let $\mathbf{j}$ be the vector $\begin{pmatrix}1\\0\end{pmatrix}$.

(a) Show $\Sigma_{i=1}^{n} \mathbf{w}_i = \mathbf{X}\mathbf{j}$
(b) Hence show $\Sigma_{i=1}^{n} \hat{\boldsymbol{\beta}}_i = \mathbf{j}$ so that the OLS estimates satisfy adding up automatically.
(c) Show that the argument can be extended to models of the form given in Exercise 1.5(b).

1.13. Suppose the utility function is $q_1^{\epsilon} q_2^{1-\epsilon}$ with $0 < \epsilon < 1$ and that the budget constraint is linear. If $\epsilon = \epsilon(p_1)$, show that the demand functions violate homogeneity, while if $\epsilon = \epsilon(p_1/p_2)$ show that they do not.

1.14. By rewriting the constant elasticity model in the form $q_i = a_i x^{e_i}$, where a_i is a function of the prices, write E_1 and E_2 (as defined in the text) as functions of x. Show that $dE_1/dx > 0$, $d^2E_1/dx^2 > 0$, $d^2E_2/dx^2 > 0$ and that $dE_2/dx_2 \rightarrow -\infty$ as $x \rightarrow 0$ and to 1 as $x \rightarrow \infty$. Hence, construct Figure 1.11.

Bibliographical notes

Nearly all the topics discussed in this chapter are taken up later in the book; models with linear budget constraints are discussed in the chapters immediately following, those with nonlinearities in Chapters 10 to 13 in particular. References to the literature are given at the end of these main chapters. A survey of the literature on transactions costs is Ulph and Ulph (1975) while Niehans (1971) discusses the role of money in similar terms. Interdependencies between decision makers are discussed and dissected by Sen (1973a) in the context of the prisoners' dilemma, which is related to the assurance game but has in addition, a conflict of interest. Public goods will only briefly reappear in this book in Chapter 9; full treatments are given in the texts by Malinvaud (1972) and Baumol and Oates (1974). See also the recent (but more difficult) paper by Groves and Ledyard (1977) on the construction of budget sets that lead to a solution of the "free rider" problem. Empirical Engel curves are discussed in an historical context by Stigler (1954), while Prais and Houthakker (1955, 2nd ed. 1971) remains the classic empirical study. See also Houthakker's (1957) survey commemorating the centenary of Engel's Law. Brown and Deaton (1972), Section III, survey the various functional forms. The conditions necessary to ensure adding up of demand functions were derived in papers by Worswick and Champernowne (1954–5) and by Nicholson (1957). Becker uses his 1962 model in his later text, Becker (1971), where he takes a view similar to our own, that the basic properties of demand functions are primarily consequences of the budget constraint rather than of preferences.

CHAPTER 2

Preferences and demand

In Chapter 1, we assumed without justification the existence of demand functions. We provide a basis for that assumption in this chapter by considering individual preferences. In so doing, we seek not only to describe rather more completely the properties of demands but also to establish a framework within which we shall operate for the rest of the book. Section 2.1 discusses the axioms of choice and how they lead to utility functions and to the system of choice described by utility maximization. Section 2.2 is concerned with the transition from utility to the demand functions; the traditional constrained maximization approach is discussed and its drawbacks enumerated. Section 2.3 presents consumer demand in terms of cost minimization rather than utility maximization. Marshallian uncompensated demand functions, defined on prices and outlay, are contrasted with Hicksian compensated demand functions, defined on prices and utility, and the central concept of the cost function is introduced. Section 2.4 uses the apparatus of cost minimization to derive the properties of demand. Symmetry and negativity (the "law of demand") are presented as is the Slutsky equation linking the price derivatives of compensated and uncompensated demands. The generality of these results is contrasted with those obtained through more traditional approaches. Section 2.5 is concerned with the meaning of "duality" in consumer theory, and we show how the cost function can be used as an alternative to the utility function as a representation of preferences. This has important empirical implications and it also enables us to discuss the "integrability" problem, the question of whether a given set of demand functions is or is not consistent with utility maximization. Finally, the optional §2.6 and §2.7 discuss two alternative approaches. The first shows how revealed preference analysis fits into the framework of utility theory while the second discusses the representation of preferences through the "distance" function. This is important in further explaining duality theory and has useful applications in describing inverse demand functions (where prices are functions of quantities) and in index number theory.

2.1 Axioms and utility

In principle, we could begin by assuming the existence of a utility function and examining its properties. However, if we wish to know exactly what is involved in such an assumption, we can try to find a set of *axioms of choice*, the acceptance of which is equivalent to the existence of a utility function. This is useful not only in its own right but also because, as we shall see, it allows us to maintain a useful distinction between preferences, on one hand, and utility functions on the other.

The axioms are defined over some field of choice. In the usual presentation (which for convenience we shall follow), individual purchases of commodities are the objects of choice. In principle, choice could be exercised over a much wider field, for example, over different life-styles, each embodying a preference system of its own. As it is, we shall interpret "commodities" rather widely, leaving the way open for application to leisure choice, intertemporal choice, social choice and so on. Even so, a clear definition can be important in practice since two apparently similar choices may in fact be very different if there are unrecognized components. For example, if we did not realize that the weather was relevant, it would be difficult to predict different leisure choices on different days. Similar difficulties arise when there are interdependencies between consumers (see §1.1). To avoid confusion, note carefully that the field of choice or choice set is to be clearly distinguished from the opportunity or budget set. The latter, as we saw in §1.1, can be restricted in all kinds of ways, whereas the consumer may well be able to formulate preferences over unattainable possibilities.

We shall discuss six axioms: reflexivity, completeness, transitivity, continuity, nonsatiation, and convexity. Not all of them are equally important; some are needed for some purposes and not for others while some have very little economic content. The part played by each should become clear as we proceed and discuss each in turn. The symbol $\gtrsim$ is used to mean "at least as good as," while superscripts on vectors, for example, q^1, will be used to distinguish different complete vectors. Hence, for example, $q^1 \gtrsim q^2$ means that the vector, or bundle, of goods q^1 is at least as good as the bundle q^2.

Axiom 1: Reflexivity. For any bundle q, $q \gtrsim q$.

Each bundle is as good as itself. This is mathematically necessary but is clearly trivial if the choice set is properly defined.

Axiom 2: Completeness. For any two bundles in the choice set q^1 and q^2, either $q^1 \gtrsim q^2$, or $q^2 \gtrsim q^1$.

This axiom says that any two bundles can be compared; the consumer can judge between any two bundles. This axiom is sometimes referred to as "connectedness" or "comparability." Note that the either/or does not exclude both; if both $q^1 \gtrsim q^2$ and $q^2 \gtrsim q^1$, we write $q^1 \sim q^2$ and say "q^1 is indifferent to q^2."

Axiom 3: Transitivity or consistency. If $q^1 \gtrsim q^2$ and $q^2 \gtrsim q^3$, then $q^1 \gtrsim q^3$.

If the consumer is prepared to accept \$10 in exchange for an orange and, at the same time, is prepared to accept a color television in exchange for \$10, we should expect him to accept the color television in exchange for the orange.

This axiom is at the center of the theory of choice and has the greatest empirical content of those axioms responsible for the existence of preferences. Nevertheless, it is quite difficult to think of satisfactory counterexamples. Many of those usually cited involve the passage of time so that preferences change during the consistency test; this is, of course, entirely beside the point. More serious cases, such as that given in Pearce (1964), depend upon the choice set not being correctly defined so that q^1, q^2, and q^3 have important components not explicitly included so that apparent inconsistencies arise when these hidden components change.

Axioms 1 to 3 define a *preordering* on the choice set; more often this is simply referred to as an ordering or *preference ordering*. Not all preference orderings can be represented by a utility function; this will only be possible if we are able to attach some numbering to bundles so that bundles with higher numbers are preferred to those with lower numbers. This can be done provided that, through every bundle q, we can draw an *indifference surface* that is the shared boundary between the set of bundles that are at least as good as q and the set of bundles all of which q is at least as good as. This will not be possible if there are sharp discontinuities in preferences, so that we can find bundles indefinitely close together that are far apart in the preference ordering. The most famous example of discontinuous preferences is the lexicographic ordering. For example, if a bundle q^1 contains more food than q^2, then q^1 is preferred to q^2 irrespective of what else q^1 or q^2 might contain. If, however, q^1 and q^2 have identical food content and q^1 has more clothing than q^2, then q^1 is preferred to q^2 again irrespective of other components. The bundles are ordered according to the principle of words in a dictionary or lexicon; food comes first in the lexicon, clothing second, and so on. In this case, each bundle has no points (other than itself) to which it is indifferent; indifference surfaces cannot be drawn and no utility function exists.

Although lexicographic orderings represent a perfectly reasonable system of choice, it is convenient to rule them out. This is done by means of the next axiom.

Axiom 4: Continuity. For any bundle q^1, define $A(q^1)$ the "at least as good as q^1 set" and $B(q^1)$ the "no better than q^1 set" by $A(q^1) = \{q | q \gtrsim q^1\}$, $B(q^1) = \{q | q^1 \gtrsim$

rules out lexicographic ordering

q}. Then $A(q^1)$ and $B(q^1)$ are *closed*, that is, contain their own boundaries, for any q^1 in the choice set.

Axioms 1 to 4 are now sufficient to allow us to "represent" the preference ordering by a utility function $v(q)$. This means that the statements $v(q^1) \geq v(q^2)$ and $q^1 \succeq q^2$ are precisely equivalent; when one holds, the other must. This allows us to treat preferences by conventional mathematical tools via the function $v(q)$ since the best choice will be that which yields the highest value of $v(q)$. In practice, it is convenient to restrict preferences so that this best choice lies on, rather than inside, the budget constraint. This is guaranteed by means of another axiom:

Axiom 5: Nonsatiation. The utility function $v(q)$ is nondecreasing in each of its arguments and for all q in the choice set is increasing in at least one of its arguments.

This completes the transition from axioms to utility; Axioms 1 to 5 reduce the consumer's choice problem to the constrained maximization of utility.

Note that we say that there exists a utility function that represents a preference ordering, not that it is unique. Indeed it cannot be unique; any other function that produces the same ordering of bundles must be just as good. Consequently, if $v(q)$ is a utility function representing an ordering, and $f(\ )$ is an arbitrary monotonic increasing function, then $f[v(q^1)] \geq f[v(q^2)]$ if and only if $v(q^1) \geq v(q^2)$. The fact that $v(q)$ and $f[v(q)]$ are, in their ordering of bundles, identical utility functions is often stated as "the utility function is only defined up to a monotone increasing transformation." This is exactly the same as saying that $v(q)$ is an *ordinal*, as opposed to *cardinal*, utility function. Its only purpose is to order bundles q; the actual values it takes are not in themselves meaningful in modeling choices.

Given this interpretation, the use of the term "utility" itself requires justification; indeed, utility functions might more appropriately be called "preference representation functions." However, when utility theory was first used by economists in the mid-nineteenth century, writers such as Gossen, Jevons, Menger, and Walras undoubtedly regarded goods as actually generating psychic pleasure, the measurement of which was accomplished by a cardinal utility function so that utility could be assessed in the same way as, for example, temperature. Since such measurements were well defined, utility could be added across people in much the same way as money income, so that the utility function of each household was the basis for a utilitarian calculus for the economy as a whole. Beginning with Pareto, these trappings of utility were gradually detached until today, the theory of consumer behavior rests on preferences and uses utility only as an ordinal concept. This does not mean that utility functions defined in a cardinal way have no part to play in welfare economics, indeed we shall argue the contrary in Chapters 7 to 9, but only that, for the theory of choice, utilitarian considerations are superfluous.

Axioms 1 to 5 and the representation of choice through utility maximization that they imply are all that is necessary for us to proceed. Before doing so, we discuss one further "axiom" that we shall use from time to time but that will not be generally assumed to hold:

Axiom 6: Convexity. If $q^1 \gtrsim q^0$, then for $0 \leq \lambda \leq 1$, $\lambda q^1 + (1 - \lambda)q^0 \gtrsim q^0$.

Equivalently, $A(q)$, the "as good as q set" defined in Axiom 4, is a convex set. This is just a formal way of saying that indifference curves are convex to the origin. For example, in Figure 2.1, q^1 and q^2 are on the same indifference curve so that any combination of the two is preferred. Counterexamples are again somewhat artificial; Bliss (1975) gives the example of a consumer who is indifferent between brown eggs and white eggs but who is superstitious and believes that terrible events will befall him if he possesses brown and white eggs simultaneously. Perhaps less fanciful is the injunction never to mix "grape and grain" which makes whisky and brandy acceptable on different nights but not on the same one. We shall frequently draw a distinction between *convexity* and *strict convexity*. Under the strict form, for $0 < \lambda < 1$, the linear combination $\lambda q^1 + (1 - \lambda)q^0$ must be strictly preferred to q^0 while, if

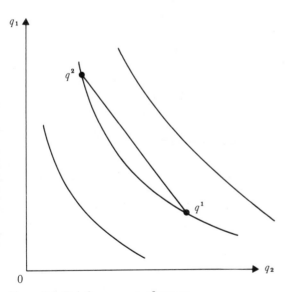

Figure 2.1. Strictly convex preferences.

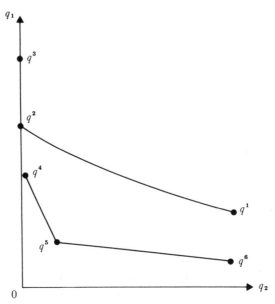

Figure 2.2. Convex but not strictly convex preferences.

the combination is indifferent to q^0, convexity itself still holds. Figure 2.2 indicates two important cases of convex preferences. On the lower indifference curve, points between q^5 and q^6 are indifferent to either so that, over the range illustrated, the two goods are perfect substitutes. Such preferences are convex but not strictly convex. The upper indifference curve joins the a_1-axis at q^2 and stops there. Points between q^3 and q^2 are strictly preferred to q^2, and so preferences are strictly convex. In such a case, there is a positive upper limit to the amount of good 1 that the consumer will give up to have even one unit of good 2; if the amount required is greater than this, he prefers to do without good 2. This would be inappropriate if good 2 were food, say, where a consumer with no food might well be prepared to trade an infinitely large amount of other goods to obtain some. But if some goods are not essential, and this is surely the general case, indifference curves will hit axes as illustrated for two goods, with good 2 inessential, in Figure 2.2.

How is the convexity of preferences translated into properties of the utility function? A scalar function $\theta(x_1, x_2, \ldots, x_n)$ of variables $x_1, \ldots, x_n, n \geq 2$ is said to be *quasi-concave* if for x^1 and x^0 such that $\theta(x^1) \geq \theta(x^0)$, and for $0 \leq \lambda \leq 1$, $\theta(\lambda x^1 + (1 - \lambda)x^0) \geq \theta(x^0)$. From this definition and from Axiom 6, it follows trivially that preferences are convex if and only if the representing utility function is quasi-concave.

Exercises

2.1. On a two-dimensional diagram to illustrate lexicographic preferences, put good 1 (the first in the lexicon) on the horizontal axis and good 2 on the vertical axis. Mark any point A with positive q_1 and q_2. Illustrate by shading the "better than A set" and show that only part of the boundary of the set is in the set. (To check, see, e.g., Phlips (1974 p. 7.)

2.2. The *linear expenditure system* for two goods comes from a utility function

$$v(q_1, q_2) = (q_1 - \gamma_1)^{\beta_1} (q_2 - \gamma_2)^{\beta_2}$$

for constants $\gamma_1, \gamma_2, \beta_1$, and β_2, where $\beta_1 > 0, \beta_2 > 0$.

(a) Can we assume that $\beta_1 + \beta_2 = 1$?
(b) Does $\beta_1 \log(q_1 - \gamma_1) + \beta_2 \log(q_2 - \gamma_2)$ represent the same preference ordering?
(c) Does $- \beta_1 \log(q_1 - \gamma_1) - \beta_2 \log(q_2 - \gamma_2)$ represent the same preference ordering?
(d) Does $q_1 q_2 + (q_1 - \gamma_1)^{\beta_1} (q_2 - \gamma_2)^{\beta_2}$?

2.3. Sketch indifference curves for the following utility functions. In each case, say whether the underlying preference ordering is (1) convex, (2) strictly convex.

(a) $v(q_1, q_2) = q_1 + \alpha q_2, \quad \alpha > 0$
(b) $v(q_1, q_2) = (q_1 - \gamma_1)^{\beta_1} (q_2 - \gamma_2)^{\beta_2}, \quad \beta_1 + \beta_2 = 1$
(c) $v(q_1, q_2) = q_1^2 + q_2^2$
(d) $v(q_1, q_2) = \min\{\alpha_1 q_1, \alpha_2 q_2\}, \quad \alpha_1, \alpha_2 > 0$
(e) $v(q_1, q_2) = \alpha - \beta_1 e^{-\gamma_1 q_1} - \beta_2 e^{-\gamma_2 q_2}$

2.4. It is sometimes argued that utility theory is tautological, having no testable implications. We shall contest this below, but can you think of any reason why a tautological system might nevertheless be useful?

2.5. Discuss the implications for the axioms of choice and for indifference curves of assuming that individuals are capable of perceiving differences in quantities only when the differences are larger than some minimum perceptible amount.

2.6. What is being assumed about preferences and indifference curves if α in Exercise 2.3(a) and γ_2 in Exercise 2.3 (b) are made increasing functions of purchases of q_2 in the period preceding the analysis?

2.2 Utility and demand

If we now combine preferences with the conventional linear budget constraint of §1.2, the choice problem reduces to the standard utility maximization problem:

$$\text{Maximize } v(q) \text{ subject to } \Sigma p_k q_k = x \tag{2.1}$$

In principle, it is clear that the solution of equation (2.1) must be the system of Marshallian demand functions

$$q_i = g_i(x, p) \tag{2.2}$$

but a general analysis of (2.2) through its derivation from (2.1) turns out to be extremely difficult.

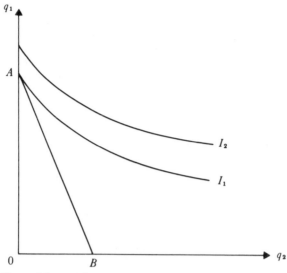

Figure 2.3. Case (1).

Consider the four diagrams Figures 2.3 to 2.6. These are examples of the sort of diagrams found in any microeconomics textbook. Two representative indifference curves I_1 and I_2 are drawn in each case; I_2 is preferred to I_1 throughout. The budget line AB represents the allowable combinations of q_1 and q_2. It is perhaps helpful to think of these diagrams as representing two-dimensional cross sections of the n-dimensional problem (2.1); not all of the n-dimensional indifference map is likely to be as shown in any one illustration.

In Case (1), good 2 is not bought at all given the budget line AB. If, however, the price of good 2 falls or if the consumer's budget increases so that AB moves outward, some of the good will eventually be purchased. Note that Figure 2.3 embodies no extreme assumptions; preferences are convex (and strictly convex since points above A on the vertical axis are better than A) and thus conform to Axiom 6 of §2.1. Indeed this must surely be the normal situation for all consumers for some part of the budget; no consumer buys some of every good. Case (2), however, does violate convexity, and we can see the consequences. Again good 2 is not purchased but in this case there will be no immediate effect of a drop in price until B reaches the other end of I_1. At this point, the consumer will jump to purchasing all good 2 and no good 1. Clearly, nonconvex preferences cause the demand functions (2.2) to be *discontinuous*. This may not be important in practice if nonconvexities are rare, but a very similar result occurs when indifference curves are straight lines. This is the case of perfect substitutes; once again, very small changes in price can

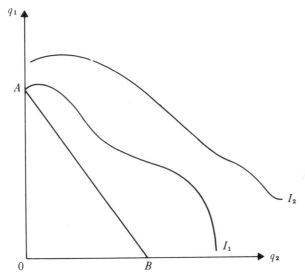

Figure 2.4. Case (2).

cause a jump from one corner solution to another. Figure 2.5 shows convex preferences with straight line segments in the indifference curves; in this case, with budget line *AB,* demand is *indeterminate* along the flat segment. At the kinks, however, changes in price will have no effect on demand, at least over a finite range. Note that kinks can occur even if preferences are *strictly* convex.

Case (4) is perhaps the most familiar one. Here, the budget line is tangent to a smoothly convex indifference curve at a single point, both goods are bought, demand is continuous, determinate, and has nonzero derivatives with respect to price. It is also the only one of the four cases that can be solved by the straightforward application of differential calculus. If this is the relevant case, we can form a Lagrangean for the problem (2.1), that is,

$$\phi = v(q) + \lambda(x - \Sigma p_k q_k) \tag{2.3}$$

where λ is a Lagrange multiplier. This has first-order conditions, for $i = 1, \ldots, n,$

$$\frac{\partial v(q)}{\partial q_i} = \lambda p_i \tag{2.4}$$

$$x = \Sigma p_k q_k \tag{2.5}$$

These are $n + 1$ equations in the $n + 1$ unknowns q and λ and their solution, when it exists, is the system of Marshallian demands (2.2). The value of the La-

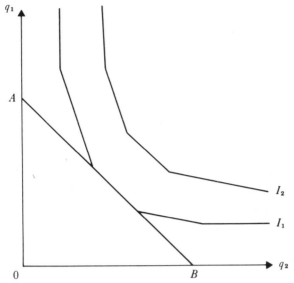

Figure 2.5. Case (3).

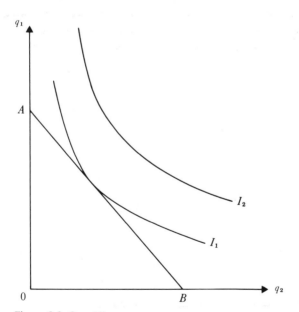

Figure 2.6. Case (4).

grange multiplier λ is the amount by which the maximand would increase given a unit relaxation in the constraint (a unit increase in x). It thus has a natural interpretation as the marginal utility of total expenditure. Of course, one must bear in mind the fact that the utility function has no observable unit of measurement so that the *amount* of utility that an extra \$1 will buy is conditional on the (arbitrary) normalization selected for the utility function.

The first-order conditions (2.4) and (2.5) can frequently be used to derive demand functions from specific functional forms, see in particular the example of the linear expenditure system in Exercise 2.7. In general, the effects of changes in p and x can be studied by totally differentiating (2.4) and (2.5) and then by matrix or determinantal manipulation to give the derivatives $\partial q_i / \partial x$ and $\partial q_i / \partial p_j$, see, for example, Hicks (1946, Appendix), Barten (1968), or Theil (1975). We shall follow a different approach here, but it is worth first looking at the standard comparative statics argument as illustrated for a rise in the price of good 1 in Figure 2.7. The original budget constraint DA moves to DB, equilibrium moves from A to B, and purchases of q_1 fall from $0Z$ to $0X$. This fall is then broken up into two parts. The first is what would have happened had only the relative price change occurred with a compensating in-

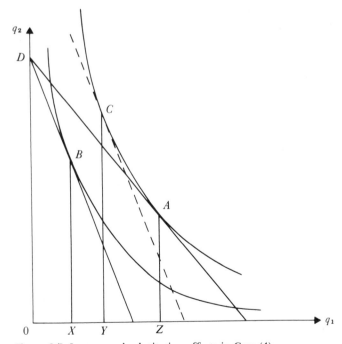

Figure 2.7. Income and substitution effects in Case (4).

crease in x to hold the consumer on the same indifference curve. This hypothetical equilibrium is at C; the move from A to C is the *substitution effect* of the price change and the change from $0Z$ to $0Y$ in the demand for q_1 is the own-price substitution effect of the price rise. To this must be added the *income effect* of the price change represented by the movement from C to B with relative prices constant. The income effect of the rise in p_1 on q_1 is thus the fall in demand YX. The crucial point about this argument is that since the indifference curves are convex, the *rise* in the relative price of q_1 must lead to a *fall* in purchases of it provided utility is held constant. Hence *the substitution effect is negative* (or at most zero if the indifference curve is kinked at A).

This argument is perfectly valid so far as it goes, but it has several important defects. First, it seems as if the nonpositiveness of the substitution effect depends on convexity of preferences. Does this mean that the substitution effect is positive in cases like Figure 2.4 or even Figure 2.3? Second, it relies on tangency arguments, and as we have seen, tangency will only *always* hold under very special assumptions, including, for example, that every consumer buys some of every good! Further, formal analysis based on (2.4) and (2.5) requires not only strict convexity of preferences but also that the utility function be "smooth" enough to be differentiated (once for (2.4) and twice for comparative statics). Nothing in our axioms will guarantee this nor can new axioms be introduced to do so without making patently unrealistic assumptions. What is thus required is a general method of examining demand functions based only on Axioms 1 to 5 of §2.1 that does not require the host of peripheral assumptions required for the validity of the first-order conditions or for the use of Figure 2.7. Such a method is the topic of the next two sections.

Exercises

2.7. Show that the utility function for the linear expenditure system given in Exercise 2.2 when maximized subject to $p_1q_1 + p_2q_2 = x$ gives demand functions

$$p_1q_1 = p_1\gamma_1 + \beta_1(x - p_1\gamma_1 - p_2\gamma_2)$$

$$p_2q_2 = p_1\gamma_2 + (1 - \beta_1)(x - p_1\gamma_1 - p_2\gamma_2)$$

By illustrating the indifference curves, explain why, if γ_1 and γ_2 are positive, the Lagrange multiplier technique will always work. What happens if γ_1 and γ_2 are both negative? Repeat your derivation using the utility function given in Exercise 2.2(b), and show that only the value of the Lagrange multiplier changes in the solution. Solve the n good problem, maximize $\Pi(q_k - \gamma_k)^{\beta_k}$ subject to $\Sigma p_k q_k = x$.

2.8. For the utility function of Exericse 2.3(a) sketch indifference curves and budget constraints for various values of α and values of p_2/p_1. Show that only q_1 is bought if $(p_2/p_1) > \alpha$ while only q_2 is bought if $(p_2/p_1) < \alpha$. Write down the maximum attainable utility in each case. What happens if $(p_2/p_1) = \alpha$? Why does the Lagrange multiplier technique not work in this case and what will happen if you try it? Discuss the type of goods for which this model might be a realistic description.

2.9. Derive the demand functions *graphically* for the utility function of Exercise 2.3(d). What goes wrong with the Lagrange multiplier technique in this case? Discuss the economic application of this model.

2.3 Cost minimization and the cost function

In production theory, we are quite used to the concept of a cost function; this has output and prices of inputs as arguments and tells us the minimum cost of producing a given output at those input prices. It is obvious enough that a firm choosing inputs to maximize output for any given input cost must be producing that output in the cheapest possible way. Cost minimization and output maximization for a fixed outlay are merely alternative ways of characterizing productive efficiency. Consumer choice can be handled in exactly the same way. In §2.2, we formulated the consumer's problem as maximizing utility for a given outlay, or cost. The solution to this problem will produce some utility level *u*, say. We can then reformulate the problem as one of selecting goods to minimize the outlay necessary to reach *u*; clearly, the vector of commodities chosen must in both cases be the same.

These two problems are often described as "dual" problems. Let us compare them systematically.

Original problem:

Maximize $u = v(q)$ subject to $p \cdot q = x$

Dual problem:

Minimize $x = p \cdot q$ subject to $v(q) = u$

where we have adopted the dot-product symbol $p \cdot q$ to denote $\Sigma p_k q_k$. We can use the same *u* and *x* in both problems since in the dual problem we simply use the *u* which is the maximum attainable in the original problem. Further, since utility maximization and cost minimization must imply the same choice, the outlay in the original problem must be the cost minimum in the dual problem. In both problems, optimal values of *q* are being sought. In the original problem, as we have seen, the solution is the set of *Marshallian* demands $g(x, p)$. In the dual problem, however, the determining variables are *u* and *p*, not *x* and *p*, so now we get the same solutions but as a function of *u* and *p*. These new cost-minimizing demand functions, which we write $h(u, p)$, are known as *Hicksian* or *compensated* demand functions. They tell us how *q* is affected by prices with *u* held constant, hence the name "compensated." Since the two solutions coincide, we have, $i = 1, \ldots, n$

$$q_i = g_i(x, p) = h_i(u, p) \tag{3.1}$$

Each of these solutions can be substituted back into their respective problems to give, first, maximum attainable utility and, second, minimum attainable cost. Hence,

$$u = v(q_1, q_2, \ldots, q_n) = v\left[g_1(x, p), g_2(x, p), \ldots, g_n(x, p)\right] = \psi(x, p) \quad (3.2)$$

$$x = \Sigma p_k h_k(u, p) = c(u, p) \qquad \qquad . \qquad (3.3)$$

The function $\psi(x, p)$, defined by (3.2) is the maximum attainable utility given prices p and outlay x. It is known as the *indirect utility function* and could be defined alternatively by

$$\psi(x, p) = \max_q [v(q); p \cdot q = x] \qquad (3.4)$$

that is, as the solution to the original problem. The function $c(u, p)$, defined by (3.3), is the minimum cost of attaining u at prices p and is known as the *cost function*. Clearly, as the solution to the dual problem it can be defined by

$$c(u, p) = \min_q [p \cdot q; v(q) = u] \qquad (3.5)$$

The cost function and the indirect utility function are intimately related. Since $c(u, p) = x$, we can rearrange or "invert" to give u as a function of x and p and this will give $u = \psi(x, p)$. Similarly, inversion of $u = \psi(x, p)$ leads directly to $x = c(u, p)$. The two functions are simply alternative ways of writing the same information. Figure 2.8 summarizes the structure so far.

The next step is to reverse Figure 2.8 and show how, starting from the cost or indirect utility functions, we can go back to demands and to preferences. First, however, we need to know more about these functions, particularly the cost function. We list five properties.

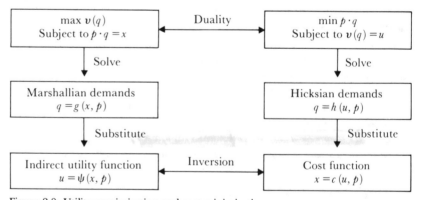

Figure 2.8. Utility maximization and cost minimization.

Property 1. The cost function is homogeneous of degree one in prices, or formally, for a scalar $\theta > 0$

$$c(u, \theta p) = \theta c(u, p) \tag{3.6}$$

This is a direct consequence of (3.5); if prices double, twice as much outlay is required to stay on the same indifference curve.

Property 2. The cost function is increasing in u, nondecreasing in p, and increasing in at least one price.

These properties follow immediately from the nonsatiation axiom. At given prices the consumer has to spend more to be better off, while increases in prices require at least as much expenditure to remain as well off.

Property 3. The cost function is *concave* in prices.

Figure 2.9 illustrates a cross section of a cost function, as a single price changes, with utility and the other prices held constant. Concavity implies that as prices rise, cost rises no more than linearly. This is essentially because the consumer *minimizes* costs, rearranging purchases in order to take advantages of changes in the structure of prices. Formally, a scalar function $f(z)$, defined on some vector z, is said to be *concave* if, for $0 \le \theta \le 1$,

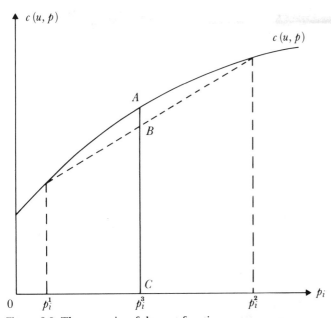

Figure 2.9. The concavity of the cost function.

$$f[\theta z^1 + (1 - \theta)z^2] \geq \theta f(z^1) + (1 - \theta)f(z^2) \tag{3.7}$$

Strict concavity occurs if we replace the $\geq$ by $>$. (Compare with Figure 2.9 where $AC > BC$.) To show that concavity holds for the cost function, consider two price vectors p^1 and p^2 and let $p^3 = \theta p^1 + (1 - \theta)p^2$. Let q^3 be the optimal choice of commodities when prices are p^3 and utility is u. Hence, by (3.3), $c(u, p^3) = \Sigma q_k^3 p_k^3 = \theta \Sigma q_k^3 p_k^1 + (1 - \theta)\Sigma q_k^3 p_k^2$ by the definition of p^3. But q^3 is not necessarily the cost minimizing bundle for u at either p^1 or p^2 so that $c(u, p^1) \leq \Sigma q_k^3 p_k^1$ and $c(u, p^2) \leq \Sigma q_k^3 p_k^2$. Hence, substituting in the expression for $c(u, p^3)$

$$c(u, \theta p^1 + (1 - \theta)p^2) \geq \theta c(u, p^1) + (1 - \theta)c(u, p^2) \tag{3.8}$$

which establishes concavity. It is important to note that this proof does not depend in any way on convexity of preferences; the cost function is concave for all the types of indifference curves illustrated in Figures 2.3 to 2.6.

Property 4. The cost function is continuous in p, and the first and second derivatives with respect to p exist everywhere except possibly at a set of specific price vectors (in technical language, this set is "of measure zero").

Mathematically, Property 4 follows from Property 3, the concavity of the cost function. We shall not attempt to provide proofs here but the geometry of cost functions, which illustrates these properties, will be taken up in §2.5. Meanwhile, Property 4 leads into Property 5:

Property 5. Where they exist, the partial derivatives of the cost function with respect to prices are the Hicksian demand functions, that is,

$$\frac{\partial c(u, p)}{\partial p_i} \equiv h_i(u, p) = q_i \tag{3.9}$$

To prove this, consider an arbitrary vector of prices p^0, a utility level u, and the corresponding vector of optimal choices q^0. Then for any other price vector p, define the function $Z(p)$ by

$$Z(p) = \sum_k p_k q_k^0 - c(u, p) \tag{3.10}$$

Since q^0 is not necessarily optimal for p, the cost of q^0 at p must always be at least as great as the cost of the optimal vector at p, that is, $c(u, p)$. Hence Z is always greater than or equal to zero. But we know that Z is equal to zero, or attains its minimum, when p is equal to p^0. Hence, if the derivative exists at p_0,

$$\frac{\partial Z(p^0)}{\partial p_i} = q_i^0 - \frac{\partial c}{\partial p_i}(u, p^0) = 0 \tag{3.11}$$

which since p^0 is quite arbitrary, proves (3.9).

The derivative Property 5, sometimes known as Shephard's Lemma, is of central importance to the approach adopted here; in terms of Figure 2.8, it allows us to move back from any known cost function to the cost-minimizing demands that underlie it. Practically, however, we also wish to be able to generate Marshallian demands from the cost function, and this is a straightforward matter of substitution. In (3.9), quantities are a function of u and p; (3.4), the indirect utility function, gives u in terms of x and p so that substitution of $u = \psi(x, p)$ in the Hicksian demands gives q in terms of x and p, that is, the Marshallian demands. Formally,

$$q_i = h_i(u, p) = h_i[\psi(x, p), p] = g_i(x, p) \tag{3.12}$$

Of course, we can do the whole thing in reverse, starting with the Marshallian demands and using the cost function to express x in terms of u and p. Hence

$$q_i = g_i(x, p) = g_i[c(u, p), p] = h_i(u, p) \tag{3.13}$$

Coupled with the derivative property, these equations establish the link between the bottom and middle rows of Figure 2.8. It is also convenient to rewrite the derivative property so as to allow us to go from the indirect utility function to the Marshallian demands. Since the cost and indirect utility functions are inverses, we have the identity

$$\psi[c(u, p), p] \equiv u \tag{3.14}$$

Differentiating with respect to p_i with u held constant and using the chain rule gives

$$\frac{\partial \psi}{\partial x} \cdot \frac{\partial c}{\partial p_i} + \frac{\partial \psi}{\partial p_i} = 0 \tag{3.15}$$

so that, from the derivative property

$$q_i = g_i(x, p) = -\frac{\partial \psi / \partial p_i}{\partial \psi / \partial x} \tag{3.16}$$

Although we shall make more frequent use of the original form (3.9), (3.16), known as *Roy's identity* is sometimes more convenient. Equations (3.9), (3.16), (3.12), and (3.13) are summarized in Figure 2.10 below. The route we shall

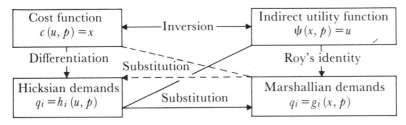

Figure 2.10. Demand, cost, and indirect utility functions.

use most often is that which starts from the cost function and has the following steps: (1) differentiate $c(u, p)$ to get the Hicksian demands, (2) invert $c(u, p)$ to get $\psi(x, p)$, and (3) substitute $\psi(x, p)$ into $h_i(u, p)$ to get the Marshallian demands.

Note on ordinality

The development of this section has followed the production analogy in that utility u has been treated analogously to output. But output is measurable in natural units while utility is not. How then are we to interpret u in, for example, $c(u, p)$, and what happens if $v(q)$ is subjected to a monotone increasing transform $f(\ )$, say? First, note that $c(u, p)$ should be thought of as "the minimum cost of reaching the indifference curve labeled u." Indifference curves are unaffected by transforms of $v(q)$ so that by moving to $f\{v(q)\}$ we simply relabel the identical indifference curves. The cost of reaching any given curve remains unchanged. If a curve is labeled u before the transform, and $f^{-1}(\ )$ is the inverse function of $f(\ )$, then $f^{-1}(u) = v(q)$ so that the new label is $f^{-1}(u)$. Hence, for the cost function, we have $x = c\{f^{-1}(u), p\}$ instead of $c(u, p)$. Since $c(u, p)$ and $c(f^{-1}(u), p)$ will always represent the same preferences and hence the same behavior, the derivative of $c(u, p)$ with respect to u, the "marginal cost of utility" or its reciprocal, the "marginal utility of total expenditure" are not objectively measurable. This is in contrast to the theory of production where returns to scale are discussed through the dependence of costs on output. In the consumer context, it is the derivatives of $c(u, p)$ with respect to p rather than u that are important. In practical work, although the ordinality of utility must always be borne in mind, a convenient choice of $f(\ )$, sometimes called the "cardinalization" or "normalization," will often simplify the algebra and the same normalization must be maintained while moving from one cell to another in Figures 2.8 and 2.10. See also Exercises 2.12 and 2.15 below.

Exercises

2.10. Use the utility function $u = q_1^{1/2} q_2^{1/2}$ and the budget constraint $x = p_1 q_1 + p_2 q_2$ to fill in the boxes in Figures 2.8 and 2.10, checking out each of the arrowed operations. Extend to $u = q_1^\beta q_2^{1-\beta}$ and $u = (q_1 - \gamma_1)^\beta (q_2 - \gamma_2)^{1-\beta}$.

2.11. Extend Exercise 2.10 to the full *linear expenditure system*, which has utility function $u = \Pi(q_k - \gamma_k)^{\beta_k}$, $\Sigma\beta_k = 1$. Check that the Marshallian demands, Hicksian demands, cost function, and indirect utility functions are as follows

$$p_i q_i = p_i \gamma_i + \beta_i (x - \Sigma p_k \gamma_k) \tag{3.17}$$

$$p_i q_i = p_i \gamma_i + \beta_i \beta_0 u \, \Pi p_k^{\beta_k} \tag{3.18}$$

$$x = \Sigma p_k \gamma_k + u \beta_0 \Pi p_k^{\beta_k} \tag{3.19}$$

$$u = (x - \Sigma p_k \gamma_k) / \beta_0 \Pi p_k^{\beta_k} \tag{3.20}$$

where β_0 is a function of the parameters only.

2.12. Repeat Exercise 2.10, using $u^* = \frac{1}{2} \log q_1 + \frac{1}{2} \log q_2$ and show that all the previous formulae hold provided u is replaced by e^{u*}.

2.13. It is often convenient to derive budget shares directly from the cost and indirect utility functions. Show that w_i is given as a function of u and p by

$$w_i = \partial \log c(u, p) / \partial \log p_i \tag{3.21}$$

and as a function of x and p by

$$w_i = \frac{\partial \log \psi / \partial \log p_i}{\Sigma\, \partial \log \psi / \partial \log p_k} \tag{3.22}$$

2.14. Using the cost function given by

$$\log c(u, p) = \Sigma \alpha_k \log p_k + u \Pi p_k^{\beta_k} \tag{3.23}$$

derive the Hicksian demands, the indirect utility function and the Marshallian demands. What conditions should the parameters α_k and β_k satisfy? What determines whether goods are luxuries or necessities?

2.15. Preferences are represented by $u = v(q)$ and a cost function, indirect utility function, and demands are calculated. If the same preferences are now represented by $u^* = f[v(q)]$ for a monotone increasing function $f(\ )$, show that $c(u, p)$ is replaced by $c[f^{-1}(u^*), p]$, $u = \psi(x, p)$ by $u^* = f[\psi(x, p)]$ and $h(u, p)$ by $h[f^{-1}(u^*), p]$. By substitution, check that the Marshallian demands are unaffected. Use these results to write down the appropriate forms of equations (3.17) to (3.20) taking natural logarithms for $f(\ )$.

2.4 Properties of demands

We are now in the position to provide a reasonably general characterization of the properties of Hicksian and Marshallian demand functions. Two of these we have seen already but restate for completeness:

Property 1: Adding up. The total value of both Hicksian and Marshallian demands is total expenditure, that is,

$$\Sigma p_k h_k(u, p) = \Sigma p_k g_k(x, p) = x \tag{4.1}$$

Property 2: Homogeneity. The Hicksian demands are homogeneous of degree zero in prices, the Marshallian demands in total expenditure and prices together, that is, for scalar $\theta > 0$,

$$h_i(u, \theta p) = h_i(u, p) = g_i(\theta x, \theta p) = g_i(x, p) \tag{4.2}$$

The Hicksian demands, by (3.9) are the derivatives of a function homogeneous of degree one and hence are homogeneous of degree zero; given the indifference curve, relative prices are all that is required to determine demand.

Property 3: Symmetry. The cross-price derivatives of the Hicksian demands are symmetric, that is, for all $i \neq j$

$$\frac{\partial h_i(u, p)}{\partial p_j} = \frac{\partial h_j(u, p)}{\partial p_i} \tag{4.3}$$

Since $h_i(u, p)$ is $\partial c(u, p)/\partial p_i$, $\partial h_i/\partial p_j$ is $\partial^2 c/\partial p_j\partial p_i$. Similarly, $\partial h_j/\partial p_i$ is $\partial^2 c/\partial p_i\partial p_j$, so that the only difference between the two lies in the order of the double differentiation. Young's theorem asserts that, given that continuous derivatives exist, this does not matter and hence the two derivatives are identical. We discuss the economic interpretation of (4.3) after the next property.

Property 4: Negativity. The n-by-n matrix formed by the elements $\partial h_i/\partial p_j$ is negative semidefinite, that is, for any n vector ξ, the quadratic form

$$\sum_i \sum_j \xi_i\xi_j \, \partial h_i/\partial p_j \leq 0 \qquad\qquad (4.4)$$

If ξ is proportional to p, the inequality becomes an equality and the quadratic form is zero. (In the technical language of linear algebra, the matrix is negative semidefinite with the price vector lying in its null-space.) This result also follows from the derivative property; $(\partial h_i/\partial p_j)$ is the matrix of second derivatives of a concave function $c(u, p)$ and so is negative semidefinite. The fact that $\Sigma_j p_j \, \partial h_i/\partial h_j$ is zero follows from homogeneity, see Exercise 2.18. (The result (4.4) can easily be generalized to the case of finite changes in prices, see Exercise 2.22.)

For convenience, we denote $\partial h_i/\partial p_j$ by s_{ij} so that the matrix is denoted by S. This is the *substitution matrix* or *Slutsky matrix* of compensated price responses; by Properties 3 and 4 it is symmetric and negative semidefinite. The negativity property places a whole series of inequality restrictions on the elements of S; most importantly, the diagonal elements must be nonpositive; for all i,

$$s_{ii} \leq 0 \qquad\qquad (4.5)$$

Thus, an increase in price with utility held constant must cause demand for that good to fall or at least remain unchanged. As for the wider restrictions embodied in (4.4), imagine that some "compound" products are sold that contain other goods in fixed proportions and that these compounds are priced according to the prices of their ingredients. These products too must then have nonpositive own-price substitution effects in terms of their own (compound) prices. Expression (4.5) is, of course, the "law of demand," that compensated demand functions can never slope upwards, which was discussed at the end of §2.2. The difference here is that (4.5) comes only from the concavity of the cost function which, as already emphasized, holds true whether preferences are convex or not. Negativity has thus nothing to do with the curvature of the indifference curve in Figure 2.7; if the indifference curves were concave to the origin, demands would be at corner solutions, not at the point of tangency.

There are thus four basic general properties of demand functions: they add up, they are homogeneous of degree zero in prices and total expenditure, and their compensated price responses are symmetric and form a negative semidefinite matrix. Adding up and homogeneity were discussed in Chapter 1, where we saw that they are consequences of the specification of a linear budget constraint. Symmetry and negativity, on the other hand, derive from the existence of consistent preferences. The symmetry of a consumer's substitution matrix is not easily interpreted without reference to the cost function; it is hardly intuitively obvious why, for example, a compensated penny per pound increase in the price of apples should increase the number of bars of soap bought by a number equal to the number of more pounds of apples bought consequent on a compensated penny per bar increase in the price of soap. Nevertheless, symmetry is a guarantee of and test of the consumer's consistency of choice; without it, inconsistent choices are made. Negativity comes from the concavity of the cost function which, as we have seen, is entirely due to the fact that costs are minimized, or equivalently, that utility is maximized. Symmetry and negativity are thus the direct consequences of Axioms 1 to 5, of rational choice.

If symmetry and negativity are to be made testable, it must be possible to observe the substitution matrix S, and this means defining it in terms of the Marshallian demands. This is done through the *Slutsky equation* which comes from differentiating the last identity in (3.13) with respect to p_j, and using (3.9),

$$s_{ij} = \frac{\partial h_i}{\partial p_j} = \frac{\partial g_i}{\partial x} q_j + \frac{\partial g_i}{\partial p_j} \tag{4.6}$$

The last term $\partial g_i / \partial p_j$ is the uncompensated price derivative of q_i with respect to p_j. To "compensate" this, an amount q_j (the derivative of minimum cost with respect to p_j) times $\partial g_i / \partial x$ (the total expenditure derivative of q_i) must be added on. Everything on the right-hand side of (4.6) relates to magnitudes that can, in principle, be directly observed by varying x and p. Hence S can be calculated experimentally and symmetry and negativity are empirically testable; the results of such tests are reported in Chapter 3. Note finally that S is unaffected by transformations of the utility function since the right-hand side of (4.6) is unaffected by them.

Equation (4.6) is usually written with $\partial g_i / \partial p_j$ on the left-hand side so that the uncompensated price response is decomposed into a substitution effect of the price change (s_{ij}) and an income effect of the price change ($-q_j \partial g_i / \partial x$). This is a taxonomic device that allows us to use our knowledge of the substitution matrix and of expenditure responses to derive properties of the observable uncompensated derivatives. For example, we can see that the law of demand does not necessarily apply to the Marshallian demand functions. Although s_{ii}, the own-price compensated response, is negative, it is possible, although unlikely, for this to be outweighted by a *positive* income effect. Thus, a positive price derivative can only occur if the good is highly inferior and if it is purchased in large quantities; such a good is known as a *Giffen good*. Note that while all Giffen goods must be inferior, the converse is not true; indeed inferior goods are quite common while Giffen goods are extremely rare, if in fact they exist at all. The substitution matrix also has an important function in classifying goods into complements and substitutes. Although other definitions are possible, Hicks' (1936) definition is now standard (although see §2.7). By this, goods i and j are *complements* if s_{ij} is negative; they are *substitutes* if s_{ij} is positive. This conforms reasonably well to normal usage of the words; if coffee becomes relatively more expensive, we may buy more of a substitute (tea) and less of a complement (cream); nevertheless, it is well to be cautious in expecting technical definitions to conform to one's preconceptions (see Exercise 2.16).

Exercises

2.16. Draw the right-angle indifference curves for the utility function of Exercise 2.3(d). Solve the demand functions graphically and show that $c(u, p) = u(\alpha_1^{-1}p_1 + \alpha_2^{-1}p_2)$. Show that $S = 0$. Would you regard goods 1 and 2 as complements in this case?

2.17. Goods 1 and 2 are often said to be "perfect" substitutes if the utility function takes the form $u = q_1 + \alpha q_2$, $\alpha > 0$ (see Exercise 2.3(a)). Show that $c(u, p) = u$ min $(p_1, p_2/\alpha)$. Show that $S = 0$ except when $p_1 = p_2/\alpha$ at which point it is not defined. Discuss the economics of the example.

2.18. Euler's theorem for a function $f(x)$ homogeneous of degree r is that $\Sigma x_k \, \partial f/\partial x_k = rf(x)$. Use the homogeneity of degree zero of the Hicksian demands to prove that, for $i = 1, \ldots, n$,

$$\sum_k s_{ik}p_k = 0 \qquad\qquad\qquad\qquad (4.7)$$

2.19. Use (4.7) and (4.5) to prove that not all goods can be complements. Relate this to Exercise 2.16.

2.20. Use the Slutsky equation (4.6) together with Cournot aggregation [Chapter 1, equation (2.5)] to show that for $i = 1, \ldots, n$,

$$\sum_k s_{ki}p_k = 0 \qquad\qquad\qquad\qquad (4.8)$$

2.21. Show that symmetric and homogeneous demand functions satisfy Cournot aggregation automatically, that symmetric demands which aggregate   are   automatically homogeneous, and that, with only two goods, homogeneous demands which add up are symmetric.

2.22. Let q^1 and q^0 be cost-minimizing vectors associated with u and p^1 and p^0, respectively. Show that concavity of $c(u, p)$ implies that

$$c(u, p^1) \le c(u, p^0) + q^0 \cdot (p^1 - p^0)$$
$$c(u, p^0) \le c(u, p^1) - q^1 \cdot (p^1 - p^0)$$

Hence show that

$$(q^1 - q^0) \cdot (p^1 - p^0) \le 0 \qquad\qquad\qquad\qquad (4.9)$$

and interpret this as a generalization of (4.4).

2.5* Duality in the theory of demand

The methods we have adopted in the previous two sections are usually referred to as "duality" methods. Many readers will be familiar with duality
from the theory of mathematical programming, and although duality in demand theory is closely related it is worth looking at it separately. The essential
feature of the duality approach is a *change of variables*. Preferences and utility
are originally defined over quantities as the objects of choice and this "primal"
formulation, of u in terms of q, is certainly the most obvious. However, if the
consumer faces a linear budget constraint, the position of this, as defined by p
and x, determines maximum attainable utility so that, in terms of economics, u
can just as well be regarded as a function of x and p (the *indirect* utility function) or, inversely, x regarded as a function of u and p (the cost function). The
manipulations of §2.3 transferred the information about preferences contained in *direct* form in $v(q)$ into the *indirect* forms $\psi(x, p)$ and $c(u, p)$. With
linear budget constraints and with convexity, preferences can be represented
by their tangents at each point.

   Figure 2.11 illustrates the relationship between indifference curves in
terms of quantities and indifference curves in terms of prices in the case

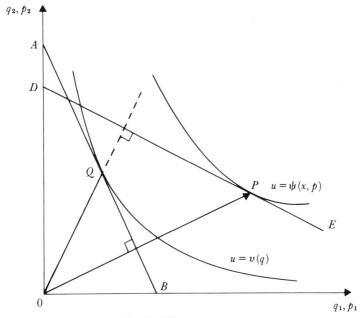

Figure 2.11. Primal and dual indifference curves.

where tangency conditions hold. Exercise 2.23 discusses other important cases. The axes in Figure 2.11 measure both prices and quantities. Start from $0Q$ representing some arbitrary quantity vector, and draw the indifference curve $u = v(q)$ through Q. By the tangency condition (2.4) the price ratio p_1/p_2 that will cause Q to be chosen is given by $(\partial v/\partial q_1)/(\partial v/\partial q_2)$, the slope of the indifference curve at Q. AB is this tangent. The line $0P$ is now drawn perpendicular to AB; the price coordinates of any point on this line are in the ratio established by the slope of AB. The point P along $0P$ is chosen so that $0P \cdot 0Q = x$, so that in price coordinates $0P$ is the price vector which, given x, causes $0Q$ to be chosen. Then P must lie on the indifference curve in price coordinates which has the same utility level as $v(q)$, i.e., u, and this curve can be drawn in by varying Q along $v(q)$ letting P trace out $\psi(x, p)$. (Note that "higher" indifference curves in q-coordinates are "lower" indifference curves in p-coordinates since $v(q)$ is increasing in q while $\psi(x, p)$ is decreasing in p.)

This procedure works in a precisely analogous way in reverse, from P to Q. Starting at P, the tangent DE has slope $(\partial\psi/\partial p_1)/(\partial\psi/\partial p_2)$ which, by Roy's identity (3.16), is q_1/q_2. Switching to quantity coordinates, $0Q$ is drawn perpendicular to DE with length such that $0Q \cdot 0P = x$. This, of course, leads us back to the original $0Q$. By this technique, if we know the indirect utility function (or, equivalently, the cost function) we can "recover" the direct utility function. The original information contained in $v(q)$ is simply recoded in the dual functions $\psi(x, p)$ and $c(u, p)$; carrying out the recoding once more takes us back to where we started. Duality is thus a mirroring technique; two reflections restore the original image. This retrievability of preferences from the dual (under conditions to be taken up below) is the "fundamental theorem of duality" sometimes referred to as the Shephard-Uzawa duality theorem.

It is at this point that convexity of preferences has an important role since, if preferences are nonconvex, the nonconvex portions will not be "encoded" in the dual and will thus not be recoverable from it. Figure 2.12 illustrates this using the cost function; the original indifference curve in Figure 2.12(a) has a nonconvex portion between A and B. Faced with a linear budget constraint, no consumer will choose points along the indifference curve between A and B since either A or B (or both) offer the same utility level at lower cost. The cost function simply "loses" the information between A and B. In Figure 2.12(b), $c(u, p)$ is illustrated as a function of p_1 with u and p_2 fixed; low values of p_1 give purchases to the right of B, while as p_1 increases, B is reached at $p_1 = \alpha p_2$ and this has identical cost to A. The points A and B are thus compressed into C in the cost function, where there will be a kink. When preferences are recreated from $c(u, p)$ the nonconvex portion between A and B will be "bridged" by a straight line giving a new indifference curve shown with shading in the diagram. Of course, provided the budget constraint is linear, the new indiffer-

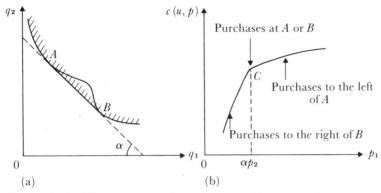

Figure 2.12. Indifference curve and cost function with nonconcavity.

ence curve is operationally equivalent to the old; only economically irrelevant information has been lost.

The fundamental theorem of duality allows us to go beyond the use of $\psi(x, p)$ and $c(u, p)$ as alternative representations of some known utility function $v(q)$. We can now start from the dual representation. In particular, any function $c(u, p)$ that satisfies Properties 1 to 4 of §2.3 can be regarded as a cost function representing some underlying preference ordering; it is not necessary to be able to write down $v(q)$ explicitly. In empirical work, this is of the greatest convenience since it is relatively easy to think of specifications for $c(u, p)$ and $\psi(x, p)$ and they can be converted immediately into demand functions simply by differentiation or use of Roy's identity. This contrasts very favorably with the frequent intractability of the first-order conditions (2.4) and (2.5).

In theoretical work, the theorem allows a straightforward solution of a problem that, historically, caused a great deal of difficulty. This is the question of the circumstances under which we can go back to preferences from a given set of demand functions, usually called the *integrability problem*. Formulated in terms of direct utility and Marshallian demands, it is far from obvious how to get from the latter to the former. However, once the maximization of utility is treated as the minimization of costs, it becomes apparent that the demand functions must allow integration into a concave, linearly homogeneous function, that is, into a cost function. It is for this reason that the conditions needed for demand functions to be consistent with preferences are known as integrability conditions. In practice, of course, the demand functions that we are presented with are Marshallian demand functions, with total expenditure and prices as arguments, while it is Hicksian demand functions that are the derivatives of the cost function and that integrate into it. This complicates the problem slightly but does not alter it in principle. Consider that we have discovered, perhaps empirically, a system of Marshallian demand functions

$$q_i = g_i(x, p) \tag{5.1}$$

We put these into the correct form by using (3.9) to write

$$\frac{\partial c}{\partial p_i} = g_i(c, p) \tag{5.2}$$

which is a system of partial differential equations to be solved for c as a function of p. Since we are integrating along an indifference surface, utility is unchanged during the integration and will emerge as a constant of integration. However, not all such systems of partial differentiatial equations have a solution. Indeed some must not since otherwise we should be able to get back to preferences from any demand functions whatever including those that do not satisfy adding up, homogeneity, symmetry, and negativity.

The mathematical conditions to ensure that a function $c(\ )$ exists which solves (5.2) turn out to be for all i, j

$$\frac{\partial g_i}{\partial x} g_j(x, p) + \frac{\partial g_i}{\partial p_j} = \frac{\partial g_j}{\partial x} g_i(x, p) + \frac{\partial g_j}{\partial p_i} \tag{5.3}$$

see, for example, Hurwicz and Uzawa (1971). But the left-hand side of (5.3) is simply the formula for calculating the substitution term s_{ij}, see the Slutsky equation (4.6). Hence (5.3) tells us that the symmetry of the Slutsky substitution matrix is the fundamental integrability condition of demand theory. Of course, for the function that results from integration to be a proper cost function, it must be concave and linearly homogeneous. This will happen automatically if the substitution matrix is not only symmetric but also negative semidefinite and satisfies the singularity property (4.7). So we come full circle. Utility maximization results in demand functions that add up, are homogeneous of degree zero, and have symmetric, negative semidefinite compensated price responses. Conversely, demand functions that add up, are homogeneous of degree zero, and have symmetric, negative semidefinite compensated price responses are integrable into a consistent preference ordering. This is a remarkable and useful result. It is empirically important because it tells us that the conditions derived in §2.4 are not simply consequences of utility maximization, they are the *only* consequences of utility maximization. If we apply them empirically, we are effectively applying a preference ordering. Conversely, if they are tested empirically and found to hold good, a preference ordering can be said to exist.

Exercises 2.25 to 2.27 below provide particular examples of integration and of integrability conditions.

Exercises

2.23. Construct the diagrams corresponding to Figure 2.11 for the following utility functions:

(a) $u = q_1 q_2$
(b) $u = \min\{q_1, \alpha q_2\}$, $\alpha > 0$
(c) $u = q_1 + \alpha q_2$ $\alpha > 0$
(d) The utility function illustrated in Figure 2.5.

2.24. Generalizing from the previous exercise, show that "flats" in the direct indifference curves turn into "kinks" in the indirect indifference curves, while "kinks" turn into "flats." (This illustrates the important proposition that strict quasi concavity of the utility function implies differentiability of the cost function, while differentiability of utility functions implies strict quasi concavity of the cost function. Concavity and differentiability are thus dual properties.)

2.25. The general homogeneous linear expenditure system is written, for parameters α_i and β_{ij},

$$p_i q_i = \alpha_i x + \sum_j \beta_{ij} p_j \tag{5.4}$$

Calculate the substitution matrix and show that it is symmetric if, for parameters γ_j, and defining the Kronecker δ by $\delta_{ij} = 1$, $i = j$, $= 0$, $i \neq j$,

$$\beta_{ij} = \delta_{ij} \gamma_i - \alpha_i \gamma_j \tag{5.5}$$

[Much harder: show that the condition is also necessary for symmetry. Answers in Stone (1954b), Deaton (1975a, pp. 22–24), or Phlips (1974, pp. 122–3).]

2.26. Substituting (5.5) into (5.4) gives the linear expenditure system

$$p_i q_i = p_i \gamma_i + \beta_i (x - \Sigma p_j \gamma_j) \tag{5.6}$$

Write (5.6) in the form (5.2), substitute $z = c - \Sigma p_j \gamma_j$, and show that $z = u \Pi p_k^{\beta k}$ for some constant u solves the equation. Hence derive the linear expenditure system cost function (3.19).

2.27. Using $w_i = \partial \log c / \partial \log p_i$, show that the demand functions

$$w_i = \alpha_i + \beta_i (\log x - \Sigma \alpha_k \log p_k) \tag{5.7}$$

integrate into (3.23). (Hint: follow the steps of Exercise 2.26.)

2.6* Revealed preference theory

One of the preoccupations of much modern work on the theory of individual choice has been the attempt to base the theory on a minimal set of axioms. In this vein is Samuelson's (1938) idea of deducing properties of demand from a simple and direct axiom on behavior. Given that the consumer always makes some choice, then we may say that a bundle of q^0 is revealed as preferred to an alternative q^1 if q^0 is chosen in a situation where q^1 is available. The axiom then says that no choice should also reveal q^1 as preferred to q^0. One immediate implication of this is a version of "the law of demand" or, more generally, of the negativity condition discussed in §2.4.

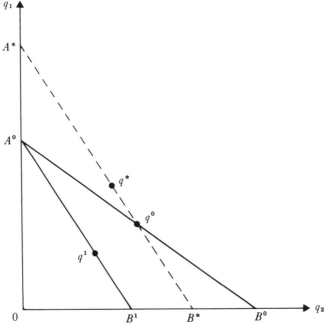

Figure 2.13. Revealed preference and the law of demand.

Consider the budget constraint A^0B^0 in Figure 2.13 on which q^0 is chosen. When p_2 increases, A^0B^0 moves to A^0B^1 and q^1 is chosen. Suppose now that the consumer receives a compensating budget increase so that the old bundle q^0 is again just attainable on the new constraint A^*B^*. In this new situation, the axiom tells us that points along A^*B^* to the right of q^0 will *not* be chosen, since q^0 has been revealed preferred to all such points by the original choice with constraint A^0B^0. Consequently, q^*, the optimal choice on A^*B^*, must either be q^0 or lie to its left, that is, $q_2^* \leq q_2^0$. In other words, a compensated increase in p_2 cannot increase the demand for q_2. If q^* is different from q^0, it cannot have been available in the original situation so that $\Sigma p_k^0 q_k^* \geq \Sigma p_k^0 q_k^0$. Since both q^* and q^0 lie on A^*B^*, $\Sigma p_k^1 q_k^* = \Sigma p_k^1 q_k^0$ and combining this with the previous inequality we have the general form of the negativity condition in this context,

$$\Sigma(p_k^1 - p_k^0)(q_k^* - q_k^0) \leq 0 \tag{6.1}$$

This form of the negativity condition is closely analogous to that given in §2.4, see in particular, (4.9). The only real difference is that here we are working with compensation defined with reference to the original bundle q^0 rather than with reference to the original indifference curve u^0. In fact the former concept of compensation is that used by Slutsky (1915), and we could define Slutsky compensated demand functions $q_i = g_i (\Sigma p_k q_k^0, p)$ rather than the Hicksian compensated functions $q_i = h_i(u, p)$. Considering a variation from the base price vector p^0, Slutsky's original formulation of the Slutsky equation was

$$
\left. \frac{\partial q_i}{\partial p_j} \right|_{\text{compensated}} = \frac{\partial g_i(x^0, p^0)}{\partial x} q_j^0 + \frac{\partial g_i(x^0, p^0)}{\partial p_j}
\tag{6.2}
$$

This equation has the same form as (4.6) and if the indifference curve through q^0 exists, it is identical to (4.6) when expressed, as in (6.2), in terms of infinitesimal changes.

So far we have discussed revealed preference with only two alternative bundles. A strong version of the axiom of revealed preference asserts that if q^0 is *indirectly* revealed preferred to q^1 through some transitive chain of comparisons through intermediate bundles, then q^1 cannot be revealed preferred to q^0. Samuelson conjectured, and Houthakker (1950) showed the validity of the conjecture, that this strong axiom implies the existence of a utility function. More recent research has established equivalences between various versions of the revealed preference axiom and properties of demand functions, for example, symmetry without negativity, negativity without symmetry, and so on. These results and related work show that some restrictions on demand functions can be obtained without going as far as assuming the existence of a utility function. For our purposes, however, we prefer the simplicity of working with utility functions and we shall relax the transitivity axiom only in specific instances, for example, by allowing habit formation to change tastes over time.

Exercises

2.28. Are indifference curves with "flats," see Figure 2.5, consistent with the (weak) axiom of revealed preference?

2.29. In Figure 2.13, illustrate the decomposition of the effect on demand of a price change into an income and substitution effect. Contrast with the decomposition in Figure 2.7.

2.30. Revealed preference is often taken to impute welfare significance to one choice over another. Discuss the validity of this procedure in the context of the assurance game in §1.1. See also Sen (1973a).

2.7** The distance function

Section 2.5 emphasizes the duality between the direct and indirect representations of preferences, between the direct and indirect utility functions. However, just as it is frequently more convenient to use not the indirect utility

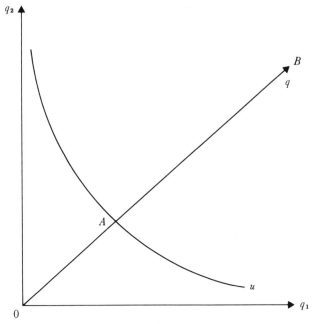

Figure 2.14. The distance function.

function, but the cost function, so is it convenient to have an inverse representation of the direct utility function. This is called the *distance function*. To define it, see Figure 2.14. $0B$ represents some arbitrary quantity vector q, u is an arbitrary indifference curve; these bear no relation to one another and, in particular, it is *not* assumed that u and q satisfy $u = v(q)$. The distance function $d(u, q)$, defined on u and q, is the amount by which q must be divided in order to bring it on to the indifference curve u. Geometrically, $d(u, q)$ is the ratio $0B/0A$. Mathematically, we can define $d(u, q)$ implicitly by

$$v[q/d(u, q)] = u \tag{7.1}$$

If q happens to lie on u so that $u = v(q)$, B and A coincide so that $d(u, q) = 1$. Hence

$$u = v(q) \quad \text{if and only if} \quad d(u, q) = 1 \tag{7.2}$$

so that we can always write the direct utility function in the equivalent implicit form. Note the analogy here with the indirect representation of preferences; $u = \psi(x, p)$ if and only if $c(u, p) = x$. We can think of $d(u, q)$ for fixed u as a scalar measure of the magnitude of q relative to u; in this sense, it is a quantity index number as we shall see in Chapter 7. Note too that, like the cost function, the value of the distance function is entirely *ordinal;* it is defined with reference to an indifference surface, not with respect to any given cardinalization of preferences.

To relate the distance function to the cost function, return to Figure 2.14 and write λ for the value of $d(u, q)(= 0B/0A$ in the diagram). Write $q^* = q/\lambda$ $(q^* = 0A)$ so that

$$d(u, q)c(u, p) = \lambda c(u, p) \leq \lambda q^* \cdot p = q \cdot p \tag{7.3}$$

for *any* u, p, and q. The inequality in (7.3) is from the definition of the cost function; q^* yields u but is not necessarily the cheapest way of doing so at p. We can rewrite this to give, for all u, p, and q, $d(u, q) \leq q \cdot p/c(u, p)$. However, if, given u and q, we choose a p that will cause the consumer to buy a vector proportional to q, the inequality in (7.3) becomes an equality. Hence, there exists at least one vector p for which $d(u, q) = q \cdot p/c(u, p)$. For any other p, this ratio is greater than $d(u, q)$. Hence

$$d(u, q) = \min_p[p \cdot q; c(u, p) = 1] \tag{7.4}$$

Now recall (3.5), the definition of the cost function. If we substitute (7.2) into this, we can rewrite the definition as

$$c(u, p) = \min_q[q \cdot p; d(u, q) = 1] \tag{7.5}$$

Clearly, then, the cost function and distance function are dual to one another. Equation (7.4) becomes (7.5) if we write q for p and c for d while, if we do so again, we return to (7.4). These two expressions are at the heart of the fundamental duality theorem discussed in §2.5 and they tell us how to move back and forward from direct to indirect representation of preferences. If we start from $v(q)$, equation (7.1) will yield $d(u, q)$. The cost function can then be evaluated by (7.5), which is just a rewritten form of the "dual problem" in §2.3, while with the cost function, (7.4) gives a "dual dual problem" that takes us back to the original problem. This can also be given an economic interpretation; just as the cost function seeks out the optimal quantities given u and p, the distance function finds the prices that will induce a vector proportional to q to be bought that achieves u. Although, initially, the distance function may not seem the obvious way to represent preferences, the relationship between (7.4) and (7.5) represents in its clearest form the basic duality result in consumer theory.

The reader can now work through the properties of the cost function in §2.3 to prove exactly analogous properties for $d(u, q)$. It is increasing in q and *decreasing* in u (the only difference), it is homogeneous of degree one in q, it is continuous and almost everywhere differentiable in q [provided (7.4) is used as a definition in which case $d(u, q)$ will represent "bridged" preferences if preferences are nonconvex], and it is concave in q. There is also a derivative property, proved in an exactly analogous way, which states

$$\frac{\partial d(u, q)}{\partial q_i} \equiv a_i(u, q) = \frac{p_i}{x} \tag{7.6}$$

The functions $a_i(u, q)$ are dual to the Hicksian demand functions and by (7.6) are compensated *inverse* demand functions; for any quantity vector and any utility level, they give the prices as a proportion of x that will cause u to be reached at a point proportional to q. Figure 2.15 illustrates. Given q and u, the $a_i(\quad)$'s are the reciprocals of the endpoints of the tangent plane to u at the point where it is cut by q. Note that the $a_i(\quad)$ functions, like the $h_i(\quad)$'s are homogeneous of degree zero in q and this can be seen in the diagram where the length of q is irrelevant. Since inverse demands frequently find their uses when prices either do not exist or are artificially distorted, the p_i's given by (7.6) are often referred to as the *shadow prices* associated with u and the ray q. They can also be thought of as the amounts of money an individual on u at proportions q is willing to pay for one more unit of each of the goods. If we wish to associate these prices directly with some q (instead of going through

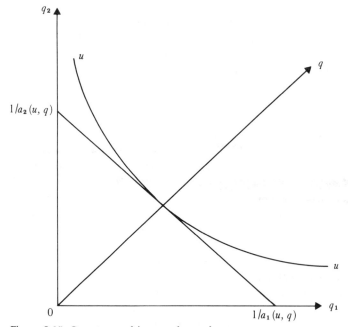

Figure 2.15. Compensated inverse demands.

u), $u = v(q)$ can be substituted in (7.6) to give *uncompensated inverse demand functions* $b_i(q)$, say,

$$p_i/x = a_i(u, q) \equiv a_i[v(q), q] \equiv b_i(q) \tag{7.7}$$

Finally, just as the second differentials of $c(u, p)$ form a symmetric negative semidefinite matrix, so too do the second differentials of $d(u, q)$. This matrix is known as the *Antonelli matrix A*, that is,

$$a_{ij} = \partial^2 d/\partial q_i \, \partial q_j \tag{7.8}$$

These terms describe the effect on the price the consumer is prepared to pay for one more unit of good i if an increase in q_j is imposed upon him given that he is maintained on the same indifference curve. Hicks (1956) has also suggested using a_{ij} to class complements and substitutes; he calls i and j "*q*-complements" if $a_{ij} > 0$ and "*q*-substitutes" if $a_{ij} < 0$. These definitions are *not* equivalent to the original definitions given in §2.4 (these are "*p*-substitutes" and "*p*-complements" in Hicks' terminology) but also are intuitively reasonable. Coffee and cream are complements if consumers are prepared to pay more for cream when they are moved along the same indifference curve but are given relatively more coffee; vice versa for substitutes. The *q*-definitions turn out to be extremely useful in the analysis of commodity taxation, see for example Deaton (1979).

As we might expect, the Antonelli and Slutsky matrices are intimately related to one another. In fact, they satisfy the following symmetrical relationships:

$$S = xSAS \tag{7.9}$$

$$A = xASA \tag{7.10}$$

so that they are *generalized inverses* of one another. These relationships and others related to them can often be used to simplify expressions involving the substitution matrix. Proofs of (7.9) and (7.10) are outlined in Exercise 2.34.

Exercises

2.31. In Figure 2.14, relabel the *q*-axes as *p*-axes, take *0B* as an arbitrary price vector and *u* an arbitrary indifference curve in price space. Define a dual distance function $d*(u, p)$ by

$$\psi[1, p/d*(u, p)] = u$$

Prove that $d*(u, p) = c(u, p)$.

2.32. The constant elasticity of substitution *CES* utility function is defined by

$$u = (\Sigma \alpha_k q_k^{-\rho})^{-1/\rho} \tag{7.11}$$

Derive the distance function and show that the cost and distance functions have identical functional forms.

2.33. A utility function is said to be *homothetic* if for some function $\theta(\ )$ homogeneous of degree one, $u = f\{\theta(q)\}$ where $f(\ )$ is monotone increasing. Show that

$$d(u, q) = f^{-1}(u)/\theta(q) \tag{7.12}$$

Using (7.5), show that

$$c(u, p) = f^{-1}(u)\phi(p) \tag{7.13}$$

where $\phi(p)$ is homogeneous of degree one.
2.34.

(a) Define $r_i \equiv p_i/x$ and show that $c(u, p) = xc(u, r)$. Hence show that $s_{ij}^* = xs_{ij} = \partial^2 c(u, r)/\partial r_i \partial r_j$.

(b) Write $\nabla c(u, r)$ for the vector whose ith element is $\partial c/\partial r_i = h_i(u, r)$ and $\nabla d(u, q)$ for $\partial d/\partial q_i = a_i(u, q) = r_i$. Show that

$$h(u, r) \equiv h\{u, \nabla d[u, \nabla c(u, r)]\}$$

$$a(u, q) \equiv a\{u, \nabla c[u, \nabla d(u, q)]\}$$

Hence, using the chain rule of partial differentiation, prove (7.9) and (7.10).

(c) Show that

$$q_i/d(u, q) \equiv h_i[u, \nabla d(u, q)]$$

Hence, prove

$$S*A = I - qr' \quad \text{and} \tag{7.14}$$

$$AS* = I - rq' \tag{7.15}$$

where a prime denotes transposition.

Bibliographical notes

It would take us a great deal of space to document the historical development of the ideas in this chapter and such discussion is outside our scope (and competence). The early history of utility is documented in Schumpeter (1954) and more succinctly in Stigler (1950). The duality approach adopted here, although it has a long history, has only been fully appreciated by the profession very recently. The papers by Diewert (1974a, 1978) offer a more advanced treatment than that given here, cover production theory by the same approach, and give a comprehensive set of references and historical notes. We mention only some of the earliest pioneers of duality, in particular the names of Antonelli (1886, translated 1971), Hicks (1946), Hotelling (1935, 1938), Konüs (1924, 1939), McKenzie (1956–7), Roy (1942), Samuelson (1947), Shephard (1953), Ville (1946), and Wold (1943–4, 1953). In several of these cases, the development is in the production rather than demand context but the differences are slight. The more conventional approach, based on first-order conditions, is usually associated particularly with the names of Slutsky (1915), Hicks (1936), Hicks and Allen (1934) and Samuelson (1947).

On supplementary reading, Baumol (1977) offers an elementary introduction to duality in consumer theory. Layard and Walters (1978) go somewhat further, but their treatment is less detailed than that given here. For more advanced treatments of duality in particular, Fuss and McFadden (1978) – in the production context – and Diewert (1981) are to be recommended. The former contains proofs of many of the propositions in this chapter, for example, that the cost function is continuous and differentiable, and of the fundamental duality theorem.

On more specific points, the proof of the differential property of the cost function we owe to (unpublished notes by) Gorman. Dixit (1976) shows that in constrained optimization problems, the optimized value of the objective generally has an analogous differential property. The integrability problem is discussed at a reasonably simple level by Samuelson (1950b) and in greater mathematical detail in the symposium edited by Chipman, Hurwicz, Richter, and Sonnenschein (1971). An empirical example is given by Deaton (1978). On revealed preference, apart from the classic papers by Samuelson (1938) and Houthakker (1950), Ville (1946, trans. 1951–2) showed that a differential version of the revealed preference axioms was equivalent to the symmetry condition on demand functions. Interested readers may again refer to the symposium edited by Chipman et al., especially Chapter 2 (Richter) and Chapter 3 (Hurwicz and Richter). The distance function also has a long history with important papers by Debreu (1951) and Malmquist (1953); a relatively straightforward exposition is given in Deaton (1979) which goes further than §2.7 above.

CHAPTER 3

The theory at work

The theory presented in Chapter 2 offers a framework within which we can attempt to organize and interpret the data. This chapter begins this task by discussing the application of four particular models, each of which seeks to describe the way in which total outlay is spent. These illustrations not only show how the theory can be made specific but also allow us to check the usefulness of the theory in empirical work. In this context, various problems and difficulties are pointed out as we go along. The identification of them provides much of the motivation for the extensions and modifications of the theory that are begun in the next three chapters.

Although we make no attempt to provide a historical survey of applications of demand theory, the studies will be presented in rough chronological order. This is natural, since there has been a steady growth in the degree to which practical work has based itself upon the theory. In §3.1, we shall discuss some of the methodology and results in Stone's justly famous 1954 monograph, *The Measurement of Consumers' Expenditure and Behaviour.* This study follows the precedent of virtually all studies up to that time in modeling commodity demands individually, equation by equation, so that, if necessary, the functional form can be varied and special explanatory variables introduced. This approach has the great advantage of flexibility and is undoubtedly the best way of modeling the demand for an individual commodity in isolation. However, as far as the theory is concerned, only the homogeneity restriction has any immediate consequence for a single equation so that, in these early studies, the theory plays a relatively minor role. When we move on to complete systems of equations, the theory becomes much more directly relevant and the rest of the chapter deals with the application to these models.

Section 3.2 is devoted to the linear expenditure system, the first practical model to be based entirely upon the theory. A more general approach, which tries for the first time to *test* the theory is introduced in §3.3. Here we meet the Rotterdam model and its competitors. Section 3.4 introduces a new model that is an extension of the Working-Leser model of §1.2 and that allows the empirical application of theory at a very general level. Finally, §3.5 gathers together the unsolved problems and difficulties that emerge from the results.

We shall not, in the text, provide any discussion of the econometric methods used to derive the estimates that we discuss. Unless indicated to the contrary, maximum likelihood principles are used since these provide a naturally integrated basis for hypothesis testing and estimation. The bibliographical notes at the end of the chapter give references for readers who wish to follow the technical background to the results.

3.1 Stone's analysis

The early history of empirical demand analysis is marked, not by an attention to theory, but by the extensive use of single equation methodology centered around the measurement of elasticities. Keynes (1933) tells us that Marshall was highly delighted at having discovered the concept of elasticity, and, ever since, Marshall's enthusiasm has been shared by the majority of applied economists. This is not surprising; elasticities are easily understood, they are conveniently dimensionless, and they can be directly measured as the parameters of a regression equation linear in the logarithms of purchases, outlay, and prices. The adding-up problems of such a model (see §1.2) have always been understood but were usually thought to be unimportant since virtually all the early studies considered only a fraction of the total budget. Nor is it particularly crucial in this context to make the careful distinction–which we have emphasized and will continue to emphasize–between income on the one hand and total expenditure, or outlay, on the other. If no attempt is made to satisfy adding up, it is possible to make a more or less pragmatic choice of whichever explanatory variable gives the better fit.

Stone's study (1954a) has its roots in this tradition, but is distinguished from it by the way in which Stone consistently uses the theory to define and modify the equations to be applied to the data. It thus forms a bridge between the old methodology and the new.

Formulation of the model

The starting point for the study is the logarithmic demand function [Chapter 1, equation 2.12)],

$$\log q_i = \alpha_i + e_i \log x + \sum_{k=1}^{n} e_{ik} \log p_k \tag{1.1}$$

where e_i is the total expenditure elasticity, and e_{ik} is the cross-price elasticity of the kth price on the ith demand. Stone wishes to use (1.1) to estimate demand functions for 48 categories of food consumption over the years 1920–38 using British data. With only 19 observations, it is imperative to keep the number of explanatory variables to a minimum (no more than five or so) whereas (1.1) contains 50. Clearly, we need some prior restrictions in order to estimate (1.1) at all. The obvious procedure, that of setting the majority of the cross-price elasticities to zero, is not an attractive one. Price elasticites contain income as well as substitution effects, and while the latter may well be zero for "unrelated goods," there is good reason to suppose the former to be nonzero. Stone solves this problem by decomposing the cross-elasticities according to the Slutsky equation; from Chapter 2, equation (4.6) in elasticity form, we have

$$e_{ik} = e_{ik}^* - e_i w_k \qquad (1.2)$$

where e_{ik}^* is the compensated cross-price elasticity and w_k, as before, is the budget share. Substitution of (1.2) into (1.1) allows us to write

$$\log q_i = \alpha_i + e_i \{\log x - \sum_k w_k \log p_k\} + \sum_{k=1}^n e_{ik}^* \log p_k \qquad (1.3)$$

Note that the expression $\Sigma w_k \log p_k$ can perfectly well be thought of as the logarithm of a *general* index of prices $\log P$, say, so that (1.3) becomes

$$\log q_i = \alpha_i + e_i \log(x/P) + \sum_{k=1}^n e_{ik}^* \log p_k \qquad (1.4)$$

This gives us demand in terms of real expenditure, on the one hand, and "compensated" prices on the other; intuitively, we can see that in going from (1.1) to (1.4), we have gone from Marshallian to Hicksian demand functions, at least approximately. This transformation will appear again in the Rotterdam model, see §3.3, and is explored in Exercise 3.4.

Stone now goes on to enforce the homogeneity restriction; from Chapter 1, equation (2.11) and (1.2) here this can be written

$$\sum_k e_{ik}^* = 0 \qquad (1.5)$$

This can then be used to allow deflation of all prices in (1.4) by the general index P. By (1.5), the following is approximately equivalent to (1.4):

$$\log q_i = \alpha_i + e_i \log(x/P) + \sum_{k \in K} e_{ik}^* \log(p_k/P) \qquad (1.6)$$

Note that the range of summation is restricted to some set K of "close" substitutes and complements. This is now perfectly acceptable since there is no reason not to rule out zero substitution between unrelated goods.

Equation (1.6) is the basis for most of Stone's analysis. However, in order to conserve degrees of freedom, the expenditure elasticities e_i are first estimated from budget studies and the estimated values used as prior information in the estimation of (1.6). Finally, in order to account for steady changes in tastes, Stone introduces a time trend $\theta_i t$, say, and takes the first differences to minimize the effects of serial correlation in the residuals. If Δ is the first-difference operator, the final equation to be estimated is thus:

$$\Delta\,[\log q_i - \tilde{e}_i \log(x/P)] = \theta_i + \sum_{k\in K} e_{ik}^* \,\Delta \log(p_k/P) \tag{1.7}$$

where $\tilde{e}_i$ is the expenditure elasticity estimated from the budget study.

Empirical results

This equation is used to model demand for 48 different goods, in most cases in several variants. The results provide fascinating reading and amply repay detailed study. Table 3.1 reproduces some sample regressions of the form (1.7) for five foods: butter, margarine, cheese, oranges, and bananas.

Note that butter and cheese appear as necessities while margarine is an inferior good. Oranges and bananas both have elasticities below 1 but are rel-

Table 3.1. *Sample results from Stone's analysis of foods. British data: budget surveys, 1937–9, and time series 1920–38*

1. Butter	Income elasticity[a]	0.37 (0.08)[b]
	Own price	−0.38 (0.16)
	Margarine price	0.06 (0.18)
	$R^2 = 0.30$ d.w. = 1.84	
2. Margarine	Income elasticity	−0.16 (0.11)
	Own price	0.06 (0.24)
	Butter price	0.67 (0.20)
	$R^2 = 0.46$ d.w. = 1.39	
3. Cheese	Income elasticity	0.21 (0.08)
	Own price	0.17 (0.11)
	Butter price	−0.60 (0.16)
	Beef and veal price	0.84 (0.23)
	$R^2 = 0.61$ d.w. = 1.74	
4. Oranges	Income elasticity	0.92 (0.17)
	Own price	−1.00 (0.26)
	Fresh green vegetables price	0.53 (0.27)
	Bananas price	0.28 (0.30)
	$R^2 = 0.56$ d.w. = 2.31	
5. Bananas	Income elasticity	0.95 (0.18)
	Own price	−0.62 (0.22)
	Oranges price	−0.41 (0.19)
	$R^2 = 0.48$ d.w. = 1.65	

[a] Stone uses income rather than total expenditure in his regressions. The imposed elasticities are 0.9 of the expenditure elasticities from the budget study.
[b] Estimated standard error.

ative luxuries among the foods. The compensated own-price elasticities for butter, oranges, and bananas are all negative as are those for most of the commodities in the analysis. Note, however, that contrary to the theory, the own-price elasticities for margarine and for cheese turn out to be *positive;* even so, in neither of the cases illustrated is the parameter significantly different from zero. It is also interesting to examine the figures in the table in the light of the Slutsky symmetry restriction [Chapter 2, (4.3)]. In elasticity form this is

$$w_i e_{ij}^* = w_j e_{ji}^* \tag{1.8}$$

Note first that this is contradicted by the fact that, while the butter price appears significantly in the cheese equation, the demand for butter is independent of the price of cheese, presumably because no significant elasticity could be found. The demands for butter and margarine do satisfy the condition, at least approximately; the value share for butter was about ten times that for margarine and $0.06 \simeq 0.67/10$. Oranges and bananas once again give problems; according to the oranges equation, bananas are a substitute for oranges, but according to the bananas equation, the pair are complements. Clearly, if complementarity and substitutability are to be measured in a consistent way, an alternative approach must be adopted.

3.2. The linear expenditure system

We may begin, once again, from the general set of Marshallian demand functions

$$q_i = g_i(x, p) \tag{2.1}$$

If we try to estimate these *without* direct recourse to the theory, we must first select a functional form and having done so, we must measure n total expenditure and n^2 price responses. In §3.1, we saw how Stone faced these problems by using a logarithmic functional form and applying the homogeneity restriction to reduce the number of parameters to be estimated. However, the major increase in degrees of freedom was achieved by deleting most of the compensated cross-price elasticities. The alternative is to impose the theoretical restrictions right from the outset. If adding up, homogeneity, and symmetry are all imposed, the $n^2 + n$ original price and outlay derivatives reduce to $(n - 1)(\frac{1}{2}n + 1)$; for a ten equation system, this represents an extra 56 degrees of freedom. In practice, this may make the difference between being able or not being able to estimate, so that it is not surprising that econometricians have increasingly made use of the theory in this way.

Once again, the crucial study is by Stone (1954b). He begins from a general linear formulation of demand, that is,

$$p_i q_i = \beta_i x + \sum_{j=1}^{n} \beta_{ij} p_j \tag{2.2}$$

and algebraically imposes the theoretical restrictions of adding up, homogeneity, and symmetry. The only form of (2.2) that satisfies these restrictions, see Exercise 2.25, is the *linear expenditure system,*

$$p_i q_i = p_i \gamma_i + \beta_i (x - \Sigma p_k \gamma_k) \tag{2.3}$$

with $\Sigma \beta_k = 1$. The cost function for (2.3) – see Exercise 2.11 – is

$$c(u, p) = \Sigma p_k \gamma_k + u \, \Pi \, p_k^{\beta_k} \tag{2.4}$$

which is concave provided all β_i's are nonnegative and provided x is no less than $\Sigma p_k \gamma_k$ so that $q_i \geq \gamma_i$ for all i. If these restrictions do not hold, $c(u, p)$ is not concave, so that we know (2.3) cannot be derived from constrained utility maximization.

Although there is no requirement that any γ_i be positive, these parameters are often interpreted as minimum required quantities, or subsistence quantities, so that (2.3) has a very simple interpretation. The committed expenditures $p_i \gamma_i$ are bought first, leaving a residual, "supernumerary expenditure" $x - \Sigma p_k \gamma_k$, which is allocated between the goods in the fixed proportions β_i. Hence, apart from the subsistence expenditure $\Sigma p_k \gamma_k$, total outlay is divided in a constant pattern between the commodities. This interpretation is reflected in the structure of the cost function; (2.4) shows a fixed-cost element $\Sigma p_k \gamma_k$, which allows no substitution at all, plus a term that allows utility to be "bought" at a constant price per unit, $\Pi p_k^{\beta_k}$. Since the β's add to unity, this last term can be thought of as a weighted geometric mean of the prices and can thus be thought of as a price index representing the *marginal* cost of living.

The direct and indirect utility functions for the linear expenditure system are, see Exercise 2.11,

$$v(q) = \Pi(q_k - \gamma_k)^{\beta_k} \tag{2.5}$$

$$\psi(x, p) = (x - \Sigma p_k \gamma_k)/\Pi p_k^{\beta_k} \tag{2.6}$$

Equation (2.5) is frequently transformed to the equivalent form $\Sigma \beta_k \log (q_k - \gamma_k)$. The indirect utility form has a clear interpretation in terms of "real expenditure." If the γ's represent subsistence requirements, only $(x - \Sigma p_k \gamma_k)$ is available for discretionary allocation and this is deflated by the weighted geometric mean of prices to give a "real" indicator of welfare.

One of the most striking features of the linear expenditure system is the fact that it has only $2n$ parameters, $(2n - 1)$ of which may be chosen independently. For n larger than 3, this is many fewer than the $(2n - 1) (\tfrac{1}{2}n + 1)$ we know are permitted by the theory, yet the passage from (2.2) to (2.3) has involved no restrictions other than those strictly required. This apparent discrepancy is because the selection of *functional form* is itself restrictive. In Chapter 1, we saw that selection of a constant elasticity functional form meant that only unitary elasticities were allowed if adding up had to be satisfied. The linearity of (2.2) causes less severe problems, but it means that the linear expenditure system is more specialized than might be needed in practice. For example (see Exercises 3.5 and 3.6), differentiation of (2.3) shows that inferiority can only occur for goods with β_i negative; but this violates concavity and, if permitted, would result in the good having a *positive* price elasticity. Similarly, if concavity is to hold, no two goods may be complements; every good must be a substitute for every other good. These restrictions do not mean that the model cannot be applied in practice, only that its application must be restricted to those cases where its limitations are not thought to be serious. Even then, care must be taken in interpreting the results and a careful distinction drawn between properties of the model, imposed a priori, and properties of the data. For example, no one can claim to have "discovered" that goods are substitutes from results obtained using the linear expenditure system.

Although the model, by definition, is linear in the variables, it is not linear in the parameters β and γ. This is hardly a problem today, but in 1954 most computers were people, not machines, and Stone found a simple algorithm that allowed him to estimate the model. If the γ parameters are known, (2.3) is linear in β and vice versa, see Exercise 3.8. Hence, from some arbitrary starting values, it is possible to iterate from β to γ and back until the parameter values stop changing. By modern standards, this method is neither very efficient nor very accurate, but it allowed Stone to apply the model to six groups of goods, again on British data from 1920 to 1938. His results are shown in Table 3.2 along with calculated values for R^2-statistics, expenditure elasticities e_i, and own-price elasticities e_{ii}. In the interwar period, consumers' expenditures in Britain did not consistently trend upwards in the way that they have done since the war, so that the R^2-statistics show a relatively good correspondence between expected and actuals. In more recent studies using postwar data from Britain, America, Belgium, and other countries, the R^2-statistics are inevitably much higher.

The expenditure and price elasticities do not conflict with prior expectations, but note one curious feature. The ordering of commodities in terms of price elasticities is identical to that by expenditure elasticities; indeed, all price elasticities are close to (minus) one-half of expenditure elasticities. The general theory of choice, as developed in Chapter 2, gives no reason to suppose that there should be any close relationship between the two kinds of elasticities. However, the results of Table 3.2 are no accident. As we shall see in Chapter 5, the linear expenditure system belongs to a class of demand models, all of which share the property of approximate proportionality

Table 3.2. *Stone's linear expenditure system results (British data 1920–38)*

	β_i	$\gamma_i{}^a$	R^{2b}	$e_i{}^b$	$e_{ii}{}^b$
1. Meat, fish and dairy	0.12	14	0.94	0.7	−0.4
2. Fruit and vegetables	0.04	3	0.94	0.9	−0.4
3. Drink and tobacco	0.06	10	0.32	0.5	−0.2
4. Household operation	0.23	11	0.66	1.2	−0.6
5. Durable goods and transport	0.30	12	0.94	1.3	−0.7
6. Other expenditure	0.25	15	0.94	1.1	−0.5

[a] γ_i's are measured in units at 1938 prices.
[b] Calculated indirectly from Stone's results.

between price and expenditure elasticities. Unless we have grounds for believing that elasticities *should* be proportional, and there is a good deal of evidence, both a priori and empirical, against such a position, even for broad groups of goods, then we have good reason for considering the linear expenditure system too restrictive and for passing on to more general models.

3.3 Testing the theory

The linear expenditure system was derived by *algebraically* imposing theoretical restrictions on a particular functional form. An obvious alternative is to use the restrictions *statistically;* a general functional form can be estimated with and without restriction, thus testing whether or not the restrictions may be validly imposed. This, of course, defeats the original purpose of the restrictions, the generation of degrees of freedom, so that the method can only be applied to a relatively small number of commodity groups. As far as we are aware, the highest disaggregation of total expenditure that has been successfully attempted in this context is the study of Barten (1969) where 16 groups are used. By contrast, the linear expenditure system can be applied to 40 or more goods, see, for example, Deaton (1975a). Nevertheless, the attempts to test the theory using a relatively coarse disaggregation are of considerable interest in their own right, and, as we shall see in Chapter 5, the analysis can be extended to finer disaggregations if we are prepared to make the assumptions necessary to support "multilevel" budgeting – whereby the group expenditures determined at the first stage can be further allocated using group expenditure and group prices as the determining variables.

The Rotterdam model

The model that has most frequently been used to test the theory was first proposed by Theil (1965) and Barten (1966) and is called, after their then domicile, the Rotterdam model. In many ways, the approach is very similar to Stone's (1954a) method, but instead of working in levels of logarithms, it works in differentials. If we totally differentiate equation (1.1), we may write

$$d \log q_i = e_i d \log x + \sum_j e_{ij} d \log p_j \tag{3.1}$$

but we now make no assumption that the elasticities e_i and e_{ij} are constant. As in the original Stone analysis, the Slutsky decomposition is used to write $e_{ij} = e_{ij}^* - e_i w_j$, for compensated cross-price elasticity e_{ij}^*, so that (3.1) becomes

$$d \log q_i = e_i(d \log x - \Sigma w_k d \log p_k) + \sum_j e_{ij}^* d \log p_j \tag{3.2}$$

which is simply the differential of Stone's equation (1.4). However, as it stands, (3.2) does not readily lend itself to the imposition of symmetry, since, by (1.8), the restrictions also involve the variable budget shares. This can be avoided by multiplying (3.2) by the budget share w_i, so that we have finally

$$w_i d \log q_i = b_i d \log \bar{x} + \sum_j c_{ij} d \log p_j \tag{3.3}$$

where

$$d \log \bar{x} = d \log x - \Sigma w_k d \log p_k = \Sigma w_k d \log q_k \tag{3.4}$$

$$b_i = w_i e_i = p_i \frac{\partial q_i}{\partial x} \tag{3.5}$$

$$c_{ij} = w_i e_{ij}^* = \frac{p_i p_j s_{ij}}{x} \tag{3.6}$$

where s_{ij} is the (i, j)th term of the Slutsky substitution matrix. The first equality in (3.4) is the definition of $d \log \bar{x}$; the second follows from the budget constraint. The quantity $d \log \bar{x}$ should be regarded as an index representing the proportional change in real total expenditure. In Exercise 3.4 below, we show that it can also be regarded as a measure of the change in utility so that, like the Stone equation, (3.3) represents Hicksian demands. Equation (3.5) shows that $b_i = w_i e_i$ is the marginal propensity to spend on the ith good.

Testing the restrictions

Equation (3.3) can be estimated provided the differentials are replaced by finite approximations and provided we are prepared to treat the b_i's and c_{ij}'s as constant parameters. At this point, however, all this may seem a rather circuitous way of repeating Stone's (1954a) analysis. But the somewhat unorthodox appearance of the Rotterdam system is more than compensated for by the simplicity with which its parameters can be related to the restrictions of the theory.

Adding up requires that the marginal propensities to spend on each good sum to unity and that the net effect of a price change on the budget be zero. Taking the latter in the form of equation (4.8) in Chapter 2 and using the definitions of b_i and c_{ij}, we have the adding-up restrictions on the Rotterdam model; for all j

$$\sum_k b_k = 1; \quad \sum_k c_{kj} = 0 \tag{3.7}$$

These are not restrictions that can be tested. Provided the data add up, as they should, (3.4) will hold so that the sum of the dependent variables in (3.3) will equal the first independent variable. In practical work, the discrete approximations to the differentials are usually chosen in such a way as to ensure that this does in fact happen. Consequently, the adding-up equations place no restriction on the explanatory power of the equations; indeed, if ordinary least squares estimation is used, the parameter estimates will automatically satisfy (3.7), see Exercise 1.12.

Homogeneity is another matter. From equation (4.7) of Chapter 2, the Rotterdam model will be homogeneous, if for all j

$$\sum_k c_{jk} = 0 \tag{3.8}$$

This can be imposed and tested equation by equation. The symmetry of the substitution matrix clearly implies that the matrix C be symmetric. Hence, symmetry is simply, for all i and j,

$$c_{ij} = c_{ji} \tag{3.9}$$

Finally, since all prices are positive, C will be negative semidefinite if and only if S is negative semidefinite. Consequently, symmetry and negativity of S can be tested by testing the same restrictions on C. (Note, however, that symmetry, adding up, and homogeneity are not independent, see Exercise 2.21.)

The first tests of homogeneity and symmetry were carried out by Barten (1967 and 1969) using Dutch data covering both prewar and postwar experience. In the earlier study, which distinguished only four broad groups and which used informal testing procedures, Barten found little apparent conflict between his data and the theory. However, the 1969 study is much more detailed, it distinguishes 16 groups, and an explicit maximum likelihood approach is adopted. This approach allows the use of the maximized likelihood values to make formal comparisons between versions of the model embodying different restrictions. Barten estimated (3.3) with the addition of intercept terms to allow for gradual changes in tastes. At the first stage, the equation was estimated without restriction, except, of course, for adding up, which is embodied in the data. Next, the homogeneity conditions (3.8) were applied. This caused a very large drop in the value of the maximized likelihood, much larger than could conceivably have arisen by chance if the data had in fact satisfied homogeneity. Barten thus concludes that, on this data, there was evidence that a proportional change in prices and aggregate expenditure will not leave the pattern of demand unchanged. He then goes on to test symmetry and, once again, finds a conflict between theory and evidence. However, there are technical grounds for doubting the validity of this particular test, see Deaton (1972a), so it may be that, *given homogeneity*, symmetry is not too severe a further restriction. These doubts do not affect Barten's conclusions on homogeneity.

Deaton (1974a) also estimated the Rotterdam model using maximum likelihood methods for a nine group disaggregation of British data from 1900 to 1970, excluding war years. The results are very similar to Barten's; homogeneity of demands is in clear conflict with the evidence, while symmetry as an *additional* restriction is not particularly damaging. Even so, this suggests that a research program based on the use of the theory to generate degrees of freedom is not a promising one. The Rotterdam model succeeds in using symmetry in a general and nonrestrictive way only to find that the much more basic postulate of homogeneity is consistently rejected. On the face of it, this would invalidate even the relatively unsophisticated methodology of Stone's (1954a) study, let alone more advanced techniques based on the Rotterdam or other formulations. We shall return to further discussion of this, but first, it is worth looking positively at the results generated by the Rotterdam model. Since we now have, for the first time, a model that has a substitution matrix estimated subject only to symmetry, it is possible to identify substitutes and complements directly from the estimation. It is also possible to see whether negativity appears to fit the evidence.

Table 3.3 shows the estimates of b, C, and the intercepts from Deaton (1974a) in the symmetric version of the Rotterdam model. Since the C matrix is symmetric, and to avoid crowding, only the lower triangle is shown; standard errors have been suppressed and those estimates which are more than twice their standard errors are marked with asterisks. The final row of the table gives the budget shares w_i in 1963; these can be used to convert the numbers to elasticities from the formula, $e_{ij}^* = c_{ij}/w_i$, see (3.6). They can also be compared with the marginal budget shares b_i in the first column; if the marginal budget share is below the average budget share, the good was a necessity in 1963 and vice versa for luxuries. Hence the table shows food, housing, travel and communication, entertainment, and services as necessities while clothing, fuel, drink and tobacco, and other goods are luxuries. Note, however, that four groups have significant intercept terms; the values shown can be interpreted as the *per annum* change in the budget share w_i, which would take place in the absence of any change in real total expenditure or in relative prices. We can thus see that, over the century, there have been trend

Table 3.3. *Symmetric Rotterdam model: U.K. 1900–70*

	b	C								
		Food	Clothing	Housing	Fuel	Drink & tobacco	Travel & communication	Entertainment	Other goods	Other services
Food	0.1516*	−0.0728*								
Clothing	0.1914*	0.0212	−0.0165							
Housing	0.0747*	0.0105	−0.0270*	−0.0160						
Fuel	0.0997*	0.0024	−0.0035	0.0001	−0.0225*					
Drink & tobacco	0.2140*	0.0107	0.0316*	−0.0045	0.0108*	−0.0622*				
Travel & communication	0.0930*	0.0421*	−0.0255*	0.0200*	−0.0051	−0.0008	−0.0465*			
Entertainment	0.0193*	−0.0140*	0.0140*	0.0022	0.0033	0.0055	0.0008	−0.0194*		
Other goods	0.0769*	−0.0014	0.0102	−0.0012	0.0016	−0.0019	0.0054	0.0013	−0.0086*	
Other services	0.0796*	0.0011	−0.0045	0.0159	0.0130*	0.0107	0.0096	0.0063	−0.0054	−0.0467*
Intercepts		0.0004	−0.0008	0.0011*	−0.0007	−0.0021*	0.0010*	0.0001	0.0002	0.0008*
Value shares		0.284	0.100	0.153	0.053	0.133	0.097	0.033	0.051	0.096

* = estimates that are more than twice their standard errors.

increases in the shares of housing, travel and communication, and services and that these have been largely offset by a trend decrease in the share of the budget going to alcohol and tobacco. These changes are perhaps the most important and obvious shifts in the pattern of demand in Britain in this century and it is sobering to discover that they cannot apparently be explained in terms of changes in real income or price structure. Any attempt to suppress the intercepts, in either this study or the earlier one of Barten, causes an unacceptable fall in the value of the likelihood.

Even so, perhaps the most interesting feature of the Rotterdam model is its ability to model the whole substitution matrix, and we can see the results on the right-hand side of the table. Note that all the diagonal terms are negative, as we should expect. None of the goods is particularly price elastic; the highest compensated own-price elasticities are around $-\frac{1}{2}$. Nor are there many significant cross-price responses. Only 9 out of the 36 off-diagonal terms have t-ratios above 2 and, once again, the implied cross-price elasticities are not particularly large. It is tempting to try to explain the patterns of substitutability and complementarity revealed by the table in terms of relations between the goods, but experience suggests that this is not particularly helpful; it is too easy ex post to justify almost any given result. The reader is nevertheless invited to speculate on whether Table 3.3 is or is not different from what might be expected. One aspect not obvious from the table is whether or not the sign conditions implied by negativity are satisfied in full since more than the negativity of the diagonal terms is required. In fact, the estimated C matrix is not negative semidefinite, but is very nearly so. Negativity implies that all the eigenvalues of C be nonpositive; this is only contradicted by one of the eigenvalues and it is not significantly different from zero. Recent studies, notably that by Barten and Geyskens (1975), have actually enforced the negativity restrictions in the estimation and have not, in general, found any great conflict with the evidence.

Undoubtedly, the Rotterdam model takes us further forward and allows us to estimate parameters and impose restrictions in a way that was not possible before. However, we are still left with the rejections of homogeneity and the question arises as to whether these rejections are specific to the Rotterdam model, being based perhaps on an unhappy approximation or choice of functional form, or whether they are indeed a genuine reflection of reality. Similar tests of the restrictions have been carried out on the double logarithmic model, notably by Byron (1970a, 1970b) who used Barten's data, and here too the results were negative. But this is not decisive. As we saw in §1.2 loglinear models cannot satisfy the theory exactly, so that rejections of homogeneity or symmetry may simply reflect the quality of the approximation rather than any inherent property of the data. Indeed, there is clear evidence of failure of approximation in Byron's work. His data add up by construction yet tests of

Engel aggregation fail and this can only be because of failings of the model, not of the theory.

A similar argument is often directed against the Rotterdam model, for example, by Phlips (1974). This is based on the discovery, originally in unpublished work by McFadden, that, if the theory is true, the Rotterdam model (3.3) cannot have b and C strictly constant unless all total expenditure elasticities are 1, all own-price elasticities are -1, and all cross-price elasticities are 0, see Exericse 3.10. This result occurs, not because the Rotterdam model violates the theory directly, but because the *differential* demand functions (3.3) are only consistent with demand functions in levels, that is, $q_i = g_i(x, p)$, under the stated conditions. Obviously, no one believes that these conditions hold in practice, but we must be extremely careful in assessing the practical relevance of the McFadden result. For example, it is not correct to argue, as does Phlips, that the use of the Rotterdam model to test the theory is an implicit endorsement of unitary elasticities. In the first place, it is perfectly obvious from Table 3.3 and from other studies using the model that the estimated elasticities are very significantly different from unity. In the second place, the argument against the Rotterdam model is valid only for a single consumer whereas, in practice, the model is estimated on aggregate data. As we shall see in Chapter 6, there is no reason to suppose that, in general, there is any stable relation between aggregate demands and aggregate total expenditure even given the validity of the underlying theory. However, as it turns out, in those cases where aggregate demand functions exist, whether or not they satisfy the theory, they are unlikely to give rise to constant b and C parameters as required by the model. So, at best, the Rotterdam model must be regarded as an approximation although it is quite possible that, over quite a wide range, the approximation will be a good one. Nevertheless, we know that the approximation is not globally valid and it may be that true, homogeneous demand functions could best be approximated, over some sample period, by a version of the Rotterdam model that does not satisfy the homogeneity restriction. Intuitively, this may not seem very likely. However, we can think of no way of naturally ruling out such cases, and it is certainly very straightforward to think of artificial cases in which the theory is true but the Rotterdam model is a very poor approximation. For example, if each household behaved exactly according to the linear expenditure system and all had the same tastes, an accurate representation under the Rotterdam system would require the C matrix to vary systematically with total real expenditure, see Exercise 3.9.

Flexible functional forms

Recently, following the important paper by Diewert (1971), a number of researchers have approached the testing problem using what have become

known as "flexible functional forms." The basic method is to approximate the
direct utility function, the indirect utility function or the cost function by
some specific functional form that has enough parameters to be regarded as a
reasonable approximation to whatever the true unknown function may be.
For example, Christensen, Jorgenson, and Lau (1975), in one of their specifications, the "indirect translog model," approximate the indirect utility function by a quadratic form in the logarithms of the price to expenditure ratios,
that is,

$$\dot{u} = \psi(x, p) = \alpha_0 + \sum_k \alpha_k \log\left(\frac{p_k}{x}\right) + \frac{1}{2} \sum_k \sum_j \beta_{kj} \log\left(\frac{p_k}{x}\right) \log\left(\frac{p_j}{x}\right) \qquad (3.10)$$

for parameters α_0, α_k, and β_{kj}. Note that, since $\psi(x, p)$ is homogeneous of degree zero, no restriction is implied by using the ratios of p to x rather than the
variables themselves. Since (3.10) can be regarded as a second-order Taylor
approximation to any arbitrary utility function, the authors argue that if the
data do not correspond to the demand functions derived from (3.10) (by
Roy's theorem in this case), then demand theory must be false. Such indeed is
the result. The authors conclude on an examination of American consumption from 1929–72 and without qualification that "Our results . . . make possible an unambiguous rejection of the theory of demand." This unambiguous
statement is false. There is no reason to suppose that utility functions are exactly "translogarithmic" either for individual consumers or in aggregate so
that (3.10) will be an approximation and, like all approximations, will be more
or less accurate. It can only be *guaranteed* to be accurate in the locality of some
point, at particular values of the price-income ratios. But the price-income
ratios are not constant over any given sample, indeed it would be impossible
to estimate the model if they were. Consequently, as far as testing the theory is
concerned, a rejection with the translog model is exactly on a par with rejections from the Rotterdam or loglinear models; we cannot know whether the
hypothesis is false or whether the approximation is inaccurate. What is impressive, however, is the uniformity of the results. The Rotterdam, loglinear,
and translog models all make different approximations and yet all obtain the
same result; the restrictions of the theory do not hold, at least on aggregate
data. There is a large number of reasons why this might be so and we shall list
some of the most important in the final section of this chapter.

Returning briefly to the methodology of flexible functional forms, note that
although it is not true that they can stand in for *any* utility function, they nevertheless provide an important way of generating *particular* utility functions,
cost functions, or demands. The indirect and direct translog forms (for the
latter, see Exercise 3.12) are not, in our view, particularly attractive members
of the class. The demand functions from (3.10) are complicated and clumsy to
estimate while the direct translog model is usually estimated under the practi-

cally nonsensical assumption that, for all goods, prices are determined by quantities rather than the other way round. In the next section, we attempt to remedy these defects by proposing a model that, although as general as the translog, is much simpler to use. As we shall see in Chapter 6, it also has great advantages when we come to consider explicitly aggregation over households. It will also give us some further insights into the validity or otherwise of the theory.

3.4* A new model of demand

In §1.2, we estimated Engel curves using a model proposed by Working and Leser. This model relates the value shares to the logarithm of total expenditure, that is,

$$w_i = \alpha_i + \beta_i \log x \tag{4.1}$$

To use this model for time-series analysis, we must extend the model to include the effects of prices. Clearly, the parameters α and β can be made functions of prices in a large number of different ways. As a first step, note that a cost function defined by

$$\log c(u, p) = a(p) + ub(p) \tag{4.2}$$

where $a(p)$ and $b(p)$ are functions of prices, always gives rise to demands of the form (4.1). (Check using $w_i = \partial \log c / \partial \log p_i$.)

For reasons that will become apparent, choose

$$a(p) = \alpha_0 + \sum_k \alpha_k \log p_k + \tfrac{1}{2} \sum_k \sum_\ell \gamma_{k\ell}^* \log p_k \log p_\ell \tag{4.3}$$

$$b(p) = \beta_0 \Pi p_k^{\beta_k} \tag{4.4}$$

where α, β, and γ^* are parameters. It can easily be checked that, for $c(u, p)$ to be homogeneous in p

$$\sum_1^n \alpha_k = 1, \quad \sum_k \gamma_{k\ell}^* = \sum_\ell \gamma_{k\ell}^* = \sum_1^n \beta_k = 0 \tag{4.5}$$

If (4.3) and (4.4) are substituted into (4.2), the budget shares w_i can be derived from $\partial \log c / \partial \log p_i = w_i$, which gives, after substitution for u,

$$w_i = \alpha_i + \sum_j \gamma_{ij} \log p_j + \beta_i \log(x/P) \quad \text{Marshallian} \tag{4.6}$$

where P is price index defined by

$$\log P = \alpha_0 + \Sigma \alpha_k \log p_k + \tfrac{1}{2} \sum_k \sum_\ell \gamma_{k\ell} \log p_k \log p_\ell \tag{4.7}$$

and the parameters γ are defined by

$$\gamma_{ij} = \tfrac{1}{2} (\gamma_{ij}^* + \gamma_{ji}^*) = \gamma_{ji} \tag{4.8}$$

The model defined by (4.6) to (4.8) is the AIDS (almost ideal demand system) of Deaton and Muellbauer (1980).

Note first that the model preserves the generality of both Rotterdam and translog models. Equation (4.6) can be thought of as a first-order approximation to the general unknown relation between w_i, log x, and the log p's. Like the Rotterdam model, the theoretical restrictions on (4.6) apply directly to the parameters. *Adding up* requires, for all j,

$$\sum_k \alpha_k = 1, \quad \sum_k \beta_k = 0, \quad \sum_k \gamma_{kj} = 0 \tag{4.9}$$

Homogeneity is satisfied if and only if, for all j,

$$\sum_k \gamma_{jk} = 0 \tag{4.10}$$

while *symmetry* is satisfied provided

$$\gamma_{ij} = \gamma_{ji} \tag{4.11}$$

Clearly, (4.9) to (4.11) are all implied by utility maximization; (4.9) and (4.10) follow from (4.5), which is required for homogeneity of $c(u, p)$, while (4.11) follows from (4.8). However, unrestricted estimation of the model (4.6) will only automatically satisfy the adding-up restrictions so that the AIDS once more offers the opportunity of testing homogeneity and symmetry by imposing (4.10) and (4.11). Note that the matrix whose elements are the γ_{ij} is *not* required to be negative semidefinite; the negativity conditions are satisfied if the matrix C defined by

$$c_{ij} = \gamma_{ij} + \beta_i\beta_j \log(x/P) - w_i\delta_{ij} + w_iw_j \tag{4.12}$$

is negative semidefinite (δ_{ij} is the Kronecker delta that is unity if $i = j$ and zero otherwise).

The most interesting feature of (4.6), from an econometric viewpoint, is that it is very close to being linear. Apart from the expression P, which involves the parameters (4.6), like the unrestricted Rotterdam system, can be estimated equation by equation using ordinary least squares. As to P, the restrictions on α and γ ensure that (4.7) defines P as a linearly homogeneous function of the individual prices. In many practical situations, where prices are relatively collinear, P will thus be approximately proportional to any appropriately defined price index, for example, that used by Stone, the logarithm of which is given by $\Sigma w_k \log p_k$. Such an index can be calculated directly before estimation so that (4.6) becomes straightforward to estimate, a situation which is in sharp contrast to the estimation of the translog models.

The β parameters of the AIDS determine whether goods are luxuries or necessities. With $\beta_i > 0$, w_i increases with x so that good i is a luxury. Similarly, $\beta_1 < 0$ for necessities. The γ_{ij} parameters measure the change in the ith *budget share* following a unit proportional change in p_j with (x/P) held constant. Note this does not imply that either the corresponding compensated or uncompensated cross-price elasticity is zero, see Exercise 3.13. It might, however, still be possible to use the γ_{ij} parameters like the e_{ij}^*'s in the original Stone model, setting to zero cross effects between relatively unrelated goods.

We do not have sufficient space here to discuss in full the results of estimating the model, see Deaton and Muellbauer (1980). Instead, we confine ourselves to a discussion of the results most relevant to the main themes of this chapter. Table 3.4 gives the relevant results for the test of homogeneity on postwar British annual data from 1954–74. These are based on a version of (4.6) in which the index P in (4.7) is approximated using $\log P = \Sigma w_k \log p_k$ in order to avoid the inherent nonlinearities. The first two columns give the R^2 and Durbin-Watson statistics for the unrestricted model. These are repeated for the homogeneous version in columns three and four. The final column gives an F-test for the validity of the single restriction for each equation; the relevant critical values are 4.84 for a significance level of 5 percent, or 9.65 for a significant level of 1 percent. Note first the *very* high values of R^2 for both versions; the dependent variables here are value shares that are much more difficult to predict than quantities or expenditures. For comparison, if the linear expenditure system is fitted to the same data, also in value share form, the R^2 for group 8 is -0.16! However, the F-ratios in the last column show that for four of the groups, the drop in R^2 is very much larger than is to be expected by chance if we are to believe in the truth of homogeneity. So, once again we must reject homogeneity, at least for food, clothing, housing, and transport. Here again, with a new model and new data the result reappears. The table contains one other very interesting piece of evidence. For every commodity group where homogeneity is unacceptable by the F-ratio, its imposition leads to a sharp drop in the Durbin-Watson statistic. In other words, the imposition of homogeneity generates positive serial correlation in the residuals. This suggests the converse proposition, that the rejection of homogeneity may be caused by an inappropriate specification of the dynamics of behavior. For example, if the model is differenced and intercepts allowed on the differenced equations, the F-statistics for homogeneity are much reduced although the inhomogeneity for food and for transport and communication remains. This suggests that time trends and possibly lagged dependent variables are omitted variables in the static model and that the price coefficients are biased by their omission. It is also likely that price expectations are more important, at least in the short run, than is generally supposed in demand analysis. Indeed, in Chapter 12 we shall argue that mistaken expectations about the prices of individual commodities can have important consequences for the aggregate consumption function, consequences that involve the abandonment of homogeneity. But this is a topic that is still subject

Table 3.4. *Tests of homogeneity on British data 1954–74*

	Unrestricted		Homogeneous		Test
	R^2	d.w.	R^2	d.w.	$F_{1,11}$
1. Food	0.999	2.33	0.998	1.74	19.4
2. Clothing	0.984	2.29	0.955	1.55	20.3
3. Housing	0.999	1.89	0.992	1.29	82.8
4. Fuel	0.883	2.25	0.870	2.03	1.2
5. Drink & tobacco	0.969	2.96	0.969	2.93	0.2
6. Transport & communication	1.000	2.24	0.992	1.36	171.6
7. Other goods	0.885	1.92	0.880	1.91	0.5
8. Other services	0.843	2.27	0.788	1.98	4.0

to research and controversy, and we have not, as yet, evolved a fully satisfactory model to explain both the phenomena studied here and those in the aggregate consumption function. Here are some fascinating puzzles awaiting solution. The model was also used to test the symmetry condition (4.11). The imposition of this led to a further but less sharp drop in likelihood especially when the model was estimated in first differences. Hence, on these data, it is unclear whether we must reject symmetry as a restriction beyond homogeneity. In the end, then, we are left with the same result that Barten found in his 1969 paper. We have looked at different models, each embodying different approximations, and these have been fitted to different data sets from several countries, but the same conclusions have repeatedly emerged. Demand functions fitted to aggregate time series data are not homogeneous and probably not symmetric.

3.5 An assessment

What general conclusions can we draw from the body of work discussed in this chapter? If the final aim of demand analysis is the establishment of a "correct" set of demand functions, complete with well-defined and precisely estimated elasticities, then we are some way from perfection. It is generally apparent from all the studies that the responsiveness of individual demands to total outlay is relatively easy to measure, and expenditure elasticities are usually established with some precision. As in budget studies, these are in most cases different from 1 so that there are well-defined luxuries and necessities. Which commodities fall into which group depends on the particular data used, but the classification rarely offends against the commonsense usages of the terms. Price elasticities, particularly cross-price elasticities, are more difficult to obtain. Even so, there is fairly consistent evidence, from the

Rotterdam model and the AIDS, that own-price elasticities are (absolutely) less than unity, at least at the sort of levels of commodity disaggregation which have been adopted here. We would expect that as more detailed commodities are distinguished and the range of potential substitutes widens price responses will be larger. Indeed, there is some evidence of this in Stone's original study, although the very high price elasticities that might be expected to arise in the presence of virtually perfect substitutes show no signs of being present. Further, there is *some* evidence of a weak association between price and expenditure elasticities. This has nothing to do with the linear expenditure system for which such results are automatic, but it is based upon wider observation in more general models. For example, the tendency is apparent in both Tables 3.1 and 3.3 and is fairly widespread in the rest of Stone's results as well as in other applications of the Rotterdam model. Such a result presumably arises from the observation that necessities tend to have few substitutes while luxuries have many.

The measurement of cross-price elasticities on time-series data seems to be a generally difficult task. In the 1954 study, Stone found clear evidence of interrelations of this sort and several of his parameter estimates appear to be quite robust. But, as was pointed out, there are clear conflicts between Stone's results and theoretical preconceptions. Attempts to correct them lead to models such as the Rotterdam system which, in the form examined here, can only deal with broad groups of goods. It is not perhaps surprising that, at this level of commodity aggregation, well-determined and credible cross-price effects are few and far between. It does not even seem possible to find a robust classification of substitutes and complements.

As far as forecasting is concerned, it must depend on the validity of the whole approach of this chapter; but given this view, the final model we discussed fits the past very well, is very easy to reestimate on new data, and, provided nonsignificant parameter estimates are set to zero, it is likely to predict well. Even so, like all the general models, it suffers from lack of degrees of freedom; and if this is overcome by imposing restrictions, we come back to the basic contradiction between these restrictions and the data. Note too that there is evidence of dynamic misspecification and that, given the importance of intercepts in the Rotterdam and AIDS first-differences models, there are important explanatory variables other than prices and total outlay.

At the methodological level, more has been learned. Both the advantages and disadvantages of Stone's original methodology can be seen and it is clear that, apart from the use of the logarithmic functional form, modeling detailed commodity demands is best done within a single equation context. We shall show in Chapter 5 how this approach can be extended to deal with small subsystems of demand functions. The overrestrictiveness of the linear expenditure system is also clear, and the model provides an important object lesson in the way that measurement can be seriously affected by unperceived theoretical restrictions built into it. The Rotterdam, translog, and AIDS models demonstrate that quite general systems can be built and estimated, at least over broadly defined groups of commodities. But these models produce a conflict with the theory. The restrictions of homogeneity and symmetry, basic to the assumptions of a linear budget constraint and the axioms of choice, are consistently rejected by the data.

In assessing this outcome, it must be recognized that in nearly all of this work, the theory is used in a highly cavalier fashion. It is called upon when convenient, ignored when inconvenient, and relatively little attention is paid to the problems of moving from theoretical abstraction to empirical reality or to the questions of which variables the theory applies to and which it does not. In this book, it would, in some ways, have been more intellectually satisfying to deal with these problems before looking at the evidence. That we did not have to do so reflects the lack of attention paid to them in the applied literature so that it is possible to describe the bulk of empirical work without reference to anything but the most basic theory. It is our view that a careful transition from theory to application is a fundamental prerequisite of sound econometric work, and we find much current empirical work profoundly unsatisfying because of the lack of such a basis. We believe that many of the problems encountered so far can be resolved by careful theoretical analysis and that better models have higher explanatory power. But it is much more than a question of finding models that fit well. The real challenge is one of intellectual honesty; we must construct models that are fundamentally credible as representations of the behavior and phenomena we are trying to understand. We shall conclude this chapter with a list of topics that have not been satisfactorily dealt with so far and that we believe are basic to an understanding of consumer behavior. In subsequent chapters, we shall take up these topics in detail.

The first problem relates to aggregation over commodities. In the theory of Chapter 2, there were simply n commodities, with n conveniently left as an algebraic abstraction. In reality, there are literally millions of commodities, and it must be clear from this chapter that econometric analysis can only hope to deal with numbers of commodities which are minute by comparison. It is thus necessary to deal, not with individual commodities, but with groups of commodities. The theory that allows us to do this and the necessary assumptions are by no means trivial and are part of the material of Chapter 5.

The second problem is potentially even more serious. All the studies referred to here treated aggregate data as if they had related to a single consumer. There is, as we shall see in Chapter 6, no general reason to suppose that this is valid. Even so, it often appears as though models that ignore aggregation phenomena fit as well as those that explicitly allow for them. This has been used by many authors as a basis for arguing that aggregation is unimportant. This is a position with which we fundamentally disagree. There are many problems for which aggregation is unimportant, but many more for which its correct treatment is at the basis of a satisfactory theoretical and empirical analysis. In Chapter 6, we shall discuss aggregation problems and theory in general terms, but the same considerations will play a vital role in the analysis of index numbers in Chapter 7, of social choice and economic inequality in Chapter 9, of labor supply in Chapter 11, of purchases of durable goods in Chapter 13, and at several other points. We believe that the confounding of the aggregate with the individual is as dangerous as it is pervasive, and much of the rest of this book is devoted to explaining why.

The third problem concerns labor supply, saving, and the definition of total expenditure. It is obviously untrue that total expenditure is given exogenously and must be spent. In Chapters 5, 11, and 12, we shall give justifications for making this assumption, but we shall also argue that it is unlikely to hold in practice. Individual expenditures are as much a determinant of the total as the other way round. A similar argument applies to the exogeneity of total *income*. Most consumers have some measure of control over the time they spend at work and a good deal more over the effort, skill, and education they bring to it. Income is thus a choice variable, and so may be affected by the prices of commodities, especially those which are specifically complementary to, or substitutable for leisure. Even when there is no choice, for example, when a worker is constrained to work a 40-hour week in a job where his salary is independent of his effort and ability, changes in circumstances of work may well affect consumption independently of income. A man put on short-time work with full salary is likely to spend his unchanged budget differently. We shall take up these issues in more detail in Chapter 11.

Fourth, empirical studies of the type discussed in this chapter are notable for the lack of special treatment for durable goods. In some cases, these are treated simply as a category like any other; sometimes they are removed altogether and treated as savings. Neither alternative is obviously satisfactory and both would require justification. Durable goods are indivisible, they have high unit cost, they last through more than one period, their consumption and their purchase are obviously not the same thing, and they are bought infrequently. All of this calls for a rethinking of how the theory of choice applies to durable purchases. We shall attempt this in Chapter 13.

Fifth, note that in Chapter 2, demands were derived as a function of prices and the empirical work adopted this formulation without question. This only makes sense if prices are set exogenously (say by manufacturers) and quantities supplied elastically to meet whatever demand emerges. This is probably the case for most goods in modern industrial societies, although food may be a partial exception and it is interesting to note that food is a commodity for which many authors have had difficulty in estimating a "sensible" price elasticity. There may also be more direct difficulties in satisfying demand in that some goods may not be available, either temporarily or, in some countries, continually, so that implicit or explicit rationing occurs. We shall discuss some of the techniques for dealing with these situations in Chapter 4.

Finally, we have said nothing about uncertainty. It might be thought that this is only a serious problem in savings behavior or in the purchase of durables, and it is indeed important in those contexts. However, there are many sources of uncertainty even in the short run. For example, consumers may frequently not know the *qualities* of goods they buy and so not know how to place them in their preference ordering. Another important source of short-run uncertainty is lack of certain information about all current prices at the time of each individual purchase; this is likely to be particularly serious when relative or absolute prices are changing unusually rapidly. In such circumstances, price expectations and the way they change through time become of crucial importance. We shall take up these issues in Chapters 12 and 14.

These are only some of the most important areas in which the simple models must be modified. There are many others which are perhaps less serious, for example, the correction of quantities for changes in the quality of commodities or models for dealing with adjustment costs. As we proceed with these and other issues, some of the problems raised in this chapter will be clarified. However, our main purpose in what follows will be to build upon our basic theory a structure that is flexible enough and realistic enough to deal with a wide range of important practical and theoretical issues. We do not believe that, at this stage, it is necessary to abandon the axioms of choice in the face of the results of this chapter. Ultimately, of course, given sufficiently convincing evidence, we should be prepared to do so. But, for reasons given in this last section, it is clear that there are many more obvious misspecifications that should be corrected first.

Exercises

3.1. Assume that for household h, expenditure on good i, $p_i q_i^h$, is a linear function of household outlay x_h and the number of persons in the household, z_h, that is,

$$p_i q_{ih} = \alpha_{ih} + \beta_i x_h + \gamma_i z_h$$

where β_i and γ_i are parameters independent of h and α_{ih} is a parameter that varies from good to good and household to household.

  (a) Show that if, in the economy as a whole, average household size remains constant over time, there will be a stable linear relation between average expenditure on good i and average total expenditure.
  (b) In a cross-section regression of $(p_i q_{ih})$ on x_h alone, would you expect to observe a linear relation?
  (c) What conclusions does this example suggest for the use of cross-section parameter estimates in time-series analysis as, for example, employed by Stone?

3.2. Give an intuitive explanation of what you mean by saying that two goods, for example, cigars and tents, are unrelated in consumption. Why is it more plausible to suggest that $e_{ij}^* = 0$ for such a pair than to suggest $e_{ij} = 0$?

3.3. For many countries, quantity series are obtained by independently obtaining value figures and price indices and dividing one by the other. Assume that both original series are measured subject to error. What bias is this likely to introduce in (a) regressions of q_i (or $\log q_i$) on p and x (e.g., the linear expenditure system), (b) regressions of w_i on p and x (e.g., the AIDS).

3.4. Totally differentiate the indirect utility function $u = \psi(x, p)$, and use Roy's identity to show that for a constant of proportionality α,

$$du = \alpha(dx - \Sigma q_i dp_i)$$

What interpretation can be given to α? Use the identities $dx \equiv xd \log x$, $dp_i \equiv p_i d \log p_i$, and so on to show that we may also write $du = \alpha^*(d \log x - \Sigma w_k d \log p_k)$ and use this to reinterpret the Rotterdam model as a system of Hicksian demand functions. Use (a) the budget constraint, (b) the first-order conditions in Chapter 2, equation (2.4) to prove the last equality in (3.4).

3.5. In the linear expenditure system, define $\phi = -(x - \Sigma p_k \gamma_k)/x$, and show that the uncompensated cross-price elasticities can be written in the form

$$e_{ij} = \delta_{ij}\phi e_i - e_i w_j - e_i \beta_j \phi$$

where $\delta_{ij} = 1$ if $i = j$ and $= 0$ if $i \neq j$. Using this equation, show that

(a) $e_{ij}^* > 0$, $i \neq j$, if $\beta_k > 0$ for all k and $x > \Sigma p_k \gamma_k$ so that all goods are substitutes
(b) $e_{ii} \simeq \phi e_i$ provided the number of goods is large
(c) e_{ij} is generally of smaller magnitude than e_{ii}.

3.6. Using the cost function for the linear expenditure system, show that $\beta_k > 0$ for all k and $x > \Sigma p_k \gamma_k$ is a sufficient condition for $s_{ii} < 0$ for all i. Hence show that inferior goods cannot occur in the linear expenditure system.

3.7. Using published studies of the linear expenditure system [e.g., Goldberger and Gamaletsos (1970), Phlips (1974), Solari (1971), Deaton (1975a), or Lluch, Powell, and Williams (1977)], see how far the published estimates of e_{ii} and e_i conform to the proportionality $e_{ii} \simeq \phi e_i$. Why is the correspondence closer when many categories are distinguished [e.g., Deaton (1975a)] than when there are few [e.g., Lluch, Powell, and Williams (1977)]? Does this mean that the linear expenditure system is less restrictive when applied to a small number of goods? Examine estimates of elasticities *not* based on the linear expenditure system [e.g., those of Stone (1954a), Goldberger and Gamaletsos (1970), Deaton (1975b)] and comment informally on whether proportionality holds in general.

3.8.* For estimation purposes the linear expenditure system may be written

$$y_{it} = p_{it}\gamma_i + \beta_i \left(x_t - \sum_k p_{tk}\gamma_k \right) + \epsilon_{it}$$

where a t suffix denotes an observation and ϵ_{it} a stochastic error. Least squares estimates of γ and β may be obtained by choosing values that minimize $R = \Sigma\Sigma_{it}\epsilon_{it}^2$. Calculate the derivatives of R with respect to β_i and γ_i, respectively, and show that by setting each to zero a scheme can be set up that allows calculation of $\hat{\beta}$ and $\hat{\gamma}$ and vice versa. [See Deaton (1975a), pp. 56–8 for why this is not an efficient computational technique.]

3.9. The Rotterdam model (3.3), if b_i and c_{ij} are *not* treated as constants, is perfectly general. Show that the linear expenditure system can be written in the form

$$w_i \, d \log q_i = \beta_i \, d \log \bar{x} - \phi \sum_j (\delta_{ij}\beta_i - \beta_i\beta_j) \, d \log p_j$$

where ϕ and δ_{ij} are as defined as in Exercise 3.5. Why is this equation not a special case of the Rotterdam model with b_i and c_{ij} treated as parameters?

3.10* (The McFadden critique of the Rotterdam model.) Using the definitions (3.5) and (3.6) plus the Slutsky equation, show that in the Rotterdam model

$$\frac{\partial q_i}{\partial x} = \frac{b_i}{p_i}, \quad \frac{\partial q_i}{\partial p_j} = \frac{x c_{ij}}{p_i p_j} - \frac{b_i}{p_i} q_j$$

Well-behaved demand functions will only exist if Young's theorem holds, that is, if $\partial^2 q_i / \partial x \partial p_j = \partial^2 q_i / \partial p_j \partial x$. From the equations above, show that this will only happen with b_i and c_{ij} constant if $c_{ij} = -(b_i \delta_{ij} - b_i b_j)$. From the Slutsky equation in the form $e_{ij} = e_{ij}^* - e_i w_j$, and using $e_{ij}^* = c_{ij}/w_i$, show that this form of c_{ij} implies that $e_{ij} = 0$, $i \neq j$, $e_{ii} = -1$ and $e_i = 1$. What demand functions correspond to these restrictions?

3.11. Houthakker (1960) suggested the indirect addilog model defined by

$$\psi(x, p) = \Sigma \frac{\alpha_i}{\beta_i} \left(\frac{x}{p_i}\right)^{\beta_i}, \quad \beta_i > 0$$

Show that under this specification, for all i and j

$$\log q_i - \log q_j = \log\left(\frac{\alpha_i}{\alpha_j}\right) + (\beta_i + 1) \log\left(\frac{x}{p_i}\right) - (\beta_j + 1) \log\left(\frac{x}{p_j}\right)$$

Differentiate this relation with respect to $\log x$ and $\log p_k$, and use Engel and Cournot aggregation to derive the total expenditure and uncompensated price elasticities. Comment on the restrictiveness of the model.

3.12. Use Roy's theorem to derive the demand functions of the indirect translog model from (3.10). Define the direct translog model using a corresponding quadratic approximation to the direct utility function $v(q)$. Using the first-order condition in Chapter 2, equation (2.4), show that $w_i = \partial v / \partial \log q_i / (\Sigma \partial v / \partial \log q_k)$ and use this to derive w_i as a function of the vector q. Interpret this equation and assess its usefulness for empirical work.

3.13. Derive the compensated and uncompensated price elasticities for the AIDS. Show that, provided $\beta_i \beta_j$ is small, $(\partial w_i / \partial \log p_j$ with $u = \text{constant})$ is approximately γ_{ij}.

3.14.* Assume that the AIDS is valid only in the long run so that (4.6) is misspecified. If the true model takes the form

$$w_{it} - \delta_i w_{it-1} = \alpha_i + \sum_{L=0}^{M} \sum_j \gamma_{ij}^L \log p_{jt-L} + \sum_{L=0}^{N} \beta_i^L \log\left(\frac{x}{P}\right)_{t-L} + u_{it}$$

where M and N are maximum lag lengths and u_{it} is a serially uncorrelated error:

(a) What values of the parameters would justify estimating the model in levels?
(b) What values of the parameters would justify estimating the model in first differences?
(c) Assuming $M = N = 0$, would you expect estimation of the AIDS in levels to lead to the rejection of homogeneity?
(d) How could you test the models discussed in the text relative to the more general model given above?

Bibliographical notes

By beginning this chapter with Stone's work, we neglect much that is excellent that predates it. Once again, Stigler (1954) is recommended for the early history while in the twentieth century the books by Schultz (1938) and by Wold (1953) are major milestones in the history of empirical demand analysis. Stone had a large number of distinguished co-workers in Cambridge in the 1950's and a large number of empirical papers on consumer behavior, by Houthakker, Prais, Brown, Tobin, Farrell, and others date from that time. These, and other developments up to 1970 are surveyed by Brown and Deaton (1972). More recent work, with slightly more emphasis on duality and coverage of the earlier literature on flexible functional forms is surveyed by Barten (1977). Most recently, Lluch, Powell, and Williams (1977) have published a massive set of applications of the linear expenditure system but their work is marred by their failure to distinguish clearly enough between the properties of the data being investigated and the properties inherent in the models being used. The Rotterdam model is treated exhaustively in the two volumes by Theil (1975, 1976), who also estimates a variant in which some prices are endogenous. The details of estimating complete systems of demand functions can be found in Barten (1969), Solari (1971), Parks (1971) and Powell (1974). Deaton (1975a, Chapter 4) considers the general issue in the context of the linear expenditure system; other models are dealt with in Deaton (1974a). The methodology of testing is discussed in Barten (1969), in Byron (1970b)–who uses Lagrange multiplier tests – and in Deaton (1978) – on "nonnested" testing applied to systems of demand equations.

Extensions to the basic model

The model of consumer behavior developed in Chapter 2 and applied in Chapter 3 is clearly limited both in scope and in realism. The process of extending and improving the model in various directions will occupy much of the rest of the book and is the particular subject matter of Part Four. In this chapter, we make a start on these extensions but only in a very limited way. In particular, in §4.1 and §4.2, we show how labor supply decisions, savings behavior, and purchases of durable goods can be handled within the framework of utility maximization subject to a linear budget constraint, provided the arguments of the utility function and the constraint are appropriately redefined. We shall refer to these models as *neoclassical*, a name we use to label the assumption of linear budget constraints with fixed, known prices. In the present context, none of the neoclassical models turns out to be very realistic and hence the substantial attention paid to their improvement in Part Four. Nevertheless, it is extremely important to understand them. First, they play an important part in much contemporary economic analysis, and it is essential to understand exactly the assumptions on which their theoretical validity depends. Second, they yield important insights that we ignore at our peril and, in Part Four, they will be the platform on which we attempt to build more realistic and relevant models.

Section 4.3 is an exposition of the theory of demand when the amounts of some of the commodities are fixed. This important extension of the model is relevant for the discussion of short-run versus long-run demand, for the analysis of rationing and of public goods, and for the understanding of much of the modern macroeconomic literature that treats consumers as being sometimes constrained to given quantities in either the goods or labor markets. We also discuss how shadow prices can be derived and how they fit into the apparatus so far developed.

4.1 The simple neoclassical model of labor supply

Our main analysis of labor supply is in Chapter 11; the following elementary neoclassical description is an essential prerequisite for the later work.

The budget constraint and preferences

We start our analysis by applying the theory of choice to the simplest neoclassical specification of constraints. Here we have an individual or a household containing a single worker faced with the choice of buying different bundles of goods at a given price vector, with these purchases being financed out of a given nonlabor income μ and labor income $\omega\ell$, where ω is the given wage rate and ℓ is the amount of time the individual chooses to work. Formally,

$$\mu + \omega\ell = \Sigma \, p_i q_i \qquad (1.1)$$

since the nonsatiation axiom guarantees an equality rather than an inequality. In addition,

$$q_i \geq 0, \quad \text{all } i \text{ and } T \geq \ell \geq 0 \qquad (1.2)$$

meaning that negative amounts of goods cannot be bought, negative amounts of work time cannot by supplied, and labor supply cannot exceed the time endowment T. If flows were measured daily, we could think of T as 24 hours minus the time necessary for sleeping and other minimal maintenance tasks. But we could also measure the flows over longer time periods such as a year or more. In some ways, a long-run interpretation would justify the neglect of saving and would overcome the criticism that in the short run, most workers have to work the hours required by the job specification: in the long run, we can argue that workers can choose their hours by choosing between different jobs. On the other hand, it then seems implausible to maintain the linearity of the budget constraint since the wage rate is unlikely not to vary with the number of hours supplied. However, let us adopt it as a simplifying approximation.

Let the utility function be

$$u = v(q_0, q_1, \ldots, q_n) \qquad (1.3)$$

where we denote leisure $T - \ell$ by q_0 to make clear that leisure is comparable to other goods with the wage rate as its price. For simplicity of presentation, we shall assume in much of what follows that there is only a single consumption good and give brief indications of how the results generalize when there are n such goods. Working with one consumption good is not quite as unrealistic as it appears: if the n relative prices are constant, we shall see in Chapter 5 that the price weighted total of the consumption vector (the "Hicks aggregate") can be treated like a single good. Since in cross sections we assume that everyone faces the same relative prices for goods, this one good model is the natural one to adopt for cross-section analysis. We can picture the problem of maximizing (1.3) subject to (1.1) and (1.2) in Figure 4.1. The attainable combinations of consumption and leisure are given by the quadri-

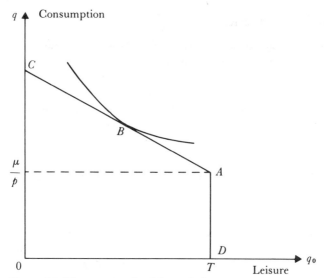

Figure 4.1. The consumption-leisure choice.

lateral $0CAD$. $0C = (\mu + \omega T)/p$ represents the maximum consumption level and is attainable by having zero leisure. Then $0D = T$ is the upper limit on leisure and $AD = \mu/p$ is the corresponding level of consumption, attainable by supplying zero hours. The amount of labor supplied is therefore measured by the distance back along the leisure axis from D. It is clear from Figure 4.1 that with differently shaped indifference curves, it might be the case that the highest level of utility is reached not at an interior solution such as B but at the corner A, where zero hours are supplied and where the usual marginal conditions for a maximum may not hold. The choice of whether to supply a positive number of hours or zero hours is usually called the "participation decision," and the analysis of it will be dealt with in Chapter 11. Meanwhile, we shall confine ourselves to interior solutions such as B.

It should be obvious that the choice problem is now similar to that analyzed in Chapter 2 with one of the goods, leisure $q_0 = T - \ell$, having price ω. There is, however, a small but significant difference that becomes immediately apparent when we rewrite the budget constraint directly in terms of q_0 and q. From (1.1)

$$pq + \omega q_0 = \mu + \omega T \tag{1.4}$$

so that ω, the price of q_0, appears not only in the normal role of a price on the left-hand side of (1.4) but also as part of the budget in valuing the time endowment T. Hence, as we shall see, a change in ω has effects on behavior over and above those of a change in the price of a good and this crucially alters the analysis of income and substitution effects. The quantity $\mu + \omega T$ represents the total purchasing power available to the consumer to be spent on leisure and goods and is usually called *full income*. We shall denote it by X since, not including saving, it is a concept more akin to total expenditure as used up to now.

Before going on, consider the effects of taxation on the budget constraint (1.4). In dealing with commodity prices, it is not necessary to separate the tax component from the producer price, but with labor supply, the situation can be more complicated since, even when only linear taxes are considered, the tax affects both labor and nonlabor income. In this case, however, ω and μ can be reinterpreted as net concepts. Suppose, for example, that the same tax rate τ applies to labor and to nonlabor income; hence,

$$\text{tax paid} = \tau(\mu + \omega\ell) - b \tag{1.5}$$

where someone with no income receives a benefit of b. This is a simple "negative income tax" system in that those below a certain threshold income receive net benefits in proportion to the shortfall of their income just as those above that level pay taxes in proportion to the excess of their income above the threshold. After-tax income is $(1 - \tau)(\mu + \omega\ell) + b$ so the budget constraint is now

$$pq + (1 - \tau)\omega q_0 = b + (1 - \tau)\mu + (1 - \tau)\omega T \tag{1.6}$$

or $\qquad pq + p_0 q_0 = \mu^* + p_0 T \tag{1.7}$

where p_0 is the net wage $(1 - \tau)\omega$ or price of leisure and μ^* is net nonlabor income $b + (1 - \tau)\mu$. Otherwise, (1.7) is identical to (1.4). Changes in the tax rate τ change the net wage and net nonlabor income so that the income effect of tax changes has an extra component compared with a change in the wage. In practice, tax systems are often not linear, and we shall discuss some of the problems this causes in Chapter 11.

Income and substitution effects and the Slutsky equation

Figure 4.2 compares the income and substitution effects of a change in the wage with the more usual ones of a change in a commodity price. If B is the starting point on the budget line AC, an increase in ω will cause an *upward* rotation around A to AF. Contrast this with the traditional case when an increase in price of the good on the horizontal axis causes the budget line to rotate *inwards*, from AC to CG. The difference between CG and FA is because of the extra income effect of the change in ω on full income X through the revaluation of T. Thus, although the *substitution* effect of the price change is, as usual, the move from B to E, the total *income* effect is the move, not from E to B_2, but

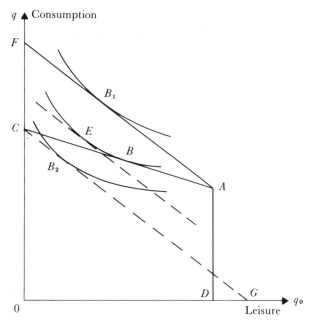

Figure 4.2. Income and substitution effects comparing the standard case with the case of a wage change.

upwards from E to B_1. Hence, the income effect of an increase in ω is *positive* on the demand for both goods and leisure (since both can be assumed to be normal) as compared with the *negative* income effect of a rise in the price of a good. On labor supply ℓ, the income effect is, of course, negative.

This analysis can be formalized along the lines of Chapter 2 using appropriately defined cost and indirect utility functions. Define the "full" cost function as

$$c(u, \omega, p) = \min_{q_0, q}\{\omega q_0 + pq;\ v(q_0, q) = u\} \tag{1.8}$$

so that, with utility maximization, $c(u, \omega, p) = X$. Similarly, maximum attainable utility is defined on $X\ (= \mu + \omega T)$, ω and p,

$$u = \psi(\mu + \omega T, \omega, p) \tag{1.9}$$

Since leisure is just another good and its price just another price, $c(u, \omega, p)$ shares all the properties of cost functions derived in Chapter 2. For example, it is concave in ω and p and the Hicksian demand functions are derived from it by differentiation:

$$q_0 = h_0(u, \omega, p) = \partial c(u, \omega, p)/\partial \omega \tag{1.10}$$

$$q = h(u, \omega, p)\ = \partial c(u, \omega, p)/\partial p \tag{1.11}$$

It is easy to see that when p and q are vectors, (1.11) becomes $q_i = h_i(u, \omega, p) = \partial c(u, \omega, p)/\partial p_i$ for $i = 1, \ldots, n$. As in Chapter 2, the solution to the problem "maximize utility (1.3) subject to (1.4)" is given by the Marshallian demand functions

$$q_0 = g_0(\mu + \omega T, \omega, p) = g_0(X, \omega, p) \tag{1.12}$$

$$q = g(\mu + \omega T, \omega, p) = g(X, \omega, p) \tag{1.13}$$

with the appropriate vector extensions. Labor supply equations are given by (1.10) and (1.12), using $\ell = T - q_0$. As in the commodity case, substitution of (1.9) for u in the Hicksian demand leads to the Marshallian demands, while writing $\mu + \omega T = X = c(u, \omega, p)$ and substituting in the Marshallian demands leads back to the Hicksian demands.

The Slutsky equations may now be derived straightforwardly. Paralleling the discussion of Figure 4.2, we wish to decompose the total effect on the leisure of a wage change into a substitution effect and an income effect. The total effect of ω on q_0 is given, via (1.12) as

$$\left.\frac{\partial q_0}{\partial \omega}\right|_\mu = \left.\frac{\partial g_0}{\partial \omega}\right|_X + \frac{\partial g_0}{\partial X} \cdot T \tag{1.14}$$

Diagrammatically this is the decomposition of the move from B to B_1 into moves from B to B_2 and from B_2 to B_1. We shall now show that the first term, the wage effect holding X constant, that is, without adjusting full income upwards for the revaluation of the time endowment, decomposes into a substitution effect and an income effect in the usual way.

From (1.12) and the cost function

$$q_0 = g_0\{c(u, \omega, p), \omega, p\} = h_0(u, \omega, p) \tag{1.15}$$

Differentiating with respect to ω gives the substitution effect as

$$\left.\frac{\partial q_0}{\partial \omega}\right|_u \equiv \frac{\partial h_0}{\partial \omega} = \frac{\partial g_0}{\partial X} \cdot \frac{\partial c}{\partial \omega} + \left.\frac{\partial g_0}{\partial \omega}\right|_X \tag{1.16}$$

The first term, which since $\partial c/\partial \omega = q_0$ equals $(\partial g_0/\partial X)q_0$, is the conventional income effect and diagrammatically is the move from B_2 to E. If leisure is a normal good, it is positive. Substituting (1.16) into (1.14) gives

$$\left.\frac{\partial q_0}{\partial \omega}\right|_\mu = \left.\frac{\partial q_0}{\partial \omega}\right|_u - \frac{\partial q_0}{\partial X} q_0 + \frac{\partial q_0}{\partial X} \cdot T = \left.\frac{\partial q_0}{\partial \omega}\right|_u + \frac{\partial q_0}{\partial X} \cdot \ell \tag{1.17}$$

Diagrammatically, the first equality in (1.17) decomposes the move B to B_1 (total effect) into B to E (substitution effect), E to B_2 (conventional income effect, negative if leisure is normal) and B_2 to B_1 (revaluation-of-time-endowment effect, always positive). Note that the total income effect cannot be negative.

This Slutsky equation can also be written in terms of labor supply as

$$\left.\frac{\partial \ell}{\partial \omega}\right|_\mu = \left.\frac{\partial \ell}{\partial \omega}\right|_u + \frac{\partial \ell}{\partial X} \cdot \ell \tag{1.18}$$

which looks (rather misleadingly) like a normal Slutsky equation. Note carefully, however, that the concavity of the cost function implies that $\partial q_0/\partial \omega|_u$ ($= \partial^2 c/\partial \omega^2$) is nonpositive so that $\partial \ell/\partial \omega|_u$ is *nonnegative*; similarly, $\partial \ell/\partial X$ is normally negative rather than positive. Hence, it is perfectly normal for the labor supply curve to be downward sloping ($\partial \ell/\partial \omega|_\mu < 0$) for at least some levels of ω and μ. One possibility is illustrated by BB' in Figure 4.3, where labor supply is measured right to left from D on the horizontal axis. Whether labor supply curves are backward bending in practice and if so, for which kind of workers, are major empirical questions and of obvious practical relevance, for example, for analyzing the incentive effects of income taxation.

Finally, we consider the effect of a change in p, the price of goods, on the supply of labor. Since full income is independent of p, differentiation of (1.15) and rearrangement gives a conventional Slutsky equation

$$\left.\frac{\partial q_0}{\partial p}\right|_\mu = \left.\frac{\partial q_0}{\partial p}\right|_u - \frac{\partial q_0}{\partial X} \cdot q \tag{1.19}$$

or, in terms of labor supply

$$\left.\frac{\partial \ell}{\partial p}\right|_\mu = \left.\frac{\partial \ell}{\partial p}\right|_u - \frac{\partial \ell}{\partial X} \cdot q \tag{1.20}$$

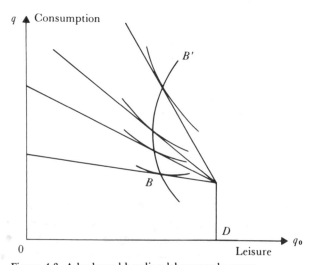

Figure 4.3. A backward bending labor supply curve.

(Note that in all these formulas, we could perfectly well replace derivatives with respect to X with derivatives with respect to μ.) If instead of one consumption good we may have many, (1.19) and (1.20) still hold with p replaced by p_i and q by q_i. Although consumption goods as a whole cannot be complementary to leisure, individual goods can be. If the ith good is complementary to leisure, the compensated demand for leisure falls as the price of the good goes up so that compensated labor supply increases. Note finally that we could generalize the approach of this section to the case where the household has initial endowments not only of time but also of some or all of the goods. This would give the individual "excess demand functions" to be found in treatments of the theory of competitive general equilibrium–see Arrow and Hahn (1971), for example. In Chapters 12 and 13, we shall see that there are two classes of goods, financial assets and consumer durables, where the value of initial endowments is important for deriving sensible econometric specifications of demand functions.

Extensions and the specification of demand functions

The simple model of the previous subsections can be extended in a number of useful ways, and we shall consider two possibilities here, both of which are consistent with the preservation of a linear budget constraint. More complex extensions are reserved for Chapter 11. Consider first the case in which there are several potential earners in a household. The family utility function is then

$$u = v(q_0^1, q_0^2, q) \tag{1.21}$$

where q_0^1 and q_0^2 are the leisure times of the two individuals. In any cross-sectional application, this utility function would also contain a vector of given household characteristics not made explicit here. In (1.21), commodities are consumed jointly rather than separated into two bundles q^1 and q^2. Such a separation is clearly possible in principle, but since q^1 and q^2, unlike the individual labor supplies, are usually unobservable, there is little point in doing so. Equation (1.21) is maximized subject to the budget constraint

$$pq + \omega^1 q_0^1 + \omega^2 q_0^2 = \mu + \omega^1 T^1 + \omega^2 T^2 \tag{1.22}$$

where ω^1 and ω^2 are the two wage rates and T^1 and T^2 the time endowments. Once again, we have a "standard" problem and it has standard solutions with, for example, the two labor supplies determined as a function of family full income, $\mu + \omega^1 T^1 + \omega^2 T^2$, price p and wage rates ω^1 and ω^2. Since q_0^1 and q_0^2 are two goods like any other, we can have substitutability or complementarity relationships between them in the usual way. Husband's and wife's leisure being substitutable in looking after children or complementary in holidaying are obvious examples. Note carefully, however, that this analysis offers little support for the position that *earnings* of the primary worker are an appropriate determinant of the labor supply of the secondary worker. This would only make sense if the primary worker's labor and leisure choices were given exogenously and not part of a joint decision within the family. Otherwise, if the model outlined above is accepted, both *wage rates* should appear in both labor supply equations.

A rather different and equally interesting extension is based on the idea that there are different types of leisure. In particular, we take up the suggestions of Lewis (1957) and Hanoch (1980), that leisure on workdays is different from leisure on nonworkdays. Further, the daily fixed cost element of travel time (and cost) to get to work suggests that it is economical to shift leisure time into full days away from work and to have only relatively brief hours of leisure during work days. Following Hanoch (1976), we can define annual hours of leisure on workdays q_0^W, as the product of the number of days worked D and the daily time endowment T, *less* travel time δT, *less* hours worked per day ℓ. Hence

$$q_0^W = D[T(1 - \delta) - \ell] \tag{1.23}$$

Analogously, q_0^N the nonworkday leisure is defined by

$$q_0^N = T(365 - D) \tag{1.24}$$

The annual budget constraint is

$$pq + p^T D = \omega D\ell + \mu \tag{1.25}$$

where p^T is the daily money cost of travel to work. If (1.23) and (1.24) are used to derive D and ℓ and the results substituted in (1.25), the budget constraint becomes, in terms of q_0^N and q_0^W,

$$pq + \left(\omega(1 - \delta) - \frac{p^T}{T}\right) q_0^N + \omega q_0^W = X \tag{1.26}$$

for full income X. Once again, the standard form appears with price of workday leisure as ω and price of nonworkday leisure $\{\omega(1 - \delta) - p^T/T\}$. Clearly, if travel time and costs, δ and p^T, are substantial, the price of q_0^N will be substantially less than the price of q_0^W. The final choice between q_0^N, q_0^W, and q will be made by maximizing $v(q_0^N, q_0^W, q)$ subject to (1.26), giving leisure demand functions in terms of the two leisure prices, the goods price and X. From (1.23) and (1.24), the supply of days function will be determined entirely by the nonworkday leisure function, while the supply of hours function will depend on both leisure demand functions.

The implementation of these models, either simple or extended, requires the specification of particular utility functions or demands in exactly the same way as was done for the commodity case in Chapter 3. Several authors have indeed estimated augmented versions of the linear expenditure system, the Rotterdam model and the indirect translog model using aggregate time series data. In our view, the simple neoclassical model of labor supply without correction for aggregation, for constraints on hours worked, for unemployment and participation decisions, is too far removed from reality for empirical results based on it to be meaningfully interpreted. Nevertheless, specific functional forms are of considerable interest, partly to add flesh to the theoretical discussion and partly as building blocks in a more complex and realistic theory.

As an immediate example, consider the linear expenditure system augmented for leisure. With one consumption good and one type of leisure, the utility function is

$$u = \alpha_0 \log(q_0 - \gamma_0) + \alpha \log(q - \gamma) \tag{1.27}$$

with $\alpha_0 + \alpha = 1$ and γ_0 and γ interpreted as "committed" leisure and consumption, respectively. Maximization subject to $\omega q_0 + pq = X$ gives demands of the LES form

$$q_0 = \gamma_0 + (\alpha_0/\omega)(X - \omega\gamma_0 - p\gamma) \tag{1.28}$$
$$q = \gamma + (\alpha/p)(X - \omega\gamma_0 - p\gamma)$$

with associated labor supply function, in terms of μ and ω

$$\ell = (T - \gamma_0) - (\alpha_0/\omega)[\mu + \omega(T - \gamma_0) - p\gamma] \tag{1.29}$$

If the time endowment is treated as a parameter to be estimated, this equation indicates that only $T - \gamma_0$, the excess over committed leisure, is identified. The γ parameters give a natural way of incorporating differences in tastes and household circumstances into cross-section labor supply functions that are usually proxied by additive dummies in (1.29) for race, sex, household size, location, and so on. The model can also be used in time series-analysis with disaggregated commodity demands by using the utility function $\alpha_0 \log(q_0 - \gamma_0) + \Sigma\alpha_k \log(q_k - \gamma_k)$ and the associated demand functions. This model is like the conventional LES in having very restricted specifications of substitution between goods (and leisure) for reasons briefly examined in Chapter 3 and to which we return in Chapter 5.

Exercises

4.1. For the indirect utility function $u = \psi(\mu + \omega T, \omega, p)$, find Roy's identity (cf. §2.3). Hence by differentiating

$$g_0(\mu + \omega T, \omega, p) \equiv h_0[\psi(\mu + \omega T, \omega, p), \omega, p]$$

derive the Slutsky equation (1.17).

4.2. In the linear expenditure system model of labor supply, equations (1.28) to (1.29), show that the labor supply curve is backward sloping if $\mu < p\gamma$ and forward sloping if $\mu > p\gamma$. Interpret this result.

4.3. Suppose that in a model of a two-earner family, the primary earner's labor supply is chosen by maximizing family welfare given by (1.21) on the assumption that the secondary earner does not work and the secondary earner's labor supply maximizes the same welfare function taking primary earnings as fixed. Show, by using the linear expenditure system utility function, that it is possible for the primary worker's labor supply to be backward sloping while the secondary worker's labor supply is forward sloping. Assess the relevance of this result for interpreting the empirical finding that hours worked by married women are more responsive to changes in their wage rate than are hours worked by men to changes in male wage rates.

4.4. In the utility function $v(q_0^1, q_0^2, q)$, let q_0^1 be husband's leisure and q_0^2 be wife's leisure. Discuss how family composition variables (e.g., number of children, ages of children, ages of parents) might affect the degree of complementarity or substitutability between q_0^1 and q_0^2. Discuss the implications for the effects of wages on family labor supply.

4.5. What considerations might tend to invalidate the model of labor supply discussed in this chapter for the case of male manufacturing workers? Is the model more appropriate for the labor supply behavior of their wives? If the husband is not free to vary the hours that he works, how should his earnings be treated in the analysis of his wife's labor supply? Will the wife work more or less if such a worker receives a pay rise?

4.6. In the analysis of optimal commodity taxes it is of interest to know the conditions under which e_{i0}^*, the compensated cross-price elasticity between leisure and good i, is independent of i. Show that if we can write the full cost function in the form $c(u, \omega, p) = \gamma \{u, \omega, \eta(u, p)\}$, the condition is satisfied. Show also that, along a given indifference curve, such a cost function implies that the budget shares are independent of ω. How might we test whether this condition holds? Much harder: show that both e_{i0}^* independent of i and w_i independent of ω imply the cost function as shown.

4.7. In empirical work on labor supply, it is sometimes convenient (e.g., for ease of aggregation, see Chapter 6) to assume that functions for labor income or "leisure expenditure" ωq_0 are linear in X and ω. Show that the cost function

$$c(u, \omega, p) = \alpha(p) + \omega\beta(p) + u\omega^\delta\gamma(p), \qquad \text{where } \delta \text{ is a constant}$$

has this property. What homogeneity conditions must the functions $\alpha(\ )$, $\beta(\ )$ and $\gamma(\ )$ fulfil? Suppose that household h has a cost function of the form

$$c_h(u_h, \omega_h, p) = \alpha(p, z_h) + \omega_h\beta(p) + u_h\omega_h^\delta\gamma(p)$$

where $\alpha(p, z_h)$ is a linear function in the characteristics vector z_h, given p. Show, given cross-section data on $\omega_h q_{0h}$, ω_h, z_h, and μ_h, that δ and the parameters relating α to z_h can be estimated by linear regression.

4.8. In empirical work on labor supply it is frequently assumed that labor supply is linear in the wage rate. Show that if $c(u, \omega, p) = -\alpha(u, p)e^{\omega/\beta(p)} + \omega\gamma(p) + \delta(p)$, then the condition is satisfied. What homogeneity conditions are required on $\alpha(u, p)$, $\beta(p)$, $\gamma(p)$, $\delta(p)$? Show that for concavity and for $c(u, \omega, p)$ to be increasing in u, $\partial\alpha/\partial u < 0$ and $\alpha > 0$. Give an example of a function satisfying these. Much harder: show that the cost function indicated is *necessary* for labor supply to be linear in ω. (Hint: note that, since ω appears both as a price and through $X = \omega T + \mu$, ℓ must be linear in both ω and X.)

4.2 Intertemporal extensions, the consumption function, and durable goods

Many of the most difficult and most important choices made by consumers involve decisions relating to the timing of purchases. In a single, timeless, period in which total expenditure is given, such problems are assumed away. In reality, expenditure today may be at the expense of expenditure tomorrow or at some unspecified time in the future, while expenditure on durable goods today will alter the conditions under which future choice is made. This section takes up these problems, again within a largely neoclassical framework. The exposition is mostly in terms of a simple, two-period model although the extensions to many periods will be indicated when appropriate.

In principle, a full neoclassical analysis would model not only the structure of demand over time but also the structure of labor supply, and the interactions of the two might well be important. For example, changes in the anticipated rate of inflation or the yield on assets may well influence the timing of a retirement decision. We shall examine these interactions in more detail in Chapter 12, but for the moment we shall follow most of the literature on the consumption function and take present and expected future income as given, on the supposition that individuals are largely unable to control the number of hours they work or, indeed, whether they work at all. We shall follow this precedent, largely because the analysis is then simpler and more familiar. It should, however, be emphasized that the two approaches yield quite different results; with labor supply exogenous to the consumer, consumption is a function of (among other things) current and expected future income, while with labor supply endogenous, the corresponding wage rates take their place. This implies, for example, that it makes little sense to build macroeconomic models in which the consumption function is defined on labor income taken as exogenous for consumers and in which the labor market is continuously in equilibrium with employment always equal to labor supply. Consumption functions of this type are characteristic of macroeconomic disequilibrium. Labor supply remains important in such contexts, but its role is quite different from that in the equilibrium setting.

Once again, the material discussed next is a prerequisite for Part Four, Chapters 12 and 13.

The budget constraint and preferences

Again, we begin with the simplest possible case. There is one nondurable consumption good, of which q_1 is consumed in period 1 and q_2 in period 2. The corresponding prices are p_1 and p_2, and incomes (paid at the beginning of each period) are y_1 and y_2. The p, q notation may invite confusion with the two-commodity, single-period case, but the analogy is virtually exact and should in fact be helpful. The two periods are linked by a single financial asset A, available in positive or negative amounts, measured at the end of each period, which pays interest at the beginning of each period. We simplify by assuming that A is fixed in money terms and not subject to revaluation; it can be thought of as an interest-bearing bank deposit or loan. We shall assume a common interest rate r, applying to both borrowing and lending; it may, however, vary from period to period so that, in general, $r_t A_{t-1}$ is paid (to or by) the consumer at the start of period t.

In modeling consumption, planning for the future is an essential element. However, if period 1 is the present, decisions for period 1 are rather different from those for period 2 (or beyond) since the former are implemented now while the latter, being planned demands, may well be revised when decision making is reassessed in the next period. The model is thus one of continuous replanning with "real" time, the present, always being period 1. This also means that all magnitudes beyond period 1, prices, incomes, or interest rates, are not known with certainty in period 1 when the plan is being made. The simplest solution, which we shall adopt in this chapter, is to assume that the consumer has single-valued expectations for all the future quantities he needs to know. However, as we shall see below, the fact that y_2, r_2, p_2 are only expected and not known is of crucial importance in interpreting and understanding the model.

If A_0 is the value of assets at the end of period 0, then for the two subsequent periods

$$A_1 = A_0(1 + r_1) + y_1 - p_1 q_1 \tag{2.1}$$

$$A_2 = A_1(1 + r_2) + y_2 - p_2 q_2 \tag{2.2}$$

where, as emphasized above, r_2, y_2, and p_2 are the values expected to prevail in period 2. This two-period model is, of course, a schematic representation of an L-period model representing the lifetime plans of the consumer. Within such a framework, assets are regarded simply as a device for transmitting purchasing power between periods so that it is appropriate to abstract from bequests by setting A at the end of the final period to be zero. In the present context, this implies $A_2 = 0$. Given this, (2.1) and (2.2) can be combined to give a two-period constraint

$$p_1 q_1 + \frac{p_2}{1 + r_2} \cdot q_2 = A_0(1 + r_1) + y_1 + \frac{y_2}{1 + r_2} \tag{2.3}$$

Equally, (2.3) can be derived directly by setting the discounted present value of consumption equal to the discounted present value of assets and income. The term $r_1 A_0$ can be thought of as "property" income, so that the y's refer to labor income only.

Since (2.3) is the basic budget constraint for the two-period intertemporal model, it is worth rewriting it in "real" as well as money terms. If we use current prices p_1 as the base, define $y_2^* = y_2/(p_2/p_1)$ as real (expected) period 2 income, and rewrite $p_2/(1 + r_2)$ as

$$\frac{p_2}{1 + r_2} = p_1 \frac{[1 + (p_2 - p_1)/p_1]}{1 + r_2} = \frac{p_1}{1 + r_2^*} \tag{2.4}$$

where r_2^* is given by

$$1 + r_2^* = \frac{1 + r_2}{1 + (p_2 - p_1)/p_1} \simeq 1 + r_2 - \frac{(p_2 - p_1)}{p_1} \tag{2.5}$$

provided $(p_2 - p_1)/p_1$ is small enough to justify the approximation. r_2^* is the money interest rate r_2 *less* the expected proportional increase in the price level and is thus the expected *real* interest rate (though this interpretation is independent of the accuracy of the approximation). Hence, substituting for y_2 and p_2 in (2.3) we have a real budget constraint

$$p_1 q_1 + \frac{p_1}{1 + r_2^*} q_2 = A_0 (1 + r_1) + y_1 + \frac{y_2^*}{1 + r_2^*} \tag{2.6}$$

Both (2.3) and (2.6) are frequently useful and both can be written in the "standard" form

$$p_1 q_1 + p_2^* q_2 = W_1 \tag{2.7}$$

where $p_2^* = p_2/(1 + r_2) = p_1/(1 + r_2^*)$ is the discounted future price and W_1, total lifetime wealth, is given by

$$W_1 = A_0(1 + r_1) + y_1 + \frac{y_2}{1 + r_2} = A_0(1 + r_1) + y_1 + \frac{y_2^*}{1 + r_2^*} \tag{2.8}$$

Preferences, as usual, are represented by the utility function $v(q_1, q_2)$ with current and future consumption as arguments so that equilibrium is reached, as illustrated in Figure 4.4, at E. The only differences from the standard analysis are (a) the position of the budget line depends on assets and interest rates as well as income, (b) the slope of the budget line varies with r through p_2^*, (c) elements of W_1 (in this case y_2) and p_2 are not known in period 1 and therefore must be anticipated in some way. We shall take up these issues next.

With the problem set up in this way, the standard apparatus can be brought into play with a cost function $c(u, p_1, p_2^*)$, Hicksian demands $h_i(u, p_1, p_2^*)$, an indirect utility function $\psi(W_1, p_1, p_2^*)$, and so on. We shall be most concerned with the Marshallian demands that take the form

$$q_1 = g_1(W_1, p_1, p_2^*) \tag{2.9}$$

$$q_2 = g_2(W_1, p_1, p_2^*) \tag{2.10}$$

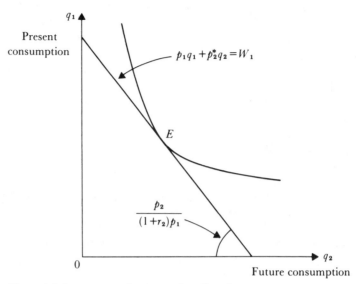

Figure 4.4. Intertemporal consumption allocation.

Note carefully that q_1, the demand for the current period, is in principle immediately *effective*, whereas q_2 is *planned* demand that may well not be realized if the consumer has a subsequent opportunity to replan.

The L-period extension of the model is straightforward. The only slight complication is in the discounting formula. If y_t is expected income in period t, the equivalent expected income in period $t - 1$ would be $y_t/(1 + r_t)$, in period $t - 2$, $y_t/(1 + r_t)(1 + r_{t-1})$, and so on. Hence the present value in period 1 of y_t is $y_t/(1 + r_t)(1 + r_{t-1}) \ldots (1 + r_2)$ which, for convenience we denote $\rho_t y_t$, where ρ_t is called the discount factor. Similarly, the real discount factor ρ_t^* is given by $1/(1 + r_t^*)(1 + r_{t-1}^*) \ldots (1 + r_2^*)$ for real interest rates r_t^*. With this, lifetime wealth W_1 over L-periods is

$$W_1 = A_0(1 + r_1) + \sum_{t=1}^{L} \rho_t y_t = A_0(1 + r_1) + \sum_{t=1}^{L} \rho_t^* y_t^* \qquad (2.11)$$

where $\rho_1 = \rho_1^* = 1$ and $y_t^* = y_t/(p_t/p_1)$ is real income in period t using period 1's prices as base. The L-period budget constraint is then

$$p_1 q_1 + p_2^* q_2 + \cdots + p_L^* q_L = W_1 \qquad (2.12)$$

where $p_t^* = p_t \rho_t = p_1 \rho_t^*$ is the discounted price for period t. The Marshallian demands (2.9) and (2.10) are then simply extended for L-periods with W_1 and the L discounted prices in each.

Income and substitution effects

The exogenous determinants of current and future planned consumption are thus present and future prices, current and future incomes, assets and interest rates. According to the basic demand functions (2.9) and (2.10), however, all these determinants act through one or more of W_1, p_1, and p_2^*. Obviously, the effects of these immediate determinants can be analyzed in the usual way, distinguishing income and substitution effects as necessary, and this offers a fruitful route for discussing the effects of the basic variables on consumption.

(a) *Changes in p_1* are the most straightforward. The income effect of an increase in p_1 depresses both q_1 and q_2, whereas the substitution effect causes substitution away from present consumption, further lowering q_1. With only two periods, substitution will be in favor of planned consumption in period 2; with more periods, or with flexible labor supply, more complex patterns of substitution or complementarity are possible. In practice, the substitution effect may be muted by the recognition that since p_2 is unknown and must be predicted, an increase in p_1 may well be projected into the future. The income effect may also be muted if y_2 is affected upwards by increases in p_1; note carefully, however, that y_1 and (especially) assets A_0 are given so that some income effect must remain. Since $y_1 + r_1 A_0$ is given, money *savings* $y_1 + r_1 A_0 - p_1 q_1$ will increase or decrease as the proportional fall in consumption q_1 is greater than or less than the proportional increase in the price level p_1.

(b) *Changes in p_2* with p_1 held constant are effectively changes in the *anticipated* rate of inflation. Substitution effects work in favor of present consumption ("buy now since it will cost more tomorrow") with income effects operating in the opposite direction ("save more to guarantee a decent standard of living at tomorrow's higher prices"). The net effect is ambiguous. On the other hand, both effects act to depress planned future consumption. Many apparently plausible but essentially partial arguments are encountered in the literature that purport to show an increased inflation rate either lowers or raises current savings. None of these arguments has any sound basis in theory and definite answers require specific functional forms and careful empirical analysis. Note finally that changes in p_2 may well be accompanied by or cause changes in other expectations, particularly expected future incomes and interest rates. These changes should be carefully allowed for in any particular analysis.

(c) *Changes in interest rates* have a wide range of effects through both p_2^* and W_1. On the former an increase in r_2 is equivalent to a decrease in p_2 (since both imply an increase in r_2^*) and has identical effects including an ambiguous effect on current saving (i.e., saving is worth more in the future but less is required to meet the same needs). On W_1, the immediate effect of an increase in

r_1 is through an increase in property income (or in the cost of servicing debt) with the budget constraint shifting in or out as A_0 is positive or negative. However, future interest rates are used to discount future incomes in constructing W_1, so that increases in interest rates will decrease the present value of future incomes in the total. If we were to relax our assumption that A is fixed in nominal value and consider the case where it is a title to a stream of future incomes (or outgoings), then changes in r_t would additionally cause capital gains or losses as the case may be. Note, however, that such capital gains and losses will affect expectations of future asset prices with further repercussions for present savings behavior; such effects are not allowed for in the present framework. One important feature of even the limited complexity allowed here is that changes in interest rates will affect different households differently. A young family with a large mortgage and with most of its lifetime earnings yet to come will be made substantially worse off by an increase in the general level of interest rates. By contrast, a young aristocrat who has just inherited a fortune in bank deposits and looks forward to a life of dissipation will benefit from an interest rate increase. (He might not be so happy, of course, if his fortune were invested in long-dated government securities.)

(d) *Changes in initial assets A_0* simply shift the budget constraint outwards and, given the normality of consumption in all periods, increase both current and planned future consumption. The magnitude of the effect on any one period will depend on how many periods are being considered so that, for example, in a life-cycle model, other things being equal, the marginal propensity to consume out of assets is likely to increase with age.

(e) *Changes in current labor income y_1* with y_2 held constant move the budget constraint in exactly the same way as do changes in A_0. Indeed, from the definition of W_1, (2.4) or (2.8), changes in y_1 and A_0 have exactly the same effects on W_1 and hence on current consumption. This has led many proponents of the theory to suggest that the short-run marginal propensity to consume out of income should be very low. However, although empirical evidence certainly supports the proposition that short-run marginal propensities to consume are considerably lower than long-run marginal propensities to consume, there is little support for the idea that assets and income have identical coefficients. To see why this is so, we must once again recognize the dependence of future expectations on current events. In particular, y_2 and in multiperiod models $y_3, \ldots , y_L$ are likely to depend on y_1. Consequently, from (2.9) and (2.10)

$$\frac{\partial q_1}{\partial y_1} = \frac{\partial q_1}{\partial W_1} \left(1 + \rho_2^* \frac{\partial y_2^*}{\partial y_1} + \cdots + \rho_L^* \frac{\partial y_L^*}{\partial y_1} \right) \tag{2.13}$$

using real incomes y_1^* $(=y_1)$, $\ldots$, y_L^* and real discount factors ρ_2^* to ρ_L^*. The right-hand side of (2.13) is likely to be much larger than $\partial q_1/\partial W_1$, the marginal propensity to consume out of assets, although by how much will depend on how expectations are formed. It is likely that expectations will be more sensitive to sustained changes in y_1 than to temporary changes so that (2.13) is consistent with a larger long-run than short-run propensity. Even in the very short run however, changes in y_1 are likely to have some effect on future expectations so that the short-run marginal propensity to consume is likely to be a good deal larger than $\partial q_1 / \partial W_1$.

The empirical modeling and formulation of the effects discussed here is a task that is of some difficulty and that has attracted a great deal of attention in the literature. We shall return to it in Chapter 12.

Some special cases and conventional consumption functions

In their famous articles on the life-cycle approach to the consumption function, Modigliani and Brumberg (1955a,b), simplified their analysis by assuming a particular form for preferences. In behavioral terms, they assumed that total resources were allocated between periods so that the ratio of each period's money expenditure to total lifetime resources was independent of the size of total resources. For example, in the two-period model, if I plan to spend two-thirds of my resources this period and one-third next, and if I receive a gift of $300, then I shall spend $200 now and $100 next period. This will be utility maximizing behavior if the indifference curves between q_1 and q_2 maintain the same shape as the utility level changes; this is the condition of *homotheticity* and we shall discuss it further in Chapter 5.

Formally, under the homotheticity assumption, (2.9) takes the form

$$p_1 q_1 = k(p_1, p_2^*) W_1 \qquad (2.14)$$

for some function $k(\ )$. Note that since q_1 must be homogeneous of degree zero in p_1, p_2^*, and W_1, k is a function of relative prices only. But referring back to the definition of p_2^* below equation (2.7), $p_1/p_2^* = (1 + r_2^*)$, so that k depends only on the real interest rate, a result that extends immediately to the L-period case. Hence, in a period in which the real interest rate is relatively constant, the observed value of k will be approximately constant and variations in q_1 will be attributable to variations in (W_1/p_1), the current price deflated value of assets, present and future discounted income. However, it is dangerous to assume that k is absolutely constant as would occur if the utility function $v(q_1, q_2)$ were of the Cobb-Douglas form $A q_1^k q_2^{(1-k)}$ with an associated elasticity of substitution between present and future consumption of unity. Consider what would happen in the case where p_2 rises relatively to p_1 with an exactly proportional increase in y_2 relative to y_1. Provided r_2 remains constant, W_1 will rise with the increase in y_2. If k is constant, (2.14) implies an increase in q_1, essentially on account of the dominant substitution effect causing present consumption to rise vis-à-vis future consumption. Although some consumers might behave in this way in response to what is effectively a fall in the real interest rate (for example debtors), it seems implausible as a general result and suggests that scope for substitution between consumption in different periods is more limited than a constant k would allow. Indeed, the extreme case of zero substitution with $v(q_1, q_2) = \min (q_1, q_2)$ is perhaps less implausible. With these preferences, consumers will plan to make $q_1 = q_2$ under all circumstances, so that to satisfy the budget constraint, we must have

$$q_1 = W_1/(p_1 + p_2^*) = \tfrac{1}{2}W_1/\tfrac{1}{2}(p_1 + p_2^*) \qquad (2.15)$$

In an L-period context, this can be thought of as giving q_1 as the Lth share of W_1 deflated by the mean of the present and future expected (discounted) price levels. Clearly, other formulations are possible, but this brief discussion should suggest (a) that the absolute constancy of k in (2.14) is implausible and (b) that the dependence of k on relative intertemporal prices is central in permitting the general income and substitution effects that are so characteristic of consumption function theory.

Most contemporary econometric work on the consumption function is based on one or other of a small number of theories. The "life-cycle" models of Fisher (1907, 1930), Ramsey (1928) and later Modigliani and Brumberg and Ando and Modigliani (1963) emphasize wealth as a determining variable and are basically consistent with our own intertemporal approach. The same is less true of empirical work based on the main alternative model, the permanent income hypothesis originating in the work of Friedman (1957), although there are many resemblances and points of similarity between the approaches. The permanent income model is usually written (although there are variants) in the form

$$q_1 = \kappa y^p \qquad (2.16)$$

where y^p is real permanent income, and κ is a quantity that is in principle variable (Friedman presents a catalog of possible determinants) but that is usually taken as fixed, at least in empirical work. A number of definitions of y^p are possible. The one that brings the permanent income model closest to the development just given makes permanent income the flow associated with the stock W_1. If the planning horizon were infinite, W_1 could generate a real income flow of r^*W_1 per period given a constant real interest rate r^*. Hence, for a consumer who expects and plans to live forever, real y^p is r^*W_1 so that substituting in (2.14)

$$p_1q_1 = k(p_1, p_2^*, \ldots, p_t^*, \ldots)y^p/r^* = \kappa(r^*)y^p \qquad (2.17)$$

since, as we saw above, $k(\ )$ is a function of real interest rates alone. In this case, the permanent income model is consistent with the theory of choice but only if the dependence of κ on the real rate of interest is explicitly recognized. In the more realistic case of a finite planning period, y^p can still be defined as that real income, at period 1 prices, which can be maintained out of W_1 over the plan. For example, in the two-period case, y^p is defined by

$$y^p + \frac{y^p}{1 + r_2^*} = W_1/p_1 \qquad (2.18)$$

so that solving and substituting into (2.14), we again have q_1 and y^p proportional, with the constant of proportionality again depending on current and future values of r^*. In the L-period case, the constant will additionally depend on L.

This is all very well, but in work using the model, not only is κ in (2.16) treated as parameter to be estimated, even in periods when prices, interest rates, and real interest rates are changing, but y^p is rarely measured as outlined above. Instead, y^p is usually modeled by some smoothing process applied to measured real income. These methods may or may not provide an adequate predictor of future incomes although, as we shall argue in Chapter 12, many of the popular methods are unlikely to do so. However, all of these, by concentrating entirely on income, omit the potentially vital effects of assets A_0. Nor can it be claimed that A_0 and y always move together so that as long as y is included, the omission of A_0 is unimportant. Obvious counterexamples are the behavior of British and American consumers after the Second World War when wartime restrictions on spending had resulted in an abnormally high ratio of A_0 to y or again in the 1970's when inflation led to an unusually low ratio. In summary then, from the point of view of the simple neoclassical theory of consumption presented in this section, we have three criticisms of much empirical work using permanent income models: (a) the proportionality constant should depend on relative prices between periods and on interest rates, (b) many standard smoothing mechanisms are likely to predict future incomes rather badly and (c) the exclusive attention paid to income ignores the potentially important contribution of assets.

In Chapter 12, we shall go beyond the simple analysis presented here as well as extend the current model further. Once other complexities are introduced, particularly the existence of borrowing constraints, of uncertainty, and of less than "perfect" aggregation, the conventional permanent income models make even less sense. However, the basic intertemporal analysis discussed here will provide an extremely useful basis for more realistic models.

Neoclassical models for durable goods

The simple neoclassical model of consumer behavior, with its linear budget constraint and assumption of perfect markets can also be extended to deal with the presence of durable goods. As we shall see, the assumptions required for this analysis are highly implausible, more so even than those required for labor supply or the consumption function, but, once again, at least one important insight is obtained.

We shall again work with a simple two-period model with one nondurable good and one durable good. The stock of durable good is denoted by S, again measured at the end of each period. In principle, utility is derived from a flow of services derived from the good and this flow might vary for a given stock with intensity of use or with inputs of other goods or labor. Here we take the simplest possible case where the service flow is proportional to S, so that S itself appears in the utility function. Hence, in the two-period model, preferences are represented by

$$u = v(q_1, q_2, S_1; S_0) \tag{2.19}$$

Here S_0 is included only after the semicolon to indicate that, although it affects preferences, it is now outside the consumer's control. Clearly, other "conditioning" variables, particularly the (exogenous) number of hours worked, could be added. The stock S deteriorates at a (not necessarily constant) rate δ per period so that S_t at the end of period t becomes $(1 - \delta)S_t$ at the end of period $t + 1$. This deterioration is of a very special type; there are no "vintage" effects of the kind usually associated with durable goods, instead a fraction δ of the stock simply "evaporates" in each period leaving a fraction $(1 - \delta)$ of identical stock indistinguishable (except in quantity) from the original stock. If this is to work at all, we must think of the stock as being measured in "efficiency units" so that, for example, if a new car is one efficiency unit, a one-year old car represents $(1 - \delta)$ units. Note too that δ represents physical deterioration, which is a different concept from the financial depreciation ascribed to real assets when their market value changes. We shall denote purchases of the durable good in period t by d_t; taking deterioration into account

$$S_t = d_t + (1 - \delta)S_{t-1} \tag{2.20}$$

which must be incorporated into the consumer's budget constraint.

The second set of assumptions relates to the market opportunities for durables faced by the consumer. The durable good can be bought and sold at the same price per unit regardless of whoever does the buying or selling. There are no indivisibilities. Second-hand goods also sell at the same price per efficiency unit as new goods although, given the type of deterioration assumed, this is not unreasonable in the absence of informational problems. Hence if a consumer invests a given amount of money in durables in period t, and if the price of durables remains unchanged into the next period, his investment will then be worth $(1 - \delta)$ of its original value. It is also assumed that, as in the case of the consumption function, the consumer can borrow and lend freely at a fixed interest rate provided only that he stays within his intertemporal budget constraint. (The relaxation of the assumptions of this paragraph will be the major task of Chapter 13.)

Given this background, the two budget constraints analogous to (2.1) and (2.2) are

$$A_1 = A_0(1 + r_1) + y_1 - p_1 q_1 - v_1 d_1 \tag{2.21}$$

$$A_2 = A_1(1 + r_2) + y_2 - p_2 q_2 - v_2 d_2 \tag{2.22}$$

where v_t is the price of a unit of the (new) durable good in period t. Since preferences are defined over stocks, we use (2.20) to eliminate d_1 and d_2 from (2.21) and (2.22), and as in (2.1) and (2.2), we assume that the value of terminal assets, $A_2 + v_2 S_2$, is zero. This makes heavy use of the assumptions of the previous paragraph since it allows, for example, that a consumer with no financial assets can borrow against his durable stock, clearing his debts at the end of the period by realizing what is left of his second-hand stock. Making the substitutions, we have the single budget constraint

$$p_1 q_1 + \left(\frac{p_2}{1 + r_2}\right)q_2 + \left[v_1 - v_2 \frac{(1 - \delta)}{1 + r_2}\right]S_1$$

$$= y_1 + \frac{y_2}{1 + r_2} + A_0(1 + r_1) + v_1(1 - \delta)S_0 \tag{2.23}$$

or by analogy with (2.5),

$$p_1 q_1 + p_2^* q_2 + v_1^* S_1 = W_1 \tag{2.24}$$

where W_1 is the right-hand side of (2.23) and now includes the valuation of the starting stock of durables $v_1(1 - \delta) S_0$ and $v_1^* = [v_1 - v_2(1 - \delta)/(1 + r_2)]$. Clearly, the utility function (2.19) and the budget constraint (2.24) define a "standard" problem within the neoclassical framework so that, once again, the apparatus of Chapter 2 can be applied.

The contribution of the neoclassical theory of durables is thus to allow us to incorporate durables into the standard analysis of nondurables. In particular, (2.23) defines a "price" v_1^* that represents the cost of holding one unit of durable stock for one period. For this reason, v^* is often referred to as the *rental equivalent price* or, more simply, *user cost*. This concept combines elements of price, capital gain, interest charge and deterioration. Consequently, if price remains constant, user cost is deterioration plus an interest charge; in the extreme case where δ is unity, $v^* = v$, and the case of a nondurable good can be taken as a limiting special case. Capital gains (losses) will result when v_2 is greater (less) than v_1, so that it is possible for user cost, unlike a normal price, to become negative. If this occurred, then, in principle, consumers would wish to hold an "infinite" quantity in order to reap "infinite" capital gains.

Note, however, that the present analysis omits not only the feedbacks on the price that such behavior might induce but also factors (such as storage costs, uncertainty about v_2 and transactions costs) that would tend to inhibit purchases in the first place.

This concept of user cost with its role of providing a price for durables is extremely important. Nevertheless, the demand functions based only on maximizing (2.19) subject to (2.24) lack plausibility, since the large scale fluctuations in demand that would be predicted by the model as a result of changes in user cost show no signs of existing in reality. There are many reasons for this, but an examination of them would take us outside the neoclassical model and is thus postponed to Chapter 13 where we shall also look at the evidence rather more systematically.

Exercises

4.9. Virtually all students, while students, have a current income which is low relative to their future expected incomes, that is, y_1 is low relative to W_1 compared to the average ratio in the population. Most are observed to maintain a consumption standard more appropriate to the current income than to W_1. Are borrowing restrictions sufficient explanation of this? What other factors might be operating?

4.10. How would you expect the ratio of y_1 to W_1 to vary over the life cycle? What implications does this have for the relationship between the savings ratio and age?

4.11. Prove that in the two-period model, if $u = \beta q_1^k q_2^{-k}$ then (2.14) holds with k an absolute constant. Why should, in contrast to the implication of (2.14), the quantities of consumption in different periods be relatively poor substitutes?

4.12. Again in the two-period model, derive (2.9) for the linear expenditure system utility function $u = \beta_1 \log(q_1 - \gamma_1) + \beta_2 \log(q_2 - \gamma_2)$. Interpret, contrast with Exercise 4.11, and discuss the plausibility of the result.

4.13. The homotheticity condition discussed in this chapter [see the paragraph before (2.14)], if applied to commodity demands, would imply unitary expenditure elasticities for each good (see also Chapter 5). Why is this condition more plausible when applied to intertemporal choice than to commodity demand analysis?

4.14. The "Leontief" utility function is written

$$u = \min(\alpha_1 q_1, \alpha_2 q_2, \ldots, \alpha_n q_n)$$

Discuss the relative plausibility of applying this function to (a) intertemporal choice and (b) commodity demand analysis.

4.15* With the utility function of Exercise 4.14, if $\alpha_1 = \alpha_2 = \cdots \alpha_n = 1$, $q_1 = W_1/(p_1 + p_2^* + \cdots + p_n^*)$ by straightforward extension of (2.15). If q_t^1, $t = 1, \ldots, n$ is consumption of period t planned in period 1, solve q_t^1 in terms of W_1 and the prices. If expectations are fulfilled, show that $q_2^1 = q_2^2$, and show that if actual consumption in period t, q_t, is given by $q_t = q_t^1$, then, barring unfulfilled expectations $q_t = q_{t-1}$. What happens if expectations are not fulfilled? In practice, would we expect q_{t-1} to be a good predictor of q_t?

4.16. The government conducts open market operations selling long-dated stocks. *Using the model of this section,* analyze the effects on consumption.

4.17. Using actual price series for some durable good and an assumed depreciation rate, calculate a time series of user cost v_t^* on the assumption that next period's price is known with certainty. Would you ever expect to observe a negative value for v_i^*? Would your answer differ according to the nature of the durable good, for example, between pasta, clothing, cars, or houses?

4.18. Suppose labor supply is endogenous in a two-period model so that in (2.1) and (2.2) y_1 and y_2 are respectively replaced by $\omega_1 \ell_1$ and $\omega_2 \ell_2$ and the utility function is $v(q_1, T_1 - \ell_1, q_2, T_2 - \ell_2)$. Contrast the resulting consumption demand equation with (2.9) and the resulting labor supply equation with leisure demand (1.12).

4.19. Suppose the consumer receives income y_1 and spends $p_1 q_1$ at the beginning of each period and that interest is paid at the end of each period on $y_1 - p_1 q_1$ as well as on A_0. Discuss how the resulting specification of the period to period budget constraint $A_t = (A_{t-1} + y_t - p_t q_t)(1 + r_t)$ alters expressions (2.3) to (2.11). Are these differences substantive?

4.20. Suppose that in Exercise 4.11, the utility function is modified to include A_2: $u = \beta q_1^{k_1} q_2^{k_2} (A_2/p_3)^{k_3}$ and $\Sigma k_i = 1$. What economic interpretation can you give this modification? What consequences does it have for the form of (2.14)?

4.21. Suppose that instead of the asset A, which is not subject to revaluation, the only financial asset in a two-period model is bonds B, where $p^B = 1/r^B$ is the price of bonds and r^B is the interest rate on bonds. Write down the period to period budget constraints analogous to (2.1) and (2.2) and discuss how expressions (2.3) to (2.11) alter. Suppose now that the two kinds of assets co-exist and continue to assume point expectations and no transactions costs. On a diagram, show the different positions the budget constraint can take for different combinations of values of r and r^B, assuming that consumers hold all their assets either in B or in A. Would a consumer ever wish to hold positive amounts of both assets? How do you think the form of asset holding would be affected by transactions costs and uncertainty?

4.3 Constraints on purchases and rationing

The theory presented so far treats all purchases as subject to consumer choice so that the quantities of all goods consumed can be varied at will provided only that the budget constraint is satisfied. In reality, a number of other constraints have to be faced, the simplest of which occur when the quantities of some goods are fixed exogenously. We have already met an extremely important example of this in §4.2 when, in analyzing the consumption function, it was assumed that consumers took their hours of employment as given. As we emphasized there, such constraints will also affect behavior outside the labor market so that the demand for goods, in effect the consumption function, will take a different form as labor is exogenous or endogenous. A similar case arises in the case of the multiple earner family considered in §1.3; it is often important to know what will happen to the labor supply of other family members if the head of the household becomes unemployed. Another case where constraints are important is in the analysis of short-run versus long-run demand. There are several goods – housing is a major example – where day to day fluctuations in consumption are not possible and, once again, this will affect the demand for other goods. The most obvious case of all is straight rationing, as in wartime, and here again, the effects on the unrationed demands is of considerable importance for government policy. Note that in this case, however, the rations are usually maxima so that the case of being forced to consume too much, which is possible in the other cases, cannot arise here. As a final example, public goods raise many of the same issues. These are provided collectively, usually, although not exclusively, without charge for use, and since it is the total amount supplied that enters each utility function, no one consumer can control the amount he consumes.

For simplicity, we shall work with one rationed good although the results generalize straightforwardly to the general case. Let the rationed good be q_1 and denote the fixed quantity to be consumed by z; for generality, a price p_1 is charged but this may be zero (provided z is finite). The central concept is again the cost function. Define the *restricted cost function* (sometimes called the conditional cost function) $c^*(u, p, z)$ as the minimum cost of attaining utility u at price vector p (including p_1) when quantity z of good 1 must be bought. Formally, if p^- and q^- are the price and quantity vectors excluding the first

$$c^*(u, p, z) = \min_q [p \cdot q; \, v(q_1, q^-) \geq u, \, q_1 = z]$$
$$= p_1 z + \min_q [p^- \cdot q^-; \, v(z, q^-) \geq u] \tag{3.1}$$

Since the presence of the constraint cannot make the consumer better off and may make him worse off, $c^*(u, p, z)$ can be no less than the unrestricted cost function $c(u, p)$. Indeed, if the ration z happened to be the amount he would have chosen in any case, $c^*(u, p, z) = c(u, p)$ and this can be used to derive restricted from unrestricted cost functions quite generally, see Exercise 4.23. Hence, we have the important property that relates the restricted to the unrestricted cost function

$$c(u, p) = \min_z c^*(u, p, z) \tag{3.2}$$

Equation (3.2) is the precise analog of the way in which long-run cost functions in theory of the firm (when capital stock is variable) "envelope" the short-run cost functions (with fixed capital); see for example, Baumol (1977, p. 291). Figure 4.5 illustrates the point when a single price $p_i, i \neq 1$, varies with the other prices and the utility level held fixed. The dotted curve represents the long-run cost function where z is variable and can be set to its cost minimizing value for each value of p_i. The short-run cost functions illustrated each show how cost increases with p_i when z is held fixed at some particular value; $z_1, \ldots, z_5$ are illustrated. From (3.2), the various short-run cost functions are never below the long-run cost function. For example, the short-run cost function with z_1 constant is everywhere above the dotted curve except at A, where z_1 is optimal for p_i; similarly for z_5 at B. The fact that the long-run or unrestricted cost function is more "concave" than any of the short-run restricted functions indicates that short-run substitution effects are always less

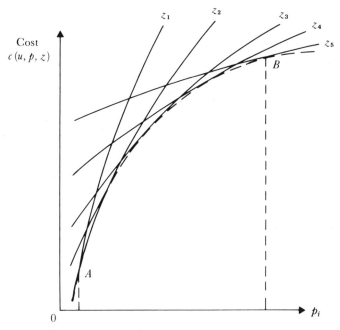

Figure 4.5. Long- and short-run cost functions.

than long-run substitution effects. This quite general result, often known as the Le Chatelier principle, was first stated in this context by Samuelson (1947) and will be demonstrated formally in equation (3.6) below. Note that it does not depend on any special relationship between the good whose substitution effects are being analyzed and the good that is being held fixed. Indeed, it is often cited in a quite general context, for example, to support the proposition that government controls and restrictions render individual behavior less flexible and responsive to changes in the economic environment.

From (3.1) we can see that the only way in which p_1, the price of the rationed good, appears in the restricted cost function is in the fixed cost term $p_1 z$. Therefore, when we derive the restricted Hicksian demand functions by differentiation with respect to p_i, the result will not depend on p_1. Denote these restricted or conditional demands by $h_i^*(u, p^-, z)$. Now if z is what the consumer would have bought without any restriction, that is, $h_1(u, p)$, the other demands must also be the same. Hence,

$$h_i^*[u, p^-, h_1(u, p)] = h_i(u, p) \tag{3.3}$$

Differentiate this with respect to p_1; thus, rearranging, provided s_{11} is nonzero,

$$\frac{\partial q_i}{\partial z}\bigg|_{u = \text{const}} = \frac{\partial h_i^*}{\partial z} = \frac{\partial h_i/\partial p_1}{\partial h_1/\partial p_1} = \frac{s_{i1}}{s_{11}} \tag{3.4}$$

where s_{i1} and s_{11} are the $(i, 1)$th and $(1, 1)$th cross-price substitution terms for the *unrestricted* demands. Note carefully that all these derivatives and the relations between them hold exactly only when the rations are set equal to what would have been bought in the absence of restrictions; this may always be guaranteed by evaluating the unrestricted demands, not at u, p_1, and p^- but at u, p_1^* and p^-, where p_1^* is the "shadow price" of z. Equation (3.4) is an important and intuitively acceptable result. Since s_{11}, the own-price substitution effect, is negative, the equation suggests that an increase in the amount supplied of the rationed good decreases the demand for substitutes ($s_{i1} > 0$) and increases the demand for complements ($s_{i1} < 0$). If we now differentiate (3.3) again, this time with respect to p_i,

$$\frac{\partial h_i^*}{\partial p_i} + \frac{\partial h_i^*}{\partial z} \cdot \frac{\partial h_1}{\partial p_i} = \frac{\partial h_i}{\partial p_i} \tag{3.5}$$

so that using (3.4) and denoting as s_{ii}^* the ith diagonal element of the restricted substitution matrix,

$$s_{ii}^* = s_{ii} - s_{i1}^2/s_{11} \tag{3.6}$$

Hence, since $s_{11} < 0$, $s_{ii}^* \geq s_{ii}$, so that the absolute size of the substitution effect is reduced under rationing. This is simply the formalization of the result shown in Figure 4.5.

So far, we have derived our results by considering what would happen if the rations and the unrationed demands coincided. An alternative and equally fruitful path is to enquire as to what price could be set that would induce the consumer to purchase the rations exactly. This is the shadow price of q_1 and we denote it by p_1^*. Provided the consumer's indifference curves are convex to the origin, the value of p_1^* is determined by dividing $\partial u/\partial q_1$, the marginal utility of good 1, by $\lambda = \partial u/\partial x$, the marginal utility of total expenditure, see equation (2.4) of Chapter 2. A precisely identical procedure is illustrated for two dimensions in Figure 4.6. A tangent drawn at the restricted optimum A defines the prices at which the current bundle, including z, will be demanded. The point B, where the tangent cuts the q_1 axis gives x/p_1^* and hence, given x, p_1^*. Note that the convexity assumption is quite crucial here and shadow prices are much less readily defined without it. By considering the relationship between the restricted and unrestricted cost functions, it can be shown that

$$\frac{\partial c^*}{\partial z} = p_1 - \frac{\partial u/\partial q_1}{\partial u/\partial x} = p_1 - p_1^* \tag{3.7}$$

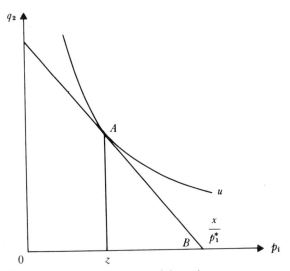

Figure 4.6. The shadow price of the ration z.

where p_1^*, the shadow price, is a function of u, p^-, and z (see Exercise 4.25). The equation is readily interpretable. The term p_1 is simply the fixed charge per unit of z, while p_1^* measures the reduction in the minimum cost of remaining on a given indifference curve consequent on a unit increase in z. Indeed, it would be perfectly sensible to *define* the shadow price through (3.7) as the money valuation (= reduction in minimum cost) of a unit of z provided at zero price. Clearly, when z is set at the level that would be freely demanded at price p_1, $p_1 = p_1^*$ and $\partial c^*/\partial z = 0$ [cf. equation (3.2)]. As the supply of z increases beyond the optimum, $p_1 > p_1^*$ with the reverse holding when the consumer goes short.

The fact that the price derivatives of the restricted cost function are quantities while the quantity derivatives are shadow prices can be used to define a remarkable set of symmetry results paralleling Slutsky symmetry as discussed in Chapter 2. First differentiate (3.7) with respect to p_i and use $\partial c^*/\partial p_i = q_i$ to give, since the order of differentiation is irrelevant,

$$\frac{\partial^2 c^*}{\partial p_i \partial z} = - \left.\frac{\partial p_1^*}{\partial p_i}\right|_u = \left.\frac{\partial q_i}{\partial z}\right|_u = \frac{\partial^2 c^*}{\partial z \partial p_i} \tag{3.8}$$

Hence, the compensated decrease in q_i of an increase in z equals the increase in the shadow price of z consequent on a unit compensated increase in p_i. This is clarified somewhat if we use (3.4) to give

$$\left.\frac{\partial p_1^*}{\partial p_i}\right|_u = \frac{s_{i1}}{(-s_{11})} \tag{3.9}$$

so that a compensated increase in p_i causes the shadow price of substitutes to rise and that of complements to fall. Finally, if there are two rationed goods z_1 and z_2, (3.7) gives

$$\left.\frac{\partial p_1^*}{\partial z_2}\right|_u = \left.\frac{\partial p_2^*}{\partial z_1}\right|_u \tag{3.10}$$

This equation is directly analogous to Slutsky symmetry but instead of exogeneous prices determining endogenous quantities, here we have exogenous quantities determining endogenous (shadow) prices. Such results have a number of possible applications, particularly in welfare economics.

Exercises

4.22. In the linear expenditure system, an amount z of good 1 must be bought. Show that, for $i = 2, n$

$$p_i q_i = p_i \gamma_i + \frac{\beta_i}{1 - \beta_1} (x - p_1 z - \Sigma p_k \gamma_k)$$

Interpret this result. Derive an expression for the restricted cost function $c^*(u, p, z)$.

4.23.* Rewrite equation (3.1) in the form

$$c^*(u, p, z) = p_1 z + \gamma(u, p^-, z) \tag{3.11}$$

where $\gamma(\ )$ is independent of p_1. Let p_1^* be the price that would induce z to be bought on the indifference curve labeled u at p^- without restriction. Show that $p_1^*(u, p^-, z)$ is the solution to $\partial c / \partial p_1 = z$. Hence, show that the restricted and unrestricted cost functions are related by the identity

$$c^*(u, p, z) = p_1 z + c[u, p_1^*(u, p^-, z), p^-] - p_1^*(u, p^-, z)z \tag{3.12}$$

4.24.* Use (3.12) (a) to check (3.2), (b) to check the restricted cost function derived in Exercise 4.22, (c) to prove (3.3) and (3.7), (d) to calculate the restricted cost function corresponding to

$$c(u, p_1, p) = u p_1 a(p^-) + p_1 b(p^-) + d(p^-)$$

for functions $a(p^-)$, $b(p^-)$, and $d(p^-)$.

4.25.* In the notation of (3.11) and (3.1)

$$\gamma(u, p^-, z) = \min_q [p^- \cdot q^-; v(z, q^-) \geq u]$$

Note that z appears only in the constraint and not in the minimand. By considering the Lagrangian associated with this problem and the associated first-order conditions, show that $\partial \gamma / \partial z = - (\partial \gamma / \partial u) \cdot (\partial v / \partial z)$. Reinterpret $\partial \gamma / \partial u$ to prove (3.7). [For further details on this type of procedure, see Dixit (1976, Chapter 3).]

Bibliographical notes

The analysis of labor supply is taken much further in Chapter 11, of the consumption function in Chapter 12, and of durable goods in Chapter 13. Fuller bibliographies are given at the ends of these chapters. The material here is comparable to that found in microeconomics texts or at least to those that deal with labor supply and consumption. Many do not, presumably because of the inherent implausibility of the simple labor supply model and because saving is regarded as the prerogative of macroeconomics. Laidler (1974) devotes a chapter to each topic. Layard and Walters (1978, Chapter 11) discuss labor supply, but not the consumption function. Macroeconomic texts discuss the latter in now standard terms [e.g., Evans (1969), Glahe (1973), Branson (1972a, 1979)] but apart from the last make little or no use of the theory of choice. Diewert (1974b) presents the neoclassical model of durable demand in terms similar to our own. Good textbooks on labor economics with a simple discussion of labor supply and some empirical examples are Fleisher (1970) and Rees (1973). On rationing, classic papers are Tobin and Houthakker (1951) and the survey paper by Tobin (1952), who covers the considerable body of theoretical and empirical work that appeared during and after the war. Mention should also be made of the earlier work on shadow prices by Rothbarth (1941) and the enunciation of the Le Chatelier principle by Samuelson (1947, 1972). Until recently, there has been relatively little interest in the topic, but see Pollak (1969, 1971b) and the applications of duality methods by Gorman (1976). A very recent important paper is that by Neary and Roberts (1978). The field is likely to expand rapidly with the current interest in macroeconomic models based on rationed behavior.

PART TWO

Separability and aggregation

Restrictions on preferences ● The theory of market
demand

CHAPTER 5

Restrictions on preferences

In Part I, we saw how the theory of choice, initially developed for application to the allocation of a fixed total expenditure over a number of goods, could be extended to deal with labor supply, the allocation of income between saving and consumption, and the purchase of durable goods. So far, we have looked at these extensions as separate problems, but in principle, each consumer has to deal with all of them simultaneously. At any given time, current assets and current and future income must be allocated over nondurable and durable goods for current and future periods, while for consumers who are free to do so, plans must be made for allocating time between work and leisure in the present and the future. There are also the complications of choosing types of real and financial assets as well as the problems of dealing with uncertainty. All of the parts of this allocation problem may interact: changes in future wage rates may alter retirement plans with important consequences for durable good purchases now; an anticipated increase in asset values three years hence may cause an elated investor to buy more of his favorite dinner, and so on. Such interactions pose formidable problems, not only for the consumer but also for the economist who attempts to describe consumer behavior. If making today's purchases requires knowledge of the price of bootlaces 30 years from now, daily living is close to impossible. Nor is there much hope of predicting behavior if all such possible interactions must be allowed for. It is thus important to find ways in which the problem can be simplified, either by aggregation, so that whole categories can be dealt with as single units, or by separation, so that the problem can be dealt with in smaller, more manageable units. For example, by making total consumption expenditure rather than its components a function of wealth, prices, and interest rates, we are aggregating; similarly in Chapter 3, expenditures on individual goods were aggregated into broad groups and these were related to group price indices and total expenditure. This latter also involves a separation of decision making since the group expenditures are related, not to their ultimate determinants (assets, wage rates, prices, interest rates) but to total expenditures within the current period. Hence, it is being assumed that the decision of how to allocate total current expenditure into various broad categories of goods can be made separately from the decision of how to arrange the intertemporal flow of expenditure. Similar assumptions about decision making are entailed when labor supply is analyzed independently of the structure of commodity demands.

There is a variety of ways in which assumptions of this type can be justified. In particular, we can place restrictions on preferences that allow separable decision making or we can restrict the allowable range of exogenous variables, particularly prices. The various possibilities and combinations are discussed in §5.1 and §5.2. The first of these is informal and presents an overview of the more detailed and more difficult material in §5.2. At first reading, the account in §5.1 of the composite commodity theorem, of two-stage budgeting, of utility trees, and of the types of preference separability will give sufficient knowledge of the more important results. Section 5.2, although still nonrigorous, goes further as well as outlining some of the derivations.

Sections 5.3 and 5.4 explore further types of restrictions on preferences. It is frequently important to know what structure of preferences will allow some property of interest to hold. Similarly, we must be aware of the empirical consequences of particular assumptions about preferences so that plausible restrictions can be used to generate degrees of freedom in econometric work while implausible ones are avoided. Section 5.3 examines strong separability or want independence; this has been heavily used in econometric work, often without a full appreciation of its consequences. Section 5.4 discusses the case of homothetic preferences which have the consequence that expenditure proportions are independent of outlay. This case is extremely easy to handle from a theoretical point of view and, as we shall see later in the book, will repeatedly appear as a necessary condition for several sorts of seemingly attractive results. However, homotheticity is of very limited applicability in econometric work, and we shall examine the important generalization that leads to linear Engel curves.

5.1 Commodity groups and separability: an elementary overview

In this and the next section, we shall revert to the model of Chapter 2, the allocation of a predetermined total over n goods, for most of the formal discussion. However, if the model is extended as in Chapter 4 to include n goods in each of N periods plus durable goods and labor supply, the analysis carries through. We shall indicate the important applications as we proceed, leaving proofs to be completed by analogy or through exercises.

Commodity groups: the composite commodity theorem

The first set of conditions for the existence of commodity aggregates we owe to Hicks (1936) although an essentially similar result was proved by Leontief

(1936). This is the *composite commodity theorem,* which asserts that if a group of prices move in parallel, then the corresponding group of commodities can be treated as a single good. We illustrate with a three-good model in which two prices always move in proportion. Write the three prices p_1, p_2, p_3, and assume that p_2 and p_3 bear some fixed ratio θ to some base period prices p_2^0 and p_3^0; that is,

$$p_2 = \theta p_2^0, \quad p_3 = \theta p_3^0 \tag{1.1}$$

where θ varies with time but is common to both prices so that the ratio p_2/p_3 remains fixed at p_2^0/p_3^0. The obvious possibility is that θ can act as a "price" for a new combined group with a "quantity" defined by weighting the individual quantities using the base-period prices p_2^0 and p_3^0. To see that this is so, define the composite quantity $p_2^0 q_2 + p_3^0 q_3$. The cost function $c(u, p_1, p_2, p_3)$ can be written $c(u, p_1, \theta p_2^0, \theta p_3^0)$ which, since p_2^0 and p_3^0 are fixed can be thought of as a function of u, p_1, and θ alone and this, say, $c^*(u, p_1, \theta)$ is the grouped cost function, that is,

$$c^*(u, p_1, \theta) = c(u, p_1, \theta p_2^0, \theta p_3^0) \tag{1.2}$$

It is left as an exercise to show that $c^*(u, p_1, \theta)$ satisfies all the properties of a "proper" cost function; it is increasing in u, p_1, and θ, homogeneous of the first degree and concave in p_1 and θ. Further, if we differentiate $c^*(u, p_1, \theta)$ with respect to θ, we have

$$\frac{\partial c^*}{\partial \theta} = \frac{\partial c}{\partial p_2} \cdot \frac{\partial p_2}{\partial \theta} + \frac{\partial c}{\partial p_3} \cdot \frac{\partial p_3}{\partial \theta} = p_2^0 q_2 + p_3^0 q_3 \tag{1.3}$$

Hence, $p_2^0 q_2 + p_3^0 q_3$ is confirmed as the quantity of the composite commodity corresponding to the price θ. Since the cost function provides a complete picture of preferences, this demonstration shows that, provided (1.1) holds, new preferences can be defined over q_1 and $p_2^0 q_2 + p_3^0 q_3$ and that these preferences lead to the same choices as the original ones. The extension to groupings of any size within a total of n commodities is straightforward, see Exercise 5.2.

The usefulness of this theorem in constructing commodity groupings for empirical analysis is likely to be somewhat limited. If we take the view that relative prices are largely independent of the pattern of demand, at least in the long run, then commodity groups should be chosen so that close substitutes in production are grouped together. For example, if two food crops require similar ratios of land, labor, and fertilizer and if progress in developing improved seed strains occurs at a similar rate, we should not expect sharp fluctuations in their relative prices. A fuller treatment of relative price constancy is contained in Exercises 5.7 and 5.8. On this basis, it might be possible to construct a relatively small number of aggregates. However, in an open economy with a floating exchange rate, considerable fluctuation in relative prices can be expected and even without this, it is not clear that we could justify the type of aggregates that are usually available. For example, the fact that the price of fish is relatively volatile would prevent its classification with other foods, and we should have to recognize that the definition of aggregates would shift with institutional changes such as alterations in tariffs or internal government policies. Fewer difficulties occur when we consider the aggregation of all purchases within each period to give total consumption as considered in §4.2. When making intertemporal choices, consumers are unlikely to have detailed information or expectations about changes in relative prices in future periods. There is thus some merit in the simplistic view that in the future, relative prices will remain unchanged, so that only variations in the expected absolute price level are accounted for. This would then allow one price and one composite commodity for each future period so that the analysis of the consumption function can proceed as in §4.2. For our purposes, this is perhaps the most useful application of the theorem.

The utility tree and two-stage budgeting

If we cannot rely on an external factor, the constancy of relative prices, to define commodity groups, we must instead ask whether or not preferences themselves might not provide some natural structuring of commodities. The first important idea in this context is that of *separability* of preferences. If this holds, the commodities can be partitioned into groups so that preferences within groups can be described independently of the quantities in other groups. For example, if food is a group, the consumer can rank different food bundles in a well-defined ordering which is independent of his consumption of housing, fuel, entertainment, and everything else outside the group. By the arguments of §2.1, this implies that we can have subutility function for each group and that the values of each of these subutilities combine to give total utility. For example, suppose there are six goods, q_1 and q_2 are foods, q_3 and q_4 are housing and fuel, and q_5 and q_6 are TV and watching sports. Then if separable groups, food, shelter, and entertainment are formed, the utility function can be written

$$u = v(q_1, q_2, q_3, q_4, q_5, q_6) = f[v_F(q_1, q_2), v_S(q_3, q_4), v_E(q_5, q_6)] \quad (1.4)$$

where $f(\ )$ is some increasing function and v_F, v_S, and v_E are the subutility functions associated with food, shelter, and entertainment, respectively. There is no reason why each subutility function could not have one or more deeper subgroupings within it, nor should we rule out the possibility that some group may only contain one good. If we put all this together, we get the *utility tree;* the individual commodities are the outermost twigs that join together to form branches that, in turn, join up to form the tree. One possibility is illustrated in Figure 5.1.

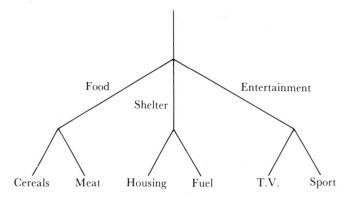

Figure 5.1. A possible utility tree.

The diagram suggests the second important idea, that of *two-stage budgeting*. This occurs when the consumer can allocate total expenditure in two stages; at the first or higher stage, expenditure is allocated to broad groups of goods (food, shelter, and entertainment in Figure 5.1), while at the second, or lower stage, group expenditures are allocated to the individual commodities. At each of these stages, information appropriate to that stage only is required. At the first stage, allocation must be possible given knowledge of total expenditure and appropriately defined group prices, while at the second stage, individual expenditures must be functions of group expenditure and prices within the group only. Both of these allocations have to be perfect in the sense that the results of two-stage budgeting must be identical to what would occur if the allocation were made in one step with complete information. This is the basic definition of two-stage budgeting, and it can be extended and modified in a number of ways. One possibility is the requirement that the decision at each stage can be thought of as corresponding to a utility maximization problem of its own. For example, different foods would be chosen so as to maximize a food subutility function subject to a food budget constraint, while the full utility function would determine the allocation to food, clothing, fuel, and so on. Note that for this latter to work we must be able to define appropriate price and quantity indices for the groups so that the synthetic utility maximization procedure can be defined. A weaker form of two-stage budgeting is to require only that once an optimal allocation has been reached, it can be maintained in the face of changes in prices and total expenditure. Note that two-stage budgeting involves both aggregation (to construct the broad groups) and separable decision making (for each of the group subproblems).

The two ideas, of separability of preferences and of two-stage budgeting, are intimately related to one another but are by no means equivalent; it is *not true* that either one implies the other. What is true, however, is that separability as illustrated in (1.4), often called *weak separability,* is both necessary and sufficient for the *second* stage of two-stage budgeting. If any subset of commodities appears only in a separable subutility function, then quantities purchased within the group can always be written as a function of group expenditure and prices within the group alone. This can be seen directly from structures such as (1.4); the maximization of utility in (1.4) must imply that v_F, v_S, and v_E are each maximized subject to whatever is spent on food, shelter, and entertainment. If this were not so, v_F, v_S, or v_E could be increased without violating the budget constraint, so that, since f is increasing in its arguments, utility cannot be maximal. Hence, the expenditures on q_1 and q_2 are the outcome of maximizing $v_F(q_1, q_2)$ subject to $p_1q_1 + p_2q_2 = x_F$, the total expenditure on food, so that we can write

$$q_i = g_{Fi}(x_F, p_1, p_2), \quad i = 1, 2 \tag{1.5}$$

for the Marshallian subgroup demands. Such demand functions possess all the usual properties of demand functions since they derive from a standard utility maximizing problem. The converse of the result, that the existence of subgroup demand functions as in (1.5) implies weak separability, is also true but is more difficult to prove: an outline is given in the next section.

If we temporarily leave aside the question of the first stage of two-stage budgeting, how useful is the result linking weak separability to the second stage? First, the separability of preferences imposes restrictions on behavior that limit the possible substitution effects between goods in different groups. We shall explore these restrictions further in the next section but the principle is clear enough from Figure 5.1. Apart from income effects, a change in the price of (say) cereals, can only affect the demand for fuel through the same channels and thus in the same way as will a change in the price of any other commodity in the food branch. This is a natural enough restriction, however, and will be satisfied if goods which bear special relationships to one another in consumption either as substitutes or complements are always kept in the same group. Given this, the separability result is important in at least four areas.

First, we may wish to assume that preferences are weakly *intertemporally* separable so that goods in each period form a closely related group with only general relations between periods. The plausibility of this assumption depends very much on the time period adopted, lunch now is rather closely substitutable with lunch twenty minutes hence. Even with longer periods, some goods, holidays, or units in an economics course, may be closely related to one another across time periods thus violating intertemporal separability. Conversely, the adoption of the assumption allows the expression of commodity demands in each period as a function of total outlay and prices in that period alone in accordance with usual practice as discussed in Chapter 3. Note too that there is no other way to justify this; regressing demands on current variables rules out any specific interaction between commodities consumed in different time periods.

Second, if leisure is weakly separable from goods, the allocation of total expenditure is independent of the decision on hours. This is clearly implausible for goods that are closely complementary (recreational goods, TV, etc.) or substitutable (travel to work, business lunches, etc.) with leisure, but may nevertheless be acceptable for the bulk of consumers' expenditure. However, since second-stage budgeting implies weak separability as well as the other way around, the allocation of *all* expenditure without regard to hours worked is only valid if *all* goods are separable from leisure.

The third important application is the obvious one; detailed commodity expenditure can be related to group outlay and prices alone. This has obvious econometric advantages since it is possible to find an explanation for behavior through a much smaller number of variables.

Fourth, and perhaps least obvious, is the application to rationing. If any good or group of goods is rationed and if some other group of goods is separable from the rationed commodity or commodities, then the only effect of the rationing on the goods in the separable group is through total group expenditure. Consequently, if only one good is rationed and all other goods are separable from it, the expenditure needed to buy the ration is simply deducted from total expenditure and the remainder is allocated amongst the other goods independently of the amount of the ration. The most important example here is leisure. If a consumer has no choice over hours worked and if goods are weakly separable from leisure, the spending of the resulting income is explicable without reference to the number of hours actually worked. The converse is just as important. If goods are not weakly separable from leisure and if the consumer is constrained in hours worked, hours worked must appear as an exogenous argument in the allocation of expenditures. These propositions and closely related arguments play an important part in the rest of this book.

The first stage of two-stage budgeting, the allocation of total expenditure into broad groups using group price indices, is more problematical than the second stage. An *exact* solution that does not require the composite commodity theorem demands conditions considerably stronger (and less plausible) than weak separability alone. Nevertheless, as we shall see in the next section, a number of useful approximations are available so that the usual (and largely inevitable) practice of working with broad groups may not involve too great an error. Even so, the existence of such key concepts as the consumption function depends upon the ability to define such aggregates, so it is worthy of note that there appear to be no theoretical assumptions that are not manifestly implausible and that will guarantee *exactly* the treatment of consumption as a single good with a single price. We shall return to this topic in Chapter 12.

Finally, while leaving the details to the next section, it must be emphasized that there are many types of separability other than the "weak" separability just discussed and that most of these different types imply or are implied by different types of two-stage budgeting. The cataloging of all the possibilities is well beyond our present purpose and is well-documented elsewhere, see Blackorby and others (1978), and only one other type is dealt with here. This is *implicit* or *quasi* separability under which not the quantities in the direct utility function but the prices in the cost function are broken up into separable groups. Implicit separability also allows a form of two-stage budgeting whereby the first stage is accomplished perfectly using group price indices that are functions of the utility level, while, at the second stage, the fractions of group outlay going to each good are a function of total utility and in-group prices alone. This structure has been relatively little used either theoretically or empirically so far, but we feel it is of sufficient potential importance to be included in some detail in the next section.

Exercises

5.1. Prove that $c^*(u, p_1, \theta)$, as defined in (1.2), is homogeneous of degree one and concave in p_1 and θ.

5.2. Assume that the price vector p can be partitioned in the form $p = (p_1, \ldots, p_G, \ldots, p_N)$, where each p_G is a subvector of prices. Assume, for all G, $p_G = \lambda_G p_G^0$, for some scalar $\lambda_G > 0$ and constant base period prices p_G^0. Following the steps in the text, define a new cost function on u and $\lambda_1, \ldots, \lambda_G, \ldots, \lambda_N$ and show that it is homogeneous and concave and that the derivative property holds for suitably defined quantity indices.

5.3. Show that for the linear expenditure system *any* group of commodities is separable from any other nonoverlapping group. What does this imply about substitutability between goods in the model? (See also §5.3 below.)

5.4. (Samuelson, 1956.) Discuss the plausibility of a model of intrafamily decision making in which each member possesses a utility function the value of which, in some suitable normalization, is an argument in an overall family utility function. Show that if no goods are consumed jointly (e.g., heating for the whole family), decentralized budgeting is possible. How might joint consumption be dealt with?

5.5. An intertemporal version of the linear expenditure has the utility function

$$u = \sum_{t=1}^{T} \sum_{k=1}^{n} \beta_{tk} \log(q_{tk} - \gamma_{tk})$$

where the t-suffix indicates the time period and the k-suffix the commodity. This is maximized (with exogenous labor supply) subject to the usual intertemporal budget constraint, see equation (2.7) of Chapter 4

$$\sum_k \sum_t p_{tk}^* q_{tk} = W_1$$

By analogy with the conventional linear expenditure system, write down the demand functions for q_{tk} in terms of the $(Tn \times 1)$ vector p^*, W_1 and the parameters. Solve this for $x_i^* = \Sigma_k p_{tk}^* q_{tk}$ in terms of the same variables, and show, by substitution, that q_{tk} can be expressed in terms of x_i^* and p_i^* alone.

5.6. The single period, linear expenditure system with utility functions $\Sigma \beta_k \log(q_k - \gamma_k)$ is separable. Good 1 is rationed to an amount z. Show that maximizing utility subject to $x = \Sigma p_k q_k$ and $q_1 = z$ is equivalent to maximizing $\Sigma_2^n \beta_k \log(q_k - \gamma_k)$ subject to $\Sigma_2^n p_k q_k = x - p_1 z$. Comment on the result.

5.7.* (On the sources of relative price changes.) Suppose that production possibilities in an economy are represented by the cost function $\Sigma c_i(r) e^{-\beta_i t} q_i$, where r is the vector of factor input prices, $c_i(r) e^{-\beta_i t}$ is the unit cost in the ith sector at time t, and β_i is the rate of technical progress in that sector. Show that efficient allocation requires that relative prices of outputs equal relative unit costs. Hence, discuss the role of factor proportions and technical progress in the determination of the relative prices of goods. How might we use an input-output table to measure the consequences for relative prices of changes in prices of primary inputs such as energy?

5.8.* (Exercise 5.7 continued.) If every consumer good price can be written as a linear combination with fixed weights of a few primary input prices, discuss how the Hicks composite commodity theorem as represented in (1.2) can be generalized. Discuss the problems of empirically implementing this approach.

5.2* Separability and two-stage budgeting: further results

The definition of separability

We begin by characterizing separability in terms of the preference ordering. If we write the vector of commodities q in the form $(q_G, q_{\bar{G}})$, where q_G is the vector in the group and $q_{\bar{G}}$ is the vector of excluded commodities, then for any arbitrary fixed vector $\bar{q}_{\bar{G}}$, say, the consumer's preferences over q will define an ordering on q_G. This is a "conditional" ordering on the goods in the group, and, in general, the position of different bundles within the group in the ordering will depend on the preselected values $\bar{q}_{\bar{G}}$. When this is not so, when the conditional ordering on goods in the group is independent of consumption levels outside the group, the group is said to be *separable*. In this case and this case only, the conditional ordering can be represented by a subutility function for the group, $v_G(q_G)$, say. If the whole commodity vector q can be partitioned into N such groups, we say that preferences are (weakly) separable. Separable preferences are represented by a utility function of the form

$$u = f[v_1(q_1), v_2(q_2), \ldots, v_G(q_G), \ldots, v_N(q_N)] \tag{2.1}$$

for subvectors $q_1, \ldots, q_G, \ldots, q_N$ and some function f which is increasing in all its arguments.

Given the argument in §5.1 above, a utility function of the form (2.1) implies subgroup demands or conditional demands of the form, for all i belonging to G

$$q_i = g_{Gi}(x_G, p_G) \tag{2.2}$$

where $x_G = \Sigma_k p_{Gk} q_{Gk}$ is total expenditure on group G. To see that (2.2) implies (2.1), consider the following heuristic argument based on Gorman (1971). Assume that the utility function $v(q)$ is *not* separable but that we partition its arguments to give $v(q_G, q_{\bar{G}})$ and that we maximize this subject to $\Sigma p_k q_k = x$ holding $q_{\bar{G}}$ constant at $\bar{q}_{\bar{G}}$, say. This is equivalent to maximizing the conditional utility function $v_G(q_G; \bar{q}_{\bar{G}}) = v(q_G, \bar{q}_{\bar{G}})$ subject to $\Sigma_{k \in G} p_k q_k = x_G = x - \Sigma_{k \in \bar{G}} p_k q_k$ and will result, for all x_G and p_G in conditional demand functions

$$q_i = f_{Gi}(x_G, p_G; \bar{q}_{\bar{G}}) \tag{2.3}$$

Since (2.2) and (2.3) hold simultaneously everywhere, the conditional demands must be identical to (2.2) and hence independent of the conditioning variables $\bar{q}_{\bar{G}}$. Thus v_G too must be independent of $\bar{q}_{\bar{G}}$ and the utility function is separable, contrary to our original assumption.

Separability and intergroup substitution

Weak separability places severe restrictions on the degree of substitutability between goods in different groups. Again, following Gorman (1971), let $i \in G$ and $j \in H$, where $G \neq H$. If we differentiate (2.2) with respect to p_j holding u constant, the only effect must be through x_G. Hence,

$$s_{ij} = \frac{\partial q_i}{\partial x_G} \cdot \frac{\partial x_G}{\partial p_j}\bigg|_{u=\text{const}} \tag{2.4}$$

But

$$s_{ji} = \frac{\partial q_j}{\partial x_H} \cdot \frac{\partial x_H}{\partial p_i}\bigg|_{u=\text{const}} = s_{ij}, \quad \text{by symmetry} \tag{2.5}$$

Thus, by division,

$$\frac{\partial x_G / \partial p_j}{\partial q_j / \partial x_H}\bigg|_{u=\text{const}} = \frac{\partial x_H / \partial p_i}{\partial q_i / \partial x_G}\bigg|_{u=\text{const}} \tag{2.6}$$

The left-hand side of (2.6) does not involve i, nor does the right-hand side involve j; hence the whole expression is independent of both and may be represented, say, by λ_{GH}. Thus

$$\frac{\partial x_G}{\partial p_j}\bigg|_{u=\text{const}} = \lambda_{GH} \frac{\partial q_j}{\partial x_H} \tag{2.7}$$

and, from (2.4), for $i \in G$, $j \in H$, and $G \neq H$,

$$s_{ij} = \mu_{GH} \frac{\partial q_i}{\partial x} \cdot \frac{\partial q_j}{\partial x} \tag{2.8}$$

where

$$\mu_{GH} \frac{\partial x_G}{\partial x} \frac{\partial x_H}{\partial x} = \lambda_{GH} \qquad (2.9)$$

Although we shall not attempt a proof here, see Gorman (1971), the relationship (2.8) is both necessary and sufficient for weak separability so that this equation summarizes the empirical implications of separability. Note that substitutability between goods in different groups is limited in a very natural way. The quantity μ_{GH} summarizes the interrelation between the groups; individual commodities must conform to this except as modified by the total expenditure responses. Since the branches of the tree are the only means of contact between goods in different groups, responses to price changes and total expenditure changes must use the same channels of communication and hence bear a close relation to one another. Thus, for example, whole groups will be substitutes or complements for one another, and barring inferiority, all pairs of goods, one from each group, must also be substitutes or complements as the case may be.

We can now interpret the terms λ_{GH} in terms of the allocation problem between the broad groups of commodities. If we multiply (2.7) by p_j and sum over all j belonging to H, we get

$$\sum_{j \in H} p_j \frac{\partial x_G}{\partial p_j}\bigg|_{u=\text{const}} = \lambda_{GH} \sum_{j \in H} p_j \frac{\partial q_j}{\partial x_H} = \lambda_{GH} \qquad (2.10)$$

Hence, λ_{GH} is the compensated derivative of expenditure on group G with respect to a proportional change of all prices in group H. The λ_{GH}'s are thus the intergroup substitution terms when each group is defined as a Hicks aggregate with fixed relative prices within the groups. If we define the elements λ_{GG} as the compensated own-price responses of each Hicks aggregate G to its own (aggregate) price, we can complete an $N \times N$ matrix out of the λ's that is interpretable as the Slutsky substitution matrix of the group aggregates under the Hicks' condition. Hence weak separability gives us a two-tier structure of substitution matrices. Within each group, no restrictions are placed on substitution and we have N completely general intragroup Slutsky matrices. Between groups, substitution is limited by (2.8), which in turn reflects a completely general pattern of substitution between groups although not between commodities. This "high-level" substitution matrix is represented by the quantities λ_{GH}. Note, however, that although the λ-matrix reflects substitution between the broad groups, we still have no allocation rule for these groups unless the conditions of the composite commodity theorem are met.

The allocation to broad groups

The correspondence between weak separability and two-stage budgeting and the existence of the subutility functions means that we can define group indirect utility functions and cost functions in the usual way. For example, we can define

$$c_G(u_G, p_G) = \min_{q_G} \left[\sum_G p_k q_k; v_G(q_G) = u_G \right] \tag{2.11}$$

which, in turn yield group indirect utility functions,

$$u_G = \psi_G(x_G, p_G) \tag{2.12}$$

All these functions have properties of homogeneity, concavity, and so on that are the exact counterparts of the properties discussed in Chapter 2. Equations (2.12) and (2.1) allow us to write total utility u as

$$u = f(u_1, u_2, \ldots, u_G, \ldots, u_N) \tag{2.13}$$

The broad group allocation problem is then solved by maximizing (2.13) subject to the budget constraint

$$\sum_1^N c_G(u_G, p_G) = x \tag{2.14}$$

In general, if no restrictions are placed on the functions c_G or ψ_G, solution of this maximization problem requires knowledge of all of the individual prices. It is thus not generally possible to replace (2.13) and (2.14) by a maximization problem involving a single price index and a single quantity index for each of the broad groups. The conditions which do permit this have been derived by Gorman (1959). One possibility is that each group cost function $c_G(u_G, p_G)$ can be written as $\theta_G(u_G) b_G(p_G)$ for some first degree homogeneous function $b_G(p_G)$ and some monotone increasing function $\theta_G(u_G)$. Making the substitution $v_G = \theta_G(u_G)$, the maximization problem becomes

$$\max u = f[\theta_1^{-1}(v_1), \ldots, \theta_G^{-1}(v_G), \ldots, \theta_N^{-1}(v_N)] \tag{2.15}$$

such that

$$\Sigma b_G(p_G)v_G = x$$

Clearly, the v_G's can be thought of as group quantity indices with corresponding price indices $b_G(p_G)$, so that (2.15) gives a perfect utility maximizing solution to the broad group allocation problem. Unfortunately, as we shall see in §5.4, this specific form for c_G implies that the budget shares within each group are independent of total group expenditure. Hence, we may never group together necessities and luxuries; everything in each group must have the same total expenditure elasticity. This condition and the composite commodity theorem are each in their own way rather restrictive and neither provides a satisfactory general basis for the allocation to broad groups.

The second solution proposed by Gorman is that the indirect utility functions ψ_G take the *Gorman generalized polar form*

$$\psi_G(x_G, \, p_G) = F_G[x_G / b_G(p_G)] + a_G(p_G) \tag{2.16}$$

for some monotone increasing function $F_G(\ \ )$, while the utility function should take an explicitly additive form between groups, that is,

$$u = v_1(q_1) + v_2(q_2) + \cdots + v_G(q_G) + \cdots + v_N(q_N) \tag{2.17}$$

In this case, (2.13) is also additive, and using essentially the same substitutions as before, that is, $v_G = x_G / b_G(p_G)$, (2.15) becomes

$$\max u = \Sigma F_G(v_G) + \Sigma a_G(p_G)$$

such that

$$\Sigma b_G(p_G) v_G = x$$

Once again, the v_G's and b_G's are interpretable as quantity and price indices while the additive structure of utility means that the functions a_G are irrelevant for the maximization and thus do not need to be known by the consumer. The Gorman generalized polar form is a good deal less restrictive with nonzero a_G's than without. Although it places restrictions on the allowable forms, see Exercise 5.13, nonlinear relationships between within-group expenditures and group outlay are permitted. However, the additivity restriction (2.17) is both severe and, in our view, unrealistic; it will be discussed more fully in §5.3. Gorman shows that, apart from the case where there are only two groups, the conditions of this or the previous paragraph are necessary and sufficient for broad group allocation within the framework of weak separability. A reasonably general solution must thus be either an approximate one or one that abandons weak separability.

An approximate solution can be derived by returning to the original problem, the maximization of (2.13) subject to (2.14). In Chapter 7 we shall discuss how the cost function can be used to define price and quantity indices. Anticipating this, choose some base price vector p^0 with associated subvectors p_G^0 and write

$$c_G(u_G, \, p_G) = c(u_G, \, p_G^0) \cdot \frac{c(u_G, \, p_G)}{c(u_G, \, p_G^0)} \tag{2.18}$$

The first term on the right-hand side of (2.18) is the money cost of reaching the utility level u_G at base period group prices p_G^0. This is itself a satisfactory measure of utility and we write it v_G so that u_G is given by $\psi(v_G, \, p_G^0)$. The second term, as we shall see in Chapter 7 is a true cost-of-living price index for group G; we write it as $P_G(p_G, \, p_G^0; \, u_G)$ to emphasize its dependence on u_G. The problem, (2.13) to (2.14), is then to maximize

$$u = f\{\psi_1(v_1, \, p_1^0), \, \ldots, \, \psi_G(v_G, \, p_G^0), \, \ldots, \, \psi_N(v_N, \, p_N^0)\}$$

such that

$$\Sigma v_G P_G(p_G,\ p_G^0;\ u_G) = x \qquad (2.19)$$

This is now very much in standard form with matching price and quantity indices v_G and P_G. In fact, in empirical work, we rarely have available physical measures of quantity and instead work with quantity and price indices. Hence, it is quite usual to think of the budget constraint in the form of (2.19). The difficulty lies in the fact that P_G is a function of u_G and if we allow for this dependency explicitly we are, of course, back to (2.13) and (2.14). Nevertheless, as we shall see in Chapter 7, it may be that the empirical variation of P_G with u_G is not very great so that indices involved in (2.19) can be approximated by Paasche or Laspeyres indices, which are exactly those indices that are involved when demand systems are estimated on national accounts data for aggregated groups. So the construct (2.19) may provide some justification for standard practice, albeit in an approximate way.

The variation of the group price indices with group utility reflects the fact that within-group Engel curves generally are not straight lines through the origin. If, however, the group cost functions take the form $x_G = a_G(p_G) + \theta_G(u_G)b_G(p_G)$ for functions a_G, θ_G, and b_G, then it will be shown in §5.4 that this gives linear, within-group Engel curves (not necessarily through the origin). With this form and only weak separability, it is easily seen (Exercise 5.14) that total group expenditure can be written as a function of total expenditure and two sets of price indices constructed from the a's and b's. Exactly this idea, assuming weak separability but working with local approximations in terms of derivatives, has been advocated by those who work with differential demand systems, see particularly Barten and Turnovsky (1966), Barten (1970) and Theil (1975). The algebra is simplest using the Rotterdam equations [Chapter 3, (3.3)] although the derivation is quite general since no parameters are being assumed constant. Equations (2.8) and (2.9) can be rewritten, for all $i \in G$ and $j \in H$, and Kronecker delta δ_{GH} (=0 for $G \neq H$ and 1 if $G = H$),

$$p_i p_j s_{ij} = \delta_{GH} s_{ij}^G p_i p_j + \lambda_{GH}\ p_i\ \frac{\partial q_i}{\partial x_G}\ p_j\ \frac{\partial q_j}{\partial x_H} \qquad (2.20)$$

to give the Rotterdam c_{ij} parameters when divided by x. Application of homogeneity to (2.20) implies that $\Sigma_{i\in G} p_i s_{ij}^G = 0$ for all j and G, see Exercise 5.10, so that substitution of (2.20) into (3.3) from Chapter 3 and summing over $i \in G$ gives

$$\sum_{i\in G} w_i\, d \log q_i \equiv x^{-1} \sum_{i\in G} p_i\, dq_i = b_G(d \log x - \Sigma w_k\, d \log p_k)$$

$$+ \sum_{j\in H} \sum_H x^{-1}\lambda_{GH} p_j \frac{\partial q_j}{\partial x_H}\, d \log p_j \qquad (2.21)$$

where $b_G = \Sigma_{i\in G} b_i$ is the marginal propensity to spend on the group. We can then define two differential group price indices by

$$d \log P_G^1 = \sum_{k \in G} \left(\frac{p_k q_k}{x_G} \right) d \log p_k$$

$$(2.22)$$

$$d \log P_G^2 = \sum_{k \in G} \left(p_k \frac{\partial q_k}{\partial x_G} \right) d \log p_k$$

one with in-group budget shares as weights, the other with in-group marginal propensities. Equation (2.21) then becomes

$$\sum_{i \in G} w_i \, d \log q_i = x^{-1} \sum_{i \in G} p_i \, dq_i$$

$$(2.23)$$

$$= b_G (d \log x - \Sigma w_G \, d \log P_G^1) + \Sigma \lambda_{GH}^* \, d \log P_H^2$$

where $w_G = \Sigma_{k \in G} p_k q_k / x$ and $\lambda_{GH}^* = \lambda_{GH} / x$. Apart from the presence of the two price indices instead of one, (2.23) is another Rotterdam system for allocating the broad groups, moreover, b_G and λ_{GH}^* may easily be shown to possess all the correct properties of such parameters in the model. Hence, (2.23) offers a method of maintaining an optimal allocation, once it is reached, requiring knowledge of only two price indices for each group. In practice, if prices move roughly together, the two price indices may well be close to one another and might be adequately proxied by a single index. Note that this result requires no restrictions beyond weak separability.

Implicit separability and two-stage budgeting

Weak separability is by no means the only type of separability nor is two-stage budgeting as so far defined the only useful form of hierarchic decision making. Implicit or quasi separability, first described by Gorman (1970), provides an alternative and, in many respects, simpler structure. Preferences are said to be implicitly separable if and only if the cost function can be written in the form

$$c(u, p) = C[u, c_1(u, p_1), \ldots, c_G(u, p_G), \ldots, c_N(u, p_N)] \qquad (2.24)$$

where, as before, the goods are partitioned into N groups with price subvectors $p_1, \ldots, p_N$. The functions $c_G(u, p_G)$ are increasing in u and p_G. Note carefully that it is *total* utility that appears in each of the functions $c_G(u, p_G)$; in sharp contrast to weak separability there are no group subutilities.

Differentiating (2.24) with respect to p_i, where good i belongs to group G,

$$q_i = h_i(u, p) = \frac{\partial c(u, p)}{\partial p_i} = \frac{\partial C}{\partial c_G} \cdot \frac{\partial c_G}{\partial p_i} \qquad (2.25)$$

Hence group expenditure x_G is given by

$$x_G = \sum_{i \in G} q_i p_i = \frac{\partial C}{\partial c_G} \sum_{i \in G} p_i \frac{\partial c_G}{\partial p_i} = \frac{\partial C}{\partial c_G} \cdot c_G(u, p_G) \qquad (2.26)$$

since each $c_G(u, p_G)$ is linear homogeneous. Thus, writing $w_G \equiv x_G/x$ for the group budget shares

$$w_G = \frac{\partial \log C}{\partial \log c_G} \tag{2.27}$$

while for the intragroup budget shares $w_{iG} \equiv p_i q_i/x_G$, from (2.25) and (2.26)

$$w_{iG} = \frac{\partial \log c_G(u, p_G)}{\partial \log p_i} \tag{2.28}$$

Provided we are prepared to revise our concepts somewhat, equations (2.27) and (2.28) show that implicit separability provides an extremely simple and perfectly consistent form of two-stage budgeting. First of all, it is clear from (2.26) that the functions $c_G(u, p_G)$ are *not* equal to group total expenditures x_G; rather they should be thought of as group price indices that depend on the level of utility u. Hence (2.24) tells us that, given implicit separability, we can define group price indices $c_G(u, p_G)$ – properly homogeneous in p_G – over which a macrocost function $C(u, \ )$ is defined. This macrocost function can be used to allocate expenditures to the broad groups in accordance with the derivative property in logarithmic form (2.27). In fact, we can go beyond this, and we shall show next that quantity indices can be defined for each group that are equal to the partial derivatives themselves. Hence, the top stage of two-stage budgeting can take place according to "macro" utility maximization and without error if preferences are such that (2.24) holds. The second, or bottom stage, is given by (2.28). The allocation within the groups can also be derived from appropriately defined cost functions and again the derivative rule works in logarithmic form. From (2.25), we see that q_i is not equal to $\partial c_G/\partial p_i$, so (2.28) is as far as we shall get. But this is really quite enough; the microallocations can be carried out using total utility and group prices alone.

Implicit separability and the distance function**

The previous discussion can be extended if we examine the implications of implicit separability for the distance function discussed in §2.7. Define (direct) implicit separability as holding if and only if the distance function can be written in the form

$$d(u, q) = D[u, d_1(u, q_1), \ldots, d_G(u, q_G), \ldots, d_N(u, q_N)] \tag{2.29}$$

for a partition of q. This is clearly dual to the definition of implicit separability through the cost function (2.24). It turns out that the two definitions are not only analogous, they are identical. Following Gorman (1976), starting from (7.4) in Chapter 2 and substituting from (2.29)

$$c(u, p) = \min_q [\Sigma \, p_k q_k; \, d(u, q) = 1]$$

$$= \min_q \left\{ \sum_G \sum_{k \in G} p_k q_k; \, D[u, d_1(u, q_1), \, \ldots, d_N(u, q_N)] = 1 \right\}$$

$$= \min_v \left\{ \sum_G \min_{q_G} \left[\sum_{k \in G} p_k q_k; \, d_G(u, q_G) = v_G \right]; \, D(u, v) = 1 \right\}$$

$$= \min_v \left\{ \sum_G \min_{q_G^*} \left[\sum_{k \in G} p_k q_k^* v_G; \, d_G(u, q_G^*) = 1 \right]; \, D(u, v) = 1 \right\}$$

$$= \min_v \left[\sum_G v_G c_G(u, p_G); \, D(u, v) = 1 \right]$$

$$= C[u, c_1(u, p_1), \, \ldots, c_G(u, p_G), \, \ldots, c_N(u, p_N)] \tag{2.30}$$

where $v_1, \, \ldots, v_N$ are a set of positive scalars, $q_G^* = q_G / v_G$, C is some function, and $c_G(u, p_G)$ is defined by

$$c_G(u, p_G) = \min_{q_G} \left[\sum_{k \in G} q_k p_k; \, d_G(u, q_G) = 1 \right] \tag{2.31}$$

A precisely similar converse argument takes us from (2.30) to (2.29). Hence, under implicit separability, the structure of separability is identical in both primal and dual formulations. No other form of separability seems to possess this extremely elegant and simple property.

From the definition (2.31), q_G would be the cheapest way of reaching u at p_G if utility were implicitly defined by $d_G(u, q_G) = 1$. Hence, compare with equation (7.3) in Chapter 2,

$$x_G = \sum_{k \in G} p_k q_k = d_G(u, q_G) \cdot c_G(u, p_G) \tag{2.32}$$

Comparing with (2.26) we have at once

$$\frac{\partial C(u, c_1, \, \ldots, c_G, \, \ldots, c_N)}{\partial c_G} = d_G(u, q_G) \tag{2.33}$$

Equation (2.33) provides the justification for claims that implicit separability provides a perfect allocation mechanism for broad groups. The expression $d_G(u, q_G)$ is a quantity index for group G, dependent on utility, but linearly homogeneous in q_G. The indices $c_1 \cdots c_N$, are price indices, one for each group, and again dependent on the utility level u. The macrocost function $C(\ )$ is then defined over these N indices and utility $u;$ it too is concave and linearly homogeneous in the indices. Finally, (2.33) shows that the quantity indices are given as the derivatives of the macrocost function with respect to the price indices. Thus, provided we can define the indices appropriately, implicit separability allows us to treat broad groups of goods as if they were single commodities.

Empirical comparisons of weak and implicit separability

We have seen how both weak and implicit separability, although different from one another, each imply schemes for two-stage budgeting. At the first level, the allocation to broad groups, there is perhaps little difference between the two structures. Implicit separability gives a theoretically "perfect" solution, but the price and quantity indices depend on the total utility level and, in empirical work, this is likely to require some approximation. Analogous approximations are required for the weakly separable scheme (2.24). Even so, detailed empirical comparisons may yet reveal unsuspected differences.

At the second stage of budgeting, the situation is quite different. In Hicksian terms, weak separability implies that *quantities* demanded are a function of *group* utility and within-group prices while implicit separability implies that *intragroup budget shares* are a function of *total* utility and within-group prices. This last implies, for example, that a compensated price increase outside the group – no matter what the good – will change all intragroup expenditures by the same proportion. This is matched, for weak separability, by the restrictions on substitution given by (2.8). These differences are important both for theory and for econometrics. In empirical work, the obvious application is to systems of demand equations. As we argued before, relating commodity demands to total expenditure x and current prices p assumes weak intertemporal separability of preferences. If instead, preferences are *implicitly* intertemporally separable, budget shares should be related not to x and p but to intertemporal utility and p. This would demand the introduction of lifetime expected wealth W_1 as well as future anticipated prices into demand systems and might have radical implications for the type of results usually obtained. This is work that remains to be done. The empirical task is complicated by the fact that we are comparing models with the same dependent variables but different explanatory variables. Conventional statistical tests designed for testing restrictions (such as homogeneity or symmetry) do not deal with this case, and instead we require tests for "nonnested" models. These tests have recently been developed in the econometric literature [for an elementary application to demand analysis see Deaton (1978)], but considerably more work needs to be undertaken before we can be certain of their properties in practice.

Exercises

5.9. The marginal rate of substitution between goods i and j is given by $MRS_{ij} = (\partial v/\partial q_i)/(\partial v/\partial q_j)$, which equals p_i/p_j at an internal equilibrium, see §2.2. Show that under weak separability, if i and $j \in G$ and $k \in H \neq G$, then MRS_{ij} is independent of k. The converse of this result is also true and is known as the Leontief separation theorem, see Leontief (1947).

5.10. Using (2.8) and the definition of λ_{GH} given by (2.10), prove that (a) $\Sigma_G \lambda_{GH} = \Sigma_H \lambda_{GH} = 0$, (b) $\lambda_{GH} = \lambda_{HG}$, (c) $\Sigma_{i \in G} p_i s_{ij}^G = 0$.

5.11. Prove that the compensated cross-price elasticity $e_{i1}^* = \partial \log q_i / \partial \log p_1|u = $ constant, is independent of i if and only if all other goods are implicitly separable from good 1.

5.12. *Indirect* weak separability is said to hold when the indirect utility function $\psi(x, p)$ written in terms of the price-outlay ratios $r = p/x$ takes the form $\psi(x, p) = \psi^*(r) = f[\psi_1(r_1), \ldots, \psi_G(r_G), \ldots, \psi_N(r_N)]$ for some partition of prices. Show that, under indirect separability, the intragroup value shares $w_{iG} = w_i/w_G$ depend only on total expenditure and group prices. What is the difference between this result and the corresponding formulation under implicit separability?

5.13. The Gorman "generalized polar form" of the indirect utility function (at the group level) is $u = \theta[x/b(p)] + a(p)$. Show, by working with the corresponding cost function, that this implies a relationship between the budget shares of the form

$$w_i = A_{ij}(p)w_j + B_{ij}(p)$$

5.14. Suppose the utility function is weakly separable and that, at the group level, preferences are given by $c_G(u_G, p_G) = a_G(p_G) + u_G b_G(p_G)$. Show that group expenditure can be written as a function of total expenditure and the price indices a_K, b_K, $K = 1, \ldots, N$. Is this result more or less general than the Barten and Turnovsky result discussed in the text?

5.15.* Using the distance function $d(u, q) = 1$ to characterize preferences, show that $MRS_{ij} = (\partial d/\partial q_i)/(\partial d/\partial q_j)$. Hence show that for $i, j \in G$ and $k \notin G$, weak separability implies that MRS_{ij} is independent of k while implicit separability implies that MRS_{ij} is independent of k *along an indifference curve*. How are we to interpret the phrase "along an indifference curve" when a single quantity is being varied? (Continued as Exercise 5.28.)

5.3 Strong separability and additive preferences

Definition of additivity

One of the most popular assumptions about preferences, and one of the most restrictive, is strong or additive separability. In this case, the direct utility function is again made up of subutility functions for each group, but unlike weak separability, they are combined additively. Hence, utility is written as

$$u = F[v_1(q_1) + v_2(q_2) + \cdots + v_N(q_N)] \tag{3.1}$$

so that under some monotone transformation, the utility function takes the explicitly additive form. Note carefully that it is preferences that are strongly or additively separable, not the utility function, hence for example

$$u = \Pi \exp[v_k(q_k)] \quad \text{and} \quad u = \Sigma v_k(q_k) \tag{3.2}$$

are both representations of the same additively separable preferences. In the case where there is only one good in each group, preferences are said to be *additive* or occasionally, that "wants are independent." The terms *strong separability* or *block additivity* are usually reserved for the case of multigood groups. In the history of consumer theory, additive preferences have played an important role. The founders of consumer theory, Gossen and Jevons, clearly thought of utility as being generated in this way, and later writers such as Marshall and Pigou made heavy use of the assumption of independent wants. In more recent writing, theorists have continued to find it a very useful assumption, while econometricians have found its restrictiveness an important aid in generating degrees of freedom for estimation. For example, by far and away the most popular demand model, the linear expenditure system, is derived from the utility function (2.5) in Chapter 3, which can easily be seen to represent additive preferences.

Empirical implications of additivity

The restrictiveness of (3.1) lies in the fact that no group occupies any special position. Since the function is additive, we can arbitrarily create new groups by combining any others, and this effectively prevents the existence of any particular relationships between pairs of groups. We shall take up this point formally at the end of this section, where we show that if i and j are two goods in different groups, the substitution effect between them can only take the form

$$s_{ij} = \mu \frac{\partial q_i}{\partial x} \frac{\partial q_j}{\partial x} \tag{3.3}$$

Note that μ is independent of the groups to which i and j belong. If preferences are additive, then (3.3) holds for all pairs of goods. It is this case that we pursue further; if preferences are block additive, our conclusions will apply to the broad groups regarded as Hicks aggregates.

Equation (3.3) defines the off-diagonal terms of the Slutsky matrix. The diagonal terms can be filled in using the relationship $\Sigma_k s_{ik} p_k = 0$ to give

$$s_{ii} = - \frac{\mu}{p_i} \frac{\partial q_i}{\partial x} \left(1 - p_i \frac{\partial q_i}{\partial x} \right) \tag{3.4}$$

In elasticity terms, using $e_{ij}^* = s_{ij} p_j / q_i$ and $e_{ij} = e_{ij}^* - e_i w_j$,

$$e_{ii} = \phi e_i - e_i w_i (1 + \phi e_i) \qquad i = 1, \ldots, n \tag{3.5}$$
$$e_{ij} = - e_i w_j (1 + \phi e_j) \qquad i \neq j$$

where $\phi = -\mu/x$ is a scalar not indexed on i. This last relation (3.5), first observed by Frisch (1959), shows why additivity is both so useful and so restrictive. Apart from the parameter ϕ, knowledge of expenditure elasticities alone is sufficient to determine all the own and cross-price elasticities. Consequently, the econometrician needs almost no relative price variation in the data in order to estimate price elasticities so that, for example, knowledge of one price elasticity is sufficient to allow cross-section household budget data to be used to "measure" price elasticities. The measurement is, of course, largely by assumption.

All this information comes at a price. Equations (3.3) and (3.4) give a particularly simple structure to the substitution matrix, and apart from very peculiar cases, the matrix will only be negative semidefinite if μ is positive (so that ϕ is negative) and if each of the expenditure elasticities is positive. Thus, inferior goods are ruled out at once, while (3.3) rules out complements permitting goods to be substitutes only. Even more severe are the consequences of (3.5). Since all the value shares are positive and add to unity, each is of the same order of magnitude as the reciprocal of the number of goods. Hence, if the number of goods – or commodity groups in the case of block additivity – is at all large, we have, to a reasonable degree of approximation, from (3.5)

$$e_{ii} \simeq \phi e_i \tag{3.6}$$

This approximate proportionality of expenditure and price elasticities, which in practice tends to be quite accurate even for eight or ten commodities, has been called Pigou's Law by Deaton (1974b) after a suggestion on the same lines by Pigou (1910). Even for broad aggregates of goods, we have no reason to suppose a priori that (3.6) is true so that, if we assume additivity, we risk severe distortion of measurement. For a fairly detailed disaggregation of commodities, the distortion is clear and is documented commodity by commodity for the case of the linear expenditure system in Deaton (1975a). In practice, the data is usually such that the variation in total outlay is much greater than that in relative prices, so the price elasticities tend to be distorted most heavily. Figure 5.2, reproduced from Deaton (1975b), illustrates this feature for a 37-commodity disaggregation of British consumers' expenditure. It shows a plot of price elasticities calculated from estimates of the linear expenditure system against those from another model that is not derived from additive preferences. These latter were cross-checked against a second nonadditive model and shown to correspond reasonably closely. Between the linear expenditure system and the nonadditive models, however, the correspondence is virtually nonexistent, as Figure 5.2 shows. This strongly suggests that additivity and its implications, (3.5) and (3.6), far from being an aid to measurement, positively hinder it.

Even so, it can be argued that for sufficiently broad groups of goods, the proportionality restriction and the absence of inferiority and complementarity are not obviously inappropriate. The evidence would seem to be against this. For example, it is possible to test (3.3) and (3.4) within the Rotterdam model. In this case, the C matrix of the Rotterdam model, see (3.6) in Chapter 3, takes the form, see Exercise 5.20,

$$c_{ij} = \phi(\delta_{ij}b_i - b_ib_j) \tag{3.7}$$

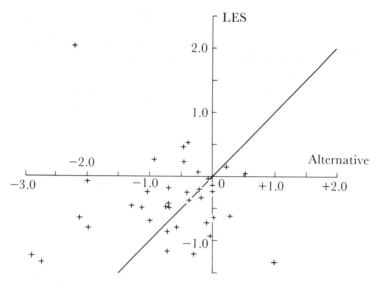

Figure 5.2. Price elasticities estimated from the linear expenditure system and an alternative model. (From A. S. Deaton, *European Economic Review,* Vol. 6, 1975.)

where ϕ is as before and b_i is the marginal propensity to spend on good i. This restriction can be tested in the same way as symmetry and homogeneity was tested in Chapter 3. Barten (1969) has done this for a 16-commodity disaggregation of Dutch data and encountered a very large drop in likelihood, indicating a sharp rejection of the additivity hypothesis. Deaton (1974a), using 9 commodities and British data, came to a similar conclusion and also found that the linear expenditure system, which is also additive, gave similar results to the additive version of the Rotterdam model. Even with highly aggregated commodities and only 4 groups, Theil (1976) does not find additivity acceptable. Further evidence using nonnested testing procedures with the linear expenditure system in Deaton (1978) further supports the conclusion. Clearly then, strong separability and additivity are too strong to be used in empirical work, despite their undoubted econometric advantages.

Additivity and the "measurement" of marginal utility

In the case where the first-order conditions $\partial v/\partial q_i = \lambda p_i$ solve for the demand functions, an alternative derivation of (3.5) is possible and this is the route followed by most previous authors. In particular, the function F in (3.1) is taken as the unit function $F(x) \equiv x$, so that normalization of utility is chosen that gives the explicitly additive form. In this normalization, marginal utility $\partial v/\partial q_i$ is a function of q_i alone, and this can be used to derive (3.5), see Exercise 5.16. Following this derivation, the quantity ϕ turns out to be the reciprocal of $\partial \log \lambda / \partial \log x$, the elasticity of the marginal utility of outlay with respect to outlay. Since the estimation of any demand system based on additive preferences will yield an estimate of ϕ, it would appear that demand analysis can provide a measure, if not of marginal utility, at least of its derivative with respect to total expenditure. As we shall see in Chapter 9, such a measure could be useful in applied welfare economics, and many authors, starting with Frisch (1932), have attempted to use additivity to make such calculations. Such applications have produced a fair uniformity of results; ϕ is usually estimated as close to -0.5, giving an estimate of -2 for the elasticity of marginal utility.

In assessing these claims, note first that our original derivation of (3.5) is quite independent of the choice for F. The equation would be the same and ϕ would be the same if, for example, utility were either $\Sigma v_k(q_k)$ or $\Pi \exp[v_k(q_k)]$. In other words, ϕ is a parameter of the *preference ordering* and is independent of the specific utility function chosen to represent it. It cannot then have anything to do with marginal utility, which varies from one normalization to another. It is certainly true that for $u = \Sigma v_k(q_k)$, $\phi = (\partial \log \lambda / \partial \log x)^{-1}$, but as soon as the utility function is nonlinearly transformed, for example to $\exp[\Sigma v_k(q_k)]$, ϕ no longer has this interpretation, although preferences, observable behavior, and the estimate of ϕ remain unchanged. Hence, we can only accept ϕ as a measure of the reciprocal of the elasticity of marginal utility if (a) we accept that consumers do actually have a utility level (i.e., the utility function has a real significance beyond the convenient mathematical representation of preferences) and (b) that consumers with additive preferences always choose to measure utility using the explicitly additive form. We see no conceivable basis for testing either (a) or (b) so that there seems to be no grounds other than assertion for assigning the marginal utility interpretation to estimates of ϕ. Nor is the uniformity in the estimates of ϕ itself surprising. According to (3.6), ϕ will be estimated at close to the average ratio of price to total expenditure elasticity. Most studies have worked with between 6 and 16 commodities and, at this level of disaggregation, an average of -0.5 is perfectly plausible.

Formal derivation of equation (3.3) *

Start from equation (3.1) and take three goods i, j, and k each belonging to a different group I, J, and K. Since a strongly separable utility function is certainly weakly separable, we can use the results of §5.2, particularly (2.8). We do this in two ways, first, recognizing the three groups and, second, combining J and K into a new group L, which because of strong separability is also separable from I. From (2.8), there exist μ_{IJ}, μ_{IL}^*, μ_{IK}, such that

$$s_{ij} = \mu_{IJ} \frac{\partial q_i}{\partial x} \cdot \frac{\partial q_j}{\partial x} = \mu_{IL}^* \frac{\partial q_i}{\partial x} \cdot \frac{\partial q_j}{\partial x} \tag{3.7}$$

$$s_{ik} = \mu_{IK} \frac{\partial q_i}{\partial x} \cdot \frac{\partial q_k}{\partial x} = \mu_{IL}^* \frac{\partial q_i}{\partial x} \cdot \frac{\partial q_k}{\partial x} \tag{3.8}$$

Hence, dividing s_{ij} by s_{ik}, $\mu_{IJ} = \mu_{IK}$ and, since J and K are arbitrary, μ_{IJ} is dependent on I only. However, by symmetry, $s_{ij} = s_{ji}$, $\mu_{IJ} = \mu_{J.}$ and so μ_{IJ} is independent of both I and J. Hence, writing $\mu_{IJ} = \mu$, (3.7) reduces to (3.3).

Exercises

5.16. Prove (3.5) from the first-order conditions (2.4) in Chapter 2 following the outline given below. Taking logarithms of (2.4) in Chapter 2 gives $\log(\partial v/\partial q_i) = \log \lambda + \log p_i$. Differentiate this with respect to $\log x$ and $\log p_j$ in turn, remembering that, under additivity, $\partial v/\partial q_i$ is a function of q_i alone. Hence, writing $\omega = \partial \log \lambda/\partial \log x$ and $\theta_i = \partial \log \lambda/\partial \log p_i$, show that $\omega e_{ij} = e_i \theta_j + \delta_{ij} e_i$. Finally, use the adding-up restrictions $\Sigma w_i e_{ij} + w_j = 0$ and $\Sigma w_i e_i = 1$ to solve for and eliminate θ_j. Check that $\phi = \omega^{-1}$.

5.17. In his original article, Pigou (1910) asserts that under additivity the proportional effect on the marginal utility of money of a one percentage increase in a single price is negligibly small. Assess this claim in the light of your solution for θ_i in the previous question.

5.18. Show that, under additivity, cross-price elasticities are always small relative to own-price and to total expenditure elasticities.

5.19. Lluch, Powell, and Williams (1978) estimate the linear expenditure system for four commodity groups (one of which is usually all food) for a large number of countries and state that they find little evidence for Deaton's (1974b) "assertion" that $e_{ii} \simeq \phi e_i$. Why might the approximation break down in this case? Does this mean that the linear expenditure system is less restrictive for very broad groups of goods?

5.20. Using (3.5), show that the Rotterdam c_{ij} parameters satisfy $c_{ij} = \phi(\delta_{ij} b_i - b_i b_j)$ under additivity. Check this for the case of the linear expenditure system, and derive an expression for ϕ in this case. How would you expect ϕ to vary over time if calculated on the basis of estimates from the linear expenditure system?

5.21. *Indirect* additivity is said to hold when the indirect utility function in terms of $p/x \equiv r$ can be written $\psi(x, p) \equiv \psi^*(r) = f[\Sigma \psi_k(r_k)]$. Show that the condition e_{ij} independent of j for all $i, j, i \neq j$ is both necessary and sufficient for indirect additivity. (Necessity is straightforward, sufficiency is harder.)

5.4 Homotheticity and quasi homotheticity

Homothetic preferences

We have already had occasion to mention homotheticity several times and the time has come to describe it more fully. Preferences are said to be homothetic, if, for some normalization of the utility function, doubling quantities doubles utility. Drawing the analogy with production theory, preferences are said to

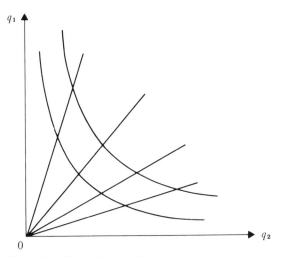

Figure 5.3. Homothetic preferences.

be homothetic if utility can be produced under constant returns to scale. In this case, each indifference curve is simply a magnified or reduced version of every other one. As illustrated in Figure 5.3, any ray through the origin will cut all the indifference curves at points where the slope is the same, which has several immediate consequences. First, because of the constant slope property, the expansion paths given by increasing x with p constant will be straight lines through the origin. Clearly, the implication is that the composition of the budget is independent of total expenditure or of utility. Hence, all expenditure elasticities are unity. The second consequence is for the structure of the cost function. If we label indifference curves along any ray through the origin such that double utility is generated by being twice as far from the origin, then the cost of reaching utility u must be proportional to u.

These two properties, obvious from Figure 5.3, can easily be demonstrated formally. First, preferences are homothetic if and only if we can write, for an arbitrary scalar $\theta > 0$

$$u = F[v(q)]; \quad v(\theta q) = \theta v(q) \tag{4.1}$$

That is, utility is a monotone increasing function of a function that is homogeneous of degree one. By ordinality, we can choose $v(q)$ itself as our representation of preferences. In this normalization $c(u, p) = \min[\Sigma p_k q_k; \; v(q) = u]$. Since $v(q)$ is homogeneous, doubling u will be accomplished by doubling q and, hence, by doubling costs. Then

$$c(u, p) = ub(p) \tag{4.2}$$

for some function $b(p)$ that is linearly homogeneous and concave in p. Again by analogy with production theory, the marginal and average costs of utility are constant and equal to one another. If we take logs of (4.2) and differentiate with respect to log p_i, we have

$$w_i = \frac{\partial \log c(u, p)}{\partial \log p_i} = \frac{\partial \log b(p)}{\partial \log p_i} \tag{4.3}$$

which, since $b(p)$ is independent of u, establishes that the budget shares are independent of u and hence of x. That all expenditure elasticities should be unity contradicts all known household budget studies, not to mention most of the time-series evidence of systematic change in expenditure patterns as total outlays increase. In consequence, the assumption of constant returns to scale is much less useful in consumption than in production theory.

Quasi homotheticity and linear Engel curves

Much of the mathematical convenience of homotheticity may be retained within the economically much more fruitful assumption of "quasi" homotheticity, exploited extensively by Gorman (1961, 1976). In this formulation, a fixed cost element is added to the cost function (4.2), so that we have the *Gorman polar form* [c.f., (2.16) with $F_G(x) \equiv x$]

$$c(u, p) = a(p) + ub(p) \tag{4.4}$$

The quantity $a(p)$ represents the cost of living when u is zero, and may thus be interpreted as subsistence expenditure. For example, in the linear expenditure system, which has a cost function of the form (4.4), $a(p)$ takes the form $\Sigma \gamma_k p_k$, so that subsistence expenditure is the cost of the subsistence quantities γ. From (4.4), the indirect utility function is given by

$$u = \psi(x, p) = \frac{x - a(p)}{b(p)} \tag{4.5}$$

which has an obvious interpretation as the real value of expenditure in excess of that required for subsistence. Differentiating (4.4) and substituting from (4.5) gives

$$q_i = a_i(p) + \frac{b_i(p)}{b(p)} [x - a(p)] \tag{4.6}$$

where $a_i(p)$ and $b_i(p)$ are the ith partial derivatives of $a(p)$ and $b(p)$, respectively. This equation shows how quasi homotheticity restricts behavior; all Engel curves are straight lines. Under homotheticity, Engel curves are straight lines through the origin, so all expenditure elasticities are unity;

under "quasi" homotheticity, the straight lines need not go through the origin, and elasticities only tend to unity as total expenditure increases. This is a significant generalization although it is still unlikely to be true for narrowly defined commodities. Even for broad groups such as food, household budget studies tend to give nonlinear Engel curves. However, such data do not, by definition, show the response of single individuals or households as outlays increase. On time-series data, albeit at an aggregate level, it is much less obvious that linear Engel curves are contradicted by the evidence for broad groups of goods.

If quasi homotheticity is valid, it offers a very convenient representation of how the pattern of demand alters with total outlay. In budget share, form (4.6) implies

$$w_i = \left(\frac{p_i a_i}{a}\right)\left(\frac{a}{x}\right) + \left(\frac{p_i b_i}{b}\right)\left(1 - \frac{a}{x}\right) \tag{4.7}$$

so that the ith value share is a weighted average of two expressions, the weights depending on the ratio of fixed costs a to total expenditure. The first expression, $p_i a_i/a$ is the ith value share when $x = a$; this term thus represents the expenditure patterns of those who can do no more than meet fixed costs, and it carries a weight of unity when $x = a$, decreasing to zero as x tends to infinity. By contrast, $p_i b_i/b$ is the ith value share at "bliss," when x is infinite, and this value carries a weight that increases from zero to one as x increases to infinity. Hence, under quasi homotheticity, actual expenditure patterns are a weighted average of value shares appropriate to very rich and very poor consumers.

Note finally that, at any given point, the cost function (4.4) imposes no restriction on price responses. The functions $a(p)$ and $b(p)$ apart from being linearly homogeneous and concave may take any form whatever, and the substitution matrix will be a utility weighted combination of their Hessians. Consequently, if we believe that poor consumers are less able to substitute between goods than are rich consumers (necessities have fewer substitutes than luxuries), it is possible to choose functions a and b so as to allow for this. The only restriction embodied in (4.4) is the linearity of Engel curves, for which quasi homotheticity is necessary as well as sufficient. And even in cases where linearity seems implausible globally, the demand functions (4.6) may still be excellent local approximations; as formally demonstrated by Diewert (1980a), the cost function (4.4) can act as a local second-order approximation to any arbitrary cost function, so that (4.6) can be regarded as a local first-order approximation to any system of demand functions. We shall return to the Gorman polar form in the next chapter, where it plays a crucial role in the theory of aggregation over consumers.

Exercises

5.22. Homotheticity implies that all expenditure elasticities are unity. What restrictions, if any, does it place on price elasticities?

5.23. Consider the quadratic utility function $u = \Sigma\Sigma(q_k - \beta_k) \alpha_{kj}(q_j - \beta_j)$ where the matrix (α_{kj}) is symmetric and negative definite. Show that these preferences are quasi-homothetic.

5.24. The marginal utility of money λ can be characterized by its reciprocal, the marginal cost of utility $\partial c/\partial u$. Show that there exists a normalization of utility such that λ is independent of u if and only if preferences are quasi-homothetic.

5.25. Show that the linear expenditure system is quasi-homothetic and that, within the model, potentialities for substitution are higher for better-off households.

5.26. (Samuelson 1965.) By combining (3.5) with the result of Exercise 5.17, show that if the same preference ordering is both directly and indirectly additive, $w_i + \phi e_i w_i$ must be independent of i. The most general condition under which this holds is $e_i = -\phi = 1$ and show that this condition is necessary and sufficient for homotheticity.

5.27.* Show that preferences are homothetic if and only if the distance function takes the form $d(u, q) = \beta(q)u$ where $\beta(q)$ is a linearly homogeneous concave function. [Hint: use equation (7.4) of Chapter 2.]

5.28.* (Exercise 5.15, cont.) Show that, in general,

$$\frac{\partial}{\partial q_k}\left(\frac{\partial v/\partial q_i}{\partial v/\partial q_j}\right) = \frac{\partial}{\partial q_k}\left(\frac{\partial d/\partial q_i}{\partial d/\partial q_j}\right) + \frac{\partial}{\partial u}\left(\frac{\partial d/\partial q_i}{\partial d/\partial q_j}\right)\frac{\partial u}{\partial q_k}$$

Hence, show that weak and implicit separability can only hold simultaneously if the subgroup utility functions are homothetic.

5.29.* By rewriting (3.3) in the form $s_{ij} = \gamma(\partial q_i/\partial u)(\partial q_j/\partial u)$, or otherwise, show that homotheticity and additivity together imply that $c(u, p) = u(\Sigma\beta_i p_i^\alpha)^{1/\alpha}$. What values can α legitimately take? [For the extension of this to quasi homotheticity, see Pollak (1971a)].

Bibliographical notes

The link between functional structure and aggregation over commodities seems to have been first drawn out in papers by Sono (1962) and Leontief (1947). Strotz's (1957) paper on the empirical implications of the utility tree prompted Gorman's (1959) characterization of the necessary and sufficient conditions for two-stage budgeting. Much of §5.2 is based on unpublished London School of Economics lecture notes by Gorman (1971) who has also published material on preferences and separability [Gorman (1968)]. Goldman and Uzawa (1964) provide a convenient listing of the empirical consequences of different separable structures. The essentially identical topic in production theory is also discussed by Bliss (1975, Chapter V). For a different approach to the same topics, see Green (1964) [summarized in Green (1976)]. A useful summary is also given by Geary and Morishima (1973). The relationship between rationing and separability is drawn out in papers by Pollak (1969, 1971b). The most complete discussion of implicit separability is an unpublished manuscript by Gorman (1970) although much of the material is in Gorman (1976). Other types of separability and their consequences are discussed by Pearce (1961, 1964) and by Blackorby et al. (1978). Additivity has a long intellectual history although the forerunner of modern analysis is undoubtedly Frisch (1932, 1959). Houthakker's (1960) paper is also important in spite of a record number of misprints. Surveys of estimates of ϕ are contained in Brown and Deaton (1972) and in Sato (1972). The empirical consequences of the additivity assumption are discussed by Deaton (1974b, 1975a, b), while the (very) special cases that allow for inferior goods are discussed by Green (1961). Linear Engel curves have their greatest theoretical importance in aggregation theory, where their history can be traced back to Antonelli (1886) and in modern times to Gorman (1953) and Theil (1954). The Gorman polar form appears in Gorman (1961) and more extensively in Gorman (1976). Homotheticity, like additivity, has long been recognized as an important special case, see, for example, the important early contribution by Bergson (1936). For an interesting application of separability theory to the analysis of international trade flows and prices, see the papers by Armington (1969a, b, 1970), Branson (1972b) and Johnson, Grennes, and Thursby (1977).

CHAPTER 6

The theory of market demand

One of the most important developments in recent applied economics has been the increased availability of data on large samples of individual households, particularly in the United States. Although the analysis of such data poses formidable problems of its own, it is possible, at least in principle, to apply the microeconomic theory of the preceding chapters. If, however, as is frequently the case, the data are available only for aggregates of households, there are no obvious grounds why the theory, formulated for individual households, should be directly applicable. The transition from the microeconomics of consumer behavior to the analysis of market demand is frequently referred to as the "aggregation problem." Aggregation is seen as a nuisance, a temporary obstacle lying in the way of a straightforward application of the theory to the data. In this view, the role of aggregation theory is to provide the necessary conditions under which it is possible to treat aggregate consumer behavior as if it were the outcome of the decisions of a single maximizing consumer; this case we shall refer to as that of *exact aggregation*. These aggregation conditions often turn out to be stringent, which has tempted many economists to sweep the whole problem under the carpet or to dismiss it as of no importance. Some economists, indeed, see for example Hicks (1956), have held the view that microeconomic theory has greater relevance for aggregate data, arguing on largely intuitive grounds that the variations in circumstances of individual households average out to negligible proportions in aggregate, leaving only the systematic effects of variations in prices and budgets. If such views are to be justified, so that the theory can be used without modification to deal with market data, clear arguments must be provided.

In general, it is neither necessary, nor necessarily desirable, that macroeconomic relations should replicate their microeconomic foundations so that exact aggregation is possible. Indeed, to force them to do so often prevents a satisfactory derivation of market relations at all. For example, most goods are not bought by all consumers, although the proportion purchasing any one good can be expected to rise as its price falls. Consequently, a decrease in price not only causes individuals who already buy the good to buy more, but also causes new consumers to purchase for the first time. A correct treatment requires that both these effects be adequately modeled, but this is impossible if aggregate demand is treated as coming from a "representative" consumer who buys some of all of the goods. Similarly, as we shall see in Chapter 11, aggregate labor supply can only be adequately modeled if we distinguish carefully between the effects of wage and income changes on the participation decision, on the one hand, and on the number of hours worked on the other. Although such situations are common, it is nevertheless of considerable interest to consider whether and under what conditions market demand functions exist which share some or all of the properties of individual demand functions. Sections 6.1 and 6.2 take up these questions in the context of the standard model, the allocation of a fixed total expenditure over a specified number of commodities. In §6.1, linear aggregation is discussed and we examine the basic results, their implications and their applicability to empirical analysis. In §6.2, *generalized linearity* is presented as an alternative method for achieving exact aggregation and we explore the possibilities it opens up for introducing distributional considerations into demand functions. Section 6.3 extends the model to the case where one price, for realism that of leisure (the wage rate), varies from one consumer to another. In all three sections, we require that aggregation be exact and that it holds no matter what happens to the distribution of total outlay over households. Section 6.4 weakens these requirements and discusses in what ways aggregation possibilities are thereby extended.

6.1 Exact linear aggregation

First, we must consider under what conditions aggregate demand functions exist at all so that it is possible to write aggregate demand as a function of prices and of aggregate outlay. If this can be done, we may then inquire further as to whether such demand can be regarded as deriving from the constrained maximization of some utility function. This aggregate utility function and the "preferences" it can be thought of as representing are in no sense the result of some process of social choice. They are merely a convenient "as if" construction which, if ascribed to a mythical representative consumer possessed of total outlay, will result in market demands identical to the sum of the individual demands. We shall assume, in this and the next section, that each household's total expenditure x^h is exogenous and varies from household to household. The n prices, however, are assumed to be the same for all consumers (at least until we consider the price of leisure in §6.3). This assumption may well not be true in practice – there is some evidence that the poor pay more, see Caplovitz (1967) and Piachaud (1974) – but it is crucial to the analysis. Its effect is to ensure that, of the $(n + 1)$ exogenous variables facing each consumer, the n prices are common to all, leaving only differences in total expenditure to be dealt with. Consequently, to get exact aggregation, we must examine how the shape of the Engel curve must be restricted. Note, however, that if individual consumers are constrained in any way, say by rationing or by transactions costs, and if these constraints differ across consumers, then we are effectively back to the situation where different consumers face different prices and the conditions for exact aggregation will be still more restrictive.

Let us denote by the superscript h magnitudes specific to the hth household so that, for example, q_i^h is the demand for good i, and we write the demand functions in the form

$$q_i^h = g_i^h(x^h, p) \tag{1.1}$$

If there are H households in all, (1.1) implies that for average demand $\bar{q}_i$, we can write

$$\bar{q}_i = f_i(x^1, x^2, \ldots, x^H, p) = \frac{1}{H} \sum_h g_i^h(x^h, p) \tag{1.2}$$

for some function f_i. Exact aggregation is possible if we can write (1.2) in the special form, for some g_i, and for all i,

$$\bar{q}_i = g_i(\bar{x}, p) \tag{1.3}$$

In general, no function such as (1.3) exists and (1.2) will be all that is possible; note too that an additional requirement that $g_i(\bar{x}, p)$ be consistent with a utility function is, in general, more stringent than that it simply exist.

To see the conditions for any form of (1.3), note that (1.3), unlike (1.2), does not depend on the distribution of expenditures x^h. Hence, for the equation to hold, a reallocation of a single unit of currency from any one to any other individual must leave market demands unchanged. This can only happen if the n different marginal propensities to spend are identical for all consumers. Rich consumers must allocate changes in their outlay in exactly the same way as do poor consumers. This observation implies that the functions (1.1) must be linear in x^h, that is, for some functions α_i^h and β_i of p alone,

$$q_i^h = \alpha_i^h(p) + \beta_i(p)x^h \tag{1.4}$$

where, although $\alpha_i^h(p)$ is indexed by h, $\beta_i(p)$ is not. Note that since the demands must be nonnegative, if either α_i^h or β_i is negative, the permitted range of x^h has to be restricted. In aggregate, we have

$$\bar{q}_i = \alpha_i(p) + \beta_i(p)\bar{x} \tag{1.5}$$

where it is assumed that none of the individual x^h's is such as to make $q_i^h \leq 0$. If, however, we do not wish to place any restriction on the range of the x^h's, and demand that aggregation be possible for all $x^h \geq 0$, we must delete the intercepts from (1.4) and (1.5) since otherwise some demands will be negative. Hence, this "global" aggregation implies that q_i^h and $\bar{q}_i$ be proportional to x^h and $\bar{x}$, respectively.

So far, we have said nothing about utility maximization and, indeed, (1.4) is necessary and sufficient for (1.3) *whether or not we require aggregate utility maximization*. Suppose now that individuals maximize utility. In this case, (1.4) will hold if and only if each household has a cost function

$$c^h(u^h, p) = a^h(p) + u^h b(p) \tag{1.6}$$

where $\beta_i(p) = \partial \log b(p)/\partial p_i$ and $a^h(p)$ satisfies $\partial a^h(p)/\partial p_i - \beta_i(p)a^h(p) = \alpha_i^h(p)$. The sufficiency of (1.6) is a simple matter of differentiation, a proof of necessity is outlined in Exercise 6.3. Similarly, the average of these cost functions is the cost function underlying (1.5), that is,

$$\bar{x} = c(u, p) = \bar{a}(p) + ub(p) \tag{1.7}$$

where $\bar{a}(p)$ is the average of the $a^h(p)$'s. Hence, provided individuals maximize and individual preferences are such as to satisfy the aggregation condition, average demands will automatically be consistent with utility maximization.

Equation (1.6) is the cost function for quasi-homothetic preferences, the properties of which were discussed in some detail in §5.4. Viewed as necessary conditions for aggregation, quasi-homothetic preferences, or equivalently, linear Engel curves, are extremely stringent. For example, any commodity not consumed at low budget levels is immediately excluded. Consequently, if linear aggregation is to work at all, it can only do so for broadly defined composites of goods. Even at this level, most people would believe that the allocation of extra expenditure among broad groups varies systematically between poor and rich consumers, and they would cite evidence from cross-section budget studies in support. However, this argument is not conclusive. Looking at (1.4) and (1.6), we see that some variation in preferences between households is allowed; the function $a^h(p)$ in (1.6) and the intercepts $\alpha_i^h(p)$ in (1.4) are indexed on h. This is of great importance because it allows, for example, household composition effects without destroying the conditions for aggregation. But it also means that linearity is difficult to check from budget data since, if the intercepts depend on household characteristics such as age, sex, and education of the household head, number of children, race, and so on, and if in cross sections these characteristics are nonlinearly related to income or total household expenditure, then quantities demanded will reveal a nonlinear relation with total expenditure alone, see, for example, Exercise 3.1. Aggregate time-series data are less obviously contrary to (1.6) although rather indirect tests carried out by Carlevaro (1976) and by Boyce and Primont (1976) would suggest that, here too, linearity is unacceptable. We shall also, in the next section, discuss some new results that support these findings. Even so, it would be a mistake to attach too much weight to these results at present, and although it remains somewhat implausible, it is not impossible that quasi homotheticity is a reasonable approximation for broad groups of goods.

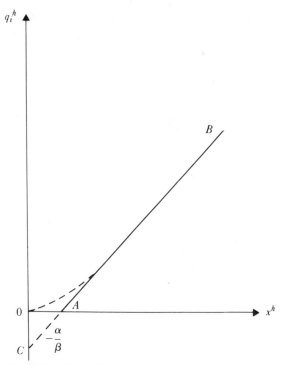

Figure 6.1. Linear Engel curve.

Note from (1.4) that goods are necessities or luxuries as $\alpha_i^h(p)$ is greater than or less than zero. For goods where $\alpha_i^h(p) < 0$, the Engel curve is illustrated in Figure 6.1. Equation (1.4) gives the line CAB, but since q_i^h cannot be negative, only AB where $x^h \geq -\alpha/\beta$ is a feasible Engel curve. If all households have Engel curves as illustrated and if all have sufficient outlay to be above A, the aggregation condition is satisfied and all goes through straightforwardly. If, however, the true Engel curve is $0AB$ rather than CAB and if some households have $x^h < -\alpha^h/\beta$, aggregation breaks down. Clearly, a redistribution of outlay from households above A to those below A will change the pattern of demand since the two types of household have different marginal propensities to spend, β for one and zero for the other. This in no way violates the theorem because $0AB$ is not linear, only "piecewise" linear. In this case, with x^h's above and below $-\alpha^h/\beta$, the average Engel curve, which shows how average demand varies with the average budget for a fixed distribution of outlays, is likely to be nonlinear as illustrated by the dotted line from 0 to B. Exercise 6.5 below works out a case in detail where the aggregate relation turns out to be quadratic.

This discussion suggests rather intuitively that, as argued, the assumption of linear Engel curves may be less plausible for a very disaggregated commodity classification. Since, at this level of detail, many consumers will be buying nothing of a particular good, much of the total expenditure response of market demand will be caused by changes at the "extensive" rather than the "intensive" margin, that is by the entry of new consumers into the market. This, as we have seen, is likely to produce a nonlinear market response. It would be an unlikely coincidence indeed if the microcurves had just that degree of off-setting nonlinearity that would render the market demands linear.

Exercises

6.1. Using any source of family budget data known to you (in the U.K., the annual Family Expenditure Survey published by the Department of Employment; in the U.S., the Bureau of Labor Statistics Consumer Expenditure Survey, e.g., for 1971–2), sketch Engel curves for a selection of both narrowly defined and broadly defined commodities. Comment on the adequacy of linear approximations to the curves you have drawn. What statistical tests are available to assess nonlinearity? What further information would be necessary before making a definitive assessment on the possibilities for aggregation?

6.2. Explain how it might be possible for market demand functions such as (1.3) to exist for some commodities but not for others. Which of the following are likely to fall into which category: (a) food, (b) aspirin, (c) cigarettes, (d) hi-fi, (e) butter, (f) steak, (g) hair grease?

6.3. Demands conform to (1.4) if and only if $\partial q_i^h/\partial x^h$ is independent of x^h. Explain why this is equivalent to $\partial q_i^h/\partial u^h$ being independent of u^h. By using $q_i^h = \partial c^h/\partial p_i$, or otherwise, show that this last condition implies that $\partial/\partial p_i (\partial c^h/\partial u^h)$ is independent of u^h. Setting $\partial c^h/\partial u^h = b(p)$ (why must this be independent of h?), prove (1.6).

6.4. Given any functions $\alpha_i^h(p)$ and $\beta_i(p)$ in (1.4), can we always find a cost function as in (1.6)? Explain your answer.

6.5. To calculate the market Engel curve in Figure 6.1, assume all households have identical piecewise linear Engel curves given by $q_i^h = 0$, $x^h \leq -\alpha/\beta$ $q_i = \alpha + \beta x^h$, $x^h \geq -\alpha/\beta$, where $\alpha < 0$, $\beta > 0$. Assume that there is a very large number of households and that x is rectangularly distributed over the interval $(\gamma, \gamma + r)$ where $\gamma < -\alpha/\beta < \gamma + r$, that is, with density function r^{-1}. Show (a) $\bar{x} = \gamma + \frac{1}{2}r$, (b) $\bar{q} = r^{-1}[\alpha(\gamma + r) + \alpha^2/\beta - \alpha^2/2\beta + \beta(\gamma + r)^2/2]$. Hence, show that $\bar{q}$ is a quadratic function of $\bar{x}$.

6.6. Show that if the cost function $c^h(u^h, p)$ takes the form $a^h(p) + F^h(u^h, p_{r+1}, p_{r+2}, \ldots, p_n)b(p)$, then exact linear aggregation is possible for goods 1 to r but not for goods $r + 1$ to n unless further restrictions are placed on F^h. More difficult: show that this form of the cost function is necessary and sufficient for exact aggregation for goods 1 to r.

6.7.* In (1.4), differences in household preferences are permitted through the term $\alpha_i^h(p)$. Show that if z^h is some household characteristic, then to aggregate the functions $q_i^h = g_i(x^h, z^h, p)$ to $\bar{q}_i = f_i(\bar{x}, z_0, p)$ for all i where z_0 is a function of $(z^1, \ldots, z^H)$, we require $q_i^h = \alpha_{i0}(p) + \alpha_{i1}(p)v(z^h) + \beta_i(p)x^h$. Show that if there are m characteristics, this generalizes to $q_i^h = \alpha_{i0}(p) + \sum_{j=1}^m \alpha_{ij}(p)v_j(z_j^h) + \beta_i(p)x^h$. What if the average demand is to depend on the average levels of each characteristic?

6.2* Exact nonlinear aggregation

In defining exact linear aggregation, it was required that average market demands should be a function of average total expenditure. The manipulation of this condition yielded the restriction that Engel curves should be linear and have the same slope for each individual. In this section, we define exact aggregation in a rather different, but still very useful way. Instead of working with the quantities, we aggregate over the different expenditure patterns of different consumers.

Let the average aggregate budget share for the ith good be $\bar{w}_i$; thus

$$\bar{w}_i = \frac{p_i \sum_h q_i^h}{\sum_h x^h} = \sum_h \frac{x^h}{\Sigma x^h} \cdot w_i^h \tag{2.1}$$

so that the market pattern of demands is a weighted average of the individual household patterns, the weights being proportional to the expenditure of each household.

In general, $\bar{w}_i$ is a function of prices and of each household's total expenditure. One approach to aggregation in this context would thus be to restrict $\bar{w}_i$ to depend on prices and *average* expenditure alone, but this leads straight back to the conditions for linear aggregation of §6.1. Instead, we require only that $\bar{w}_i$ depend on prices and a *representative* level of total expenditure x_0, say, which itself can be a function of the distribution of expenditures and of prices. If this holds, the market pattern of demand can be thought of as deriving from the behavior of a single representative individual endowed with total expenditure x_0 and facing prices p. Note that this individual is representative only of *market* behavior and is not representative in any *democratic* sense.

Formally, we say that a representative consumer exists if we can define some utility function $\psi(x, p)$ with corresponding cost function $c(u, p)$, so that for some $u_0 = \psi(x_0, p)$,

$$\bar{w}_i = w_i(u_0, p) = \frac{\partial \log c(u_0, p)}{\partial \log p_i} = \sum_h \frac{x^h}{\Sigma x^h} \frac{\partial \log c^h(u^h, p)}{\partial \log p_i} \tag{2.2}$$

where $c^h(u^h, p)$ is the cost function of household h, with $u^h = \psi^h(x^h, p)$. Having defined the requirements of exact nonlinear aggregation, (2.2) can be manipulated by changing u^h, for example, while keeping u_0 constant. This gives certain partial differential equations that can then be integrated to give the cost functions and preferences necessary to guarantee the existence of the representative consumer. It turns out that for household h, the cost function must take the form

$$c^h(u^h, p) = \theta^h[u^h, a(p), b(p)] + \phi^h(p) \tag{2.3}$$

where $a(p)$, $b(p)$ and $\phi^h(p)$ are linearly homogeneous functions of prices, and θ^h is linearly homogeneous in a and b. Given that $\theta^h(\ )$, $a(\ )$, and $b(\ )$ are increasing functions in their arguments, we would expect $\theta^h(\ )$ to be concave in a and b and the latter to be concave in p so that each cost function as a whole is concave over some relevant range of x. Over all consumers the $\phi^h(p)$ functions must add to zero, so that the representative cost function takes the form

$$c(u_0, p) = \theta\,[u_0, a(p), b(p)] \tag{2.4}$$

for the same functions $a(p)$ and $b(p)$. These functions can be thought of as the "prices" of two intermediate goods that together with utility, define the macro-cost function (2.4), an interpretation that is also available for the special case of linear aggregation, equation (1.7). From (2.4), the representative value shares take the form

$$\bar{w}_i = w_i(u_0, p) = \frac{\partial \log \theta}{\partial \log a} \cdot \frac{\partial \log a}{\partial \log p_i} + \frac{\partial \log \theta}{\partial \log b} \cdot \frac{\partial \log b}{\partial \log p_i} \tag{2.5}$$

Since θ is homogeneous of degree one in a and b, $\partial \log \theta / \partial \log a = 1 - \partial \log \theta / \partial \log b$ so that (2.5) can be written as

$$\bar{w}_i = (1 - \lambda)\frac{\partial \log a}{\partial \log p_i} + \lambda \cdot \frac{\partial \log b}{\partial \log p_i} \tag{2.6}$$

where $\lambda = \partial \log \theta / \partial \log b = \lambda(x_0, p)$, substituting out for u_0. Hence, as in the case of quasi homotheticity, the value shares are a weighted sum of the value shares associated with the two functions $a(p)$ and $b(p)$, with the weights depending on representative utility or total expenditure and prices but being the same for all goods. Consequently, at constant prices each value share $\bar{w}_i$ is a linear function of every other; given time-series data without relative price variation, this could be tested very directly. At the microeconomic level, the presence of the expression $\phi^h(p)$ prevents such a straightforward test, but (2.3) still places strong restrictions upon Engel curves; note, for example, that for each household the slopes of the different Engel curves will vary linearly with one another as total expenditure changes at constant prices. This does not, of course, imply that the Engel curves themselves are linear.

Since these linear relations occur and since (2.3) is an evident generalization of the linear cost function (1.7), the name given to the conditions for consistent nonlinear aggregation is *generalized linearity* (GL). Thus (2.4) is the macro GL cost function with microcost functions of maximum allowable taste variation given by (2.3). By definition, representative expenditure x_0 will be some point in the expenditure distribution, the position of which is determined by the degree of nonlinearity in the Engel curves and by the price vector p. A particularly interesting special case occurs when the representative expenditure level is independent of prices and depends only on the distribution of expenditures. This case, known as *price independent generalized linearity* (PIGL) occurs when the microcost functions take the form

$$c^h(u^h, p) = k^h[a(p)^\alpha(1 - u^h) + b(p)^\alpha u^h]^{1/\alpha} \qquad (2.7)$$

for scalars k^h and α, with a representative cost function

$$c(u_0, p) = [a(p)^\alpha(1 - u_0) + b(p)^\alpha u_0]^{1/\alpha} \qquad (2.8)$$

The weighting between the two indices is even more explicit in the PIGL form; (2.8) gives the cost function as the utility weighted mean of order α between the two indices. When α tends to zero, (2.8) becomes

$$\log c(u_0, p) = (1 - u_0) \log a(p) + u_0 \log b(p) \qquad (2.9)$$

This logarithmic form is known as PIGLOG. We have already discussed examples in Chapter 2, Exercises 14 and 27, and the new model of demand in §3.4. Also see Exercise 6.11 below for the relationship to §5.2's Gorman generalized polar form.

The parameter α is crucial in determining the nonlinearity of the Engel curves and hence, as we shall see, in determining the relationship between representative and average expenditures. Clearly, when α is 1, the cost function takes the linear form and the Engel curves are linear. In general, the Engel curves take the form

$$w_i = \gamma_i + \eta_i(x/k)^{-\alpha} \qquad (2.10)$$

or

$$w_i = \gamma_i^* + \eta_i^* \log(x/k) \qquad (2.11)$$

in the PIGLOG case, where γ_i and η_i are functions of prices only. Hence, Engel curves are quadratic when $\alpha = -1$, have linear and hyperbolic terms when $\alpha = 2$, and so on. Representative expenditure can be found by summing the individual value share equations and equating the result to the original functional form using representative, rather than household or average expenditure. Taking the case where k^h is unity to illustrate, and using (2.10)

$$w_i = \sum_h \frac{x^h}{\Sigma x^h} \cdot w_i^h = \gamma_i + \eta_i \sum_h \frac{(x^h)^{1-\alpha}}{\Sigma x^h} = \gamma_i + \eta_i x_0^{-\alpha} \qquad (2.12)$$

Hence, representative expenditure x_0 is given by

$$x_0 = \left[\frac{\sum_h (x^h)^{1-\alpha}}{\Sigma x^h} \right]^{-1/\alpha} \qquad (2.13)$$

This formula is only available in the PIGL case but it is still general enough to be of interest. Note that it is linearly homogeneous in the x's so that, for example, we can write $x_0 = \kappa_0 \bar{x}$, where κ_0 summarizes the combined effects of nonlinear Engel curves and an unequal distribution of expenditures. Indeed, for any given α, κ_0 can be interpreted as an indicator of dispersion with precise functional form dictated by α. For example, when α is -1, so that Engel curves are quadratic, κ_0 is given by

$$\kappa_0 = 1 + \sigma^2/\bar{x}^2 \tag{2.14}$$

where σ^2 is the variance of the expenditure distribution. When α is zero (PIGLOG), we have

$$\kappa_0 = H/Z \tag{2.15}$$

where H is the number of households and $\log Z$ is Theil's (1967) entropy measure of dispersion. Z takes its maximum value of H when all x's are identical; otherwise $\kappa_0 > 1$. In general, κ_0 is decreasing in α so that representative expenditure is above average expenditure if and only if α is less than unity, and it is this case that seems to be empirically important.

So far, we have taken the PIGL case where each household's preferences are identical. But as (2.7), (2.10), and (2.11) indicate, the parameter k^h can vary over households. This reminds us that differences in household budgets are not the only important differences between households and we would expect k^h to vary significantly with household size and demographic composition. In fact, this seems a rather plausible way of incorporating such effects: deflating x^h by k^h is similar to taking the household budget on a per capita basis, except that k^h can take into account the lower consumption requirements of children and economies of household size rather than crudely counting heads. In Chapter 8 we will meet this idea and its extension again. For the present, note that if we allow for these effects, x_0 takes into account changes in the demographic composition as well as in the distribution of budgets, that is, (2.13) becomes

$$x_0 = \left[\frac{\sum_h (x^h/k^h)^{1-\alpha}}{\sum x^h} \right]^{-1/\alpha} \tag{2.16}$$

What then are the implications of this analysis for the empirical estimation of demand systems using aggregate time-series data? As we saw in §6.1, when the expenditure distribution can vary, average expenditure may only be used as a regressor if Engel curves are linear, and even then individual total expenditures must be high enough to ensure nonnegative demands. Generalized linearity goes beyond this and allows nonlinear Engel curves at the price of introducing representative rather than average expenditure. From the previous discussion, if the expenditure distribution and, given differences in k^h, the demographic composition remain constant, κ_0 is constant, so that representative is proportional to average expenditure. Thus, provided the parameter multiplying expenditure is reinterpreted, and provided the distribution of expenditures and the demographic composition really are constant, aggregate expenditure patterns can be related to average expenditure without error. But this is a rather negative view. More excitingly, representative expenditure allows a straightforward and extremely elegant way of introducing distributional and demographic considerations into demand equations. One possible methodology would be to estimate α and the k^h's from household budget data and use the result, together with expenditure distribution data, to calculate the distributional parameter κ_0 and hence x_0. This could then be used in aggregate demand functions such as Chapter 3, equation (4.6), instead of $\bar{x}$. Unfortunately, few countries have data on the distribution of total expenditure (as opposed to income) of sufficient quantity and quality to make such a scheme feasible. The authors have carried out some indirect experiments but not with any notable success; it is quite possible that the distribution has been sufficiently stable in Britain over the last two decades for the error involved in approximating x_0 by $\bar{x}$ to be small compared with other errors of misspecification or measurement. [Somewhat similar experiments, but using the distribution of income as a proxy, are reported by Berndt, Darrough, and Diewert (1977).] Consequently, empirical work with PIGL forms has so far been confined to aggregate models such as that discussed in §3.4. However, we are in little doubt that the extra generality allowed in the Engel curves will prove to be of great empirical significance even on time-series data. For example, using the forms $a(p) = \Sigma a_k p_k$ and $b(p) = \beta_0 \Pi p_k^{\beta k}$, the demand functions from (2.7) were fitted to postwar British data from 1954 to 1974 for eight groups of goods. The estimate of α was very close to -1, implying close to quadratic Engel curves over time, while a test of the hypothesis that α was $+1$, that Engel curves were linear, was decisively rejected. This not only supports the evidence against linear Engel curves cited in §6.2, but also shows that PIGL offers a substantial improvement, even without exploiting its ability to introduce distributional effects.

Exercises

6.8. Using the same source of data as in Exercise 6.1, investigate the empirical usefulness of (2.3) with $\phi^h = 0$ by drawing scatter diagrams of w_i against w_j for various i and j and testing for linearity.
6.9. Sketch the Engel curves (q_i against x) implied by the equations (2.10) and (2.11) for various values of α. What restrictions, if any, are placed on the range of x by (a) the need to ensure $0 \le w_i$, (b) the concavity of (2.7), (c) the requirement that $\partial c / \partial u > 0$?
6.10. Using (2.13), (a) prove (2.14) when $\alpha = -1$, (b) find an explicit formula for Z when $\alpha = 0$ and prove that $Z = H$ when all x's are identical and that this is its maximum, (c) show that $\kappa_0 = 1$ when $\alpha = 1$.
6.11.* The generalized Gorman polar form $u = \phi [x/b(p)] + a(p)$ was discussed in the

context of two-stage budgeting, see Chapter 5, equation (2.16). Show, by suitable choice of θ, b, and a, that PIGL is a special case of the generalized Gorman polar form. Show that the latter is in turn a special case of GL.

6.12.* Show how the budget shares implied by the GL cost function (2.3) aggregate to the form (2.6) and show how λ depends on the distribution of total expenditure.

6.13.* Suppose that for each household the demand function for each good can be written as a polynomial in the budget, that is, $q_i = g_i(x, p) = \sum_{j=1}^{m}\beta_{ij}(p)x^{\alpha_j}$, where $\sum \alpha_j = 1$. Show that average demand now depends upon up to m functions of the vector $(x_1, \ldots, x_H)$ instead of only two as in the GL or PIGL cases. More difficult, see Gorman (1980) or Lau (1980): what additional restrictions are imposed on the β_{ij}'s and α_j's if each household optimizes?

6.3 Aggregation with endogenous labor supply

To extend the analysis to include labor supply, we use the full cost function introduced in §4.1. To recall, write this

$$c(u, \omega, p) = \omega T + \mu = X \tag{3.1}$$

where ω is the wage rate, T the time endowment and μ is "unearned" or transfer income. X is referred to as full income. Since, in this framework leisure is simply another good with price ω, it is immediately clear that if all consumers face the same wage rate but differ in time endowment (some consumers need more sleep than others) or in transfer income, perfect linear aggregation is possible if $c(u, \omega, p)$ has the form of (1.6), that is,

$$c^h(u^h, \omega, p) = a^h(\omega, p) + u^h b(\omega, p) \tag{3.2}$$

Average leisure demand $\bar{q}_0$ would then be a function of average full income $\bar{X}$, the wage ω and prices p in exactly the same way as the commodity demands (1.3). To state the problem this way shows clearly why labor supply has to be treated differently from the other commodities: whereas p can be assumed to be the same for all households, the price of leisure ω clearly varies from consumer to consumer. The problem that this creates is seen from (3.2); if ω is indexed on h, $b(\omega, p)$ varies from household to household. Hence, the marginal propensity to consume good i, $\partial \log b/\partial \log p_i$, will also depend on h so that exact aggregation will be impossible. This situation can only be rectified if the functions in (3.2) are further restricted.

In fact, it is not very useful to look for an aggregate demand for $\bar{q}_0$. Instead, it is more fruitful to aggregate, not over q_0^h, but over its money value $q_0^h\omega^h$. If T is the same for all consumers, this is equivalent to aggregating over $(T - q_0^h)\omega^h = \ell^h\omega^h$, which is earnings. Hence, if it were possible to believe that relative wage rates reflected the relative efficiencies of workers, $\omega^h\ell^h$ would be proportional to labor supply measured in efficiency units and would be the natural variable over which to aggregate. We shall also require, in the spirit of the rest of this chapter, that exact aggregation be possible over goods and leisure simultaneously (for weaker conditions see Exercise 6.17 below). This is possible if and only if (ω^h, p) is restricted to take the form $(\omega^h)^\delta b(p)$ for some scalar δ, while $a^h(\omega^h, p)$ must have the linear form $a^h(p) + \omega^h d(p)$, that is,

$$c^h(u^h, \omega^h, p) = a^h(p) + \omega^h d(p) + u^h(\omega^h)^\delta b(p) \tag{3.3}$$

where $a^h(p)$ and $b(p)$ are homogeneous of degree one and $d(p)$ is homogeneous of degree zero. The aggregate preferences resulting from (3.3) are given by

$$c(u, \bar{\omega}, p) = \bar{a}(p) + \bar{\omega} d(p) + u \bar{\omega}^\delta b(p) \tag{3.4}$$

As far as commodity demands are concerned, (3.3) and (3.4) are not notably more restrictive than (1.6) and (1.7) although demands must be linear in *both* the wage rate *and* full income. Differentiation of (3.3) and substitution from the indirect utility function gives

$$q_i^h = a_i^h(p) + \omega^h d_i(p) + [b_i(p)/b(p)][X^h - a^h(p) - \omega^h d(p)] \tag{3.5}$$

where the subscripts on a_i, d_i, and b_i denote partial differentiation with respect to the ith price. The labor supply equation is perhaps more restrictive; earnings are given by

$$\omega^h \ell^h = (1 - \delta) \omega^h[T - d(p)] - \delta\mu^h - \delta a^h(p) \tag{3.6}$$

so that the derivatives of earnings with respect to unearned income and the value of the time endowment are the same for everyone and their difference must be unity. Nevertheless, (3.6) is certainly not without empirical interest and is no more restrictive than the typical functional form used in labor supply studies. Furthermore, if T is taken as unob̌servable, (3.6) permits unrestricted linear estimation on cross-section data with the function $a^h(p)$ allowing an entry for the effects of specific household characteristics.

The analysis in this section is not only applicable to aggregation with endogenous labor supply but can be used when any single price varies over consumers. The extension to many prices varying is also possible; each such price must be "extracted" from the general functions in (3.3) and dealt with as is ω^h in that equation. Not surprisingly, the more such prices there are, the more restrictive are the resultant functional forms required for exact aggregation. Finally, we note that generalized aggregation with endogenous labor supply is also possible, and this permits both nonlinear Engel curves and labor supply equations more general than (3.6).

Exercises

6.14. The "augmented" linear expenditure system has utility function $u = \beta_0 \log(q_0 - \gamma_0) + \Sigma\beta_k \log(q_k - \gamma_k)$ and this is maximized subject to $\omega q_0 + \Sigma p_k q_k = X$. Write down the commodity demand functions, the labor supply equation, and the full cost function.

Show that it is not possible to aggregate exactly over either q_0^h or ℓ^h in the model. Show that exact aggregation is possible for $\omega^h q_0^h$ or $\omega^h \ell^h$, and show that the augmented linear expenditure system is a special case of (3.5).

6.15. Show that the augmented linear expenditure system requires that all goods be substitutes for leisure and that this is not so for the general form (3.5).

6.16. Check that (3.3) implies (3.6). What interpretations can you suggest for $d(p)$, $a^h(p)$, and δ?

6.17. Show that if the cost function $c^h(u^h, \omega^h, p)$ can be written in the form $a^h(p) + \omega^h d(p) + F^h(u^h, p) (\omega^h)^\delta b(p)$ then exact linear aggregation is possible for labor supply but not for individual commodity demands without further restrictions on $F^h(\ )$ (cf. Exercise 6.5). Show that, because of the budget constraint, exact linear aggregation is still possible for total expenditure on all goods (other than leisure) and discuss the usefulness of the previous result for analyzing cross-section data.

6.4 Aggregation under restrictions

Although the previous sections have suggested some interesting and useful functional forms, they are all undoubtedly extremely special compared with the almost infinite range of functional forms we might wish to use to model actual behavior. It is natural to ask, therefore, whether exact aggregation might not be asking too much. For example, why insist that aggregate demand patterns should be themselves derivable from an "as if" utility maximization exercise? Alternatively, we might demand exact aggregation only when the expenditure distribution remains unchanged or is at least subject to some, hopefully mild, restriction. Finally, there is the intuitive notion that if preferences are identical, then aggregation must become easier. We take up these possibilities in this final section.

Let us begin by asking whether exact aggregation is easier when it is not required that aggregate demands be consistent with a utility function. The simple answer to this is "yes, sometimes," particularly when restrictions are placed on the expenditure distribution. Given that all consumers face the same prices, the possibilities for exact aggregation are determined by the shape of Engel curves. Sometimes it happens that the restrictions on individual Engel curves required by exact aggregation are left unchanged by the additional requirement of utility maximization. Examples of this are exact linear aggregation and exact generalized linear aggregation. In §6.1, the linearity of the Engel curves was derived without reference to maximizing behavior and no extra restrictions on the Engel curves are imposed by maximizing. Similarly, the linear relationship between slopes of Engel curves under generalized linearity is the basic condition for the existence of a representative expenditure level and has no essential connection with utility maximization. In the nonmaximizing case, we cannot, of course, talk about cost functions so that the aggregation conditions must be written in a different form. But this is straightforward enough. The representative, not necessarily maximizing, consumer exists if and only if household budget shares take the form

$$w_i^h = \gamma_i(p) + \eta_i(p)\xi^h(x^h, p) + \delta_i^h(p)/x^h \tag{4.1}$$

for some functions $\gamma_i(\ )$, $\eta_i(\ )$, $\xi^h(\ )$, and $\delta_i^h(\ )$, while the special case of $x_0 = \bar{x}$ occurs when $\xi^h(x^h, p) = 1/x^h$. It is a simple matter to check that these are simply the shares resulting from the GL and linear cost functions, respectively, although in the not necessarily maximizing case, the functions of p need not be integrable. The restrictions on the Engel curves are, however, identical in the maximizing and not maximizing cases. However, under the condition that the representative level of total expenditure x_0 be price independent, without maximizing behavior, the budget shares for household h must satisfy

$$w_i^h = \gamma_i(p) + \beta_i(p)\,(x^h/k^h)^{-\alpha} + \delta_i^h(p)/x^h \tag{4.2}$$

This integrates, under maximizing behavior, to the PIGL cost function (2.7) for $\alpha \neq 1$. But the implied budget shares of this have $\delta_i^h = 0$ for all i and h. Hence, in this case, integrability actually restricts the form of the Engel curves for individual households. On the other hand, the δ_i^h terms cancel out at the aggregate level so that no further restriction on the aggregate Engel curves is entailed by assuming that the representative consumer is a maximizer.

Placing restrictions on changes in the expenditure distribution turns out to be rather more fruitful and results in a dramatic contrast between the maximizing case and the not necessarily maximizing case. Start from the case where consumers are maximizers. Imagine first, that by a system of continuous and instantaneous lump-sum transfers the government can hold the *utility* distribution constant. Hence, for some completely arbitrary level of "representative".utility u_0, there are constants π^h such that $u^h = \pi^h u_0$ at all times. We can then define an aggregate cost function $c^*(u_0, p)$ by

$$\sum_h c^h(\pi^h u_0, p) = c(u_0, p; \pi^1, \ldots, \pi^H) = c^*(u_0, p) \tag{4.3}$$

which has all the correct properties and clearly generates aggregate demands. Of course, the perfect compensation case is not very realistic; governments do not work in such a way nor could they if they so wished. However, this special case makes it clearer why it is that a constant *expenditure* distribution is not enough for the perfect aggregation of utility maximizing consumers. In this case, changes in prices have effects on utility levels so that the restrictions on the Engel curves of the representative consumer are very similar to those in the general case. Indeed, the necessary conditions for consistent maximizing aggregation with a fixed expenditure distribution turn out to be very close to generalized linearity.

If, however, with a fixed expenditure distribution we abandon maximization in aggregate, aggregation itself is always possible. We may write $x^h = \delta^h \bar{x}$ for constants δ^h so that, paralleling (4.3),

$$\sum_h g_i^h(x^h, p) = \sum_h g_i^h(\bar{x}\delta^h, p) = g_i(\bar{x}, p; \delta) = g_i^*(\bar{x}, p) \tag{4.4}$$

However, note that implicitly the joint distribution of household characteristics and expenditure is being held constant here – otherwise the form of $g_i^*(\ )$ would change over time. Also, note that there is no reason to suppose that the functions $g_i^*(\bar{x}, p)$ will satisfy any of the restrictions of demand theory other than adding up and homogeneity, even if all the functions $g_i^h(x_h, p)$ are derived by maximizing behavior. In fact, when aggregate demand functions $g_i^*(\bar{x}, p)$ exist under whatever conditions, there is no reason to suppose that these will bear any obvious relation to the microfunctions that generated them. Recent theoretical work has demonstrated that *any* set of demand functions $g_i^*(\bar{x}, p)$, satisfying only adding up, can be generated by some configuration of preferences and expenditure distribution. To emphasize the point, Exercise 6.18 below constructs an example in which although two goods are perfect substitutes for each and every consumer with no consumer buying both, in aggregate, the data will show both goods being bought with apparently smooth substitution between them. The opposite can also occur with no substitution for any individual but apparent substitution in aggregate, see Exercise 6.19. The basic point is that, in general, "micro" and "macro" functional forms can tell us relatively little about one another. In particular, it is extremely dangerous to deduce microeconomic behavior on the basis of macroeconomic observations, particularly if such deductions are then used to make judgments about economic welfare. We shall return to this point on several occasions in the next three chapters.

A useful alternative approach to that of a fixed expenditure distribution and one that employs rather weaker assumptions is a stochastic formulation. Write differential household demand functions as

$$dq_i^h = \frac{\partial q_i^h}{\partial x^h} \cdot dx^h + \sum_h \frac{\partial q_i^h}{\partial p_j} dp_j \tag{4.5}$$

which, after substitution using the Slutsky equation, may be written

$$dq_i^h = \frac{\partial q_i^h}{\partial x^h} \cdot \left(dx^h - \sum_k q_k^h dp_k\right) + \sum_j s_{ij}^h dp_j \tag{4.6}$$

where s_{ij}^h is the i, jth term in the hth household's Slutsky matrix. Average demand is given by

$$d\bar{q}_i = \frac{1}{H} \sum_h \frac{\partial q_i^h}{\partial x^h} \left(dx^h - \sum_k q_k^h dp_k\right) + \sum_j \bar{s}_{ij} dp_j \tag{4.7}$$

Equation (4.6) is a differential Hicksian demand equation with changes in utility being proxied by the terms $(dx^h - \Sigma q_k^h dp_k)$. Now, since $\bar{S}$ will be symmetric if each of its components S^h is, (4.6) will give perfect aggregation to average expenditure $\bar{x}$ if

$$\frac{1}{H} \sum_h \frac{\partial q_i^h}{\partial x^h} \cdot \left(dx^h - \sum_k q_k^h \, dp_k \right) = \frac{\partial \bar{q}_i}{\partial \bar{x}} \, (d\bar{x} - \Sigma \, \bar{q}_k \, dp_k) \qquad (4.8)$$

We have already met two conditions under which this takes place: when $\partial q_i^h / \partial x^h$ is independent of h – parallel linear Engel curves – or when the utility distribution is fixed so that $(dx^h - \Sigma_k q_k^h \, dp_k)$ is independent of h. But if changes in the distribution of total expenditure and in prices are such and Engel curves are such that (4.8) holds in any case, then aggregation will be possible. Essentially, marginal propensities to spend must be distributed over the population independently of the distribution of changes in real income so that, if the number of consumers is large, the covariance approximates to zero.

In general, there is no reason to suppose that this will work, although, by giving us one more aggregation condition, it may well be useful in special cases. The main objection to supposing (4.8) to hold is the same as that against linear Engel curves. Rich consumers almost certainly spend marginal increments in their total outlays differently from poor consumers, so that aggregation will only work through (4.8) if changes in prices and the distribution of expenditures are such as to affect their welfare equally. It is implausible to suggest that this condition has been satisfied for either the United States or Great Britain for more than a few isolated periods this century. We have little doubt that the same applies to other economies.

Finally, we take up the question of imposing identical tastes. There is no doubt that this eases the derivation of aggregate functions given microfunctions. If expenditure x^h is the only source of differences between households, we may write $\bar{q}_i$ as $\Sigma_h g_i(x^h, p)/H$. Suppose that the distribution of expenditure can be well represented by some distribution function governed by only a few parameters, say θ_1, θ_2. Then in aggregate we have $\bar{q}_i = f_i(\theta_1, \theta_2, p)$, which may bear no resemblance to $g_i(\ )$. Without identical tastes, we would need the much larger informational requirement of the joint distribution of x^h and the vector of relevant household characteristics to proceed in this way without restricting the forms of $g_i^h(\ )$. If, however, we want exact aggregation in the sense of existence conditions for a representative consumer, there are no particular gains from the assumption of identical tastes. In §6.2, the generalized linear cost function (2.3) was given as the necessary and sufficient condition for the existence of the representative consumer. This clearly does *not* imply that all consumers have identical tastes but taste variation is limited to the functions $\theta_h(\ )$ and $\phi_h(\ )$; the functions $a(p)$ and $b(p)$ must be identical across consumers. If we began from the assumption of identical tastes, we should simply come back to (2.3) but with $\theta(\ )$ rather than $\theta_h(\ )$ and $\phi_h(\ )$ suppressed. The intuitively plausible idea, that identical tastes makes exact aggregation easier, is founded on the misapprehension that identical tastes are equivalent to identical expenditure patterns. Nothing could be further from the truth. A rich man and a poor man may have identical tastes, but they are unlikely to buy the same commodities out of their very different outlays.

Exercises

6.18. Assume that for each consumer, goods 1 and 2 are perfect substitutes and that choice between them is made so as to maximize $u = q_1 + aq_2$, $a > 0$, subject to $p_1q_1 + p_2q_2 = x$. Sketch the individual demand curve for q_1 as a function of p_1 and show that it is discontinuous at $p_1 = p_2/a$. If a varies continuously over households with density function $\beta a^{\alpha-1}$ for constants α, β, show that, if all consumers have identical outlay x, $\bar{q}_1$ is a continuous function of p_1, p_2, and x. Explain the discrepancy between the behavior of q_1 and $\bar{q}_1$.

6.19. Assume that for each consumer, goods 1 and 2 are perfect complements and that choice is made so as to maximize $u = \min\{q_1/a_1, q_2/a_2\}$ subject to $p_1q_1 + p_2q_2 = x$. Show that for each consumer, the Hicksian demands are independent of p_1 and p_2 and derive the Marshallian demands. Again, assuming x the same for all consumers but that $\alpha = a_1/a_2$ is rectangularly distributed over (α_0, α_1), show that

$$\bar{q}_2 = \frac{x}{p_1(\alpha_1 - \alpha_0)} \log\left\{\frac{p_1\alpha_1 + p_2}{p_1\alpha_0 + p_2}\right\}$$

and derive the corresponding expression for $\bar{q}_1$. Show that these are *not* the demand functions for goods that are perfect complements in aggregate and explain why the aggregation process apparently introduces substitution.

6.20. Why do consumers with identical tastes not always behave identically? What type of identical tastes would give identical behavior?

6.21. Assume that all households have parallel linear Engel curves that do not pass through the origin. Show that it is possible for the total expenditure elasticities of each aggregate demand to be unity. Conversely, if each household has total expenditure elasticities equal to unity, will the aggregate elasticities also be unity?

6.22. For the AIDS model, which is in the PIGLOG class [see Chapter 3, equation (4.6)]

$$w_i = \alpha_i + \sum_j \gamma_{ij} \log p_j + \beta_i \log(x/P)$$

If the expenditure distribution is fixed, discuss which of the parameters α_i, γ_{ij}, and β_i could be allowed to differ across households without destroying exact aggregation.

Bibliographical notes

Until recently, aggregation theory has been a rather neglected branch of consumer theory. Many authors simply dismiss the topic as unimportant, e.g., Phlips (1974), while we find in a book as good as Green (1976) a statement to the effect that it is impossible to state what the aggregation conditions are. The linear Engel curve condition is first given by Antonelli (1886), see the translation in Chipman et al. (1971), and was certainly known to such economists as Wicksell and Keynes. However, although a related problem had been analyzed by Samuelson (1952b), Gorman (1953) is the first really systematic statement of the problem of what conditions are necessary for market demands to correspond to a utility function and its solution. Gorman (1961) makes the implications for the form of the cost function explicit. Mention should also be made of Theil's (1954) work on linear aggregation in general. The concept of generalized linearity we owe to Muellbauer (1975b, 1976) although the PIGLOG Engel curve has appeared earlier in the literature in a different context and an example given by Diewert (1974a) turns out to be a special case. For linear and nonlinear aggregation with endogenous labor supply or with several prices varying, see Muellbauer (1981b), Simmons (1979) and Muellbauer (1978b). On aggregation with the utility distribution held constant, see Samuelson (1956). Chipman (1974) has also shown that with the distribution of x's fixed, homothetic tastes guarantee aggregate utility maximization, but this is by no means the most general assumption that guarantees the result. To illustrate the point, Pearce (1964) gives a quadratic Engel curve example that aggregates exactly. Theil (1975, 1976) and Barten (1974) have consistently advocated stochastic aggregation and these ideas have been extended recently by Barnett (1979). Gorman (1980) and Lau (1980) have investigated conditions under which the market demands can be written in terms of several functions of vectors of total expenditure and household characteristics.

PART THREE

Welfare and consumer behavior

Consumer index numbers • Household characteristics, demand, and household welfare comparisons • Social welfare and inequality

CHAPTER 7

Consumer index numbers

Index numbers of prices, output, and welfare are part of the common parlance of economic debate. Yet the theory of economic index numbers, which has attracted some of the best minds in economics over the years, had until very recently been rather unfashionable. Few modern texts include more than passing references to index number theory, and the topic seems to be regarded as a rather unimportant backwater. However, the increase in rates of inflation in recent years has brought renewed interest in the measurement of price indices, while the realization that inflation affects different groups differently had rendered the quantification of these differentials an important element in assessing inequality between households or individuals.

In the context of consumers, economic index numbers attempt to construct a single ratio that measures one of two things. The first, the cost-of-living index, measures the relative costs of reaching a given standard of living under two different situations, while the second, the real consumption index, compares two different standards of living in some appropriate units. As we shall see, the most convenient scale with which to measure welfare is the expenditure necessary, at constant prices, to maintain the various welfare levels being considered. These concepts, which use money to measure changes in welfare, can only be applied to situations where money and welfare are uniquely linked. This will not be the case where goods that are important for consumers' well-being are not purchased through the market; examples are health care, public parks, clean air, a noise-free environment, or some kinds of education. Hence, the index numbers discussed in this chapter are limited, as are most countries' consumer prices indices, to the measurement of quantities and prices that arise in the market.

Our general approach in this book makes the theory of index numbers very straightforward. It is no accident that the concept of the cost function of which we make so much use, first appeared in recognizable form in the literature on cost-of-living index numbers in the pioneering contributions by Konüs in the 1920's and 30's. In §7.1, the Konüs price index, or true cost-of-living index, is defined and the famous inequalities with the Paasche and Laspeyres indices explained. The variation in the true index between rich and poor households is discussed, and we present an empirical example designed to show how the indices can be calculated and how inflation rates have affected different income groups differently in Britain over the last decade. Section 7.2 deals with the problem of measuring real consumption or welfare; this is done, first, through the cost function and, second, with respect to some reference bundle of goods. Section 7.3 discusses the theory of subindices. Conventional price and quantity indices include only current variables, yet it is clear that in principle, expectations about the future can affect current welfare levels. If a consumer unit's standard of living depends on how much it expects to consume next period as well as on present consumption, its cost of living goes up if next period's expected prices go up, other things being equal. Even so, we might have doubts about making price index numbers dependent upon individuals' subjective expectations about the future, so that it is desirable to be able to construct subindices for the current period that are independent of future variables. The conditions under which this is possible are discussed in this section and the analysis is also applied to the construction of price and quantity indices for subgroups of goods. Finally, in §7.4, consumer surplus is discussed and related to the welfare measures based on index numbers.

7.1 The true index of the cost of living

Cost-of-living index numbers are devices for reducing the comparison between two complete price vectors such as p^1 and p^0 to a single scalar. If the two vectors are proportional to one another, so that, for example, p^1 is 5 percent greater than p^0, then we have no difficulty in saying that prices at 1 are 5 percent higher than prices at 0. However, when relative prices change, some standard of comparison is required. Almost by definition, an index of the cost of living uses a measure of the standard of living as reference. One such measure would be some reference commodity bundle q^R, say. This technique, that of the fixed "shopping basket," yields a price index

$$P(p^1, p^0; q^R) = p^1 \cdot q^R / p^0 \cdot q^R \tag{1.1}$$

where to minimize notation, we have adopted the "dot-product" symbol $p \cdot q$ to denote $\Sigma p_k q_k$. Clearly, (1.1) expresses the price level corresponding to p^1 relative to that at p^0 as the relative costs of buying the fixed basket q^R at the two sets of prices. However, a single bundle is an unnecessarily restrictive interpretation of what is meant by a constant standard of living, and the obvious alternative is to take a specific indifference curve as the reference concept that is to be held constant. On this interpretation, the cost-of-living index is the ratio of the minimum expenditures necessary to reach the reference indifference curve at the two sets of prices. Hence, if u^R is the label of the indifference curve taken as reference, the true cost-of-living index number is given by

$$P(p^1, p^0; u^R) = c(u^R, p^1) / c(u^R, p^0) \tag{1.2}$$

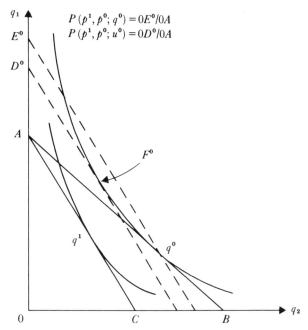

Figure 7.1. Base-weighted true and Laspeyres price indices.

If the index numbers (1.1) or (1.2) are to be used to compare a large number of different prices on a consistent basis, some convenient "representative" q^R or u^R can be chosen. If, however, only two different price situations are being compared, the natural choices for reference are q^0, u^0 or q^1 and u^1. The two resulting index numbers are illustrated in Figures 7.1 and 7.2 for the case of a rise in p_2 with p_1 held constant.

In both diagrams, the original budget line AB rotates, with the rise in p_2, to AC. In Figure 7.1, the budget line necessary to buy q^0 at the new prices cuts the vertical axis at E^0; however, an identical standard of living can be obtained at F^0 and the corresponding budget line cuts OE^0 at D^0. Since p_1 is unchanged, distances along OE^0 are proportional to total expenditures; hence, the base quantity weighted index, or *Laspeyres* price index is given by OE^0/OA while the base utility referenced index is OD^0/OA. Clearly, the former exceeds the latter. Figure 7.2 illustrates the corresponding situation with the current weighted indices. The current quantity weighted index is the *Paasche* price index, and this can be no more than the current utility referenced index $P(p^1, p^0; u^1)$.

The inequalities illustrated in the diagrams are easily shown to hold, in general. The bundle q^0 is one way of reaching u^0 but not necessarily the cheapest when prices are p^1; hence, $p^1 \cdot q^0$, the cost of q^0 at p^1, is greater than or equal to

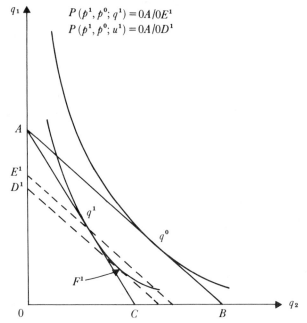

Figure 7.2. Current-weighted true and Paasche price indices.

$c(u^0, p^1)$, the minimum cost of u^0 at p^1. But, by the definition of q^0, $p^0 \cdot q^0$ is equal to $c(u^0, p^0)$. Hence, we have at once that

$$P(p^1, p^0; q^0) = \frac{p^1 \cdot q^0}{p^0 \cdot q^0} \geq \frac{c(u^0, p^1)}{c(u^0, p^0)} = P(p^1, p^0; u^0) \qquad (1.3)$$

Similarly, since q^1 is *one* way of obtaining u^1 at p^0, $p^0 \cdot q^1 \geq c(u^1, p^0)$ so that, since $p^1 \cdot q^1 = c(u^1, p^1)$,

$$P(p^1, p^0; q^1) = \frac{p^1 \cdot q^1}{p^0 \cdot q^1} \leq \frac{c(u^1, p^1)}{c(u^1, p^0)} = P(p^1, p^0; u^1) \qquad (1.4)$$

Note that these inequalities, which date back to Konüs (1924), do *not* imply that the true index lies somewhere between the Paasche and the Laspeyres. In general, there is no unique true index and the base-weighted utility index that has the Laspeyres index as an upper limit is a different number from the current weighted utility index that is no less than the Paasche index. Indeed, it is even possible for the Paasche index to exceed the Laspeyres!

The dependence of the true cost of living (1.2) on u^R means that, even for a single individual obeying the axioms of choice, it is not generally possible to talk about *the* price index. Consequently, changes in prices will affect the cost of living differently for different individuals, even if they have identical tastes, if their total expenditure levels differ. It is only under very special circumstances that these differences do not arise. In §5.4, we saw that if preferences are *homothetic*, so that all indifference curves are the same shape and expenditure patterns do not vary with outlay, the cost function is proportional to utility, that is, $c(u, p) = ub(p)$ for some function $b(p)$. If we substitute this into (1.2), the utility based price index is simply $b(p^1)/b(p^0)$, which is independent of u. It is also clear that this is the *only* case in which this happens, so that homotheticity is both necessary and sufficient for the existence of *the* price index. This is also the only case in which it is always true that the true index lies between the Paasche and the Laspeyres. As we have already seen, homotheticity is unlikely to be true in reality, so that it will always be necessary to allow for the effects of welfare on cost-of-living indices. We return to the issue below in an empirical context.

Measuring price indices

The true cost-of-living index numbers $P(p^1, p^0; u^0)$ and $P(p^1, p^0; u^1)$ can be calculated straightforwardly using (1.2) if we know the cost function $c(u, p)$. The closest we are likely to approach this is through the estimation of a complete system of demand equations. As was seen in Chapter 3, such an exercise requires a great deal of data if generality is to be preserved and, even if these are available, the results do not always conform to theoretical preconceptions. It is thus natural to inquire whether it is possible to do with less information. Calculation of true indices $P(p^1, p^0; u^R)$ involves two separate issues. The first relates to the dependence of the index on u^R which, as we saw above, results from the nonhomotheticity of preferences. Changes in prices affect different households differently if they have different patterns of expenditure. To deal with this, we need information on Engel curves and on how family composition affects consumption. We take up these effects below. The second issue relates to substitution effects consequent on relative price changes. In Figures 7.1 and 7.2, the differences between the Laspeyres index, the Paasche index, and the corresponding true indices was caused by substitution effects, and these are generally present whether or not preferences are homothetic.

It can be assumed that, at a minimum, there will be information on p^0, q^0, p^1, and q^1, the prices and quantities in the two situations. Since both Paasche and Laspeyres indices require only this, they can always be easily evaluated and they are both used freely in practice. They will be exactly equal to their corresponding true indices if there is no substitution between commodities, that is, when the cost function takes the form

$$c(u, p) = \sum_k a_k(u)p_k \tag{1.5}$$

for quantities $a_k(u)$. This result may easily be checked, see Exercise 7.3, or can be seen directly from Figures 7.1 and 7.2 in the case of right-angle indifference curves. Even if (1.5) does not hold, the Laspeyres will offer a first-order approximation to the true index. Taking the first two terms of a Taylor expansion of $c(u^0, p^1)$ around u^0, p^0 yields

$$c(u^0, p^1) = c(u^0, p^0) + \Sigma q_k^0 (p_k^1 - p_k^0) + \tfrac{1}{2}\Sigma\Sigma s_{kj}^0 (p_k^1 - p_k^0)(p_j^1 - p_j^0) \qquad (1.6)$$

since $\partial c(u^0, p^0)/\partial p_i = q_i^0$. Hence, if p^1 is fairly close to p^0, or if p^1 is almost proportional to p^0 (recall $\Sigma s_{kj}^0 p_j^0 = 0$), or if substitution is limited, the last term will be small so that

$$P(p^1, p^0; u^0) = \frac{c(u^0, p^1)}{c(u^0, p^0)} \simeq \frac{q^0 \cdot p^1}{q^0 \cdot p^0} = P(p^1, p^0; q^0) \qquad (1.7)$$

Similarly, the Paasche index can be shown to give a first-order approximation to the current weighted true index. These approximations offer considerable encouragement to the use of Paasche and Laspeyres indices although it is important to be aware of cases where substitution is likely to be significant, for example, in comparisons between different countries.

There have been frequent attempts to improve on the Paasche and Laspeyres formulas without extending the information required. Following recent work by Diewert (1976a), perhaps the most useful of these is the Törnqvist (1936) price index defined by

$$\log P(p^1, p^0; T) = \sum_k \tfrac{1}{2}(w_k^1 + w_k^0) \log(p_k^1/p_k^0) \qquad (1.8)$$

where w^1 and w^0 are the budget shares in the two situations. Diewert shows that if the logarithm of the cost function is a quadratic form in the logarithms of prices and utility, then the Törnqvist index is the true index $P(p^1, p^0; u^*)$, where the reference utility u^* is the geometric mean of u^0 and u^1. If we are willing to accept the reference indifference curve labeled by u^* as the relevant one, this property of the Törnqvist index is attractive since the quadratic specification can provide a second-order approximation to any arbitrary cost function. However, without knowing the parameters of the cost function, we lack more specific information about the reference indifference curve (such as what budget level and price vector corresponds to it), and the result is of no help in constructing a constant utility cost-of-living index series with more than two elements. A chained series of pairwise Törnqvist indices can always be constructed, but this has a different reference indifference curve for every link in the chain.

An alternative approach to approximation is via the construction of Divisia indices. Instead of comparing two discrete price situations, these indices work by analyzing the continuous effects of price changes on the cost of living.

Denote the proportional rate of change of the price level by $d \log P(p; u)$; this is equal to $d \log c(u, p)$, so that

$$d \log P(p; u) = d \log c(u, p) = \Sigma w_k(u, p) \, d \log p_k \qquad (1.9)$$

Hence, for any fixed utility level u, we can always write

$$\log P(p^1, p^0; u) = \int_{p^0}^{p^1} \Sigma w_k(u, p) \, d \log p_k \qquad (1.10)$$

This suggests constructing a price index that replaces $w_k(u, p)$ in (1.9) and (1.10) by the actually observed budget shares w_k, and this index is the Divisia index comparing p^1 and p^0. However, unless preferences are homothetic, the utility constant budget shares are not equal to the actual budget shares, and the variation of u over the integration means that, if prices were to change through time so as to return after some variation to an earlier value, then the calculated integral will not generally give $P(p^0, p^0) = 1$. In practice, neither the quantities nor the prices are continuously observable, so that (1.9) would have to be approximated by some formula containing finite changes; the Törnqvist index (1.8) is an obvious possibility, but there are many others. Such differential price indices can then be "chained" to give an approximation to (1.10).

Price indices for different households

Finally, we return to the question of how the true index can vary between households of differing standards of living. This is a phenomenon that exists independently of the degree of substitution between goods and can be seen, for example, by considering the Törnqvist index (1.8). If we assume that $\log(p_k^1/p_k^0)$ is the same for all households, differences in the index will exist if the average budget shares $\frac{1}{2}(w_k^1 + w_k^0)$ vary from household to household. But with nonhomothetic preferences, richer households will have larger budget shares for luxuries and smaller budget shares for necessities, so that if changes in prices involve relative price changes between luxuries and necessities, the cost-of-living index will differ systematically between poor and rich households.

We illustrate these effects using true indices calculated from an assumed cost function the parameters of which are econometrically estimated. In Chapter 6, the class of price-independent generalized linear preferences was discussed. The logarithmic form of this class (PIGLOG) has the cost function

$$\log c(u, p) = (1 - u) \log a(p) + u \log b(p) \qquad (1.11)$$

where $a(p)$ and $b(p)$ are positive linearly homogeneous concave functions of prices. This gives a particularly simple form for the base-weighted, true cost-of-living index,

$$\log P(p^1, p^0; u^0) = (1 - u^0) \log \frac{a(p^1)}{a(p^0)} + u^0 \log \frac{b(p^1)}{b(p^0)} \tag{1.12}$$

where u^0, the base utility level is equal to $\log[x^0/a(p^0)]/\log[b(p^0)/a(p^0)]$. Hence, across different households facing the same prices, u^0 is a linear function of $\log x^0$. Equation (1.12), which is of course specific to the PIGLOG model, shows very clearly how the price index varies with the standard of living of the household. Rich households have cost-of-living indices closer to $b(p^1)/b(p^0)$, while $a(p^1)/a(p^0)$ is more relevant for the less affluent.

The cost function (1.11) can be differentiated to give the commodity demands and if specific forms are chosen for $a(p)$ and $b(p)$, in this case $\Sigma \alpha_k p_k$ and $\beta_0 \Pi p_k^{\beta k}$, respectively, the model can be estimated and the cost-of-living indices calculated. Pooled time-series and cross-section British data for four different households types over the years 1965 to 1976 were used; the resulting index numbers, using the 1970 utility level as a base and expressed as annual rates of growth, are shown in Table 7.1 for the four household types and four different expenditure levels.

From 1965 to 1971, inflation was relatively neutral. In fact, on these figures, for families with children it was if anything slightly biased against the rich. But from 1971, sharply rising food prices impart a strong "anti-poor" bias to these indices. As the figures indicate, even the food subsidies that the British Government introduced in 1974 could not stem the tide and when they were eventually dismantled in the course of 1975 and 1976, the food price rises together with fuel price rises produced some of the strongest and most sustained regressive relative price changes that have been seen in British postwar history.

For Britain, a number of studies, Allen (1958), Brittain (1960), Tipping (1970), Piachaud (1978), and Muellbauer (1977a), suggest that the postwar period can be divided into well-defined phases by the degree of bias in price changes. The war years saw a substantial bias in favor of the poor, but after the war, relative price changes were substantially antipoor until 1961. Until 1966, the bias was smaller but in the same direction, vanishing altogether from 1966 to 1971. In an open economy, we would expect these episodes to be associated with shifts in the international terms of trade. For the United States, there is evidence, see Hollister and Palmer (1972), that in the 1950's and 1960's inflation was relatively neutral, so that, for this period, a single price index is an adequate measure of the cost of living. However, in the 1970's relative prices moved against the poor, see Williamson (1977) and the BLS Monthly Labor Review. This also appears to have been the case for Canada, see Afriat (1977). But even these changes seem trivial by comparison

Table 7.1. *The distributional impact of inflation in the U.K. 1965–76: annual average percentage rates of inflation for four household types and four levels of expenditure*

1970 weekly expenditure levels

	£15				£30				£50				£80			
	Two adults with respective number of children															
	0	1	2	3	0	1	2	3	0	1	2	3	0	1	2	3
1965–71	5.52	5.35	5.36	5.36	5.43	5.39	5.41	5.41	5.36	5.43	5.44	5.44	5.30	5.46	5.48	5.47
1971–5	14.17	14.18	14.34	14.45	13.82	13.94	14.07	14.14	13.56	13.77	13.88	13.93	13.33	13.58	13.68	13.70
1974–5	24.66	24.69	24.88	25.09	24.41	24.50	24.53	24.57	24.24	24.36	24.27	24.18	24.06	24.23	24.03	23.84
1975–6	16.39	16.39	16.53	16.94	15.42	15.55	15.64	15.85	14.69	14.94	15.95	15.05	14.05	14.38	14.40	14.33

with some episodes that have occurred in underdeveloped countries where there are often structural reasons that permit drastic fluctuations in the prices of staple foods relatively to other goods. Sen (1977a) has documented the consequences of the huge increases in the prices of staple foods that occurred in the Great Bengal Famine of 1943 in which between three and five million people died. Clearly, in such a case, the price system can bring about a drastic change in the distribution of real consumption that we would not perceive by looking at money income or money expenditure. In such a case, the simplification of working with a single price index is a very dangerous one.

Exercises

7.1. Show that the price index $P(p^1, p^0; u^R)$ satisfies the following propositions and interpret each of them:

    (a) $P(\lambda p^0, p^0; u^R) = \lambda$

    (b) $P(p^0, p^0; u^R) = 1$

    (c) $P(p^1, p^0; u^R) = 1/P(p^0, p^1; u^R)$

    (d) $P(p^0, p^1; u) P(p^1, p^2; u) = P(p^0, p^2; u)$

    (e) $\min(p_i^1/p_i^0) \leq P(p^1, p^0; u^R) \leq \max(p_i^1/p_i^0)$

    (f) Hence, show that upper and lower bounds can be derived for both true indices, that is,

$$\min(p_i^1/p_i^0) \leq P(p^1, p^0; u^0) \leq P(p^1, p^0; q^0)$$

$$P(p^1, p^0; q^1) \leq P(p^1, p^0; u^1) \leq \max(p_i^1/p_i^0)$$

7.2. Show that the cost-of-living index number $\log P = \Sigma w_k \log (p_k^1/p_k^0)$ is equal to $\log P(p^1, p^0; u)$ if preferences are Cobb-Douglas.

7.3. Show that the cost function (1.5) gives the Laspeyres index as a true cost-of-living index number, and interpret the result in terms of the shape of the indifference curves. Harder: is (1.5) *necessary* for the true index to be Laspeyres?

7.4. Show that the Laspeyres index $P(p^1, p^0; q^0)$ can be written in the form $\Sigma w_k^0(p_k^1/p_k^0)$. If the budget shares take the PIGLOG form $w_i^0 = \alpha_i^0 + \eta_i^0 \log x^0$, where α_i^0 and η_i^0 are functions of p^0, show that $P(p^1, p^0; q^0)$ takes the form $P_A + P_B \log x^0$. How might P_A and P_B be relevant in assessing the differential effects of price changes on households of differing standards of living?

7.5. (Exercise 7.4, cont.) Assuming that different households have the same parameters α_i^0 and η_i^0 but different levels of x^{0h}, find the Laspeyres index $P(p^1, p^0; q^0)$, where $q^0 = (1/H)\Sigma_{h=1}^H q^{0h}$, which corresponds to market expenditure. Show that it is identical to the Laspeyres index for a representative consumer with a budget level $x^* > \bar{x}$ where $\bar{x} = (1/H)\Sigma x^{0h}$ (cf. §6.2). What implications follow from this result for the interpretation of published aggregate price indices?

7.6.* Show that if preferences are homothetic and the cost function is $c(u, p) = u(p \cdot Ap)^{1/2}$ for a negative definite matrix A, the Fisher "ideal" index – the geometric mean of the Paasche and the Laspeyres – is the true index. [This result is related to Bu-scheguennce's (1925) famous theorem proving that Fisher's index is the true index if the *utility function* is quadratic; see Afriat (1977) and Diewert (1980) for further details.]

7.7.* (Diewert 1976a.) Prove that if $\log c(u, p) = \alpha_0 + \Sigma\alpha_k \log p_k + \frac{1}{2}\Sigma\Sigma\alpha_{kj} \log p_k \log p_j + \beta_0 \log u + \frac{1}{2}\Sigma\beta_k \log p_k \log u + \frac{1}{2}\gamma(\log u)^2$, the Törnqvist index (1.8) is the true index for $u^* = (u^0 u^1)^{1/2}$.

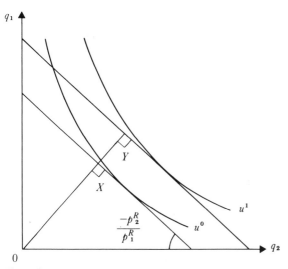

Figure 7.3. Money metric utility.

7.8.* All the other results in this set of exercises require that tastes remain unchanged from 0 to 1. Assume, instead, that the consumer is steadily becoming more efficient as a "utility machine," has homothetic tastes, and a cost function indexed on time t, $c_t(u, p) = e^{-\alpha t}ua(p)$ for $\alpha > 0$. Interpret the "cardinal" cost-of-living index number $P_c(p^t, p^{t-1}, u)$ given by $c_t(u, p^t)/c_{t-1}(u, p^{t-1})$ and compare its properties to those of the more usual index. [See Phlips (1974), Muellbauer (1975a) and Pollak (1976a) for further discussion.]

7.2 Quantity indices and real consumption indices

Money metric utility

The cost function can be used not only to construct price indices but also to construct real consumption or utility indices. Since we already have a scalar measure of welfare, utility itself, the problem of constructing real consumption indices is essentially one of choosing a convenient utility function, or equivalently, of choosing a convenient system for labeling indifference curves. Figure 7.3 illustrates for two indifference curves, u^0 and u^1, say. Choose any reference price vector p^R; this establishes the slope $-p_2^R/p_1^R$ as illustrated. We can then calculate, for any indifference curve, the minimum cost of reaching it at the reference prices and this becomes our money measure of utility itself. In common parlance, the welfare level u^1 might correspond to a "\$20,000-a-year-family" while u^0 is a "\$15,000-a-year-family," the two sums being the minima necessary to reach the respective standards of living. The real consumption or welfare index number for u^1 relative to u^0 is the ratio $0Y/0X$; we call this the "welfare index" (rather than utility index, a term often used to refer to the utility function itself).

Formally, money metric utility at reference prices p^R is $c(u, p^R)$, which, since $c(u, p)$ is increasing in u and p^R is constant, is a monotone increasing function of u itself and can thus be taken as a utility indicator in its own right. The welfare *index* u^1 and u^0 is written $U(u^1, u^0; p^R)$ and is defined by

$$U(u^1, u^0; p^R) = c(u^1, p^R)/c(u^0, p^R) \tag{2.1}$$

Note the parallels and contrasts between (2.1) and (1.2); the price index is measured by the variation in $c(u, p)$ as p changes with u held constant while the welfare index takes u as variable with p fixed at its reference level. As before, with only two utility levels to compare, the natural candidates for p^R are p^0 and p^1 giving base-weighted and current-weighted welfare indices, respectively. These are straightforwardly related to the two true price indices through the expenditure index x^1/x^0. The following can be checked by straightforward substitution from (1.2) and (2.1)

$$P(p^1, p^0; u^0) \cdot U(u^1, u^0; p^1) = x^1/x^0 \tag{2.2}$$

$$P(p^1, p^0; u^1) \cdot U(u^1, u^0; p^0) = x^1/x^0 \tag{2.3}$$

Hence, the expenditure index divided by the base-weighted price index gives the current-weighted welfare index, while the expenditure index divided by the current-weighted price index leads to the base-weighted welfare index.

Given full information on preferences, we can immediately apply these concepts to obtain a comparison of indifference curves on a ratio scale. However, a considerable part of the literature on economic index numbers is concerned with obtaining weaker results in cases where less information is available. For example, given only the two price and quantity vectors (p^0, q^0), (p^1, q^1) and no other information, we might look for an indicator of whether q^1 is at least as good as q^0. One approach to this is via the concept of revealed preference, see §2.6: q^1 is at least as good as q^0 if q^1 is chosen when q^0 is available at no greater cost. Hence, q^1 is at least as good as q^0 if $p^1 \cdot q^1 \geq p^1 \cdot q^0$, that is, if the Paasche quantity index is greater than or equal to unity. Similarly, if $p^0 \cdot q^0 \geq p^0 \cdot q^1$, that is, if the Laspeyres quantity index is no greater than unity, we can rank q^0 as at least as good as q^1. If neither condition holds, we have insufficient information to rank the bundles, see, for example, Samuelson (1938, 1947), Little (1957). Ranking bundles seems a weaker requirement than comparing indifference curves on a ratio scale. But the two apparently different approaches to measuring index numbers are fundamentally the same. As we saw in Exercise 7.1, upper and lower bounds for each of the two cost-of-living indices $P(p^1, p^0; u^0)$ and $P(p^1, p^0; u^1)$ are easily derived. Since the corresponding welfare indices are obtained from (2.2) and (2.3), we can immediately write down corresponding bounds for them. The width of these reflects the limited information that is available, and Afriat (1967, 1969) has shown how the bounds can be brought closer together if we have more than two price and quantity vectors consistent with the same preference ordering. With many data points, we can estimate demand functions that will give an approximate representation of the underlying cost function, and in the limit, this will lead to full information on preferences.

Quantity metric welfare and quantity indices

The welfare indices defined here are by no means the only way of measuring real consumption. One important alternative is not to label indifference curves by the costs required to reach them but rather by their relative distances from the origin along some reference quantity bundle. For example, in Figure 7.4 the welfare index for u^1 and u^0 referenced on q^R is $0B/0A$ while that referenced on q^S will be $0B'/0A'$. In general, these will be different, although, as is intuitively clear, the index will be independent of q^R if preferences are homothetic.

This technique can also be used in reverse, to define quantity indices with reference to some base indifference curve. To illustrate, let this be u^0 in the diagram. An index of q^R relative to q^S is constructed by comparing the amounts by which each vector has to be scaled down to reach u^0. In this case q^R must be divided by $0C/0A$ and q^S by $0C'/0A'$ so that the quantity index $Q(q^R, q^S; u^0)$ is measured by $0C/0A \div 0C'/0A'$. These index numbers, which

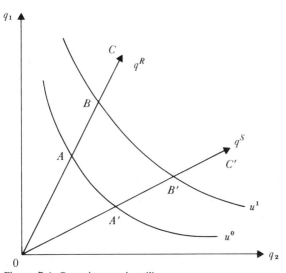

Figure 7.4. Quantity metric utility.

were first defined by Malmquist (1953), are dual to the true price indices discussed in §7.1 above. Note however, that unlike the welfare indices $U(u^1, u^0; p)$, these concepts do not require the intermediation of prices at all. They thus have the advantage of being applicable independently of the existence of prices, for example, under rationing or with nonlinear budget constraints. A formal discussion requires use of the distance function of §2.7 and is carried on in Exercise 7.12 below.

Exercises

7.9. The Paasche and Laspeyres *quantity* indices are defined by $p^1 \cdot q^1/p^1 \cdot q^0$ and $p^0 \cdot q^1/p^0 \cdot q^0$, respectively. Show that the Paasche quantity index is less than or equal to $U(u^1, u^0; p^1)$ and that the Laspeyres quantity index is greater than or equal to $U(u^1, u^0; p^0)$. Show that the Paasche and Laspeyres quantity and price indices are related by equations analogous to (2.2) and (2.3). When are the indices $U(u^1, u^0; p^R)$ independent of p^R?

7.10. By totally differentiating outlay x, show how a Divisia quantity index can be defined analogously to the Divisia price index in (1.9).

7.11. Draw the "dual" diagram to Figure 7.4 by labeling the axes $r_1 = p_1/x$ and $r_2 = p_2/x$ and marking in the indifference curves corresponding to the indirect utility function. Following Figure 7.4, select a reference indifference curve and two arbitrary normalized price vectors (r_1^0, r_2^0) and (r_1^1, r_2^1). How is the ratio of "reducing factors" necessary to bring r^0 and r^1 to the reference utility u^R related to the true cost-of-living index number $P(p^1, p^0; u^R)$?

7.12.* The formal definition of the Malmquist quantity index is $Q(q^1, q^0; u^R) = d(u^R, q^1)/d(u^R, q^0)$. The corresponding welfare index is then $U(u^1, u^0; q^R) = d(u^0, q^R)/d(u^1, q^R)$. Show that the following hold and interpret each:

(a) $Q(q^1, q^0; u^0) = U(u^1, u^0; q^1)$

(b) $Q(q^1, q^0; u^1) = U(u^1, u^0; q^0)$

(c) $Q(q^1, q^0; u^0) \leq Q(q^1, q^0; p^0)$

(d) $Q(q^1, q^0; u^1) \geq Q(q^1, q^0; p^1)$

(e) $U(u^1, u^0; q^0) \geq U(u^1, u^0; p^0)$

(f) $U(u^1, u^0; q^1) \leq U(u^1, u^0; p^1)$

(g) For some λ, $0 \leq \lambda \leq 1$, and $u^* = \lambda u^0 + (1 - \lambda)u^1$, $P(p^1, p^0; u^*)Q(q^1, q^0; u^*) = x_1/x_0$.

These theorems are Malmquist's (1953); more readily accessible proofs are given in Deaton (1979) and Diewert (1980b).

7.3 Cost-of-living subindices

In many contexts, we wish to be able to refer, not merely to a general index of prices, but also to particular components. "Food prices" as well as "rents" are always regarded as indices that are particularly important politically, while for descriptive purposes it is often important to be able to ascribe changes in the overall index at some particular time to one or more of its components. More fundamentally, as Pollak (1975) has persuasively argued, even the general price index is itself a subindex in the context of intertemporal decision making, although, as we pointed out in the introduction, ignorance of the future makes a full intertemporal index highly subjective. Two closely related questions arise in constructing subindices. First, can we design them in such a way as to allow the aggregate index to be derived from its components? Second, what meaning can we attach to individual subindices independently of what is happening elsewhere? To take a very important example, can we define a conventional market good cost-of-living index without explicitly taking account of the consumer's situation in the labor market or his access to public goods?

In §7.1, the existence of preferences was the essential prerequisite to our defining cost-of-living index numbers. Similarly, a cost-of-living index for a subgroup of commodities requires the existence of preferences for that subgroup. As we saw in Chapter 5, such preferences depend in general on the consumption of goods outside the group and will only be independent of variation in such consumption if the subgroup is separable from other goods. This is the only case where we can define a subgroup utility function $v_G(q_G)$, say, and with this can be associated a cost function $c_G(u_G, p_G)$ defined in the usual way as the minimum expenditure on the group required to reach a group utility level of u_G. Given this, the true group price index $P_G(p_G^1, p_G^0; u_G^R)$ is given by

$$P_G(p_G^1, p_G^0; u_G^R) = c_G(u_G^R, p_G^1)/c_G(u_G^R, p_G^0) \qquad (3.1)$$

analogously to (1.2). Note that any attempt to construct such an index if preferences are *not* separable will result in the group price index varying with variations in prices of goods outside the group. This can be seen by constructing a partial conditional cost function, cf. (3.11) of Chapter 4, as the minimum expenditure on the set of included goods necessary to reach a given level of overall utility for some preset levels of the other goods. If these preset levels are constant, price indices for the goods included can be constructed from these partial cost functions in the usual way. If, however, such indices are to be independent of the conditioning variables, weak separability is required and we return to (3.1).

Although (3.1) gives a perfectly satisfactory group price index that can be applied to individual periods in an intertemporal context or to subgroups of commodities, it is not generally possible to combine the individual P_G's into the overall index $P(p^1, p^0; u)$, see Exercise 7.15. Nor is it even possible, unless preferences are homothetic, to combine the subcost functions into the overall cost function. It appears that these problems can be lessened to some degree by working with *implicit* rather than *weak* separability, see Blackorby and Russell (1978), but even in this case, severe restrictions have to be placed on the cost function before aggregation of indices is possible, see Primont (1977).

Finally, we note that, just as separability simplified this analysis of the demand for rationed goods, see §5.1, the same assumption allows the construction of subcost-of-living indices for unrationed goods in the presence of rationing. In the more general, nonseparable case, cost functions can still be used to measure the impact of rationing. For example, at a given budget, an increase in prices, caused for example, by a supply reduction, makes the household worse off. If price controls are instituted together with rationing of the goods in short supply, it may well be that the government's price index shows no increase and yet households are worse off. If preferences are known, we can compare the utility levels in the rationed and unrationed situations and price them using the unconditional cost function, see Exercise 7.16.

Exercises

7.13. The group Laspeyres price index is given by $p_G^1 \cdot q_G^0 / p_G^0 \cdot q_G^0$. Show that knowledge of these group indices plus the base period budget shares for each group is sufficient for the construction of the overall Laspeyres index. Does a similar result hold for Paasche price indices?

7.14. In the case of additive preferences, with only one good in each group, the group price indices are the price ratios p_i^1 / p_i^0. Show, by choice of a suitable example, that it is not generally possible to calculate $c(u, p^1)/c(u, p^0)$ knowing only the price ratios p_i^1 / p_i^0.

7.15. (Pollak 1975.) Under weak separability, see Chapter 5, $c(u, p) = \Sigma c_G(u_G, p_G)$ for category cost functions $c_G(u_G, p_G)$, category utility u_G and price subvector p_G. Show that $c(u^0, p^1) \leq \Sigma c_G(u_G^0, p_G^1)$ so that we have the Laspeyres type inequality $P(p^1, p^0; u^0) \leq \Sigma w_G^0 P_G(p_G^1, p_G^0; u_G^0)$, where P_G is given by (3.1) and w_G^0 is the budget share devoted to group G in the base period.

7.16.* Let $c^*(u, p, z)$ be the minimum cost of attaining u at prices p when quantity z has to be bought, see Chapter 4 (3.1). How would you interpret the index $c^*(u, p, z)/c(u, p)$ regarded as a function of z with u and p held constant? If $\psi^*(x, p, z)$ is the indirect utility function corresponding to $c^*(u, p, z)$, interpret $c[\psi^*(x, p, z), p]/c[\psi(x, p), p]$, again regarded as a function of z. Taking z as leisure, discuss how these concepts could be used for measuring the welfare loss from unemployment [see Hurd (1976), Ashenfelter (1980), for an example]. How satisfactory would such a measure be?

7.4 Consumer surplus

The basic idea of consumer surplus is to attach a monetary value to the change in welfare resulting either from a change in consumption or from a change in prices and the budget. For example, we might ask how much a household would pay rather than do without some particular good or how much it would have to be paid to compensate it for a price increase. The early formulation by Dupuit (1844) in terms of marginal utility was later replaced by Marshall's (1890) idea of taking the area under the Marshallian (uncompensated) demand curve to define consumer surplus (see Figure 7.5). However, as early as (1947) Samuelson realized that consumer surplus is essentially superfluous to the theory of consumer behavior. As we shall see, correct

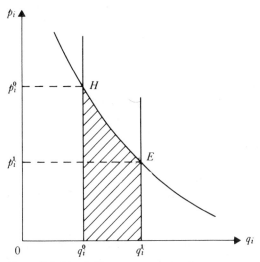

Figure 7.5. Marshallian consumer surplus.

formulations have precise equivalences in terms of the index numbers already discussed but this is not always appreciated, and the use of consumer surplus as an analytical tool frequently seems to lead to errors and confusion.

The intuitive rationale for Marshall's idea is clear enough. From the first-order conditions for utility maximization, $\partial v(q)/\partial q_i = \lambda p_i$, the total differential of utility can be written $du = \Sigma \lambda p_i dq_i$. If it can be assumed that λ, the marginal utility of total expenditure, is constant, and if we think of p (the price the consumer is prepared to pay for a marginal unit) as a function of q, then we can integrate utility changes over the interval q^0 to q^1 to give the total welfare change as λ times the sum over all goods of the areas like that shaded in Figure 7.5. Alternatively, we could start from the indirect utility function and equation (3.16) from Chapter 2: $-\lambda q_i = \partial \psi(x, p)/\partial p_i$ with $\lambda = \partial \psi(x, p)/\partial x$. In this case, we would integrate the differential $du = -\Sigma \lambda q_i \, dp_i$ over the interval p^0 to p^1 taking q as a function of p, and again assuming λ to be constant. This would give λ times the sum over all goods of the areas like $p_i^0 H E p_i^1$ in Figure 7.5. However, as was realized as early as Pareto (1892), the constancy of λ is impossible since it would imply, for example, that maximum attainable utility be independent of prices. It turns out that whether we integrate over prices or over quantities, the only circumstance in which *either* the area $p_i^0 H E p_i^1$ *or* the area $q_i^0 H E q_i^1$ is a valid measure of welfare change is if preferences are homothetic, see, for example, Chipman and Moore (1976) and Exercise 7.20.

One answer to the problem is to take areas under the *compensated* or Hicksian demand curves and over a price rather than a quantity change. Since the Hicksian demand functions are the derivatives of the cost function, integration gives the *difference* in costs of reaching the same indifference curve at two different price vectors. This perfectly correct use of consumer surplus can be described in terms of the cost function, but instead of having index numbers based on *ratios*, as in the earlier sections, we have "equivalent" and "compensating variations" in terms of *differences*. These will yield actual cash sums as opposed to the pure numbers of index number theory and this can occasionally be useful if, for example, it is required to compare the welfare effects of two mutually exclusive government policies.

Hicks (1956) defines the compensating variation (CV) as the minimum amount by which a consumer would have to be compensated after a price change in order to be as well off as before. Hence, and compare (1.2),

$$CV = c(u^0, p^1) - c(u^0, p^0) \tag{4.1}$$

Alternatively, CV may be defined implicitly through the indirect utility function; clearly, $\psi(x^0 + CV, p^1) = \psi(x^0, p^0)$ is equivalent to (4.1). The equivalent variation (EV), on the other hand, is the maximum amount the consumer would be prepared to pay at the budget level x^1 to avoid the change from p^0 to p^1. Clearly, $\psi(x^1 - EV, p^0) = \psi(x^1, p^1)$ so that

$$EV = c(u^1, p^1) - c(u^1, p^0) \tag{4.2}$$

Clearly, CV and EV are the exact analogs in difference form of the base and current-utility weighted true price indices $P(p^1, p^0; u^0)$ and $P(p^1, p^0; u^1)$. It is to emphasize this analogy that we have adopted the definitions given rather than those more frequently met in the literature which are (4.1) and (4.2) with signs reversed. Similar differences can be defined to give the money value of the utility change using both p^1 and p^0 as reference; this gives four consumer surplus type concepts in all. Since these concepts are nearly always used in situations where x is being held constant while prices change, CV and EV can also be used as measures of welfare change. For example, using p^0 as reference, the money metric utility change is $c(u^1, p^0) - c(u^0, p^0)$, which, since $c(u^0, p^0) = c(u^1, p^1) = x$, is $c(u^1, p^0) - c(u^1, p^1) = -EV$. Similarly, with fixed x, $c(u^1, p^1) - c(u^0, p^1) = -CV$. This makes perfect sense; if positive compensating or equivalent variations are required, welfare after the change must be lower than in the original situation.

A considerable literature exists on methods for evaluating these concepts that parallels the comparable discussion for price indices, see §7.1 above. As before, complete information on the cost function, or equivalently on a utility-based system of demand functions, is sufficient to calculate CV and EV exactly. However, just as the Paasche and Laspeyres price indices act as first-order approximations to the true price indices, parallel formulas exist in

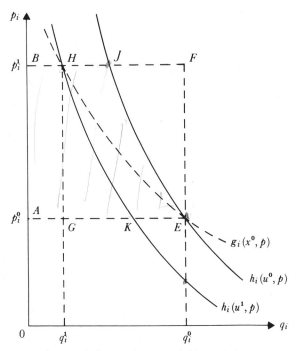

Figure 7.6. Equivalent and compensating variations.

the present case. If we expand $c(u^0, p^1)$ around $c(u^0, p^0)$ and $c(u^1, p^0)$ around $c(u^1, p^1)$, we get [cf. (1.6) and Exercise 7.18]

$$\mathrm{CV} \simeq q^0 \cdot (p^1 - p^0), \qquad \mathrm{EV} \simeq q^1 \cdot (p^1 - p^0) \qquad (4.3)$$

We illustrate these formulas for single price change in Figure 7.6. The initial situation is at point E where q_i^0 is bought at a price p_i^0 and at a total expenditure x^0. This is to be compared with the situation after p_i^0 has gone up to p_i^1 and we want a measure of the fall in the consumer's welfare. CV measures this by the area $EJBA$ under the Hicksian demand curve $h_i(u^0, p)$ lying between EA and JB. The approximation (4.3) is shown by the area $EFBA$ and this clearly exceeds CV. The equivalent variation EV is conditional upon the reference utility level u^1, which in this diagrammatic illustration is below u^0. It is thus the area $KHBA$ under the Hicksian demand curve $h_i(u^1, p)$ lying between KA and HB and this is approximated (understated) by the rectangle $ABHG$.

We may note that there appears to be a widespread impression in the literature that computation of CV or EV is intrinsically more difficult or requires more information than calculating the area under Marshallian demand functions; see, for example, Burns (1973), Seade (1978) or Willig (1976)–who provides formulas for the maximum error involved in approximating CV and EV by the Marshallian measure. In fact, this is not so, and there exist several straightforward methods of calculation for CV and EV based only on knowledge of the uncompensated demand functions, see Vartia (1983). Of course, if we do not know the demand functions, we are back to the case of more limited information discussed in §7.1 and §7.2 and not much more remains to be said. When the only information is on the base and current price and quantity vectors, we saw in §7.1 that one true index number is bounded above by the Laspeyres index while the other is bounded below by the Paasche index and that this fact had tempted many economists to take the combination of Paasche and Laspeyres as being in some sense "better." Similarly, in the consumer surplus literature, averages based on (4.3) have been proposed. Consider the indicator of the change in purchasing power with total outlay held constant given by

$$H^* = \tfrac{1}{2}(q^1 + q^0) \cdot (p^1 - p^0) = -\tfrac{1}{2}(p^1 + p^0) \cdot (q^1 - q^0) \qquad (4.4)$$

where the second equality depends on $p^1 \cdot q^1 = p^0 q^0$. The first of these measures was suggested by Hicks (1946), the second by Harberger (1971). There seems little point in trying to interpret H^* as an approximation to either CV or EV (although note that it is the area $BHEA$ if H and E are joined by a straight line), since, as already defined, CV and EV measure two quantities that are conceptually distinct. However, H^* may be of interest in its own right if all we wish to do is tell whether, with x constant, the move from p^0 to p^1 has increased or decreased welfare. Since an increase in welfare will always cause both CV and EV to be negative (see Exercise 7.18), any combination of them will do as well, and as can be seen from (4.3), H^* is a first-order approximation to $\tfrac{1}{2}(CV + EV)$. Further, it is easily shown, see Exercise 7.18, that when the price change indices in (4.3), $q^0 \cdot \Delta p$ and $q^1 \cdot \Delta p$ agree with one another, H^*, which is their average, gives the correct direction for welfare change. When the evidence for welfare change is ambiguous, Diewert (1976a) shows that H^*, and indeed Fisher's "ideal index," will indicate the direction of change correctly if preferences can be locally approximated by some quadratic but not necessarily homothetic utility function, see also Exercise 7.18.

Note, finally, that all the discussion in this chapter, whether of index numbers or of consumer surplus, is in the context of a single household. It cannot be emphasized too strongly that the extension to many households is far from trivial. For example, the widespread practice of interpreting index numbers constructed from aggregate data as measures of aggregate welfare is justifiable only under very special assumptions. We return to these matters in Chapter 9 below.

Exercises

7.17. Using some convenient utility function and its associated demand functions, derive expressions for EV and CV and the various approximations to them given an increase in a single price. Discuss the practical problems of evaluating these expressions. Does H^*, as given by (4.4), indicate utility correctly for your model?

7.18. (a) Show that if $u^1 > u^0$, $c(u^1, p) > c(u^0, p)$ for all price vectors p. Hence show that CV and EV always have the same sign. (b) Suppose that total outlay is given. Denote $q^0 \cdot (p^1 - p^0) = \Delta P_L$ (for Laspeyres or base-weighted price change) and $q^1 \cdot (p^1 - p^0) = \Delta P_P$ (for Paasche or current-weighted price change). Why is $\Delta P_P \geq$ CV and $\Delta P_P \leq$ EV? Show that ($\Delta P_P > 0$, $\Delta P_L < 0$) violates the axioms of choice (and of revealed preference), that ($\Delta P_P \geq 0$, $\Delta P_L > 0$) means welfare has fallen, that ($\Delta P_L \leq 0$, $\Delta P_P < 0$) means welfare has risen, and that ($\Delta P_L \geq 0$, $\Delta P_P \leq 0$) is consistent with an increase or decrease in welfare. What implications follow for the usefulness of $H^* = \frac{1}{2}(\Delta P_L + \Delta P_P)$?

7.19.* Show that if $c(u, p) = [p \cdot B(u)p]^{1/2}$ for some matrix B, the elements of which depend on u, then H^* will indicate u correctly. What conditions are required on $B(u)$ and how do you justify them? (See Diewert (1976a) for further discussion of this and the previous exercise.)

7.20.* Show that if preferences are homothetic then the sum of the areas under the Marshallian demand curves,

$$\int_{p^0}^{p^1} \sum_i g_i(x^0, p) \, dp_i$$

is a valid welfare indicator. [Hint: show that with the cost function $c(u, p) = ub(p)$, the integral is $x^0 \log[b(p^1)/b(p^0)]$, which is a monotonic function of CV.]

7.21. Given a utility function $u = q_1 + \phi(q_2)$, show that the Hicksian and Marshallian demand functions for q_2 coincide. Show that, in this case, the Marshallian concept of consumer's surplus can be formally justified. Discuss how q_1 can be extended to a Hicks aggregate or to a linearly homogeneous function of goods other than q_2.

Bibliographical notes

The approach presented in this chapter is often known as the *economic* theory of index numbers as opposed to more obviously statistical approaches or the "test" approach originated by Irving Fisher (1922). The early survey paper by Frisch (1936), which makes these distinctions, retains its classical status. The textbook by Allen (1975) is very useful on historical as well as practical and theoretical aspects of index numbers. The survey paper by Sen (1979) on national income measurement contains not only a useful survey of index number theory but makes useful distinctions on the relationship between index numbers and welfare at the individual as well as social level. Pride of place in the economic theory of indices must go to Auspitz and Lieben (1889) and to Konüs (1924, trans. 1939), see also Konüs and Buscheguennce (1925) and Konüs (1939). Other important references are Allen (1949) and, more recently, Afriat (1972, 1977), Pollak (1971c), Samuelson and Swamy (1974), and Diewert(1976a).The paper by Malmquist (1953) is of quite fundamental importance and originality but is not easily accessible. A straightforward discussion of his results is in Deaton (1979) while Diewert (1980b)provides an excellent survey of the whole area. The term *money metric utility* we owe to Samuelson (1974). The calculations of price index numbers given in §7.1 are from Muellbauer (1977a); for an example of the methodology of Exercise 7.4 applied to price comparisons of the United States, the United Kingdom, and Hungary, see Muellbauer (1978a). The problems associated with subindices were first raised by Pollak (1975); for further discussion and related results, see Blackorby and Russell (1977), Primont (1977), and Vartia (1976). An early discussion of the measurement of the cost of living in the presence of rationing is given by Nicholson (1942–3), who also gives an empirical estimate of the correction to the official price index in wartime Britain. In the older literature, consumer surplus is usually associated with the names Dupuit and Marshall though Jevons (1871) and Auspitz and Lieben (1889) made important contributions. In the more recent past, Hicks (1946, 1956) and Samuelson (1942, 1947) are the classic sources. Amongst a large and not very edifying literature, and apart from the papers cited in the text, useful references are Samuelson (1947), Silberberg (1972), Hause (1975), Chipman and Moore (1976), and Mishan (1977).

CHAPTER 8

Household characteristics, demand, and household welfare comparisons

Households differ in size, age composition, educational level and other characteristics and, in general, we would expect households with different characteristics to have different expenditure patterns. Just as we are interested in modeling the effects on demands of differences in prices and budget levels, so is it legitimate and useful in summarizing a great deal of information to model the effects of household characteristics. In cross-section studies, either rather aggregated data for a few household types are available or, more rarely, a great deal of truly microeconomic information. Modeling the effects of household characteristics is useful in both situations provided that the model is plausible: in the former case, we obtain more precise estimates of the price and budget responses by pooling scarce data; in the latter, the model provides a convenient way of summarizing information that otherwise would take the form of a different demand system for each of the many household types.

In general, we can model differences in behavior by making demand depend not only on prices and total expenditure but also on some list of household characteristics. Most frequently modeled are the effects of household composition, the number, types, and ages of household members, but in principle any other characteristics can be included. As we shall see, this can be done in a wide variety of ways. One of the crudest, other than ignoring such effects altogether, is to deflate both demands and total outlay by household size so that, in per capita terms, consumption is the same function of the budget and prices for all households. Such an approach raises the question of whether such per capita demand functions can form a basis for welfare comparisons between households, and indeed, much of the literature on household characteristics has been motivated by the search for such a basis. It is certainly tempting to conclude that if the per capita budget is relevant for demand patterns it should also reflect welfare levels. However, it always must be borne in mind that such welfare comparisons are being made *across* households so that, by making the leap from behavior to welfare, we are assuming that two households who behave identically have identical welfare levels. We can accept this assumption or not, but a behavioral basis has been sought for the making of welfare comparisons for many years, and we must therefore investigate what systematic foundation can be given to such an approach.

One obvious basis is to extend the notions of index numbers developed in the last chapter to cover comparisons of welfare or real income across households of different sizes and compositions. The index numbers through which these comparisons are made are called *equivalence scales*. These are to welfare comparisons between households with different characteristics what cost-of-living indices are to welfare comparisons for a given household facing different prices. And, in the same way that cost-of-living indices are based on the assumption of unchanging tastes, equivalence scales are based on the assumption that the only differences in tastes between households are because of variations in observable characteristics.

In many contexts, it is important to know how well off the members of one household are relative to those of another. Given that both face the same prices, one way is to compute and compare per capita budget levels as suggested above. However, this ignores the variation of need with age: babies need less than adults. Also there are likely to be opportunities for economies of scale in consumption. Three people do not need proportionately more bathrooms or cars than two people; buying and cooking food in bulk is cheaper; clothes can be handed down from older to younger children. Household equivalence scales are deflators that are more sophisticated than mere head counting and by which the budgets of different household types can be converted to a needs-corrected basis. They play a fundamental role in government welfare policies. For example, in income maintenance programs, families with many children or older children generally receive larger benefits than those with fewer or younger children. Equivalence scales also play a central role in defining the poverty line, since minimal consumption standards certainly vary with household composition.

The question of what numerical values these scales have or should have has received much attention over the years. Briefly, the alternative sources for equivalence scales may be said to be (a) nutritional and physiological studies, (b) the haphazard interaction of pressure group politics, voting, and administrative conventions and (c) empirical investigations of the expenditure behavior of households. Method (a) has been widely attacked on the same grounds as physiological definitions of poverty: as Atkinson (1975) points out, need is a social concept. Method (b) clearly begs the question of what equivalence scales *should* be. This leaves (c). An extensive literature has accumulated ever since Engel's (1895) pioneering work. References will be found in Brown and Deaton (1972), Prais and Houthakker (1955), and at the end of the chapter.

8.1 Engel's approach

Our first model goes back to Engel's famous observation that, for poorer households, a higher share of total expenditure goes on food than is the case for richer households. He also observed that the same was true for large households over small households at the same level of total expenditure. This suggested to him that the share of food (and perhaps of other commodities whose shares vary systematically with total expenditure) could be used as an indirect indication of welfare. Thus, two households with the same food share must have the same level of real income, irrespective of differences in size. Hence, comparison of their *money* incomes at the same foodshare will yield an index of the cost of maintaining the larger relative to the smaller family and this is the equivalence scale.

Before formalizing this model and working out its implications, let us introduce some notation. Let m^h be the minimum cost of maintaining household h at some welfare level expressed as a multiple of the minimum cost of maintaining some standard reference household at the same welfare level. On a simple view, we may take m^h to be a function of household characteristics only, assuming it to be independent of prices and the level of welfare. Hence, we may write

$$m^h = m(a^h) \tag{1.1}$$

where a^h is a vector of characteristics of household h. Typically, the first component of a^h might be the number of children under five; the second, the number of school age children; the third, the number of adults; and so on. If the reference household were one containing only a single adult, then in its crudest form, $m(a)$ could just be a counting function and m^h would simply be the number of people in household h. But, of course, this is absurd; two adults and a child with three times the expenditure of a single adult would be much better off. This can be recognized by expressing m^h not as the number of persons, but as the number of *adult equivalents* with children only counting fractionally. Several sets of weights exist; Table 8.1 shows the Amsterdam scale used by Stone (1954a) in his chapter on food expenditures. Hence, a

Table 8.1. *The Amsterdam scale*

Age group	Male	Female
under 14 years	0.52	0.52
14–17 years	0.98	0.90
18 years and over	1.00	0.90

man and wife are 1.90 equivalent adult males; a couple with a small child 2.42 equivalents, and so on. Though these scales are, in principle, based on nutritional "requirements" determined by experts, they could also be determined behaviorally as we now show.

As we have seen, the assumption $m^h = m(a^h)$ is simply a sophisticated way of head counting. Therefore, the demand functions, the direct and indirect utility functions, and the cost function are the same across households once expressed in equivalent adult per capita terms. Thus, the cost function can be written

$$c^h(u^h, p, a^h) = m(a^h)c(u^h, p) = x^h \tag{1.2}$$

where $c(u, p)$ is the per capita cost function, which is that of the reference household (for which $m = 1$). Similarly, the direct utility function is

$$u^h = v^h(q^h, a^h) = v(q^h/m(a^h)) = v(q^{h*}) \tag{1.3}$$

where $q_i^{h*} = q_i^h/m(a)$. The demand functions then have the per capita form

$$q_i^h/m(a^h) = g_i(x^h/m(a^h), p) \tag{1.4}$$

which in budget share form becomes

$$w_i^h = \frac{p_i q_i^h}{x^h} = \frac{p_i g_i(x^h/m(a^h), p)}{x^h/m(a^h)} \tag{1.5}$$

which is a function of $x^h/m(a^h)$ only and not of x^h or $m(a^h)$ separately. Hence if h is a household with characteristics a, if k is the reference household for which $m(a^k)$ is unity, and if h and k have the same budget share, we must have

$$\frac{x^h}{m(a^h)} = \frac{x^k}{m(a^k)} = x^k \tag{1.6}$$

so that

$$m(a^h) = x^h/x^k \tag{1.7}$$

Figure 8.1 illustrates the method diagrammatically for a large household relative to a smaller reference household. The diagram suggests that, in general, the scale might well be different if we select, not $0A$, but some other budget share. This can easily be allowed for by permitting the equivalence scale to depend on the utility level. The direct utility function is then defined implicitly by

$$u^h = v[q^h/m(u^h, a^h)] \tag{1.8}$$

or even more intuitively, the cost function (1.2) becomes

$$c^h(u^h, p, a^h) = m(u^h, a^h)c(u^h, p) \tag{1.9}$$

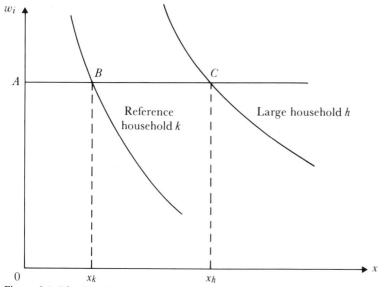

Figure 8.1. The Engel model for measuring equivalence scales.

Engel's method has been widely used. For example, Muellbauer (1977b) estimated scales using British data from the Family Expenditure Survey under
the hypothesis for (1.1) that

$$m = 1 + \delta_1 a_1 + \delta_2 a_2 \tag{1.10}$$

where δ_1 and δ_2 are parameters, a_1 is the number of children between 0 and 5
years, and a_2 is the number of children between 5 and 16 years. In this case, a
two-adult household without children was taken as reference so that the m's
are not "adult" equivalents but equivalent numbers of childless couples. For a
household of two adults and a young child, we get an equivalence scale of 1.08
(with a standard error of 0.016); for two adults with an older child, this rises
to 1.21 (0.008). Muellbauer gives a number of technical reasons for believing
that these figures may be underestimates even if the Engel model is correct,
but they nevertheless reinforce the belief that older children have greater
needs than younger children. Though the figures are conditional on the
validity of the rather restrictive form assumed for the scale in (1.10), the
goodness of fit of the corresponding demand functions is vastly improved
compared with making no allowance for household size or deflating by the
number of individuals in the household.

Exercises

8.1. Show that if the utility function is $u = v^*[f(q/s), s]$ where s is household size, $q_i/s = g_i(x/s, p)$ which is the same as for the utility function $u = f(q/s)$. Hence, comment on the implicit assumptions of regarding x/s as the appropriate money measure of welfare.

8.2. Using any source of family budget data (see Exercise 6.1 for references to U.S. and U.K. data), use Engel's method based on the food share to calculate equivalence scales relative to a two-adult household for (a) a single-adult household, (b) a two-adult-plus-one-child household, (c) a two-adult-plus-two-children household. How does your scale vary with the total outlay considered? Interpret your results. Is it possible for two to live (nearly) as cheaply as one? In such studies, it is often observed that the marginal effect of the second child is much larger than that of the first. Why might this be? What happens if you repeat the exercise using the share of some commodity other than food?

8.3. Show that if the cost function takes the form $c(u, p) = p_1^{f(u)} g(p_2, \ldots, p_n, u, a)$, where good 1 is food, and where $f(\ )$ is monotonic decreasing in u and $g(\ )$ is homogeneous of degree $1 - f(u)$ in prices, then the budget share of food gives a unique welfare ranking across households irrespective of prices. Discuss how the method discussed in Figure 8.1 would be used in this case. How might this case be generalized? [Hint: consider the consequences of replacing $f(u)$ by $f(u, p_2, \ldots, p_n)$.] How plausible empirically do you find such restrictions on preferences?

8.4. * Assuming the Engel model of equivalence scales to be correct, derive a formula for $m(a^h)$ using the distance function.

8.2 Commodity specific generalizations of Engel's model

In one important respect, Engel's model lacks plausibility. Effectively, it assumes that the needs of children relative to adults and the economies of scale in consumption are the same for every commodity. In reality, however, a household with young children is likely to be "equivalent" to more single adults in, say, ice-cream consumption, than in tobacco or alcohol consumption. This was recognized first by Sydenstricker and King (1921) whose approach was later taken up by Prais and Houthakker (1955). The Engel curve (1.4) is generalized to

$$\frac{q_i}{m_i} = g_i \left(\frac{x}{m_o} \right) \qquad (2.1)$$

where m_0 is a general scale and is defined as some weighted average of the individual commodity scales m_i. Note that the interpretation of (2.1) remains much the same as in the Engel model; quantity per equivalent capita is related to total expenditure per equivalent, but we now have a more general definition of equivalents. As before, we have all the m_i's and m_0 set at unity for the reference household. By analogy with the Engel model in §8.1, it might seem that, given (2.1), a household with m_i times as much of each q_i as the reference households would be as well off. The direct utility function would then be written

$$u = v \left(\frac{q_1}{m_1}, \frac{q_2}{m_2}, \ldots, \frac{q_n}{m_n} \right) \tag{2.2}$$

and this hypothesis was first put forward by Barten (1964). However, the analogy is correct only in a special case and the Barten and Prais-Houthakker formulations are not in general equivalent. Let us see why.

In the Barten model, define, as in §8.1, $q_i^* = q_i/m_i$. The budget constraint for (2.2) is $\Sigma p_i q_i = x$, which, if $p_i m_i = p_i^*$, can be written $\Sigma p_i^* q_i^* = x$. Thus, the Barten problem reduces to: maximize $v(q^*)$ subject to $\Sigma p_i^* q_i^* = x$. The cost function is thus given by

$$c(u, p^*) = x \tag{2.3}$$

In this form, Barten's analysis is a recognizable generalization of the Engel model. But this cost function yields a very important insight; changes in family composition act so as to modify prices, not only absolutely – as in the Engel model – but relatively. Having children makes ice cream, milk, and soft drink relatively more expensive and makes whisky or cigarettes relatively cheaper. In Gorman's (1976) words, "a penny bun costs threepence when you've a wife and child." The point of this, of course, is that changes in relative prices might be expected to cause substitution away from the relatively expensive goods. But none of this appears in the Prais-Houthakker model. In (2.1), q_i^* is only a function of the welfare level, x/m_0; the relative price effects of the different commodity scales are absent. Given that the m_i's differ across goods, the Prais-Houthakker model is thus consistent with the theory of consumer choice only in the case where the utility function permits no substitution between goods (but see Exercise 8.8). The indifference curves that produce this result must be as illustrated in Figure 8.2. Note that the fact that indifference curves are right angles does not necessarily imply that the expansion path $0A$ is a straight line through the origin. Indeed, apart from ruling out inferiority, such preferences do not restrict the shape of the Engel curve in any way.

Since there is no substitution in the Prais-Houthakker model, the Hicksian demand functions do not depend upon prices. Hence, for some functions $\beta_i(u)$

$$q_i^* = \beta_i(u) \tag{2.4}$$

so that the cost function for the model is given by

$$c(u, p, a) = \sum_i p_i^* \beta_i(u) = \sum_i p_i m_i \beta_i(u) = x \tag{2.5}$$

Equation (2.5) says that minimum cost is simply the cost of buying the given bundle $\beta(u)$; contrast this with the cost function of the Barten model as given by (2.3).

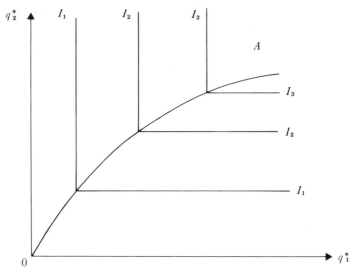

Figure 8.2. The indifference curves for the Prais-Houthakker model.

The Prais-Houthakker cost function (2.5) offers us a direct way of defining the general equivalence scale m_0 in (2.1). In a cross section in which prices are constant for all households, the relative cost of living for household h relative to the reference household k is given by $\Sigma p_i m_i^h \beta_i(u) / \Sigma p_i \beta_i(u)$ for some reference utility level, usually u^h or u^k. Hence, the natural choice for the deflator in (2.1) for household h is

$$m_0^h = \frac{\Sigma p_i m_i^h \beta_i(u^h)}{\Sigma p_i \beta_i(u^h)} = \Sigma v_i^h m_i^h \tag{2.6}$$

where

$$v_i^h = \frac{p_i \beta_i(u^h)}{\sum_k p_k \beta_k(u^h)} \tag{2.7}$$

Hence, m_0 is a weighted sum of the individual m_i's, and from (2.4), we see that the weights are the budget shares of the reference household *evaluated at the utility level u^h*. To actually evaluate (2.6) at the budget x^h, which yields utility level u^h at scales m_i^h, we note that $\Sigma\, p_i m_i^h \beta_i(u^h) \equiv x^h$ and $\beta_i(u^h) = g_i(x^h/m_0^h)$, which gives

$$\frac{x^h}{m_0^h} = \Sigma\; p_i g_i \left(\frac{x^h}{m_0^h}\right) \tag{2.8}$$

and this can be solved numerically for m_0^h. Note that if we wanted to compare costs for the two households evaluated at the utility level u^k, which the refer-

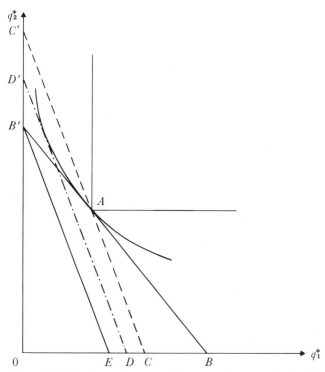

Figure 8.3. The change in the equivalence scale comparing the Barten and the Prais-Houthakker models.

ence household (with $m_i = 1$ all i) gets from budget x^k, we use $x^k = \Sigma p_i \beta_i(u^k)$ and $\beta_i(u^k) = g_i(x^k)$ to evaluate the relative costs as $\Sigma p_i m_i^h \beta_i(u^k)/\Sigma p_i \beta_i(u^k) = \Sigma p_i g_i(x^k) m_i^h /x^h = \Sigma w_i^k m_i^h$ for *actual* budget shares w_i^k of the reference household (i.e., at x^k). Note that if we use pooled time-series and cross-section data so that the reference household is defined not only for reference characteristics but also for reference prices, the cost-of-living ratio between h and k is now $\Sigma p_i m_i^h \beta_i(u)/\Sigma p_i^0 \beta_i(u)$ for reference prices p^0, which is an index number containing both a price index and an equivalence scale.

We are now in a position to illustrate from a simple diagram the difference that arises from the application of the Prais-Houthakker and Barten models. Figure 8.3 is similar to the diagrams already discussed in Chapter 7. Suppose that there are two goods, q_1 and q_2 and that the arrival of a child increases m_1 leaving m_2 unchanged. Since the axes are measured in terms of q_1^* and q_2^*, the arrival of the child shifts the budget line from $B'B$ to $B'E$. Assume that, originally, consumption was at the point A. The right-angled indifference curve at A is for the Prais-Houthakker model, while the smooth curve shows the

Barten model indifference curve. The cost-of-living index or equivalence scale for the former is the expenditure as given by $C'C$. For the Barten model, however, substitution takes place and the line $D'D$ is now sufficiently far from origin to restore the original utility level. Since m_2 is unchanged, the scale can be read off from the vertical axis; the Prais-Houthakker scale is $0C'/0B'$ and the Barten scale is $0D'/0B'$.

If we have the same starting point and the same two sets of m_i's to be compared, the equivalence scale of the Barten model is, in general, below that of the Prais-Houthakker model precisely because of the substitution it permits. This result is, of course, analogous to the demonstration in Chapter 7 that true cost-of-living index numbers are less than Laspeyres price indices, given the same base for each.

The formal analogy in the Barten model between prices and equivalence scales allows an extremely interesting characterization of the effects of changes in family composition. For example, the arrival of an extra child will have two quite separate effects on demand. Since

$$q_i = m_i(a)g_i(x, p^*) \tag{2.9}$$

there will be a direct effect through the shift in m_i; the child needs milk, warmth, toys, and so on. There is also an indirect effect through the impact on the "adjusted" prices p^* that will lead to some substitution away from children's goods according to the price elasticity of demand. In general,

$$\frac{\partial \log q_i}{\partial \log m_j} = \delta_{ij} + e_{ij} \tag{2.10}$$

where δ_{ij} is the Kronecker delta and e_{ij} is the Marshallian (uncompensated) price elasticities of good i with respect to the jth price. To take the example illustrated in Figure 8.3 where the arrival of the child affects m_1 only, we have

$$\frac{\partial \log q_1}{\partial \log m_1} = 1 + e_{11} \tag{2.11}$$

Since e_{11} could, in principle, be below -1, it is possible that even though the "need" for good 1 is increased as a consequence of the child's arrival, purchase of it may actually fall. This is very unlikely to happen in the Prais-Houthakker model. There, if m_1 increases, from (2.1)

$$\frac{\partial \log q_1}{\partial \log m_1} = 1 - e_1 \frac{\partial \log m_0}{\partial \log m_1} \tag{2.12}$$

where e_1 is the expenditure elasticity of good 1. From differentiation of (2.5) and (2.8), we see that the elasticity of m_0 with respect to m_1 is the budget share w_1, so that it is hardly conceivable that there would exist a commodity for which (2.12) could be negative.

In some respects, both models are rather extreme whether as ways of modeling household composition effects or for estimating equivalence scales. One allows no substitution while the other implies what is likely in practice to be excessive substitution in response to changes in household composition. In §8.4, we consider some alternative possibilities.

Exercises

8.5. It is frequently observed that the average consumption of alcohol in households with many children is larger than that in households with few children. What alternative explanations might be advanced for this phenomenon?

8.6. Incorporate Barten-type household composition effects into the linear expenditure system. Show that the marginal effects of variations in household composition are independent of the budget level and that the marginal propensities to spend are independent of household composition. How plausible do you find these features? [See Parks and Barten (1973) for an application.]

8.7. Consider the PIGLOG cost function

$$\log x = (1 - u) \log a(p) + u \log b(p)$$

Discuss the consequences for the role of household composition effects in demand functions of each of the following two assumptions:

(a) both $a(p)$ and $b(p)$ are Cobb-Douglas
(b) $\log b(p)/a(p) = \gamma_0 \Pi p_i^{\gamma_i}$.

Relate (b) to the AIDS model of Chapter 3.

8.8. It can be shown that there is an additive class of preferences that yields Engel curves of the form (2.1), but without the interpretation of x/m_0 as a utility indicator or m_0 as an equivalence scale defined as $c(u, p, a)/c(u, p, a^0)$. The following is an illustration: Show that the cost function

$$c(u, p, a) = \Sigma \alpha_i p_i m_i + u \Pi p_i^{\gamma_i m_i/\Sigma_j \gamma_j m_j}$$

where $m_i = m_i(a)$ yields demand functions that satisfy (2.1). Show that

$$x/m_0 = \frac{x - \Sigma \alpha_i p_i m_i}{\Sigma \gamma_i m_i} + \Sigma \alpha_i p_i$$

and that m_0 is not of the form $c(u, p, a)/c(u, p, a^0)$. Contrast this way of putting household composition effects into preferences with the Barten model in the context of the linear expenditure system.

8.9. Suppose that there are two goods with $p_1 = p_2 = 1, x = 20,000, m_1 = 3$, and $m_2 = 2$ and

$$g_1(x/m_0) = -0.15(x/m_0) \log (x/m_0) + 2 (x/m_0)$$

and

$$g_2(x/m_0) = 0.15(x/m_0) \log (x/m_0) - (x/m_0)$$

Compute general equivalence scales $\Sigma p_i m_i^h \beta_i(u)/\Sigma p_i \beta_i(u)$ using both reference and actual utility as weights.

8.3 Empirical applications

On the face of it, it would appear that, given a specification for the equivalence scales in terms of household characteristics, budget data can be used to estimate either the Prais-Houthakker model (2.1) and (2.5) or the Barten model (2.9). Unfortunately, this is not the case. It turns out that for either model, using only a single cross section of households, the equivalence scales for each commodity are identified only *relatively to each other* and not in absolute terms. A formal explanation of the lack of identification will not be attempted here; the reader may consult Cramer (1969) and Muellbauer (1974b, 1980a); also see Exercise 8.11. Intuitively, however, the problem is that we are trying to identify n parameters m_i, which vary with household composition, by examining n different Engel curves. But Engel curves must satisfy the adding-up restriction, and so will yield only $n - 1$ independent pieces of evidence. This leaves us one short for the full identification of the scales. This means, for example, that Barten's original suggestion of using his model to estimate price elasticities from budget data is not possible without further restrictions. Similarly, the identification of the scales themselves requires some additional information.

For the Barten model, some variation in relative prices is sufficient so that a natural solution is the use of pooled time-series and cross-section data. But this does not help for the Prais-Houthakker model because, with zero substitution, the role that price changes play is exactly the same as that of changes in total expenditure. Only absolute, not relative, price changes matter. Identification thus requires prior information such as the sort of nutritional requirements data with which we began, or, more attractively, such restrictions as "children do not drink or smoke." Unfortunately, budget data on alcohol and tobacco consumption are notoriously unreliable and this prevents use of this particular proposal.

The Barten model is estimated using pooled cross-section and time-series data for 1968–73 from the British Family Expenditure Survey in Muellbauer (1977b) using a PIGLOG specification (see §6.2) of the cost function (2.3). It is assumed that $m_i(a) = 1 + \delta_{1i}a_1 + \delta_{2i}a_2$, where $m_i = 1$ for two adults, a_1 is the number of children aged 0 to 5 and a_2 is the number of children aged 5 to 16. All the households in the sample contain two adults and the number of children ranges from none to four or more. Having estimated the δ's for food for the Barten model, the Prais-Houthakker model is estimated on the same data conditional upon these same food scales. Table 8.2 reports the commodity scales for each model for two adults with respectively one child aged 0 to 5 and one aged 5 to 16. Also given are the (asymptotic) standard errors and the general equivalence scales, evaluated at three different budget levels, namely weekly expenditure levels at 1975 prices for a reference household of two adults of £20, £40, and £70.

Table 8.2. *Commodity specific and general equivalence scales from the Barten and Prais-Houthakker models for households with a young child and households with an older child*

	Barten Model		Prais-Houthakker Model	
	2 adults + 1 child (0–5) years)	2 adults + 1 child (5–16 years)	2 adults + 1 child (0–5 years)	2 adults + 1 child (5–16 years)
Fuel and light	1.12 (0.10)	1.27 (0.06)	1.03 (0.02)	1.17 (0.01)
Food	1.25 (0.11)	1.47 (0.08)	1.25 (fixed)	1.47 (fixed)
Alcohol	0.89 (0.17)	1.20 (0.13)	1.25 (0.21)	2.19 (0.14)
Tobacco	1.36 (0.13)	1.27 (0.08)	1.41 (0.06)	1.17 (0.04)
Clothing	1.50 (0.27)	1.48 (0.30)	1.36 (0.21)	2.74 (0.15)
Durables	0.80 (0.27)	1.09 (0.14)	1.48 (0.28)	2.49 (0.19)
Miscellaneous goods	1.34 (0.15)	1.09 (0.07)	1.40 (0.07)	1.80 (0.04)
Private transport	0.81 (0.19)	0.90 (0.06)	1.82 (0.44)	3.53 (0.31)
Public transport	1.17 (0.26)	1.44 (0.17)	1.17 (0.14)	1.54 (0.09)
Services	0.80 (0.20)	0.98 (0.09)	0.95 (0.14)	2.22 (0.08)
General equivalence scale:[a]				
at low expenditure	1.16	1.30	1.24	1.82
at medium expenditure	1.09	1.22	1.36	2.00
at high expenditure	1.04	1.17	1.46	2.15

Note: Standard errors are shown in parentheses.
[a] Low expenditure £20, medium expenditure £40, high expenditure £70, all per week at 1975 prices for a reference household of two adults.

Perhaps the most obvious feature of Table 8.2 is the striking difference between the results for the two models; the Barten model gives typically much lower values for both commodities and general scales, while the latter decrease with total outlay. The single commodity with the largest difference in scales is private transport, and it is most revealing to interpret this finding in terms of the underlying theory we have discussed. In the data, it is apparent that, holding the budget constant, households with a child and especially an older child have considerably higher private transport expenditures than households without children. In the Prais-Houthakker model, this can happen only if this commodity has a higher than average commodity scale. But in the Barten model, this need not be the case; as we saw, if a commodity's own-price elasticity is large enough, then a *smaller* than average commodity scale is consistent with the observed expenditure pattern. And indeed, private transport has a higher estimated substitution response than most of the other goods. The same phenomenon in a less extreme form also suggests why the commodity scales for services, durables, and alcohol are so much higher in the Prais-Houthakker estimates than in the Barten estimates. And this also explains why the general equivalence scale falls with the budget in the Barten model and rises with the budget in the Prais-Houthakker model: goods whose budget shares increase with the budget (luxuries) have commodity scales lower than average in the Barten model and higher than average in the Prais-Houthakker model.

The lack of substitution in the Prais-Houthakker model and its embarrassing consequences – even at medium expenditure the general scales implausibly suggest that it costs twice as much to support a couple with an older child than one without children – seems sufficient to suggest that it is *not* a suitable model of household composition effects. The Barten model, on the other hand, seems more plausible, though we would not place too much weight on the estimates in Table 8.2. One immediate problem is that the expenditures on goods such as household durables and private transport contain investment elements, and as we saw in §4.2, it is not appropriate to treat these goods as nondurables. We shall have more to say on this general question in §8.4. Nevertheless, we can attempt to test the Barten model by comparing the goodness of fit of demand functions, which incorporate its restrictions fitted to data pooled across different household types with the goodness of fit of demand functions fitted separately for each household type and hence not imposing the Barten restrictions. This is done in Muellbauer (1977b) and two conclusions are drawn. First, the goodness of fit is very substantially worse when the Barten restrictions are imposed. Second, it appears that when they are imposed, there is a general tendency for the estimated substitution responses to fall and this would seem to suggest that the quasi-price substitution responses associated with household composition differences are different from the substitution responses associated with changes in actual prices. However, until these tests are repeated on better data, this conclusion should be regarded as tentative.

Finally, it may be of some interest to compare the equivalence scales estimated for the Barten model with those used in the British supplementary benefit systems that help households with low incomes. In 1975, the benefits paid imply scales of 1.18 when there is one child aged 0 to 5, 1.21 for age 5 to 10; 1.26 for age 11 to 12 and 1.32 for age 13 to 15. Our estimates at low expenditure are quite close to these figures, but in view of the problems already discussed, we should not put too much weight on this similarity.

Exercises

8.10. Incorporate the Barten composition effects into the AIDS model discussed in Chapter 3. In what sense can we say that the household composition effects in the model are independent of the budget effects? Compare with the results from the linear expenditure system in Exercise 8.6.

8.11.* For the Prais-Houthakker model show that

$$\frac{\partial \log (p_i q_i)}{\partial \log a} = \frac{\partial \log m_i}{\partial \log a} - \frac{\partial \log (p_i q_i)}{\partial \log (x/m_0)} \frac{\partial \log m_0}{\partial \log a}$$

or $f_i = h_i - \eta_i h_0$ in obvious notation,

and $\dfrac{\partial \log m_0}{\partial \log a} = \Sigma \, w_j \dfrac{\partial \log m_j}{\partial \log a}$ or $h_0 = \Sigma \, w_j h_j$

Treating the f's (elasticities of demand with respect to number of children), η's (budget elasticities) and w's (budget shares) as observables, investigate whether a unique solution for the unknown h_i, $i = 0, 1, \ldots, n$ can be obtained. [Hint: show that in matrix form $f = (I - \eta w')h$, and consider the implication of $\Sigma \, w_i = 1$ for the rank of the matrix $(I - \eta w')$ – see Muellbauer (1980a).] Show that if one h_i is known, then the others can be identified.

8.12.* How would you attempt to generalize the result of the previous question to the Barten model where substitution between goods is allowed and all the data refer to a single cross section? [See Muellbauer (1974b).]

8.4 Equivalence scales in perspective

The most general way of incorporating household composition effects in demand functions that result from optimizing behavior is simply to write the cost function as $c(u, p; a)$. Any general equivalence scale is then simply a constant utility, constant price, cost-of-living index relating the cost of living at household characteristics a to that for some reference household with characteristics a^R. Thus, for reference utility level u^R and prices p^R, if $c(u^R, p^R; a^h)$ is the minimum cost of attaining u^R at prices p^R given characteristics a^h

$$m^h = \frac{c(u^R, p^R; a^h)}{c(u^R, p^R; a^R)} \tag{4.1}$$

One cost function more general than Barten's that is less likely to suffer from excessive substitution has been proposed by Gorman (1976). It simply adds some fixed costs, which vary with household characteristics, to the Barten cost function; thus,

$$c(u, p, a) = \Sigma \gamma_i(a)p_i + \hat{c}(u, p^*)$$ (4.2)

where $p_i^* = p_i m_i(a)$ as before. Pollak and Wales (1979) have compared the goodness of fit of two special cases of (4.2): one is the Barten hypothesis in which $\gamma_i(a) = m_i(a)$, all i; in the other, $m_i(a) = 1$, all i, and all the composition effects work through the γ's. The former hypothesis appears to fit much better.

We should also note that a number of alternative approaches to family decision making have been proposed based on the use of separability concepts; see in particular, Samuelson (1956) and Muellbauer (1975a).

Leisure and intertemporal choice

So far in this chapter, we have restricted ourselves to composition effects and equivalence scales for current, conventional market goods conditional upon household composition, that is, treating household composition as exogenous. Maintaining the last assumption, it is certainly possible to extend the notion of equivalence scales to wider classes of goods. For example, taking the full cost function (see §4.1), which includes wage rates, a general equivalence scale is defined analogously to (4.1) as

$$\frac{c(u^R, p^R, \omega^R; a^h)}{c(u^R, p^R, \omega^R; a^R)}$$ (4.3)

This assumes, of course, that the budget constraint for leisure, particularly that of the second worker in the household, is linear. This is not always realistic, but at least it does offer a way of making some allowance for the known sensitivity of labor supply, especially that of wives, to the presence of children. Whether the multiplicative specification of the Barten model is fully appropriate for leisure is unclear, but it at least tends to give the right sign to the effect. The leisure elasticity with respect to the leisure scale is 1 plus the wage elasticity of leisure and only in the rare cases where the latter is less than -1 will the effect of an extra child be to increase rather than reduce labor supply.

To illustrate the issues raised by intertemporal choice, consider the two period utility function given by

$$u = v(q_1, q_2; a_1, a_2)$$ (4.4)

where q_t is the (nondurable) consumption vector in period t and a_t is the household composition vector in period t. Conditional upon the a's, the decision variables are q_1 and q_2 and the budget constraint is that of equation (2.3) in Chapter 4.

The corresponding cost function is defined on the utility level and on current and future expected discounted prices, and it is conditional upon a_1 and a_2. In principle, we could certainly define through it a general equivalence scale that corresponds to the long-run planned notion of utility entailed in (4.4). However, it would depend on the somewhat subjective expectations of prices or incomes that appear either directly in the cost function or indirectly through the utility level. Estimation of the parameters of such a function through the intertemporal demand functions would clearly require strong prior parameter restrictions.

An alternative, simpler approach is possible if the utility function is intertemporally separable:

$$u = v[v_1(q_1; a_1), v_2(q_2; a_2)] \tag{4.5}$$

If $u_t = v_t(q_t; a_t)$ then, as we saw in §5.2, two-stage budgeting is possible and we can write subcost functions for each period as

$$c_t(u_t, p_t; a_t) = x_t \tag{4.6}$$

This is the best way of interpreting the static demand functions and cost functions discussed so far in this chapter. The concept of utility or welfare that is entailed is, of course, a fairly narrow one, but then so is the concept of utility that underlies the index numbers of prices or real consumption considered in Chapter 7. In regard to equivalence scales from the point of view of income maintenance policies, most governments define need in terms of current income rather than long-term wealth and support current consumption levels rather than allow households either to repay debts or build up their asset position.

As we saw in §4.2, when markets are perfect, durable goods pose no special problems as long as we define their prices to be rental prices [as in Chapter 4, (2.24)], the quantity to be the service flow from the stock or the stock itself, and define the current period budget correspondingly. For example, for period 1,

$$x_1 = p_1 q_1 + v_1^* S_1 \tag{4.7}$$

which gives $c_1(u_1, p_1, v_1^*; a_1)$ as the corresponding period 1 cost function given separability as in (4.5). The difficulty is that in many budget surveys the current purchase of durables $d_1 = S_1 - (1 - \delta)S_0$ [cf. Chapter 4, (2.20)] is all that is known. While the rental price v_1^* can be reasonably well approximated, S_1 is unknown without knowledge of initial stocks. Unless the expected value in cross sections of d_1 is proportional to S_1, biases will occur in using d_1 instead. Households with children are quite likely to have higher than average purchase to stock ratios, and this would tend to bias the estimated household composition effects if expenditures on durable goods rather than stock data are used.

Where do children come from?

The answer in this context, "Storks bring them," is not as frivolous as it might seem. So far in this chapter, we have considered demand functions and cost functions conditional upon household composition. If household composition is not exogenous (as presumably it would be if storks were responsible), one potential problem is statistical bias. After all, if households decide simultaneously on the number of children and purchases of goods, then explaining one by the other is using one endogenous variable to explain another and hence will lead to biased estimates. In practice, these biases may not be very serious, especially if the equations fit well. The number of children is much less endogenous in the short run than are purchases of goods, and in any one day or year, relatively few households are at the margin of deciding whether to have another child. The children that households have were often planned when households found different circumstances and had different expectations of the future. This is perhaps especially so for the kinds of households for whom income maintenance policies are particularly relevant: as Tobin (1973) points out, children are not chattels that can be readily sold or otherwise disposed of. This has sometimes been forgotten in the literature on the economics of fertility that has been burgeoning since the 1960's – see for example Becker (1960), T. P. Schultz (1969), the 1973 symposium edited by T. W. Schultz, and Leibenstein (1974).

Apart from the question of statistical bias, there is the question of how endogeneity of the household composition affects the welfare interpretation of equivalence scales estimated on the assumption of their exogeneity. Pollak and Wales (1979) argue that such scales have no relevance whatsoever for welfare comparisons, but this seems to us to be too negative a position. The cost function conditional upon household composition has the clear interpretation of being the cost of reaching a given level of utility associated with the consumption of marketed goods given household composition. As the number of dependents increases, given the prevailing household ethics and household technology for their maintenance (of which the equalization of utility levels within the household is but one possible characterization),the cost of reaching a given utility level must increase. As a measure of the cost of children, the conditional cost function is a particularly attractive tool for analyzing the full decision problem of adults in deciding on the number of children. This can be illustrated in a highly simplified and stylized planning model. Let us collapse the present and the future into a single period and let

$$W = F[v(q; a), a] \tag{4.8}$$

be the adults' utility function; $u = v(q; a)$ is the utility of goods given the number of children a and is assumed to be decreasing in a. However, given u, for a mixture of motives based on selfishness, altruism or religious tradition, $F(u, a)$ is typically increasing in a, at least over some range. The simplest form of the budget constraint is $x = p \cdot q$, where x might conceivably depend upon a if children contribute to market income. The maximization of (4.8) with respect to q and a subject to the budget constraint can be broken into two stages. At stage one, the adults find the best budget allocation over goods, given a, the solution to which can be expressed through the cost function $x = c(u, p; a)$. The second stage is then to choose u and a as functions of x and p to maximize $W = F(u, a)$ subject to $x = c(u, p; a)$. The solution to this problem is illustrated in Figure 8.4. The conditional cost functions can reasonably be supposed to be similar for different adult couples as illustrated. If we assume that u is normalized to measure the real value of consumption, see §7.2, the x contours will be convex to the origin while the W contours will have the usual shape, see Exercise 8.16. If we can assume that the welfare function $F(\ )$ is also similar across adult couples, then it would provide the basis for the making of welfare comparisons. Given this, we can speculate on the nature of the biases that occur if welfare comparisons are made on the basis of u rather than W. It seems reasonable that the lower the level of u, the smaller should be the increase in welfare from an increase in the number of children, and below some critical level of u^*, as illustrated in Figure 8.4, it is optimal not to have children. As can be seen from the figure, the poorest adults would plan to have no children unless children actually contributed to market income. However, given the irreversibility of children, adults may have children as a result of mishaps in contraception or overoptimistic forecasts of income potential. Let us compare the levels of the budget required to sustain a given level of welfare for two sets of adult couples with and without children as illustrated in Figure 8.5. The couple with no children has a budget x^0 that yields u^0 and the indifference curve labeled w_0. A couple with children a^* needs a budget x^1 to reach the same level u^0. But this budget gives an inferior welfare level $w_1 < w_0$. This argument suggests that the conventional equivalence scale $x^1/x^0 = c(u^0, p; a^*)/c(u^0, p; 0)$ underestimates the compensation x^{11}/x^1 such a poor couple with children requires to be as well off as one without children. It is easy to see that above u^* the conventional equivalence scale overestimates the cost, while around the u^* the bias will be small.

   Given the estimated conditional cost function, we could, in principle, estimate the indifference curves from planned fertility behavior and combine the two to give the full cost comparisons. However, apart from various other problems, there are likely to be substantial variations in the preferences of

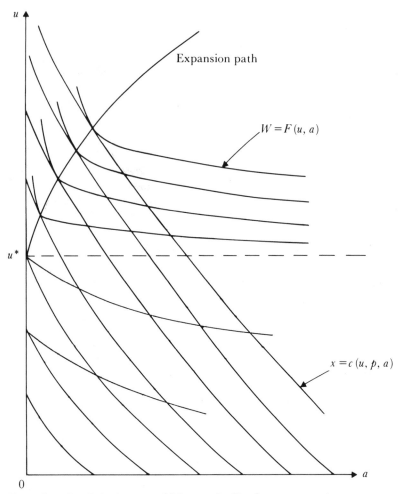

Figure 8.4. The choice between children and utility from consumption.

adult couples that makes welfare comparisons difficult. If we argue that the object of the exercise is to find a summary statistic of the relative budget constraints faced by different households rather than "welfare comparisons" as such, then we can overcome the difficulty by choosing some set of reference preferences at which to make the comparison. In any case, the estimated conditional cost function is vital information for such an exercise.

We have seen that one argument in favor of the use in income maintenance policy of conventional equivalence scales as estimated from the conditional cost function is that if the minimum standard of living of the adults, which it is

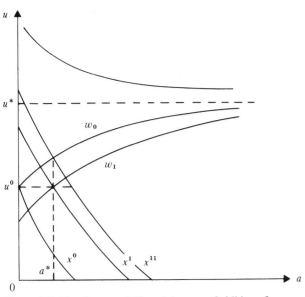

Figure 8.5. The downward bias of the cost of children for poor families.

the purpose of the policy to support, is in the region of u^*, then there will be little bias even if the relevant welfare concept is W rather than u. But there is an alternative argument.

Consider the welfare of the children. The children did not participate in the family planning decision and for them the welfare concept W is not relevant. What is relevant is the welfare concept u since that effectively determines how much consumption of goods they can engage in, and the money metric measure of u is derived through the conditional cost function. If, therefore, the only way of distributing income to children is through the adults and the aim of the income maintenance policy is to ensure that no child falls below a certain minimum, the relative benefits paid to couples with various numbers of children is given by the equivalence scales (4.1) defined by the conditional cost function. In this particular case, there is a coincidence between policy and welfare comparisons that, in general, we could not expect. For example, in designing a tax system, the government may well take into account not only the effects of taxes on the supply of labor and other factors but on fertility. Hence we would not expect two households judged to be at the same standard of living necessarily to be paying the same share of income in income tax.

This completes our account of household welfare comparisons. Our discussion of fertility was highly stylized in order to clarify the basic issues. However, it can be modified to make it more realistic and bring in explicit consideration of the intertemporal planning problem; the technology of birth control; the allocation of time and investment in education in the household; the discreteness of the number of children and their irreversibility, their potential contribution to household production; as well as uncertainty about the future part of the budget constraint, about the survival rates of both parents and children, about the effectiveness of methods of birth control, and about the biological fertility of the parents. These are all points that have been discussed in the literature on the economics of fertility. For the one-period notion of the conditional cost function to be applicable in such an intertemporal framework, we have to assume weak intertemporal separability of the welfare planning function in market goods, given household composition, see (4.5) above. With this assumption, the one-period conditional cost function remains a useful tool in the analysis of fertility.

Exercises

8.13. In the Gorman model (4.2), suppose that the cost function is $c(u, p, a) = \Sigma \gamma_i(a)p_i + \hat{c}(u, p)$. Show that the total effect on each demand is the sum of a direct and a budget effect and contrast this result with the decomposition of the total effect for the Barten model $c(u, p, a) = \hat{c}(u, p^*)$.

8.14. Into the linear expenditure system augmented for leisure, incorporate the Barten composition effects. Discuss the effect on labor supply of the addition of a child. Contrast the general equivalence scale when labor supply is held fixed with the case where labor supply varies. What would you think of the proposal that the earnings lost by the wife are an appropriate measure of the cost of a child?

8.15. Discuss the argument that parents' revealed choices in the presence of children indicate that the chosen alternative is better than the ones not chosen and hence that in income maintenance policy there are no grounds for giving higher grants to those with children.

8.16. Assume that the Engel model of composition effects is correct and use the framework to discuss the sign of d^2u/da^2 along the contours $c(u, p; a) = $ const. in Figures 8.4 and 8.5. What is the importance of economies of scale in numbers of children? Discuss the effects of the choice of normalization for u with special reference to the possibility of using money metric utility.

Bibliographical notes

In line with our approach throughout this book, we have presented all the models of equivalence scales in terms of utility theory. It must be emphasized however that neither Engel (1895) nor Sydenstricker and King (1921) nor indeed Prais and Houthakker (1955) originally put forward their models in this framework.

Indeed, Barten's (1964) model was the first to explicitly apply utility theory to the equivalence scale problem; the contrast between Barten's (heroic) matrix algebra and the simplicity of the cost-function approach is one of the best illustrations of the power of duality methods. After Engel and Sydenstricker and King, important early studies of the "cost" of children are those of Nicholson (1949) and Henderson (1949–50a, b).

Brown (1954) put forward a way of introducing household composition effects in log-linear Engel curves that turns out to be exactly consistent with the Barten form of the loglinear demand functions. However, until recently, Prais and Houthakker's (1955) study remained the most influential. Prais and Houthakker seem to have been unaware of the identification problem, while many later authors, e.g., Singh (1972), Singh and Nagar (1973), Blokland (1976), and McClements (1977, 1978), face the issue but in the words of the Scottish preacher, pass on. However, the issue is discussed by Forsyth (1960) and Cramer (1969), who gives an excellent general discussion of the whole area. A formal proof of the identification problem is in Muellbauer (1974b) for the Barten model and in Muellbauer (1980a) for the Prais-Houthakker model. A discussion of the utility basis of the Engel and Prais-Houthakker methods is given in Muellbauer (1977b).

A somewhat different way of introducing household composition effects into demand functions is suggested by Lau, Lin, and Yotopoulos (1978). Basically, they suggest using a flexible functional form including household composition variables of the indirect utility function. Their particular formulation, however, turns out to be equivalent to the Barten model.

As a practical matter, where equivalence scales used in policy actually have a single empirical basis, it appears to be either some form of the Engel model, e.g., Jackson (1968) or else the scales are based on detailed, published, budget plans drawn up by panels of experts. The latter is the case, for example, in West Germany, while the official United States definition of the poverty line for different household types is based on a set of food plans that are scaled up by a fixed proportion to make an allowance for the remaining commodities.

CHAPTER 9

Social welfare and inequality

The preceding two chapters have been concerned with the analysis and measurement of the welfare of individual households. We now turn to questions of the welfare of society as a whole. The two topics which make up the title of this chapter are both major fields of economic investigation in their own right, and we cannot hope to give more than an outline of them here. Indeed, we are more concerned with illustrating one of the major themes of the book, that consumer theory as we have presented it is of great analytical value in other branches of economics. Social welfare functions have obvious conceptual links with individual utility functions and we shall explore these ideas in §9.1. We shall use our previous analysis to discuss possible structures for social welfare functions, and we shall argue that the index number concepts discussed in Chapters 7 and 8 can be used to provide natural units for making interpersonal comparisons of welfare. Section 9.2 is concerned with the measurement of inequality. The approach described is based on an explicit link with social welfare, pioneered by Kolm (1969, 1976) and Atkinson (1970) and we show how the analysis of §9.1 can be used to adapt the conventional measurement of income inequality to the more fundamental purpose of measuring welfare inequality.

9.1 Social welfare functions and their arguments

The social welfare function is an essential tool of welfare analysis and this section is concerned with its development and its properties. It will be used in §9.2 in specific practical contexts. We begin by discussing what a social welfare function does *not* do, and we relate the type of social welfare function we shall use to the results of Arrow's (1951b) analysis of the impossibility of basing social choice on individual values. After discussing various methods of making interpersonal comparisons, we go on to suggest that the price index numbers and equivalence scales of Chapters 7 and 8 provide a natural method of correcting incomes so as to serve as a reasonable basis for welfare comparisons, at least within the confines of inequality measurement.

Arrow's impossibility theorem

The impossibility of basing social choice on individual preferences is a fact known to every student of economics. However, the implications of Arrow's result for welfare economics are not always clearly understood. While making no attempt to provide a full exposition of the result – for that see Arrow (1963) or Sen (1970) – we briefly summarize the result and its implications for our later analysis. In presentation, we follow the useful framework suggested by Sen (1977b) following d'Aspremont and Gevers (1977), whose work, in turn, links back to Sen (1970), especially Chapters 7 and 8.

Preferences, both individual and social, are defined over a set of social "states," $s_1, s_2, \ldots, s_m$, say where m may be infinite. For example, each state might be an Hn-vector listing the consumption levels of each of the n-goods by each of the H-households. Each household or individual (we shall explore the distinction below) has preferences over the social states that, we shall assume, can be represented by utility functions $v^h(\ \ )$ defined over the space of social states. The preferences of the individuals, which are the basic data of the problem, are thus represented by the list of functions $v^1(\ \ )$, $v^2(\ \ ), \ldots, v^H(\ \ )$. In Arrow's framework, social choice must depend only on individual preferences, not on their particular representations. Hence, any *social* preference ordering based on the $v^h(\ \ )$'s must be unaffected if each $v^h(\ \ )$ is transformed by any arbitrary monotone-increasing transform, $\phi^h(\ \ )$, say, which can be different for each h. One way of expressing this is to say that individuals are *ordinally noncomparable* within an Arrow social choice rule. If this is so, the utility functions $v^h(\ \ )$ act only as representations of the underlying preference orderings of each individual separately so that they can provide no basis for making any sort of welfare comparisons between *different* individuals. In the usual language, interpersonal comparisons are impossible. Given this, what we are looking for is some rule that takes us from the list of individual utility functions to a social preference ordering. If, for the moment, we think of this latter as being representable by a social utility function, the social choice rule is a procedure that creates a function taking a whole list of other functions (the individual utility functions) as arguments. The inputs to the rule or, as Arrow (1977) calls it, a "social constitution," are thus the preferences or beliefs of individuals as represented by their preferences, not the values of individual utilities, while the output is itself a preference ordering; the rule is thus not merely a procedure for ranking vectors of individual welfare levels, it is a device for creating social preferences from individual ones. Mathematicians call such a rule a *functional* (or function of functions) and it must be clearly distinguished from the more familiar *function* that associates one number with a list of other numbers. To take a very simple example, consider a society that is trying to design an income tax system. Each individual has a $v^h(\ \ )$ defined over the different possible designs that reflects (presumably) his views, not only about his own welfare under the various systems but also about that of others and of what he regards as socially desirable, just, or whatever. The social welfare *functional,* or SWFL for short, would then define, from the individual preference orderings, a social preference ordering over the various tax systems, and this could be used, under various circumstances, to design a tax system and to modify it as necessary. This is much more general than the procedure with a social welfare *function* (SWF) that would take as arguments, not the individual utility functions, but the values of those utility functions under the alternative tax regimes. In this case, social choice consists simply of weighting the individual welfare levels in some way. Clearly, SWF's are special cases of SWFL's, and for much of our discussion in this chapter the narrower framework will be adequate. However, what might be regarded as the essential issues of social choice, such questions as liberty and fairness, can only be dealt with using the richer structure of SWFL's.

What properties can a SWFL be expected to possess? One possibility, that of ordinal noncomparability, has already been discussed. Others are imposed by the requirement that the SWFL should actually produce an ordering satisfying completeness, reflexivity, and transitivity in the usual way. In general, this rules out such SWFL's as the method of majority voting whereby s_i is preferred to s_j if more votes are cast in its favor. Without restrictions on preferences, this can easily lead to s_i being socially preferred to s_j, s_j to s_k, and s_k to s_i, that is, to severe violations of transitivity. Arrow requires four further conditions, which he suggests are necessary – although not necessarily sufficient – for a satisfactory SWFL. The first, the condition of unrestricted domain, is that the SWFL or social choice rule should work for any conceivable list of preferences $[v^1(\ \ ),\ v^2(\ \ ),\ \ldots,\ v^h(\ \ )\ \ldots\ ]$. This is almost definitional, since by only considering societies in which, for example, all consumers have identical preferences and identical endowments, we should make the social choice problem much easier. As another example, the possibility of intransitivity inherent in the method of majority voting is removed if individuals order states only by reference to a single one-dimensional characteristic of each; this is the condition known as *single-peakedness,* see, for example, Arrow (1963, pp. 75ff). The second condition embodies the (weak) Pareto principle that if $v^h(s_1) > v^h(s_2)$ for all h, so that all individuals strictly prefer state 1 to state 2, then s_1 is socially preferred to s_2. Third, there should be no dictatorship; no one single consumer's preferences should determine social choice independently of what anyone else prefers. Finally, choice between any two states s_1 and s_2 must depend only on individuals' preferences between s_1 and s_2 and not on anything else. This condition, the condition of independence of irrelevant alternatives, would require, for example, that if household preferences change without actually changing the individual rankings of two relevant states s_1 and s_2, then if s_1 were socially preferred to s_2 before the change, it must be so afterwards and vice versa.

The Arrow theorem states that these conditions make a mutually self-contradictory set. No SWFL exists which preserves ordinal noncomparability, which has unrestricted domain, which is Paretian and nondictatorial, and which makes choices independently of irrelevant alternatives. How we react to this result depends very much on the use we wish to make of social choice theory, and much of the literature is concerned with exploring the types of SWFL's that result from the various possible relaxations of the assumptions. For the purposes of this chapter, by far the most fruitful approach is to abandon the ordinal noncomparability requirement and to inquire in some detail as to how interpersonal comparisons can be made and in what sort of units meaningful measurements of welfare can be compiled. For many years, the majority of economists took the position that the making of interpersonal comparisons, if not impossible, was certainly no part of the economist's trade. In view of Arrow's theorem, such a view leaves very little for welfare economics to do, and much of the so-called new welfare economics of the 1940's and 1950's that embodied this position makes sterile reading by contemporary standards. Modern approaches, by contrast, are firmly based on explicit interpersonal comparisons.

Interpersonal comparisons

The substantive issue is thus not *whether* interpersonal comparisons should be made, but *how,* and this issue will occupy us for much of this section. Sen (1977b) sees the issue as one of specifying exactly what information about individual preferences is or is not admissible in the construction of the SWFL. In deriving the impossibility theorem, it was required that monotone transformations of each $v^h(\ )$ should leave social preferences unchanged and this clearly rules out much potentially useful information. It is thus natural to begin by weakening this ordinality condition in various directions.

One approach that turns out not to be very helpful is to require only that the SWFL be invariant with respect to positive *linear* transformations of individual utility functions. Hence, if for $\beta^h > 0$ each $v^h(\ )$ is replaced by $[\alpha^h + \beta^h v^h(\ )]$, we require that the social welfare function is unchanged. Each individual is thus endowed with a *"cardinal"* rather than ordinal utility function and this is to be taken into account in constructing the SWFL. This approach could only work if utility functions could be measured up to a linear transformation rather than up to a nonlinear transformation. It is often claimed that the assumption of additive preferences allows such a cardinalization to be deduced from observable behavior but, as was argued in §5.3, measurements of the "marginal utility of money" or its elasticity have no sound basis in such models and are derived from essentially arbitrary and untestable assumptions. Exactly the same is true of measurements based on Von Neumann-Morgenstern "cardinal" utility as we shall show in §14.2. But such measurements are not only ill-founded, they are also irrelevant, since, even under "cardinal" noncomparability, the Arrow impossibility result holds. There is thus no validity in claims that attempted measurements of marginal utility from consumer behavior have any useful role in making interpersonal comparisons.

Useful interpersonal comparisons require stronger assumptions. One that does generate a possible SWFL is what Sen calls *cardinal unit comparability*. This makes the assumption that somehow we can measure *changes* in welfare in comparable units. We still cannot say anything about *levels* of welfare between individuals, but statements such as "the change from s_1 to s_2 will increase household h's welfare by twice as much as it decreases household j's welfare" are taken to be meaningful. Clearly, with this information, we can construct a *utilitarian* SWFL by adding up utilities; s_1 is socially preferred to s_2 if the total difference in utilities between s_1 and s_2 is positive and such choices are unchanged if we transform each $v^h(\ )$ to $\alpha^h + \beta v^h(\ )$ for $\beta > 0$ and the same for all h. It also turns out that provided we strengthen our previous conditions slightly – nondictatorship to anonymity (so that only welfare levels matter, not whose they are) and the Pareto principle so that if one person is better off without anyone being worse off, the state is socially preferred – then the utilitarian SWFL is the *only* (strongly) Paretian SWFL characterized by cardinal unit comparability, unrestricted domain, anonymity, and independence of irrelevant alternatives, see d'Aspremont and Gevers (1977), Sen (1977b). Figure 9.1 illustrates a social welfare function defined on the values u^1 and u^2. Curve AB illustrates the feasible combinations of u^1 and u^2, and $I_n I'_n$ is an indifference curve for a general nonutilitarian welfare function $V(u^1, u^2)$, say, and $I_u I'_u$ is an indifference curve for the utilitarian welfare function $u^1 + u^2$. If $v^h(\ )$ is now transformed so that u^h is given by $\alpha^h + \beta v^h(\ )$ for some $\beta > 0$, then relabeling the axes as $\tilde{u}^h = (u^h - \alpha^h)/\beta$ leaves the utility possibility frontier unchanged. But switching from u^h to $\tilde{u}^h$ will generally change the shape of the indifference curves $V(u^1, \ldots, u^h, \ldots) = $ constant unless $V(\ )$ takes the utilitarian form of simply adding up utilities, see also Exercise 9.5.

A utilitarian rule is, of course, a classic procedure for making social choices. Goods (and income) are distributed to where they make the sum of utilities as large as possible and many would find this desirable. Consider, however, the effects within the utilitarian framework of extending our assumptions so that we can compare *levels* as well as *changes* in welfare, and we only allow transformations such as $\tilde{v}^h(\ ) = \alpha + \beta v^h(\ )$ for $\beta > 0$ with *both* α and β identical for all h. Then, if we are interested in the distribution of resources between

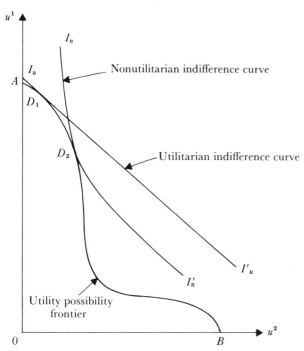

Figure 9.1. Utilitarian and nonutilitarian social welfare functions.

households and wish our social rule to favor equal over unequal distributions of welfare, other things being the same, utilitarianism is not likely to be very useful. For example, if it is true that policies promoting equality tend to be costly in terms of output, then the utility possibility frontier may well be as illustrated in Figure 9.1. In such a case, utilitarianism will nearly always imply an extremely inegalitarian distribution of welfare. Another classic example is that of allocating a fixed total of resources between two individuals, one of whom is sensitive and possesses a highly developed system for sensory enjoyment (the "aesthete") while the other is insensitive and uncultivated (the "boor"). As Figure 9.2 illustrates, the utilitarian outcome is extremely inegalitarian and this may well be thought to be undesirable. Of course, if we stick to the cardinal unit comparability assumption only, comparison of levels is impossible and such issues do not arise.

An informational assumption that is an alternative to cardinal unit comparability and that can be used to give quite different results, is that it is possible to make *ordinal comparisons of welfare levels* between individuals. We can thus recognize whether any two individuals are better off, worse off, or equally well off even if we are unable to measure their welfare levels or the differences

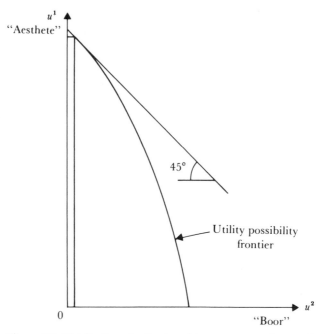

Figure 9.2. Distribution of a fixed total between an aesthete and a boor on utilitarian principles.

between them. If social choice is to be possible in this case, social preferences must be unaffected if each $v^h(\ )$ is transformed by a *common* monotone-increasing function $\phi(\ )$ since such a transformation will not affect ordinal comparisons of levels. Given this and the previous conditions, plus some condition embodying a preference for equity (for example, if everyone except two individuals are indifferent between two states and these two disagree, some priority should be given to the views of the worse off), the SWFL is of a type that leads to a "dictatorship" of the worst-off nonindifferent individual. This is the *leximin* [or Rawlsian, see Rawls (1971)] SWFL under which states are compared as follows: if the worst-off individual in state s_i is better off than the worst-off individual in state s_j (whether they are the same individual or not), s_i is socially preferred to s_j. If the worst-off individual(s) in s_i and s_j have the same welfare level, we pass on to the second worst off, and so on. Note that the leximin SWFL is strongly Paretian, if $v^h(s_i) \geq v^h(s_j)$ for all h with the strict inequality holding for at least one h, s_i is preferred to s_j. This does not hold for the related but simpler *maximin* criterion under which social choice is concerned *only* with the welfare of the worst off. This latter is illustrated by the right-angle indifference curves in Figure 9.3. The utility possibility fron-

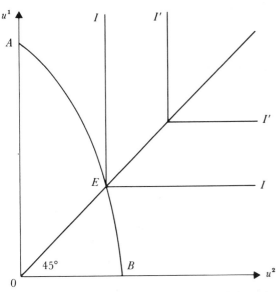

Figure 9.3. Rawlsian social welfare contours and the unimportance of cardinality.

tier AB illustrates possible combinations of $u^h = v^h(\ )$. As in Figure 9.2, relabeling the axes as $\phi^{-1}(\bar{u}^h)$ will give the possibility frontier for $\bar{u}^h = \phi[v^h(\ )]$. But since $\phi(\ )$ is monotone increasing, the contours of $\min(\bar{u}^1, \ldots, \bar{u}^h, \ldots,) = $ constant are always identical to those of $\min[\phi^{-1}(\bar{u}^1), \ldots, \phi^{-1}(\bar{u}^h), \ldots] = $ constant so that the indifference curves are unchanged. Hence, with the Rawlsian SWFL, and only in this case, social choice is invariant with respect to common (nonlinear) monotone-increasing transforms of individual utility functions. In Figure 9.3, a position of complete equality is always optimal and this will be the case provided the utility possibility frontier crosses the 45-degree line.

Note that the leximin is not dictatorial in the true sense, since the worst-off nonindifferent individual is anonymous. A leximin SWFL is not equivalent to the maximization of utility of one specific individual; rather, it embodies an extreme concern with the least favored members of society, whoever they may be. The leximin social ordering, like the lexicographic individual ordering discussed in §2.1, is not continuous, so that small changes in states can provoke large changes in social choice and this might be taken as a serious objection to its use, see Arrow (1977). For example, a change that leaves the welfare position of the worst off unchanged but brings great benefits to everyone else is socially desirable under leximin. However, an almost identical change with a barely perceptible worsening of the position of the worst off would be socially undesirable under the same criterion. Most people are likely to find this unacceptable and to prefer some social rule that permits some trade-off between welfare levels. Nevertheless, we shall be paying considerable attention to issues of equity in the next section, and the leximin or maximin social welfare function will provide an important limiting case of extreme concern with poverty.

Equivalence scales and interpersonal comparisons

In practice, the problems discussed in the previous two subsections will be "solved" by the government, the planning authority, or any interested individual working with a welfare function that represents that agent's views of how social choice ought to be made. Although for many purposes, it is the government's view of social welfare that is important, social welfare functions are by no means confined to this use. As we shall argue in §9.2, social welfare functions are useful concepts in the measurement of inequality and aggregate social consumption so that the study of social welfare functions is important for clarifying individual as well as social ethics.

One fairly general formulation of a social welfare function is over the consumption vectors of each of the individuals, that is,

$$W = f(q^1, q^2, \ldots, q^h, \ldots, q^H) \tag{1.1}$$

Although this allows the expression of views about what each individual should or should not consume, without being further restricted, it ignores most of the considerations discussed in the previous subsections since it bears no necessary relation to individual preferences. The most obvious restriction of (1.1) is thus

$$W = V(u^1, u^2, \ldots, u^h, \ldots, u^H) \tag{1.2}$$

where $u^h = v^h(q^h), h = 1, \ldots, H$. This is the Bergson-Samuelson social welfare function; when (1.1) takes this form, social welfare is sometimes said to be individualistic since it is based on individual preferences. It should not need repetition at this point that this kind of social welfare function embodies a greatly restricted view of social choice compared with the SWFL's with which we began. Not only does the ranking of social states depend only on individual welfare *levels* but we are assuming full comparability of utility, so that these levels are themselves expressed in units that can be meaningfully compared across individuals. Although it is clearly of interest to compare the different social choices that result from adopting different cardinalizations of the $v^h(.)$'s, the social choice involved is not, in general, invariant with respect to such changes. It is thus not very useful to talk about Bergson-Samuelson welfare functions being defined over *ordinal* utilities.

Contours of the utilitarian and maximin forms of (1.2) have already been illustrated in Figures 9.1 to 9.3, and it is straightforward to construct cases intermediate between these. For example,

$$
W = \frac{\sum_h [v^h(q^h)]^{1-\epsilon}}{1 - \epsilon} \quad \text{for } \epsilon \neq 1
$$

$$
= \sum_h \log v^h(q^h) \quad \text{for } \epsilon = 1
$$

(1.3)

is frequently used since, with ϵ zero it is utilitarian, while as ϵ becomes very large the social indifference curves become more and more like right angles. Note that the form of (1.2) is reminiscent of the form of weakly separable preferences, see Chapter 5, although in the latter the q^h's form a partition of commodities whereas here, each q^h contains all the commodities (potentially) but is consumed by only one household. However, just as in the weakly separable case, maximization of W in (1.2) necessarily implies maximization of each of the $v^h(\ )$ functions within it subject to whatever total expenditure is socially optimal for that household. Hence, the adoption of (1.2) means that the planner need only be concerned with the distribution of total expenditure (or income) between the households, while each individual household can be relied upon to allocate that total exactly to the planner's tastes (as well as its own). Thus, (1.2) respects households' preferences at least to the extent of the planner assuming the household knows best how to allocate its own expenditure. In spite of first appearances, however, life is not necessarily much easier for the planner since, in order to allocate the optimal expenditure to each household, full knowledge is required of each household's preferences. This is exactly the same problem encountered in Chapter 5 when trying to find the optimal allocation among broad groups at the first stage of two-stage budgeting. In the present case, there is an additional problem posed by the existence of public goods that are consumed jointly by many consumers and that will not fit into the decentralization process in any straightforward way.

It is not only the planner whose choices are restricted by taking (1.1) to have the form (1.2). By defining each individual's utility function over only that individual's consumption vector, we rule out of consideration many interesting and important phenomena. Many authors have argued that welfare results not only from individual consumption but also from consumption relative to that of others, so that utility is a function not only of q_i^h but of $q_i^h/\bar{q}_i$, say. From the welfare point of view, such phenomena, if true, mean that (1.2) will give a seriously biased picture of social welfare. Similarly, policies based on (1.2), for example the pursuit of economic growth, may well be far from optimal. We shall return to these points briefly at the end of §9.2 and discuss related interdependence effects in Chapters 12 and 13; meanwhile, although we continue in an individualistic framework, it should be emphasized that there is no inherent impossibility in handling the more general case within the framework of SWF's.

For many purposes, a social welfare function of the form $V(u^1, u^2, \ldots, u^h, \ldots, u^H)$ may be sufficiently well specified. For example, results involving only Pareto efficiency require no further detail, nor do the *form* of many results in optimal tax theory. However, if we wish actually to calculate optimal tax rates or if we wish to compare a given income distribution with the ideal, then more precision in the specification of the u^h's is required. If we believe that differences in tastes are caused by differences in characteristics, we may take a common utility function for all households but make this a specific function of household characteristics a^h, say. Hence,

$$u^h = v(q^h, a^h) = \psi(x^h, p, a^h) \tag{1.4}$$

with corresponding cost function $c(u^h, p, a^h)$. By taking common functions $v(\ )$, $\psi(\ )$, and $c(\ )$, we ensure that households with the same characteristics and the same total expenditures are regarded as equally well off. By itself, this is rather a weak assumption, but by limiting the characteristics included in a^h, it can be made much stronger. If, for example, some households are more efficient than others (with otherwise similar characteristics) at "extracting utility" from identical bundles, then by disallowing "efficiency as a utility machine" from the list of characteristics, we effectively impose the same cardinalization on each utility function. In any case, given the common functional form, we are free to choose any convenient units to measure utility. As usual, a money measure at constant prices is convenient, and as in Chapters 7 and 8, we label indifference curves by the minimum amount of money needed to reach them at some reference prices for a household with reference characteristics. Hence, if the reference prices and characteristics are p^0 and a^0, respectively, we replace (1.4) by

$$u^h = c[\psi(x^h, p, a^h), p^0, a^0] \tag{1.5}$$

Note, for example, that if $p = p^0$ and $a^h = a^0$, then $u^h = x^h$, so that if prices never change and if all households are identical, we can simply represent welfare by money income or total expenditure. More generally, however, we can rewrite (1.5) as

$$\begin{aligned} u^h &= x^h \cdot \frac{c[\psi(x^h, p, a^h), p^0, a^0]}{c[\psi(x^h, p, a^h), p^0, a^h]} \cdot \frac{c[\psi(x^h, p, a^h), p^0, a^h]}{c[\psi(x^h, p, a^h), p, a^h]} \\ &= x^h/m^h P^h \end{aligned} \tag{1.6}$$

where m^h is an equivalence scale given by the reciprocal of the first ratio (= the number of equivalent standard, or reference, adults that are equivalent to a household, or individual, with characteristics a^h) and P^h is household h's true cost-of-living index number given by the reciprocal of the second ratio (see

Chapter 7 and 8 for details). The use of this index number measure of utility thus gives us the attractive possibility of using total expenditure deflated by index number of prices and of household size and characteristics as a conceptually straightforward measure of welfare. Note in particular the importance of prices; as we saw in Chapter 7, since consumers at different welfare levels have different patterns of consumption, relative as well as absolute price changes affect welfare.

If, indeed, differences in tastes can be ascribed to differences in the characteristics a, then (1.6) provides a direct measure of welfare that is an excellent candidate for the making of comparisons between individuals. But what if tastes cannot be explained this way, if as Arrow (1977) claims "reducing an individual to a specified list of qualities is denying his individuality in a deep sense"? If this is so, then we can still mount a good defense for (1.6), since it can reasonably be argued that what we are concerned with in making interpersonal comparisons or in measuring inequality is not comparisons of welfare levels but of the objective circumstances – the constraints – faced by each individual. On this interpretation, if all individuals share the same preferences, the welfare level of each individual is merely a convenient scalar measure of the constraints he faces. In fact, if all faced the same prices and other circumstances other than the budget x^h, we may as well base interpersonal comparisons on the budgets that are complete scalar indicators of the circumstances faced by each individual. Indeed, under these circumstances we might well argue that if there were taste differences between individuals, we should reject comparisons based on the individual welfare levels in favor of comparisons based on the individual budget levels.

As it is, prices and characteristics do vary, and by taking (1.6), we are effectively using some reference tastes as a way of evaluating different prices and characteristics and correcting the budget for their influence. Hence, although each individual may well have truly individual tastes, (1.6) will still tell us what his budget would be worth to a consumer with standard tastes given the individual's objective characteristics and the prices he faces. Indeed, some such basis inevitably lies behind conventional measurements of "real" income or "real per capita" income; all that (1.6) does is to formalize these notions using the theory of choice. However, it must be pointed out that with u^h defined by (1.6) to call (1.2) a "social welfare function" might be misleading: it is better thought of as an aggregate weighting function of the individual opportunity sets faced by the different individuals with whom we are concerned.

If the characteristics a^h are directly measurable (e.g., numbers of children, age, hair color), econometric analysis of the type described in Chapter 8 can estimate the parameters of (1.5), at least to the extent that preferences and behavior patterns are affected. Equivalence scales and price indices can then be calculated, and in full knowledge of these the planner can maximize social welfare $V(u^1, \ldots, u^H)$ by setting the appropriate values of x^h by a system of taxes and subsidies. Unfortunately, this ideal is unlikely to be attainable, although, as we shall see in §9.2, equivalence scales can still play an important role in measurement.

The problems of going beyond measurement to optimization are three-fold. First, the relationship between the cost at given prices of reaching a given living standard and the household characteristics is likely to be a stochastic one so that, for example, although in general tall people are better off, the relationship is far from universal. It is thus doubtful as to whether it is even possible to tax people on the basis of such characteristics without reference to their ability to pay. In the second place, many of the elements of a^h are at least partially under the control of the household, in the long run if not in the short, children being the obvious example. This not only causes difficulties (although not insuperable ones) for the econometric analysis, see §8.4, but more seriously, it means that the taxes and subsidies set by the government will alter the characteristics as consumers alter their behavior in response to the tax and welfare system. This may well mean that full compensation is no longer desirable since, for example, family allowances to compensate for children may result in an undesirably high growth rate of population. The third problem is somewhat similar and arises because many important characteristics are either unmeasurable or can only be measured by direct appeal to the individual concerned. The classic example is "ability," which affects both the earning power of the individual and his preferences. Econometric analysis is now much more difficult since data on the basic independent variables are lacking, although modern advances in estimating equations with unobservables – see, for example, Goldberger (1972, 1974), Griliches (1974) or Joreskøg (1973) – may in time allow us to measure both the unobservable and its effects simultaneously. However, even if in some random sample we manage to measure ability and its effects and we use this information to design taxes and subsidies based on ability, the implementation of the system in the population as a whole is still likely to be impossible. The reason is that such analyses generally rest on identifying ability through behavioral traits (e.g., you can tell an able man by the way he drinks his wine), and once these rules become known, the individual can once again alter behavior so as to manipulate the system to his or her own benefit.

We note, finally, a source of some difficulty in the treatment of children. So far, we have cavalierly ignored the distinction between households and individuals, treating the two terms more or less interchangeably. Our preference in analyzing behavior is to treat the *household* as the basic decision-making unit, modeling the behavioral impact of family composition through the equivalence scales m^h. If the social welfare function has as its arguments family welfare levels, then this approach goes through with family per capita equivalent real income as the welfare indicator for each household. But this is not entirely satisfactory. Social welfare is formed over individual welfares so that society is not likely to be unconcerned about how members of families are treated even if, in some sense, the family regards itself as well off. The social welfare function should thus have a "slot" for each individual, and if each family member has the same welfare level, the family per capita equivalent real income can be used as the welfare indicator of each member of the family. For example, if social welfare is utilitarian, this procedure is equivalent to weighting size-deflated family incomes by the number of individuals in each family. Intermediate between these two extremes is the case where social weightings reflect the equivalence scales. Although this last may be a sensible compromise in practice, none of these alternatives is entirely satisfactory without a theory of (or at least some assumption about) allocation *within* the household.

Exercises

9.1. If the SWFL is utilitarian so that $W = \Sigma u^h$, and if we write $\gtrsim$ for "is socially preferred to," show that if $s_1 \gtrsim s_2$ for $u^h = v^h(s)$, then $s_1 \gtrsim s_2$ for $u^h = \tilde{v}^h(s) = \alpha^h + \beta v^h(s)$, $\beta > 0$. What can we say about equity in s_1 versus s_2? Why does the result not work if β is replaced by β^h?

9.2. (Condorcet's paradox.) Show that if for three individuals, and three states s_1, s_2, and s_3, $v^1(s_1) > v^1(s_2) > v^1(s_3)$, $v^2(s_2) > v^2(s_3) > v^2(s_1)$, and $v^3(s_3) > v^3(s_1) > v^3(s_2)$, then majority voting leads to the "preference cycle," $s_1 \gtrsim s_2 \gtrsim s_3 \gtrsim s_1$.

9.3. (The Borda rule.) Let there be m social states, s_1, s_2, . . . , s_m and assume m is finite. Define $\rho^h(s_i)$ as the number of social states to which s_i is preferred by individual h and let the Borda SWFL be defined by $s_i \gtrsim s_j$ if and only if $\Sigma_h \rho^h(s_i) \gtrsim \Sigma_h \rho^h(s_j)$. Show that the Borda rule satisfies ordinal noncomparability and unrestricted domain, is Paretian and nondictatorial, but is not independent of "irrelevant" alternatives. [See Sen (1970, p. 39; or 1977b, p. 1544).]

9.4. If society makes all decisions by means of a sacred book of rules existing from time immemorial, which of the Arrow conditions does the resulting SWFL satisfy or violate?

9.5. In a two-individual economy, there is a constraint $q^1 + q^2 = Q$ for the consumption of each individual and total consumption Q. Social welfare is given by $W = u^1 + u^2$. Show that if in case (a) $u^h = \theta^h \log q^h$ and in case (b) $u^h = \alpha^h + \beta \theta^h \log q^h$, then in both (a) and (b), $q^1 = \theta^1 Q/(\theta^1 + \theta^2)$ and $q^2 = \theta^2 Q/(\theta^1 + \theta^2)$. Is the distribution of utilities the same in both cases? If, instead, case (b) had been $u^h = (q^h)^{\theta^h}$, would you obtain the same results? State the general principle that governs these results.

9.6. Using the same constraint as in Exercise 9.5, but using the social welfare function $W = \min(u^1, u^2)$ and cases (a) $u^h = \theta^h \log q^h$, (b) $u^h = \alpha^h + \beta \theta^h \log q^h$, and (c) $u^h = (q^h)^{\theta^h}$, show that, in contrast to the allocation in Exercise 9.5, the socially optimal allocations of Q are identical in (a) and (c) but different in (b) unless $\alpha^h = \alpha$ for all h.

9.2 Social welfare and inequality

The Bergson-Samuelson social welfare function developed in the previous section can be used as the basis both for the *measurement* of welfare and for the

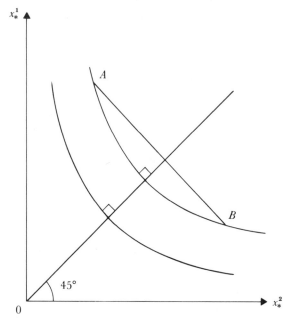

Figure 9.4. An anonymous homogeneous social welfare function.

design of policies to improve it. In this section, we take up the former issue, focusing particular attention on the decomposition of social welfare into its component parts. Our starting points are equations (1.2) and (1.6) which may be combined to give social welfare W as

$$W = V(x_*^1, x_*^2, \ldots, x_*^H) \tag{2.1}$$

where $x_*^h = x^h/m^h P^h$, is real equivalent per capita expenditure for family h. If prices are being held constant, $P^h = 1$, while if each household has identical needs, $m^h = 1$. This is the special case where social welfare can be defined over total expenditures, or if an intertemporal dimension is added, over incomes or lifetime present values.

Figure 9.4 illustrates two contours of a typical social welfare function. These are drawn to be symmetric around the 45-degree line, cutting it at right angles. This means that the value of social welfare is unaltered if only the names of the different households are altered; no attention is paid to who has the given welfare levels. This property is known as *anonymity* (or symmetry) and would be quite inappropriate if (2.1) were defined over expenditures alone since different households have different needs. As it is, the x_*'s are corrected both for needs through the m^h's and for the effects of differential price changes through the P^h's, and anonymity seems appropriate. The geometry can easily be checked by noting that, with anonymity, the reflection of each point in the 45-degree line must lie on the same indifference curve. Two other important properties have been assumed in Figure 9.4. First, we have taken $V(\ )$ to be quasi-concave so that the social indifference curves are convex to the origin. In this context, and given anonymity, quasi concavity implies a preference for a more equal distribution of the x_*'s. Hence, points between A and B, each of which involves an unequal allocation, are preferred to either. The second property is *homotheticity* which, by ordinality of $V(\ )$, we may as well take as *linear homogeneity:* if each household's x_* doubles, so does social welfare, with the implication that the shape of the social welfare contours is unaffected by the increase. No doubt objections could be made to this property, but in this context it has the advantage of permitting the inequality of a distribution to be measured independently of its mean. (The reader of §2.7 will find it a straightforward exercise to generalize the following analysis to the nonhomogeneous case, see also Exercise 9.12.)

By homogeneity, we can rewrite (2.1) as

$$W = \bar{x}_* \cdot V\left(\frac{x_*^1}{\bar{x}_*}, \ldots, \frac{x_*^h}{\bar{x}_*}, \ldots, \frac{x_*^H}{\bar{x}_*}\right) \tag{2.2}$$

where $\bar{x}_*$ is mean real per capita equivalent expenditure. If the x_*'s are equally distributed, W is simply proportional to $\bar{x}_*$, the constant of proportionality being $V(1,1, \ldots, 1)$. If this constant is not equal to unity, we can conveniently make it so by rescaling the original social welfare function so that under perfect equality we have

$$W = \bar{x}_* \tag{2.3}$$

Social welfare is measured by average real (equivalent) per capita total expenditure. This (conventional) measure will usually be a considerable overstatement of social welfare since, as can be seen from Figure 9.4, the quasi concavity and symmetry of V means that equal distributions are always preferred. Hence, by the homogeneity of V and using $V(1, 1, \ldots, 1) = 1$,

$$\begin{aligned}\bar{x}_* &= \bar{x}_* V(1, 1, \ldots, 1) \\ &= V(\bar{x}_*, \bar{x}_*, \ldots, \bar{x}_*) \geq V(x_*^1, x_*^2, \ldots, x_*^H) = W\end{aligned} \tag{2.4}$$

The inequality in the distribution of the x_*'s reduces W below its theoretical maximum of $\bar{x}_*$, so that we can measure *equality* by the ratio of W to $\bar{x}_*$, its theoretical maximum. Hence, from (2.2), write

$$W = \bar{x}_* E \tag{2.5}$$

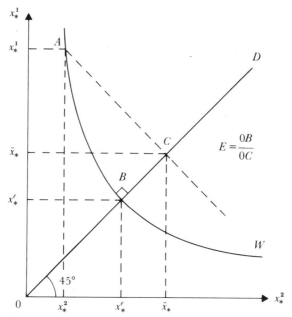

Figure 9.5. The measurement of inequality.

where

$$E = V\left(\frac{x_*^1}{\bar{x}_*}, \ldots, \frac{x_*^H}{\bar{x}_*}\right)$$

$$= \frac{V(x_*^1, x_*^2, \ldots, x_*^H)}{\bar{x}_*} = \frac{V(x_*^1, x_*^2, \ldots, x_*^H)}{V(\bar{x}_*, \bar{x}_*, \ldots, \bar{x}_*)}$$

(2.6)

Thus, equality E is defined as the ratio of social welfare as it is to what it would be at perfect equality; it takes a maximum value of unity (perfect equality) and a minimum value of zero (depending on the precise social welfare function used).

Our exposition of the equality index E is based on the *quantity metric* index number approach, see §7.2. In this approach, indifference curves are labeled by their relative distance from the origin along some reference ray, here the line of complete equality $0D$ in Figure 9.5, rather than by the relative costs required to reach them. Thus, we compare the existing distribution at A in the figure with a *hypothetical* egalitarian distribution along the line of complete equality $0D$. It is very important to realize that there is no implication that complete equality is either attainable or desirable; extremely special cases apart, attempts to achieve complete equality will reduce the total amount available for distribution, while, in an important class of problems, complete equality is not even attainable. To see how the equality measure works, start from the point B where the indifference curve through A cuts the 45-degree line. At this point, each consumer has x_*^e, say, so that social welfare is $V(x_*^e \cdots x_*^e) = x_*^e$, which is equal to social welfare at A, that is, $V(x_*^1, x_*^2, \ldots, x_*^H)$. Hence, by (2.6), E is $x_*^e / \bar{x}_*$ or $0B/0C$. The quantity x_*^e is referred to as the "equally distributed equivalent" real expenditure and is, clearly, by the quasi concavity of $V(\ )$ less than or equal to $\bar{x}_*$. Hence, rewriting (2.5) in terms of x_*^e

$$W = \bar{x}_* E = \bar{x}_* (x_*^e / \bar{x}_*) = x_*^e \qquad (2.7)$$

so that we are essentially measuring social welfare by reference to the points at which the social indifference curves through the existing distribution cut the 45-degree line.

It is interesting to compare this approach with the exposition in Atkinson (1970) or Sen·(1973b) that is analogous to the more usual "money metric" index number approach. In this, we compare the minimum aggregate cost of reaching the contour through A with the actual aggregate cost of reaching A. Provided that the budget constraint is always symmetric about the line $0D$, the cost minimizing point is B so that the cost ratio $E = 0B/0C = x_*^e / \bar{x}_*$. Whichever one of the two verbal interpretations we adopt, the resulting equality index is exactly the same. However, the second interpretation is less appealing than the first, since as already argued it is most unlikely that the aggregate budget constraint could be symmetric about the equality line.

Figure 9.5 also illustrates how the measurement of equality depends on the type of SWF being considered and, in particular, on the degree of concavity of the indifference curves. If we are concerned with only the welfare of the poorest, indifference curves will be right angles with the corner at B, and perceived inequality will be larger than shown, even if the actual distribution is the same. By contrast, if $V(\ )$ is utilitarian and is simply the sum of the x_*'s, indifference curves are parallel straight lines at 90 degrees to the 45-degree line so that inequality is always zero and social welfare is identical to $\bar{x}_*$. This dependence of the measurement of inequality on social preferences may seem inappropriate in a situation where an objective measure seems called for, but as we shall see, the use of conventional "objective" measures of inequality merely serves to disguise implicit value judgments.

In many contexts, we wish to measure *inequality* rather than equality and this is accomplished straightforwardly be defining I by

$$I = 1 - E \qquad (2.8)$$

and this is the measure proposed by Kolm (1969, 1976) and Atkinson (1970). Clearly, I, like E, lies between 0 and 1. Note carefully too that although $V(\ )$ is ordinal in the sense that only indifference curves matter, both E and I are independent of which cardinalization of $V(\;)$ is actually used, provided that homogeneity is maintained.

In §9.1 above, it was shown how the individual measure of welfare proposed, $c[\psi(x, p, a), p^0, a^0]$, could be decomposed into total expenditure, price, and family composition indices. The same technique can be used with social welfare. From (2.5), we have immediately, for two periods 1 and 0

$$\frac{W_1}{W_0} = \left(\frac{\bar{x}_*^1}{\bar{x}_*^0}\right) \cdot \left(\frac{E^1}{E^0}\right) \tag{2.9}$$

For simplicity of exposition, taking only the case where all families are the same so that a^0's and a^h's vanish,

$$\frac{\bar{x}_*^1}{\bar{x}_*^0} = \frac{\sum_h c^h(u^{1h}, p^0)}{\sum_h c^h(u^{0h}, p^0)} = \frac{\sum_h c^h(u^{1h}, p^0)}{\sum_h c^h(u^{1h}, p^1)} \cdot \frac{\bar{x}^1}{\bar{x}^0} \tag{2.10}$$

The expression $[\Sigma_h c^h(u^{1h}, p^1)]/[\Sigma_h c^h(u^{1h}, p^0)]$ is an aggregate price index using current utility levels as weights comparing p^1 with p^0, so that (2.10) decomposes $\bar{x}_*^1/\bar{x}_*^0$ into a money expenditure index divided by an aggregate price index. By an exactly analogous procedure, E^1/E^0 can be split into a money equality index divided by a price deflator measuring the extent to which price changes are biased towards or against the rich or the poor. These distinctions can be important in practice; we have already discussed in Chapter 7 how relative price changes affect different income groups differently, and if, for example, prices move against the poor as they did in Britain and America in the early 1970's, the approach adopted here would show an increase in inequality even though the distribution of money expenditures were to remain unchanged. Similar considerations apply in comparing distributions of income or expenditure across countries when relative price structures differ widely. The approach discussed here would proceed by comparing the inequality measures obtained for a single country, using for reference both its own prices and those of the other country. Comparison of the two measures would then indicate which country's price structure was the more or less egalitarian. Exactly parallel remarks apply to differences in family composition; identical distributions of income do not imply the same degree of inequality if the incomes are received by families of different sizes or needs.

How then do such measures of inequality relate to conventional summary statistics of dispersion such as the Gini coefficient or the coefficient of variation? As we shall see, such measures can be thought of as resulting from specific social welfare functions, given the principles discussed previously. By making these implicit social welfare functions explicit, we can thus see more clearly exactly what view of distributional justice is implied by the use of each individual measure. Before doing this, it is useful to consider the alternative

Cumulative
percent of x_*

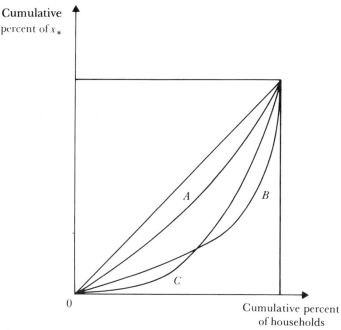

Cumulative percent
of households

Figure 9.6. Intersecting and nonintersecting Lorenz curves.

approach to inequality measurement that starts, not from a social welfare function, but from an axiomatic approach to the direct measurement of inequality.

Three particular axioms command reasonably wide assent, at least in practice. The first of these is *mean independence*, that inequality should not depend on the *level* of expenditures or incomes, only on their distribution, and this assumption is analogous to our earlier postulate of homogeneity in the social welfare function context. The second axiom, of *anonymity*, is again familiar and, as before, will be reasonable if expenditures are needs and prices corrected. The third axiom, first proposed by Dalton (1920), is the *principle of transfers*, which requires that transfers of expenditure from a better off to a poorer individual must decrease inequality, provided only that the transfer is not large enough to change their relative positions. This can be illustrated using the familiar Lorenz curve, or plot of the cumulative percentage of total x_* against the cumulative percentage of population. Figure 9.6 shows three distinct Lorenz curves, *A*, *B*, and *C*. Distribution *B* has a Lorenz curve entirely outside that of distribution *A* so that, by the definition of the Lorenz curve, it would be possible to pass from *B* to *A* by a series of transfers from richer to poorer households. Hence, *any* inequality measure satisfying the principle of transfers will show less inequality in A than in B. Similarly, C is more unequal than A. However, since B and C intersect, their ranking will depend on the precise measure used and it is easy to see why ranking B and C involves more complex ethical judgments than does ranking A vis-à-vis either B or C. Distribution C is more equal at the top of the distribution than is B, while B is more equal at the bottom. Which sort of inequality is worse is a matter of social welfare judgment over and above that encompassed by the principle of transfers, and if the deadlock is arbitrarily resolved by choosing one inequality measure over another, we implicitly make value judgments of exactly this type.

If we go back to our original definition of inequality I, equation (2.8), then as we shall illustrate, if the construction is based on a homogeneous quasi-concave social welfare function, the index will automatically satisfy the principle of transfers. For our present purposes, we may also take the converse as being true, that any mean independent, anonymous inequality measure satisfying the principle of transfers can be used to construct a homogeneous quasi-concave social welfare function. To illustrate, consider the Gini coefficient in two equivalent forms

$$\gamma = \frac{1}{2H^2\bar{x}_*} \sum_{1}^{H} \sum_{1}^{H} |x_*^h - x_*^k| = 1 + \frac{1}{H} - \frac{2}{H^2\bar{x}_*}(x_*^1 + 2x_*^2 + \cdots + Hx_*^H) \quad (2.11)$$

where the x_*'s are arranged in descending order so that $x_*^1 \geq x_*^2 \geq \cdots \geq x_*^H$. When there is perfect equality, that is, $x_*^h = \bar{x}_*$, $\gamma = 0$, while with perfect inequality, $x_*^1 = H\bar{x}_*$ and $\gamma = 1 - 1/H \simeq 1$ if H is large. Hence, γ is interpretable as $1 - E$ in (2.8), so that from (2.7) the social welfare function is

$$W_\gamma = \bar{x}_*(1 - \gamma) = x_*^1 + 3x_*^2 + \cdots + (2h - 1)x_*^h + \cdots + (2H - 1)x_*^H \quad (2.12)$$

where, as before, the x_*'s are ordered. The indifference curves for $H = 2$ are illustrated in Figure 9.7. Note that, although the SWF is quasi-concave, it is not strictly so, and the social marginal utility of x_* to each household depends only on its rank in the distribution rather than on the more obvious criterion of how much x_* it already has. Figure 9.7 also illustrates the SWF for the coefficient of variation. The inequality index is

$$C = \left[\frac{1}{H} \Sigma(x_*^h - \bar{x}_*)^2\right]^{1/2}/\bar{x}_* \quad (2.13)$$

and satisfies the three axioms as it stands. At $x_*^h = \bar{x}_*$, $C = 0$, while if $x_*^1 = H\bar{x}_*$, $C = (H - 1)/(H)^{1/2}$ so that, if C is divided by $(H)^{1/2}$, $C/(H)^{1/2}$ lies between the same limits as the Gini coefficient. Hence, applying (2.7) as before

$$W_C = \bar{x}_* - \frac{1}{H}[\Sigma(x_*^h - \bar{x}_*)^2]^{1/2} \quad (2.14)$$

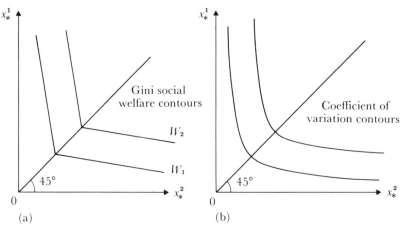

Figure 9.7. Social welfare contours for two inequality indices.

the contours of which are parabolas symmetric about the 45-degree line as illustrated. Similar exercises can be performed for other measures of inequality.

Further implications of inequality indices in terms of social welfare have recently been obtained in work by Blackorby and Donaldson (1978) who draw three-dimensional diagrams corresponding to Figure 9.7. It is particularly important to do this since the case of only two consumers is very special; for example, with only two consumers, Lorenz curves can never intersect, and the principle of transfers by itself is sufficient for judging relative inequality, leaving only a very limited role for the specific social welfare function. Consider, for three households, the triangular plane or "simplex" defined by $x_*^1 + x_*^2 + x_*^3$ = constant, see Figure 9.8. This corresponds to a three-dimensional version of Figure 9.7, viewed down the 45-degree axis from the top right. Once again, it must be emphasized that these points are neither necessarily attainable nor desirable; rather we shall use the simplex merely as a convenient plane through which to take a cross section of the social indifference curves. Starting from the given distribution S, Blackorby and Donaldson point out that all points within the central irregular hexagon $SABCDE$ (see Figure 9.8) must be preferred according to any quasi-concave anonymous social welfare function. This also shows why quasi concavity implies the principle of transfers; any equalizing transfer from S must lead into the hexagon and hence to points which are preferred to S independently of which specific SWF is being used. Although the six vertices of the hexagon will be indifferent for all SWF's, the exact indifference contours in the simplex will vary

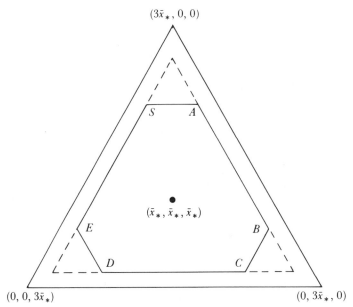

Figure 9.8. Simplex for three households.

from SWF to SWF. Again, the Rawlsian welfare function is an interesting limiting case and, using this criterion, any point within the triangle completed in broken lines is preferable since it involves an improvement in the position of the worst off. Non-Rawlsian criteria involve more "rounded" contours because the worst off are allowed to be made worse off if the trade-off is sufficiently good. Figure 9.9(a) illustrates the actual contours for the Gini SWF (the hexagons) and for the coefficient-of-variation SWF (the circles), and these correspond to the view looking "down" the 45-degree line in Figure 9.7. The concentricity of both sets of figures in Figure 9.9(a) show that both the Gini and the coefficient-of-variation are what Blackorby and Donaldson call "distributionally homothetic," inasmuch as the shape of the contours does not alter as we move away from the central point of equality. (Note that this property has nothing to do with mean independence or homotheticity of the social welfare function.) Figure 9.9(b) illustrates the contours of what might be considered a more plausible SWF; in this, the central circles become more triangular as we move outwards, indicating that the more unequal the distribution, the more are we concerned about the welfare of the poorest. Contours such as these are produced by a SWF of the constant elasticity of substitution form

$$W = \left(\sum_{1}^{H} \frac{1}{H} x_*^{h\rho} \right)^{1/\rho}$$

(2.15)

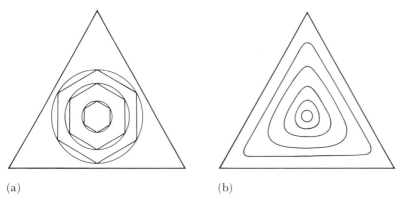

(a)   (b)

Figure 9.9. Social welfare contours in the three-household simplex.

among others, including the SWF based on Theil's (1967) entropy inequality measure, for example, and the distributional homotheticity of the Gini and the coefficient of variation can be regarded as an argument in favor of these other types of indices.

It is possible to go on to consider a wide range of other properties of inequality measures both from the axiomatic and from the social welfare points of view and some guide to the literature dealing with this is given at the end of the chapter. However, we must conclude this section with a warning on the range of applicability of the concepts discussed here. We argued in the previous section that in many ways distributional comparisons are best interpreted as being defined over the objective opportunity sets faced by individuals and that the individual *welfare level* is merely a convenient scalar summary measure of each individual's opportunity set. The *social welfare function* is then merely an aggregate weighting function of the individual opportunity sets as represented by the needs corrected real expenditure of each individual given by (1.6). Such an approach clearly excludes such phenomena as envy or altruism.

However, we may wish to take a wider view of welfare and recognize such effects. Consider, for example, the case where each household's welfare depends on its own consumption through $v^h(q^h)$ as usual, but also on social welfare as a whole. Hence,

$$u^h = \phi^h[v^h(q^h), W] \tag{2.16}$$

In this separable form, the allocation of goods will still be done so as to maximize $v^h(q^h)$ so that, as before, $v^h(q^h)$ can be replaced by a function of x^h, p, and a^h. Social welfare is again defined over the u^h's but because of (2.16) takes the implicit form

$$W = V\{\phi^1[v^1(q^1), W], \ldots, \phi^h[v^h(q^h), W], \ldots, \phi^H[v^H(q^H), W]\} \qquad (2.17)$$

With this form, in principle, we could proceed exactly as before, defining x_*'s that allow for the impact of social welfare W. In practice, it is hard to see how this could be accomplished given the separability assumption, because variations in W will not affect the composition of spending. This highlights one of the major difficulties of this type of approach, that a rather precise specification of how the interdependences work is required before real progress can be made. Note, however, that the structure of (2.17) allows us to "solve" for W as

$$W = V^*[v^1(q^1), v^2(q^2), \ldots, v^H(q^H)] \qquad (2.18)$$

for some function $V^*(\ )$ since the $v^h(q^h)$'s are the only variables involved. However, V and V^* are quite different functions, and inequality measured through (2.18) would be quite different from that measured by (2.17); this is obvious enough – variations in social welfare are of different value to different individuals.

A number of other caveats should also be mentioned. The x_* measures are based on cost functions and are thus limited by the range of the market and by the appropriateness of assuming a linear opportunity set. Once again, however, corrections could be made as required by recognizing the effects of constraints on the cost function, for example, unemployment or rationing of certain goods. We have also said little about the time period over which expenditures are measured, whether a year or a lifetime, although this issue is of great importance in the practical analysis of inequality.

Exercises

9.7. Many economists would take an individual's welfare as representing that individual's own personal interests only and would exclude phenomena such as envy or altruism from social welfare formulations. Do you agree with this view? If envy and altruism are recognized, what difference is there in the optimal allocation of goods in the economy?

9.8. Prove that Dalton's principle of transfers is satisfied for inequality measurements based on a strictly quasi-concave social welfare function. Does a utilitarian social welfare function satisfy the principle?

9.9. One possible inequality measure is the variance of logs given by $V_L = H^{-1}\Sigma(\log x_*^h - \overline{\log x_*})^2$. Show that if $x_*^j > x_*^i$, then a small amount transferred from i to j will increase V_L if $(\log x_*^j - \overline{\log x_*})/x_*^j > (\log x_*^i - \overline{\log x_*})/x_*^i$. By writing $x_*^i = (1 + \theta)x_*^j$, show that by keeping a fixed ratio between x_*^i and x_*^j, but by increasing both, this inequality will eventually be satisfied. What conclusions do you draw for the use of V_L as an inequality measure? If it were known that x_*'s were lognormally distributed, would V_L be a suitable device for comparing distributions?

9.10.* Show that the ranking of two distributions induced by using different inequality indicators based on different (strictly) quasi-concave symmetric social welfare functions will always be the same if the associated Lorenz curves do not cross.

9.11. What is the inequality index associated with the social welfare function defined by (2.15)? Discuss how this varies with ρ, and explain the part played by ρ in (a) the recognition of inequality and (b) the amount of distributional nonhomotheticity.

9.12.* In Chapter 7, the distance function $d(u, q)$ was used to define the quantity index numbers $Q(q^1, q^2; u)$ by $d(u, q^1)/d(u, q^2)$. Defining $d(W, x_*)$ as the distance function for the social welfare function $W = V(x_*)$, show that the equality measure E is given by $E = Q(x_*, \bar{\iota}\bar{x}_*; W)$, where $W = V(x_*)$ and ι is the vector of ones. Show that, given homogeneity of $V(\ )$, E does not depend on W. Conversely, discuss the question of measuring inequality when W is *not* homothetic, that is, when the shape of social indifference curves alters systematically with national well-being. Is this likely to be an important case?

9.13. Suppose that we have a nonhomothetic social welfare function, $W = \log (x_*^1 - \alpha) + \log(x_*^2 - \alpha)$, where $\alpha > 0$ and $x_*^h > \alpha$, all h. Show that if we continue to define E as $x^e/\bar{x}$, where $W(x_*^e, x_*^e) = W(x_*^1, x_*^2)$, and if both budget levels double, the index increases. Do you think that this should be a general feature of equality indices? Suppose that the subsistence standard α depends upon past consumption levels, what are the consequences for intertemporal and cross-sectional distributional comparisons?

9.14. Show that the welfare function $W = \alpha - \Sigma \exp(-\gamma x_*^h)$ has the property that if an amount k is added to every individual's budget, the equality index is unaffected while that for a homothetic social welfare function increases, see Kolm (1976). What happens to equality given by the two social welfare functions if there is an equiproportional increase in budgets? Kolm calls the first social welfare function "leftist" as opposed to homothetic social welfare functions he calls "rightist." In the context of equal absolute or equiproportional budget reductions, how well does this interpretation stand up?

9.15. Is one minus the coefficient of variation (2.13) "leftist" or "rightist" in Kolm's sense? How well does it correspond to your own ethical views on distribution?

Bibliographical notes

The literature on social choice theory is vast, and we can do no better than to refer the interested reader to Arrow (1963) and to the excellent text by Sen (1970). Modern developments, which we have tried to summarize, work much more directly with utility functions than did the original contributions and this has brought the subject into much closer contact, not only with consumer theory but also with the rest of welfare economics. Sen's (1977b) Walras-Bowley lecture gives an excellent exposition and bibliography on which we have leaned heavily. However, in addition to the seminal work of d'Aspremont and Gevers, we should like to note the work by Hammond (1976a), Strasnick (1975), Maskin (1978), Deschamps and Gevers (1978), and Roberts (1980a, b); see also Arrow (1977) for a much shorter but very useful review. Our discussion of inequality is based on the work of Kolm (1976), Atkinson (1970), and Sen (1973b), although we have tried to use the results of earlier chapters to extend and unify the analysis. There is a long history of empirical measurement of inequality but the explicit link with social welfare is much more recent. For further reading on a number of topics related to inequality, see Cowell (1977). For discussion of the effects of prices and household composition and for a practical example, see Muellbauer (1974d) and (1978a), respectively.

PART FOUR

Extensions and applications

The quality of goods and household production theory • Labor supply • The consumption function and intertemporal choice • The demand for durable goods • Choice under uncertainty

CHAPTER 10

The quality of goods and
household production theory

To newcomers to economics, utility theory often appears as a vacuous subject. One of our chief concerns in this book is to show how appropriate assumptions on preferences and the constraints households face are required in different contexts to put flesh on utility theory, to gain insights into particular kinds of behavior, and to justify particular empirical procedures. We have already had many good examples of this, ranging from the selection of easy to handle but general functional forms for Engel curves and demand functions to assumptions that permit groups of goods to be treated as one good and groups of households to be treated as a single household. The borderline between whether restrictions are to be placed on preferences or on the constraints faced by the household is sometimes a subtle one. For example, in Chapter 8, we saw that to be able to place a welfare interpretation on cost-of-living comparisons across households with different compositions, we had to assume that the differences in preferences between households could be fully characterized through certain parameters which could be given a price or cost interpretation. In one example, the cost function common to all households was defined on "corrected" prices, which are the product of the actual market prices and parameters that increase with household size and reflect the higher "equivalent prices" larger households have to pay for their consumption goods. In a sense, these parameters are preference parameters, and yet they can be interpreted as measures of the different constraints faced by different households.

Perhaps the most general way in which special assumptions can be incorporated into models of household behavior is through what is generally known as household production theory: Gorman (1956), Becker (1965), Lancaster (1966a, b) are the classic early references. In this approach, it is assumed that the household obtains utility from some underlying goods that cannot be bought in the market but are instead produced in the household from inputs of market good and leisure time. Stigler and Becker (1977) have made much of the power of this approach in explaining phenomena that economists otherwise would simply leave unexplained by citing taste changes or differences. Thus, they explain addiction to music (or drugs) in terms of the accumulation of human capital specific to skill in music (drug) appreciation, the existence of habits and customs in terms of the search costs associated with nonhabitual behavior and the specificity of the stock of accumulated human capital, the effects of advertising on behavior through changed knowledge about the household production function, and fashions and fads through the existence of a good called social distinction that is produced from the fashion goods bought by the household and reduced by those bought by other households. We certainly sympathize with their methodology of assuming as far as is possible that everyone has the same stable underlying preferences but that households differ in the constraints they face. Our only qualm is that, when the intervening variables are not observable, there may be little cutting edge to the distinction between preferences and constraints, and the "explanations" offered by the approach can sometimes be complicated ways of making rather simple points.

The analysis of quality and of choices between goods differing in observable characteristics has probably been the area of economics where the household production approach has been most applied but, as we shall see in §10.3, a more direct analysis of these topics analogous to that in Chapter 8 is often more convenient. The analysis of quality is an important topic in economics. For example, when a new good is introduced, national income statisticians need to make corresponding adjustments in their price indices. Effectively, this will involve finding some way of comparing the new good with existing goods, ideally by finding the indifference locus linking them. Another important policy issue is at what level to provide a public good (such as a recreational facility) which is not to be fully charged for. Again, this involves making indirect deductions about households' indifference curves by relating observable behavior to the demand for the publicly provided good. For example, costs of travel to and from the recreational site and other costs such as equipment (skis, fishing rods, etc.) and hotel costs, can be used to make deductions about the valuation of the recreational facility. One way in which we can link indifference curves between existing and new goods or goods for which market transactions cannot be directly observed is through the use of measurable specification variables associated with these goods. Transport mode choice and the choice of housing distinguished by location are examples where such measurable specifications illuminate the quality dimensions of choice. We shall examine two different ways in which such information can be used.

In §10.1, we summarize household production theory, discuss some of its empirical implications, and in §10.2 apply it to the measurement of quality change. In §10.3, we take an alternative approach that we suggest is often more relevant than household production theory to the choice of varieties of a good, for example, a brand of toothpaste. Both it and the household production model suggest ways of using specification information. Section 10.4

contains a brief nontechnical review of some of the other issues raised for economic analysis by the existence of different qualities.

10.1 Household production theory

Household production theory is an integration of the theory of the consumer with that of the firm. The latter is relevant to that part of household decision making that is concerned with the efficient use of market goods, time, and human capital as inputs in the production of utility-yielding, nonmarket goods. For example, suppose that there are two nonmarket goods produced at levels z_1 and z_2. In Figure 10.1, we illustrate the production possibility frontier: the largest combinations of z_1 and z_2 that can be produced from a given budget. As we shall see, the efficient production problem can also be thought of as a cost minimization problem such as is standard in the theory of the firm. Indeed, the cost function defines the production possibility frontier: at a point such as z^0, the marginal rate of transformation between the outputs is the ratio of the marginal cost of output 2 to that of output 1. These marginal costs π_2, π_1 are often called the *shadow costs* or *shadow prices* of the outputs. Given the production possibility frontier, what remains is for the household to choose that combination of z_1 and z_2 that maximizes utility. In Figure 10.1, this occurs at z^0 where the highest attainable indifference curve just touches the production possibility frontier. Since this is, in general, nonlinear, this upper-stage optimization problem is likely to be rather more complicated than the lower-stage problem of computing the minimum cost of a given z_1, z_2, and the derived demand functions for the outputs and inputs will be correspondingly complicated. As we shall see, the shadow prices are quite helpful in reducing to manageable proportions both the conceptual computations and the econometric estimation of derived demand functions. In §10.2, we shall examine the role of the shadow prices in another context: the construction of price indices to correct for changes in the technology.

We begin discussing the lower-stage optimization by thinking of the consumer as a firm. The firm produces an output vector z from a vector of material inputs q, a vector of labor inputs ℓ_0, and a vector of capital inputs k. The objective is to minimize short-run cost, $x = p \cdot q + \omega \cdot \ell_0$ subject to the constraint imposed by the technology given z and k. We neglect intertemporal considerations such as would be raised by including costs of investment. The solution is a function

$$x = C(p, \omega, z; k) \tag{1.1}$$

This cost function has similar properties to the consumer cost function derived in Chapter 2 and much used in previous chapters. It is positive linear homogeneous, and concave in p and ω, increasing in z and nonincreasing in k.

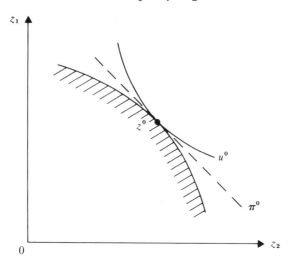

Figure 10.1. Choice in the household production model.

As before, its price derivatives,

$$q_i = \partial C(p,\ \omega,\ z;\ k)/\partial p_i = q_i(p,\ \omega,\ z;\ k) \tag{1.2}$$

and

$$\ell_{0r} = \partial C(p,\ \omega,\ z;\ k)/\partial \omega_r = \ell_{0r}(p,\ \omega,\ z;\ k) \tag{1.3}$$

are the derived input demand functions for good i and the rth type of labor conditional upon the output and capital vector. The derivative with respect to z_j,

$$\pi_j = \partial C(p,\ \omega,\ z;\ k)/\partial z_j = \pi_j(p,\ \omega,\ z;\ k) \tag{1.4}$$

has the interpretation of being the shadow price of output j: it measures the marginal cost of a small increase in z_j. If the technology has constant returns to scale in the short run, the cost function (1.1) is linear homogeneous in z; doubling all outputs doubles the cost of producing them. Then, by Euler's theorem,

$$C(p,\ w,\ z;\ k) \equiv \sum_j \pi_j(p,\ \omega,\ z;\ k)z_j \tag{1.5}$$

Now consider a household that obtains utility from nonmarket goods in quantities z, which it produces from market goods in quantities q, together with a vector of time inputs ℓ_0 and a vector k of stocks of human capital and consumer durables. We can divide the overall optimization problem into two stages. At the lower stage, the cost of producing the vector z is minimized. Just as for the firm, the solution is (1.1) where, for the consumer, x is "full income": the value of the exogenous time endowment plus nonlabor income. Given x, (1.1) implies a possibility frontier in z-space illustrated in Figure 10.1. The slope of the dotted tangent at z^0 is $-\pi_2(p, \omega, z^0; k)/\pi_1(p, \omega, z^0; k)$, which is the marginal rate of transformation of output 2 into output 1.

The upper stage of the household optimization problem is then to choose z to maximize

$$u = v(z) \quad \text{such that} \quad x = C(p, \omega, z; k) \tag{1.6}$$

This is illustrated in Figure 10.1 by the tangency of the indifference curve labeled u^0 to the budget constraint (1.1). An important assumption about the treatment of time should be made explicit here. Let ℓ be the vector of labor time supplied to the market. Then $\mu + \omega \cdot \ell = p \cdot q$ is the market constraint. Let ℓ_0 be the vector of labor time in household production and $F(q, \ell_0, z) = 0$ be the joint production function. If T is the vector of time endowments, then $T - \ell_0 - \ell$ is the leisure vector and this is implicitly treated as part of the vector z. Note also that (1.6) is quite general in the sense that some of the z's can be identical with some of the market goods. In some applications of the approach, it is assumed that $v(z)$ is a separable subutility function, and that none of the market goods from which z is produced appear in the rest of the utility function. Then x is the total expenditure on the market goods that produce z and, following the analysis of Chapter 5, two-stage budgeting is possible; that is, given x, the optimal allocation of z and the inputs that produce it can be made independently of other household decisions.

In some contexts, the household production approach is not merely a clever or elegant way of looking at household decisions but the only appropriate way. This occurs when the household consists essentially of a small business or firm together with one or more consumers; family farming or shopkeeping are obvious examples. In this case, we can make rather more than a conceptual distinction between production and consumption. For production, efficiency is guaranteed if the farm or shop maximizes profits for any given inputs, while for consumption, the farmer or shopkeeper will maximize utility taking the profits as a constraint. Such a framework would be the obvious way of analyzing the behavior of, for example, subsistence farmers in a developing country.

The role of shadow prices

In general, the budget constraint in the space of nonmarket goods is nonlinear. However, at the optimum point z^0, the dotted line labeled π^0 is a separating hyperplane between the indifference and budget constraint loci. Moreover, under the assumption of constant returns, which is almost invariably assumed in the household production literature, (1.5) holds true, and then we can restate the problem as selecting z to maximize

$$u = v(z) \quad \text{such that} \quad x = \sum_j \pi_j(p, \omega, z^0; k)z_j \tag{1.7}$$

Note that here we have already replaced the π_j functions by their optimal values, and this allows us to treat the shadow prices π_j as if they were exogenous. The solution of the problem (1.7) can thus be written in the form

$$z_j = \hat{z}_j(x, \pi) \tag{1.8}$$

while bearing in mind that $\pi_j = \pi_j(p, \omega, z; k)$. Hence, in (1.8), demands depend on the shadow prices π_j which, in turn, depend on demands. The endogeneity of the π's differentiates (1.8) from the ordinary consumer demand functions, where prices are exogenous to the individual consumer (although in a full general equilibrium system they would of course be endogenous to the system in much the same way as they are here). However, given the two-stage procedure, we can take (1.8) as a behavioral equation, albeit one linking endogenous variables to both exogenous and other endogenous variables. It is thus one of the structural equations of a model, which is completed by adding the equations for q, ℓ, and π, that is, (1.2) to (1.4). The advantage of looking at it this way is that equations (1.8) are yielded by a standard optimization problem subject to a *linear* budget constraint. This means that a corpus of ready-made theory, possible functional forms, and developed intuition is available to aid in their interpretation and estimation. In contrast, the reduced form, which is obtained by solving (1.6) for

$$z_j = z_j(x, p, \omega; k) \tag{1.9}$$

and substituting into (1.2) and (1.3) to obtain

$$q_i = q_i[p, \omega, z(x, p, \omega; k); k]$$
$$\ell_r = \ell_r[p, \omega, z(x, p, \omega; k); k] \tag{1.10}$$

will typically be *very* nonlinear.

The shadow prices π_j and the demand functions (1.8) have been heavily emphasized in applications of the household production model by Becker (1965), Michael and Becker (1973), Becker (1976), and others, see the applications in Terleckyj (1976). For example, Grossman (1972, 1976) explains the negative relationship between medical care and health (why people who are less healthy spend more on medical care) as follows: the higher rate of depreciation on health capital raises the shadow price of health and causes the quantity of health *capital* demanded to fall. However, the demand for medical care from which health capital is produced increases as long as the price elasticity of demand for health capital is less than one. Sometimes, indeed, the shadow prices are treated like exogenous prices that are independent of the amounts of the nonmarket goods consumed. In general, this is possible only under restrictive assumptions on the technology. The question of independence of the shadow prices π from z is, as we shall see, also important for quality measurement. Muellbauer (1974c) points out that, unless restrictions are placed on preferences, the budget constraint in Figure 10.1 must be linear, and this occurs only with a cost function of the form

$$x = \Sigma \; \hat{C}_j(p, \; \omega; \; k)z_j \tag{1.11}$$

where the individual $\hat{C}_j$ functions give the unit cost of producing one unit z_j. This is a consequence of theorems by Samuelson (1966) and Hall (1973a) relating to nonjoint production and in fact (1.11) corresponds to constant returns production functions of the form

$$z_j = f_j(q_j, \; \ell_{0j}; \; k) \qquad \text{where} \; \sum_j q_j = q \; \text{ and } \; \sum_j \ell_{0j} = \ell_0 \tag{1.12}$$

This nonjointness assumption means that market goods and time inputs can be additively split up between separate production processes for each output j. As Pollak and Wachter (1975) remark, nonjointness is a very restrictive assumption, implying that time spent in household production cannot yield direct utility or disutility except in so far as it reduces the amount of the leisure vector that remains. If nonjointness were valid, the power of the model would be clear: the budget constraint in z-space takes the linear form, and the dimensionality of the consumer choice problem has been reduced from the many market good inputs to the fewer nonmarket goods. The implications of changes in wage rates, in prices, or in technology can then be relatively easily analyzed. In particular, the usual demand systems corresponding to a linear budget constraint can be defined for the z's for each individual household. Even in this case, though, the shadow prices can depend upon wage rates and stocks that differ between households, and aggregating demand functions across households is unlikely to be straightforward. However, Pollak and Wachter go too far in implying that in the more complicated case of joint production the shadow prices are not analytically useful. As we saw, the structural equations (1.2) to (1.4) and (1.8) are all readily derivable from the specification of preferences and the cost function (1.1). As Barnett (1977) points out, estimating the structural parameters is likely to be both easier and more readily interpretable by fitting (1.2), (1.3), and (1.8) using methods (such as instrumental variables) to overcome simultaneity bias than by attempting to fit the very nonlinear reduced form (1.9) and (1.10). In other words, the two-stage decomposition of the household's decision problem has its analog in econometric estimation even under joint production. To apply it, however, requires microdata not only on quantities purchased of market goods but on the amounts z produced of the nonmarket goods as well as on ω and k.

Without data on z, we would not, in general, expect to identify the structural parameters from the part of the reduced form given by (1.10). Note finally, however, that over situations in which the technology is unchanged, the household production approach is formally equivalent to the standard utility maximization problem. After all, the budget constraint is linear in the market goods and we can, in principle, always define a utility function in market goods by maximizing $v(z)$ with respect to z subject to z being producible for a given q-vector. Of course, when the technology changes, this is formally equivalent to a change in "tastes" in the utility function defined on q. And indeed, one of the main points of the household production approach is to avoid such arbitrary attribution whenever possible.

The linear characteristics model

Let us now turn to a model that incorporates joint production and yet has some attractively simple features. This is the linear production model first suggested for the analysis of diets, in which contexts it dates back to Cornfeld, Stigler (1945), and Dantzig; see Dorfmann, Samuelson, and Solow (1958). In its present form, it was developed in Gorman (1956) and extensively discussed by Lancaster (1966a,b, 1971). Here the production functions are

$$z_j = \sum_i b_{ji} q_i \tag{1.13}$$

This means that one unit of each good contains b_{ji} units of the nonmarket good j. It is often referred to as the linear characteristics model since each market good embodies various characteristics that ultimately yield utility. The diet example is particularly instructive: think of z_1 as the total amount of calories, z_2 as the amount of protein, z_3 as the amount of vitamin C, and so on. Incidentally, note that if goods $n_1 + 1, n_1 + 2, \ldots, n$ are bought for themselves rather than any embodied characteristics, we can simply write $z_{k+1} = q_{n_1+1}$, $z_{k+2} = q_{n_1+2}$ and so forth, which is a special case of (1.13).

In this model, the cost minimization problem, the solution to which defines the budget constraint, is a standard linear programming problem, see Exercise 10.5. Consider instead the maximization of $u = v(z)$ with respect to q subject to $x = \Sigma\, p_i q_i$. For purchased market goods, this gives the first-order condition, in the absence of corner solutions,

$$\sum_j (\partial u/\partial z_j) b_{ji} = \lambda p_i$$

Since $1/\lambda$ is the marginal cost of utility, the shadow price is given by $\pi_j = (\partial u/\partial z_j)/\lambda$, so that we have

$$p_i = \sum_j \pi_j b_{ji} \tag{1.14}$$

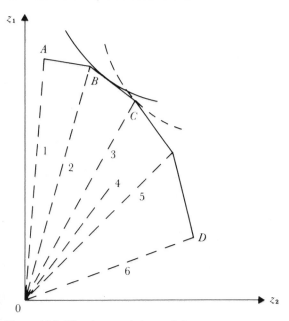

Figure 10.2. The characteristics model.

The characteristics model is illustrated in Figure 10.2. The rays labeled 1 to 6 indicate the proportions of characteristics 1 and 2 present in each market good. With a given budget, the locus AD gives the attainable combinations of z_1 and z_2. For example, if the whole budget is spent on good 1, then the point A gives the available z_1, z_2. Note that good 4 is inefficient: a combination of goods 3 and 5 will give good 4's characteristics more cheaply. The frontier may not be defined for small values of z_1 and z_2 if it is impossible to dispose of unwanted characteristics in market goods. With the indifference curve tangential at B, the optimal solution is to purchase some of good 2 and some of good 3 and none of the other goods. For the purchased goods 2 and 3, $p_2 = \pi_1 b_{12} + \pi_2 b_{22}$ and $p_3 = \pi_1 b_{13} + \pi_2 b_{23}$ from which π_1 and π_2 can be computed. In the absence of corner solutions, a single consumer will buy as many goods as there are characteristics and given that the b_{ji} are exactly observable, we can always compute the π_j by solving such a system of simultaneous equations. However, with the dotted indifference curve at C, only good 3 is purchased and the marginal rate of substitution at C, $(\partial v/\partial z_1)/(\partial v/\partial z_2)$, exceeds the shadow price ratio to the left of C, but is less than the shadow price ratio to the right of C.

The existence of corner solutions raises difficulties for econometric applications of the characteristics model to the study of demand for market goods at both the aggregate and the individual household level. Without corner solutions, we could compute the π_j's (which, for goods bought for themselves rather than their characteristics, are just the market prices), and with a specification of $v(z)$, estimate the implied demand functions for the z's conditional upon the observed choice of those market goods from which characteristics are assembled. However, the endogenity of this observed choice even then causes statistical problems. When there are corner solutions, which occur if fewer market goods are bought than there are characteristics, the resulting discrete choice problem ought, in principle, to be explicitly faced, which is by no means easy. In practice, we might well take the shadow costs from one of facets adjoining a corner, or some average of them, and proceed as for the case where there are no corner solutions. An alternative procedure would be to approximate the frontier AD by some nonlinear function and take the full structural approach of estimating (1.8) or (1.9).

The characteristics model has some interesting implications. One concerns price effects. Suppose that in Figure 10.2, good 3 becomes more expensive. The point C moves inward until eventually a combination of goods 2 and 5 becomes more efficient at which point purchases of good 3 drop to zero while those of good 5 become positive. This effect indicates that at the individual household level, the derived demand for individual market goods is likely to be rather unstable and, at certain points, very sensitive to small changes in relative prices. Similar sorts of effects can occur with nonhomothetic indifference maps as the budget expands: if initially the solution is at B, a continuous expansion of the budget will, as the shape of the indifference curve changes, sooner or later bring about a corner solution. At a microlevel, inferior goods can therefore be quite common, as indeed can Giffen goods, see Lipsey and Rosenbluth (1971). Suppose that in Figure 10.2 p_2 increases, pushing the point B in the direction of the origin. It is easy to draw indifference curves such that marginal reductions in the budget increase the ratio z_1/z_2, and this can easily cause purchases of good 2 to actually *increase* when p_2 rises.

One advantage of the characteristics model relative to the general nonlinear model is that the z's are comparatively easily measured; in fact, the specification of the production function (1.13) really defines how the z's are to be measured given that the b_{ji} can be observed. However, without modification, it is not very suitable as a theory of the allocation of labor time within the household. Suppose that characteristic j is protein. Protein is produced from combining various foods with cooking and shopping time, given the stocks of human capital and household durables. With one kind of labor, the linear model is

$$z_j = \sum_{i=1}^{n_1} b_{ji}q_i + b_{j0}\ell_0 \tag{1.15}$$

where n_1 is the number of foods. However, to simply extract protein from labor time in this way independently of what foods are bought is unreasonable. More reasonable, but more complicated, would be to make the b_{ji} functions of both the physical protein content of the various foods and of time taken in preparing food.

Exercises

10.1. Give a formal demonstration of Grossman's point about the demand for medical care and the shadow price of health capital.

10.2. Suppose that, instead of the linear characteristics model (1.13), we had multiplicative generation of the z's by $z_j = \Pi_i q_i^{\beta_{ji}}$ [see Gorman (1956, 1976)]. Show that for purchased goods, in the absence of corner solutions, $p_i q_i = \Sigma_j \gamma_j \beta_{ji}$ and interpret the γ_j's. Discuss the plausibility of the assumption that different households face the same γ's. Is this model any better or worse than the linear characteristics model in this respect?

10.3. The treatment of labor time in the linear characteristics model was criticized above. Suppose that

$$z_j = \sum_{i=1}^{n_1} b_{ji} q_i + \beta_{j0} \ell_{0j}$$

where ℓ_{0j} is the amount of total household production time ℓ_0 devoted to the production of the jth nonmarket good, $\Sigma_j \ell_{0j} = \ell_0$, and β_{j0} is a constant but unobservable parameter. Discuss the role of wages in governing the shape of the transformation frontier, the determination of the π's, and the choice of market goods.

10.4. Explain intuitively and/or formally why we should expect the budget constraint in Figure 10.1 to be convex to the origin. What assumptions are being made about the technology to produce the result? Are these restrictive?

10.5. Set up the cost-minimizing problem for the characteristics model as a linear program, and show how the solution can be used to produce the budget constraint in the generalization of Figure 10.2.

10.6. Suppose that one of the nonmarket goods is "child services," which reflects the number and "quality" of children, and that its production requires market goods and time, especially the wife's time. Discuss potential effects on fertility of increases in the female wage rate relative to the male – see Becker (1960) and the special issue on fertility of the *Journal of Political Economy* (1973), edited by T. W. Schultz.

10.7. Easterlin, Pollak, and Wachter (1979) have criticized what they regard as the excessive focus by the "Chicago-Columbia school" on monetary aspects of household technology, especially the opportunity cost of a wife's time. They believe that the approach neglects the importance of taste factors and the basic technology of fertility. Discuss the issues with particular relevance to the economics of fertility in underdeveloped countries.

10.8. Contrast the analysis of addiction in the household production framework with the assumption of endogenous tastes – see Stigler and Becker (1977), Chapter 13 or, Phlips (1974, Ch. 10), or Pollak (1978).

10.9. Construct a diagrammatic illustration of how Giffen goods can arise in the linear characteristics model.

10.10. Suppose the nonjoint production functions (1.12) have the Cobb-Douglas form with constant returns in q_j and ℓ_{0j}. Derive the shadow price functions $\pi_j = \pi_j(p, \omega)$.

10.11. Suppose the nonjoint production functions (1.12) with a single labor input have the form $z_j = \Sigma_i \beta_{ji} q_{ij} + \beta_{j0} \ell_{oj}$, where $\Sigma_j q_{ij} = q_i$ and $\Sigma_j \ell_{oj} = \ell_0$. Derive the shadow price functions and contrast this linear model of production with the linear characteristics model.

10.2 The relevance of household production theory to quality measurement

We shall discuss quality measurement in the context of the construction of a quality corrected price index. Given such an index, the corresponding "volume" index, which combines both quantity and quality, can be constructed by dividing an index of money values by the quality corrected price index.

In 1961, the Price Statistics Review Committee of the United States Congress reported: "If a poll were taken of professional economists and statisticians, in all probability they would designate (and by a wide majority) the failure of the price indexes to take full account of quality changes as the most important defect of these indexes." Since 1961, which also saw the publication of the influential article by Griliches (1961), there has been a great deal of research on the subject, primarily in the United States, and this is well reviewed in Triplett (1975). Contrary to common belief, Triplett shows that it is by no means the case that official price indices are automatically biased by procedures that take little explicit account of quality changes. Most such indices are based on frequent chain linking of indices based on highly disaggregated price information so that, to the extent that quality changes take place by one good replacing another, bias is avoided (see also Exercise 10.12).

Empirical work on quality corrected price indices is mostly based on a procedure referred to as the *hedonic technique* and this is usually justified in terms of household production theory. The view is taken that the quality of a good is related to measurable specification variables such as size and performance. Stone (1956), for example, uses alcoholic content as a way of comparing prices of different alcoholic beverages. The empirical applications typically regress prices or the logs of prices of the different varieties of a type of good on such specification variables. However, there are two main variants of the empirical forms that have been used: single year cross-section regression and pooled (over at least two years) time-series/cross-section regressions. The first variant is our main concern in this section, and we shall see in the next section that the second variant corresponds better to a rather different view of quality change.

The first variant claims to estimate the "shadow prices" of the "characteristics" of the goods in question for a given year. These shadow prices are then used to price some average bundle of characteristics in the two years that are being compared. If, say, the base year's bundle is used, an index that looks similar to a Laspeyres price index can be constructed. For example, the following regression is typical

$$p_{it} = \sum_j \pi_{jt} b_{jit} + \epsilon_{it} \tag{2.1}$$

where p_{it} is the price of the ith good at time t, b_{jit} is the level of the jth specification variable of the ith good at time t, π_{jt} is the shadow price of the jth specification variable, and ϵ_{it} is a disturbance term. For example, in studies of refrigerators by Burstein (1961) and Dhrymes (1971) the b_{ji}'s are variables such as total cubic capacity, capacity of the freezer section, and various zero–one variables measuring the presence of features such as egg shelves, automatic defrosting, and two doors. The quality-corrected Laspeyres price index, which is based on such estimates, is then given by

$$\sum_j \hat{\pi}_{jt} Z_{j0} / \sum_j \hat{\pi}_{j0} Z_{j0} \tag{2.2}$$

where the aggregate base period level of the jth specification variable is $Z_{j0} = \Sigma_i b_{ji0} Q_{i0}$, and Q_{i0} is the aggregate level of sales of good i in the base period.

We have purposely used the notation to make clear the parallels between (2.1) and (1.14) and between (2.2) and (1.5) and, indeed, the characteristics model of household production is the one that best seems to correspond to such an empirical procedure. However, let us begin with the general household production model and discuss in that context the theory of cost-of-living index numbers. As we saw in Chapter 7, a constant utility cost-of-living index compares the costs of reaching some reference indifference curve at two different price vectors. The household's full cost minimization problem has as its solution the cost function

$$x = c(u, p, \omega; k) \tag{2.3}$$

This is obtained from the first stage cost function $x = C(p, \omega, z; k)$ by replacing z by its Hicksian demand functions with arguments u, p, ω, and k. Since quality change in the household production framework is treated as a change in the household technology, both types of cost functions (2.3) and (1.1) need to be given a time subscript to indicate which technology they refer to.

Cost-of-living indices, which take account of changes in technology, can be defined in different ways, depending upon what informational requirements we wish to demand. With a knowledge of preferences and of the current and base technology, the constant utility index with the base indifference curve as reference is

$$c^t(u^0, p^t, \omega^t; k)/c^0(u^0, p^0, \omega^0; k) \tag{2.4}$$

where we assume the stocks of human capital and durable goods are held constant in the comparison. Knowledge of preferences is unlikely to be available, so it is therefore interesting to consider as an approximation to (2.4) an upper bound for it:

$$C^t(p^t, \omega^t, z^0; k)/C^0(p^0, \omega^0, z^0; k) \qquad (2.5)$$

The denominator in both (2.4) and (2.5) is x^0 while $C^t(p^t, \omega^t; z^0, k) \geq c^t(u^0, p^t, \omega^t, k)$, since with nonmarket goods at the levels z^0 the indifference curve labeled u^0 can certainly be reached, though given the new prices and technology z^0 will not, in general, be the cheapest combination of nonmarket goods that will do so. If we weaken the informational requirements further to local knowledge only, as conveyed by the shadow prices, of the current and base technology, we now ask, is the measure

$$\sum_j \pi_j^t z_j^0 / \sum_j \pi_j^0 z_j^0 \qquad (2.6)$$

a satisfactory approximation to (2.4) in the sense of having a known bounding relationship to it? Let us confine ourselves to constant returns technologies so that the total shadow cost adds up to the cost by (1.5). Then as Muellbauer (1974c) shows, there is still a difficulty in establishing the connection between (2.6) and (2.4). Consider Figure 10.3. The index (2.4) is x^*/x^0 as illustrated. It is defined by the relative positions of the transformation loci A^0B^0 and A^*B^*, the latter being given by the new technology and prices but tangential to the base indifference curve. Of those tangents shown in the diagram, that labeled π^0 is tangential to the base frontier at z^0; that labeled π^t is the tangent between the frontier A^*B^*, which corresponds to the new technology and prices, and the base indifference curve. Given constant returns,

$$x^0 = C^0(p^0, \omega^0, z^0; k) = \sum_j \pi_j^0 z_j^0 \qquad (2.7)$$

$$x^t = C^t(p^t, \omega^t, z^t; k) = \sum_j \pi_j^t z_j^t \qquad (2.8)$$

and

$$x^* = C^t(p^t, \omega^t, z^*; k) = \sum_j \pi_j^* z_j^* \qquad (2.9)$$

The index (2.4) is

$$x^*/x^0 = \Sigma\pi_j^* z_j^*/\Sigma\pi_j^0 z_j^0 \leq \Sigma\pi_j^* z_j^0/\Sigma\pi_j^0 z_j^0 \qquad (2.10)$$

since z^0 yields utility u^0, although z^* is the cheapest way of reaching u^0 at shadow prices π^*. But the final term in (2.10) is still not the observable index (2.6) since π^* and π^t may differ.

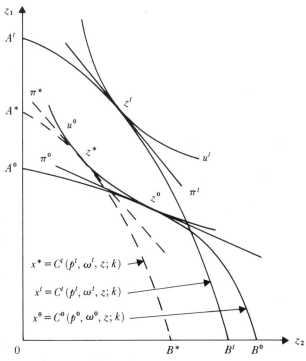

Figure 10.3. Bias in the Laspeyres index based on shadow prices.

There are two circumstances in which, under constant returns to scale, the problem does not exist and $\pi^* = \pi^t$. The first is the nonjoint technology discussed in the previous section that has a cost function (1.11) such that shadow prices are independent of z. The second occurs when preferences are homothetic. Given a homogeneous technology and homothetic preferences, the expansion path is a ray through the origin and the tangents at z^0 and at z^t must have identical slopes. Under constant returns to scale, it also follows that the shadow prices π^* at z^0 with the frontier A^*B^* will be the same as the shadow prices π^t at z^t with the frontier A^tB^t. However, we also need to assume either that the stocks k are the same in the two periods or that they do not enter the shadow prices.

The motivation for this analysis is two-fold. First, it has been argued that hedonic regressions compute the local values of shadow prices in a general model of household production without the need to identify the whole technology. Second, in the linear characteristics model, which can be more directly related to the hedonic technique, the relationship (1.14) is a local one:

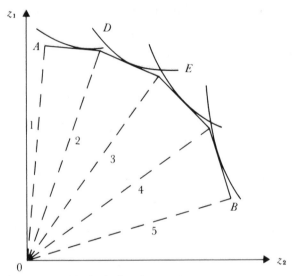

Figure 10.4. The hedonic price schedule for consumers with different tastes.

it picks out the facet on which the consumer is located and gives no information on the rest of the frontier. The implication of homothetic preferences in this case is obvious: it guarantees that the facet on which z^t is purchased is parallel to the facet on which z^* is purchased. If they are not, then local information is not enough and we need to know more of the frontier in order to compare the costs.

We must now acknowledge the fact that the data on which hedonic regressions are computed – lists of prices and associated specifications – are generated in a market situation where there are many consumers with different budgets and tastes. Let us suppose that the linear characteristics model is valid and that we have the situation illustrated in Figure 10.4. With four households with differently shaped indifference curves, some of all five goods are bought. Note too that if all households have identical but nonhomothetic preferences, variations in budget levels have the same effect. If then we are adventurous and fit a fairly general, not necessarily linear relationship between the prices p_i and the specification variables b_{ji}, for the most part, the results we obtain will reflect not just the evaluation by different households of different specifications but also the technology of firms in producing them and, in imperfect competition, the pricing strategies of firms. Note that which market goods are produced, in what quantities and at what prices, is a complicated general equilibrium problem that requires an analysis of the interactions between firms and households and is not answered by taking a "snap-shot" of AB at some particular time.

For the estimated schedules AB in the base and the current periods to be used in the construction of quality-corrected, cost-of-living indices, the aggregation problem needs to be faced explicitly. In general, different segments of the market will have moved differently between the two periods. In Chapter 7, Exercises 7.4 and 7.5, we noted that the usual official (Laspeyres) indices $P_L = \Sigma_i p_i^t \Sigma_h q_{ih}^0 / \Sigma_i p_i^0 \Sigma_h q_{ih}^0$ are weighted averages of the individual household indices $P_h = \Sigma_i p_i^t q_{ih}^0 / \Sigma_i p_i^0 q_{ih}^0$ of the form $P_L = \Sigma_h x_h P_h / \Sigma_h x_h$, that is, weighting by the relative purchasing power of each household. "Undemocratic" though this may be, to be consistent with this methodology, the non-linear schedules AB should, in principle, be matched up with data on the distribution of household budgets to determine the relative aggregate purchasing power of households in different segments of AB. Needless to say, this is not a widespread empirical practice! However, as a first approximation, we might weight the observations in (2.1) by some increasing function of sales of the good in question, and this kind of weighted regression has in fact sometimes been used.

The question arises: under what circumstances does this aggregation problem not exist? If all households have identical, homothetic preferences, then firms are forced to price the market goods according to the common facet. For example, if all households have indifference curves of the same shape as DE in Figure 10.4, then the relative prices of the different goods will be forced to adjust so that the vertices lie along a straight line. In this case, many different combinations of market goods yield the same combination of characteristics, so every household faces the same shadow prices and linear regression is the appropriate hedonic technique.

Since these conditions are unlikely to be fulfilled, in general, we will frequently observe market segmentation in the sense that different products with different shadow prices for characteristics will be produced for different types of consumers. In such circumstances, it will clearly be more appropriate to fit some nonlinear or piecewise linear function AB according to some plausible segmentation of goods into groups. If there are increasing returns to scale in production, for example, because of fixed set-up costs, then as Schmalensee (1978) has suggested, imperfect competition is likely to be the outcome because in each segment there is room for only a few producers, and the combination of quantities and qualities produced is unlikely to be a Pareto efficient one. However, that is not our main concern here.

Finally, it should be noted that for many goods such as large durables to which these techniques are most often applied, purchases are confined to integers, most often 0 or 1. Although we can impose the additional restriction of integer purchases on the linear characteristics model, it wipes out most of the relevance of the linear facets – the existence of which requires the possibility of combining various quantities of the different market goods. This is one reason for investigating an alternative, simpler approach in the next section.

Exercises

10.12. In the construction of official price indices in most countries, new goods are chained in as they appear and disappear. For example, for the introduction of color television sets, the T.V. set inflation rate from one year to the next is measured by some average of price relatives, perhaps by size of set, and weighted by relative sales in each size group. In the first year color sets come on sale, the T.V. set inflation rate includes the color T.V. price relative weighted by sales, and the overall inflation rate is chained to those of previous years to get the index. As ownership of color sets spreads and the price drops because of scale economies, technical change, and competition, their weight in the index grows. Have you any criticisms of this procedure? Discuss how the hedonic approach might be used to do things differently.

10.13. Given the nonjoint Cobb-Douglas technology of Exercise 10.10, discuss how technological differences between households and technical change over time affect the shadow prices (and the cost function). What kind of data and empirical procedures would you need to apply this model to estimating quality-corrected price indices for the market goods?

10.14. In the light of hedonic studies for one particular kind of good, evaluate the extent of quality bias in the corresponding official indices. What are the chief difficulties in such a comparison? [See Triplett (1975).]

10.15. Suppose the cross-section regression $\log p_{it} = \Sigma_j \alpha_{jt} \log b_{jit} + \epsilon_{it}$ is run separately for each of a number of years. Discuss how a Laspeyres-type index analogous to (2.2) could be constructed. Are there any a priori grounds for preferring either the logarithmic or the linear regression?

10.3 An alternative view of quality

Rather than specify household production functions and rationalize a role for specification variables through them, we are going to look at an alternative. One that has many advantages for the analysis of different varieties of a good is to introduce quality parameters, and through them, specification variables, directly into the utility function. As we shall see, such an approach can be used to justify the second variant of the hedonic technique – which cannot be easily interpreted in terms of household production theory. Here pooled time-series/cross-section regressions are run, usually of the log prices on specification variables that control for quality while time-dummy variables pick up differences in the general price level for the varieties in question.

The simple repackaging model for a single good

To give the background, let us return to a question posed and answered by Fisher and Shell (1971). Assume quality change occurs in one good only, say in good 1. Higher quality gives higher utility, and this suggests introducing a quality parameter θ directly into the utility function:

$$u = v(q_1, q_2, \ldots, q_n, \theta) \qquad (3.1)$$

where θ is supposed to depend upon the observed specifications of the good. Fisher and Shell propose to adjust p_1 in such a way that the constant utility cost-of-living index correctly takes quality change into account. They ask variants of the question: under what conditions is the adjustment in p_1 "simple," for example, independent of the amounts of the q's consumed. Corresponding to (3.1) is a cost function

$$x = \bar{c}(u, p_1, p_2, \ldots, p_n, \theta) \qquad (3.2)$$

Suppose θ is initially 1, then we can always define a quality corrected p_1^* so that

$$\bar{c}(u, p_1^*, p_2, \ldots, p_n, 1) \equiv \bar{c}(u, p_1, p_2, \ldots, p_n, \theta) \qquad (3.3)$$

Suppose we require that the quality correction to p_1^* for a small change in θ, $\partial p_1^*/\partial\theta$, be independent of all q and u. This turns out to require that

$$\bar{c}(u, p_1, p_2, \ldots, p_n, \theta) = c(u, p_1/h(\theta), p_2, \ldots, p_n) \qquad (3.4)$$

Since $h(\theta)$ serves just as well as an index of quality as does θ, with no loss of generality we can change the notation writing θ for $h(\theta)$ and

$$x = c(u, p_1/\theta, p_2, \ldots, p_n) \qquad (3.5)$$

This implies demand functions $q_1 = (1/\theta)g_1(x, p_1/\theta, p_2, \ldots, p_k)$ and $q_i = g_i(x, p_1/\theta, p_2, \ldots, p_n)$ for $i \neq 1$ and corresponds to the utility function

$$u = v(q_1\theta, q_2, \ldots, q_n) \qquad (3.6)$$

In fact, (3.5) and (3.6) have a striking similarity with the multiplicative model of equivalence scales proposed by Barten (1964), $u = v(q_1/m_1, q_2/m_2, \ldots, q_n/m_n)$ and $x = c(u, p_1m_1, p_2m_2, \ldots, p_nm_n)$, and discussed in Chapter 8. Fisher and Shell call (3.6) the "simple repackaging" specification of quality change. Just as in Chapter 8, we see that the trick is to write preference parameters in such a way that they have a ready price or cost equivalent interpretation. Here, a quality improvement is exactly equivalent to getting a larger package of the old good at the same price or having to pay less per unit of the old good. This idea has, in fact, considerable previous history. Prais and Houthakker (1955) drawing on Theil (1952–3) suggest that purchases of a good can be thought of as the product of quantity (in kilos say) and quality (measured in price per kilo relative to some standard variety).

The simple repackaging model: the case of varieties

The case of a single good is a highly simplified one, and the simple repackaging model can be extended to the more realistic case where there are avail-

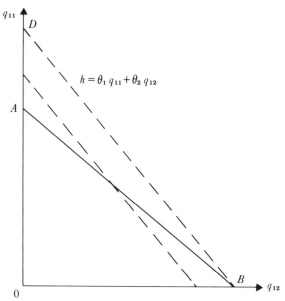

Figure 10.5. Perfect substitutes.

able a number of varieties of the same kind of good from which the household chooses one. To ensure this result, assume that there are linear indifference curves between the different varieties (i.e., that they are perfect substitutes), but that there is less than perfect substitution between them and other goods:

$$u = v\left(h\left(\sum_{i=1}^{r} \theta_i q_{1i}\right), q_2, \ldots, q_n\right) \tag{3.7}$$

Figure 10.5 illustrates two indifference curves giving combinations of the two varieties that will yield the same level of subutility h from good 1. The budget constraint for fixed expenditure on good 1 is AB and the highest indifference curve that can be reached is DB, which involves buying variety 2 and none of variety 1. The simple repackaging model, however, does not explain why richer households systematically tend to buy different qualities than do poorer ones. But there is an important generalization of the model to nonhomothetic repackaging that can explain this. Suppose that in (3.7) we write $h = \Sigma \theta_i(u) q_{it}$, which corresponds to replacing θ by $\theta(u)$ in (3.5). Under this specification, the linear indifference curves between varieties change slope as households become better off, and this explains the different choices made by rich and poor, as well as rationalizing the "quality elasticities" estimated by Prais and Houthakker (1955). In practice, we would expect household composition variables as well as the utility level to enter θ.

Returning to the somewhat unrealistic case where all households' indifference curves have the same slope, it is clear that it is impossible for both varieties to be bought if the ratio p_{12}/p_{11} differs from θ_2/θ_1. If the ratios are identical, utility theory cannot tell us how individuals choose the combination of varieties, but it is not unreasonable to assume that in this case, some of both varieties are bought, at least in aggregate. Thus, in a cross section of varieties for which all households have the same $h = \Sigma\theta_i q_{1i}$ functions, the relative values of the quality indices for purchased goods must equal their relative prices. When there are many varieties, there is a multiplicative relationship of the form $p_{1it} = \theta_i p_{1t}$, where p_{1t} is the price of some reference variety that can serve as a measure of the general price level for all the varieties of good 1. With the extra assumption that the quality index θ_i is a function of the specification variables b_{ji}, we find

$$\log p_{1it} = \log p_{1t} + f(b_{1i}, b_{2i}, \ldots, b_{ki}) \tag{3.8}$$

Adding a disturbance term and with the frequently adopted assumption that $f(\ )$ is loglinear in the specification variables, we obtain an equation that exactly corresponds to the second variant of the hedonic technique as defined earlier. In a pooled time-series/cross section, the $\log p_{1t}$ terms are measured as the coefficients on zero–one time-dummy variables, one for each year except the reference year. These coefficients then pick up price changes relative to the reference year.

This technique is subject to the same market segmentation qualifications discussed in the previous section and so is unlikely to work well if applied to all the varieties of a good purchased by the entire cross section of households. Using an idea originally proposed by Cagan (1966) and developed by Hall (1971), the model can be extended to used durables for which age effects, measuring relative depreciation, are included in addition to the specification and time effects. To give an illustration of the technique in practice, Table 10.1 shows the results of such a hedonic regression fitted to British price data for the late 1950's and the 1960's on 150 models of used cars (aged between one and three years) produced by nine main manufacturers. The implied quality corrected price index for cars is some 8 percent lower in 1969 than in 1958.

To take an example from the table, a coefficient of 0.370 on brake horsepower means that, other things being equal, we would expect a 1 percent increase in brake horsepower to increase the price by 0.37 percent. The standard error is 0.023 percent. The range of 101.7 to 106.0 for the presence of power brakes is a 95 percent confidence interval and indicates that we can be confident that cars with this feature do command higher prices, other things being equal. Some of the problems that tend to arise with the hedonic technique are illustrated by the negative coefficients on interior size and miles

Table 10.1. *A hedonic regression for the British used car market*

		Manufacturer effects		
		---	---	---
Specification elasticities		Quality percentages		Age
Brake horse power	0.370			
	(0.023)	BMC	100	0.131
Length	0.415			
	(0.068)	Ford	87.3–92.9	0.125
Miles per gallon	−0.064			
	(0.041)	Vauxhall	93.4–100.9	0.157
Width	0.264			
	(0.082)	Rootes	99.6–106.5	0.136
Interior size	−0.146	Standard		
	(0.094)	Triumph	102.2–109.7	0.137
		Volkswagen	103.8–113.9	0.119
Dummy coefficients (%)		Humber	117.3–127.4	0.177
Extra gear	101.8–107.0%	Rover	155.3–169.6	0.145
Luxury trim	85.6–91.2	Jaguar	135.3–147.7	0.189
Power brakes	101.7–106.0			

per gallon and the price reduction suggested by the presence of luxury trim. What may be happening is that with length and width present, a high interior size may be indicating restricted luggage space given design constraints. The problem here is that crude size variables are positively associated with price, and yet households may attach a positive value to small size and maneuverability. This is so particularly for weight, which has been used in a number of the American studies: a manufacturer who by clever design or the use of more expensive material holds weight down is given no credit by the estimated cross-section equation even though the price of a particular model may reflect the market's positive evaluation of the design. We should not thus be surprised if the coefficient on weight were rather sensitive to which other size related variables are included in the regression. Similarly, luxury trim is present mostly in cars produced by Humber, Rover, and Jaguar, who command substantial price premiums once the specification effects have been taken into account. The negative effect of luxury trim may then reflect a negative market valuation of luxury trim when (rarely) present in the models produced by the other manufacturers. Finally, the age effects give the proportionate annual fall in price of two- and three-year-old cars relative to one-year-old cars. These have standard errors mostly between 0.01 and 0.03, which suggests significant differences between some manufacturers.

The point made about market segmentation is supported by the results of comparing the goodness of fit when separate regressions are run for different manufacturers with that of the pooled regression reported. The appropriate F-statistic is 9 while the critical value is 1.2 at the 5 percent level. This means that we can reject the hypothesis of a homogeneous relationship over the whole range of models.

A competitive equilibrium theory of hedonic price functions

As we have seen, the strong assumption that all households have identical marginal rates of substitution between the specification variables is needed if a hedonic price function is to reflect only household preferences. In the context of this section's model, to ensure that different varieties are then actually produced, there must be variations between firms in the costs of producing goods with a given set of specifications. Conversely, if marginal rates of substitution differ over households but all firms have the same marginal rates of transformation between specifications and operate under competitive conditions, the hedonic price function will reflect only the marginal rates of transformation. In between these extreme cases, we would expect the hedonic price function in market equilibrium to reflect both the distribution of marginal rates of substitution over households and the distribution of marginal rates of transformation over firms. This is the point made in an excellent paper by Rosen (1974b), and we shall adapt his analysis using duality methods for the repackaging model for varieties.

The cost function for the utility function (3.7), where $h = \Sigma \theta_i q_{1i}$ and $\theta_i = \theta(b_i)$, takes the form (3.5)

$$c(u, p_1^*, p_2, \ldots, p_n) = x \qquad (3.9)$$

where $p_1^* = \min(p_{1i}/\theta_i)$. Now suppose that because of diminishing returns for firms, many varieties are produced and there is therefore a continuum in specification space over which households can choose. This greatly eases the mathematics of the analysis. The choice of the optimal combination of specifications by the household is made by minimizing p/θ. The household has to take the market equilibrium hedonic price function $p_1(b)$ as given and minimizing $p_1(b)/\theta(b)$ with respect to b implies marginal conditions

$$\partial \log p_1(b)/\partial b_j = \partial \log \theta(b)/\partial b_j \qquad (3.10)$$

These are illustrated in Figure 10.6, where the partial variation of the log hedonic price function and of the log quality index with the jth specification variable are shown. Since $\theta(b)$ varies over households with differences in household composition and, in the case of nonhomothetic repackaging, with the utility level, there is a whole family of log $\theta(b)$ curves all tangential to the log hedonic price schedule log $p_1(b)$. In fact, log $\theta(b)$ can be interpreted as the maximum the household is prepared to pay for one unit of the variety with

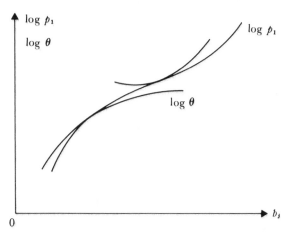

Figure 10.6. The envelope property of the hedonic price schedule.

specification b and such curves can be defined for more general cases than re-packaging. As Rosen (1974b) shows, analogous reservation supply prices for firms are defined and one is illustrated in Figure 10.6 above the hedonic price schedule.

With microdata for firms and households on varieties produced and consumed by each and shift variables such as income and household composition and factor prices for firms, the structural relations that underlie the hedonic price schedule can be identified. For households, the obvious way of modeling the choice of varieties is to estimate the market hedonic price schedule and then use (3.10) to give the variety choice subject to it.

For example, if we take the following simple structures

$$\log \theta(b) = \sum_j \left(\sum_s \beta_{js} a_s \right) \log b_j \qquad (3.11)$$

$$\log p_1(b) = \sum_j \alpha_j b_j \qquad (3.12)$$

where a_s is the sth household variable – for example, composition and income. Then (3.10) implies

$$b_j \alpha_j = \sum_s \beta_{js} a_s \qquad (3.13)$$

which defines a household demand function for the jth specification variable b_j. With appropriate error terms, both stages of the estimating procedure can then be carried out by linear regression methods.

One area where such models are particularly relevant is the demand for housing. Among the specifications will be such variables as distance from the

ity center and rapid transport, measures of house size, density, and so forth, although one complication here is that some of the variables will be of a zero–one type (a garage is present or it is not), and this calls for special statistical techniques, as we shall see. There are a number of empirical studies of cross-section housing demand that can be rationalized at least loosely along these lines – see, for example, the survey by Ball (1973) and also King (1976), Ball and Kirwan (1977), and Quigley (1976).

Discrete choice among varieties

Although the assumption of continuity in specifications space permits rather elegant results to be derived, it is often unrealistic, particularly when nonconvexities on the production side restrict the number of varieties produced. One classic example is the choice of transport mode, to the analysis of which the utility function (3.7) is extremely well suited. When households choose between two discrete alternatives, the relevant measure of demand to be empirically explained is the *probability* of choosing one or the other. The reason for this can be easily understood when it is remembered that in a continuous econometric demand function it is the *expected value* of the quantity purchased that is explained, the difference between the observed value and the expected value being the unobserved stochastic error term. Thus, if we write 1 when a particular variety (e.g., traveling to work by bus) is chosen and 0 otherwise, the expected value of the variable is analogously P, the probability of choosing that variety.

While the probability distribution of the unobserved stochastic error term is usually little emphasized in studies of continuous demand, in discrete choice, the unobserved stochastic elements are rather important for selecting the functional form for the probability function to be estimated. To show why, consider the choice between two varieties with utility function (3.7) with the function h given by

$$h = \theta_1(b_1, a, \epsilon_1)q_{11} + \theta_2(b_2, a, \epsilon_2)q_{12} \tag{3.14}$$

where a is the vector of household composition and budget variables and ϵ_1 and ϵ_2 are unobserved elements in either the household characteristics or the specifications of the two varieties or both. As we have seen, variety 1 is chosen if $\theta_1/p_{11} > \theta_2/p_{12}$ and variety 2 is chosen if the reverse inequality holds. Thus variety 1 is chosen if $\log \theta_1 - \log \theta_2 > \log p_{11} - \log p_{12}$. Now suppose that we can write $\log \theta_i = \log \theta^0(b_i, a) + \epsilon_i$. Hence, variety 1 is chosen if

$$\epsilon_1 - \epsilon_2 > [\log \theta^0(b_2, a) - \log p_{12}] - [\log \theta^0(b_1, a) - \log p_{11}]$$
$$= v_2 - v_1 \tag{3.15}$$

Thus, if P is the probability of choosing variety 1, $P = 1 - F(v_2 - v_1)$, where $F(\ )$ is the frequency distribution of $\epsilon_1 - \epsilon_2$, that is $F(v_2 - v_1) = P(\epsilon_1 - \epsilon_2 < v_2 - v_1)$.

As well as choosing a reasonable but convenient form for $\theta^0(\ )$, we must do the same for $F(\ )$. As Domencich and McFadden (1975) show in their excellent book on discrete choice in urban travel demand, there are many good reasons for assuming that ϵ_i follows the Weibull or extreme value distribution. Among them is the fact that the distribution is quite flexible and can, for example, approximate a normal distribution very closely, the fact that P is a logit and easy to fit (much easier than the normal distribution), and finally, that when there are n varieties instead of 2 the generalization to the multinomial logit follows immediately and is also easy to fit.

A random variable ϵ_i follows the Weibull distribution if

$$F(v) = P(\epsilon_i < v) = e^{-e^{-(v+\alpha)}} \tag{3.16}$$

where α is a parameter that governs the location of the distribution. As Domencich and McFadden show, if both ϵ_1 and ϵ_2 have the Weibull distribution with parameters α_1 and α_2,

$$P(\epsilon_1 - \epsilon_2 > v_2 - v_1) = \frac{e^{v_1 - \alpha_1}}{e^{v_1 - \alpha_1} + e^{v_2 - \alpha_2}} = \frac{1}{1 + e^{(v_2 - \alpha_2) - (v_1 - \alpha_1)}} \tag{3.17}$$

which is the logistic function with argument $v_2 - v_1$. The probability of choosing variety 1 out of n available varieties is analogously multinomial logit:

$$P* = \frac{e^{v_1 - \alpha_1}}{\sum_{i=1}^{n} e^{v_i - \alpha_i}} \tag{3.18}$$

To apply (3.17), suppose we observe a sample of $I_1 + I_2$ households, where the first I_1 choose variety 1 and the rest variety 2. Then the joint probability or likelihood of observing the sample is

$$\mathcal{L} = \prod_{h=1}^{I_1} P_h \prod_{h=I_1+1}^{I_1+I_2} (1 - P_h) \tag{3.19}$$

where P_h is the probability of household h choosing variety 1 and is given by (3.17) after substitution for $v_1 - v_2$. Expression (3.19) is maximized with respect to the parameters α_1, α_2, and those in $\theta^0(\ )$. For applications of this and further discussion of the logical foundations of discrete choice, see Domencich and McFadden (1975) and Quandt (1970).

One of the virtues of the utility function (3.7) is that besides serving as a vehicle for modeling the probabilities of discrete choice, it also determines *how much* of the variety is purchased, given that a choice of quantity is possible. For example, in noncommuting travel, the frequency of use as well as the type of mode may be open to choice. In this case, consider the implications of (3.7) for the variety demand functions when prices of varieties change. For two varieties, the demand curve for variety 1 is discontinuous at $p_{11} = p_{12}\theta_1/\theta_2$. However, the variations in ϵ_1 and ϵ_2 across households mean that in terms of Figure 10.5, the line BD has a different slope for different households so that aggregate demand for variety 1, unlike individual demand, will be a smooth continuous function of prices as new households switch from one to the other variety. A specific example of the demand function for a variety in these circumstances is given in Exercise 10.22 below.

Exercises

10.16. Given simple repackaging quality change, when does an increase in the quality of a good reduce and when does it increase the number of units bought of that good? Show how it depends upon the own-price elasticity and illustrate using the linear expenditure system.

10.17. Show in the context of (3.3) that if the quality correction $\partial p_1^*/\partial b$ is to be independent of $u, p_3, p_4, \ldots, p_n$ but can depend upon p_2, then the cost function must take the form

$$c(u, \theta(p_2, b)p_1, p_2, \ldots, p_n)$$

Discuss the consequences this has for the effect of quality change in the first good as the demand for the other goods – see Muellbauer (1975b, p. 281). How might you interpret the model if p_2 is the wage rate?

10.18. What would you regard as the main factors altering the shape of the hedonic price schedule from year to year? Discuss the pros and cons of adjacent year pooling of regressions such as (3.8) and chaining the year to year changes versus pooling data for many years in a single regression.

10.19. Suppose you regress b_j on a vector of household composition and budget variables according to (3.13). Discuss the economic interpretation of the "reduced form" parameter β_{js}/α_j as opposed to the "structural form" parameter β_{js} as an appropriate measure of the effect of variations in a_s on b_j. What are the implications for the interpretation of the (majority of) studies that have used the reduced form?

10.20. How might you generalize the structural hedonic relations (3.11) and (3.12)? Discuss the estimating procedure for your model.

10.21. Under what circumstances do the linear characteristics model of §10.2 and the simple repackaging model coincide? [See Muellbauer (1974c, p. 990).]

10.22. In Exercise 6.18, we have $h = q_{11} + \theta q_{12}$ in current notation and θ has a distribution across households with density $\beta\theta^{\alpha-1}$. Find $E(q_{11})$ and $E(q_{12})$ for a single household when the underlying utility function for all goods has the form $\log u = \gamma_1 \log(q_{11} + \theta q_{12} - \delta_1) + \Sigma_2^n \gamma_i \log(q_i - \delta_i)$, which generates the linear expenditure system. Hence, find $E(p_{11}q_{11} + p_{12}q_{12})$. Suppose p_{11} and p_{12} always move in the same proportion and the distribution of θ is constant. Discuss the consequences for demand studies of regarding total expenditure over all varieties of good 1 deflated by some variety price index as the appropriate quantity variable.

10.23.* (Exercise 10.22 cont.) Holding the mean of the distribution of θ constant, discuss how changes in the dispersion of the distribution affect the own-price effect and the cross-price effect from variety 2 on mean demand for variety 1. Can you draw any general conclusions for the relationship between the "closeness" between varieties and the degree of substitution between them?

10.24. In the context of (3.17), suppose that mode 1 is traveling by car while mode 2 is using red buses. If a third mode, traveling by blue bus, which otherwise has the same characteristics as traveling by red bus is introduced, show that the probability of traveling by car falls. What happens if red and blue buses are treated as the same mode? Contrast the cases where the frequency of service (one of the mode specification variables) alters and does not alter as a result of introducing blue buses.

10.24. In the utility function $u = v(z_1, q_2, \ldots, q_n)$, suppose z_1 is "produced" by $z_1 = \Sigma \theta_i q_{1i}$, where θ_i depends on variety i's specifications. Discuss the usefulness of the shadow price π_1 as defined in §10.1. Suppose we generalize the production function to $z_1 = \Sigma \theta_i \min(q_{1i}, \beta_i \ell_{0i})$, where ℓ_{0i} is the household time input. Discuss the applicability of this model to transport mode and house location choice when different households face different wage rates.

10.4 Other aspects of quality

Many of the most interesting aspects of the notion of quality of goods in economics fall outside the coverage of this book. One of these is the supply of quality; rather than taking an exogenously given list of goods and asking how much of each is produced, we inquire *which* goods are produced. Until quite recently, the supply of quality was a relatively neglected question, although closely related topics have long been studied in spatial economics and the theory of monopolistic competition. In quality space, competition is likely to be localized: small changes in price or quality affect the demand only of goods that are qualitatively similar. Quality space can be defined in terms of the characteristics in §10.2 or in terms of the specification variables in §10.3. Given scale economies over at least some initial production range, firms will then be oligopolists and a variety of questions that have been studied in oligopoly theory arise. Will there be a collusive solution with an entry preventing strategy? What governs the entry barriers? Does advertising constitute a barrier to entry? How suboptimal is the unregulated solution? What form could regulation take? The reader is referred to Spence (1975, 1976), Sheshinski (1976), Dixit (1979), and Schmalensee (1978) for discussion and further references.

Another major issue in the analysis of quality is information. Again, the major interest has been in the implications for the performance of markets. Much work has followed the line suggested by Akerlof's (1970) study of the market for "lemons" – used cars that the sellers know to be of low quality but the buyer does not. The point made by Akerlof is something as follows: the potential seller of a used car has alternative uses for it and will only sell if the used car price matches or exceeds the worth of the alternative uses. The seller knows accurately the quality of his car but potential buyers do not: they are informed only about the average quality of cars on the used car market and will only offer a single price that reflects this average. But, at this price, some of the potential sellers of high quality cars stay out of the market. Suppose that initially the price is too high for the average quality sold. As buyers realize this, the price drops and more potential sellers of above-average quality cars drop out. This drives the price down further, and it is theoretically possible that it could be driven to a point at which no trade takes place. This is an extreme possibility – Gresham's Law of "bad money" driving out "good money" – and the assumption of complete buyer ignorance is obviously too extreme; for example, it may be possible to have tests carried out at a cost, or the seller may offer a guarantee or have a reputation to protect. But the general point is that the informational asymmetry results in an externality that causes some degree of market failure. In the simple case just discussed, the marginal seller in equilibrium sells a car of above-average quality: this must be so to balance the sales by nonmarginal sellers of below-average quality cars. The opportunity cost to him is higher than the marginal benefit to the buyer, and if the informational asymmetries were removed, traders on both sides of the market could be made better off.

This raises the question of imposing licensing standards from outside or, indeed, of the sellers getting together to set up their own licensing standard to guarantee a minimum quality level – see Leland (1979). If buyers are not completely ignorant, models of how they learn, search, and are influenced by advertising are required – see Grossman and Stiglitz (1976) and Kotowitz and Matthewson (1979). One possibility is that they may judge quality by price – see Scitovsky (1945), Alcaly and Klevorick (1970), and Pollak (1977). This has consequences that are fairly simple to handle with the approach in §10.3. For example, b in (3.11) and (3.12) can be replaced by $b_0^{1-\gamma}(\hat{p}_{12}/\hat{p}_{11})^\gamma$ with $0 < \gamma < 1$, where $\hat{p}_{12}/\hat{p}_{11}$ is the normal price ratio of the two varieties and b_0 has some distribution over households. The closer γ is to 1, the more households' quality perceptions are dominated by the normal price ratio. Given that normal prices are weighted averages of past prices, this introduces price lags into the variety demand functions and creates a distinction between short- and long-run price responses. Perhaps even more interesting would be to analyze the implications of judging quality by price for market equilibrium in an oligopolistic industry.

Bibliographical notes

Much of the literature has already been referenced in the text. Among the antecedents of household production theory is Leontief's (1947) article on weak separability. He interprets the subutility levels of the commodity groups similarly to the z's in $u = v(z)$, but note that weak separability means that each z_j is produced from nonoverlapping groups of market goods. Related but not fully formalized approaches can be found in the spatial economics and housing literature – e.g., Alonso (1964), where urban rent gradients use analogous shadow-price notions and where time costs are an important consideration – and in the transport mode choice, for example, the mode attribute model of Quandt and Baumol (1966). The literature on the demand for recreation, see Clawson (1959), has also emphasized the cost of travel time as a major determinant of the underlying price of recreation.

The hedonic regression idea appears to have been used first by General Motors economist Court (1939). Other studies for cars not mentioned in the text are Ohta and Griliches (1976) for second-hand American cars, Cowling and Cubbin (1971, 1972) and Cubbin (1975) for new British cars. Gordon (1971) surveys analogous studies for producer durables. The notion of a hedonic price shcedule as a market phenomenon appears fairly explicitly in Houthakker (1952). Implications of the linear characteristics model for quality measurement are also discussed in R. E. B. Lucas (1975), Triplett (1976), and Klevmarken (1977). Ohta (1975) interprets hedonic price functions in a specific context as reflecting the technology and pricing practices of producers. The simple repackaging model originates with Fisher and Shell (1971); Muellbauer (1975a), using duality methods, simplifies, proves, and extends their results. Further extensions are in Davies (1974).

There are two other sets of literature to which we have not referred. One is in psychology where there is a literature on scaling and measurement that is related to utility theory and the introduction of attributes of goods. This and the closely related marketing literature, where product attributes, socioeconomic, and attitudinal variables are widely used to explain very specific microeconomic phenomenon, are surveyed in Hansen (1972) and Woodside, Sheth, and Bennett (1977) and with particular emphasis on stochastic aspects of buying behavior by Massy, Montgomery, and Morrison (1970). Some of these phenomena such as repeat buying behavior for specific brands should, one would have thought, be quite interesting to economists. Conversely, there has been some interest in the marketing literature in the linear characteristics model, but though market segmentation is widely applied, in practice, the economic literature on household production, quality, and location has so far not penetrated very widely. Perhaps part of the reason is the propensity in the marketing literature to think of consumers as malleable and to search for the points at which pressure can be applied. This is more alien to economists who think of consumers as basically rational and incline towards an exogenous view of preferences. Still, there is certainly scope for more trade in ideas between the economics of quality and taste change and the marketing literature.

CHAPTER 11

Labor supply

No part of economics is more contentious and more interconnected with the rest of the subject than is labor economics. We shall here attempt to separate the analysis of labor supply from labor economics as a whole, but it is inevitable that, to some extent, we shall be drawn into wider issues. One aspect of the contentiousness of the subject is the range of different approaches to it, from the institutionalists, on the one hand, to those who apply a narrow version of the neoclassical paradigm, on the other. Our approach is analytical, but we think not narrow and, as throughout the book, our aim is to formulate models relevant for good empirical work.

The chapter is divided into three sections. The first extends Chapter 4's discussion of the basic neoclassical model of labor supply to deal with the case where the individual chooses not to work at all. The choice between working and not working is referred to as the *participation decision,* and in §11.1, we show how it can be analyzed in terms of the divergence between the actual and an appropriately defined "shadow" wage rate. We also discuss the implications of this theoretical analysis for econometric studies of participation rates and of the labor supply of those who do work. Section 11.2 considers the effects of abandoning the linear budget constraint of the neoclassical model and takes a more realistic view of the constraints faced by households. This section deals with nonlinearities caused by complex tax and social security systems, with constraints on hours worked imposed by employers, and most importantly of all, with unemployment regarded as a constraint on hours. Section 11.3, which concludes the chapter, is devoted to labor supply in the long run, particularly as concerns the choice of education, training, and occupation. We discuss critically the human capital approach, its links to the theory of household production in Chapter 10, and its role in providing an economic theory of the distribution of earnings. The section concludes with a discussion of the role of education as a "screen" for ability.

11.1 The participation decision

The simple neoclassical model of labor supply discussed in §4.1 is limited, by its simplistic assumptions, to workers who are free to vary the hours they

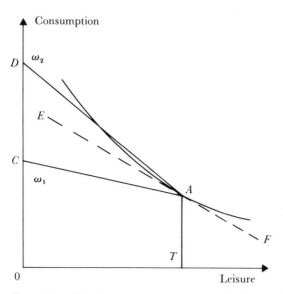

Figure 11.1. The minimum wage necessary to induce participation.

work. An important group for whom this may be a fair approximation consists of secondary workers in the household, particularly married women. However, many potential second workers choose not to work, a case we ruled out by assumption in the earlier discussion. In Figure 11.1, budget constraints corresponding to two wage rates, ω_1 (CAT) and ω_2 (DAT) are illustrated. The indifference curve through A has been drawn in and its tangent at A is the broken line EF. Let the slope of EF be ω^*/p; since this is the marginal rate of substitution between goods and leisure at A, ω^* is the shadow wage rate at A, see Gronau (1973) and Heckman (1974). Clearly, if the *actual* wage rate is less than ω^*, for example, ω_1, the worker will remain at A and will not choose to participate in the work force. Equally, if, as with ω_2, the actual wage is above ω^*, positive hours will be offered. In the intermediate case of $\omega = \omega^*$, the worker "participates" but offers zero hours.

Formally [from Chapter 4, equation (1.12)], leisure demand q_0 is given by $g_0(\mu + \omega T, \omega, p)$ for unearned income μ, time endowment T, and wage rate and price level ω and p. The shadow wage ω^* is that value of ω that makes q_0 equal to T, that is,

$$T = g_0(\mu + \omega^*T, \omega^*, p) \tag{1.1}$$

To fix ideas and to give specific solutions, we illustrate throughout with the linear expenditure system augmented for leisure as discussed in §4.1. This model has the labor supply function, ignoring the requirement that hours worked be positive, given by

$$\ell^* = (T - \gamma_0)(1 - \alpha_0) - \frac{\alpha_0}{\omega}(\mu - p\gamma) \tag{1.2}$$

where the asterisk emphasizes that the nonnegativity restriction has not been accounted for. The shadow wage for the model is defined by setting $\ell^* = 0$, so that solving

$$\omega^* = \alpha_0(\mu - p\gamma)/(1 - \alpha_0)(T - \gamma_0). \tag{1.3}$$

Hence, actual labor supply ℓ is given by

$$\ell = \ell^* = (T - \gamma_0)(1 - \alpha_0) - (\alpha_0/\omega)(\mu - p\gamma) \quad \text{if } \omega \geq \omega^* \tag{1.4}$$

$$\ell = 0 \quad \text{if } \omega \leq \omega^* \tag{1.5}$$

Equations (1.3), (1.4), and (1.5), or analogs derived from another utility function, are the basis in theory for the analysis of labor supply and the participation decision in the neoclassical model. As we shall see, the main source of difficulty in empirical work is the inequality $\omega \leq \omega^*$ that determines which of (1.4) and (1.5) is actually observed.

Note carefully the equation for the shadow wage (1.3). To illustrate this we can consider a family in which the primary worker's hours are institutionally given and we are interested in the participation decision of the secondary worker. The earnings of the primary worker can be absorbed in exogenous income μ. As they increase, so the shadow wage rate ω^* increases and participation becomes less likely. This would also apply to variations in assets in an intertemporal model. Conversely, the shadow wage will be reduced if μ contains a large negative component, for example, commitments to the repayment of debt or interest. The parameter γ_0 can be interpreted as committed leisure and so will vary across households with the number and ages of children and with tastes. Note that a high γ_0, as would occur with young children, increases ω^* and reduces the probability of participation.

Until quite recently, and in many studies even now, equations of the type (1.4) are used to estimate hours worked as a function of the wage rate in both cross-section and aggregate time-series studies. In the latter, the participation ratio and the number of hours worked have sometimes even been used as interchangeable measures of labor supply to be explained by wage rates and income, see, for example, the pioneering study by Mincer (1962) on participation of married women. Other studies such as Owen (1969, 1971), Abbott and Ashenfelter (1976), and Phlips (1978) have used individual labor supply equations conditional on participation, for example, (1.4), as vehicles for the interpretation of aggregate data. The approach taken here indicates one reason why such studies are likely to be misleading even if individuals are free to adjust their hours worked and face exogenous wage rates. Changes in aggregate labor supply in response to changes in ω and μ are the result not only of changes in the supply by those who are already working – equation (1.4) – but of the changes brought about through individuals joining or leaving the labor force as ω^* changes relatively to ω. Nevertheless, the aggregate time-series evidence is consistent in showing a long-run decline in both hours worked and in the participation ratio by men, with a strong secular increase in the participation of women. Most time-series studies attribute both these effects to rising real wages. For men, whose shadow wage is low and who work relatively long hours, the income effect is dominant so that the labor supply curve is backward sloping, at least in the observed range. For women however, the high value of time spent in the home sets a relatively high shadow wage and both participation and hours at work are lower than for men. With shorter working hours, the income effect is necessarily relatively unimportant, so that rising real wages account for greater labor supply by married women through increased participation and longer hours. Note carefully the importance in this context of analyzing labor supply within a family context.

In cross-section studies, questions of participation and of hours worked conditional on participation have usually been dealt with as two separate studies. Much of the work on hours has used a linear specification of ℓ as a function of ω and μ, and it is possible to justify this in terms of utility theory, see Exercise 4.8. The interested reader can find an excellent sample of this literature in the volume edited by Cain and Watts (1973). Many of the issues – the measurement of leisure, of unearned income, and of wage rates, the treatment of simultaneity, the inclusion of other variables – would take us beyond our present scope. Perhaps not surprisingly, such studies give a wide range of results; for example, Cain and Watts quote compensated wage elasticities for women from zero to over two. However, the backward-bending supply curve for males seems to be broadly consistent with the evidence. Studies of participation rates have focused not only on the effects of wages, but also on such factors as household composition, age of the worker, education, work experience, husband's wage and/or income, and so on. In cross sections of households, workers either participate or they do not so that the participation variable is of the dichotomous 1 or 0 type. In some studies, this dichotomous variable is simply regressed against the determinants of participation, see for example, Boskin (1973), Greenhalgh (1980). This can be justified as an approximation and gives apparently sensible results, but a much better procedure uses the explicit participation equation directly. Here we follow Gronau (1973), although we continue our example of the linear expenditure system.

Let γ_0, the committed leisure demand, be written for individual h by

$$\gamma_0^h = a_0 + b_0 z^h + \epsilon^h \tag{1.6}$$

where z^h is a composition variable (in practice, a vector of such variables) and ϵ^h an "error" term specific to the individual. If ω^h is the wage offer to h, h will participate if $\omega^h > \omega^{*h}$, that is, if

$$\omega^h > \alpha_0(\mu^h - p\gamma)/(1 - \alpha_0)(T - a_0 - b_0 z^h - \epsilon^h) \tag{1.7}$$

assuming for convenience that α_0, T, γ, and p do not vary over households. Rewriting this as a condition on ϵ^h, participation takes place if

$$(1 - \alpha_0)\epsilon_h < (1 - \alpha_0)(T - a_0 - b_0 z^h) - (\alpha_0/\omega^h)(\mu^h - p\gamma) \tag{1.8}$$

Hence, if ϵ is assumed to have some convenient density function, typically normal, the inequality (1.8) gives the probability of participation in terms of the distribution function, the variables z^h, ω^h, and μ^h and the parameters. If this probability is π^h and we have a sample of H individuals, the first R of whom work, the likelihood of the sample is

$$\mathscr{L} = \prod_{h=1}^{R} \pi^h \prod_{h=R+1}^{H} (1 - \pi^h) \tag{1.9}$$

and given data on z, ω, and μ, the parameters can be estimated by nonlinear techniques. In the case where ϵ follows a normal distribution, this estimating technique is called Probit analysis. In Gronau's (1973) study, which followed these principles using American 1960 census data on participation of married women, μ was found to exert a strong positive influence on the shadow wage, as did young children (with an opposite effect for older children), while women who had received college educations were more ready to participate. These sorts of conclusions have been replicated in other studies.

Although there is no doubt that much useful empirical work has been done modeling participation and hours worked separately, the neglect of the full set of equations such as (1.3) to (1.5) creates a number of problems, the discussion of which provides an excellent illustration of the interaction between economic theory and econometric practice. These all have to do with the existence of the inequality conditions in (1.4) and (1.5). One of the most interesting is a "sample selectivity" bias first noticed by Gronau (1974). It takes two main forms. The first concerns studies that analyze cross sections of hours while ignoring the participation decision, and the second concerns the lack of observations on the wage offers received by individuals who do not participate in the labor force. We deal with each problem in turn.

To illustrate the first sample selectivity bias, take the linear expenditure system form (1.4) with γ_0 given by (1.6), that is,

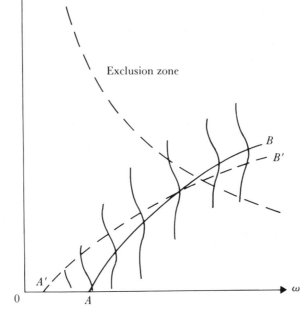

Figure 11.2. Selectivity bias in a cross section of hours worked.

$$\ell^h = (T - a_0 - b_0 z^h)(1 - \alpha_0) - (\alpha_0/\omega^h)(\mu^h - p\gamma) - (1 - \alpha_0)\epsilon^h \quad (1.10)$$

The participation decision is given by (1.8), so that labor supply is given by (1.10) if the right-hand side is positive and is zero otherwise. The deterministic part of (1.10) is illustrated for fixed z^h and $\mu^h(>p\gamma)$ in Figure 11.2 by the kinked curve $0AB$. A study of participants only would attempt to fit AB on the basis of (1.10), and this will give biased parameter estimates as we now illustrate. The problem is that the error term $-(1 - \alpha_0)\epsilon^h = v^h$, say – has a nonzero mean that is correlated with ω^h (and μ^h and z^h). This occurs because the inequality (1.8) effectively removes the lower end of the distribution of v^h and the amount removed depends on the values of the exogenous variables. The vertical lines in the figure represent, say, two standard deviations of u around $AB;$ these are cut off at the lower end from somewhere to the right of A. If the predicted value of ℓ^h is high, the inequality has little effect, but near A as illustrated, close to half the distribution is being removed. Note also that some individuals with exceptionally low leisure preference will work at wages below $0A;$ these individuals cannot, of course, be balanced by observations *below* the axis. A hypothetical scatter is shown together with the biased regression line $A'B'$, which would result from estimation; in this case, the effect of wages on hours worked is understated. This type of bias will be made worse if, as sometimes happens, the sample survey is confined to "poor" households for whom $\omega^h \ell^h + \mu^h$ falls below a certain level. In Figure 11.2, individuals falling in the exclusion zone illustrated would not be observed so that, once again, part of u is removed, but this time the higher values at higher values of ω and ℓ. As illustrated, this will decrease even further the slope of the estimated regression although, in principle, a different bias is possible.

These problems can be overcome by making full use of both participation and hours information simultaneously. Again, we can illustrate using the linear expenditure system. Let us write v^h for $-(1 - \alpha_0)\epsilon^h$ and let $f(v)$ and $\dot{F}(v)$ be the density and distribution functions of v, respectively. The basic data are the numbers of hours worked for R participating individuals plus income and characteristics variables for all H participants and nonparticipants. Given the linear expenditure system and inequality (1.8), the probability that individual h participates

$$\pi^h = 1 - F[(\alpha_0/\omega^h)(\mu^h - p\gamma) - (1 - \alpha_0)(T - a_0 - b_0 z^h)] \qquad (1.11)$$

while, since the Jacobian of the transformation is unity, the density of $\ell^h(\ell^h > 0)$ is simply $f(v)$. The likelihood for the entire sample is thus

$$\mathcal{L} = \prod_{h=1}^{R} f(v^h) \prod_{h=R+1}^{H} (1 - \pi^h) \qquad (1.12)$$

which combines information for both participants and nonparticipants. Note that the difference from (1.9), which (1.12) resembles, is that (1.12) incorporates the hours worked by those who participate while (1.9) does not.

Let us now turn to the second sample-selectivity problem, namely the lack of observations on the wage offers received by the nonparticipants. We have only observations on that part of the distribution satisfying $\omega > \omega^*$, which is by no means a random or representative selection. In consequence, observed wage rates cannot be straightforwardly used, for example, by regression on the personal characteristics of those who work, to make inferences about the complex distribution of wage rates. Hence, the independent variables determining participation, for example, the number of children, exert an indirect influence through the participation rate on the mean of the observed wage distribution, and this will give biased measurement both of the effects of wages and of children on participation. Similar biases will affect even quite straightforward comparisons of wages. For example, as emphasized by Gronau, if white women place a higher value on time at home than do black women, then even if both face the same uncensored distribution of wages, the observed distribution will show significant "discrimination" against blacks.

The problem of missing observations on ω^h can be solved by means of a supplementary equation for the observed wage in terms of education, age,

Table 11.1. *Estimated probabilities of working*

No. of children	Years of schooling				
under six years old	8	10	12	14	16
0	0.30	0.39	0.47	0.56	0.66
1	0.09	0.13	0.18	0.25	0.32
2	0.013	0.025	0.04	0.065	0.09

Source: J. J. Heckman (1974), "Shadow prices, market wages and labour supply," *Econometrica*, Vol. 42, pp. 679–94.

and experience, which since the participants are included in the sample, can be estimated simultaneously, see Heckman (1974) and (1979). Applying these techniques to a 1967 American sample, Heckman (1974) finds that the inclusion of the nonparticipants compared with a regression confined to participants renders the effect of children on annual hours worked (by the participants) insignificant. Its significance in the participants-only regression, with a t-ratio of 9.4, appears to be entirely because of sample-selection bias. Heckman's results also enable estimates to be made of π^h, the probability of working as a function of individual characteristics; one of his tables is reproduced as Table 11.1. For British evidence, see Layard, Barton, and Zabalza (1979).

Exercises

11.1. How would (11.1) have to be modified if there were fixed costs of participating in the labor market? Give a graphical illustration and discuss the consequences for observing small levels of hours of labor supply per day or per week.

11.2. Using the relationship $\partial c(u, \omega, p)/\partial \omega = T$ to define the shadow wage rate $\omega^* = \omega^*(T, u, p)$, show that, if leisure is a normal good, $\partial \omega^*/\partial u$ is positive. Show that $\partial \omega^*/\partial p_i$ is positive if good i is a substitute for leisure and negative if it is complement. Interpret these results. How might we interpret the derivative $\partial \omega^*/\partial T$?

11.3. In Exercise 4.8, the cost function $c(u, w, p) = -\alpha(u, p)e^{\omega/\beta(p)} + \omega\gamma(p) + \delta(p)$ is shown to give labor supply functions linear in μ and ω. Calculate ω^* in this model and interpret it. Can ω^* be negative?

11.4. The existence of substantial debts in the household (e.g., mortgage, loans) is often cited as a reason why increases in income tax rates should be associated with increased labor supply. Assess this view in the light of the foregoing analysis. Are short-run responses likely to differ from long-run responses?

11.5.* For the cost function analyzed in Exercise 4.7, wage income is a linear function of μ and ω, so that in a cross section, we have $\omega^h \ell^h = \alpha + \beta\omega^h + \gamma\mu^h + \epsilon^h$. Assume that this model is correct, that the ϵ^h are independently identically distributed as $N(0, \sigma^2)$ but that a sample is drawn in which households are excluded if total income $\omega^h \ell^h + \mu^h$ is greater than some fixed amount z. Derive a formula for $E(v^h)$, where v^h is the disturbance term in the sample relationship, and show that it is a declining function of both ω^h and μ^h. Discuss the resulting bias in the estimates of β and γ when the relationship is estimated on the sample information using ordinary least squares.

11.6. Assume that in (1.8) the random variable ϵ has a Weibull distribution with the standardized frequency function $P(\epsilon \leq v) = e^{-e^{-v}}$, see §10.3. Derive the elasticity of the probability of participation with respect to the wage for a given household.

11.7. For a given household whose behavior is governed by (1.10) and for which ϵ^h follows a standard normal distribution, derive the expectation of the hours of labor supplied [see Tobin (1958a), section 2].

11.2 Nonlinear constraints and restrictions on hours

Nonlinear constraints

The linear budget constraints that we have used so far will only be appropriate for simple tax systems with lump sum benefits and constant proportional tax rates. In fact, most Western economies have complex tax and social security systems. Typically, income tax systems are nonlinear with marginal rates rising with income, see Figure 11.3. The shape of the budget constraint depends on the particular circumstances of the individual or the household, for example on the amount and composition of unearned income and on the number of dependents. For those individuals who are beyond or close to retiring age or are, for other reasons, eligible for special benefits, the nonlinearities are often even more severe. One of the most widely discussed and controversial examples in almost all Western economies is the so-called poverty trap. To give a British example, if a household is eligible for Family Income Supplement (FIS) because its earnings are below a certain limit, it is also

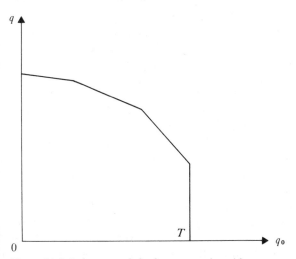

Figure 11.3. Leisure-goods budget constraint with a progressive income tax.

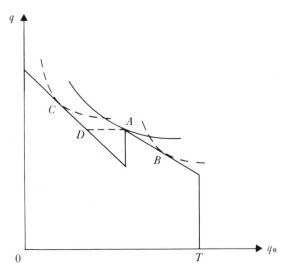

Figure 11.4. The poverty trap.

eligible for a number of other means-tested benefits such as not paying National Health Service prescription charges, free school meals, and rent rebates
in public housing. The larger the household, the greater the value of the benefits. Because the tax floor has not been adjusted upward to fully compensate
for inflation, many families eligible for FIS are also liable for income tax.
Since FIS makes up 50 percent of the gap between actual earnings and the
earnings limit, extra earnings are taxed at 50 percent plus the standard rate
of income tax plus National Insurance contributions (a social security tax), a
total marginal rate close to 90 percent. And if the extra earnings take the
household over the eligibility limit, the budget constraint has a sharp kink as
illustrated in Figure 11.4. The poverty trap operates at point A which will be
the best choice for a large number of families; indeed, no rational, fully informed household that values leisure will choose any point between A and D.

   In empirical analysis, such kinks have to be explicitly modeled using techniques similar to those discussed in the context of the participation decision
above. In the case illustrated, maximum attainable utility is calculated for
both linear segments, for example, at C and B, as well as at the kink A. As before, individuals are assumed to vary in characteristics or tastes so that, given
the distribution of an approximately defined variable reflecting taste differences, we can calculate the probabilities that a randomly selected individual will be at each of the three types of points. The likelihood function for any
given sample is a straightforward generalization and can be maximized to
give estimates of the parameters.

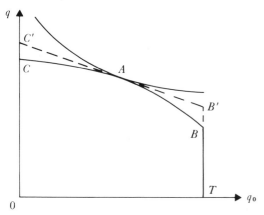

Figure 11.5. Linearizing a convex budget constraint.

Where kinks and other nonconvexities do not arise, as in Figure 11.5, Hall (1973b) has suggested that the nonlinear budget constraint for an individual at A be replaced by a linear constraint corresponding to the tangent at A. Clearly, behavior corresponding to the constraint TBC is identical to that for $TB'C'$. The problem here is that the slope of $C'B'$ depends on the observed labor supply so that, in estimation, causality runs not only from the net wage to hours but also in reverse. Hence individuals with low preference for leisure will face a low net wage and the estimated effect of wages on hours will be biased downwards. In principle, simultaneous equation estimation methods, by recognizing the supply and the wage rate as mutually dependent endogenous variables, can be used to overcome this problem, see also §10.1.

Restrictions on hours

Many workers do not have complete flexibility in choosing the hours they work and it is often argued that, at least in the short run, the effective choice is between working a standard day, week, and year or not working at all. To see the implications of this, we neglect the days, weeks, year distinction and treat the weekly number of hours as fixed at $\bar{\ell}$. If the individual decides to work, the budget constraint is $pq = \omega\bar{\ell} + \mu$ so that the maximization of $v(q, T - \bar{\ell})$ subject to this gives a conditional utility maximum (using the indirect utility function conditional on hours) of $\psi(\omega\bar{\ell} + \mu, p, T - \bar{\ell})$. A binary comparison between this and the utility of not working, $\psi(\mu, p, T)$, determines whether it is preferable to work or not to work. The aggregate number of individuals prepared to work a standard work week depends, via such binary comparisons, on the joint distribution of wage rates, nonlabor income,

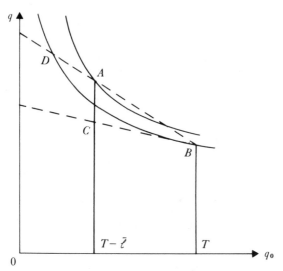

Figure 11.6. Restricted hours.

and observable and unobservable characteristics entering the utility function. Note that, in general, the indifference curve is not tangential to AB at A. In the case illustrated in Figure 11.6, the worker is working more hours at A than would have been chosen had all of AB been available. However, in fact, B is the only alternative and this is even worse. This situation gives the employer considerable flexibility in varying the required number of hours. In the case illustrated, the worker will only choose not to work at the given wage if hours worked are above $D;$ he will accept any number of hours between A and B.

Involuntary unemployment can also be regarded as a restriction on hours. However, a satisfactory definition is no easy matter. Keynes in the *General Theory* (1936, p. 15) writes "the equality of the real wage to the marginal disutility of employment . . . corresponds to the absence of 'involuntary' unemployment." The equality implied is, of course, the tangency of the linear budget constraint to the goods-leisure indifference curve, so that Keynes' negative definition only really works when any point on the budget constraint can be chosen. In the context of Figure 11.6, the most obvious definition would be that the worker is involuntarily unemployed if he would have chosen A in favor of B had A been offered but because it is not, has been forced to B. However, suppose that the choice is between B and C, not B and A. Is the worker who *chooses* B to be regarded as involuntarily unemployed? Relative to A it would appear so, while relative to C he has "volunteered" unemployment. This can only be resolved by recognizing the existence of "normal" wages for particular skill levels. If the normal rate for his skill is that at A, then a worker at B would, by social convention, be regarded as involuntarily unemployed, even though C might be available. An individual with different tastes who accepts the less skilled job at C would not normally be regarded as unemployed, and yet in a certain sense is so.

If we look at this analysis from the viewpoint of the worker, unemployment may simply be the result of imperfect information about the range of job opportunities available. In this situation, it may well pay a worker to turn down known opportunities that are superior to unemployment if he believes that further search will reveal more attractive options. Clearly, the optimal amount of search will vary from worker to worker and the potential explanation for unemployment that this offers has drawn some economists into denying that involuntary unemployment exists at all. However, there is considerable evidence that most search activity is carried out on the job and that a large proportion of workers leaving jobs do not quit voluntarily. Further, it has been suggested, see Spence (1973) and Stiglitz (1975b), that with imperfect information, firms may treat a worker's state of unemployment as an indication of his (unobservable) competence. It is argued that workers who are relatively unproductive, given the standard rate for their claimed skill class, are the most likely to be laid off by employers who from experience have observed their productivity. Thus in a random sample of individuals, the unemployed will have lower than average productivity. Hence, a worker who is involuntarily laid-off suffers a utility loss that is greater than indicated by the indifference curves, for example, between A and B in Figure 11.6, and that is caused by the negative effect on his prospects of future employment. Some of this loss is also incurred by a worker who quits *voluntarily* without having another job and this provides a basis for the superiority of on-the-job search over search while unemployed. However, similar arguments also account for part of the incentive for continued search on the part of involuntarily laid-off workers. The characteristics of the previously held job are a signal to potential employers about the quality of the applicant. Thus the unemployed worker has an incentive not to take a worse job than the previous one but to continue searching. Thus, these arguments would not deny the empirical insights of search theory, for example, that, *abstracting from effects on aggregate demand or on long-term labor mobility*, an increase in unemployment benefits, by decreasing the cost of off-the-job search, might increase measured unemployment. However, in Britain and the United States, the benefit systems are so designed that workers whose participation is sensitive to shifts in nonlabor income, for instance, secondary workers in the family, are typically not eligible. Even so, some workers doubtless take vacations between jobs and they, when unemployed, will be more selective about taking a new job if the opportunity cost of remaining unemployed a little longer is reduced, see Nickell (1979a).

Similarly, among those unemployed with similar skill and experience backgrounds, we should expect those with larger accumulated assets to remain unemployed rather longer. But in Britain, at least, there can be little doubt that the involuntarily unemployed who do not register as unemployed because they are ineligible for benefits outnumber those who do register but are "voluntarily" unemployed. For example, substantially fewer than half the women who in the Population Census or in household surveys say they are unemployed are officially registered as unemployed.

This difficulty of making hard and fast distinctions also applies to the situation of institutionally fixed hours. For example, there may be scope for some choice of hours between different jobs offering different hours per day, days per week, or weeks per year. Hence, choice in the long run is between a set of distinct points representing job opportunities. However, given the costs of moving and that workers have more information about the job they have rather than the jobs they do not, risk-averse individuals are likely to stay in the job they have even if the hours they would have freely chosen at that wage rate diverge significantly from the hours set by the employer. There are, of course, limits to the divergence, but it seems likely that for short-run analysis there are many types of jobs in which it is more realistic to take hours as given or at any rate set by employers. To some extent, this is even true in jobs where overtime at a higher wage rate is common. The explicit or implicit contract between employer and employee often specifies that the employee works the overtime hours required by the employer, so that it is variations in demand conditions and not in supply that account for variations in hours. After all, firms typically operate quite inflexible overtime payment rates and, given specific production plans, cannot continuously vary the overtime rate to bring the labor supply that would then volunteer into balance with its requirements.

The theory of labor contracts, see Gordon (1974), Baily (1974), and Azariadis (1975), suggests that not just hours but even unemployment may be part of the package that workers "buy" when they take a particular type of job with a particular type of firm. Given that workers are informed about the associated probability of unemployment but differ in attitudes to risk and other job characteristics, it is argued that compensating differentials in the wage and other job characteristics will emerge so that a kind of cross-sectional equilibrium in job packages emerges. From this point of view, simple market theory of supply and demand in hours with flexible wages to clear the market is simply inappropriate. Instead, the theory of choice among goods with different bundles of specifications, see §10.2 and §10.3, would seem to be relevant to study the market for job packages. This suggests that apart from the nonlinearity in the budget constraint because of taxes and overtime, there is a second fundamental reason for not treating the wage rate as exogenous in cross-section studies of the supply of hours. In a market cross section, hourly wage rates reflect to some extent the other specifications of the package of which they are a part. Following the two-stage estimation procedure discussed in §10.3, this suggests fitting the market schedule that connects the hourly wage rate with the job specification variables. Assuming that individual workers choose hours and other job specifications subject to this market constraint, the structural equations can then be estimated using the fitted market schedule. In principle, we could even use such a model to cover the cross-sectional choice of the probability of unemployment. However, note that, in a time series in which the average unemployment rate over firms varies, this model does *not* imply that unemployment is "chosen" by workers.

Restrictions on hours and aggregate time-series labor supply studies

The analysis of the previous subsection has important implications for attempts to estimate labor supply equations in time-series data by regressing average hours worked on wage rates, prices, and full income. Consider Figure 11.7, which illustrates for a typical employee the minimum and maximum number of hours per day he would be willing to work at each wage rate. At the normal wage, if fewer hours than at A are offered, the worker will quit. Overtime wages are paid if more than $0N$ hours are worked and, again, if more hours than at B are required, the worker will quit. The "true" labor

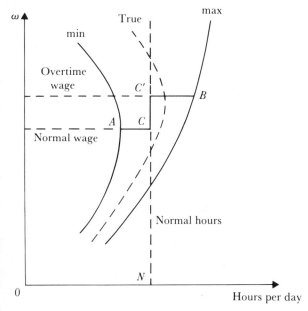

Figure 11.7. Flexibility in hours with an overtime premium.

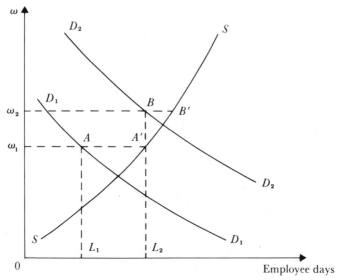

Figure 11.8. A sectoral labor market with excess supply.

supply curve illustrates the hours the worker would supply if he had a perfectly free choice. As illustrated, the minimum and maximum curves diverge
as ω increases; this may not necessarily occur, but is plausible if better paid
workers are more flexible. Given the economic environment, including the
state of the goods market and the availability of extra labor at the normal
wage, the *employer* chooses points along $C'B$ (when the demand for goods is
strong and the market for new employees is tight) or along AC (otherwise).
Aggregating over firms, each facing different market conditions, the
"stepped" wage function is smoothed out, so that in aggregate we observe a
smooth, upward-sloping aggregate relationship between hours per day and
the average wage rate. The relationship between this and the true (unobserved) supply curve is quite arbitrary and the observed relationship is
neither a supply nor a demand curve.

   Problems also arise in the analysis of a sectoral market for employee days.
Suppose that the real wage in the market is higher than that which would
clear the market. Labor markets are not auction markets and there are many
reasons why wage rates may be sticky. For example, unions attempt to pre-
serve differentials with other occupations and hence prevent downward
movements in wages. Even without this, unemployed workers who are imper-
fectly informed can quite rationally *not* bid down the wage by offering their
services at less than the going rate, see §14.5. Whatever the reason, in Figure
11.8, the real wage ω_1 produces employment $0L_1$ given by labor demand

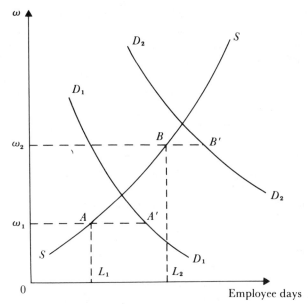

Figure 11.9. A sectoral labor market with excess demand.

(since firms cannot be forced to hire more than this amount) and unemployment AA'. Suppose now that demands shift up to D_2 and that the expansion of economic activity raises the real wage in the sector to ω_2. Employment rises to $0L_2$ and a straightforwardly fitted curve would go through A and B; only by coincidence would it resemble the supply curve, for example, if overtime unemployment were constant or independent of labor supply.

The basic problem in the example in Figure 11.8 is that with excess supply of labor and an exogenously determined real wage, labor supply plays no part in determining employment, and no amount of employment and wage data can help to identify it. Not all economists would agree that labor markets work in this way but the model illustrated in the figure seems more realistic than one in which the wage rate adjusts to clear the market before transactions take place and which could thus be analyzed in terms of the standard econometric model of simultaneous price and quantity determination. If, however, markets are consistently in excess demand, employment will be determined by the supply curve as shown in Figure 11.9. However, there are very good reasons for supposing that labor markets generally are not in excess demand since resistance to increases in wage rates is likely to be small compared with resistance to decreases under excess supply.

From Figure 11.8, it is clear that, under excess supply, labor supply is the sum of employment and unemployment, and that this identity will hold true even if we aggregate over submarkets, some of which may have unfilled vacancies and hence zero unemployment. If unemployment can be correctly measured, we can thus take employment plus unemployment as the dependent variable in the labor supply regression.

Involuntary unemployment has repercussions on labor supply itself and not just on its measurement. Two kinds of effects are discussed in the literature, usually referred to as the "added-worker" effect and the "discouraged worker" effect. The former suggests that secondary workers in a family are more likely to seek work if the primary worker becomes unemployed. This is partly because of the income affect of a reduction in family income on the participation decision, see §11.1, and partly because of the substitution effects associated with rationing, see §4.3, whereby the primary worker's nonmarket time can be substituted for that of the secondary worker – for example, in housekeeping, freeing the latter for labor force participation. This effect depends to some degree on social security institutions; in Britain, the wife of an unemployed husband loses substantial state benefits if she takes a job and the net effect may well be to discourage additional participation. Another reason, somewhat more loosely based in theory, for a "discouraged worker" effect is that with high unemployment, unemployed workers take a more pessimistic view of the probability of getting a job and hence search less actively or even withdraw from the labor force altogether. However, there is yet another factor involved that may well dominate and that can be put on a more formal footing by taking an intertemporal view of labor supply. Workers observing a rising unemployment rate are likely to take this as a sign that the labor hours to which they will be rationed next period are likely to fall. Even without the fuller probabilistic setting that seems appropriate here, it is likely that they will want to work more and accumulate additional financial assets by saving more in the present.

There are spillovers for the demand for goods not only from expected future unemployment but also from current unemployment. A promising start in the direction of integrating the latter with the more appropriate measurement of labor supply as employment plus unemployment has been made by Ashenfelter (1980). He takes preferences as intertemporally separable to justify focusing on only the static budget constraint $\mu + \omega(T - q^0) = \Sigma p_k q_k$. In such a context, $-\mu$ is saving that although endogenous is decided at a different stage of the budgeting decision. To this must be added the additional restriction $T - q^0 = \bar{\ell}$, which is operative for workers rationed in employment. Using the augmented linear expenditure system, for a completely unconstrained worker, superscript s (for supply), goods demand, and labor supply equations are

$$p_i q_i^s = p_i \gamma_i + \alpha_i [\mu + \omega(T - \gamma_0) - \Sigma p_k \gamma_k]$$
$$\omega \ell^s = \omega(T - \gamma_0) - \alpha_0 [\mu + \omega(T - \gamma_0) - \Sigma p_k \gamma_k]$$

$$(2.1)$$

A constrained worker (superscript c) is limited to $\bar{\ell}$ days (possibly but not necessarily zero) and chooses goods demands so as to maximize the restricted utility function $v(T - \bar{\ell}, q)$. The augmented linear expenditure system has the convenient property, see Exercise 11.10, that constrained commodity demands are linked to unconstrained demands by the intuitively simple form

$$p_i q_i^c = p_i q_i^s - [\alpha_i / (1 - \alpha_0)] \omega(\ell^s - \bar{\ell}) \tag{2.2}$$

so that the shortfall in the budget caused by the restriction is shared between the goods in the same proportions as is "supernumerary" expenditure in the unconstrained demands. If, at any time a fraction σ of workers are constrained and if the α parameters are identical over households , *average* observed employment and commodity expenditures, $p_i q_i^M$ and $\omega \ell^M$, are given by

$$p_i q_i^M = p_i q_i^s - [\alpha_i / (1 - \alpha_0)] \sigma \omega(\ell^s - \bar{\ell})$$
$$\omega \ell^M = \omega \ell^s - \sigma \omega(\ell^s - \bar{\ell})$$

$$(2.3)$$

Since employment is labor supply less unemployment, the unemployment rate u should, *in theory*, measure $\sigma(\ell^s - \bar{\ell})/\ell^s$, since $(\ell^s - \bar{\ell})$ multiplied by the number of unemployed is the number of days lost through unemployment while ℓ^s multiplied by total work force is full employment days. In practice, measured unemployment is rather different. For example, in Britain, unemployment is measured by the number of people registering at unemployment exchanges, and there is considerable direct and indirect evidence, for example, Godley and Shepherd (1964) and Joshi (1981), that not all workers register, that the proportion registering is particularly low for married women and others with limited or zero eligibility for unemployment benefits, and that this proportion increases as registered unemployment increases. Even in the United States where unemployment is measured more directly, the theory and practice diverge and Ashenfelter goes no further than postulating a relationship of the form

$$\sigma(\ell^s - \bar{\ell})/\ell^s = a_0 u + a_1 u^2 \tag{2.4}$$

for the measured unemployment proportion u. Ashenfelter substitutes (2.4) into (2.3) and estimates using American data from 1930 to 1967. He finds that the inclusion of the unemployment terms in the augmented linear expenditure system increases the likelihood substantially and significantly. Further, the parameter α_0, which plays a major role in determining the response of labor supply both to wages and to transfer income, is reduced by almost 50 percent compared with the model that does not allow for involuntary unemployment.

Note that this study, like many others, on both time series and cross section takes labor supply as conditional upon saving, whereas derivation of uncond: tional demand would require analysis of a full intertemporal model. Sinc changes in wage rates are likely to affect anticipations about the future savings behavior and labor supply will be jointly endogenous and ignorin this will produce measurements that cannot be clearly interpreted as eithe short-term or long-term responses.

Restrictions on hours and cross-section studies

In cross-section estimates of labor supply, the problem of involuntary unem ployment is in principle just as serious as it is in aggregate time series. It is fai to say that most studies in the past have ignored the problem, although som of the more recent ones have been able to exclude individuals who claimed t be working more or less hours than they wished. If individuals questioned i sample surveys give a correct estimate of the degree to which they are ur deremployed or overemployed, then the data can be corrected to give actus labor supply. If this information is not available, one approach is to specif the degree of underemployment theoretically and to use only the fact of ur deremployment rather than its amount in the estimation. Let us see how th can be done.

Suppose that ℓ_h hours are reported for an individual whose voluntary labo supply is ℓ^s. There are three possibilities: he can report that he is underem ployed, in which case $\ell_h^s \geq \ell_h$; he can report that he is overemployed, i which case $\ell_h^s \leq \ell_h$; or he can report that he is unrationed in either directior in which case $\ell_h^s = \ell_h$. If we specify the labor supply function as $\ell_h^s = \ell^s(X_h) + \epsilon_h$ and ϵ_h has a distribution function $F(\ )$ and a density functio $f(\ )$, we can write the three events and their probabilities (or densities) a shown in Table 11.2.

Suppose that observations 1 to R_1 refer to underemployment, $R_1 + 1$ to R refer to overemployment and $R_2 + 1$ to H refer to no rationing. Then th likelihood (the joint probability density of the sample), assuming that ϵ_h i independent of X_h and independent across households, is

$$\mathcal{L} = \prod_{h=1}^{R_1} [1 - F(\ell_h - \ell^s(X_h))] \prod_{h=R+1}^{R_2} [F(\ell_h - \ell^s(X_h)]$$

$$\prod_{h=R_2+1}^{H} [f(\ell_h - \ell^s(X_h))] \quad (2.5$$

This is the approach of Ham (1977) who uses data from the University o Michigan Income Dynamics Survey. This is a longitudinal survey, and there fore gives some idea about the incidence over time of rationing. Of th sample of males aged between 25 and 50 in 1967, only 28 percent exper able 11.2. *Employment states and probabilities*

vent	Conditions	Probability or density
nderemployment	$\ell_h^* \geq \ell_h \equiv \epsilon_h \geq \ell_h - \ell^s(X_h)$	$1 - F[\ell_h - \ell^s(X_h)]$
veremployment	$\ell_h^* \leq \ell_h \equiv \epsilon_h \leq \ell_h - \ell^s(X_h)$	$F[\ell_h - \ell^s(X_h)]$
o rationing	$\ell_h^* = \ell_h \equiv \epsilon_h = \ell_h - \ell^s(X_h)$	$f[\ell_h - \ell^s(X_h)]$

ıced no form of rationing at any time during 1967–74. The annual percent-
ge underemployed or unemployed varies from 3½ percent to 7 percent.
Ience, the incidence of rationing is by no means negligible. Ham contrasts
ıe results of fitting a linear specification of $\ell^s(X_h)$ by ordinary least squares to
ıe whole sample and to the censored sample, on the one hand, with the max-
num likelihood results on the other. Although the latter give very similar
ᴇsponses to the man's own wage and his wife's wage, the coefficients on race,
ducation, number of children, and age are substantially different. With the
ıaximum likelihood approach explicitly taking rationing into account, race
ecomes insignificant, while with the full and the truncated sample it is signif-
antly negative. This suggests that the lower labor supply for blacks than
hites estimated in earlier studies is at least partly spurious, with race serving
s a proxy for underemployment or unemployment. The fall in the estimated
ffect of education can be similarly interpreted since the more educated have
smaller probability of being unemployed. Generally then, the change in the
ffects of the background variables suggests that the estimates of these vari-
bles in earlier studies are likely to have been heavily biased.

.xercises

1.8. Assume that a secondary worker has preferences represented by $u = (q_0 - z + $
ıq, where z is a variable that increases with the number of children in the household
ınd ϵ is a random variable representing taste differences from worker to worker. The
ᴏrker has the choice of not working or of accepting a job with wage ω and fixed hours
. Show that $\omega > \mu/(T - \overline{\ell} - z + \epsilon)$ is necessary for the job to be accepted and contrast
ᴠith the condition for participation when hours can be freely chosen. What happens if
here are several jobs with $\omega_1, \overline{\ell}_1, \omega_2, \overline{\ell}_2, \ldots$, etc.? Explain, in principle, how the pro-
ᴏrtions of workers accepting each type of job could be derived. What role is played
ᴠy z?

1.9. A worker with utility function $u = (q_0 - \gamma)q$ is employed by a firm who pays wage
ate ω and requires h hours of work per week. Another firm offers employment at ω^*
ᴏr ℓ hours. There are no other jobs. Show that the worker will work for the first firm

only if $h_1 \leq h \leq h_2$ and derive formulas for h_1 and h_2. What effect will the institution of overtime payments have on $h_2 - h_1$?

11.10. For the augmented linear expenditure system [Chapter 4, (1.27)], extended for many goods, write down the unrationed demand functions as well as those that result from imposing the additional constraints of fixed working hours. Show that the two sets of functions are related by equation (2.2).

11.11. In a model of family supply, $u = v(q_0^1, q_0^2, q)$, where q_0^1, q_0^2 are the husband's and wife's leisure, show that making worker 1 unemployed with full compensation will cause worker 2 to work more or less as q_0^1 and q_0^2 are substitutes or complements. Discuss how and whether unemployment compensation should depend on the extent of substitution. How might you expect the relationship between q_0^1 and q_0^2 to vary with household age?

11.12. Following Exercise 4.26, discuss how the cost function for $v(q_0^1, q_0^2, q)$ may be transformed into the restricted cost function appropriate when worker 1 is unemployed. Interpret carefully each of the functions and magnitudes that appear in the analysis.

11.13. Suppose that a quadratic tax schedule is imposed so that the budget constraint becomes $p \cdot q = \mu + \omega\ell(1 - \tau - \frac{1}{2}\alpha\omega\ell)$ for some positive parameter α. Using the augmented LES [Chapter 4, (1.27)] show that it is possible to define a wage rate $\bar{\omega}$ as a function of ℓ that, when substituted into the usual demands, will give the correct choice. Illustrate geometrically why the unearned income parameter μ, also has to be adjusted. Suggest an estimation technique for such a model that does not involve solving explicitly for ℓ.

11.3 Labor supply in the long run

We now turn to the long-run choices of occupation and of length and type of education that entrants to the labor force have to make if only by default. We shall have a good deal to say on "human capital theory," but the focus on decision making will give it a somewhat different perspective than is usual in the literature on earnings functions where this theory has most frequently been applied. For the moment, let us abstract from the nonpecuniary advantages or disadvantages of particular occupations and assume that different amounts of education result in different earnings streams over the working life. Like investment in capital by firms, investment in education in the human capital story involves both a cost and a stream of benefits that accrues over a long period.

Human capital under present value maximization

Ignoring the possibility that education might be a consumption good as well as an investment good, the trade-off for the consumer is between the income foregone and cost of education, on the one hand, and the future stream of returns on the other. Assuming that the individual can borrow at a given interest rate, the intertemporal utility function defined on *consumption of goods* is maximized in two stages. At stage *A*, the individual chooses education to max-

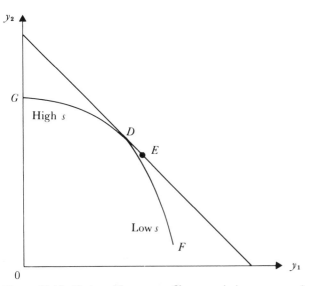

Figure 11.10. Choice of income profile to maximize present value.

imize the present value of future discounted purchasing power, while at stage B, the individual makes an intertemporal consumption plan given the present value from stage A. Figures 11.10 and 11.11 represent these two stages for a simplified two-period example. If length of schooling is s and $y_2(s)$ is income in period 2, which depends positively on s, increases in s move the consumer to the left along the income possibility frontier FDG. By definition, present value of earning power is $W = y_1(s) + y_2(s)/(1 + r)$, where r is the interest rate, and this is maximized with respect to s at the point D. Since this point involves low current income compared with future income, it is optimal to borrow an amount $pq_1 - y_1$ to reach E, where utility is maximized subject to the constraint that present value of earning power be equal to present value of purchasing power: if p_2 is the expected value of the price level in period 2, this takes the form

$$W = A + p_1 y_1^R(s) + \frac{p_2 y_2^R(s)}{1 + r} = p_1 q_1 + \frac{p_2 q_2}{1 + r} \tag{3.1}$$

where A is initial assets, y_1^R and y_2^R are real income levels defined by y_1/p_1 and y_2/p_2. The equation can be divided through by p_1 to give a problem with a fixed price level and real interest rate r^* defined by $1/(1 + r^*) = p_2/p_1(1 + r)$.

As Irving Fisher originally pointed out, it is the linearity of the intertemporal budget constraint that allows the separation of the problem into two

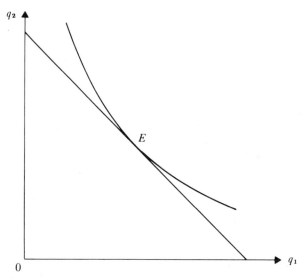

Figure 11.11. Choice of consumption profile to maximize utility.

stages so that the marginal rate of substitution of consumption over time ha
no bearing on the choice of s at the first stage. The assumption of preser
value maximization is almost universal in writings on human capital. Hov
ever, it is only valid if another implicit assumption of the model holds, namel
that leisure time is fixed in both the present and the future, so the choice
limited to the allocation of the remaining time between work and schooling. I
leisure time is set by convention or other means–for example, if the co
sumer must choose how to allocate an eight-hour day between work and edu
cation, maximization of present value is correct. In general, however, this wi
not be the case, as can be seen from the full two-period budget constraint in
volving leisure. This constraint takes the form, assuming that the only costs c
schooling are earnings foregone,

$$A + \omega_1(s)(T - q_{01} - s) + \frac{\omega_2(s)}{1 + r}(T - q_{02}) = p_1 q_1 + \frac{p_2}{1 + r} q_2 \qquad (3.\text{?}$$

where A is the level of initial assets, ω_1 and ω_2 are wage rates, hours of wor
are $\ell_1 = T - q_{01} - s$ and $\ell_2 = T - q_{02}$ for time endowments T, and q_{01} and q_0
are leisure hours. This can be rewritten as

$$A + \omega_1(s)(T - s) + \frac{\omega_2(s)T}{1 + r} = \tilde{W} = p_1 q_1 + \omega_1(s)q_{01} + \frac{p_2 q_2}{1 + r} + \frac{\omega_2(s)q_{02}}{1 + r} \qquad (3.\text{?}$$

but maximization of $u = v(q_1, q_{01}, q_2, q_{02})$ will not be achieved by choosing s t maximize $\tilde{W}$ and then selecting leisure and consumption for fixed $\omega_1(s)$ and $\omega_2(s)$. However if q_{01} and q_{02} are exogenously given, they can be taken over to the left-hand side of (3.3) and present value maximization will again be optimal. Even so, the possibility that schooling itself yields welfare is another reason for arguing that present value maximization is too simple an objective. Note, however, that time itself introduces some separation into decision making since, once the individual is past the initial schooling phase, s becomes fixed parameter, although this ignores opportunities for adult education and training that is not costless to the individual.

In Becker's household production theory [see Becker (1975, Chapter 3, especially Appendix)], the possibility that present value maximization may not be a step in utility maximization is recognized, at least in principle. As we saw in the previous chapter, one or more of the final household goods on which utility is defined and which are produced from inputs of purchased market goods including leisure may be durable. So quite generally, educational investments may be made with leisure and other market inputs. Indeed, the goods and services which make up expenditure on medical care could also be considered as inputs into human capital. We can still make a conceptual separation of optimization into two stages, with minimizing the market cost of reaching a given vector of final household goods being one stage, see §10.1, but this is a different procedure than maximization of present value.

To some extent, the literature on human capital breaks into two branches. In one (in particular, the work in the tradition of Mincer) the major focus is the analysis of earnings distributions using earnings functions, which are the analog of the "hedonic" price–characteristics functions we discussed in the previous chapter. Almost everyone working in this branch has assumed present value maximization. The focus of the other branch [see, for example, Ghez and Becker (1975)] has been the explanation of consumption expenditure and labor supply for individual households. In these studies, life-cycle budget constraints that are generalizations of (3.2) lie at the heart of the analysis, and as we have seen, present value maximization is not useful in this context (see also §12.1).

arnings functions in the absence of postschool investment

Despite the restrictive assumptions behind the present value maximizing model, let us pursue it beyond the two-period form. The choice open to an individual about to end the legally minimal schooling requirement is to decide on the level of s further years of schooling. Note that the present value approach does not deny the obvious fact that choice is made subject to advice from parents and teachers as well as being influenced by the examples of contemporaries and siblings, provided, of course, that such factors are thought of as containing information relevant to the maximization decision. Assume that during the schooling period earnings are zero and are afterwards given by $y_\tau(s)$. The objective, even if it emerges through some kind of cultural osmosis rather than a private calculus, is to maximize present value W with respect to s. Assuming a constant real interest rate and measuring earnings in real terms,

$$W = A + \sum_{\tau=1}^{s} \frac{0}{(1 + r)^\tau} + \sum_{s+1}^{L} \frac{y_\tau(s)}{(1 + r)^\tau} \tag{3.4}$$

where A is the initial level of financial assets and L is the retirement date. Suppose that real annual earnings after $\tau - s$ years at work are expected to be starting salary $y(s)$ multiplied by the factor $g(\tau - s)$. Then net present value V, excluding initial assets, is given by

$$V = W - A = \sum_{s+1}^{L} y(s) \frac{g(\tau - s)}{(1 + r)^\tau} \tag{3.5}$$

$$= \frac{y(s)}{(1 + r)^s} \left[\frac{g(1)}{1 + r} + \frac{g(2)}{(1 + r)^2} + \cdots + \frac{g(L - s)}{(1 + r)^{L-s}} \right]$$

$$= \frac{y(s)}{(1 + r)^s} G(L - s, r) \tag{3.6}$$

If the real interest rate is relatively large and years of schooling beyond the minimally required level are small relative to the work span, then $G(\ )$ differs by negligible amounts as s varies. Since $\log V = \log y(s) - s \log(1 + r) + \log G$ and $\log(1 + r) \approx r$, we can write as a reasonable approximation

$$\log V \approx \log y(s) - rs + \text{constant} \tag{3.7}$$

Note that the same approximation for $\log V$ can be obtained by working in continuous time, see Exercise 11.14.

In the early days of human capital theory and especially in the work of Mincer (1958, 1970, 1974, 1976), equation (3.7) became the basis for regressing the logarithm of earnings on schooling as an "explanation" of earnings and as a "theory" of the distribution of earnings. The argument goes as follows: in addition to the simplifying assumptions made about preferences, including the irrelevance of nonpecuniary benefits of different jobs and the assumption that each individual can borrow at a given interest rate, assume that the interest rate is the same for everyone, that labor markets are perfectly competitive and always clear instantaneously, that individuals foresee future earnings correctly and that higher ability individuals get no extra benefit from education but get multiplicatively higher earnings. Then Adam Smith's theory of equalizing net advantage suggests that V will be the same for everyone of the same ability. The reasoning is as follows: if for anyone of a given ability a higher V could be reached by choosing a different level of schooling, the extra flow of maximizing individuals acquiring that level of schooling would drive earnings down, so that in equilibrium, for individuals of equal ability, the same V is attained. Note that equalization will only be obtained for those levels of schooling at which some firms wish to hire workers. If we assume further that the age-earnings profile $g(\ )$ is the same across individuals, then since every individual of the same ability expects to attain the same present value V,

$$\log y(s) = \text{constant} + rs + \epsilon \tag{3.8}$$

where ϵ represents multiplicative ability differences and the effect of temporary aberrations from equilibrium. Since after $\tau - s$ years on the job $y_\tau(s) = y(s)g(\tau - s)$, equation (3.8) implies

$$\log y_\tau(s) = \text{constant} + rs + \log g(\tau - s) + \epsilon \tag{3.9}$$

Fitting the regression

$$\log y_\tau(s) = \beta_0 + \beta_1 s + u \tag{3.10}$$

Mincer (1976) finds for the United States that $\beta_1 = 0.070$ (s.e. $= 0.0016$) and $R^2 = 0.067$. The sample comes from a subsample of the census and consists of the annual earnings and schooling of 30,000 United States white nonfarm men in 1959 who had some earnings and were neither students nor retired. Psacharopoulos and Layard (1979) for Britain find $\beta_1 = 0.053$ (0.004) with $R^2 = 0.031$ for annual earnings of a sample of 7,000 employed men taken from the 1972 General Household Survey.

However, crude formulations such as (3.10), in contrast to (3.9), ignore variations of earnings with age or labor market experience. Indeed, adding $(\tau - s)$ to the equation improves the fit dramatically. This is often done in the regression

$$\log y_\tau(s) = \beta_0 + \beta_1 s + \beta_2(\tau - s) + \beta_3(\tau - s)^2 + \bar{u} \tag{3.11}$$

since it is observed that the profile is not constant over the work cycle but tends to decline so that β_3 is negative. The terms in $(\tau - s)$ are often interpreted as "on the job training" or "postschool investment," but could equally well reflect anything that gives earnings a time profile. We return to this issue next. Mincer (1976) finds $\beta_1 = 0.107$ (0.0015), $\beta_2 = 0.081$ (0.0011), and $\beta_3 = -0.0012$ (0.000022) and $R^2 = 0.285$. Psacharopoulos and Layard (1979) for British males find $\beta_1 = 0.097$ (0.0030), $\beta_2 = 0.091$ (0.0020), $\beta_3 = -0.0015$ (0.000039) and $R^2 = 0.316$. Note that in equation (3.10) $\hat{\beta}_1$ gives a clearly biased estimate of the rate of return r because of the omission of the $(\tau - s)$ terms. So it is not surprising that estimating (3.11) should give higher values of $\hat{\beta}_1$, which in that equation does have the interpretation of being the rate c return.

Even on its own terms, as Adam Smith made clear in 1776, the principle c equalizing net advantage should take into account nonmonetary job chara‹ teristics such as the noise level, repetitiveness of tasks, and so on. Luc‹ (1977), who includes such variables in earnings regressions and also makes a‹ allowance for whether or not the job is unionized, finds that not all of the jo characteristics have the anticipated sign and that unionization has a high‹ significant positive effect on earnings. On the face of it, this would seem ‹ cast some doubt on the competitive assumption implicit in Smith's principl‹

Earnings functions with postschool investments

The human capital interpretation of earnings functions can be even more e: plicitly derived in terms of investment theory, and this kind of derivation used by Mincer and others to incorporate postschool investments into th model. First, note that in (3.4) we can explicitly think of earnings foregone being the amount of investment in the period $\tau = 0$ to s, and we write y_τ as‹ function of the stock K_s of human capital accumulated during this period ar‹ assume that from period $s + 1$ no further investment takes place. Thus,

$$W = A + \sum_{\tau=0}^{L} (y_\tau(K_\tau) - I_\tau)/(1 + r)^\tau \tag{3.1}$$

with $y_\tau = I_\tau$ for $\tau = 0$ to s, $I_\tau = 0$ for $\tau = s + 1$ to L and $K_\tau = K_{\tau-1} + I_{\tau-1}$ ‹ $\delta K_{\tau-1}$, where δ is the rate of deterioration of stock of human capital, whic‹ completes the recursive relationship by which the stock is built up. Note, hov‹ ever, that (3.12) has no empirical implications beyond those of (3.4): it simp‹ tells the same story in somewhat different words and symbols and typically w‹ would not be able to disentangle the separate effects of income growth an‹ deterioration. To extend it to postschool investments is easy enough forma‹ by allowing $I_\tau > 0$. These investments have been used to rationalize the dow‹ turn in the age income profiles in the latter part of the working life cycle. ‹ individuals approach retirement with its enforced departure from the lab‹ market, it becomes less and less productive to invest in further accumulati‹ of capital since the earning lifetime of the stock gets shorter and shorter, ‹ the deterioration element dominates and the earnings profile turns dow‹ The difficulty with the theory is that the concept of postschool investment difficult to relate to anything observable except "experience" $(\tau - s)$, and seems implausible to suppose that all individuals with $\tau - s$-periods of lab‹ market experience have all received the same degree of on the job trainin‹ On the other hand, periods of further or part-time adult education can be o‹ served, and there have been attempts to estimate their effects.

If the cost of investment in on the job training is reflected in earnings in the short run being lower than they would otherwise be, then *observed* earnings are not gross earnings $y_\tau(K_\tau)$ but net earnings $y_\tau(K_\tau) - I_\tau$. This makes it difficult to measure $y_{s+1}(K_{s+1})$, which is the most immediate measure of the productivity of schooling. However, if the principle of equalizing net advantage holds, then someone who engages in no postschool investment and with (say) a flat earnings stream of $y_{s+1}(K_{s+1})$ per year should have the same present value as someone who accepts lower initial earnings compensated by higher later earnings, as would occur with positive postschool investments. Thus, the earnings streams must cross and Mincer argues that they tend to do so after about ten years experience which he calls the "overtaking" point. He therefore suggests that the cohort with around ten years experience should give satisfactory estimates of the rate of return computed from regressions of the logarithm of net earnings on years of schooling. In support of his case, he cites American evidence that suggests that R^2 for different experience cohorts is indeed largest for the cohort centered around ten years experience. However, a rigorous demonstration of a single overtaking point requires, not only the principle of equalizing net advantage but also special assumptions on the postschool investment profiles for which there is no particular basis. Psacharopoulos and Layard find no regular inverted u-pattern in the R^2's for experience cohorts in Britain and therefore question the usefulness of the "overtaking" concept for isolating the effect of school investments from that of postschool investments.

A structural approach to earnings functions and educational investment

So far, we have stayed close to the Mincerian development of earnings functions, but in what follows we shall no longer do so. Even if we could accept the long list of assumptions required to justify the earnings functions already examined, those assumptions no more constitute a theory of distribution than the equilibrium condition – supply equals demand is a theory of price and quantity in a given market. As has become increasingly recognized, structural equations for both supply and demand are needed for the determination of earnings and of the distribution of schooling levels. So let us return to our examination of the structure of supply of educated labor.

We begin by relaxing some of the very restrictive assumptions we have made, although to ease the analysis, we shall abstract from the complications posed by the existence of postschool investments. Returning to (3.4), we now allow each individual h an ability vector a_h. Even in some kind of long-run equilibrium in which individuals embarking upon schooling somehow managed to foresee correctly the future earnings associated with a given ability vector and various levels of schooling, one would expect the log (earnings)

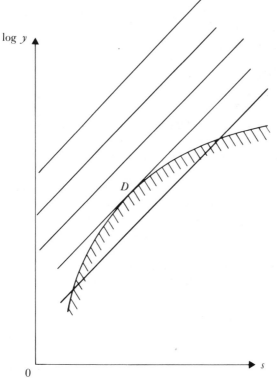

Figure 11.12. Present value maximization subject to a perceived earnings function.

function, conditional on ability, offered by the market to be concave as in Figure 11.12. For the purposes of this analysis, we measure earnings immediately after leaving school, that is, $y(s)$. Now consider the problem of maximizing net present value V subject to the perceived market earnings function. Define *indifference lines*, the parallel lines in Figure 11.12, each of which represents a different level of V and is given by (3.7) with log V held constant. The perceived constraint takes the form $\log y = \log y(a, s)$, which is the concave curve. V is maximized at D, where we have the marginal condition $r = d \log y(a, s)/ds$. To take a specific example, suppose

$$\log y = s(\beta_0 + \beta_1 a + v) - \tfrac{1}{2}\beta_2 s^2 \tag{3.13}$$

where v represents unobserved ability and $\beta_2 > 0$ captures the concavity of the relation. Then $\beta_0 + \beta_1 a + v - \beta_2 s = r$ and

$$s = (-r + \beta_0 + \beta_1 a + v)/\beta_2 \tag{3.14}$$

This structural schooling equation makes explicit that if one estimates an equation of the form (3.13), there is a potentially major simultaneous equation bias even if measured ability were exogenous because the level of schooling is endogenous. Regressions such as (3.11) suffer both from this bias and that which is introduced by omitting ability measures that are positively correlated with schooling. This suggests that "the rate of return" on schooling is likely to be significantly overestimated by (3.11).

Another important modification, which has received considerable attention since Becker and Chiswick (1966), is relaxing the assumption that everyone faces the same interest rate. Strictly speaking, if there are borrowing constraints or credit worthiness requirements, which are usually given as the reasons for interest rate differences between households, the schedule of marginal investment funds is upward sloping, so the interest rate varies with how much is borrowed. But then the separation illustrated in Figures 11.10 and 11.11 between the schooling investment decision and intertemporal consumption allocation is not possible. The correct approach, then, would be to take a specification of preferences and of the nonlinear interest rate schedule as a function of observable family background variables such as wealth and to compute the utility maximizing demand for schooling from it. Recent authors such as Rosen (1977) and Rosen and Willis (1979) do not allow for these complications and use the linear form (3.7), but with r a function of family background variables z. Substituting $r = \alpha_0 + \alpha_1 z + v_1$ into (3.14), for example, the schooling equation becomes

$$s = (-\alpha_0 - \alpha_1 z - v_1 + \beta_0 + \beta_1 a + v_2)/\beta_2 \tag{3.15}$$

where v_1 and v_2 are unobserved error terms. With panel data and the assumption that individuals or their advisers make unbiased forecasts of the earnings function, the reduced form (3.15) can be used to predict s and this prediction used as an instrument in place of observed s in estimating the earnings function (3.13) without incurring the simultaneous equation bias.

In practice, one of the most important American sources of panel data, the NBER-Thorndike sample, consists of men all of whom completed high school. For the population of all men, from which the sample is drawn, the indifference lines and constraints as illustrated in Figure 11.12 have distributions that generate a distribution of years of schooling, part of which is below completion of high school. The censoring of this part of the sample means that estimates for such data need to be corrected for sample selection bias as discussed in §11.1 above. However, even an uncensored sample is likely to have a much higher proportion of those who just complete high school but do not go beyond than can be explained with the smooth concave constraint of Figure 11.12. It is likely that for someone who is six months short of completing high school, the return on that six months is likely to be well in excess of a

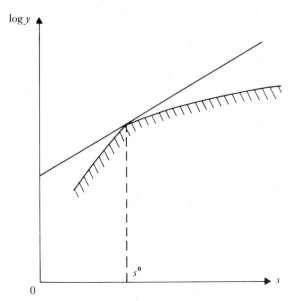

Figure 11.13. Earnings function kinked at high school completion.

limited period of six months spent in higher education beyond high schoo
Thus, as illustrated in Figure 11.13, there is likely to be a kink in the earning
function at high school completion s^0, and since indifference curves with
range of slopes will be tangents at s^0, this feature accounts for the high fr
quency at s^0. This analysis, as well as dealing with sample selection bias, coul
serve as a motivation for the elegant study by Rosen and Willis (1979) of th
NBER-Thorndike sample. For simplicity in exposition, we assumed that th
earnings-experience profile $g(\tau - s)$ is the same across individuals. This
highly unlikely and Rosen and Willis permit g to vary, which gives an extr
structural equation in addition to the earnings function. Since they do not us
information on the level of schooling of those beyond s^0, they can use Prob
analysis to model the probability that a given individual chooses between th
simple alternatives $s > s_0$ and $s = s_0$. They do not, however, attempt to mod
s when $s > s_0$.

The choice of schooling, and especially the discrete choice of whether c
not to complete high school, is formally very similar to the choice of occupa
tion which in turn is closely related to the choice among varieties of goods ar
alyzed in §10.3. The combination of job characteristics, family backgroun
variables, monetary rewards, and unobserved differences in both individual
and jobs is exactly analogous to the role in Chapter 10, equation (3.15) c
specification variables, household characteristics, prices, and random compc

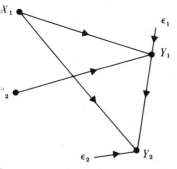

Figure 11.14. Simple illustration of path analysis.

ents. We could therefore take over this analysis and use it to model choice of occupations at the individual level, and by aggregating over individuals, derive the aggregate supply curve to each occupation. These supply curves are highly interrelated and their shapes depend not only on the population distribution of family background variables and the characteristics of available occupations but on the shapes of the distributions of the unobserved differences.

The structural approach that gets away from earnings functions of the Mincer type begins to permit connections to be made with another systematic structural approach common in socioeconomic modeling. This is *path analysis*, the term noneconomists in the social sciences use for a recursive statistical model. Consider a simple example:

$$Y_1 = \alpha_0 + \alpha_1 X_1 + \alpha_2 X_2 + \epsilon_1$$
$$Y_2 = \beta_0 + \beta_1 Y_1 + \beta_2 X_1 + \epsilon_2 \tag{3.16}$$

here Y_1 = son's test score (e.g., on an IQ test), X_1 = father's education, X_2 = father's socioeconomic background, Y_2 = son's schooling, and ϵ_1 and ϵ_2 are independently distributed random variables. Figure 11.14 traces the paths of determination from X_1 and X_2 to Y_2 through Y_1. In practice models such as those estimated by Jencks and others (1972) are much larger, and by using standardized (mean zero, variance one) data, researchers are able to combine information from several distinct samples. One preoccupation in this literature that there has been much controversy about has been the attempt to distinguish the influence of genetically inherited ability from other family background and chance influences. One lesson from it is that test scores are biased measures of exogenous ability. This suggests that measurement errors could be a serious source of correlation between the error terms and the explanatory variables such as a and z in schooling equations of the type (3.15). On the other hand, structural models of the type discussed previously raise questions about whether the schooling equation is really recursive relative to the earnings function, which is typically the final equation in a path analysis. We have already discussed the simultaneity caused by people making schooling plans conditional upon their estimate of the earnings function. Work is beginning on models with both simultaneity and measurement errors, and this is an area that will certainly develop further.

We conclude by discussing another issue that has generated considerable controversy. Some of the early literature on human capital attempted to interpret the estimated rate of return r from Mincer-type earnings functions as a measure of the marginal social efficiency of education. We have already seen the upward bias in this coefficient caused by the omission of ability variables and the endogenity of schooling. Quite closely related is the point made by Arrow (1973), Stiglitz (1975b), and other writers on the economics of information, that part (or in principle, even all) of the return to education is a purely private return that results from "screening" individuals through educational credentials into high- and low-ability groups. To take an extreme position, it might be that education does not alter the marginal productivity of the individuals who go through it but simply labels them. Of course, the value of this information to society would not be zero since it helps fit workers into suitable slots, but it is not measured by the coefficient on schooling in an earnings function. If different jobs were the same in the degree to which screening by educational qualifications is an appropriate predictor for firms of the marginal productivity of employees, there would be no particular implications for the structural model for schooling we have discussed. However, as Riley (1979) has pointed out, if jobs differ in this respect, there are potential empirical differences that should be observable.

Exercises

11.14. Repeat the analysis of (3.4) through to (3.7) using continuous time and show that identical results are achieved.

11.15. Using the investment model of (3.12) with human capital investment allowed at any age, calculate the optimal time path for I_t and discuss the earnings profile that results. For what type of occupations do you think this model might provide a reasonable description?

11.16. In many occupations, there are age-related incremental pay scales. Can these be "explained" in terms of human capital theory? What are the implications of your results for the estimation of equations such as (3.7) and (3.11)?

11.17. What would be the implications for the existence of a market in human capital?

11.18. Assume that apart from providing consumption benefits to those engaged in it, the only role of a university or college education is to act as a screen. What are the implications (a) for the type of courses and assessment procedures that should be instituted and (b) for the optimal amount of higher education in the society as a whole?

11.19. Contrast the analysis represented in Figures 11.12 and 11.10. How might the discussion of competitive determination of the provision of varieties of goods with different specifications in §10.3 be applied to earnings functions without making the assumption of present value maximization?

11.20. If labor markets are competitive, then within each group of workers with common family background variables and abilities, the principle of equalizing net advantage asserts that (assuming common tastes are shared) there is fundamental equality. Under what assumptions does this extend to workers with varying abilities? Discuss the idea that variations in family background are the fundamental cause of "noncompeting groups." What other sources of noncompeting groups can you suggest?

11.21.* How might the analysis that underlies the illustrative equations (3.13), (3.14), and (3.15) be extended if the earnings-experience profile varies cross sectionally – in at least one parameter? See Rosen and Willis (1979).

Bibliographical notes

It is a reflection of the dramatic development of the subject that so little of the material in the first two sections of this chapter is covered in the otherwise excellent text by Fleisher (1970). That both the extensive and the intensive margin needed to be taken into account in computing the aggregate labor supply elasticity was made explicit as early as Douglas (1934). The fact that in cross-section studies of participation the probability of participation is the relevant variable has long been acknowledged and, for example, Cain (1966) fitted linear probability functions. Although Probit and Tobit (Tobin (1958a)) estimation procedures had been applied to the demand for durables and transport mode choice, they were slow in entering empirical labor economics. Not until the 1970's was the labor participation decision widely seen as a corner solution, with consequent sample selection problems for hours and the wage rate – see Gronau (1973), Ben-Porath (1973), Cain and Watts (1973), Heckman (1974) and much subsequent work. Another development that we have only touched on (see Exercise 12.10) is the analysis of labor force participation decision over time; see Heckman and Willis (1977), Heckman (1978), Lillard (1977), and Heckman and McCurdy (1980) for further work on this.

For further reading on nonlinearities in the budget constraint and estimating labor supply functions that deal with them, see Greenberg and Kosters (1973), Hall (1973b), H. Rosen (1976), and Hanoch and Honig (1978). For British evidence on nonlinearities caused by the poverty trap, see Kay and King (1978) and the Royal Commission on the Distribution of Income and Wealth (1978). The effects of hours constraints and unemployment on male labor supply in a sample from the National Longitudinal Survey sampled at dates one year apart have been considered and found to be important by Kalacheck, Mellow, and Raines (1978). Moreover, they argue that time-series and cross-section variations in wage rates play very different roles in labor supply and quite misleading labor supply estimates are obtained unless allowance is made for these different roles. Ashenfelter and Ham (1979) have taken both elements into account in analyzing longitudinal data from the Michigan Income Dynamics Survey.

The idea that the acquisition of education and skills in human beings could be regarded as a form of investment in a factor of production is not new – see, for example Marshall (1890). Closely related ideas are in Friedman and Kuznets (1954) and the empirical literature begins to accelerate after Mincer (1958) and Schultz (1960). Becker

(1964) is a classic reference that extends the theoretical foundations. Since then, a vast literature has accumulated. An excellent critical review is Blaug (1976). A survey of the empirical research with a more detailed discussion of models, data, and econometric procedures is S. Rosen (1977). Rosen (1972, 1974) has further discussion of the interaction of supply of and demand for human capital. Cain (1976) has surveyed the contrasts of the competitive approach to labor markets followed by most writers on human capital with that of noncompeting groups and the hypothesis of labor market duality of which Doeringer and Piore (1971) are major proponents. Atkinson (1975) has a good discussion of the implications for income distribution of labor market economics.

For a simple account of choice of occupation, see Friedman (1962) who draws on his well-known study, Friedman and Kuznets (1954). The application of the analysis of discrete choice to choice among occupations using panel data is still in its infancy, but will, no doubt, become an important research area.

As we have remarked, path analysis does not specifically rest on the assumptions of competitive labor markets, but focuses on genetic and family background influences on earnings. There has been considerable controversy about the measurement of the genetic component, and Griliches (1979) surveys sibling studies that attempt to identify the genetic component. Goldberger (1977, 1978) has shown that virtually all of the early studies have critical defects.

CHAPTER 12

The consumption function and intertemporal choice

We have already discussed, in Chapter 4, the straightforward extension of the neoclassical utility maximizing model to problems involving choice over consumption in different time periods. In this chapter, we extend the analysis in several directions. Section 12.1 considers various aspects of intertemporal planning, especially in the context of the individual's life cycle. First, the model is extended to allow simultaneous choice of consumption and labor supply, and we discuss how, given freedom of choice, we might expect consumers to vary their work and consumption levels in response to variations over the life cycle in prices and wages. We then turn to the more conventional case of constrained labor supply as discussed in Chapter 4, and illustrate the derivation of the consumption function with a model based on the AIDS of Chapter 3. The relationship between the consumption function and systems of demand equations is also briefly considered. Liquidity constraints in the form of borrowing restrictions or different rates of interest on borrowing and lending are then discussed, and their influence in raising the marginal propensity to consume is emphasized. Finally, we discuss the implications of the analysis for the relationship between the aggregates of consumption, income, and wealth. Section 12.2 considers the dynamics of the link between income and consumption, not only within the full intertemporal model but also taking into account other explanations and the econometric evidence. Section 12.3 is concerned with questions of imperfect information. The discussion is informal, in contrast to the more thorough treatment of uncertainty in Chapter 14. However, we show that imperfect information about price changes in times of rising inflation may act systematically to increase the savings ratio. Finally, §12.4 is concerned with the question of consistency in intertemporal choice: will a consumer, with unchanged preferences in an unchanged and perfectly foreseen economic environment, always choose to validate today's decisions for tomorrow when tomorrow actually comes? Like most paradoxes, the problem is based on a misunderstanding. Even so, consideration of the questions involved raises other, genuinely important issues.

12.1 Intertemporal planning and the life cycle

For nearly all of this chapter, we shall work with a single commodity q, subscripted to indicate the period in which it is consumed. It is perhaps simplest to think of it as a Hicks aggregate and, indeed, without specific information to the contrary, it will often make sense for a consumer to assume that the relative prices of goods in the future will not be subject to change. Alternatively, the consumer can be thought of as allocating in two stages according to weak intertemporal separability as discussed in Chapter 5: total consumption first and, conditional on this, the details of commodity expenditures. However, given the doubtful verdict on such systems of equations in Chapter 3, it is important to explore other approaches and we shall look at these briefly below.

Consumption and labor supply over the life cycle

Consider a single consumer at the beginning of the economic life cycle who is free to plan consumption and leisure supply for the present and the future up to some terminal future date. If we abstract from the existence of more than one consumer-worker in the household and if, as before, period 1 is the present and L is the terminal period, the relevant utility function can be written

$$u = v(q_{01}, q_1, q_{02}, q_2, \ldots, q_{0L}, q_L) \tag{1.1}$$

where q_{0t} is leisure time and q_t is consumption both in period t. The budget constraint is the intertemporal extension of equation (1.4) in Chapter 4 and requires that the present discounted value of expenditure on goods and leisure should equal the present value of "full wealth," the latter defined as assets plus the discounted present value of the time endowments. Hence, for discount factors ρ_t defined by

$$\rho_t = 1/(1 + r_t)(1 + r_{t-1}) \cdots (1 + r_2), \quad t = 2, \ldots, L \tag{1.2}$$

and $\rho_1 = 1$, the budget constraint is

$$\sum_1^L \rho_t p_t q_t + \sum_1^L \rho_t \omega_t q_{0t} \doteq \tilde{W}_1 \tag{1.3}$$

where ω_t is the wage rate in period t, and full wealth $\tilde{W}_1$ is given by

$$\tilde{W}_1 = (1 + r_1)A_0 + \sum_1^L \rho_t \omega_t T \tag{1.4}$$

assuming a common time endowment T in each period.

Equations (1.1) and (1.3) define a standard neoclassical utility-maximizing problem with a linear budget constraint. Note that this relies crucially on the assumption that households are free to lend and borrow at an identical rate of interest. The intertemporal plan thus consists of a set of consumption demand and labor supply functions ($\ell_t \equiv T - q_{0t}$)

$$q_t = \bar{g}_t(\bar{W}_1, \rho_1 p_1, \ldots, \rho_L p_L, \rho_1 \omega_1, \ldots, \rho_L \omega_L) \tag{1.5}$$

$$\ell_t = f_t(\bar{W}_1, \rho_1 p_1, \ldots, \rho_L p_L, \rho_1 \omega_1, \ldots, \rho_L \omega_L) \tag{1.6}$$

These equations are of the standard type and can be analyzed in the usual way. Note carefully that (1.5) is *not* a consumption function in the usual sense, even for q_1, consumption in the current period. Consumption is linked, not to income, assets, and prices, but to future time endowments, assets, wages, and prices. Incomes are endogenous to the model and are chosen by the consumer; they cannot thus appear on the right-hand side of (1.5). It is also important to realize that, since $t = 1$ is the beginning of the life cycle, the index t in (1.5) is an index of age rather than of "real" time.

Provided it is thought reasonable to suppose that individuals actually achieve such life-cycle plans, (1.5) and (1.6) can be empirically implemented, using data from individuals of different ages. In practice, the model is usually considerably restricted in order to yield firmer predictions. One possibility is to make the utility function (1.1) directly additive, that is,

$$u = \sum_1^L v_t(q_{0t}, q_t) \tag{1.7}$$

This limits substitutability between consumption in different periods in exactly the same way as, in the static context, additivity restricts substitutability between goods, see §5.3. However, in intertemporal choice, we should perhaps not expect very strong specific substitutabilities and complementarities between periods, so that in this context additivity is likely to be more acceptable. Further, since consumption in different periods is comparable in a way that consumption of different goods is not, the functions $v_t(\ )$ can be given a similar functional form. In particular, it is often assumed that (1.7) can be written

$$u = \sum_1^L \delta^{(t-1)} v^*(q_{0t}, q_t) \tag{1.8}$$

for a common function $v^*(\ )$ not indexed on t. The parameter δ, $0 < \delta < 1$, is interpreted as reflecting impatience on the part of consumers so that the benefits of future consumption and leisure are more heavily discounted the further into the future they occur. To relate δ to an interest rate, we can think of i defined by $\delta = 1/(1 + i)$ as the *rate of time preference*.

The utility function (1.8) and the budget constraint (1.3) readily yield their empirical implications. At an interior solution, using suffixes to denote partial differentiation, we have first-order conditions

$$v_1^*(q_{0t}, q_t) \delta^{(t-1)} = \lambda \omega_t \rho_t$$
$$v_2^*(q_{0t}, q_t) \delta^{(t-1)} = \lambda p_t \rho_t \tag{1.9}$$

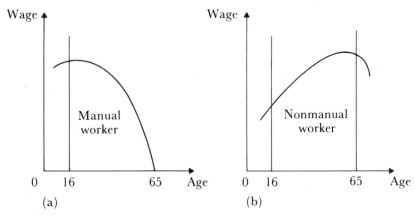

Figure 12.1. Life-cycle wage profiles for typical manual and nonmanual workers.

for some (positive) Lagrange multiplier λ. Hence, inverting (1.9)

$$q_{0t} = \phi(\lambda\omega_t\rho_t/\delta^{(t-1)}, \lambda p_t\rho_t/\delta^{(t-1)})$$
$$q_t = \theta(\lambda\omega_t\rho_t/\delta^{(t-1)}, \lambda p_t\rho_t/\delta^{(t-1)})$$

(1.10)

For specific functional forms, (1.10) for $t = 1, \ldots, L$ plus the budget constraint (1.3) will give an expression for λ that on substitution will give the conventional demand functions (1.5) and (1.6). However, (1.10) is extremely useful as it stands. The functions ϕ and θ are not indexed on t, nor is the quantity λ, which represents the influence of $\bar{W}_1$ as well as of all wages and prices other than those in period t. Hence, for a given consumer, life-cycle variations in labor supply and consumption depend entirely on life-cycle variations in $\omega_t\rho_t/\delta^{(t-1)}$ and $p_t\rho_t/\delta^{(t-1)}$. In the case where the $v^*(\ )$ functions are additively separable in the two arguments, v_1^* will depend only on $\omega_t\rho_t/\delta^{(t-1)}$ and v_2^* only on $p_t\rho_t/\delta^{(t-1)}$ so that q_{0t} through ϕ will be governed entirely by variations in $\omega_t\rho_t/\delta^{(t-1)}$ while q_t will be determined by $p_t\rho_t/\delta^{(t-1)}$. More generally, there will be cross effects in (1.10), and it can be shown, see Exercise 12.11, that ϕ_2 and θ_1 – the derivatives of ϕ and θ with respect to their second and first arguments – will be positive if leisure and consumption are substitutes or negative if leisure and consumption are complements. In any case, ϕ_1 and θ_2 are always negative.

Consider, then, the wage profiles illustrated in Figure 12.1. Since such profiles occur rather frequently, it is interesting to use them together with (1.10) to draw predictions for leisure and consumption behavior over the life span. Hence, if $p_t\rho_t/\delta^{t-1}$ is constant with age, life-cycle labor supply patterns will have the same general shapes as the curves, and empirical evidence not inconsistent with this has been presented, for example, by Ghez and Becker (1975).

Consumption, on the other hand, will be constant with age in the additive case, will have a similar pattern to labor supply if leisure and consumption are substitutes, and an inverse pattern if they are complements. The major determinant of consumption variations, however, is likely to be the term $p_t \rho_t / \delta^{t-1}$ which, according to the degree of substitution implicit in the utility function, will shift consumption towards periods where it is relatively cheap. As an example, if interest rates are constant, ρ_t / δ^{t-1} is simply $[(1 + i)/(1 + r)]^t$, so that, for constant prices, consumption will grow steadily with age if $r > i$ (the external rate of return overcoming impatience) and decline if $r < i$.

This model can be extended to make the wage rate a function of time spent in education and thus to yield predictions about education patterns and human capital formation over the life cycle, see Ghez and Becker. Note, however, that the model's ability to generate firm conclusions depends heavily on the specific form assumed for the intertemporal utility function. This may be plausible enough but the conclusions already discussed are not generally valid and are not implicit in the general solutions (1.5) and (1.6).

Consumption with constrained labor supply

In many circumstances, it is more reasonable to assume that consumers take their labor supply decisions as given and determine their intertemporal consumption conditional on expected future income streams rather than on wage rates. If we write $\overline{\ell}_1, \overline{\ell}_2, \ldots, \overline{\ell}_L$ for the number of hours the consumer expects to work in each period, then the decision problem is still given by (1.1) to (1.4) if we add the L constraints, $q_{0t} = T - \overline{\ell}_t$, rendering q_{0t} exogenous. Given this, we can rewrite (1.3) and (1.4) as

$$\sum_{1}^{L} \rho_t p_t q_t = W_1 \tag{1.11}$$

$$W_1 = (1 + r_1)A_0 + \sum_{1}^{L} \rho_t \omega_t (T - \overline{\ell}_t) = (1 + r_1)A_0 + \sum_{1}^{L} \rho_t y_t \tag{1.12}$$

where y_t is earned income in period t. This is the standard model analyzed in Chapter 4, see equation (2.11) there, and we need not repeat the earlier analysis. The consumption demand function (1.5) is replaced by

$$q_t = g_t(W_1, \rho_1 p_1, \ldots, \rho_L p_L, \overline{\ell}_1, \overline{\ell}_2, \ldots, \overline{\ell}_L) \tag{1.13}$$

Note specifically that since W_1 is defined over assets and incomes, the determining variables in (1.13) are quite different from those in (1.5). Second, the wage rates in (1.5) are replaced by the exogenous $\overline{\ell}$'s in (1.13). Changes in these hours will have income effects through W_1 – see (1.12) – but, in general, must appear in their own right in (1.13). For example, an unemployed consumer and an employed consumer with differing amounts of assets might have identical W_1's but quite different lifetime consumption plans. The ℓ's will be absent from (1.13) only in the (unlikely) event that leisure is weakly separable from consumption in (1.1), see §5.1. For notational convenience only, we shall usually suppress these arguments when presenting consumption function equations, but unless stated to the contrary, they should always be taken as implicitly present.

Once again, the life-cycle consumption plan given by (1.13) is best illustrated by a specific example, albeit a fairly general one. Since the maximization problem involves a linear budget constraint, preferences can be characterized by the intertemporal cost function $c(u, p^*)$ for discounted prices $\rho_t p_t = p_t^*$; for a utility maximizing consumer, this will take the value W_1. The *intertemporal AIDS* is thus defined by

$$
\log W_1 = \log c(u, p^*) = \alpha_0 + \sum_1^L \alpha_t \log p_t^*
$$
$$
+ \frac{1}{2} \sum_1^L \sum_1^L \lambda_{ts}^* \log p_t^* \log p_s^* + u \prod_1^L p_t^{*\beta_t}
$$

(1.14)

Differentiating and rearranging [cf. Chapter 3 (4.6)], the intertemporal consumption plan viewed from $t = 1$ is given by

$$
p_t^* q_t = \alpha_t W_1 + \beta_t W_1 \log \frac{W_1}{P^*} + \sum_{s=1}^L \gamma_{ts} W_1 \log p_s^*
$$

(1.15)

where P^* is a price index encompassing all the discounted prices $p_1^*, \ldots, p_L^*$. The α_t's, which add to unity over the life cycle, can be thought of as reflecting the pattern of needs over the life span; if, for example, these were equally spread, we should have $\alpha = 1/L$. Each of the last two terms in (1.15) adds to zero over the life cycle. The first represents the way in which increasing wealth causes rearrangements of the desired life-cycle profile of consumption; this seems likely to be small in most cases. The final term reflects intertemporal rearrangement of consumption to take advantage of relatively low-price periods. If $\beta_t = 0$ and $\gamma_{ts} = 0$, the model reduces to Cobb-Douglas $p_t q_t = \alpha_t W_1$, which as discussed in Chapter 4 implies unrealistically high intertemporal substitution. This can be reduced in (1.15) if $\gamma_{tt} > 0$ for each t.

The effects of replanning

Models such as this can be used to compare consumption behavior of different age groups conditional on wealth and prices as described for labor supply and consumption taken together. Alternatively, as we shall see below,

(1.13) can be aggregated over age groups to derive implications for the economy as a whole. However, note that equations such as (1.13) are derived by the consumer at the beginning of the life cycle, presumably in full knowledge of all future incomes and prices. This is clearly unrealistic, and we might expect that such equations will give actual demands only for the first period of the plan. Subsequently, as new information becomes available, expectations of the future will be revised and new plans will be calculated. Consider, in particular, the variable W_1 as defined by (1.12). As time passes, the consumer will observe actual incomes and discount rates, so that at each point in the life cycle, W_1 can be recalculated and these estimates will generally differ, since it is only at time L that the final value of W_1 becomes known with certainty. The same is true of the price variables in (1.13) and (1.15). In consequence, at each point in the cycle, there is a different complete life-cycle consumption plan associated with the then best estimates of W_1 and prices. But such plans will generally involve the recognition that previous consumption levels are not optimal, given the new information, and since the past cannot be altered, the actual consumption function will not simply be (1.13) with the current estimates of W_1 and prices, but will be further modified by the influence of past consumption. This influence, which is comparable to that of rationing (see §4.3), takes two forms; on the one hand, previous consumption levels affect current asset levels and thus exert income effects on present and future consumption, while on the other hand, there may be substitution effects as the consumer compensates for previous consumption levels that now appear to be too high or too low.

Such effects cannot easily be illustrated in the AIDS, but if we take the Cobb-Douglas case, $p_t^* q_t = \alpha_t W_1$ represents optimal planned consumption at age t as seen from age 1. This can more accurately be written

$$p_t^* q_t^1 = \alpha_t E_1(W_1) \tag{1.16}$$

where the superscript denotes planning time and $E_\tau(\ )$ is the (point) expectation held at time τ. When the consumer actually reaches age t, the plan for t will become effective as q_t^t and this will be calculated by maximizing utility subject to (1.12) as perceived at t and subject to $q_1, \ldots, q_{t-1}$ taking their *actual* values $q_1^1, \ldots, q_{t-1}^{t-1}$. In the Cobb-Douglas case, utility is given by $\Sigma_1^L \alpha_\tau \log q_\tau$, so that the life-cycle problem, as seen at time t, is to maximize this subject to the new perception of the lifetime budget constraint, $E_t(W_1) = \Sigma_1^L p_\tau^* q_\tau$, and the previously fixed levels, $q_\tau = q_\tau^\tau, \tau = 1, \ldots, t-1$. In general, of course, the expectation of prices will also have changed, but we ignore this for simplicity of exposition. Since the Cobb-Douglas function is additively separable over time, we can ignore the presence of the first $(t-1)$ terms in utility, which are now fixed, so that the consumers life-cycle problem as seen at time t can be rewritten as, choose $q_t, \ldots, q_L$ to maximize $\Sigma_t^L \alpha_\tau \log q_\tau$ subject to

$E_t(W_1) - \Sigma_1^{t-1} p_\tau^* \, q_\tau^\tau = \Sigma_t^T p_\tau^* q_\tau$, which has solutions

$$p_t^* q_t^t = \alpha_t^* \left[E_t(W_1) - \sum_1^{t-1} p_\tau^* q_\tau^\tau \right] \qquad (1.17)$$

where $\alpha_t^* = \alpha_t/(1 - \Sigma_1^{t-1} \alpha_\tau)$. This equation gives *actual* consumption for an individual at t if preferences have the Cobb-Douglas form. Of course, such an example is very special but it suggests generalizations for rewriting (1.17) in two other forms. First, consider the consumption levels for $\tau = 1, \ldots, (t - 1)$ which, with hindsight at time t, are seen to be optimal; these are written q_τ^t, $\tau = 1, \ldots, t - 1$, and in the present case are equal to $\alpha_\tau E_t(W_1)$. Using this, we can rearrange (1.17) to

$$p_t^* q_t^t = \alpha_t E_t(W_1) + \alpha_t^* \sum_1^{t-1} p_\tau^*(q_\tau^t - q_\tau^\tau) \qquad (1.18)$$

The first term of (1.18) is the original plan for $p_t^* q_t$ reevaluated at $E_t(W_1)$ rather than $E_1(W_1)$, while the second term shows the modifying influence of what, with hindsight, are seen to be "errors" in past consumption. In general, the relationship between actual consumption and the optimal lifetime plan re-calculated with current perceptions will be much more complex than (1.18), but the idea is clear enough and indicates the errors that can be involved in applying optimal consumption plans to real data.

An alternative form of (1.17) comes from the recognition that $E_t(W_t)$, the current expectation of the current discounted wealth position, is linked to $E_t(W_1)$ via the identity $\rho_t E_t(W_t) \equiv E_t(W_1) - \Sigma_1^{t-1} p^* q_\tau^\tau$, see Exercise 12.6. Substituting this into (1.17) gives

$$p_t q_t = \alpha_t^* E_t(W_t) \qquad (1.19)$$

Hence, in this simple case, current actual consumption levels are related to the current wealth position, and the influence of past consumption levels is confined to the latter. However, as we shall see in §12.4, (1.19) depends on the fact that the Cobb-Douglas utility function is intertemporally separable, and in general, actual consumption at age t will depend on both W_t and past values of consumption. Note that even in the simple formulation (1.19), α_t^* is not equal to α_t in (1.16) or the first term of (1.18). Nevertheless, basing actual consumption functions on life-cycle plans such as (1.13) and allowing for the effects of new information, provides us with important information on the relationship between consumption and age that can be exploited in both micro-economic and macroeconomic studies.

Before concluding this section, note the relationship between aggregate consumption models such as (1.19) or the AIDS applied as in (1.14) and (1.15) to Hicks aggregates of goods at different times, on the one hand, and to systems of demand equations on the other. Note first that the existence of such models as the LES or AIDS defined on p_t and x_t and discussed in Chapter 3 depends on weak intertemporal separability to justify making commodity demands depend on within-period prices and total expenditure alone. Weak separability also is an approximate alternative to the assumption that prices in each period move in parallel, which is needed to define Hicks aggregates: as we saw in §5.2 it can be used to give aggregate equations such as (1.19) and (1.15) a justification as approximations. Of course, there is no need to use the same cost function for both levels of the hierarchy. Thus we might well use AIDS at the detailed commodity level and a CES or some other relatively simple form at the level of intertemporal aggregates. However, consumption functions such as (1.13) or (1.15) can result from a much wider range of assumptions than weak separability (e.g., implicit separability or the example in Exercise 12.9). Acceptance of these would imply that the standard static models linking q_t to x_t and p_t would have to be abandoned, but given the empirical evidence on such models, this would probably be a healthy development.

Consumption functions with liquidity constraints

The models considered so far all relate consumption behavior to wealth, in the form of either financial assets or discounted future income. Current income is important only in so far as it contributes to the latter either in its own right as a component part or through the formation of expectations about future income (see Chapter 4). However, much of the literature on the consumption function emphasizes not wealth but rather liquidity, the immediate means of paying for consumption. For consumers who cannot borrow, or can only do so at penal rates of interest, consumption expenditures are likely to be closely tied to income receipts. To model these effects, the life-cycle model already discussed must be modified to allow for constraints limiting the negativity of assets.

In some cases, the lifetime consumption plan (1.13) may be unaffected. A consumer who is fortunate enough to inherit large amounts of financial assets with which to begin the life cycle or one who expects to be most highly paid at the beginning of his career may be a net creditor throughout his life. However, for consumers with income profiles derived from the wage-age relationships in Figure 12.1b, a relatively even distribution of consumptin needs throughout life will imply that it is optimal to accumulate debts early in the life span. For many consumers, a good deal of this can be accomplished by borrowing for house purchase through specialized institutions such as building societies or savings and loan associations. However, if these needs are not met, consumption will be below what it would have been with borrowing allowed in the early years of the life span; this can be made up by higher con-

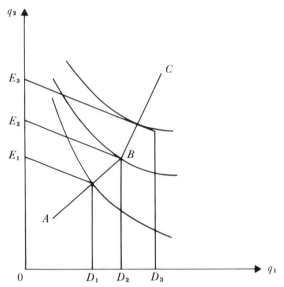

Figure 12.2. The effect of a borrowing constraint.

sumption later, but at a net cost of welfare because of the forced intertemporal rearrangement. Correspondingly, given the standard earnings profiles, net asset holdings for borrowing constrained consumers will always be at least as high as those of unconstrained consumers whether or not the constraints are actually binding at that moment. However, perhaps the most important effect of borrowing constraints is to increase the marginal propensity to consume for the economy as a whole. Clearly, for consumers who are constrained to borrow less than they would wish, any increase in available resources will be spent.

We can illustrate this for a two-period model in Figure 12.2. Assume the borrowing constraint means that assets at the end of period 1, $A_1 \geq \bar{A}_1$ for some given $\bar{A}_1$. Since $A_1 \equiv (1 + r_1)A_0 + y_1 - p_1 q_1$, the restriction implies that $p_1 q_1 \leq y_1 + (1 + r_1)A_0 - \bar{A}_1$; that is, that current consumption expenditures be limited to current income plus (less) the value of current assets (debts) including interest receipts (payments). The presence of this inequality induces the vertical segments on the lines $E_1 D_1$, $E_2 D_2$, and $E_3 D_3$. If instead of an absolute borrowing constraint we assume that borrowing is always possible, albeit at a rate higher than the lending rate, the vertical segments are replaced by segments more steeply sloped than the left-hand side of the budget constraint. However, in both cases, the budget constraints are kinked. Those illustrated each correspond to a different value of y_1, so that ABC is the expansion path as current income increases. The constrained consumer is at the kink on the budget constraint and as long as he remains so, increases in y_1, for example, from D_1 to D_2, are translated directly into increases in q_1. Eventually, however, above D_2, increases in current income will be large enough to overcome the borrowing restriction and points along the unrestricted slope will be reached.

The issue of which consumers are constrained and which unconstrained is thus of considerable importance in determining the degree to which current income determines consumption in the economy as a whole. Clearly, those with high initial assets or high current income are unlikely to wish to borrow (or to have difficulty doing so should they wish). Conversely, high future expectations of earnings may well induce the need to borrow. To take a concrete example, suppose the first period's unconstrained consumption plan is $p_1 q_1 = \alpha_1 W_1$. This can be rationalized either by a Cobb-Douglas utility function or by any homothetic intertemporal utility function, for example, the homothetic form of AIDS with $\beta_t = 0$, all t in (1.15), as long as expected intertemporal prices are constant. Then borrowing will be required if $\alpha_1 W_1 \geq y_1 + (1 + r_1)A_0 - \bar{A}_1$. Substituting for W_1 from (1.12), the condition for the borrowing constraint to be binding is that

$$\sum_2^L \rho_t y_t > \frac{(1 - \alpha_1)}{\alpha_1} [y_1 + (1 + r_1)A_0 - \bar{A}_1] \tag{1.20}$$

Note that since $(1 - \alpha_1)/\alpha_1$ decreases with α_1, which measures current consumption needs, whether or not a household is constrained depends on a balance of expectations, needs, income, and assets. As y_1 increases, borrowing becomes less likely since the right-hand side of (1.20) increases, see Figure 12.2. However, the expected future values of income are likely to rise with increases in current income, and this will magnify the increase in y_1 needed to remove the constraint, see Exercise 12.4.

In a world of imperfect information, there are likely to be other reasons why consumers face borrowing restrictions. Lenders may be unable to assess the ability of potential clients to repay their loans and are likely to fall back on easily observable characteristics that are thought to be correlated with this unobservable quantity. In consequence, consumers who are unemployed may find they cannot borrow, even if their future earning potential is in fact good. Similarly, access to funds may be denied on grounds of sex, age, color, or social status. In line with the theory, we should thus expect systematic differences in savings and consumption behavior for such groups because of the liquidity constraints. Without such a realization, such differences may be ascribed to "tastes," and this is another excellent example of the importance of modeling constraints correctly if we are to understand behavior.

Implications for aggregate consumption

It should be clear from the foregoing discussion that, for the consumption function, there is little point in attempting to find conditions under which aggregate behavior will mirror the behavior of some representative consumer. As we saw in Chapter 6, perfect aggregation in the single-period model depended on all prices being the same for all individuals with only variations in income allowed. As soon as prices were allowed to vary as well as incomes, aggregation became much more difficult and the conditions permitting it correspondingly more stringent. With intertemporal choices, not only do consumers differ in their incomes and asset positions, but they differ in age, in expectations about future prices and income, and in the extent to which they are constrained. Some consumers can vary their working hours, others cannot; some can borrow, others cannot or only at very high rates of interest. Faced with these complications, one approach is to follow Dolde and Tobin (1971) in the use of computer simulation based on "realistic" assumptions about population structure, income, and asset distributions and the incidence of constraints to construct a macroeconomic consumption function. This can be used to gauge the importance of these effects and as a complement to further econometric work at the micro and macro levels. Alternatively, we can draw out a series of isolated effects, each of which is likely to play a part in determining overall behavior and this is the approach we follow here.

The macroeconomic implications of the life-cycle model are perhaps the most familiar. If we ignore bequests, savings and asset accumulation exist only to transmit purchasing power from one period to another, and since there are few grounds to suppose that increasing wealth causes some periods of the life cycle to be differentially favored over others (i.e., it is plausible that preferences over time are approximately homothetic), the hypothesis suggests that savings, consumption, and wealth will grow proportionately over time (provided there are no major upsetting factors such as radical changes in distribution or in the extent of constraints). Since, for a given growth rate of income, income and wealth are proportional in the long run, this gives the famous result of the secular constancy of the savings ratio. The empirical evidence in favor of this proposition is not as conclusive as many writers suppose. Certainly, Kuznets (1962) found not only that the ratio had been virtually constant over a century or so in the United States but also that in virtually all long time-series data available to him, savings increased much less with income than would be supposed from looking at either short-run time series or cross-section data from individual households. However, it has been suggested that the American result is the consequence of a number of disturbing forces that are mutually offsetting, see Friedman (1957, pp. 119–124), and for most European countries, the savings ratio shows evidence of some upward trend over time, although this can undoubtedly be explained on other grounds, see, for example, Deaton (1975c).

The life-cycle model also tells us a great deal about the link between demographic variables, income growth, and savings. Although neither income flows nor consumption needs are evenly spread over the life cycle, the latter are likely to be more stable than the former with income flows following the sort of patterns illustrated in Figure 12.1. In particular, household consumption needs are highest in the years of family formation while income flows are lowest after retirement. Consequently, the early years of the life cycle are likely to be ones of low saving or dissaving. Later on, savings become positive reaching a peak sometime before retirement, after which point there is dissaving. Consequently, the aggregate relationship between consumption and income depends both upon the age structure of the population and on the relative incomes of different age groups within it. Hence, if incomes are growing rapidly, then in the absence of a major redistribution from the young to the old, the old will be dissaving out of relatively small accumulated assets while the young (or middle-aged) will be saving out of relatively large incomes. This results in a larger overall savings ratio than for an economy with lower long-term growth in incomes. This effect is likely to be reinforced in an economy with a larger proportion of income profiles as in the first half of Figure 12.1 since people with such profiles are likely to do more saving during their working lives and more dissaving in retirement. Similarly, a rapidly growing population is one in which a small proportion is in the retirement phase and, hence, is one with a high aggregate savings ratio, other things (including per capita real income) being equal. A temporary baby boom is likely to cause a small temporary reduction in the aggregate savings ratio as these former babies pass through the family formation stage, an increase in the ratio as they reach the peak of their earnings potential, and then later, a longer and larger reduction in the ratio as they go through the retirement phase. Note finally that, in the absence of a bequest motive, the life-cycle model suggests that in a stationary economy, with neither population nor income growth, the savings ratio should be zero. The saving of the young is exactly offset by the dissaving of the old. These "rate of growth" effects have been documented by a number of economists [see, e.g., Modigliani and Brumberg (1955b), Farrell (1959, 1970), Tobin (1967), Russell (1977)], and there exists a good deal of empirical evidence for them, both from observing cross-country savings ratios [Modigliani (1970), Surrey (1974)] and from drawing out the implications of time-series results for individual countries [see the tabulations in Stone (1966) or Deaton (1972b)]. Exercise 12.5 provides an example of how simple formulas for such effects can be derived in rather special cases.

All this analysis has to be modified when we take into account the differing types of constraints facing different consumers. For example, as we saw, consumers who are free to alter their labor supply will have different types of consumption functions from those whose labor supply is predetermined. The extent of the difference will depend on the extent of the constraint, hence, in aggregate, the proportion of self-employed workers is likely to be important in determining consumption, while, for those who are constrained, variables such as unemployment expectations will have important influences on current savings and spending decisions. Liquidity constraints are also important in aggregate. As we saw, an economy with a less developed financial system is likely to be one with a higher average savings ratio since liquidity constraints will limit dissaving via borrowing for many consumers. The aggregate marginal propensity to consume will also depend crucially on the proportion of consumers who face borrowing restrictions. In aggregate, this proportion will depend, through inequalities such as (1.16) on the distribution in the population of assets, needs, income, and expectations. Although such relationships are hard to model formally, some general points are clear. If there are borrowing constraints, the full life-cycle model is unlikely to have much relevance at the lower end of the income distribution when, for example, there is a temporary fall of income. If borrowing is impossible, consumers without assets are in no position to maintain consumption. Even here, however, the life-cycle model may give the same result. If expectations linking future to current income are highly elastic, then, even at the beginning of a recession, since expectations of future income fall with the fall in current income, the proportion of households who actually wish to borrow and are prevented from doing so may be quite small. Hence, the implications of a high elasticity of expectations and of borrowing constraints are the same: a high marginal propensity to consume. Note that to the extent that borrowing constraints are binding, many consumers with substantial assets may be affected if these are illiquid in the sense of being difficult or costly to encash or unacceptable as collateral for short-term loans. This applies not only to such obviously illiquid assets as used consumer durables but could well extend to equities or government bonds. If interest rates are temporarily high or the stock market temporarily low, the costs of unplanned liquidation may be high enough to enforce a cut in consumption in response to a temporary cut in current income. All these considerations suggest that the marginal propensity to consume is a complex function of current economic conditions but they certainly provide no basis for the supposition that, in accord with the crudest interpretation of the life-cycle model, the marginal propensity to consume out of current aggregate income should be very small.

Another important modifying influence on the life-cycle consumption theory is the provision of savings institutions and public goods by the state. In aggregate these are paid for out of taxes so that there is no net income effect of such provisions, although this may disguise important distributional changes. In addition, however, many of these provisions act as a substitute for private expenditures or private provision for future expenditures. In recent years, there has been much discussion of the so-called ultrarational view, that consumers have full information about and discount correctly all such government activities, particularly those linked to intertemporal decision making [see, e.g., David and Scadding (1974) and Feldstein (1976b)]. Hence an increase in taxes is fully offset by a reduction in savings if the former is used by the state to accumulate real wealth which supposedly reduces consumers' needs for their own assets in the future. These views are central to the debate on the "crowding-out" effects of fiscal policy, a debate that goes back to the early arguments between monetarists and Keynesians and has its roots in the controversies of the interwar years on how to cure unemployment. For recent and earlier references, see Buiter (1977), Hancock (1960), and Cochrane (1970). One problem with the approach in its extreme form is the "fallacy of composition" which it embodies; an individual may know that social wealth is created with the taxes he pays but he has no guarantee that he personally will benefit from it. This and the (clearly invalid) assumption made about the amount of information that consumers possess are the two main objections to the position. However, this does not invalidate the idea that when state pension schemes or state insurance arrangements are extended, it is plausible that some reduction in private saving will take place. Indeed, many of the long-term developments in the structure of consumer demand can be accounted for by developments of this kind, see again Kuznets (1962). Yet, even in these cases, where the information available to consumers is excellent (at least in the long term), we would not necessarily expect a one-for-one reduction.

Exercises

12.1. In Ghez and Becker's version of the consumption-leisure model, utility is defined solely on commodities $q_1^*, \ldots, q_L^*$ which are produced by leisure and market consumption according to constant returns to scale production functions $q_t^* = F(q_{0t}, q_t)$. Is this model substantively different from that discussed in this section? How does the interpretation differ?

12.2. Using Figure 12.2, or otherwise, analyze the income and substitution effects of a change in r_t in the presence of liquidity constraints as compared with the unconstrained case discussed in §4.2.

12.3. Using the AIDS consumption function (1.15), analyze the effects of future price expectations on the likelihood of a borrowing constraint actually binding. If the Barten model of household composition effects can be used in an intertemporal context (see §8.4), discuss what type of families are most likely to be constrained. Is it likely that the proportion of liquidity constrained consumers will remain constant over time?

12.4. Using the inequality (1.20) and assuming that $\alpha_1 = 1/L$, show that expectations elasticities are unlikely to be high enough so that increases in y_1 increase the left-hand

side more than the right-hand side. How robust do you think this conclusion is likely t
be with respect to respecifications of the utility functions? Discuss the implications fo
the effects of changes in current income on the proportion of consumers who are l
quidity constrained.

12.5. Assume that in an economy with zero population growth and a zero interest rate
there is a rectangular distribution of ages, that all individuals are the same, that retire
ment takes place after N years in the labor force and death $(L - N)$ years later. As
sume that all individuals have identical tastes, that for each individual's working life ir
come is constant, that all choose to spread consumption evenly over the L years of life
that there is steady growth of incomes at rate g (i.e., between age groups so that all ind
viduals of age 0 have constant lifetime income $e^{\tau g}$ times that of an individual of age
where $\tau \leq N$) and show that the savings ratio is

$$1 - \frac{N}{L}\left(\frac{1 - e^{-Lg}}{1 - e^{-Ng}}\right)$$

Show that, for reasonable values of N and L, this is close to the relationship $1 - e^{-5}$
found by Davidson, Hendry and others (1978), see below.

12.6. Define the *current* discounted wealth at age t by

$$W_t = A_{t-1}(1 + r_t) + y_t + \rho_t^{-1}\sum_{t+1}^{L} y_\tau \rho_\tau \qquad (1.21)$$

show that if expectations are fulfilled, $W_t = (1 + r_t)(W_{t-1} - p_{t-1}q_{t-1})$. Now write η_t fo
the change in discounted income prospects between t and $t - 1$, that is,

$$\eta_t = E_t\left(y_t + \rho_t^{-1}\sum_{t+1}^{L} y_\tau \rho_\tau\right) - E_{t-1}\left(\rho_{t-1}^{-1}\sum_{t}^{L} y_\tau \rho_\tau\right) \qquad (1.22$$

Show that W_t is linked to W_1 via the identity

$$E_t(W_t) \equiv \rho_t^{-1}\left[E_1(W_1) - \sum_1^{t-1} p_\tau^* q_\tau^\tau + \sum_2^t \rho_\tau \eta_\tau\right] \qquad (1.23$$

12.7. The intertemporal LES has utility function $\Sigma_1^L \beta_t \log(q_t - \gamma_t)$. Derive the life-cycl
consumption plan viewed from the beginning of life, that is , equation (1.13). Show
that, with such preferences, the life-cycle hypothesis does *not* predict a constant long
run savings ratio. Why is this and do you consider the result evidence against the likel
hood of a constant ratio?

12.8. Show that if expectations are not always fulfilled, the *actual* consumption level o
an individual of age t with LES preferences as above is given by

$$p_t^* q_t^t = \alpha_t^*\left[E_1(W_1) - \sum_1^{t-1} p_\tau^* q_\tau^\tau + \sum_2^t \rho_\tau \eta_\tau\right] - \alpha_t^* \sum_t^L \gamma_\tau E_t(p_\tau^*) + \gamma_t p_t^* \qquad (1.24$$

where $\alpha_t^* = \alpha_t/(1 - \Sigma_1^{t-1}\alpha_\tau)$ and η_t is as defined in Exercise 12.6. Rewrite (1.24) usin
(1.23) and interpret the resulting relationship between consumption and curren
wealth.

12.9. If we distinguish individual commodities in each period so that q_{ti} is the deman
for i in period t, then the full intertemporal AIDS is given by

$$\frac{p_{ti}^* q_{ti}}{W_1} = \alpha_{ti} + \sum_s \sum_j \gamma_{tisj} \log p_{sj}^* + \beta_{ti} \log\left(\frac{W_1}{P^*}\right)$$

for parameters α_{ti}, γ_{tisj}, and β_{ti}, $s,t = 1, \ldots, L$, $i,j = 1, \ldots, n$. By analogy wit
(4.6) and (4.7) of Chapter 3 derive and interpret a form for P^*. Interpret the restrictio

$\iota\beta_{ti} = 0$ and suggest other plausible restrictions on the parameters. Derive a consumption function from the equation and compare your result with (1.15).

2.10. A household maximizes the life-cycle utility function

$$u = \sum_1^L \alpha_t \log q_t + \sum_1^N \beta_t \log q_{0t} + \sum_{N+1}^L \beta_t \log T$$

where the periods $N + 1$ to L represent the retirement phase and where $\Sigma_1^L \alpha_t + \Sigma_1^N \beta_t =$. It faces the neoclassical, life-cycle budget constraint $W = \Sigma_1^L \rho_t p_t q_t + \Sigma_1^N \rho_t \omega_t q_{0t}$. Suppose that the only type of corner solution possible is that, for some or all periods, the household may not participate in the labor force. Show that the first-order conditions for the optimization problem are given by

$$q_t = \alpha_t / \lambda \rho_t p_t$$

and $\quad q_{0t} = \beta_t / \lambda \rho_t \omega_t \quad$ if $q_{0t} < T$ (i.e., participation > 0)

$\qquad q_{0t} \leq \beta_t / \lambda \rho_t \omega_t \quad$ if $q_{0t} = T$ (i.e., participation $= 0$)

For which periods do the household plans make participation least likely? Contrast λ in the case where the household plans to participate for all N-periods with the case where it plans to retire at $N_1 < N$.

2.11. Rewrite (1.9) in the form

$$v_1^*(q_{0t}, q_t) = \lambda \omega_t \rho_t / \delta^{t-1}$$

$$v_2^*(q_{0t}, q_t) = \lambda p_t \rho_t / \delta^{t-1}$$

Totally differentiate both equations, and solve the resulting simultaneous equations for dq_{0t} and dq_t. Hence, derive the signs of ϕ_1, ϕ_2, θ_1, and θ_2 in equation (1.10) above. Discuss the use of the words "complements" and "substitutes" in the foregoing presentation of life-cycle variations of consumption.

2.2 The dynamics of income and consumption

The empirical implementation of the consumption functions discussed in Section 1 is far from straightforward. Apart from the problems of aggregation already discussed, there are formidable data problems. Although income, consumption, prices, and interest rates are adequately measured, at least in principle, this is not true of assets or of expectations. For several countries, asset data are available, derived either from accumulated savings figures or from inferences based on assets left at death. However, such figures are nearly always admitted to be highly unreliable, if only because it is frequently impossible to accurately allow for the large proportions of private wealth owned, not by households, but by charities, trusts, or small owner-run businesses. This suggests that, even where asset series are available, it may be preferable to rely on proxies or on methods that do not require the use of asset data. The situation is even more difficult for expectations, and although some recent work has attempted to use the results of consumer surveys, the vast majority of studies have relied on some proxying technique. In particular, since the behavior of past incomes is likely to contain relevant information about their likely future course, much attention has been focused on modeling the dynamics of the relationship between consumption and income. Although other variables are undoubtedly important, the vast majority of empirical consumption functions ever estimated draw a high percentage of their explanatory power from the link between consumption and income. It is thus of great importance to understand the implications of the various theories for the nature of this relationship and to see how the empirical estimates confirm or disconfirm them.

Direct estimation of life-cycle models

In his famous study of the consumption function, Friedman (1957) uses a model of the form

$$q_t = k y_t^p + \epsilon_t \tag{2.1}$$

where ϵ_t is transitory consumption, assumed uncorrelated with real permanent consumption $k y_t^p$. The quantity y_t^p, is "permanent" income, which as we saw in §4.2 can be thought of as that quantity which, if received as a constant stream over the life cycle, has a real present value equal to W_1. As already argued, this interpretation is likely to imply that, at the very least, k should be a function of real interest rates. However, here we are more concerned with the interpretation of y_t^p and its relation to W_1. One of the crucial issues is how such a construct models the elasticity of future income expectations with respect to changes in current income. Friedman makes the assumption that permanent income is uncorrelated with "transient" income (permanent income plus transient income = measured income), which can only occur if the elasticity is close to zero. Hence, to the extent that such a supposition is built into the empirical work, the issue of the size of the short-run marginal propensity to consume is being essentially prejudged in favor of a very low value. However, Friedman leaves the construction of y_t^p to "empirical observation" and in his own econometric work, after allowing for a trend rate of growth, constructs permanent income from the rule

$$y_t^p = \lambda \left[\left(\frac{y_t}{p_t} \right) + (1 - \lambda) \left(\frac{y_{t-1}}{p_{t-1}} \right) + (1 - \lambda)^2 \left(\frac{y_{t-2}}{p_{t-2}} \right) + \cdots \right] \tag{2.2}$$

that is, as a weighted average, with geometrically declining weights, of current and past real incomes. Since, if λ is not too close to zero, $(1 - \lambda)^t$ rapidly becomes small, the infinite series in (2.2) can be truncated after a finite number of terms. (Friedman, in fact, goes back 17 years, although for his estimated value of λ of one-third, only the first six to nine have significant weight.)

The proxy (2.2) has been very widely used, often together with (2.1), but usually without the correction for trend used by Friedman. Such a procedure is fraught with theoretical difficulties. One argument often put forward for (2.2) is that, under certain circumstances such a scheme will generate an "optimal" forecast of future real income. Indeed, Sargent (1977) has shown that if real income follows the pattern

$$(y/p)_t = (y/p)_{t-1} + a + u_t - (1 - \lambda) u_{t-1} \tag{2.3}$$

where u_t is a serially independent error process, then the expectation of $(y/p)_{t+1}$ calculated at time t, $E_t[(y/p)_{t+1}]$ is given by $y_t^p + a/\lambda$, see Exercise 12.15. Hence, if we add an intercept to (2.1), the formulation (2.2) can be regarded as modeling expectations of future income, at least one period ahead. The weaknesses of such an approach are obvious: there is no reason to suppose that real income does obey (2.3), at least without testing, nor is income one period ahead the relevant theoretical quantity that permanent income is supposed to represent. Consequently, formulas such as (2.2), even corrected for growth in incomes (the a in 2.3), are likely to give poor forecasts of variables that are in any case only a part of the relevant magnitude. For example, the *rate of change* of income is likely to be an important variable in determining expectations of the future, and perhaps the simplest formulas for expected future income would involve both current income and its rate of change. But if this is so, the lag structure of income in the consumption function may contain terms with *negative* weights, so that neither (2.2) nor any other representation involving essentially positive weights can possibly be appropriate. This criticism applies not only to declining geometric lags such as (2.2) but to the whole range of low-degree Almon polynomials that are frequently used in the consumption function. Distributed lags are certainly required in the consumption function, but it is essential that their form not be overly restricted a priori and that estimated forms be tested against more general alternatives.

Another weakness of distributed lag formulations of models such as (2.1) is their incompleteness. No account is taken of expectations about unemployment nor about the effects of current inflation rates upon anticipated future levels of income. Similarly, there may be available at particular times specific information that is highly relevant: for example, a government incomes policy under which no one can have pay increases exceeding 10 percent. Perhaps most serious, however, is the ommission of assets that is implicit in replacing y_t^p by a measure depending only on incomes. Not only does this mean that the independent effects of A are confused with those of y, but also, since assets are related through saving to past incomes and expenditures, that the lag structure between consumption and income is further distorted. Note too that we lose the important error correction mechanism that assets provide in their role as a link between the past, present, and future. If, in period 1, the consumer makes mistakes so that, for example, consumption is higher than de-

sired, assets will be lower than their desired level and subsequent consump
tion will be lowered in compensation [see, e.g., (1.17) and (1.18)]. No such
error correction exists in models such as (2.1) and (2.2), which omit assets en
tirely.

Assets are accorded an explicit role in the important paper by Ando and
Modigliani (1963). They start from the homothetic model in which at con
stant prices consumption is proportional to W_1 for each age group and ag
gregate by assuming that the distributions of assets, income, and expected in
come are each invariant with respect to age structure. This gives rise to an
equation in terms of aggregate variables, given

$$p_t q_t = \beta_1 y_t + \beta_2 y_t^e + \beta_3 A_t \qquad (2.4$$

where y_t^e is an aggregate measure of expected future incomes and β_1, β_2, and
β_3 are parameters. Ando and Modigliani make two alternative assumptions
about y_t^e, first that it is proportional to y_t and second that it is related both to y
and to y_t weighted by a factor that depends on the current unemploymen
rate. This is intended to capture the lower income expectations of the unem
ployed. On annual American data for 1929–59, excluding 1941–6, and de
fining consumption to include the services of durables (see §4.2), it was
found that differencing was required to remove positive first-order serial cor
relation in the residuals. Upon doing this, the short-run (one-year) marginal
propensity to consume out of current disposable labor income is found to be
0.55 or larger, while the coefficient on assets is estimated between 0.05 and
0.08 suggesting a planning horizon (average life cycle) of from 10 to 20 years
Clearly, this procedure is much closer to the spirit of the theory than is
Friedman's. However, note that once again the proxy for future income ex
pectations, although more plausible, remains untested, and there must re
main doubts over the measurement of assets. At the same time, the strong
first-order autocorrelation in the residuals of the levels equation suggests tha
these problems may be having serious effects. We shall return to both issues

The role of lagged dependent variables

From a very early stage in the literature on the consumption function, it was
found that the use of lagged consumption as well as current income as a re
gressor yielded a considerable increase in explanatory power as well as giving
a model that seemed consistent with both short-term and long-term evidence
Indeed, the consumption function

$$q_t = \beta_0 + \beta_1(y_t/p_t) + \beta_2 q_{t-1} + u_t \qquad (2.5$$

with y_t usually including asset income ($r_t A_{t-1}$), first estimated by Brown (1952)
has been more frequently estimated and more frequently used than any

ther. It can be found either directly or in some modification, at the heart of most Keynesian macroeconometric models. Nor is theoretical backing for 2.5) difficult to find; indeed, the greatest difficulty is in discriminating between the profusion of possible explanations. We shall follow a number of disparate lines here, each has some insight to offer, even if not all are compatible.

The most immediate justification for the formulation is that consumption responds only slowly to changes in current income; today's consumption is largely determined by yesterday's consumption although this year's consumption has much more to do with this year's income than with consumption a year or a decade ago. Hence, the balance between β_1 and β_3 depends on the length of the observation period. Similarly, since $0 \leq \beta_2 < 1$, the short-run marginal propensity to consume (β_1) is less than or equal to the long-run propensity $\beta_1/(1 - \beta_2)$. If the time period is very short, such phenomena must exist; consumers can hardly respond to changes in constraints that have not yet been observed, nor, to put it another way, would we expect a close link between consumption and income on a day-to-day basis. Over the longer period, such phenomena can be described as "habit persistence," as in Brown's study, or as "consumption inertia." A closely argued case for similar effects has been put in the classic study by Duesenberry (1949). He, although not denying the relevance of income expectations, assets, unemployment, and the kind of life-cycle effects discussed, places greatest weight on the influence of past consumption levels to which consumers have become accustomed. To quote, "when high-income families suffer a loss of income . . . they continue to live in the same kinds of neighbourhoods and maintain their contacts with others of the same socio-economic status . . . they can absorb a considerable reduction of income by reducing saving without cutting consumption too deeply" (p. 87). Hence, in Duesenberry's formulation, current consumption is related to current income and to the highest consumption standard previously reached. With a strong upward trend in consumption over time, this gives an equation virtually identical to (2.5).

Note too that (2.5) is closely linked to the Friedman model (2.1) and (2.2). Using (2.5) lagged one period to substitute for q_{t-1} in the original equation and repeating, we have

$$q_t = \frac{\beta_0}{(1 - \beta_2)} + \beta_1 \left[\left(\frac{y_t}{p_t}\right) + \beta_2 \left(\frac{y_{t-1}}{p_{t-1}}\right) + \beta_2^2 \left(\frac{y_{t-2}}{p_{t-2}}\right) \cdots \right] + v_t \qquad (2.6)$$

$$v_t = u_t + \beta_2 u_{t-1} + \cdots = \beta_2 v_{t-1} + u_t \qquad (2.7)$$

which, apart from the intercept and the autoregressive error, is identical to 2.2) substituted into (2.1). Hence, from our theoretical standpoint, (2.5) suffers from the same drawbacks as does the Friedman model. (Note, however, that the two models are *not* identical. Even allowing for the intercept, if we were certain that one or other model were correct, it would be a simple matter to discriminate between them on the basis of the difference in error structures, see Exercise 12.17).

An alternative approach that leads to the same conclusion can be based on the sociological motives so important in Duesenberry's analysis. Although we have said little about what determines preferences, there is nothing in utility theory used as a descriptive device that precludes interactions between the behavior and tastes of different consumers. On the contrary, it seems unrealistic to suppose that preferences are exogenous, God-given, and unchangeable. Rather they are socially inherited and conditioned and are governed by the conventions of technology and social institutions. At the same time, goods have social functions, particularly in communicating between people, see for example Becker (1974). Individuals need to define themselves vis-à-vis others and to communicate these definitions so that they are treated as they would wish; a consumption life-style is thus part of this definition of identity. Since belonging to certain social groups and not belonging to others is part of the sense of identity, it is inevitable that, to some extent, households will pattern their consumption and market behavior on that of other households. Conversely, there will be some kinds of behavior from which a household will consciously wish to dissociate itself. This idea of a social function of goods is not unlike the idea explained in §10.1 that market goods are bought, not for themselves, but for the characteristics that they yield. This patterning of behavior by households on other households takes time, particularly since there are recognition lags in perceiving what is the behavior of the group with which the individual identifies. These lags in interactions result, when aggregated, in current purchase levels being dependent on past ones. A simple formulation of such effects is possible using, for example, a linear consumption function (though y could just as well be replaced by W). Assume that for household h

$$q_t^h = \gamma_t^h + \beta y_t^h \tag{2.8}$$

where γ_t^h reflects "needs" in period t. Assume that h identifies with some reference group H, of which it is a member, and that group consumption $q^H = \Sigma q^h$ is observed only after a one period lag. The simplest assumption is

$$\gamma_t^h = \gamma_0^h + \theta^h q_{t-1}^H \tag{2.9}$$

so that, aggregating over the group,

$$q_t^H = \gamma_0^H + \beta y_t^H + \theta^H q_{t-1}^H \tag{2.10}$$

which has the same form as (2.5). (Note, however, that this example was formulated to give this result, and theoretically more satisfying forms of (2.8) and (2.9) can easily be formulated.)

Finally, it is instructive to examine the implications of the life-cycle model for the role of lagged consumption. Consider first a stationary economy, with neither income nor population growth, in which dissaving is just balanced by new saving so that net saving is zero. For such an economy, consumption will be constant, and if, for simplicity, consumption needs are spread equally over the life cycle, the same will be true for each citizen. Hence, at both the individual and aggregate levels, there is a perfect relationship

$$q_t = q_{t-1} \tag{2.11}$$

in which income plays no role whatever. Suppose now that incomes are not constant but change over time in any fashion whatsoever *provided only that changes are fully anticipated by those who receive them.* If we continue to assume an even spread of needs, then (2.11) will continue to hold for each consumer (although there will now be growth or decline in *aggregate* consumption if the expectations of new entrants to the life cycle are systematically different from those who die). Hence, fully anticipated changes in income have no role in the consumption function once a lagged dependent variable is included. Clearly, such an argument can be extended to include the effects of other types of information such as prices or assets, and this leads to the situation where, apart from lagged consumption, the only variables relevant to current consumption are those quantities whose values were unknown in the previous period.

Hall (1977) has shown that, given rational expectations for income and other assumptions, the foregoing analysis implies that conditional on q_{t-1}, the expectation of q_t formed in period $t-1$ is a function of q_{t-1} alone so that, if the function is linear, consumption follows the *random walk*

$$q_t = \beta_2 q_{t-1} + v_t \tag{2.12}$$

where v_t is independent of variables dated earlier than t. If income expectations are rational, v_t which reflects unanticipated income changes must be independent of all past information including lagged values of income y_{t-1}. Hence, (2.12) is consistent with (2.5), since y_t is likely to contain information unknown in $t-1$, although it does no justify the omission of unanticipated changes in assets, price levels or other variables relevant to the prediction of income. Hall's derivation of (2.12) depends both on the assumption of intertemporal additivity of preferences and on various approximations that guarantee the linearity of the relationship. The specific form is unlikely to be valid in general, and it seems difficult to produce manageable results under less restrictive assumptions. However, the general points are of undoubted validity and owe much of their force to the budget constraint rather than to specific forms of preferences. A consumer reconsidering his wealth position at time t will have discounted wealth W_t given by

$$W_t = A_{t-1}(1 + r_t) + \rho_t^{-1} E_t\left(\sum_t^L \rho_t y_t\right) \tag{2.1}$$

Assets are governed by the equation

$$A_{t-1} = A_{t-2}(1 + r_{t-1}) + y_{t-1} - p_{t-1}q_{t-1} \tag{2.1}$$

Combining (2.13) and (2.14) gives

$$W_t = (1 + r_t)(W_{t-1} - p_{t-1}q_{t-1}) + \rho_t^{-1}\left[E_t\left(\sum_t^L \rho_\tau y_\tau\right) - E_{t-1}\left(\sum_t^L \rho_\tau y_\tau\right)\right] \tag{2.1}$$

Consumption is determined by wealth and prices so that, if we can substitu for W_t and W_{t-1}, (2.15) establishes a relationship between q_t, q_{t-1}, prices, d count rates, and the change in expectations. For example, in the simplest po sible case of $p_t q_t = \alpha W_t$, (2.15) gives

$$p_t q_t = (1 - \alpha)(1 + r_t)p_{t-1}q_{t-1} + \alpha\rho_t^{-1}\left[E_t\left(\sum_t^L \rho_\tau y_\tau\right) - E_{t-1}\left(\sum_t^L \rho_\tau y_\tau\right)\right] \tag{2.1}$$

which is similar in form to (2.12) and is likely to be consistent with it on a gregate data. Note that the last term in (2.16) reflects unanticipated revisio in income expectations.

Expressions such as (2.16), although considerably oversimplified by t omission of changes in price expectations and revaluations of financial asse are consistent with the empirical success of (2.5), at least for much of the po war period, but point rather clearly to its inadequacies. On the positive sid the random walk hypothesis predicts that further lags in (y_t/p_t) and q_t a unnecessary in (2.5) and Hall, in his empirical work on the hypothesis, fin no significant role for higher lags on quarterly, seasonally adjusted, postw American data. On the other hand, (2.5) will only be a good proxy for (2.16) the innovative elements in y_t bear a constant relationship to y_t itself, a although this may have been true from the fifties to the late sixties, it unlikely to have been true since. Similarly, (2.16) might explain why, on Br ish data, variables representing the real value of wealth are much more sign icant if included in equations like (2.5) when more recent data are used. It quite possible that changes in the real value of assets, particularly liquid asse were well anticipated until the rapid rise in the inflation rate in the early se enties and have been rather poorly anticipated since. At the same time, t direct estimation of equations such as (2.16) poses formidable problems constructing proxies for the changes in anticipations. In the face of these di ficulties, and given the ambiguity of interpretation of the lagged depende variable, it might be tempting to revert to the estimation of models, such those of Friedman and of Ando and Modigliani, which relate consumptic directly to its ultimate determinants – dispensing with the lagged depende

riables and transformations intended to remove autoregressive elements.
owever, such a procedure is extremely dangerous. Consumption, income,
ices, and assets all share largely common trends, so that correlations
tween them and significant regression coefficients may simply be because of
e *nonsense correlation* problem. The high *t*-values and low Durbin-Watson statics that are usually associated with such consumption functions should act
a warning [see, e.g., Granger and Newbold (1974)], but are frequently ig-
red. Given the large autoregressive element in the consumption data series,
e inclusion of the lagged variable will largely protect investigators against
e most obvious spurious correlations. However, the frequent exclusion of
gged dependent variables on the grounds that their entry causes the rela-
nship to "collapse" is a testimony both to the effectiveness of the cure and
the greater difficulty of finding a theoretically satisfactory relationship that
tperforms a simple autoregression.

rther empirical evidence

e recent British empirical evidence on the dynamics of the relation
tween consumption and income has been studied in a notable paper by
vidson, Hendry and others (1978). These authors begin with only loose
eoretical preconceptions but provide a systematic and sophisticated treat-
ent of the time-series estimation so that their results are ideal for comparing
th prior theoretical preconceptions. The study uses quarterly, *seasonally un-
justed* data; the period from 1958(i) to 1970(iv) is used for estimation with
e subsequent 20 observations 1971(i) to 1975(iv) kept for forecast tests. Pre-
ction of these five years outside of the sample period can be regarded as a
vere test; indeed many economists would claim that the British economy
perienced major structural change between the two periods. The use of
asonal data raises difficult questions for the implementation and testing of
eoretical models in which the length of time periods is left conveniently ab-
ract. Since the change in expectations in equations like (2.16) only becomes
fective when the consumer makes new plans, the essential question is the
riod after which consumers reassess their situation. Although many con-
mers may replan more often, the year seems by far the most likely alterna-
e. Anything shorter than this involves the consumer in making seasonal
rrections for income, prices, or other variables, and even when plans are re-
ade frequently, comparisons with the situation of a year before are likely to
ay an important role. Hence, when we look at quarterly data, the lagged
pendent variable may just as well be q_{t-4} as q_{t-1} and it is important to allow
r the possibility of both. The alternative of using seasonally adjusted data is
t attractive; published series given in adjusted form are invariably adjusted

separately so that the adjustment procedure can produce systematic biases in the estimated dynamic structure, see Wallis (1974).

Davidson, Hendry, and others considered a number of previously published, quarterly consumption functions including several variants of (2.5). The following are estimated on their own data:

$$\hat{q}_t = 2556 + 0.20(y/p)_t + 0.35q_{t-1} + 16.3t + z_1$$
$$\quad\;\; (537) \quad (0.05) \qquad (0.12) \qquad (3.7) \tag{2.17}$$

where t is a time trend and z_1 includes a dummy (for 1968, first quarter) plus trending seasonals. Alternatively, with z_2 including only the dummy and constant seasonals and excluding the time trend

$$\hat{q}_t = 509 + 0.18(y/p)_t + 0.75q_{t-1} + z_2$$
$$\quad\;\; (142) \quad (0.08) \qquad (0.11) \tag{2.18}$$

Finally, using q_{t-4} rather than q_{t-1} and adding $\Delta_1(y/p)_t$, the quarter-to-quarter, backward first-difference

$$\hat{q}_t = 734 + 0.28(y/p)_t - 0.09\Delta_1(y/p)_t + 0.59q_{t-4} + z_3$$
$$\quad\;\; (112) \quad (0.06) \qquad (0.06) \qquad\;\; (0.08) \tag{2.19}$$

where z_3, once again, includes the dummy and constant seasonals (in each case the seasonal dummy for quarter four is zero). All three of these models fit rather well, the lowest R^2 being 0.990; the short-run marginal propensities to consume are very similar (0.20, 0.18, and 0.19) as are the long-run propensities for the last two models (0.72 and 0.68). The first has a long-run marginal propensity of only 0.31 reflecting the importance ascribed to the time trend in modeling the long-run evolution of consumption. In (2.19), the inclusion of $(y/p)_{t-1}$ through $\Delta_1(y/p)_t$ proves insignificant, which might be interpreted in favor of the random walk model.

However, all three of these models are found to be unsatisfactory. The first and second equations suffer from pronounced fourth-order autocorrelation in the residuals, while the third has strong positive first-order autocorrelation. Moreover, all three models fail the forecast test; the three ratios of mean square forecast error to squared standard error of estimation over the sample are 6.5, 9.5, and 6.45, respectively. The authors thus search for an alternative model that will both explain the evidence [including why (2.17) to (2.19) are wrong] and pass the forecast test. Finally, after an impressive piece of applied econometric detective work, the following equation is reached:

$$\Delta_4 \log q_t = 0.47\,\Delta_4 \log(y/p)_t - 0.21\,\Delta_1\,\Delta_4 \log(y/p)_t - 0.10 \log(pq/y)_{t-4}$$
$$\qquad\qquad (0.04) \qquad\qquad\quad (0.05) \qquad\qquad\qquad (0.02)$$
$$\qquad + 0.01\,\Delta_4\,D_t - 0.13\,\Delta_4 \log p_t - 0.28\,\Delta_1\Delta_4 \log p_t \tag{2.20}$$
$$\qquad\quad (.003) \qquad\quad (0.07) \qquad\qquad (0.15)$$

where Δ_4 is the difference compared with the same quarter one year previously, D_t is the dummy, and seasonals were found to be unnecessary. This equation meets the desired criteria, both explaining the previous results and passing the forecast test. It also cannot be rejected against a model in which $\log q_t$ is regressed on $\log q_{t-1}$, $\log q_{t-2}$, up to $\log q_{t-5}$, $\log(y/p)_t$ up to $\log(y/p)_{t-5}$ and $\log p_t$ up to $\log p_{t-5}$. In consequence, it can safely be taken as an econometrically satisfactory specification of the lag structure. The terms in the annual inflation rate and its rate of change (which are crucial for the forecasting test) were introduced following earlier theoretical work by Deaton (1977) which will be discussed in the next section. However, we have already suggested why unanticipated price changes might be important in determining consumption, and those terms in (2.20) can also be interpreted in this way.

Interpreted loosely, (2.20) is not inconsistent with the predictions of the life-cycle model. For example, in the long term, the savings ratio is $(1 - e^{-5.3g})$, where g is the annual growth rate of real income, which is consistent with the theoretical order of magnitude for rate of growth effects, see also Exercise 12.5. In the short run, the lagged term $\log(pq/y)_{t-4}$ acts as an error correction or asset term; according to both (2.16) or the first-difference of the Ando-Modigliani model (2.4) – see Exercise 12.12 – the coefficient on the lagged dependent variable measures the effects of assets on consumption. However, the implied estimate of the marginal propensity to consume out of assets at 0.1 per quarter suggests either an unrealistically short planning horizon, $2\frac{1}{2}$ years, or that one of the other explanations for the lagged dependent variable is operating. The complete dynamics can be seen by "disentangling" (2.20) term by term; the elasticities of q_t with respect to $(y/p)_t$ at respective lag lengths are: at 0, 0.26; at 1, 0.21; at 2, 0; at 3, 0; at 4, -0.16; and at 5, -0.21. This pattern of weights is implausible on the hypothesis that only the unanticipated element of income should be important in determining consumption and would thus seem to disconfirm a strict interpretation of the random walk hypothesis.

Note, finally, that (2.20) pays little attention to other information that may be relevant in calculating future income. In particular, it may well be that terms proxying liquidity conditions could improve the equation still further. Bean (1978), taking (2.20) as his starting point has found that $\Delta_1\Delta_4 \log$ (unemployment) with a negative sign improves the explanatory power of the model, and this is in line with rising unemployment decreasing future income expectations and so cutting current consumption.

Exercises

12.12. Show that, if asset income is included in current income, assets satisfy $A_t = A_{t-1} + y_{t-1} - p_{t-1}q_{t-1}$. Hence, by first differencing the Ando-Modigliani equation (2.4) derive a relationship in p_tq_t, $p_{t-1}q_{t-1}$, y_t, y_{t-1}, and discounted expected future incomes.

Show that if the first difference of consumption expenditure is regressed on incom
and lagged expenditure, the coefficient on the latter provides an estimate of (minu
the marginal propensity to consume out of assets.

12.13. Approximating the Ando-Modigliani form by $p_t q_t = b_1 y_t + b_2 A_t$, derive t
long-run ratio of assets to income. Do the parameter estimates given in the text show
sensible value for this ratio?

12.14. It has been argued that models of social interaction such as (2.8) to (2.10) a
more convincing for single commodities (e.g., new electrical gadgets) than for all
consumption. Do you agree?

12.15. Assume that $(y/p)_t$ satisfies the relation (2.3). Defining y_t^* by $E_{t-1}[(y/p)_t]$, sho
that (a) $y_t^* = (y/p)_t - u_t$, (b) $y_t^* - y_{t-1}^* = a + \lambda u_{t-1}$, (c) $y_t^* - y_{t-1}^* = a + \lambda[(y/p)_{t-1} - y$
Thus, prove the relationship between y_t^* and y_t^p given by (2.2).

12.16. Using the *actual* consumption function for the intertemporal LES, (1.23), deri
a consumption function linking q_t to q_{t-1} and the change in expectations. Discuss t
role of unanticipated price changes on the savings ratio.

12.17.* To compare the permanent income model (2.1) with the adjustment mod
(2.5), write z_t for $(y/p)_t$ and c_t for $p_t q_t$ so that the competing models are

$$H_0: c_t = \alpha + k\lambda \sum_1^\infty (1 - \lambda)^r z_{t-r} + \epsilon_t$$

$$H_1: c_t = \beta_0 + \beta_1 z_t + \beta_2 c_{t-1} + u_t$$

where ϵ_t and u_t are assumed to be serially uncorrelated error processes with varianc
σ_0^2 and σ_1^2 and H_0 and H_1, respectively. Show that, if H_0 is true, $\beta_0 = \alpha\lambda$, $\beta_1 = k$
$\beta_2 = (1 - \lambda)$, and $\sigma_1^2 = \sigma_0^2[1 + (1 - \lambda)^2]$ and that u_t is, in fact, a moving average err
Hence, derive the plims of the OLS estimates of β_0, β_1, and β_2, given the truth of H
Similarly, derive expressions for α, k, λ, and σ_0^2, given H_1, derive the properties of
and calculate plims of the OLS estimates of α, k, and λ as a function of β_0, β_1, and β
[This analysis can be used to test the models. First, obtain maximum likelihood or oth
consistent estimates of the parameters of each hypothesis, assuming each to be true
turn. These can then be used to calculate estimates of the plims of the other mod
using the formulas from the exercise and compared with the estimates actually o
tained. In this manner, we shall reject H_0, H_1, both H_0 and H_1, or neither. For a conce
tually similar exercise, see Pesaran and Deaton (1978).]

12.3 Information

Nowhere is the problem of imperfect information so acute as in interten
poral planning. We shall provide a formal analysis of choice under unce
tainty in Chapter 14, but for the moment we consider informally some of t
problems that are likely to arise.

Errors and replanning

In one sense, the intertemporal models discussed so far contain an erro
learning mechanism in that they are planning models in which replannin
occurs at every period on the basis of new experience and new informatio

nsider, for example, the consequences of an error in the estimate of the fu-
re rate of inflation. A consumer at the beginning of his life cycle obeying
13) has current and future planned consumption

$$q_t = g_t(W_1, \rho_1 p_1, \ldots, \rho_L p_L, \overline{\ell}_1, \ldots, \overline{\ell}_L) \qquad (3.1)$$

w suppose that $\rho_2 p_2$ and all future discounted future price levels have been
derestimated by $\epsilon_2 > 0$, $\epsilon_3 > 0$, and so on. Hence, q_1 should have been

$$q_1 = g_1(W_1, \rho_1 p_1, \rho_2 p_2 + \epsilon_2, \rho_3 p_3 + \epsilon_3, \ldots, \rho_L p_L + \epsilon_L,$$
$$\overline{\ell}_1, \ldots, \overline{\ell}_L) \qquad (3.2)$$

ovided present and future consumption are gross complements (comple-
ents in uncompensated terms), (3.1) for $t = 1$ implies a greater value for q_1
an does (3.2). But having mistakenly followed (3.1.), the household starts
riod 2 with smaller assets than it would have liked. Period 2 consumption is
erefore lower than it would have been for two reasons: real lifetime
ending power has been cut and the household is not in the asset position it
uld have liked, had it correctly foreseen inflation. Hence, the savings ratio
creases. In a period of accelerating inflation, it seems likely that the next
riod's price level will be underestimated for several periods in succession.
 this case, each error will cause the savings ratio to be higher than it would
ve been had the rate of inflation been correctly foreseen. The effect of
ese cumulative errors is likely to persist for some time even after inflation
pectations are back on course. However, if and when the inflation rate falls,
e opposite effect is likely to operate, offsetting the cumulative errors made
rlier.

certainty about current prices

though the most obvious form of uncertainty about prices is that relating to
e future, even the current price level is unlikely to be known with any cer-
nty. Consumers typically do not purchase all their goods simultaneously so
at they have immediate, up-to-date knowledge only on the prices of goods
at they are currently buying. At the same time, the general price index (or
solute price level) is not instantaneously observable; true indices, as dis-
ssed in Chapter 7, require a full round of purchases, while official indices
e published only with a considerable lag. In consequence, at least in the first
stance, individual consumers have no possible means of distinguishing rela-
e price movements from absolute price changes. In particular, unantici-
ted absolute price changes will first be observed in unexpected price
anges in individual commodities, and some of this change will inevitably be

interpreted as a relative price change. Consider, then, the case of an unex
pected increase in the rate of inflation. At any time, different consumers wil
be buying different goods, each of which appears to have become relatively
more expensive. As a consequence, consumption will fall and, if real income is
maintained, saving will rise.

A model of savings along these lines has been constructed by Deaton
(1977). We assume weak intertemporal separability so that, in period t, the
consumer wishes to allocate x_t among the n goods q_{ti} and can do so as a func
tion of x_t and $p_{t1}, \ldots, p_{tn}$ alone. Hence, if tildes denote planned or expected
values

$$\tilde{q}_{ti} = g_i(\tilde{x}_t, \tilde{p}_{ti}, \ldots, \tilde{p}_{tn}) \tag{3.3}$$

in the usual way. On the purchase of good i, however, an actual price p_{ti} is en
countered so that actual demand q_{ti} is

$$q_{ti} \cong g_i(\tilde{x}_t, \tilde{p}_t) + (p_{ti} - \tilde{p}_{ti})\frac{\partial g_{ti}}{\partial p_i} \tag{3.4}$$

Equation (3.4) is then aggregated over goods by aggregating at a single in
stant over different consumers, each purchasing different commodities. On
the assumption that the differences $(p_{ti} - \tilde{p}_{ti})$ are entirely because of mistaken
expectations about the absolute price level $(p_t - \tilde{p}_t)$, the aggregate form of
(3.4) is approximately

$$\log x_t \cong \log \tilde{x}_t + (1 + \phi)(\log p_t - \log \tilde{p}_t) \tag{3.5}$$

where ϕ is a negative quantity equal to $\Sigma \tilde{w}_k e_{kk}$ for desired budget shares $\tilde{w}_k$
and own-price elasticities (conditional on $\tilde{x}_t$) e_{kk}. The quantity $\tilde{x}_t$ can be interpreted as $p_t q_t$ from an aggregate intertemporal consumption function so that
(3.5) suggests the addition of a term in unanticipated prices to whatever form
of the consumption function we would choose on other grounds.

As we have already seen, a consumption function containing terms in unanticipated inflation explains British experience very well and similar models
work well for other countries, including the United States, see Deaton (1977
and Howard (1978). Indeed, the increase in the savings ratio in nearly al
Western economies in the early 1970's can hardly be explained without some
such term. However, as our discussion of the life-cycle model showed, such
terms may arise simply from the revision of plans as new information about
prices becomes available. Such effects include the unanticipated downward
revaluation of real assets that accompanies an unanticipated rise in the price
level. Since both explanations rest on unanticipated changes in prices, it i
very hard to see how it would be possible to devise a test that distinguished
between them in any very reliable way.

The calculation and implementation of optimal plans

Another important issue closely linked to the problem of lack of information is the question of how consumers actually calculate utility-maximizing demand functions. Conceptually, this is a problem even in the single-period analysis of Chapter 2, but it becomes particularly acute in the intertemporal context. Obviously, as every elementary textbook reminds us, consumers are not observed making calculations on the backs of shopping bags, nor indeed, to bring the observation up to date, are pocket calculators sophisticated enough to perform multiperiod multicommodity optimization calculations. Instead, these problems, if they are solved at all, are solved by a process of trial and error. A consumer who wishes he had spent more on books and less on beer is likely to alter his behavior accordingly the next time around; similarly, everyone has had the experience of overrunning a budget and not being able to buy something more desirable than something else already bought. It is easy enough to see that an iterative process of this kind can be designed that will lead to optimal demand functions; indeed, as we have already seen, the presence of assets (or of lagged dependent variables) acts as an error correction mechanism causing, for example, past overspending to decrease future spending.

Even so, *trial and error takes time* and optimal decisions to new stimuli are not reached instantaneously. Once this is recognized, we must also admit that exogenous factors, prices and incomes, may change before full adjustment has taken place to the previous levels. This is particularly likely to occur if the full optimization requires a great deal of information, some of which is difficult to come by. For example, in the Deaton model of inflation and saving, the fact that all prices are not known, even in a one-period model, means that equilibrium may never be reached since it takes time to observe true prices and to correct mistakes. In general, behavior will depend on exactly how the trial and error procedure takes place, or to borrow a mathematical term, on what type of algorithm the consumer employs to solve his optimization problem. But note that it is possible that the outcome of attempting to optimize may be so far from optimal that it may pay the consumer not to try, but instead to follow some less demanding and perhaps less costly behavioral rule. In the intertemporal problems discussed in this chapter, all these difficulties are particularly acute partly because of the great amount of information required (future prices, incomes, interest rates, etc.) but also because of the complexity of the optimization process itself in this context. Unlike the single-period case, there is no question of having several attempts at the same problem; intertemporal problems, by definition, change as time passes, the same time that is required to solve them. Even armed with a solution, only the very beginning

of the plan is likely to be used since, with new information, replanning in sub
sequent periods will usually produce a different result. And as we shall see in
Chapter 14, the formal recognition of uncertainty increases the complexity a
great deal further.

We make no attempt to minimize the importance of these problems. In
deed, attempts to specify plausible trial and error mechanisms and to exam
ine how these interact with the way in which consumers obtain information
are likely to provide fruitful areas for further research. But if optimal behav
ior is close to the actual outcomes, consumers must be able to simplify
problems of choice. One way this can be done is by the use of Hicks ag
gregates so that, for example, in planning future consumption, the structure
of relative prices is assumed not to change. Alternatively, separability helps to
define index numbers on which strategic assumptions can be formed and
under appropriate assumptions, future consumption can be represented by
an index, akin to real wealth, which appears along with current consumption
in the utility function. In this way, complex problems can sometimes be re
duced to simpler ones that appear to be within the powers of consumers to
solve.

Exercises

12.18. How is it possible, in practice, for a consumer to decide on whether to buy
chocolate bar now when, even though he expects to live for more than ten years, th
price of soap ten years ahead is completely unknown? Why is this problem less seriou
than the current purchase of a car when future petrol prices are unknown?

12.19. Interpret the Davidson and others equation, that is, (2.20) as an algorithm fo
reaching an appropriate relationship between consumption and income. If income ha
been growing for a long time at 3 percent per annum and there is a sudden drop to
percent per annum, what will the short-run and long-run reactions of consumers be

12.20. In the Deaton (1977) savings model, the inflation effect depends on the size o
the quantity $\Sigma \bar{w}_k e_{kk}$. Since, typically, own-price elasticities become absolutely larger a
more finely disaggregated commodities are distinguished, the inflation effect will b
larger at higher levels of disaggregation. Why should this be so? What defines the de
gree of disaggreation in the model?

12.4 Consistency in intertemporal choice

The actual consumption levels that would come out of the models discusse
in this chapter result from a process of continual replanning. In each period
the consumer looks into that period and into the future, makes plans for th
entire future, but carries out only that part of the plan that refers to the cur
rent period. After the period has elapsed, this planning process repeats itself
From the past, the consumer inherits stocks of financial and other assets an
this links the past to the present. However, that may not be all the consume

inherits from the past since his tastes themselves are likely to be formed by past experiences. This has given rise to considerable discussion in the literature about the question: when is behavior intertemporally consistent? One reason, of course, why behavior might be intertemporally inconsistent is that the consumer may have incorrect or incomplete information about the future. Then he would not, in general, stick to the plans he made for the current period at an earlier date. However, even if the consumer has full information, behavior can result that is in a *certain sense* intertemporally inconsistent.

We begin by discussing the case where no consistency problem can arise. This turns out to be the most natural starting point since, in the most fundamental sense, the problem is an artificial one. Suppose that at time 1, the utility function is

$$u = v^1(q_1, q_2, \ldots, q_L) \tag{4.1}$$

here q_t is the consumption vector in period t. Let the intertemporal constraint take the general form

$$G(q_1, q_2, \ldots, q_L) = 0 \tag{4.2}$$

maximize with respect to $q_1, q_2, \ldots, q_L$ (4.1) subject to (4.2) and let q_t^* be the optimal consumption vector of period t. Then the problem

$$\max u = v^1(q_1^*, q_2^*, \ldots, q_{s-1}^*, q_s, q_{s+1}, \ldots, q_L) \tag{4.3}$$

with respect to $q_s, \ldots, q_L$ subject to

$$G(q_1^*, q_2^*, \ldots, q_{s-1}^*, q_s, q_{s+1}, \ldots, q_L) = 0 \tag{4.4}$$

has exactly the same solution vectors as before, that is, $q_s^*, q_{s+1}^*, \ldots, q_L^*$. The reason is clear: $v^1(q_1^*, q_2^*, \ldots, q_{s-1}^*, q_s^*, \ldots, q_L^*)$ is by definition the highest level of utility obtainable. The implications of this are obvious enough but are nevertheless interesting. Provided the consumer actually fulfills the optimal plan until $s - 1$, then at time s, the relevant utility function to be maximized in (4.3) and the relevant constraint is (4.4) with a solution for $q_s, \ldots, q_L$ identical to the solution from the original plan. If we wish, we may relabel (4.3) as $v^s(q_s, \ldots, q_L)$ so that the original problem is replaced by a series of time-dependent maximization problems, each with their own budget constraint and each with a solution consistent with the original, given that information is unchanged.

Note that, in general, the utility functions $v^s(q_s, \ldots, q_L)$ depend on the conditioning variables $q_1^*, \ldots, q_{s-1}^*$. This implies that if two individuals face the same remaining planning horizon $s, s + 1, \ldots, L$, with the same intertemporal preferences represented by (4.1) and the same constraint on q_s, $q_{s+1}, \ldots, q_L$ but with different consumption histories, they will, in general, have different utility functions and will act differently during periods s, $s +$ 1, . . . , L. By the same token, a consumer's current and future consumption history will depend, not only on his current wealth position W_t and current and expected future prices but also on his past consumption levels. This gives yet another justification for the presence of lagged dependent variables in life-cycle consumption functions. Formally, since consumption plans cannot be retrospectively altered once effected, past consumption decisions act as rations and the analysis of §4.3 can be applied to determine the modifications they cause to the optimal unconstrained plan. However, if consumption levels q_2, . . . , q_L are weakly separable from q_1 so that (4.1) takes the form $v[q_1, v^2(q_2, . . . , q_L)]$, then the "conditional preferences" defined by (4.3) are $v[q_1^*, v^2(q_2, . . . , q_L)]$, which, by ordinality, give the same behavior for q_2, . . . , q_L as does the utility function $v^2(q_2, . . . , q_L)$. If this has to be true for each time period, then q_3, . . . , q_L must also be separable in $v^2(\ )$, q_4, . . . , q_L in $v^3(\ )$, and so on. Hence, the time-specific utility function must take the form

$$v^s(q_s, q_{s+1}, . . . , q_L) = F^s \{q_s, F^{s+1}[q_{s+1}, F^{s+2}(. . .)]\} \tag{4.5}$$

This condition is known as *strong recursivity*, see Blackorby and others (1978), but follows immediately from assuming that at all times the future is separable from the past. Even in this case, of course, past consumption levels have income effects, or more appropriately asset effects, since variations in past consumption will affect the future through variations in current assets. However, given the current wealth position, past consumption levels have no effect on current or future plans if (4.1) is such that $v^s(\ )$, defined by (4.3), has the strongly recursive form (4.5).

It is also possible to look at the replanning problem in a different way, and it is here that inconsistencies can arise. In this alternative approach, it is simply assumed that at time s, the consumer solves the maximization problem

$$\max \tilde{v}^s(q_s, q_{s+1}, . . . , q_L) \quad \text{subject to} \quad \sum_s^L \tilde{\rho}_t q_t p_t = W_s \tag{4.6}$$

for suitable discount factors $\tilde{\rho}_t$. Put like this, it is not surprising that, with changing preferences, plans change from period to period even conditional on the same information. The inconsistency may *seem* more surprising if we take specific forms for $\tilde{v}^s(\ )$. For example, in the article by Strotz (1956) that started the debate

$$\tilde{v}^s(q_s, q_{s+1}, . . . , q_L) = \sum_{t=s}^L \tilde{v}(q_t) \delta_{t-s} \tag{4.7}$$

where $\delta_0, \delta_1, . . . , \delta_{L-s}$ are a series of *constant* discount factors reflecting impatience. In fact, for general discount factors, since s moves forward through time, the marginal rate of substitution between any two *fixed* time periods, say 1978 and 1979, will change depending on whether they are viewed from three years before or four years before so that (4.7) is inconsistent with the existence of a stable underlying preference structure such as (4.1). Hence, for the intertemporal choice of a single consumer, (4.6) is not a very sensible way of modeling behavior. Even so, such a formulation may be appropriate for other problems and has, in fact, been studied in the context of social choice with succeeding generations planning for the future, see Pollak (1976a), Blackorby and others (1973) and Hammond (1976b). In such a context, the question of when (4.6) does produce consistent choice becomes important, and not surprisingly, given the necessity and sufficiency of weak separability for consistent two-stage budgeting, the condition is that $\tilde{v}^s(\ )$ must be strongly recursive. However, we must emphasize that such a view of the problem is of limited interest in the present context.

Exercises

12.21. Using the Cobb-Douglas or the LES, follow through (4.1) to (4.4), defining new period by period utility functions and checking that, with unchanged information, decisions always replicate themselves.

12.22. Using (4.1) and (4.3), show that both the Cobb-Douglas utility function $\Sigma \beta_t \log q_t$ and the intertemporal LES $\Sigma \beta_t \log(q_t - \gamma_t)$ are strongly recursive. Hence, using the analysis of (1.17) and (1.18) for the Cobb-Douglas and (1.23) for the LES, check by example that past consumption levels have only income effects in present and future decisions when information changes.

12.23. If intertemporal choice is fundamentally rational and consistent over time, why do consumers enter into contracts to prevent themselves from doing something that they know now they later will wish to do? (For example, a man going to a party who pleads with a friend to *make* him leave – against his will – at some specific time; or the problem of the millionaire's Marxist son who knows that, when he is old enough to inherit his fortune, he will be wise enough not to wish to donate it to the Party.)

Bibliographical notes

It would be impossible to even begin to give a comprehensive review of the literature on the consumption function. For excellent bibliographies see Evans (1967), Mayer (1972), Ferber (1973), and Blinder (1975). See also Tobin (1968) for an excellent overview. The life-cycle model upon which we have focused has its origins in Fisher (1907, 1930) and Ramsey (1928) but modern work with the model begins from the classic papers by Modigliani and Brumberg (1955a, 1955b). See Ando and Modigliani (1963) and Modigliani (1975) for later restatements. Our choice of this framework reflects our belief that this is the only fully coherent model of intertemporal choice. The permanent income hypothesis of Friedman (1957), although it has had enormous influence on subsequent work, has so many different interpretations that it is unsuitable as a basis for a general theory. We are conscious that our approach probably does scant justice to the important work of Duesenberry (1949) but, as we have tried to indicate, we do not regard his approach as in any way contradicting our own.

Although most of the important references are given in the text, the following indicators to background material might be useful. The distinction between consumers who are free to vary their labor supply and those who are rationed is an immensely important one for macroeconomic analysis. The recent recognition of this and its justification for the existence of the Keynesian consumption function begins with Clower (1965), see also Barro and Grossman (1976), Malinvaud (1977), and Muellbauer and Portes (1978) for further developments and references. The constraints implied by liquidity have been emphasized by Tobin (1951, 1972) and Flemming (1973). Discussion of the dynamics of the consumption function is part of a much wider debate on the question of the appropriate economics and econometrics of lag structures. On the economic side, the work on "rational expectations" in particular, see, e.g., Lucas (1976), has posed quite fundamental problems about even the possibility of modeling consumers' responses to changes in government policy, and Hall's (1978) paper is in this tradition. Econometricians are also beginning to emphasize the importance of working with very general lag structures and of *testing* theoretical preconceptions, see in particular, Mizon (1977), Mizon and Hendry (1979), Davidson, Hendry et al. (1978), Hendry (1979), and, on a rather broad tack, Sims (1979). On a number of smaller points, on the ultrarationalist position and the particular issue of the substitutability of public and private saving, see Cagan (1965), Feldstein (1974, 1976a,b) and for the United Kingdom, Hemming (1978) and Threadgold (1978). On the problems of calculating optimal plans and on the consequences of their recognition, see Simon (1955, 1978a,b). On intertemporal consistency, an approach we have not discussed is that of explicitly making utility functions depend on past consumption, see the rather different approaches taken by Gorman (1967), Pollak (1970), Von Weiszäcker (1971), Peston (1967), and Phlips (1972); in the first three of these, the issue of consistency arises in the form of whether or not there exists a long-run stable utility function. We shall return to this in the next chapter.

CHAPTER 13

The demand for durable goods

Developing good theoretical models for applied work in economics is a difficult task and perhaps nowhere more so than in the modeling of the demand for durables, especially in aggregate time series data. On the one hand, a good model ought to be complete; on the other, the essence of a model is abstraction: choosing a small number of characteristics that are supposedly central to behavior. Abstraction is necessitated not only by the need to communicate ideas and information but by the limited discriminatory power of most aggregate time-series data. In the area of the demand for durables, a number of really very different and seemingly contradictory approaches have been put forward, and agreement is far from universal as to what are the central issues.

Perhaps the best way of seeing how complex are the problems is to begin by listing various themes or special features of the demand for durables, all of which have been emphasized by different economists working in the area.

(1) There is an extremely important distinction to be made between *purchases,* on the one hand, and *consumption,* on the other. Purchases are regarded as adding to *stocks,* while consumption, which is rendered possible by the existence of the stocks, is responsible for their depletion or physical deterioration. Although it is often assumed that consumption is proportional to the stock of the durable and that the latter physically depreciates at a constant, proportional rate, this is only one particular formulation.

(2) The presence of stocks that last through more than one time period means that past decisions affect present behavior just as present decisions set constraints on future action.

(3) The purchasing decision can be advanced or postponed in the light of new information.

(4) Consumer confidence and income and price expectations are important determinants of purchases.

(5) Purchases of durable goods are particularly volatile.

(6) A useful and perhaps important distinction should be drawn between new demand and replacement demand.

(7) The decision whether or not to buy a durable good is a choice between

two discrete alternatives. It is thus different, in principle, from a non-durable purchase where choice is exercised over a continuous range.

(8) Discrete choice causes difficult aggregation problems. We may know what we mean when we say "the representative household buys 0.2 cars per year," but it would not make a great deal of sense to model the decision to buy one-fifth of a car.

(9) Many durable goods are either new to the market or are subject to a high level of technical change. Hence, information about them may take time to diffuse through the population.

(10) Stocks of durables and "stocks" of habits play a similar role in linking past, present, and future decisions and ought to be analyzed using the same tools.

(11) Markets for durable goods are often imperfect; for example, developed, second-hand markets do not always exist and the information possessed by buyers and sellers may be quite different. Such phenomena give rise to complex constraints facing consumers and are likely to affect behavior.

(12) There are adjustment and/or transactions costs that may give rise to a lagged adjustment of actual to desired stocks.

(13) Because of the volatility of purchases, markets for durables are more liable to excess demand episodes where suppliers cannot meet demand yet do not raise prices to clear the market. Then some purchasers will be informally rationed by having to wait for delivery while the demand of others may be shifted to some available but less preferred alternative.

(14) Markets for new and used durables interact in complicated ways unless different vintages of durables are perfect substitutes *ex ante*. This is unlikely to be true if, for example, there are information problems in judging the quality of used durables.

Not all of these issues are specific to durable purchases alone but most arise more acutely in that case. The fact that the list lacks coherence is simply a reflection of the state of the literature. We certainly would not claim that each of the points is equally important (or even consistent with the others) but, between them they cover the most commonly mentioned issues in the analysis of durable purchases. We shall take them all up at some point in this chapter, but it is clear that the very variety of these themes precludes their simultaneous investigation.

The plan of the chapter is as follows. The first five sections will all abstract from the problems of discrete choice, not because it is unimportant, but because its relevance will be more clearly seen when we have dealt with some of the other problems. Further, discrete choice is particularly important for cross-section studies, and we prefer to leave to the end the special problems for the theory posed by cross-section data. Section 13.1 extends the introduction in §4.2 to neoclassical models of the demand for durables in which it is assumed that markets operate perfectly. At the very least, this gives a coherent framework in which to discuss the distinction between stocks and flows, purchases, and consumption. Section 13.2 is devoted to the stock adjustment model, which has been and still is very popular in applied studies. Among other things, we look at the relationship between it and an approach, such as that discussed in §13.1, which is explicitly based on optimizing behavior. In particular, we shall examine whether adjustment costs can give rise to the stock adjustment model. Section 13.3 considers an alternative model, called the *discretionary replacement* model, which attempts to improve on the rather unconvincing explanation of replacement investment in the stock adjustment model. In §13.4, we return to the problem of liquidity constraints which was discussed, for example, in §12.2 in the context of the effect of borrowing restrictions on the consumption function. Durable goods are in many cases illiquid assets, and it may be very difficult to sell them at anything like their replacement cost. We shall see that the behavior implied by the neoclassical model of §13.1 is very substantially modified by the recognition of these liquidity constraints and that their presence goes someway towards accounting for the empirical anomalies mentioned in the final section.

The phenomenon of discrete choice of durables and the role of the diffusion of durable ownership within the population of consumers is the subject of §13.5. Section 13.6 takes up the closely related topic of habits in consumption; as we shall see, habits can be thought of as stocks that may depend upon the consumption of the household itself, on that of other households, or on other external stimuli such as advertising. Although it is no doubt true that economists have sometimes attributed empirical significance to habit effects when these are, in fact, standing proxy for other omitted variables, such effects remain theoretically plausible, especially when thought of as arising out of the social interaction of households.

13.1 Neoclassical models

We have already discussed in §4.2 a two-period neoclassical model in which there is a single durable good whose service flow is proportional to the stock. We maintain all the assumptions made there but extend the horizon as in Chapter 12 to the life cycle. We had an extensive discussion there – see §12.1 and §12.4 – of planning and the replanning that takes place every period and of simplifying conditions on preferences that limit the effects of past decisions to the budget constraint. Including stocks of durables in the utility function leaves that analysis unchanged. For the present, we shall merely consider the period 1 decision with the utility function

$$u = v(q_1, q_2, \ldots, q_L, S_1, S_2, \ldots, S_L, A_L/p_L; \bar{q}_{01}, \ldots, \bar{q}_{0L}) \quad (1.1)$$

where q_t is an aggregate of nondurable purchases at time t, L is the planning horizon and A_L/p_L is the real value of financial assets at the end of period L which, together with S_L, represents the consumer's bequest. As in Chapter 12, we could begin by assuming that the leisure in period t, q_{0t} is freely variable and solve for demands with wage rates as independent variables. Here, however, we pass over this case and take the hours constrained case with $q_{0t} = \bar{q}_{0t}$. We can thus treat the y_t's, wage incomes in period t, as exogenous variables in the budget constraint. As in Chapter 12, the constants $\bar{q}_{01}, \ldots, \bar{q}_{0L}$ become part of the utility function and will appear as conditioning variables in the commodity demands, see for example, Chapter 12, equation (1.13). However, this issue was fully discussed in Chapter 12 and, since we have nothing further to add here, we shall ignore the $\bar{q}_{0t}$'s, assuming the separability of leisure from consumption in formal justification for their omission. On the assumption that all markets are perfect so that consumers face parametric prices, the period-to-period budget constraint takes the following form as in Chapter 4, equation (2.21).

$$
\begin{aligned}
A_t &= (1 + r_t)A_{t-1} + y_t - p_t q_t - v_t d_t \\
&= (1 + r_t)A_{t-1} + y_t - p_t q_t - v_t[S_t - (1 - \delta)S_{t-1}]
\end{aligned} \quad (1.2)
$$

since purchases are related to stocks by [Chapter 4, (2.20)], $S_t = d_t + (1 - \delta) S_{t-1}$. Equation (1.2) can be used to write A_{L-1} as a function of A_L, A_{L-2} as a function of A_{L-1}, and so on recursively until we have an intertemporal budget constraint linking A_0 to A_L. This takes the form

$$\sum_{t=1}^{L} \rho_t p_t q_t + \sum_{t=1}^{\tau} \{\rho_t v_t^*\}S_t + \rho_L A_L = W_1 \quad (1.3)$$

and

$$W_1 = v_1(1 - \delta)S_0 + (1 + r_1)A_0 + \sum_1^{L} \rho_t y_t \quad (1.4)$$

where $\rho_t = 1/\Pi_{s=2}^{t}(1 + r_s)$ is the discount factor as defined in §12.1, and

$$v_t^* = [v_t - v_{t+1}(1 - \delta)/(1 + r_{t+1})] \quad (1.5)$$

is the user cost of durables, which is a rental equivalent price as explained in §4.2. Note that the present value of wealth over the life cycle W_1 includes the initial market value of durable stock.

The maximization of (1.1) subject to (1.3) is now a standard problem with solutions, in period 1,

$$
\begin{aligned}
q_1 &= g_1(W_1, \rho_1 p_1, \ldots, \rho_L p_L, \rho_1 v_1^*, \ldots, \rho_L v_L^*) \\
S_1 &= f_1(W_1, \rho_1 p_1, \ldots, \rho_L p_L, \rho_1 v_1^*, \ldots, \rho_L v_L^*)
\end{aligned} \quad (1.6)
$$

Purchases of the durable good are given by

$$d_1 = f_1(W_1, \rho p, \rho v^*) - (1 - \delta)S_0 \qquad (1.7)$$

where ρp and ρv^* are the vectors of length L of discounted prices and user costs.

We can see immediately from equation (1.6) that the neoclassical approach, by defining appropriate flows and prices, transforms the demand for durable goods into a form precisely analogous to the demand for nondurable goods. This analogy, which is implied by (1.6), is a very great convenience, but we must emphasize again the price at which it is bought. Among other things, it is assumed that consumers can lend or borrow quite freely at a constant and identical rate of interest, that purchases or sales of the durable are allowed at a common price, and that purchases are continuously variable in amount.

Disaggregating nondurable consumption and durable stocks does not alter the neoclassical form of the budget constraint (1.3). Therefore, we can apply the notions of budgeting and separability discussed in Chapter 5. With weak intertemporal separability, for example, Exercise 5.5, the demands in any period can be written as functions of prices and total expenditure in that period. Then, provided we define the user costs v_t^* correctly, the neoclassical model allows us to incorporate durable stock demands even into the static single-period models considered in Chapters 2 and 3 of this book, see Exercise 13.1. Note, however, that the user cost concept (1.5) introduces a genuine intertemporal element into all these equations so that, in particular, the budget in each period will depend on the *stock* of durables, a fact not taken into account in Chapter 3. To the extent that many goods have some element of durability, the incorrect definition of the current period budget and the omission of the price expectations implicit in user cost may be further reasons why conventional conditional demand functions turn out to be both statistically and theoretically ill-specified, particularly in their consistent rejection of the homogeneity condition. These problems can only be avoided if, in addition to intertemporal separability, we are prepared to assume separability between durable and nondurable goods, so that expenditures on the latter can be written as a function of total nondurable expenditures alone. In practice, this is unlikely to hold; for example, most fuels bought by households are used as complements to specific durable goods, while in contrast, expenditure on public transport is a substitute for car ownership and so on.

Although we believe that the insights offered by the neoclassical model are genuine, it is not possible to take either equations (1.6) or their single-period counterparts entirely seriously. One immediate problem relates to the rental price v_t^*. As was pointed out, expected capital gains to holding the durable good can reduce v_t^* so that it may even become zero or negative. According to the theory, this would lead to consumers demanding infinite quantities of the

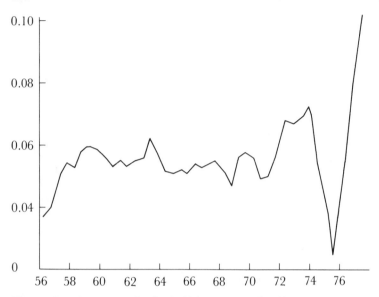

Figure 13.1. User cost series for British consumer durable stock for 1955–1976, as computed in Muellbauer. (From "Testing neoclassical models of the demand for durables," in A. S. Deaton, ed., *Essays in the Theory and Measurement of Consumer Behaviour*, Cambridge: Cambridge University Press, 1981a.)

good in order to realize the expected capital gains. Even allowing for uncertainty on the part of consumers and for quantity constraints on the supply side, price fluctuations could well imply powerful advancement and postponement effects in purchases. Even a cursory look at some of the price changes, which, at least in Britain, have taken place in durables markets in the last twenty-five years, suggests that, unless expectations of price increases are quite insensitive to actual changes, service prices have at times reached quite low levels. Yet these periods do not, by and large, coincide with large booms in sales. Figure 13.1 shows a graph of these data: v_1^* was constructed by assuming that next quarter's price v_2 is forecast by applying the most recently experienced annual rate of change, see Muellbauer (1981a) for details. Using the actual data on v_2 makes the series even more volatile.

In the context of changing prices, we must briefly discuss the question of the exogeneity of prices in the neoclassical theory of the demand for durables. According to the model, new and used durables are perfect substitutes so that in a simple supply and demand model for durables, total market supply is $(1 - \delta)S_0 +$ new supply. Suppose that new supply is $F(v_1$, costs of production). Then in market equilibrium $(1 - \delta)S_0 + F(v_1$, cost of production$) = f_1(W_1, \rho_1 p_1, \ldots, \rho_L p_L, \rho_1 v_1^*, \ldots, \rho_L v_L^*)$, where $v_1^* = v_1 - (1 - \delta)$

$\rho_2 v_2$ and $f_1(\quad)$ is the aggregate demand equation for the stock. This can be solved to give v_1 and $S_1 = f_1(\quad)$ as functions of $(1 - \delta)S_0$, W_1, $\rho_1 p_1$, . . . , $\rho_L p_L$, $\rho_2 v_2$, $\rho_2 v_2^*$, . . . , $\rho_L v_L^*$ and costs of production. If we believed this model, these reduced form equations are the ones to estimate. However, the model lacks plausibility except perhaps in the long run. Prices of new durables such as cars tend to be fixed in the short run with inventory changes, production changes and import changes taking up demand fluctuations. And even when they do change it seems to be more in response to cost conditions than to demand conditions, except perhaps perversely as increasing excess manufacturing capacity raises unit cost. For example, in Britain prices of cars rose sharply relative to other goods in the recession of 1974–7. In a quarterly model, therefore, it seems reasonable to regard prices of durables as exogenous.

Muellbauer (1981a) looks at the evidence more systematically. He estimates the extended linear expenditure system version of (1.6) applied to quarterly British data on nondurable purchases and stocks of durables. One implication of this version of (1.6) lies in the restrictions across equations on various parameters. These are, however, rejected by the data. Moreover, (1.6) implies that all the elements that make up long-run purchasing power are wrapped up in the variable W_1. These include existing financial and real assets, current income, and discounted expected labor income. Because the same W_1 appears in both equations, the parameters that reflect the proxying of income expectations ought to be the same in both equations. Even this hypothesis by itself, without the further restrictions on parameters stemming from the linear expenditure system can be strongly rejected. Further, although the neoclassical theory has no place for borrowing restrictions, a variable that captures the tightness of official credit restrictions plays an important role in the durables equation. These pieces of evidence, together with severe autocorrelation found in the durables equation throw serious doubt on any claim the neoclassical model might have as offering a complete explanation of the demand for durables and nondurables. We shall suggest some possible explanations of these empirical phenomena in subsequent sections.

Exercises

13.1. What are the demands (1.6) if (1.1) takes the form

$$u = \sum_{i=1}^{n} \sum_{t=1}^{L} \alpha_{it} \log(q_{it} - a_{it}) + \sum_{t=1}^{L} \gamma_t \log(S_t - b_t) + \lambda \log A_L \tag{1.8}$$

where $\Sigma_{i=1}^{n}\Sigma_{t}^{L}\alpha_{it} + \Sigma_{1}^{L}\gamma_t + \lambda = 1$? Derive the demands in period 1 conditional upon total expenditure in period 1. Contrast the budget constraint $\Sigma_1^n p_{i1}q_{i1} + v_1^* S_1 = x_1^*$ with the budget constraint $\Sigma_1^n p_{i1}q_{i1} + v_1 d_1 = x_1$. Discuss the likely consequences of fitting a static form of the linear expenditure system when, in fact, (1.8) is valid.

13.2. Suppose that (e.g., from an intertemporal Cobb-Douglas utility function) the stock demands take the form $v_1^* S_1 = \beta_1 W_1$ and $v_0^* S_0 = \beta_0 W_0$. Substituting into purchases $d_1 = S_1 - (1 - \delta)S_0$, discuss the role of unanticipated price and income changes in determining purchases of durables.

13.3. With $v_1^* S_1 = \beta_1 W_1$, assuming that $(1 - \delta)/(1 + r_2) = 0.9$ and $v_1 = 1$, compute the elasticity of stock demand with respect to expected price v_2 with W_1 constant. Hence discuss possible orders or magnitude of the elasticity of purchases d_1 with respect to v_2. How plausible do you find these results?

13.2 Stock-adjustment models and costs of adjustment

Models based on the partial adjustment principle have been widely applied to the demand for durables ever since the work of Stone and Rowe (1957), Chow (1957), and Nerlove (1956, 1958). It offers a ready, if ad hoc way of justifying the introduction of lags into behavioral equations. Begin by writing the stock-flow relationship [Chapter 4, (2.20)] in the form

$$d_t = (S_t - S_{t-1}) + \delta S_{t-1} \tag{2.1}$$

Gross purchases are equal to net additions to stock plus physical deterioration. The stock-adjustment model assumes the existence of some desired stock $\tilde{S}_t$, say, and postulates that, in any given period, actual net investment is a fixed proportion of the net investment required to bring the stock to its desired level. Hence, $(S_t - S_{t-1}) = k(\tilde{S}_t - S_{t-1})$ for some k between 0 and 1, so that, from (2.1)

$$d_t = k(\tilde{S}_t - S_{t-1}) + \delta S_{t-1} \tag{2.2}$$

Typically, the desired stock $\tilde{S}_t$ is taken to be some function of disposable income y^d, prices, and other relevant economic variables. In the absence of data on stocks, S_{t-1} is frequently eliminated from (2.2) using the Koyck transformation. For example, if $\tilde{S}_t = \alpha + \beta y_t^d/p_t$, and since $d_{t-1} = S_{t-1} - (1 - \delta)S_{t-2}$

$$d_t - (1 - \delta)d_{t-1} = k\alpha\delta + k\beta\left[\frac{y_t^d}{p_t} - \frac{(1 - \delta)y_{t-1}^d}{p_{t-1}}\right] + (\delta - k)[S_{t-1} - (1 - \delta)S_{t-2}]$$

$$= k\alpha\delta + \frac{k\beta y_t^d}{p_t} - \frac{k\beta(1 - \delta)y_{t-1}^d}{p_{t-1}} + (d - k)d_{t-1}$$

so that, finally

$$d_t = k\alpha\delta + k\beta\frac{y_t^d}{p_t} - k\beta(1 - \delta)\frac{y_{t-1}^d}{p_{t-1}} + (1 - k)d_{t-1} \tag{2.3}$$

For example, if this is estimated for motor cars on British data from 1954 to 1975 we have, with standard errors in brackets, $k\alpha\delta = -763(287)$; $k\beta = 0.187(0.050)$; $-k\beta(1 - \delta) = -0.146(0.042)$ and $(1 - k) = 0.200(0.226)$. The R^2 and Durbin-Watson statistics are 0.913 and 1.34, respectively. Hence, the adjustment coefficient k is estimated as 0.80 while the estimated depreciation rate is 0.22. Equation (2.3) can be extended by allowing $\tilde{S}$ to depend on other factors. In the present context, the price of cars relative to the overall price index was tried as was a variable representing the tightness of government restrictions on consumer credit; these have frequently been significant in durable goods equations generally [see, e.g., Deaton (1976) and Muellbauer (1980b)], but although correctly signed here, neither variable was significant. Nevertheless, many investigators have considered results similar to (2.3) to be reasonably satisfactory and the model is widely used. Note, however, that this estimation technique is not really satisfactory. If (2.2) holds apart from a serially independent error, the Koyck transform will generate a moving-average error process in (2.3) and, given the presence of the lagged dependent variable, this will cause bias, inconsistency, and inefficiency. If autocorrelation already exists in (2.2), the Koyck transform will further complicate the situation, except in the purely fortuitous situation when the original error is a first-order autoregressive process with parameter $(1 - \delta)$.

An alternative and more appropriate estimation technique is to use the definition (2.1) to construct an artificial stock series around some arbitrary fixed point (which can be absorbed into the intercept). This can be done for a range of alternative values for δ to select that value which gives the lowest residual sum of squares. Using the same data as before and estimating (2.2) directly, we again find relative price and credit terms correctly signed but insignificant, while the optimal values of δ and k are 0.15 and 0.31, respectively. This last value is rather far from 0.8 and with a Durbin-Watson statistic of only 0.81, serious misspecification is suggested. Although first- or higher-order autocorrelations could be allowed for, this would merely treat the symptoms of the disorder. Instead, we interpret these results as showing that d_t is linked to (y_t^d/p_t) and S_{t-1} merely by common trends and that the simple stock-adjustment model offers a far from adequate explanation of the dynamic behavior of durable purchases.

These empirical problems with the stock-adjustment model throw considerable doubt on its validity as a tool for aggregate time-series analysis of durable purchases. But then in the form in which we have presented it, following empirical tradition, it is not a very sensible model. Two obvious criticisms are the following. First, it is really rather crude to suppose that the adjustment coefficient k is independent of economic variables. For example, it is not sensible to introduce credit variables through desired stock. Credit restrictions, if they act at all, are likely to work through the adjustment process but, in the simple stock-adjustment framework, desired stocks are the only channel through which economic variables can act. Second, while we might not want to take the neoclassical theory in §13.1 entirely seriously, the insight from the user cost concept, that it is an advantage to buy now if capital gains can be expected, is one that it would be hard to deny. Even so, investigators of consumers' demand for durable goods have generally used static ad hoc formulations of the stock-adjustment model which seldom include such effects. In the context of the theory of the firm, however, it has been argued that stock-adjustment models can be given a sound intertemporal basis in terms of maximizing subject to constraints when allowance is made for costs of adjustment. For example, Eisner and Strotz (1963) and Nerlove (1972) have shown how maximizing profits over time with a quadratic adjustment cost term in investment gives investment demand equations not unlike those of the stock-adjustment form except that the target level to which adjustment takes place is a distributed lead of expected exogenous variables. A similar result exists for household behavior if it can be assumed that S_0 enters the utility function in such a way that utility depends not only on the current stock S_1[plus the other variables in (1.2)] but also declines, the larger the gap between S_1 and S_0. This can be interpreted as a type of adjustment cost, although not one that explicitly enters the budget constraint in money terms (see Exercise 13.5 for an illustration).

Even so, the rationale for adjustment costs needs further development. Are they supposed to arise from transactions costs, from search costs, from supply constraints, from the inability to borrow, or from the inability to liquidate used durables without substantial loss? Certainly, if the last three causes are important, it makes more sense to attempt to model these effects as part of the constraints faced by consumers rather than as an impressionistic addition to the utility function. Note too that this approach runs into severe difficulties if adjustment costs do not increase more than proportionally with the adjustment gap. If adjustment costs have a considerable fixed-cost element, which is extremely plausible, consumers will not invest at all in response to a small disequilibrium in stocks, but will adjust completely when it is worthwhile doing so. With aggregation, these discontinuities may well be smoothed out, but this process needs to be modeled explicitly rather than assigned to a mythical representative consumer. All this evidence argues for an approach in which nonlinear constraints are modeled explicitly, and we shall suggest in §13.4 that such an approach also allows us to overcome, at least in principle, some of the major empirical drawbacks of the neoclassical model, whether with or without adjustment costs.

Exercises

13.4. Quadratic adjustment costs are symmetric and stock adjustment is correspondingly symmetric for positive and negative deviations from the desired stock. If stock adjustment is a proxy for "disequilibrium," discuss the plausibility of symmetric upward or downward speeds of adjustment.

13.5. Consider the following quadratic life-cycle utility function with quadratic adjustment costs:

$$u = \sum_{1}^{L} \frac{1}{(1 + \gamma)^t} \left[v(q_t, S_t) - \frac{c}{2} \{S_t - (1 - \delta)S_{t-1}\}^2 \right]$$

where

$$v(q_t, S_t) = \alpha_1 q_t - \frac{\alpha_2}{2} q_t^2 + \alpha_3 S_t - \frac{\alpha_4}{2} S_t^2$$

This is to be maximized subject to (1.3) with terminal assets $A_L = 0$, where W_1 is defined by (1.4). Show that the marginal condition for S_t is a linear equation in S_{t+1}, S_t, S_{t-1} and λv_t^*, where λ is the Lagrange multiplier. Show that the solution for S_1 conditional on S_0 is linear in λ and involves expected rental prices up to the horizon L. Show that q_1 is also linear in λ and hence discuss the different dynamic structure of the equations for durables and nondurables.

13.6. In the light of the distinctions in Chapter 10 between quality and quantity, would you expect short-run responses to income and price changes of aggregate quality to be the same as short-run responses of numbers of units sold, for example, in the new car market? Would you regard the stock-adjustment model as equally suitable (or unsuitable) for the two dimensions?

13.3 The discretionary replacement model

In the context of durable goods, the word *replacement* can refer either to the making good of physical deterioration or to the actual physical replacement of one good with another. The stock-adjustment model of §13.2, to the extent that it recognizes replacement at all, does so in the first sense and equates purchases for replacement with δS_0, almost as a matter of definition. However, if we think of one of the most important of durable goods markets, the market for cars, we usually think of replacement in the second sense, as trading one vehicle for another. In Britain and the United States, nearly all new cars are bought by households who are replacing a previously owned vehicle. Modeling this as a fixed proportion of existing stock is liable to cause several problems. First, replacement of an existing vehicle can be advanced or postponed through time, depending on current economic variables; this means that the proportion of stock actually replaced in any year may be quite different from the proportion that is lost because of deterioration. Second, households who buy new cars are not those who scrap old ones. Evidence, based on the Michigan Surveys as presented by Smith (1975) shows that new cars are largely bought by higher income groups who replace them by new cars after anything from one to four years. Hence, there is a "trickling down" of used cars to lower income brackets or to more affluent households as second or third cars. In equilibrium with a stationary stock, this structure of the market would be relatively unimportant; new cars bought by the rich would balance old ones scrapped and the two types of replacement would be equal,

Table 13.1. *Age of cars traded in by new car buyers*

	1966	1968
1 year or less	13.3%	11.8%
1 to 2 years	22.6	21.2
2 to 3 years	20.5	22.8
3 to 4 years	15.1	16.7
4 to 5 years	9.1	10.7
5 to 6 years	7.4	6.1
6 years or more	12.0	10.7

Source: R. P. Smith (1975), *Consumer Demand for Cars in the U.S.A.*, Cambridge: Cambridge University Press, p. 92.

advancements or postponement aside. But if total stock is growing, as it is in nearly all countries, replacement of old by new cars will be both larger and more volatile than physical deterioration. This clearly offers scope for both bias and confusion in naive interpretations of the stock-adjustment model.

These arguments suggest that there may be considerable returns to modeling the discretionary element in advancing or postponing replacement. Smith (1974, 1975) and Westin (1975) have put forward discretionary replacement models that are in many ways attractive alternatives to the stock-adjustment model. Smith's (1975) model can be explained as follows: let R_t be the replacement demand for a durable good. He writes

$$R_t = k_t R_t^* \tag{3.1}$$

where R_t^* is normal replacement demand and k_t represents the deviations owing to current and expected economic conditions of actual from normal replacement demand. Smith suggests that survey data can be used to make R_t^* a function of the stock of cars with parameters fixed a priori.

From survey data such as that cited in Table 13.1 for the United States, we can discover the normal proportion of each age group of the durable due to be replaced in any year, so that given knowledge of past purchasing behavior, normal replacement R_t^* can be calculated. Since whether k_t is greater than or less than unity depends on whether postponement or advancement took place in the recent past, k_t can be made a function of current variables such as real disposable income, relative prices, consumer confidence, or unemployment rates (as a proxy for income expectations) and of differences or ratios of current levels of these variables to those in the recent past.

This is basically Westin's (1975) argument except that he writes the model in additive rather than multiplicative form,

$$R_t = k_t + R_t^* \tag{3.2}$$

To this we can add a term to represent new demand that depends on the current levels of some or all of the variables in k_t as well as on past stocks to capture the depressing effect that large, inherited stocks have on current purchases. Westin estimates the resulting model, choosing to estimate the parameters of R^* rather than impose them from survey information, and carries out a systematic comparison of his results with those of the stock-adjustment model. The dependent variable in each case is aggregate annual numbers of new passenger cars purchased in the United States from 1953 to 1972. Two representative equations estimated by Westin:

Stock-adjustment model

$$= 9.8 + 0.025 \; YD - 12.3 \; PCR - 0.144 \; UE + 0.070 \; ATT + 0.296 \; STRIKE$$
$$(3.84) \qquad (-2.94) \qquad (-1.23) \qquad (3.58) \qquad (2.25)$$
$$- 0.35 V_{-1} - 0.20 V_{-2} - 0.11 V_{-3} - 0.08 V_{-4} - 0.08 V_{-5} - 0.07 V_{-6} - 0.06 V_{-7} \tag{3.3}$$

The standard error of the regression is 0.355.

Discretionary replacement model

$$= 19.1 + 0.018 \; YD - 9.4 \; PCR - 0.321 \; \Delta UE + 0.030 \; \Delta ATT + 0.476 \; STRIKE$$
$$(3.36) \qquad (-2.79) \qquad (-3.76) \qquad (1.83) \qquad (4.00)$$
$$+ 0.03 V_{-1} - 0.03 V_{-2} - 0.08 V_{-3} - 0.12 V_{-4} - 0.14 V_{-5} - 0.13 V_{-6} - 0.08 V_{-7} \tag{3.4}$$

The standard error of the regression is 0.322, and t-statistics are given in parentheses. The variables are defined as follows: YD = disposable income in 1958 dollars, PCR = relative price of new cars, UE = unemployment rate, ATT = Index of Consumer Sentiment, V_{-i} = number of i-year-old cars in use at the beginning of the year, while $STRIKE$ is a dummy variable for strikes. A three-parameter Almon lag was used to restrict the coefficients of the various vintages subject to the restriction that, after seven periods, the polynomial is zero.

In the stock-adjustment model, only levels of the exogenous variables appear since these must be justified as the determinants of the desired stocks, whereas in (3.4), first differences appear as the determinants of postponements and advancements. If we attempt to interpret (3.3) in terms of the strict stock-adjustment model, we should expect a declining geometric progression on the coefficients of successively older vintages reflecting their declining value in efficiency rather than absolute units. If we take the coefficients on V_{-1} and V_{-2} as representative, then the results imply a deterioration coefficient of rather more than 0.4 per annum and an adjustment coefficient of close to

0.75. This deterioration rate is unrealistically high. However, if we turn to (3.4), we see that the negative coefficient on V_{-1} in (3.3) reflects the fact that high purchases in one year depress demand in the next, and that when the shift factors ΔUE and ΔATT are explicitly accounted for, this effect vanishes. Note that both ΔUE and ΔATT have the correct sign in (3.4) so that, if in the previous year confidence was low and unemployment high, new car purchases would have been postponed, reinforcing the effect of any improvement this year. The improvement in·fit in (3.4) compared with (3.3) is not dramatic, suggesting that past vintages are reasonably successful in (3.3) in picking up the effects of discretionary purchases. It is worth noting that the joint hypothesis that the coefficients on the stocks of all past vintages are zero in (3.4) is statistically acceptable. Although we would expect some effect through true deterioration, it is plausible that this is so trendlike as to be absorbed in the other variables. Note, finally, that although the two models have quite similar long-run price and real income responses, (3.3) implies much higher short-run effects. No doubt the stricter form of the stock-adjustment model, in which vintages were not disaggregated, would have gone even further astray in capturing these effects.

Although (3.4) is clearly superior to (3.3), we would not wish to imply that it is an ideal formulation. It does not have a role for speculative buying in response to price expectations and we may question whether the advancement-postponement phenomenon can take place only over one year. Nevertheless, the basic idea of the discretionary replacement model is an attractive one that deserves to be taken at least as seriously as the stock-adjustment model, since it overcomes the rigid and naive view of replacement investment in the latter. It suggests lagged stock has a dual role in durables equations. One is that of the trend element in replacement investment and in long-run saturation effects as ownership spreads. The other role is that of a proxy for economic conditions in the recent past. If conditions were very favorable then, the resulting advancement of purchases will, for a time, have a depressing effect on current purchases. We would not expect the two effects always to be in fixed proportions, and the fact that past vintages in (3.3) pick up both effects obscures the measurement of short-run dynamics. So it makes sense to explicitly allow for other variables that pick up the second of the two roles, the proxy for recent economic conditions. However, it remains to be seen whether the discretionary replacement model can be given a firmer rationale in terms of more systematic economic theory.

Exercises

13.7. Contrast the short-term and the long-term price responses estimated in (3.3) and (3.4).

13.8. How inconsistent is (3.3) with the assumption of geometric deterioration in the simple stock-adjustment equation (2.2)?

13.9. In a model of new and second-hand car markets, prices of new cars are set by manufacturers, while those of used cars are determined competitively in the used car market. Discuss whether the interactions between new and second-hand markets are likely to be stabilizing for the number of new cars sold. What is the role of the trade-in price of fairly young used cars in your analysis?

13.4 Constraints on sales and on borrowing

If the neoclassical model discussed in §13.1 were correct, we should expect pronounced volatility in purchases in response to changes in economic conditions. For example, suppose that income y_1 and future income expectations $y_1^e = \Sigma_2^L \rho_t y_t$ drop. The demand for the stock S_1 will also fall, and if the decline is more than δS_0, the physical deterioration, purchases become negative. In the neoclassical model, it is assumed that liquidation of the stock is possible and that sales can take place at the current price v_1.

Consequently, if consistent aggregation is possible and sales by some consumers are simply purchases by others, the final form of the aggregate equation is the same whether some consumers are selling the durable good or not. Of course, in such a world, it may be somewhat implausible to assume that the price of the durable is exogenous, since, if it were so, all the burden of adjustment would fall on purchases and sales, which are likely to be unrealistically volatile. Nevertheless, even with some price adjustment, a once and for all drop in income or expected income will lead to an immediate reduction in purchases, which would later gradually increase as deterioration reduces stocks. Similarly, a rise in income will cause a sharp rise in sales, declining thereafter. As we saw in §13.1, identical effects will also be induced by fluctuations in the expected future prices of durable goods. Thus, the neoclassical model is likely to generate quite powerful advancement and postponement effects in response to changes in the economic environment.

In a model formulated in continuous time, the lack of realism entailed in the assumption of instant adjustment of stocks is particularly apparent. A discrete jump of income in such a model generates a rate of flow that, for an instant, is infinite. But even in our discrete time formulation, which precludes this extreme case, full adjustment within the period seems implausible. In §13.2, we saw that such changes will be damped by the presence of certain types of adjustment costs. While these can be rationalized to a certain extent, for example, by the costs associated with transactions, we argued that the usual specification was largely ad hoc and, in requiring that costs increase more than proportionately with the change, somewhat unrealistic.

We now consider illiquidity constraints, which have a role somewhat similar to that of adjustment costs, but have a much more explicit microeconomic foundation in the form of the budget constraint faced by consumers. The two most obvious illiquidity constraints are restrictions on sales of used durables and restrictions on borrowing. We have already seen the importance of borrowing restrictions in §12.1 in the context of demand for nondurables, and in many ways, they are even more obviously relevant in the context of durables. Even if a consumer expects that the price of the durable good will be much higher next period and could therefore make a big capital gain by buying now, he will be prevented from taking advantage of this opportunity if in the absence of a large stock of liquid financial assets, he is limited in how much he can borrow.

Restrictions on sales of used durables also very substantially dampen the advancement of purchases caused by expected price increases of durables. This is because they prevent the realization of capital gains so that consumers will only make advance purchases of durables that they intend to keep. Of course, restrictions on sales of used durables are not usually absolute. Instead, the price at which sales can be made is usually very substantially less than the price at which goods can be bought even for obviously transferable items such as cars. The reason why a recently purchased car sells for much less than it cost is not that the car buyer experiences such a surge of utility as he drives it out of the showroom that the car deteriorates greatly. Rather, it is Akerlof's (1970) "lemon effect," see also §10.4, which points out that there is an asymmetry of information between seller and potential buyer about the quality of the car. The latter fears that the reason the owner wishes to sell is because the car is a "lemon," while even if it is not, there is no way the owner can give this information to the buyer. The lemon effect has consequences that are very similar to not being able to sell at all or more generally to having to pay transactions costs both on purchases and sales, see Exercises 13.15 and 13.16. In particular, the lemon effect limits or prevents decumulation of stocks in the current period.

We begin by illustrating the consequences of restrictions on borrowing and on sales for the choice between durables and nondurables in the current period. Suppose that in the utility function we hold everything but q_1 and S_1 constant. If no borrowing whatever is allowed, we must have $A_1 \geq 0$, which implies

$$A_1 = (1 + r_1)A_0 + y_1 - p_1 q_1 - v_1[S_1 - (1 - \delta)S_0] \geq 0 \qquad (4.1)$$

Similarly, the absolute selling constraint $d_1 \geq 0$ implies $S_1 \geq (1 - \delta)S_0$. However, the importance of this constraint is not so much in that it restricts consumption, but that it implies that if consumers give up some durable stock, they get nothing in return. In economic terms, the selling price of durables is zero. To these two constraints must be added the intertemporal budget constraint that, with future plans fixed, takes the form

$$W_1 - \text{planned future expenditure} = p_1 q_1 + v_1^* S_1 \qquad (4.2)$$

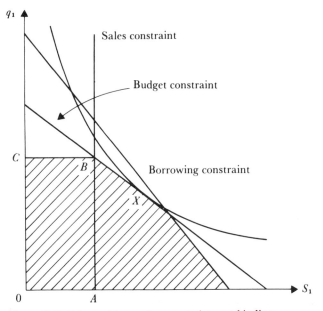

Figure 13.2. Sales and borrowing constraints not binding.

Since $v_1^* < v_1$, the intertemporal constraint (4.2) is less steep than the borrowing constraint (4.1). Figure 13.2 illustrates the positions of the various constraints with attainable set shaded. Note that the area $0ABC$ is shaded; the consumer can consume as little of S_1 as he wishes simply by not using it. Selling it, however, produces no return, and between B and C the boundary of the attainable set becomes horizontal. In Figure 13.2, the consumer chooses point X so that, in this case, neither borrowing nor sales constraint is binding. In Figure 13.3, on the other hand, perhaps because of a greater preference for durables or because of lower initial assets, the borrowing constraint becomes binding although the sales constraint is not. Figures 13.4 and 13.5 illustrate the remaining two possibilities, with the sales constraint alone binding and with both binding, respectively.

It is also worth illustrating the case in Figure 13.6, where the selling restriction takes a less extreme form [cf. Exercise 13.16]. Suppose that the selling price is substantially less than the buying price. In this case, at the point X, it is now possible, by giving up durable stock, to obtain some nondurables in return. However, the amount is substantially less than has to be given up to get the same increment of durable stock by buying it new to the right of the point X. Comparison of Figures 13.5 and 13.6 suggests that if the gap between

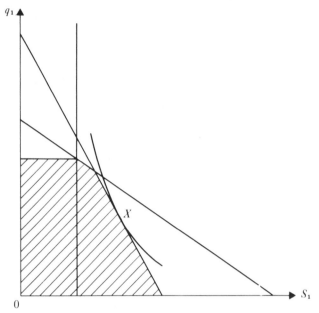

Figure 13.3. Borrowing constraint binding, sales constraint not binding.

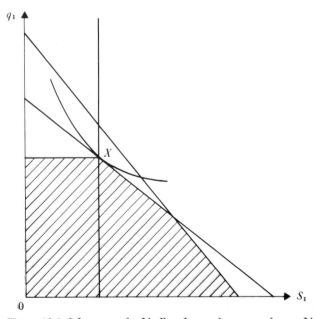

Figure 13.4. Sales constraint binding, borrowing constraint not binding.

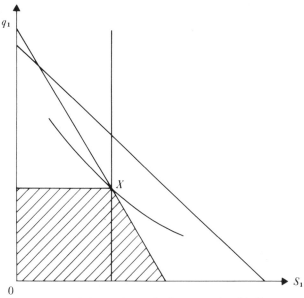

Figure 13.5. Both borrowing and sales constraints binding.

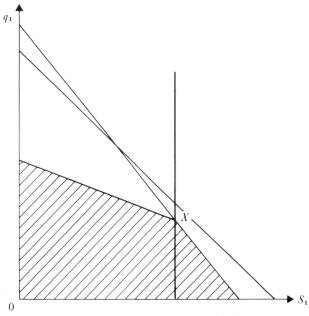

Figure 13.6. Borrowing and sales constraints binding when the buying price exceeds the selling price.

buying and selling prices is substantial, it is a good approximation simply to assume that selling takes place at a zero price as in Figure 13.5.

We can thus see that the two kinds of illiquidity restriction strongly dampen flow changes caused by expectations of changes in prices of durables or in income. There is an interesting difference here between nondurables and durables. Borrowing restrictions cause income reductions to be quickly transmitted into reductions in nondurable consumption expenditure for those with few financial assets. Thus, in contrast to the permanent income hypothesis, in which such shocks are assumed to be largely absorbed, borrowing restrictions make the nondurable consumption more volatile than it would be in their absence. For purchases of durables however, borrowing restrictions and sales restrictions, by dampening adjustment, have exactly the opposite effect.

The two kinds of restrictions are formally rather similar to the analyses of borrowing restrictions in §12.1 and of households rationed or unrationed in the labor market in §11.2. However, because quantity constraints can arise in two markets, a larger number of distinct regimes is possible. In a multiperiod model in which households expect not to be quantity constrained in period 2 and beyond but where these constraints can occur in period 1, four regimes are possible, which we have illustrated in Figures 13.2 to 13.5. However, this is not enough for a minimum of realism since it does not exclude the case in which a consumer, expecting next period's price of durables to be substantially higher than this period's, buys vast amounts of durables in order to realize the capital gains. Thus, we also need a restriction on selling in the *second* period, where it is understood that restrictions on selling are merely a simplified way of saying that the household believes that it will not be able to sell its durable goods at anything like the new price. If we also wish to take into account *borrowing* restrictions in the second period, 16 different regimes would have to be considered, though treating sales restrictions like transactions costs, see Exercise 13.16, does simplify the analysis. However, since borrowing restrictions next period are likely to arise mainly if it is expected that incomes or durable prices will be substantially higher in period 3 than in period 2, consumers may take the simplistic view that period 3 will be similar to period 2.

Since the classification of regimes depends on preferences, on assets, on expectations and on incomes, it is likely that at any moment different households will be in different behavioral regimes. For example, if current income falls, and with it expectations of future income, some households–particularly those with stocks of durables that are large relative to their financial assets–are likely to wish to sell some of their durable stocks at the price prevailing for new durables. Inasmuch as they cannot, the constraint $S_1 \geq (1 - \delta)S_0$ is likely to be binding so that the behavioral equations for these households will be different from those for households that are wealthier in financial assets, since for them, this constraint will not be binding. It is likely that the difference between the nondurable consumption functions for the two kinds of households will be less than the difference in the durable purchase or stock demand functions, and the same result follows if sales constraints on durables are treated as (nonconvex) transactions costs. In the aggregate, the deviation from the conventional form of the nondurable consumption function is likely therefore not to be as large as will be the case for durables. For the latter, aggregate purchases will be a complex weighted average of zero and the conventional not sales-rationed equation with the weighting factor itself very sensitive to income changes. Thus the income dynamics in the aggregate nondurable consumption function will to a great extent be those of the wealth term W, while those in the aggregate durables equation will be quite different. This is a plausible explanation for the empirical finding mentioned above, that the income dynamics of the two equations are very different.

There is empirical support too for the importance of restrictions on hire purchase lending (or loans) for the demand for durables in Britain. These operate by altering the number of households for whom borrowing is a possibility, and their effectiveness is a testimony of the importance of liquidity constraints.

This brings us finally to the question of how the applied economist should use these insights, convincing as we believe them to be. The data requirement for the successful estimation of aggregate multiple regimes models is quite unlikely to be met. One possible answer is simulation in order to get some idea of how the pattern of dominant regimes and the aggregate demands themselves change with economic conditions. Indeed, in Chapter 12, we have already referred to one such study, by Dolde and Tobin (1971), although not applied to durables. Such experiments can perhaps be combined with estimation in order to suggest how far the ideas discussed here are likely to take us in modeling reality. Such work remains to be done.

Exercises

13.10. With the utility function of Exercise 13.5, contrast the forms of the equations for q_1 and S_1 when the restriction $S_1 \geq (1 - \delta)S_0$ is binding and when it is not binding, under the assumption that no borrowing restrictions hold and that no sales restrictions are expected in the next period. (You need not obtain analytical solutions for the Lagrange multiplier λ, which attaches to the intertemporal budget constraint.) Discuss the factors that determine the aggregate proportion of households that at any one time fall in the sales constrained regime.

13.11. Assuming now that sales constraints on durables do not bind and are not expected to bind, carry out a similar analysis to that in Exercise 13.10 for the impact of hire purchase restrictions. For simplicity, assume that at the level of the individual

household these take the form $A \geq \bar{A}$, so that net financial assets cannot fall below some lower limit, and assume that they are not expected to be binding next period.
13.12. In empirical work on the time-series demand for durables, investigators often include the volume of hire purchase lending as an explanatory variable. Discuss the validity of this procedure and suggest possible alternatives.

13.5 Discrete choice, diffusion, and cross-section analysis

In the analysis of cross-section microeconomic data, it is not possible to maintain the pretense of continuously variable stocks of durables in the way we have been doing so far. For many durable goods, the choice is between ownership and nonownership and, in this situation of discrete choice, it is often argued that conventional demand analysis is irrelevant. In this section, we introduce in the simplest possible way the basic notions involved in modeling this type of choice.

To keep the analysis as simple as possible, we take the example of car ownership and assume that ownership can be had for the payment of an annual rental v^*. The single-period budget constraint, conditional on total expenditure, is then

$$pq + v^*S = x \tag{5.1}$$

where p is the price and q the quantity of the nondurable, and $S = 1$ if a car is owned with $S = 0$ if a car is not owned. Let the single-period utility (or subutility) function be

$$u = v(q, S, \epsilon) \tag{5.2}$$

where ϵ is a parameter (or more generally a vector of parameters) that differs from household to household and that picks up differences in tastes or in circumstances such as family composition, which are not reflected in the budget constraint.

Figure 13.7 illustrates the choices made by two households 0 and 1 with indifference curves I_0I_0 and I_1I_1, respectively. If the households choose not to own a car, nondurable consumption is x/p, while with ownership, it falls to $(x - v^*)/p$. If u_0 and u_1 are the utility levels associated with nonownership and ownership, respectively, we have

$$u_0 = v\left(\frac{x}{p}, 0, \epsilon\right) \tag{5.3}$$

$$u_1 = v\left(\frac{x - v^*}{p}, 1, \epsilon\right) \tag{5.4}$$

Households for which $u_1 > u_0$ will own a car while those for which $u_0 > u_1$ will not. Which households fall into which category depends upon the values

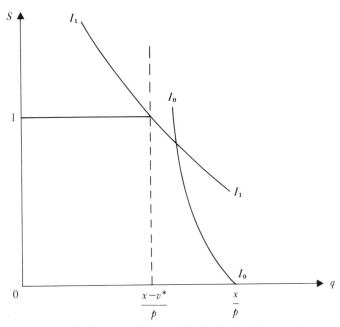

Figure 13.7. Choices of two households faced with binary choice.

of x and ϵ, which are the only variables that differ across households. If we consider for a moment households with the same taste parameter ϵ but different total expenditure x, then it is clear that for poorer households u_0 is likely to be greater than u_1. When nondurable consumption is low, the marginal disutility of any further drop is large compared to the benefits of car ownership. However, as x increases, so will nondurable consumption, until eventually, provided preferences do not turn against motoring as welfare increases, the disutility of a decrease in v^*/p is outweighed by the benefits of ownership. This is illustrated in Figure 13.8 at the point $x_T(\epsilon)$, often called "threshold" expenditure. Thus, when household of type ϵ reaches $x_T(\epsilon)$, that household will become an owner; at lower income levels, nonownership is preferred.

To take a specific example, if utility is given by $u = (S + a + \epsilon)^\alpha q^{1-\alpha}$, for parameters a and α, then the durable will be owned (see Exercise 13.13) if $[(1 + a + \epsilon)/(a + \epsilon)] > (x/x - v^*)^{(1-\alpha)/\alpha}$. For simplicity, take $\alpha = \frac{1}{2}$. The ownership condition can thus be written either $\epsilon < x/v^* - 1 - a$ or $x/v^* > a + 1 + \epsilon$. Given x, the former tells us which families of a given expenditure class will own a car and this depends on family composition, region, rural or urban residence, and so on, which can all be part of ϵ. Given ϵ, the latter tells us the

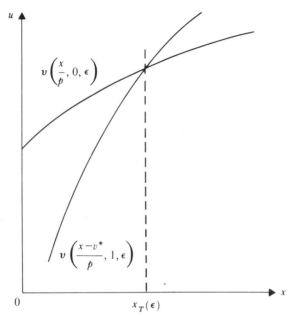

Figure 13.8. The derivation of threshold expenditure $x_T(\epsilon)$.

threshold expenditure of a family of given type. Note that the durable price v^* and total expenditure x always appear together in the expression x/v^*; we could thus just as well have defined a threshold price below which purchase will take place.

In general, if $f(x, \epsilon)$ is the joint density function of x and ϵ, the proportion of households with expenditure x who own the durable $g(x)$, say, is given by

$$g(x) = \int_{-\infty}^{\phi(x/v^*)} f(x, \epsilon)\, d\epsilon \bigg/ \int_{\infty_-}^{\infty} f(x, \epsilon)\, d\epsilon \qquad (5.5)$$

where $\phi(x/v^*)$ is a increasing function of x/v^*, $(x/v^* - 1 - a)$ in the example, defining the highest level of ϵ that results in ownership. Equation (5.5) gives a basis in utility theory for "quasi" Engel curves linking ownership in any income bracket to the income level. These have been widely estimated – see Cramer (1969) for a good discussion of their properties and Aitchison and Brown (1957), Pyatt (1964), and Bonüs (1973) for examples of their applications. In the traditional formulation, x is usually interpreted as income and ϵ itself as the threshold income level above which ownership occurs; hence, $S = 0$ if $x < \epsilon$ and $S = 1$ if $x \geq \epsilon$. If, for example, we assume that ϵ is distributed independently of x and that it has the lognormal distribution with parameters μ and σ^2, then (5.5) is replaced by

$$g(x) = \text{prob}(S = 1; x) = \int_{-\infty}^{x} f(\epsilon; \mu, \sigma^2) \, d\epsilon = \Lambda(x; \mu, \sigma^2) \qquad (5.6)$$

where $\Lambda(x; \mu, \sigma^2)$ is the cumulative distribution function of the lognormal distribution. Note that (5.5) is considerably more general than (5.6) and that the former has the advantage of giving a systematic basis for the inclusion of variables such as prices or household characteristics as well as suggesting explicit forms for the threshold income level, given some convenient form of the utility function.

Using microeconomic survey data on individual households, such models can be estimated directly by the principle of maximum likelihood. If we ignore taste differences other than those captured by ϵ, then $g(x)$ from (5.5) is the probability of a randomly selected household owning the durable conditional on household expenditure x. Suppose that in our sample of n households, n_1, with outlays $x_1, \ldots, x_{n_1}$, do not own the good, while the remainder do. The parameters of the model can then be estimated using the same techniques used in §10.3 for the choice of varieties or in §11.1 for labor participation. In this case, the likelihood is [cf. Chapter 10, (3.19) and Chapter 11, (1.9)],

$$\mathscr{L} = \prod_{i=1}^{n_1} [1 - g(x_i)] \prod_{i=n_1+1}^{n} g(x_i) \qquad (5.7)$$

since $[1 - g(x)]$ is the probability of nonownership. If $g(x)$ is derived from a utility function as in (5.5), it will depend on the parameters of the utility function and they can be estimated by maximizing (5.7) by nonlinear techniques.

On macroeconomic data, we may be more interested in the proportion of all households that own the good and how this moves over time with aggregate income, prices, and so on. From (5.5), integrating over x,

$$\text{Proportion of owners} = \int_{0}^{\infty} \int_{-\infty}^{\phi(x/v^*)} f(x, \epsilon) \, d\epsilon \, dx \qquad (5.8)$$

which will take a simpler form if x and ϵ are independently distributed. Even in the general case, however, it is clear that, as average income increases, or the durable price falls, the proportion of owners will follow an increasing S-shaped or sigmoid curve. In any income group, some proportion will have sufficiently low thresholds to be owners and this proportion will increase the higher the income group. Hence, as average income increases, and the whole distribution moves upwards, households are lifted into higher income groups and over their individual thresholds. At first, when incomes are low, few people are rich enough to be above their thresholds and increases in average income only enable rich people, who are few, to purchase. Later, as income increases further or the price becomes lower, so that many households are close to their thresholds, changes in income will have a much larger effect. In the final stages, the "poor" tail of the income distribution is reached, and although this may be much thicker than the rich tail, eventually saturation is reached and ownership once again becomes unresponsive to changes in income and price. Figure 13.9, reprinted from Deaton (1975c), illustrates all these phases for the spread of television ownership for various European countries; here the characteristic sigmoid shape appears very clearly. It is worth noting that, using (5.8), an explicit connection can be drawn with the distribution of incomes. Clearly, if incomes are very unequally distributed, diffusion of ownership can be expected to be long and slow, only proceeding rapidly in the very final stages. Conversely, with great equality, the sigmoid becomes very sharp and in the limit approaches a right-angled step shape. As far as we are aware, no attempt has been made to compare international diffusion and income distribution patterns, perhaps because of lack of data on the latter; even so, it remains a promising research topic.

The diffusion of ownership as rising real incomes allow more and more people to purchase is only one of several processes that produce the sigmoid curves illustrated in Figure 13.9. Another important case occurs when a new good is introduced and information about its existence and characteristics is the barrier to the spread of its ownership, rather than a high unit cost. Many minor items of household hardware would come into this category as well as some traditional nondurables which once were unknown; Ironmonger (1972)

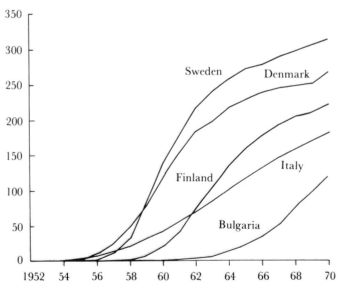

Figure 13.9. Television ownership per 1,000 population in selected countries.

gives many examples for Britain, including such (surprising) items as tea, bananas, ice cream, and milk. A useful model in this context is the "epidemic" model, which draws an analogy between the spread of information and the spread of an infectious disease. If N is the number of consumers who are potential owners (not immune), while ν is the number who are already owners (carriers), then the rate of change of ownership is assumed to be proportional both to the number of owners and the number of nonowners. Hence, we have, for some constant k.

$$\frac{d\nu}{dt} = k\nu(N - \nu) \tag{5.9}$$

Alternatively, income rather than time can be assigned the driving role on the assumption that changes in income induce larger changes in ownership when there are both large numbers of carriers and uninfected but infectable consumers. Equation (5.9) can easily be solved by substituting $z = \nu/(N - \nu)$ so that (5.9) becomes $d \log z/dt = Nk$ with solution, after substitution,

$$\nu = \frac{N}{1 + \alpha e^{-Nkt}} \tag{5.10}$$

for some constant α. Equation (5.10), like (5.8), makes ownership a sigmoid function of time with $\nu = 0$ when $t = -\infty$ and $\nu = N$ when $t = \infty$. This can be modified in various ways by replacing t by income or some function of income and prices. Since, by suitable choice of independent variables, (5.10) can approximate (5.8) very closely, and vice versa, it is likely to be difficult in practice to disentangle diffusion processes associated with discrete choice problems from those associated with the spread of information. This may not matter very much since, in many cases, such as the television example cited both phenomena are likely to be present.

The discrete choice which we have examined in this section is of a peculiarly simple kind and, in practice, would need considerable modification. For example, it can be argued that purchase of a durable, for example, a car, is not merely a (0, 1) choice but involves a decision whether to spend nothing or to spend more than some minimum level necessary to own the cheapest version of the good. Such a choice can be modeled either as discrete choice between alternative varieties as discussed in §10.3 or in the same way as the decision on labor force participation and hours worked discussed in §11.1, and we do not repeat the analysis here. It is also necessary to modify our simple static framework. In an intertemporal model, however, one difficulty is that discrete decisions can be remade next period, and so the number of discrete decisions multiplies even with perfect markets and without the liquidity constraints discussed in §13.4. For example, a household considering whether to buy a new car or not may have the options of holding on to its used car until next period, of selling it now and not buying a replacement, or of buying a less old used car.

In our view, for the understanding of *aggregate* dynamics, the discreteness of these choices as such is probably not of central importance. What *is* central is the existence of the liquidity constraints we have discussed and the distinct regimes to which these lead. The fact that these regimes are different from one another means that even if durables are perfectly divisible, on cross-section data we would need to apply discrete choice models in order to determine in which constraint regime a given household found itself. We saw in §13.4 that whether a given household is in the quantity nonconstrained regime or in the regime in which new purchases are constrained to zero depends on an inequality involving wealth and lagged stock. In a micromodel, we would need to include a random taste term in the utility function and hence in this inequality. The resulting probability model is similar to the treatment of kinked budget lines in the analysis of labor supply mentioned in Chapter 11.

Exercises

13.13. Suppose utility is given by $u = (S + a + \epsilon)^\alpha q^{1-\alpha}$ for parameters a and α and the household faces the budget constraint $pq + v*S = x$. If the durable is owned $S = 1$, if not, $S = 0$. Show that the durable will be owned if $[(1 + a + \epsilon)/(a + \epsilon)] > [x/(x - v*)]^{(1-\alpha)/\alpha}$

13.14. (Exercise 13.13, cont.) If $\alpha = \frac{1}{2}$, show that the ownership condition is $\epsilon < x/v* - 1 - a$. Hence, see §10.3, find the probability that a household with a total outlay of x owns the durable good if ϵ follows a Weibull distribution. If the distribution of ϵ and x over households are independent and each follow the Weibull form, find the proportion of households that own the durable.

13.15. Suppose that the amount of the durable good that can be owned is continuously variable but that every time a transaction is made a fixed charge c per unit change in the stock is made. Then the one-period budget constraint that is relevant when preferences are intertemporally separable is $pq + v_1^*S_1 + c|S_1 - (1 - \delta)S_0| = x$. Illustrate this budget constraint diagrammatically. Given the utility function in Exercise 13.13, show under what conditions the stock is increased, stays the same, or is decreased. Discuss the implication of such a model for the replacement decision of households.

13.16. Discuss whether fixed per unit transactions costs, as defined in Exercise 13.15, are a reasonable approximation to the effect of the differential faced by households in buying and selling prices of durable goods (which was discussed in §13.4). Discuss the alternative specification of transactions costs as $c_1S_1 + c_0S_0$ if $S_1 \neq (1 - \delta)S_0$ and zero if $S_1 = (1 - \delta)S_0$, and illustrate it diagrammatically. Repeat the analysis and discussion requested in Exercise 13.15 for this specification. How well does such a model explain why most households do not change houses every year?

13.17. In the light of the discussion of the interaction of new and second-hand durable markets in §13.1, of constraints in §13.4, of discrete choice in §13.5, and of transactions costs in Exercise 13.16, suggest how a model for the behavior of second-hand house prices might be constructed. Does house price inflation itself cause the volume of transactions to increase? How is the size of this effect likely to be altered by limiting tax relief on interest payments or taxing the subsidy some households receive in below market interest rates?

13.6 Habits and lags

We now turn to some general issues relating to the dynamics of consumer's expenditure equations, with particular reference to the presence of lagged dependent variables. These issues are taken up here because habits that develop as a consequence of past behavior are very much like stocks of durable goods, which analogously, are built up from past purchases. "Dynamic" demand equations are most obviously required for durable goods, but are·far from confined to this limited area of consumer behavior, given the pervasiveness of habits.

We have already met in this chapter, but especially in §12.2, several reasons for the presence in demand equations of lagged values of the dependent variable. The most obvious of these is through the role of stocks of financial and nonfinancial assets in the wealth constraint applicable to intertemporal decision making. In Chapter 12, we saw that if consumer durables and asset revaluations are ignored, the consumption function can be transformed using the period-to-period budget constraint, which governs the change in the level of financial assets so that assets are replaced by last period's nondurable consumption. When durables are included, the period-to-period budget constraint is (1.2), which includes the term $v_t d_t$. It can easily be shown that the transformation analogous to Chapter 12, equation (2.16) results, for example, with Cobb-Douglas preferences, in a nondurable consumption function with not just last period's purchases of durables and nondurables but stocks from two periods back.

A second reason why lagged dependent variables appear in demand equations was examined in the discussion in §13.2 of costs of adjustment, and these costs may apply to some nondurables as well as to durables. Search costs are one example that have a tendency to make people act as they did before rather than to continually reevaluate alternative courses of action. Also, costs of adjustment in durables may well be reflected by the presence of lagged values of nondurable consumption. Consider a household that installs an electric central heating system, only to face a large increase in price of electricity relative to, say, natural gas. If it had the opportunity of starting again from scratch, it would install a gas-fired plant and would consume no electricity for heating. Nevertheless, because the electrical heating equipment that has been installed is costly to remove and worth little on the second-hand market, it may well be optimal to hold on to it until it falls apart, thus continuing to consume expensive electricity at a high level for some time to come. In time-series data on electricity expenditure, this will show up as a positive coefficient on lagged electricity consumption, and adjustments to relative price changes will take a long time to work themselves out. There are a number of other examples where complementarities between nondurable commodities and stocks of durables induce such lagged responses.

A third explanation for lagged endogenous variables, at least in the case of stocks of durables, lies in liquidity constraints as analyzed in §13.4. There we gave an example where some households have zero purchases of durables and others have positive purchases and where the lagged stock of durables relative to wealth, income, and price variables plays an important role in determining the weights given to these two components of aggregate purchases.

There is a fourth explanation of lagged dependent variables that has received a good deal of attention in the literature, see Peston (1967), Pollak (1970, 1976a, 1978), Von Weizsäcker (1971), and Gorman (1967), and has been used in empirical applications by, for example, Houthakker and Taylor (1966, 1970) and Phlips (1972, 1974). This is that tastes are affected by previous consumption experience. The usual model is one of "myopic" habit formation in an individualistic context, myopic because households do not look ahead to the future effects when making their present decision. A popular version of the model is a modified version of the linear expenditure system in which committed consumption levels are made functions of lagged consumption. A system of this form was first estimated by Stone and Croft-Murray as long ago as 1959, although they give the model a rather different interpretation in terms of partial adjustment of actual to desired quantities, as given by the conventional linear expenditure system. This is a good example of the general difficulty of deducing empirically which theory is responsible for generating the lagged responses in the first place.

It has sometimes been claimed that such "dynamized" demand models are appropriate vehicles for treating the demand for durable goods, but since they are usually derived from a one-period utility function maximized subject to a one-period budget constraint, such models cannot take account of the important expectational factors present even in the simplest model discussed in §13.1. Intertemporal models in which tastes in each period depend upon past consumption and in which this is foreseen by the consumer are technically very difficult to handle and, by making no concession to imperfect knowledge or to questions of calculation, are extremely implausible as descriptions of observed behavior. However, there is another justification for a kind of habit formation that does not raise this problem and this we explained in §12.2.

Goods have social functions in communicating between people. The spread of goods and fashions is a symptom of the consequent lagged patterning of behavior by one household on other households. In §12.2, we saw in the context of a simple linear example how, by aggregating across households, lags *between* households become lags common to the aggregate of households. By aggregation, we get the same kind of behavior that Phlips (1972), Pollak (1970), and others specify at the individual level. But there is one advantage to the "social" rather than individualistic formulation. In the latter, there is the difficulty that a self-conscious individual will realize that his behavior will alter his subsequent preferences and will attempt to take this into account. He who does not might justifiably be thought to be myopic. But a nonmyopic formulation of the intertemporal problem is exceedingly complicated. The advantage of the social formulation is that even if the planning problem is set up intertemporally, each household is so small that it can safely ignore the feedback from its actions through group actions back to its own preferences. So a fully intertemporal demand model at the aggregate level can well exhibit the kind of lagged responses that, if true at the individual level, we would have to call myopic. Our demonstration of this model works out nicely because of the linear functions we have chosen but the point is a more general one.

Let us for comparison, briefly examine the individualistic formulation taken, for example, by Phlips (1972). The linear expenditure system utility function is modified by allowing the intercepts to vary over time:

$$\log u_t = \Sigma \alpha_i \log (q_{it} - \gamma_{it}) \tag{6.1}$$

where γ_{it} depends upon $q_{it-1}, q_{it-2}, \ldots$. Phlips defines

$$\gamma_{it} = \gamma_{i0} + \gamma_{i1} \theta_{it} \tag{6.2}$$

where θ_{it} represents the stock of habits for good i and is defined by $\dot{\theta}_{it} = q_{it} - \delta_i \theta_{it}$, where δ_i is the rate of decay of habits. A discrete time approximation to this is

$$\Delta \theta_{it} = q_{it-1} - \delta_i \theta_{it-1} \tag{6.3}$$

which implies $\theta_{it} = q_{it-1} + (1 - \delta_i)q_{it-2} + (1 - \delta_i)^2 q_{it-3} + \cdots$. [Houthakker and Taylor (1970) suggest a more sophisticated approximation than (6.3), but this does not affect the essence of the argument.] If (6.1) is maximized subject to the static linear budget constraint, we obtain the standard demand functions of Chapter 3.

$$q_{it} = \gamma_{it} + \frac{\alpha_i}{p_{it}} (x_t - \Sigma \gamma_{jt} p_{jt}) \tag{6.4}$$

but where

$$\gamma_{it} = \gamma_{i0} + \gamma_{i1}[q_{it-1} + (1 - \delta_i)q_{it-2} + (1 - \delta_i)^2 q_{it-3} + \cdots] \tag{6.5}$$

and estimate the γ's, α's, and δ's by nonlinear maximum likelihood methods. For annual American data for 1929 to 1970, Phlips finds that out of 11 goods including several categories of durables, all γ_{i1}'s except for automobiles and parts and furniture and household equipment are positive, which he inter-

prets as positive habit formation. The negative γ_{i1}'s for these two categories of
durables are consistent with the stock adjustment principle, which also pre-
dicts a negative coefficient on θ_{it} in an equation explaining purchases, since θ_{it}
can be literally interpreted as a stock measure in the case of durables. The δ_i's
lie mostly between about 0.05 and 0.4, indicating fairly long lagged responses
for most goods.

One interesting feature of this model that has been discussed by Von
Weizsäcker (1971), Pollak (1970, 1976a), Gorman (1967), and others is the
question of "long-run preferences." It can be shown for $0 < \delta_i < 1$ that if
prices and total expenditure are constant over time, then eventually the demands will settle down to long-run quantities. Further, these quantities are
actually consistent with a static form of the original utility function but with
different parameters. This is obvious enough: in the long run, $q_{it-1} = q_{it-2} =$
$\cdots = q_i^*$, say. So $\gamma_{it} = \gamma_i^* = \gamma_{i0} + (\gamma_{i1}/\delta_i) q_i^*$. For the utility function given
by (6.1), the first-order conditions for an optimum are

$$\alpha_i/(q_{it} - \gamma_{it}) = \lambda_t p_{it} \tag{6.6}$$

which, in the long run becomes $\alpha_i/(q_i^* - \gamma_{i0} - \gamma_{i1}q_i^*/\delta_i) = \lambda p_i$. But this is
identical to

$$\alpha_i^*/(q_i^* - \gamma_i^*) = \lambda p_i \tag{6.7}$$

with $\alpha_i^* = \alpha_i/(1 - \gamma_{i1}/\delta_i)$ and $\gamma_i^* = \gamma_{i0}/(1 - \gamma_{i1}/\delta_i)$ as the parameters of the
"long-run utility function."

Pollak (1976a) has considered more general conditions under which such
long-run utility functions exist, and these turn out to be very restrictive. This
is one reason to be critical of Von Weizsäcker's (1971) interpretation of the
long-run utility function as in some sense representing "true" preferences. A
more down-to-earth criticism is that there are a number of other important
reasons, which we have discussed, why in empirical work on demand, lagged
endogenous variables should appear, and it would seem highly dangerous to
base welfare judgments on estimates contaminated, say, by omission of financial assets from the budget constraint. Nevertheless, attempts have been made
to "correct" various index numbers for dynamic effects. One such is Phlips'
(1974) construction of what he calls "cardinal index numbers" of the cost-
of-living. The general idea of these can be illustrated as follows. The cardinal
cost-of-living index is the ratio $c_t(u_0, p_t)/c_0(u_0, p_0)$, where $c_t(u_0, p_t)$ is the minimum cost at prices p_t of reaching u_0 at parameter values γ_{it}, where $c_0(u_0, p_0)$ is
the same concept evaluated at p_0 and γ_{i0}. Phlips finds that the γ_i's, which reflect committed consumption, mostly increase over time. In consequence, the
consumer needs more money to be as well off as before even if prices and
total expenditure are constant. Thus, Phlips' cardinal index shows a much
greater increase in the cost of living over time than does a conventional index
based on fixed tastes.

The general question of welfare measurement when tastes are truly endogenous is a tricky one, especially on the interpretation given of endogeneity of tastes as a result of social interaction. Hirsch (1977) has criticized the individualism of conventional welfare economics, which he argues gives a quite misleading evaluation of the benefits of economic growth and of the efficiency of the market economy. He argues that externalities in consumption are much greater than is conventionally accepted and, moreover, tend to increase with economic growth. As is well-known, such externalities introduce a divergence between private and collective rationality. Further, there are many goods that he calls "positional goods" whose supply cannot be increased – for example land used for leisure purposes – which economic growth as such will never bring within the reach of the mass of population and to which access will always be regulated by one's relative position in the distribution of purchasing power. Their existence suggests that a substantial part of individual welfare rests on *relative* rather than absolute consumption. One implication is that in the trade-off between growth and distribution, the latter may well be more important than individualistic welfare functions would lead us to expect.

Exercises

13.18. Define the lag operator B such that $Bx_t \equiv x_{t-1}$, and by writing

$$A_t = \frac{y_t - p_t q_t - v_t d_t}{1 + (1 + r_{t+1})B}$$

and $\quad S_t = \dfrac{d_t}{1 - (1 - \delta)B}$

show that W_t is a function of W_{t-1}, W_{t-2} and of lagged values of labor incomes, expenditures on durables and nondurables, and expectations of discounted future incomes.
13.19.* (Exercise 13.18 cont.) Hence, discuss the implications of the presence of durable goods, even when there are perfect financial markets, for the Hall result discussed in §12.2.
13.20. Stigler and Becker (1977) have argued, see §10.1, that most cases economists label as "taste change," for example, habit formation, are better analyzed as changes in the constraints. Contrast their example of the accumulation of music appreciation-specific human capital with a model of habit formation such as (6.1) and (6.2) in which goods such as concert tickets, and other musical material, have an associated taste parameter influenced by past consumption levels. Discuss whether the two approaches have different welfare implications.
13.21.* How does knowledge that goods are habit forming affect future planning? See Phlips (1974, Chapter 10).
13.22. Phlips (1972) suggests essentially the following estimation procedure: write (6.6) as $q_{it} = \gamma_{it} + (\alpha_i)/(\lambda_t p_{it})$, and in order to eliminate the unobservable components in γ_{it}, apply the Koyck transformation $\gamma_{it} - (1 - \delta_i)\gamma_{it-1} = \gamma_{i0}(1 - \delta_i) + \gamma_{i1}q_{it-1}$. Estimate the resulting least squares treating the series on λ_t as known data to be updated after each round of estimation. How, given a first set of estimates of the α's and γ's, would you compute a series on λ_t? Contrast the assumption on the stochastic error terms implicit

in this procedure with that implicit in estimating (6.4) after substituting (6.5) by least squares.

13.23. Suppose that in Exercise 13.14 the utility function at time t is $u = (S_t + a(1 - P_{t-1}) + \epsilon_t)^{1/2} q_t^{1/2}$, where P_{t-1} is the proportion of households in the population at time $t - 1$ who own the durable. Is this a reasonable model of the spread of the "disease" of owning the durable? Show mathematically and graphically how P_t is related to P_{t-1} with x constant. Hence, discuss how the speed of response of P_t with respect to an increase in the average level of x in the population is altered by comparison with Exercise 13.14.

13.24. Generalize the model of social interaction discussed in §12.2 to the case of specific goods, using the linear expenditure system.

Bibliographical notes

The neoclassical theory of the demand for durables parallels the growth of neoclassical investment theory, see Fisher (1907, 1930), Hirshleifer (1958), Haavelmo (1960), Eisner and Strotz (1963), Lucas (1967), Jorgenson (1967), Gould (1968). A useful book of readings on investment of firms is Helliwell (1974), and Nickell (1979b) is the best text on the subject. Tintner's (1938a, b) exposition of the life-cycle theory was extended to stocks of durables by Cramer (1957), though Theil (1951) had earlier discussed the role of stocks in consumer theory. A good recent exposition of the consumer equivalent to firms' investment decisions is in Diewert (1974b), and an empirical investigation explicitly based on neoclassical theory is in Hess (1977).

The partial or stock-adjustment model goes back to Goodwin (1951), Chenery (1952) and Koyck (1954), in turn, being a generalization of the much older investment accelerator of, for example, Clark (1919). Among the best known applications of it to the demand for consumer durables are Chow (1957, 1960) and Stone and Rowe (1957, 1958); other applications can be found in Harberger (ed.) (1960). Williams (1971) is an empirical study on British data that is more than usually careful about the stochastic specification of the equations. A precursor of the discretionary replacement model is Brems (1956), who was involved in a debate with Nerlove (1957), a proponent of the stock-adjustment model. There has been some debate about the use of attitude measures such as the Michigan Survey Research Center's indices, see Evans (1969, Chapter 6), Juster and Wachtel (1972), and Smith (1975).

Following Keynes (1936), liquidity constraints have been fairly widely discussed in the postwar literature. Tobin (1951, 1972) and Dolde and Tobin (1971) are key references. The closely related issue of nonconvex transactions costs but in the context of general equilibrium theory has been surveyed by Ulph and Ulph (1975), and its consequences for consumer behavior have been investigated by Zabel (1973), who does so in the context of behavior under risk. Because we have left portfolio theory for Chapter 14, we have omitted from the present chapter consideration of the demand for durables as merely part of a spectrum of assets with different degrees of appreciation or depreciation, maturity dates, and risk. Apart from the references in Chapter 14 on portfolio theory, Watts and Tobin (1960) and Evans (1969, §6.5) contain empirical applications, including consumer durables, while Hamburger (1968) among others has estimated closely related demand functions for financial assets.

Analysis of cross-section data on ownership or purchases of durables has always had to face up to the discreteness of owning or not owning. De Wolff (1938) is one of the earliest applications of sigmoid Engel curves. The Probit technique for analyzing zero−one variables developed in biometric applications in the 1930's, see Finney (1947), and saw its first systematic application to the demand for durables in the classic paper by Farrell (1954). Not only does he analyze discrete choice in terms very close to the utility theory we discussed in Chapter 11 but his model takes seriously the interactions of new and used markets. We have mentioned in the text some of the more recent references and to these should be added Cramer (1962), Bain (1964), Wu (1965), Cragg and Uhler (1970), who take an explicit characteristics approach, and Cragg (1971). Priority patterns – regularities in the order of acquisition of household durables – have been analyzed by Pyatt (1964) and Paroush (1965). The latter, for example, finds that radio, gas cooker, refrigerator, and washing machine is the most common priority pattern.

The suggestion that the parameters of the utility function could be made to depend on past consumption was originally made in Stone's (1954b) classic paper on the linear expenditure system. Further reading on habits and endogenous preferences will be found in the 1976 symposium in the *Journal of Economic Theory*, in Leibenstein (1950, 1974), Gaertner (1974), and Gintis (1974). Apart from Phlips (1974), discussions of how to estimate such models are in Houthakker and Taylor (1966, 1970), Phlips (1972), and Taylor and Weiserbs (1972).

CHAPTER 14

Choice under uncertainty

The problems faced by consumers when there is uncertainty have frequently arisen in our discussion to date. Indeed, uncertainty is pervasive in almost all decision making and is inevitable whenever an action or decision and its consequence are separated by a space of time, however short. Even for consumption decisions involving the most highly perishable commodities, some uncertainty is always present. An ice cream may melt before it can be eaten; its quality or flavor may be very different from that anticipated, or it may or may not cause indigestion at some unpredictable time after consumption. All these are trivial enough, but become of the greatest importance in considering any sort of intertemporal decision making, whether buying a car, planning savings, or choosing the assets in which to hold wealth. Because of such considerations, a fully satisfactory treatment of consumers' behavior would allow for uncertainty right from the start. However, as we shall see, although a consistent and well-articulated theory for choice under uncertainty does exist, its applications to date are partial in coverage and are very considerably more complex than the corresponding results under certainty. Moreover, the omnipresence of uncertainty does not imply that it is always important.

Only in the last twenty years, dating essentially from the work of Savage (1954), has a full, axiomatic treatment of choice under uncertainty been available, although, as in the case of the axioms of choice under certainty, there has been considerable refinement by later writers. A good survey of alternative approaches to the subject prior to these developments is available by Arrow (1951a). At that time, the work of Von Neumann and Morgenstern (1947) had popularized an approach based upon the maximization of *expected* utility, but there were many critics. Many economists felt that, as suggested by Knight (1921), there is an important distinction between "risk" – a situation where probabilities are known or at least knowable, and uncertainty proper, where it is not obvious that probabilities can even be meaningfully defined. Tied up with this is the question of "repeatability"; if a situation recurs many times, probabilities can be defined in terms of the relative frequencies of various events, and at least intuitively, expected utility seems a relevant criterion in that the average utility obtained is likely to approach its expectation as the number of repetitions increases.

The axiomatic approach renders most of this discussion irrelevant, and although the axioms of choice under uncertainty have not gone unchallenged and are certainly much stronger than the axioms discussed in Chapter 2, there now seems to be a fair consensus of opinion among economists. Certainly, those who still do not accept the expected utility approach do not seem to be able to support their position with generally convincing objections to the axioms. Consequently, we are able to present in this chapter "the" theory of choice under uncertainty.

Section 14.1 discusses how uncertainty is formalized and is essentially preparatory material for the sections that follow. Here we introduce the concepts of acts, states, and consequences and discuss briefly the most general approach to choice under uncertainty, state-preference analysis. Section 14.2 contains an extremely nonrigorous introduction to the axiomatic approach. Each of the crucial axioms is briefly discussed, and we try to indicate intuitively how these axioms lead to the definition of "subjective" probabilities and to the expected utility theorem. Readers who are prepared to accept the expected utility approach on trust and, in particular, do not feel the need for an axiomatic justification of attaching subjective probabilities to uncertain events can omit this section and proceed straight to §14.3. That section presents some of the classic applications of expected utility theory to insurance and gambling and to the allocation of wealth among different risky assets. The concept of risk aversion is discussed and applied. Section 14.4 returns to what for us is a more central concern, the effects of uncertainty on savings within the context of intertemporal choice theory. General results in this area are somewhat rare, and we proceed by means of a particular example; although simple, this allows a wide range of possible behavior and provides some very suggestive results. It is also intended as a practical example of how the expected utility model can be used to generate specific, testable functional forms. Finally, §14.5 discusses another important application of the expected utility model to consumer behavior; this is the area of search, when a consumer wishes to buy at the lowest price (or to become employed at the best wage), and has to spend time searching to discover the prices actually available.

14.1 The characterization of uncertainty

In our discussion of choice under certainty in Chapter 4, the objects of choice were bundles of commodities. No distinction was made between the act of choice, on the one hand, and its consequence on the other. Indeed, since the act is the choice of a commodity bundle and the consequence its receipt, only a trivial distinction is possible. Under uncertainty, on the other hand, the consequences of any given act will vary according to the outcomes of events

Table 14.1. *Payoff matrix*

	States		
Acts	1	2	3
1	γ_{11}	γ_{12}	γ_{13}
2	γ_{21}	γ_{22}	γ_{23}

beyond the control of the individual. These outside events, which determine the consequences of actions, are usually referred to as *states of nature,* states of the world, or sometimes simply *states.* Obvious examples might be the weather tomorrow – dry or wet, the state of the stock market, the outcome of a government decision, and so on. The essential feature is that states of the world are outside the control of the individual making the uncertain choice. Hence, uncertainty is characterized as an aspect of nature, external to individuals.

We thus have three central concepts, acts, consequences, and states. An act may be thought of as a function, or mapping, which attaches to each state a consequence. Thus, if we had three states and two acts, we might draw up a "payoff matrix" as in Table 14.1. Then γ_{ij} is the consequence of act i if state of the world j occurs. We could, of course, have continuously variable acts and states, and this could be illustrated as in Figure 14.1. Both acts illustrated assign a numerical consequence to a given value of the state variable; note that in Figure 14.1 act 2 is a "constant" act in that its consequence is independent of the state of the world.

States are used to characterize all possible outcomes of nature. Hence, the set of all states of the world contains everything that can possibly happen. For most practical examples, this is too fine a classification and we wish to deal with only relevant events. This can be done straightforwardly by defining events as subsets of the set of all states of the world. For example, the states of the weather would include every conceivable conjunction of wind, rain, sun, humidity, and temperature, whereas these may be grouped into two sets, "dry" or "wet," which may be all that is relevant to the choice at hand. More often than not, the columns of the payoff matrix will relate to mutually exclusive events rather than to the primitive states themselves.

With this framework set up, the most general approach to choice under uncertainty is to write utility as a function of the usual variables for all possible states of the world. To fix ideas, index the s-states of nature by $\theta = 1$, $2, \ldots, s,$ and assume that, if state θ occurs, a vector or range of consequences $\gamma(., \theta)$, say, becomes available. The particular element of $\gamma(., \theta)$, or particular value, will depend on the act α chosen by the consumer. Hence, we can write a general utility function,

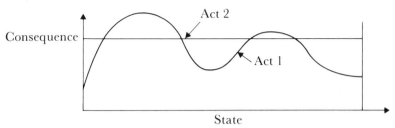

Figure 14.1. Continuous state and consequence variables.

$$u = \zeta[\gamma(\alpha, 1), \ldots, \gamma(\alpha, \theta), \ldots, \gamma(\alpha, s)] \qquad (1.1)$$

to emphasize the dependence of consequences on acts and states, or more succinctly and analogously to choice under certainty,

$$u = \zeta(\gamma_1, \ldots, \gamma_\theta, \ldots, \gamma_s) \qquad (1.1')$$

The consumer will then choose an act, or set of acts, from those available to him, so that (1.1) is maximized. Note the analogy between (1.1) and the household production model of Chapter 10; the consequences in the various states are analogous to the characteristics, the actions to the market commodities, and the functions $\gamma(\alpha, \theta)$ to the production technology.

It is important to see a distinction between (1.1') and the certainty or ex post utility function. If the consumer had the opportunity to rank different γ vectors under certainty, knowing which state occurs, the relevant utility function would be $v(\gamma)$ as in other chapters. Further, note that (1.1) is quite consistent with the special case

$$u = f[\pi_1 v(\gamma_1) + \pi_2 v(\gamma_2) + \cdots + \pi_s v(\gamma_s)] \qquad (1.2)$$

where $\pi_1, \ldots, \pi_s$ are some positive numbers which can be made, arbitrarily, to add to unity. Equation (1.2) is simply an additive version of the general utility function (1.1), so that, in this context, $v(\ )$ is merely a subutility function within the general form. Clearly, if (1.2) holds, if we can argue that probabilities of states (or of events) have any meaning, and if the π's can be regarded as these probabilities, then it makes sense to talk about expected utility maximization. We shall attempt to justify each of these "ifs" in the next section, but for the present, note simply how specialized (1.2) is compared with the general form (1.1).

Although most modern analysis uses (1.2), it is worth seeing how far we can get using (1.1) alone. This general approach is usually labeled *state-preference* theory. The standard example, see Green (1976) for a more detailed exposition, concerns the allocation of a portfolio between a risky and a safe asset.

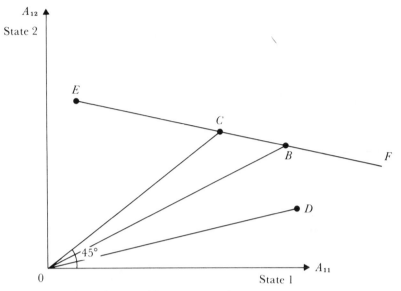

Figure 14.2. The budget set with two states and two assets.

Utility is assumed to be entirely a function of the total worth A and of terminal assets in the two states $\theta = 1$ and $\theta = 2$. This can be thought of as taking up the problem left in Chapter 12, that of allocating the portfolio between different assets. Note that severe separability assumptions are being made so that utility should be only a function of terminal assets, or put another way, so that the composition of the portfolio should be independent of consumption decisions. We shall examine some possible justifications for this view in §14.4.

The consumer has a fixed initial worth A_0 to be allocated between money, which has no return, and a bond, which either makes a profit (in State 1) or a loss (in State 2). Figure 14.2 illustrates the situation; the axes are the values of terminal assets in each of the two states. The line $0C$ is at 45 degrees to both axes and, since points along it have equal values in either state, it represents the line of complete certainty. In this case, there is an asset whose value is certain, so that if the whole portfolio is invested in money, the outcome is C. The point B represents the outcome when all assets are invested in bonds, assuming the profit under State 1 is greater than the loss under State 2. Clearly, points along CB represent a portfolio composed of bonds and money, while points such as F correspond to borrowing money to buy bonds, and points such as E represent selling bonds short (for delivery at the end of the period) in order to hold cash.

Note the similarity (apart from projecting CB in either direction) with the linear characteristics model of §10.1. The states correspond to the characteristics and the securities to the goods. Hence, the existence of securities with different characteristics (they have different yields in different states of the world) allows consumers to "span" state space and thus to minimize the effects of uncertainty. Indeed in some circumstances, it will be possible, although not necessarily desirable, to eliminate uncertainty altogether. For example, in Figure 14.2, bonds bought in combination with a third type of asset lying on the other side from bonds of the certainty line $0C$ will enable $0C$ to be reached. Indeed, any two assets that have distinct lines in state space will enable the certainty line to be reached provided there are no restrictions on borrowing or on short sales. Similarly, with n-states of nature, the same proviso will allow certainty to be attained with n linearly independent assets. We can also use other results of §10.1's linear characteristics model to characterize behavior of investors in security markets. For example, consumers will never hold more assets than there are states of the world. Similarly, some assets are inefficient (D in Figure 14.2 if there are no borrowing constraints) and will thus not be held. Conversely, in equilibrium, the market prices of all securities must adjust so that none that are actually held are inefficient in this sense.

Portfolio equilibrium in the state-preference approach simply requires the addition of indifference curves to Figure 14.2. However, these are sufficiently different from the usual indifference curves for us to give them some further discussion. The basic point is that utility functions such as (1.1) represent not only the consumer's preferences among the various outcomes, but also his evaluation of the relative likelihood of the various states or events. It is perfectly rational to prefer a conditional gift of one hundred dollars if it rains rain tomorrow than a gift of one thousand if it rains fire and brimstone. This allows us to make some interesting deductions from the shapes of the indifference curves which will become quite crucial in the next section. Assume, and this is an assumption to which we shall return, that the consequences of his acts are specified in sufficient detail so that the consumer has preferences only among the consequences, independently of the states in which they occur. In the context of Figure 14.3, we assume that the same total of terminal assets are equally valuable in both states. This would not apply if, for example, the states were "dry" and "wet" and we were dealing, not with wealth but, say, umbrellas. Taking this assumption as valid, consider the slope of an indifference curve at the point where it intersects the certainty line. In Figure 14.3, the slope of II' at C is given by the line AB whose slope gives the rate at which the consumer, starting from a position of certainty, is prepared to trade one unit of wealth payable in State 1 for one unit of wealth payable in State 2. Since wealth means the same in either state, any deviation of the slope from unity indicates that the consumer believes one state is more likely to occur than the other. In Figure 14.3, the slope of AB is steeper than (minus) one

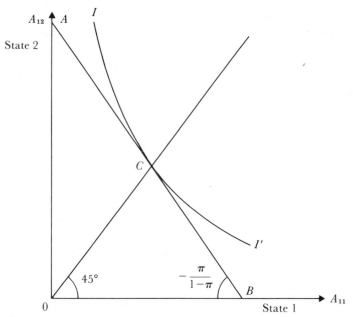

Figure 14.3. Risk-averse indifference curve.

and reflects a belief that State 1 is more likely than State 2. In cases where these likelihoods can acceptably be characterized by probabilities, and if π is the probability of State 1 occurring, then the slope of AB is given by $-\pi/(1 - \pi)$, the odds for State 1. This sort of argument will be developed further in the next section.

Note, finally, that given the consumer's subjective beliefs about the relative likelihoods of the two states, positions on AB represent "fair" bets on his own terms, that is, alternatives with the same expected value as the point C. However, with a quasi-concave utility function (1.1), the indifference curves are convex to the origin, as in Figure 14.3, and the consumer will not accept fair bets even on his own assessment of the odds. We can thus equate convex indifference curves with risk aversion; such consumers will pay to avoid uncertainty. Conversely, indifference curves that are concave to the origin characterize consumers who like risk – they will accept even unfavorable bets – while straight-line indifference curves represent risk neutrality.

Exercises

14.1. Define as precisely as you can the "states," "consequences," and "acts" in each of the following problems of choice under uncertainty:

(a) a game of cards (think of specific examples)
(b) voting at an election
(c) deciding which type of car to purchase
(d) deciding whether to purchase a car at all
(e) deciding whether to read any more of this chapter.

14.2. A fruit machine costs one coin per play, and pays either zero or ten coins in return. A consumer has a utility function given by (1.2) with $v(\gamma) = \log(\gamma + b)$, where b is a constant > 1. Show that if the fruit machine is programmed to make profits for its owner, the consumer will refuse to play. For what sort of specification of $v(\ )$ would the consumer wish to play?

14.3. There are two assets $i = 1, 2$ which pay γ_{ij} in state j, $j = 1, 2$ for each investment of one unit. Show that if the matrix formed by the γ_{ij}'s is singular and if the assets are not identical, then only one will be held. What is the generalization of this result to n assets? Discuss the view that, in practice, the near singularity of the γ matrix effectively limits consumer choice among assets.

14.4. If the indifference curves associated with (1.1) and illustrated in Figure 14.3 are symmetric around the 45 degree line, what can we say about beliefs? Discuss the problems with this interpretation if such indifference curves are nonhomothetic.

14.5. Show that the additive utility function (1.2) implies that the consumer's assessment of the relative likelihood of any two states is independent of the consequences of other states. Show that this is not the case for the more general function (1.1). Is it sensible to talk about probabilities of states if the condition is not met? (For further discussion, see §14.2.)

14.2 The axioms of choice under uncertainty and expected utility maximization

The maximization of expected utility is an extremely simple approach to choice under uncertainty and has a number of immediate advantages. It is the most obvious extension of the utility approach followed so far, and few would dispute that expected utility should be at least one goal of the rational consumer. The relative simplicity and empirical content of (1.2) over (1.1) is an added attraction.

The hypothesis has also a long pedigree of use in explaining various behavioral phenomena. The earliest application, preceding utility theory itself by more than a century, is by Daniel Bernouilli to the St. Petersburg paradox. The "paradox" runs as follows. Peter contracts to pay Paul 1 ducat, if, at the first throw, a fair coin falls heads; he will pay 2 ducats if heads first appears at the second throw, 4 ducats at the third, and so on to 2^{n-1} ducats at the nth. How much will Paul pay Peter to be allowed to play the game? The expected value of Paul's winnings is given by

$$E \text{ (winnings)} = \tfrac{1}{2} \times 1 + \tfrac{1}{4} \times 2 + \tfrac{1}{8} \times 4 + \cdots$$
$$= \tfrac{1}{2} + \tfrac{1}{2} + \tfrac{1}{2} + \cdots = \infty \tag{2.1}$$

The paradox arises because Paul, or at least his typical real counterpart, is unwilling to pay more than some relatively small and certainly finite sum to be permitted to play. The expected utility resolution comes about by taking some concave subutility function v (wealth), so that if Peter's initial assets are A_0, the amount $P(A_0)$, which he is willing to pay to play, is given by

$$v(A_0) = \sum_{1}^{\infty} \left(\frac{1}{2}\right)^r v(A_0 - P(A_0) + 2^{r-1}) \tag{2.2}$$

The left-hand side of (2.2) is Peter's utility if he does not play; in this case, he receives A_0 with certainty. The right-hand side is the expected utility, having paid $P(A_0)$; each utility outcome is weighted by its respective probability. If $P(A_0)$ is the maximum amount Peter will pay, these two expressions must be equal. For example, if, as suggested by Bernouilli, the utility function is given the logarithmic form, then for $A_0 = 100$, say, (2.2) yields a value of only 4.4 for $P(A_0)$.

We shall see, in §14.3, that similar applications have been made to the analysis of insurance and bets in general. The paradox given will serve as illustration for the time being.

In spite of its advantages, there are two objections to the expected utility approach that appear to have considerable force. The first questions the relevance of expected utility as the sole aim of maximization, while the second, more fundamental objection, denies that the requisite probabilities either exist or can be meaningfully defined. If we take these in turn, we can first assume that probabilities are well defined for a given situation, say a game of cards. Consider then an individual who plays only one "hand" of the game. Why should his expected utility be the sole object of attention when, in practice, this is only one of many possible outcomes? If the hand is repeated many times, total winnings divided by the number of hands will certainly approach the expected value of winnings, but even then, it is the *total* of winnings (which is more, not less, risky), rather than the average, that concerns the player. The only way the expectation becomes the outcome is when the number of replications goes to infinity *and* the stake becomes infinitesimal. But in this case, the risk can be made arbitrarily small so that even a risk-averse individual will, in the limit, be indifferent between certainty and fair bets at infinitesimal risk. If the stake becomes small enough and the number of replications large enough, Paul will pay Peter increasingly large sums to play the St. Petersburg game (although whether or not Peter will agree to play is quite another matter). But for this result, expected utility maximization is unnecessary; the maximization of wealth will do just as well.

The objections to the characterization of uncertainty in terms of probabilities are much deeper and raise fundamental issues of philosophy. The debate is essentially the same as that between Bayesian and classical statisticians as to whether we can attach probabilities to the truth or falsity of hypotheses. In the present context, the distinction is usually drawn, after Knight, between risk, on the one hand (probabilities well defined – example, games of chance), and uncertainty, on the other (probabilities unknown or undefinable). Thus the probability of being dealt a full house at poker is meaningful and calculable, but the probabilities of there being a man on Mars by the year 2000 or of the Einsteinian general theory of relativity being true are meaningless and thus unknowable. It is these problems that the axioms are designed to surmount.

Before discussing the axioms directly, we must restate two important conditions on our basic concepts. The first of these is that the state that occurs is independent of the actions of the individual making the decision. This will rule out of consideration the important class of problems usually grouped under the title, moral hazard. The outcome of a tennis match in which the decision maker is a participant is not a state of "nature" nor a subset of states of nature and cannot be included in the analysis. The term *moral hazard* arises as the reason for an insurer not being prepared to give insurance in such cases. The second is that consequences be fully specified so as to contain everything of interest to the agent. We discussed this condition briefly in §14.1, and as the analysis there showed, this proviso is quite crucial in that it means that, given the same consequences, consumers are quite indifferent between different states. The decision maker must only be concerned with consequences and not with the events that produce them. It is, of course, always possible to specify consequences widely enough to meet this proviso, but this may involve costs in terms of excessive generality and lack of empirical content.

Let us introduce some simple notation; as in (1.1) we write acts as α_1, $\alpha_2, \ldots$, consequences by γ_i, and states of the world by θ. An event, a specified subset of states will be denoted by E so that $\theta \in E$ means that for state of the world θ, E can be said to occur.

The axioms fall into four groups. The first group corresponds to the axioms in Chapter 2 and allows us to define a utility function over acts such as (1.1). We assume that the consumer can define an ordering over all possible acts, which satisfies completeness (or connectedness), transitivity, and continuity. Thus, if α_1 and α_2 are two acts, then in view of their consequences under all possible states of the world, we have, where $\gtrsim$ means "is at least as preferred as,"

(a) $\alpha_1 \gtrsim \alpha_2$ or $\alpha_2 \gtrsim \alpha_1$

(b) $\alpha_1 \gtrsim \alpha_2$ and $\alpha_2 \gtrsim \alpha_3$ implies $\alpha_1 \gtrsim \alpha_3$

(2.3)

We shall not give a formal definition of continuity here, see Arrow (1973) for details. But, as in Chapter 2, continuity implies that acts that have consequences close to one another must be close to one another in preference. This is by no means an innocent assumption and the example given by Arrow is worth quoting: "Let action α_1 involve receiving one cent with no risk of life, α_2

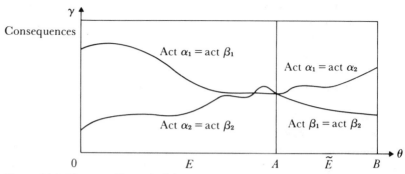

Figure 14.4. The sure-thing principle.

receiving nothing with no risk of life, and α_3 receiving one cent with an exceedingly small probability of death. Clearly, α_1 is preferred to α_2. Continuity would demand that α_3 be preferred to α_2 if the probability of death under α_3 is sufficiently small." As Arrow comments, this is not so outrageous as it seems. Most of us accept significant risks of death every day to gain quite small ends; we drive to work or cross the street to buy a bar of chocolate. If we accept this and (2.3) we can define a utility function over acts, but this takes us only as far as (1.1).

The second axiom goes under various names, conditional preference (Arrow, 1970a), the strong independence axiom (Samuelson, 1952a), or the sure-thing principle (Savage, 1954). This is perhaps the most controversial of the axioms and is responsible for allowing us to give (1.1) an additive structure. As we saw in Chapter 5, additivity is both very strong and very powerful and it is of great importance to understand why, in contrast to the certainty case, it should be acceptable in the present context. Begin by considering some event E and its complement $\tilde{E}$; E happens if $\theta \in E$, E does not if $\theta \in \tilde{E}$. In Figure 14.4, the horizontal axis is partitioned at point A to illustrate this. Consider two acts α_1 and α_2, which have different consequences if E happens but the same consequences if E does not. Take another pair of acts β_1 and β_2 such that, as illustrated, β_1 and β_2 have identical consequences to α_1 and α_2 if E occurs, and identical consequences to one another (but different from those of α_1 and α_2) if E does not occur. Then the strong independence axiom asserts that $\alpha_1 \gtrsim \alpha_2$ if, and only if $\beta_1 \gtrsim \beta_2$. If this holds, we can draw up a conditional ordering of acts, "given E" since consequences on $\tilde{E}$ make no difference and this conditional ordering will satisfy completeness, transitivity, and continuity, just as did the original unconditional ordering of acts. The justification lies in the fact that E and $\tilde{E}$ are mutually exclusive. Either E occurs, in which case $\alpha_1 \gtrsim \alpha_2$, or E does not occur, in which case they are equivalent. Since only one of the two is possible, we have no need to know what exactly are the conse-

Table 14.2. *The lottery*

Case (1)			Case (2)		
	State			State	
Ticket	Democrat	Republican	Ticket	Democrat	Republican
A	$100	$200	A	$100	$500
B	IBM share	$200	B	IBM share	$500

quences of α_1 and α_2 on $\bar{E}$ in order to be able to order them on E. Put even more clearly, if we know an event will not occur, we should pay no attention to the consequences of that event in choosing among the acts available to us.

This is perhaps even more obvious if we specialize Figure 14.4 to an example involving simple discrete choice. Assume a consumer has to choose between two lottery tickets, A and B. In A, he receives $100 if a Democrat is elected president in 1992 and $200 if a Republican is elected. With B, he receives a single share in IBM if a Democrat is elected and $200 if a Republican. Call this Case (1) as in Table 14.2. Case (2) is identical except that both tickets pay $500 rather than $200 if the Republican wins. Now, since the two events are mutually exclusive (there is no possibility of both a Republican and Democratic president), and since in both cases, A and B have exactly the same payoff if a Republican wins, then only the outcomes if the Democrat wins should be taken into account. Since these are identical in the two cases, if A is preferred to B in Case (1), it must also be in Case (2) and vice versa.

Intuitively, it is this mutual exclusivity of the various events that allow us to impose an additive structure on the utility function. Note that the situation is quite different from choice under certainty; additivity as discussed in Chapter 5 demands (in our view) a quite unacceptable degree of independence between commodities within preferences. For example, if Table 14.1 referred to commodities instead of states (Democrat = cars, Republican = shoes), and the payoffs were different combinations of commodities, then consumption would involve *both* cars and shoes. Hence, there is no reason why preferences over shoes should be independent of how many cars one possesses. As it is, however, only one state actually occurs, and additivity of preferences between mutually exclusive alternatives is perfectly acceptable.

We now need to be able to use our ordering of acts to derive an ordering of consequences, this latter being necessary for our final axiom, which allows the interpretation of the additive structure in terms of *subjective probabilities*. Since we already have an ordering on acts, valued in terms of their consequences, we can order consequences through the acts that produce them. In particular, we assume the existence of (possibly hypothetical) constant acts so that for every consequence there exists a constant act that will yield that consequence for all possible states of the world. (See Figure 14.1 for an illustration of a constant act.) Since these acts are already ordered, so are all consequences. Note that this ordering of consequences requires our initial assumption that consequences are specified in sufficient detail for states per se to have no value for the agent.

The final group of axioms relate to the ordering of events and the definition of the probabilities. A number of fairly technical assumptions are necessary at this point, see Arrow (1970a, pp. 69–88); we shall not discuss these, confining our attention to the way in which events themselves are ordered. In this case we are dealing, not with a preference ordering, but with a likelihood ordering. Imagine two consequences γ_1 and γ_2 such that $\gamma_1 \gtrsim \gamma_2$. We can think of these as cash prizes, with γ_1 the larger. The agent must then choose one of two courses of action; in the first, he receives γ_1 if event E_1 occurs and γ_2 if it does not, while in the second, he receives γ_1 if event E_2 occurs and γ_2 if it does not. If he consistently chooses the former over the latter, we say that E_1 is revealed as least as likely as E_2, and vice versa. The crucial axiom here is that the relationship "is revealed as likely as" defined by this experiment defines an ordering on the space of all events. Thus, if E_1 is revealed as likely as E_2 using some consequences γ_1 and γ_2 as prizes, then it will be revealed as likely as E_2 using any pair of consequences. This will not be satisfied if, once again, different consequences have different values in different states.

These four groups of assumptions are sufficient to prove what Drèze (1974) calls the "moral expectation theorem" whereby a utility function and probabilities of events are *simultaneously* defined such that optimal choice involves maximization of expected utility. Thus, if α_1 and α_2 are acts with consequences $\gamma_{1\theta}$ and $\gamma_{2\theta}$ in state of the world $\theta = 1, 2, \ldots, s$, then given the axioms, we can define probabilities $\pi_\theta \geq 0$ with $\Sigma\pi_\theta = 1$, and a "subutility" function $v(\gamma)$, such that $\alpha_1 \gtrsim \alpha_2$ if and only if

$$\Sigma\pi_\theta v(\gamma_{1\theta}) \geq \Sigma\pi_\theta v(\gamma_{2\theta}) \tag{2.4}$$

The function $v(\ )$ is defined up to an increasing *linear* transformation, and the reader can easily be satisfied that arbitrary increasing monotone transformations of $v(\ )$ can be found that will reverse the inequality. Hence, it is often said that utility functions for choice under uncertainty are "cardinal" as opposed to the ordinal utility functions we have considered up to this point. This is rather misleading. Clearly, neither (1.1) nor (1.2) are cardinal in our earlier sense, and if optimal choice is achieved by maximizing the expectation of $v(\ )$, then so will it by maximizing *any* monotone increasing function of the expectation of $v(\ )$. Thus, although $v(\ )$ itself may be cardinal, the relevant maximand is not. Hence, for any monotone increasing function $f(\ )$, we may write utility in the general form (1.2), that is

$$u = f\left[\sum_1^s \pi_\theta v(\gamma_\theta)\right] \tag{2.5}$$

The simultaneous axiomatization of utility and probability is a remarkable result and the theorem provides a powerful and robust defense against the arguments considered at the beginning of this section. Note, however, that the probabilities π_θ are called such because they satisfy all the properties of probability and can thus be manipulated according to all the usual rules of probability calculus. Readers who wish to reserve their position to the extent of not giving full recognition to the π's as probabilities are perfectly entitled to do so. Several writers use the term *subjective* probabilities, others the title *degrees of belief;* indeed, this latter corresponds closely to the discussion of the final set of axioms. In any case, these probabilities are clearly part of *preferences;* they are embedded in the general functional form (1.1) and are "extracted" with the aid of the last three sets of axioms.

We have already discussed some of the practical advantages of the expected utility formulation (2.3) in terms of simplicity and strong empirical content. It is worth adding that the formulation in terms of subjective probabilities or degrees of belief allows us to model the fact that agents are likely to learn as they make decisions under uncertainty. Indeed, it would be a fundamental flaw in any theory of choice under uncertainty not to have this feature. Learning in the expected utility framework takes the form of "updating" the probabilities π_θ as events occur. Hence, after an event occurs, the *prior* probabilities π_θ are modified to *posterior* probabilities π_j^* according to the rule of Bayes' theorem; see, for example, Mood, Graybill, and Boes (1974, p. 36)

$$\pi_j^* = \text{prob}(\theta = j|E) = \frac{\text{prob}(E|\theta = j)\pi_j}{\sum_k \text{prob}(E|\theta = k)\pi_k} \tag{2.6}$$

In (2.6), the prior probabilities π_j are modified by the sample information through the likelihood function $\text{prob}(E|\theta = j)$, hence the posterior probabilities are a combination of prior beliefs and observed evidence. As behavior evolves through time, the posterior beliefs will become the new priors and will be further modified, and so on. In many cases, if it is possible for consumers to learn about their environments, and if these environments are reasonably stable, we would expect the posterior probabilities to converge onto some objective "correct" probabilities, at least in cases where these are well defined. By such a process, the subjective probabilities of the theory (which are likely to be different for different consumers) may be brought into conformity with common objective probabilities. In other cases, however, uncertainty may be such as to prevent any convergent process on beliefs taking place.

As to the disadvantages, we have already repeatedly emphasized the crucial assumption that consequences are sufficiently well specified so as to make the decision maker indifferent between the states in which a given consequence occurs. It is our impression that many applications would not strictly satisfy this proviso. There has also been some debate as to whether the theory can really be used as a description of actual behavior as opposed to a prescription for ideal behavior. This question could also be raised about our treatment of choice under certainty, but we have taken the view in this book that, although the axioms of choice under certainty may be false, it is a much more promising research strategy to accept the axioms unquestioningly, at least for the time being, and examine closely the nature of the constraints facing consumers. In the present context, such a position is still tenable, but is less defensible. The crucial problem is that probabilities are part of preferences and not part of the objectively verifiable constraints. At the same time, consumers are not well trained in the calculus of probabilities; indeed, anyone who has ever had to perform exercises in probability with packs of cards, dice, and colored balls in urns will know how tedious and complex such calculations can be. We must thus accept that consumers will frequently accept unfair bets or make decisions that are clearly not optimal simply because uninformed intuition suggests that probabilities are different from what the rules of probability would reveal. Consider, for example, the case quoted by Haber and Runyon (1973, p. 189). A room contains 30 people and bets are offered on the event that two or more have the same birthday. Many individuals, although accepting the basic premise that each birth date is equally likely, would not readily accept its logical consequence that the probability of the event is 70 percent. Under subjective probability, this would show up as inconsistency of choice. A consumer making choices under certainty can only be cheated if his preferences are nontransitive. Cheats flourish much better with a good dose of uncertainty.

Exercises

14.6. We owe the following example originally to Allais. Consider the two payoff matrices (in \$, say):

States		1	2	3
Problem 1	α_1	1,000,000	1,000,000	1,000,000
Acts	α_2	5,000,000	1,000,000	0
Problem 2	α_1	1,000,000	0	1,000,000
Acts	α_2	5,000,000	0	0

Assume that, in both problems, the probabilities of the states are 0.1, 0.89, and 0.01, respectively. Show that the sure-thing principle implies that $\alpha_1 \gtrsim \alpha_2$ in problem 1 if and only if $\alpha_1 \gtrsim \alpha_2$ in problem 2. Do you agree with Allais (and many others) in finding this a counterintuitive result, that is, that $\alpha_1 \gtrsim \alpha_2$ in problem 1 and $\alpha_2 \gtrsim \alpha_1$ in problem 2 is more likely to be chosen? Is this alternative choice irrational?

14.7. In Exercise 14.2, show that the result is unchanged if $v(\gamma)$ is replaced by $a + bv(\gamma)$ for $b > 0$, but that it is not invariant if we replace $v(\gamma)$ by $\exp[v(\gamma)]$. Does this mean that, under uncertainty, utility functions are cardinal?

14.8. A university teacher of economics knows that, of his current audience, a proportion p or $(1 - p)$ (where p is known) is mathematically trained, but has forgotten which. He assigns prior probabilities of 0.5 to each of the alternatives and determines to decide the issue by random sampling. Show, using Bayes' rule (2.6), that if a random sample of one produces a mathematician, the posterior probability that the proportion is p is p and that, if a random sample of n produces r mathematicians, the posterior odds against p are $(p/1 - p)^{n-2r}:1$.

14.9. Consider the following well-known theorem, see, for example, Leamer (1978, p. 55). If, conditional on parameters μ and σ^2, x is a vector of n independently and identically distributed normally distributed variables each with mean μ and variance σ^2, and if μ has a prior normal distribution with mean m_a and variance v_a, then the posterior distribution of μ given x and σ^2 is normal with mean m_b and variance v_b given by

$$m_b = (v_a^{-1} + (\sigma^2/n)^{-1})^{-1} (m_a v_a^{-1} + m(\sigma^2/n)^{-1})$$
$$v_b = (v_a^{-1} + (\sigma^2/n)^{-1})^{-1}$$

where m is the sample mean of x. Interpret these formulas in terms of "learning from experience." Discuss how the new posteriors can become priors at the next stage and show how m_b converges on μ. What are the relative contributions of prior and sample information to these formulas? What might be the difficulties of applying such models to learning about economic magnitudes, for example, the rate of inflation.

14.3 Some standard applications:
risk aversion and the allocation of wealth

The most straightforward and best-known applications of expected utility theory are to cases where utility is defined on a single magnitude, whether it be wealth, money, income, or consumption. We have already seen one example of this in our brief discussion of the St. Petersburg paradox in the previous section. If we take assets A as the relevant variable, so that A_θ is the value of assets if state θ prevails, then the consumer is concerned to maximize

$$u = Ev = \Sigma \pi_\theta v(A_\theta) \tag{3.1}$$

or the corresponding integral if the state variable is continuous.

It is not immediately obvious how such a formulation can be consistent with the role that we have previously assigned to assets, of linking consumption in different periods. However, as we might expect, (3.1) can be justified under sufficient separability assumptions. Take, for example, the case of a two-period consumption model with consumption vectors q_1 and q_2 where there is weak separability in q_2. Hence, we write

$$u = v[q_1, v_2(q_2)] \tag{3.2}$$

which is to be maximized subject to $p_2 \cdot q_2 = (A_0 + y_1 - p_1 \cdot q_1)(1 + r) + y_2$ or, more briefly, $p_2 \cdot q_2 = A_1 + y_2$. Given the weak separability of q_2, the second period demands are a function of $A_1 + y_2$ and p_2 alone; hence, we have the mixed direct-indirect utility function

$$u = v[q_1, \psi(A_1 + y_2, p_2)] \tag{3.3}$$

If we assume that uncertainty is confined to A_1, which is in the spirit of the models we are about to consider, then expected utility maximization of (3.3) will involve the necessity of (3.1) if (3.3), and thus (3.2) are additively separable in q_1 and q_2. In this case, treating u^* as the expected value of v in (3.3), the consumer must maximize, for some functions v_1 and v_2^*

$$u^* = v_1(q_1) + \Sigma \pi_\theta v_2^*(A_{1\theta} + y_2, p_2) \tag{3.4}$$

Treating y_2 and p_2 as constants, whatever value is optimal for q_1, overall maximization must imply that A_1 is allocated such as to maximize the second term on the right-hand side, which in turn can be thought of as equivalent to (3.1). Note that this formulation does not claim that the optimal choice of q_1 and of savings in period 1 is independent of the prospects for assets but only that whatever level of savings is optimal, the resulting assets must be allocated so as to maximize the second term on the right-hand side of (3.4).

A crucial role in this specification is played by the concavity or convexity of the function $v(\ )$ in (3.1). As we shall see, the important case of risk aversion occurs when the function is concave; note that this is consistent with our earlier definition of risk aversion in §14.2. If we consider the different A_θ's as different goods, the concavity of $v(\ )$ will guarantee the quasi concavity of the function as a whole, so that in state space, indifference curves are convex to the origin.

We can illustrate (3.1) with risk aversion for the case of insurance. Assume that the consumer is considering buying fire insurance for a house and let A_2 be assets if no fire occurs and A_1 ($< A_2$) if the house is burned down. The situation is illustrated with a concave $v(A)$ function in Figure 14.5. If we write π for the probability of fire, EA the expected value of assets is given by

$$EA = \pi A_1 + (1 - \pi)A_2 \tag{3.5}$$

Expected utility is given by the point D on the line BC; since $v(\ )$ is concave, Ev is *less* than the utility of expected assets, $v(EA)$. In fact, for all concave functions, the function of the expectation is no less than the expectation of the function (sometimes called Jensen's inequality), so that any consumer with a concave utility function will prefer the certainty of the expectation of a

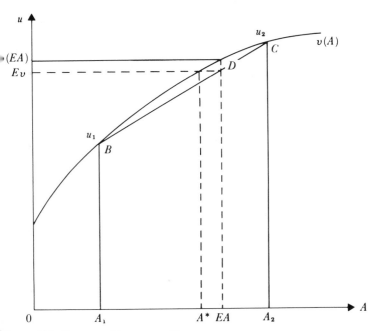

Figure 14.5. Concave, risk-averse utility.

random variable to the uncertain prospect itself. Another way of putting this is that such a consumer will pay to avoid uncertainty.

In Figure 14.5, the certainty of A^* gives the same utility as the uncertain prospect of A_1 and A_2; hence, the consumer will pay a "premium" of up to $A_2 - A^*$ in order to persuade an insurance company to provide complete compensation if a fire occurs. The fact that $EA > A^*$ indicates that there are profits to be made in insurance. The maximum expected profit for the insurance company is premium less expected payout, $A_2 - A^* - \pi(A_2 - A_1) = EA - A^* > 0$.

Before going on to formalize this analysis, consider the case when $v(A)$ is convex rather than concave. Clearly, such a consumer will not only not reject fair bets, he will even be prepared to accept some unfair ones. Uncertainty is sufficiently attractive to be paid for. Such behavior is, of course, observed and, in many cases, is observed in the same individual who carries life or fire insurance. This behavior has prompted Friedman and Savage (1948) to suggest that the typical utility function is neither entirely concave nor entirely convex but is as illustrated in Figure 14.6; concave for low values of A becoming convex as A increases. This would explain the coexistence of insurance against the remote possibility of large loss, with gambling for the

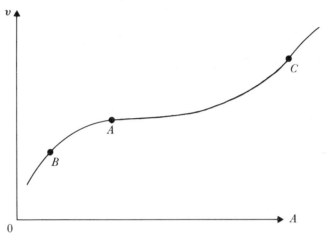

Figure 14.6. A Friedman-Savage utility function.

remote possibility of a large gain, for example, a consumer at A considering B and C, respectively. However, this kind of construct can imply quite unreasonable behavior at other levels of wealth, such as a rich man at C not insuring himself against possibilities of the major loss of a move to A. It can also be argued that gambling is an activity that is enjoyed for its own sake and that it is a mistake to try to bring it into this framework. Certainly, most recent work takes risk aversion as a working hypothesis and assumes that it applies, more or less strongly, at all levels of wealth.

Measures of risk aversion have been provided in work by Arrow (1970b) and by Pratt (1964). Looking at Figure 14.5, we can see that (minus) the second derivative of $v(A)$ is a measure of concavity, but this by itself is not invariant even under linear transformations of $v(\ )$. Instead, Pratt defines the absolute risk aversion ρ_A by

$$\rho_A = -\frac{v''(A)}{v'(A)} = -\frac{d\log v'(A)}{dA} \tag{3.6}$$

A simple interpretation can be given to this by considering a risk averter faced with a small fair bet. Again, let A be assets and B a random variable such that $E(B) = 0$ is the value of the bet. Let $P(A)$ be the *premium* that the consumer will pay in order to avoid the bet. Then, by definition

$$v[A - P(A)] = E[v(A + B)] \tag{3.7}$$

If we expand both sides of (3.7) around their values at A, we have

$$v[A - P(A)] = v(A) - P(A)v'(A) + \cdots \tag{3.8}$$

$$E[v(A + B)] = v(A) + \tfrac{1}{2}E(B^2)v''(A) + \cdots \tag{3.9}$$

since $E(B) = 0$. Hence, combining (3.8) and (3.9)

$$P(A) = -\frac{1}{2}\,E(B^2)\,\frac{v''(A)}{v'(A)} = \frac{1}{2}\,\sigma_B^2\,\rho_A \tag{3.10}$$

where σ_B^2 is the variance of the bet. Thus, ρ_A, the measure of absolute risk aversion, is twice the maximum premium the individual will pay to avoid one unit of variance for very small risks. Note carefully that ρ_A, like $P(A)$, depends on A. Intuition would suggest that the rich are more tolerant of risks than the poor, hence, the hypothesis of decreasing absolute risk aversion.

Analogously to absolute risk aversion, relative risk aversion ρ_R is defined by

$$\rho_R = -\frac{Av''(A)}{v'(A)} = -\frac{d\log v'(A)}{d\log A} = \rho_A A \tag{3.11}$$

Similarly to (3.7), ρ_R can be shown to be twice the premium per unit of variance of a bet when both premium and bet are expressed as proportions of assets.

These two concepts of risk aversion have been extensively used by Arrow (1970b) to analyze the question of how an individual ought to allocate a given total wealth between a riskless asset (money), on the one hand, and a risky asset (bonds), on the other. If A_0 is initial assets, M is money, and r is the stochastic rate of return on bonds, then the level of final assets A_1, is given by $M + (1 + r)(A_0 - M)$, so that the consumer chooses M to maximize

$$E[v(A_1)] = E\{v[A_0 + r(A_0 - M)]\} \tag{3.12}$$

For an interior solution, $0 < M < A_0$, we must have

$$E\{v'[A_0 + r(A_0 - M)]r\} = 0 \tag{3.13}$$

We can differentiate (3.13) with respect to A_0 to give, after minor rearrangement

$$\frac{\partial(A_0 - M)}{\partial A_0} = -\frac{E[v''(A_1)r]}{E[v''(A_1)r^2]} \tag{3.14}$$

Since the denominator of (3.14) is negative (v is concave), the sign of the derivative is the same as that of the numerator. Assume that decreasing absolute risk aversion holds, so that $\rho_A(A)$ is a declining function of A. But, since bonds are held in positive quantities, $r > 0$ implies that $A_1 > A_0$, so that $\rho_A(A_0) \geq \rho_A(A_1)$ which, by definition is $-v''(A_1)/v'(A_1)$. Thus, we must have $rv''(A_1) \geq -rv'(A_1)\rho_A(A_0)$. If we take expectations of this inequality, we have, by (3.13), $E[v''(A_1)r] \geq 0$. Conversely, if $r < 0$, $A_1 < A_0$ so that, following through the argument, once again $E[v''(A_1)r] \geq 0$. Similarly, it can be shown that *increasing* absolute risk aversion implies that $E[v''(A_1 r] \leq 0$. Hence, the risky asset is or is not an inferior good as absolute risk aversion is an increasing or decreasing function of wealth. Common sense would suggest that decreasing absolute risk aversion is the rule. Arrow also shows that the wealth *elasticity* of the demand for money is greater than, less than, or equal to unity as *relative* risk aversion is an increasing, decreasing, or constant function of wealth. Arrow interprets the empirical finding that money is a luxury good as evidence in favor of increasing relative risk aversion, although it is not difficult to think of alternative explanations.

One implication of this analysis is that quadratic utility functions are inappropriate tools for modeling normal behavior. To see why, write, for parameters α_0, α_1, α_2,

$$v(A) = \alpha_0 + \alpha_1 A - \tfrac{1}{2}\alpha_2 A_1^2 \tag{3.15}$$

where, to ensure concavity, $\alpha_2 > 0$. Note immediately that, at best, this can only apply over a limited range since, for $A > \alpha_1/\alpha_2$, $v'(A)$ becomes negative. More generally, however, we have

$$\rho_A = -\frac{v''(A)}{v'(A)} = \frac{\alpha_2}{\alpha_1 - \alpha_2 A} \tag{3.16}$$

which is an *increasing* function of A. Hence, quadratic utility implies that the rich insure more heavily than the poor against the same risk and that the rich hold more cash and less risky assets (absolutely) than do the poor. In spite of the deficiencies of the Arrow-Pratt analysis, which we are about to discuss, this argument should be sufficient to remove quadratic utility from serious consideration.

The problems in using ρ_A and ρ_R to characterize behavior towards risk arise when we try to extend the analysis to cover many assets. Cass and Stiglitz (1970) have constructed an example with one safe and two risky assets in which an investor with increasing relative risk aversion allocates a larger proportion of his wealth to the two risky assets together as wealth increases. This means that we cannot interpret the "bond" in the foregoing analysis as a representative risky asset and that, in general, knowledge of risk aversion alone may not be very helpful in describing behavior. In fact, Hart (1975) has shown that it is only in the case where the optimal mix between risky assets is independent of wealth that the Arrow results hold for money versus risky assets as a whole.

It is not our impression that more general models with many assets or many periods have produced very much in the way of clear-cut results. Certainly most work has been concerned with deriving qualitative conclusions of the type discussed so far in this section. The problem of generating concrete specific functional forms for systems of demand functions for assets, is the diffi-

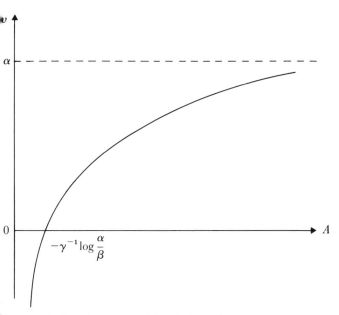

Figure 14.7. Negative exponential utility function.

ulty of finding specific utility functions and specific distribution functions, which, when combined, will yield a tractable expression for expected utility. Hence, as we shall see, most empirical work has focussed on the mean-variance approach discussed next. One avenue does, however, lead a certain way and has links with the mean-variance model. This is the use of a negative exponential utility function. It can be written in the form

$$v(A) = \alpha - \beta e^{-\gamma A} \tag{3.17}$$

for some constants α, β, γ and is illustrated in Figure 14.7. Note that $v(A)$ is everywhere concave, is bounded above by the asymptote α and has constant absolute risk aversion, $\rho_A = \gamma$. If we now assume a particular distribution function for A, $F(A)$, say, expected utility is given by

$$u = \int v(A)dF(A) = \alpha - \beta \int e^{-\gamma A} \, dF(A) = \alpha - \beta m(-\gamma) \tag{3.18}$$

where $m(t) = \int e^{tA} \, dF(A) = E(e^{tA})$ is known as the "moment generating function" of the distribution of A; see, for example, Mood, Graybill, and Boes (1974 p. 72). Such functions are extremely useful in mathematical statistics and their forms are well-known for a wide range of theoretical distributions. Hence, this technique allows easy derivation of functional forms for expected utility. As we shall see, the technique can be straightforwardly applied when there are many assets. For example, Saito (1977) has used the method together with the gamma distribution to derive a linear expenditure system for assets and presumably other distributions will yield other similar models. There is, however, a considerable artificiality about the technique. The utility functions and distributions are chosen for their properties of manipulation rather than their correspondence with economic theory, so that it is perhaps not surprising that models such as Saito's do not appear very convincing. However, this remains a promising avenue for research and may yet generate useful results.

The alternative, practical, approach is the mean-variance model associated particularly with the names of Tobin (1958b, 1965) and Markowitz (1959). Indeed, many of the results on the demand for money and bonds under uncertainty first appeared in Tobin's classic 1958 paper. The basic idea is to simplify the complexities of expected utility by assuming that the consumer is concerned with two quantities only, expected yield, on the one hand, and risk on the other. Risk is defined as the standard deviation (or variance) of the distribution of yields. Hence, the consumer maximizes some function of mean and variance subject to the constraints provided by the variances and covariances of the assets available to him.

Clearly, it is not generally true that a ranking of portfolios in terms of their means and variances alone will always be able to reproduce the "true" rankings of the complete distributions by expected utility. If however, risks are small in some sense, see Samuelson (1970) for details, we may hope that a mean-variance approach will yield a suitable approximation. The mean-variance model can only be exact, however, under one of two conditions, see Borch (1969) and Feldstein (1969). Either the utility function must be quadratic, or the distribution of yields must be normal. We have already seen how unattractive is the quadratic utility model and, in practice, the distribution of yields rarely appears to be normal. Hence, neither of these justifications gives much general support to the approach.

Nevertheless, the model is relatively simple to use. Consider Figure 14.8, where the expected-yield/risk combinations for three assets A, B, and C are illustrated. Indifference curves for a risk averter are as illustrated; for a risk lover, they would slope downwards to the right and be concave to the origin. The point that can be reached by allocating a given total of wealth between A, B, and C will depend on how the distributions of the yields on the three assets are correlated. Take the pair AB first. Assume that A has yield k_1 and variance σ_1^2, B has k_2 and σ_2^2, and that the covariance between the yields of A and B is σ_{12}. If the portfolio is allocated with fraction λ to A and $(1-\lambda)$ to B, then the portfolio yield is $\lambda k_1 + (1-\lambda)k_2$ and the standard error is $[\lambda^2\sigma_1^2 + 2\lambda(1-\lambda)\sigma_{12} + (1-\lambda)^2\sigma_2^2]^{1/2}$. By varying λ for different values of σ_{12}, we can trace out the various combinations on Figure 14.8. If the yields on A and B are per-

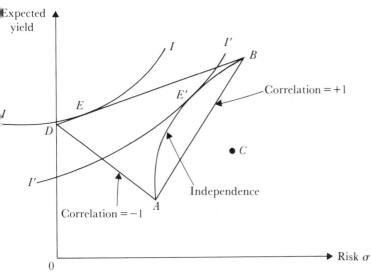

Figure 14.8. Portfolio choice in the mean-variance model.

fectly positively correlated, so that $\sigma_{12} = \sigma_1\sigma_2$, linear combinations of the two give linear combinations of risk and yield; hence, in this case, the line AB is the feasible set. On the other hand, if the correlation is perfect and negative, $(\sigma_{12} = -\sigma_1\sigma_2)$, a 50:50 combination will eliminate risk at the point D (a perfect hedge) and the locus of combinations is ADB. Independence of yields $(\sigma_{12} = 0)$ is the intermediate case $AE'B$ with equilibrium at E' corresponding to E on ADB. Note that the point C as illustrated is inefficient and such a security would not be held.

The general approach can be illustrated formally by going back to the negative exponential utility function and assuming yields to be normal. Let a be the vector of assets held and write k for the vector of returns, that is, $k_i = 1 + r_i$, where r_i is the (stochastic) yield on asset i. Expected utility is thus

$$Ev = E(\alpha - \beta e^{-\gamma k \cdot a}) \tag{3.19}$$

If k is assumed to have a multivariate normal distribution with mean $\bar{k}$ and covariance matrix C, then $k \cdot a$ is normally distributed with mean $\bar{k} \cdot a$ and with variance, given by the quadratic form $a \cdot Ca$. Thus, from the moment generating function of the normal distribution [see Mood, Graybill, and Boes (1974, p. 109)],

$$Ev = \alpha - \beta \exp\left[-\frac{\gamma}{2}\bar{k} \cdot a + \left(\frac{\gamma}{2}\right)^2 a \cdot Ca\right] \tag{3.20}$$

Hence, maximization of expected utility is precisely equivalent to

$$\text{Max } \overline{k} \cdot a - \frac{\gamma}{2} a \cdot Ca \qquad\qquad (3.21$$

It might have been more in the spirit of the mean-variance approach to star at this point and maximize (3.21) directly, but the example illustrates the rol of the normality assumption. However justified, the consumer's problem is t choose a to maximize (3.21) subject to $\Sigma a_i = A_0$ and whatever inequality con straints (e.g., $a_1 \geq 0$) are imposed by allowing or not allowing short sales, bor rowing restrictions, and so on. This transforms the complex maximization o expected utility problem into a standard problem in quadratic programmin that can be solved by standard methods. Note that, in general, as in Figur 14.8, some assets will be inefficient and will not be held. If we eliminate thes and restrict (3.21) to efficient assets only, we can derive the system of deman equations straightforwardly; see Exercise 14.14. The asset demands will be linear function of expected returns and of total wealth. The matrix of deriva tives of asset demands with respect to yields is symmetric and positive definit while the derivatives with respect to wealth are all positive. In theory, if w know the variance-covariance matrix C, we can calculate all the responses apart from the parameter γ, but in practice we might prefer to estimate C o the grounds that it is the investors' perception of C that is important rathe than its true value.

This example is, of course, special even within the mean variance approac in that (3.21) is a peculiarly simple mean-variance utility function. Neverthe less, more general models have a very similar flavor and have been used no only to describe the behavior of households but also of institutional investor see, for example, Markowitz (1959), Hester and Tobin (1967), and Parki (1970).

Exercises

14.10. In a single period, a consumer receives uncertain outlay x_θ in state θ and is con cerned to maximize expected utility $\Sigma \pi_\theta \psi(x_\theta, p)$ for indirect utility function $\psi(x, p)$ an certain prices p. Show that if $\psi(\ )$ has to show constant relative risk aversion ρ, that is so that ρ is neither a function of x nor p, the associated cost function must take the PIG form (cf. §6.2), $c(u, p) = [a(p)u + b(p)]^{1/(\rho+1)}$ for $a(p)$ and $b(p)$ homogenous of degre $(\rho + 1)$. Can you think of an intuitive reason why the imposition of constant relativ risk aversion should impose restrictions on the way in which outlay is allocated amon goods? [See Hanoch (1977).]

14.11. A consumer has $v(A)$ given by $\alpha_0 + \alpha A - \frac{1}{2}\beta A^2$ and starts from a total W to be al located between money M, return 0, and bonds $(W - M)$ with risky return r, that is, th value of the portfolio is $M + (1 + r)(W - M)$. Show that the optimal amount of M i $W - (\alpha - \beta W)\bar{r}/\beta E(r^2)$, where $\bar{r}$ is the mean of r. Discuss the plausibility of this result i the light of the remarks made in the text, and explain why a concrete result is obtain able without a complete knowledge of the distribution of r. Is the mean-variance analy sis applicable here and, if so, why?

4.12. For the same problem as in Exercise 14.11, but assuming that $v(A) = e^{-\gamma A}$ and assuming that r is distributed as $N(\bar{r}, \sigma^2)$, show that M is given by $W - 2\bar{r}/\gamma\sigma^2$. Compare this result with that of the previous exercise and discuss which is the more satisfactory.

4.13. In the mean-variance approach illustrated in Figure 14.8, show that when the correlation between the yields is -1 that the riskless point D is achieved when λ, the proportion of the portfolio in asset 1, is given by $\sigma_2/(\sigma_1 + \sigma_2)$. By setting $\sigma_{12} = \sigma_1\sigma_2$ and $\sigma_{12} = -\sigma_1\sigma_2$ in turn, derive the equations for the sides of the triangle ADB and show that the diagram is correctly drawn.

4.14. Show that the maximization of (3.21) subject to the budget constraint $\iota \cdot a = A_0$ for initial assets A_0 and unit vector ι, gives demands

$$a = \gamma^{-1}\left(C^{-1} - \frac{C^{-1}u'C^{-1}}{\iota'C^{-1}\iota}\right)\bar{k} + \frac{C^{-1}\iota}{\iota'C^{-1}\iota}A_0$$

Confirm the statement in the text that "the matrix of derivatives of assets demand with respect to yields is symmetric and positive definite, while the derivatives with respect to wealth are all positive." What happens if C is singular or close to singular? Show that the model cannot be valid for indefinitely large A_0.

4.15. Use the concepts of the degree of risk aversion to discuss how you might measure the degree of inequality aversion of an additive social welfare function. Relate your discussion to Exercise 9.14 and to the welfare function (2.15) constant elasticity of substitution of Chapter 9.

14.4 Intertemporal consumption decisions under uncertainty

All the examples discussed in §15.3 were concerned with maximizing the expected utility of wealth within a single period. Inevitably, such models have rather limited applicability, although several studies concerned with multi-period extensions, for example, Samuelson (1969), Merton (1969), and Fama (1976) have shown that many of the characteristics of single-period behavior will reappear in the more general context. However, a number of very important questions in consumer behavior do not fit into this framework. In particular, we wish to recognize that utility is generated by consumption, not by wealth, and we want to be able to analyze the effects of uncertainty on the choice between consumption and saving. A general solution to this problem is hardly even conceivable; in reality, intertemporal decision making is carried out in spite of uncertainty about present and future prices, about future income, about rates of return, and even about tastes themselves. There is also a bewildering variety of assets with yields, rates of growth, maturities, and other characteristics tailored to meet the specific needs of particular groups of individuals. As Stiglitz (1970) has forcefully pointed out, even the distinction between relatively safe short bonds and relatively risky long bonds may be highly misleading. If a consumer is planning now for several periods ahead, it may be possible to avoid risk altogether only by holding the appropriate mixture of short and longs. Indeed, income flows may be such (e.g., steadily declining) that only longs will be held by a risk-averse consumer. In such a context, "speculation" may just as easily imply speculating in shorts as speculating in longs.

Evidently, the best we can hope to do is to analyze some very simple situations. Perhaps the most important of these is a two-period consumption model in which income in the second period is uncertain. Consider first the following heuristic argument on the effects of increasing uncertainty on savings. A greater degree of uncertainty about future income makes the risk-averse consumer worse off, since the possibility of gain is outweighed by the possibility of loss. Thus, if present consumption is a normal good, the individual will consume less out of an unchanged present income, so saving more. This argument is, as we shall see, substantially correct, although it ignores one potentially crucial aspect of the problem. Indeed, Sandmo (1970) has defined a two-period analog of decreasing absolute risk aversion that he shows is a sufficient condition for increasing uncertainty about future income to increase saving. However, the full story is a good deal more complex and more interesting.

The crucial point is that since today's consumption takes place today before future income is known, future consumption becomes a random variable while present consumption is nonstochastic. Hence it is not possible, in general, for the usual equating of marginal rates of substitution and relative prices to take place. The two budget lines in Figure 14.9 illustrate two possible states for y_2 with $y_{21} > y_{22}$. If y_{21} were known with certainty, consumption would be at E_1; similarly for y_{22} at E_2. The situation is that the consumer must choose q_1 and await the outcome. If he chooses q_{11}, he reaches either E_1 or E_{12}; in the latter case, he finishes on the very low indifference curve u_4. Similarly if he chooses q_{12}, he will receive u_3 or u_2; note u_2 is higher than u_3 but not as high as u_1. Most risk-averse consumers would probably feel that q_{12}, the high saving strategy, is preferable; this would certainly be the maximin strategy since any other choice for q_1 involves the possibility of falling below u_3, for example, q_1^*. In general, however, such extreme risk aversion might well be considered too costly, especially if the higher income is adjudged more probable. Hence, some value q_1^* will be chosen depending on what particular numbers are attached to the indifference curves, these numbers representing the consumer's attitude to risk.

A simple example may illustrate the point further as well as acting as a counterexample to the proposition that increased uncertainty always increases savings. Assume that present and future consumption are perfect complements and that risk aversion is represented by the logarithmic form. Hence,

$$u = \log[\min(q_1, q_2)] \tag{4.1}$$

where, for simplicity, we have not allowed for any time preference. Similarly

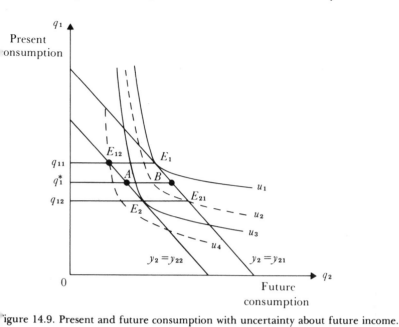

Figure 14.9. Present and future consumption with uncertainty about future income.

ssume that the interest rate is zero so that, for initial assets A_0, the budget onstraint is, for example,

$$q_2 = A_0 + y_2 + y_1 - q_1 = q_2(y_2, q_1) \qquad (4.2)$$

.et us compare the case of certainty, $y_2 = \bar{y}_2$, with an uncertain prospect with he same expectation, $y_{21} = \bar{y}_2 + \epsilon$ with probability $n/(1 + n)$ and $y_{22} = \bar{y}_2 - \epsilon$ with probability $1/(1 + n)$. The idea is that n is large so that the consumer aces a small probability of unemployment, say, (y_{22}) and a much larger hance of staying in employment with a small bonus. By keeping the mean onstant at $\bar{y}_2$ we can isolate the effects of the introduced uncertainty.

Clearly, under complete certainty,

$$q_1 = q_2 = \tfrac{1}{2}(A_0 + y_1 + \bar{y}_2) = \tfrac{1}{2}W_1 \qquad (4.3)$$

Jnder uncertainty, q_1 must be chosen to maximize

$$Eu = \left(\frac{n}{1 + n}\right) \log\{\min[q_1, q_2(y_{21}, q_1)]\}$$

$$+ \left(\frac{1}{1 + n}\right) \log\{\min[q_1, q_2(y_{22}, q_1)]\} \qquad (4.4)$$

t is clear (from a diagram similar to Figure 14.9 but with right-hand angle ıdifference curves) that q_1 must satisfy

$$q_2(y_{21}, q_1) \geq q_1 \geq q_2(y_{22}, q_1) \tag{4.5}$$

since if q_1 lies outside these bounds, both min expressions can be simulta neously increased. Substitution of the bounds in (4.2) gives the explici bounds for q_1 itself

$$\tfrac{1}{2}(W_1 + \epsilon) \geq q_1 \geq \tfrac{1}{2}(W_1 - n\epsilon) \tag{4.6}$$

Further, using (4.5) we can write expected utility (4.4) as

$$Eu = \left(\frac{n}{1+n}\right) \log q_1 + \frac{1}{1+n} \log(A_0 + \bar{y}_2 - n\epsilon + y_1 - q_1) \tag{4.7}$$

Now, $\partial Eu/\partial q_1 > 0$ for all $q_1 < (n/n + 1)(W_1 - n\epsilon)$ so that, provided $W_1 > n$ so that positive consumption is possible in even the worst eventuality, the solu tion for q_1 is, using (4.6),

$$q_1 = \left(\frac{n}{1+n}\right)(W_1 - n\epsilon) \qquad \text{if } W_1 \leq \xi n\epsilon \tag{4.8}$$

$$q_1 = \tfrac{1}{2}(W_1 + \epsilon) \qquad \text{if } W_1 \geq \xi n\epsilon \tag{4.9}$$

where $\xi = [(2n^2 + n + 1)/(n^2 - n)] \simeq 2$ if n is large. Hence, consumers for whom W_1 is more than twice $n\epsilon$, so that the consequences of unemploymen are mild relative to their assets, will actually *increase* their consumption (anc thus decrease saving) in response to increased uncertainty. The increase ir consumption over the position of certainty is small and occurs so that presen and future consumption stand in the right relation to one another in the event of the much more likely occurrence. To increase saving, although de creasing risk, would involve a high probability of being off the indifference curve that can very likely be reached and this, like risk itself, is costly. For poorer households, the risk is too great relative to wealth and the (high chance of higher utility is abandoned in favor of risk aversion and greate saving.

Although this example is rather special, we believe that it illustrates some quite general principles. Increased income uncertainty may increase rather than decrease present consumption and although increased saving decreases risk, the benefits of this must be offset against lost benefits of intertemporal optimization. Note too the aggregation implications of the example. In creased uncertainty about employment prospects will affect mainly poorer consumers and is thus likely to decrease consumption by more than would be anticipated by the decline in expected net worth alone. On the other hand, in creased uncertainty about, for example, income tax rates at high income levels may well increase rather than decrease consumption.

This analysis covers only the case of income uncertainty, ignoring the many other sources of risk. Uncertainty about rates of return on saving can be ana-

.yzed in much the same way, again see Sandmo (1970). Fluctuations in rates of return generate income effects, see, for example, §4.2, and to this extent the analysis of the effects of uncertainty is similar to that dealt with previously. However, in the rate of return case, if the consumer responds to increased uncertainty by saving more, this can actually increase the risk because the uncertainty has a larger base on which to operate. Hence, even in this simple case, it is very difficult to generate concrete solutions of any general applicability. However, these analytical difficulties should not obscure the fact that for consumers, asset demand, whether for money, bonds, or real estate, should be modeled as intertemporal consumption choice under uncertainty. In particular, demand functions for money or bonds that do not recognize the future consumption that is represented by stocks of such assets are theoretically unsatisfactory and likely to be empirically misleading. The construction of models that are tractable in practice and that deal adequately with uncertainty about rates of return and future incomes is a difficult but important task for further research. For the present, we content ourselves with the simplified and incomplete analysis already given (but see also Exercise 14.18).

Exercises

14.16. The two-period linear expenditure system has utility function $u = \phi[\beta_1 \log(q_1 - \gamma_1) + \beta_2 \log(q_2 - \gamma_2)]$ and the budget constraint is $A_0(1 + r_1) + y_1 + y_2/(1 + r_2) \equiv W_1 = p_1 q_1 + p_2 q_2/(1 + r_2)$. Deflate by p_1 to get W_1^* and real interest rate $(1 + r_2)p_2/p_1$ and show that u as a function of q_1 is given by $u = \phi\{\beta_1 \log(q_1 - \gamma_1) + \beta_2 \log[(1 + r^*)(W_1^* - q_1) - \gamma_2]\}$. Viewed from period 1, which variables are subject to uncertainty? Formulate the consumer's problem in selecting q_1. What role is played by the function $\phi(\ )$: (a) under certainty and (b) under uncertainty? How would you go about solving this problem?

14.17. Contrast and discuss the following arguments:

(a) "Increased uncertainty about the future will cause saving to fall since savings are more likely to be lost through bank failures, theft, or just inflation."

(b) "Increased uncertainty about the future will cause savings to rise since assets are the only protection against disaster."

Can the conflict be resolved through the recognition of "income" versus "substitution" effects?

14.18. Suppose a household maximizes expected utility over a two-period horizon. Let the budget constraint be

$$p_2 q_2 = m_0 + B_0 + y_1 - p_1 q_1 + k_1 B_1 + k_2 y_1$$

where m_0 is the initial money holding, B_0 is the initial bond holding, $k_1 B_1$ is total capital gains received in period 2 from holding B_1 of bonds in period 1, and $k_2 y_1$ is income in period 2. Note that k_1 and k_2 are stochastic variables but p_2 is not. The utility function is

$$u = \alpha - \beta_1 e^{-\gamma_1 q_1} - \beta_2 e^{-\gamma_2 q_2}$$

Assuming that k_1 and k_2 have a joint normal distribution with means $\bar{k}_1$, $\bar{k}_2$ variances and covariance σ_1^2, σ_2^2, and σ_{12}, find $E(u)$ as a function of q_1 and B_1. Maximize with respect to q_1 and B_1 and show that the solution implies that $B_1 = (\bar{k}_1/\gamma_2 - y_1\sigma_{12})/\sigma_{12}^2$. What implications does this example have for the way in which point expectation proxies for the rate of capital gains $\bar{k}_1$ and income growth $\bar{k}_2$ enter the consumption function? Using the same utility function, contrast this model with the case discussed in §4.2 where there is no uncertainty and the asset yields a return r but is not subject to revaluation.

14.5 Other applications: the theory of search

Just as almost all economic decisions are affected by uncertainty in one respect or another, so then is there almost no limit to the areas of economic theory that can be modified by this recognition. In recent years, a considerable literature has grown up that attempts, in a diversity of approaches, to model the fact that agents possess a good deal less than the complete information assumed by perfectly competitive theory. One important consequence that has received a good deal of attention is the fact that, in many situations, it will pay a consumer to *search* for fuller information.

The seminal paper in this context is Stigler's (1961) "The Economics of Information." Stigler models a consumer who faces a distribution of prices for the same good. Different retail outlets charge different prices, and although the consumer is assumed to know the distribution of prices, he has no means of knowing, without searching, which outlet charges the lowest price. A conceptually identical situation exists when an unemployed worker is looking for work and must visit employers to ascertain the wages offered. Search itself has a cost in time and in foregone earnings, while its benefits are likely to diminish as the search becomes more and more complete.

Stigler models each "search" as an independent random drawing from a known distribution. Hence if p_i is the price observed at the ith search, and $F(P)$ is the distribution function,

$$\text{prob}(p_i \le P) = F(P) \qquad \text{for all } i \tag{5.1}$$

Hence, in n searches,

$$\text{prob}[\min(p_1, p_2, \ldots, p_n) \le m] = 1 - \text{prob}(p_i \ge m, \text{ all } i)$$
$$= 1 - \prod_i \text{prob}(p_i \ge m) \tag{5.2}$$
$$= 1 - (1 - F(m))^n$$

which gives us the distribution of m_n, say, the minimum price after n searches. The expected value of m_n is then given by [see, e.g., Mood, Graybill, and Boes (1974, p. 65)],

$$E(m_n) = \int_0^\infty [1 - F(x)]^n \, dx \tag{5.3}$$

Stigler then considers the expected gain g_n of searching one more time given that n searches have been completed. Clearly,

$$g_n = E(m_n) - E(m_{n+1}) = \int_0^\infty [1 - F(x)]^n F(x)\, dx \qquad (5.4)$$

Both elements in the integrand of (5.4) are positive, while the first, which is raised to the power n is always between 0 and 1. Hence g_n is a declining function of n, while the costs of search c_n may be either constant or rising, if, for example, previous offers of employment stay open. Thus, an equilibrium will be reached at some positive value of n, possibly zero, at which search will not continue.

In this formulation, the gain function g_n is simply taken to be the expected reduction in price. This could easily be made more realistic by making g_n the expected rise in (indirect) utility as a consequence of the reduction in price. This would then allow for the fact that consumers search longer when contemplating the purchase of a car or of hi-fi equipment than when buying ice cream. Note too that Stigler sets up the model so that the optimal number of searches can be determined before search begins. McCall (1965, 1970) and Nelson (1970) have pointed out that a better strategy is to use the information of the search as it comes to hand, since if the consumer knows the distribution function, he can recognize a good price when he sees one. Again, let m be the minimum price so far observed. Then the expected decrease in m from one more search is given by

$$\int_0^m (m - x)\, dF(x) = \int_0^m F(x)\, dx = g(m) \qquad (5.5)$$

where the second integral is derived by integrating by parts. Now, if $c > g(m)$, it does not pay to search any further. Hence, if c is constant, we can derive an R such that $g(R) = c$, and the optimal strategy is to search until a price below R (a wage above R) is found. For obvious reasons, R is known as the *reservation price or wage*. Note that R is a function of search costs, on the one hand, and the shape of the distribution of prices or wages, on the other.

The assumption that the distribution function $F(\ )$ is known is clearly crucial to both these approaches. If this knowledge is lacking, further search is likely to be profitable since this will give valuable information that can then be fed into one of the other rules. Hence, an optimal strategy might well be to search for at least some fixed number of searches and then to set a reservation price, conceivably one that has already been observed.

Search models have been applied to a number of areas of economics but most notably to the analysis of the behavior of unemployed workers in the labor market, see, for example, Mortenson (1970a, b), Phelps (1970) and Lucas and Rapping (1970). A full analysis requires, however, that such models be set in a general equilibrium framework and that the behavior of sellers as well as buyers be taken into account. Such an extension would take us well beyond our intended scope in this book.

Exercises

14.19. An unemployed worker is searching for a job. He knows that wages w have a legal minimum w_0 and that $\xi = (w - w_0)$ is exponentially distributed, that is, has density $f(\xi) = \alpha^{-1}e^{-\xi/\alpha}$ for parameter α. The cost of one more search is the maximum wage so far discovered. Show that, if the worker stops when the cost is greater than the expected value of one more search, search will stop when the maximum wage found is 0.57α greater than the legal minimum. Can you formulate a more realistic stopping rule?

14.20. Contrast the stopping rule in the previous exercise with that which would result if the Stigler procedure were followed.

14.21. Why do consumers spend a great deal of time "searching" for, say, hi-fi systems when they spend relatively little time "searching" for food even though expenditure on food is much higher that expenditure on hi-fi systems?

Bibliographical notes

The modern approach to the economics of choice under uncertainty begins with Ramsey (1931). The treatments by de Finetti (1937) and von Neumann and Morgenstern (1947) are closely related, but it was only after Savage's (1954) *Foundations of Statistics* that the axiomatic approach discussed in this chapter began to be widely accepted in economics. The state of play before the publication of Savage's book is reviewed in a classic paper by Arrow (1951a). The papers by Samuelson (1950a, 1952a and c), conveniently republished together in the Samuelson collected papers, provide fascinating documentation of the "conversion" of one economist and are extremely helpful in clarifying the crucial role of the "sure-thing" principle. Modern discussions of the axiomatic approach can be found in Drèze (1974) and Arrow (1970a); the latter, in particular, reflects the technical difficulty of the subject. Elementary discussions of choice under uncertainty can be found in several texts, e.g., Baumol (1977) and Green (1976). These make the crucial simplification of known probabilities; this certainly makes the exposition easier, but carries little conviction with anyone skeptical of the notion of subjective probabilities. The account by Raiffa (1968) is both general and readily accessible. See also De Groot (1970) and Raiffa and Schlaifer (1961) for applications. Simon (1978b) provides a useful discussion and list of references on whether consumers actually do maximize expected utility and on the applicability of Bayes' rule as a description of actual learning.

The subjective interpretation has implications well beyond economic theory and the associated Bayesian approach to statistical inference has much important work to its credit. For an elementary view of the issues as they concern inference, see Barnett (1973). Bayesian methods in econometrics have been particularly associated with the names of Drèze (1972) and Zellner (1971), see also the important recent volume by Leamer (1978). Note, however, that subjective probability in economic theory and subjective probability in econometrics and statistics need not go together; for example, it would be quite logical to accept the analysis of this chapter as far as decision analysis is concerned but to refuse to see statistical inference in this way.

On various specific topics, and apart from references given in the text, the St. Petersburg paradox and the associated literature is discussed in Samuelson (1977). The Allais counterexample to the "sure-thing" principle, see Exercise 14.6, is discussed by both Drèze (1974) and Raiffa (1968). The state-preference approach briefly discussed here is fully presented and applied, mostly diagrammatically, by Green (1976), see also Malinvaud (1972). The question of "spanning" is discussed by Leland (1973) and by Ekern and Wilson (1974). The collected essays on risk-bearing by Arrow (1970b) contain not only those already referred to but also papers on risk aversion and on moral hazard; on the last, see also Pauly (1968). Hanoch (1977) has a good discussion of the implications for preferences of constancy of each of the several concepts of the degree of risk aversion when there are many goods. The general life-cycle models of consumption with uncertainty of Samuelson (1969) and Merton (1969) are given a lucid exposition by Flemming (1974); in this paper, and also in Flemming (1978), good use is made of the negative exponential utility function. Sandmo (1974) provides a review and further references on intertemporal choice under uncertainty. Sibley (1977) has examined the implications for the permanent income hypothesis. The search models of the final section are surveyed in Rothschild (1973), Spence (1974), Lippman and McCall (1976), and Stiglitz (1975a).

Abbott, M., and O. Ashenfelter (1976), "Labour supply, commodity demand, and the allocation of time," *Review of Economic Studies*, Vol. 43, pp. 389–411.

Afriat, S. N. (1967), "The construction of utility functions from expenditure data," *International Economic Review*, Vol. 8, pp. 67–77.

(1969), "The method of limits in the theory of index numbers," *Metroeconomica*, Vol. 21, pp. 141–65.

(1972), "The theory of international comparisons of real income and prices," in D. J. Daly (ed.), *International Comparisons of Prices and Outputs*, pp. 13–69, New York: National Bureau of Economic Research (NBER)

(1977), *The Price Index*, Cambridge: Cambridge University Press.

Aitchison, J., and J. A. C. Brown (1957), *The Lognormal Distribution*, Cambridge: Cambridge University Press.

Akerlof, G. (1970), "The market for lemons", *Quarterly Journal of Economics*, Vol. 84, pp. 488–500.

Alcaly, R. E., and A. K. Klevorick (1970), "Judging quality by price, snob appeal, and the new consumer theory," *Zeitschrift für Nationalökonomie*, Vol. 30, pp. 53–64.

Allen, R. G. D. (1949), "The economic theory of index numbers," *Economica*, Vol. 16, pp. 197–203.

(1958), "Movements in retail prices since 1953," *Economica*, Vol. 25, pp. 14–25.

(1975), *Index Numbers in Theory and Practice*, London: Macmillan.

Alonso, W. (1964), *Location and Land Use*, Cambridge: Harvard University Press.

Ando, A., and F. Modigliani (1963), "The 'life-cycle' hypothesis of saving: aggregate implications and tests," *American Economic Review*, Vol. 53, pp. 55–84.

Antonelli, G. B., (1886), *Sulla teoria matematica della economia politica*, Pisa: Nella Tipografia del Fochetto, (trans. Chapter 16 of J. S. Chipman, L. Hurwicz, M. K. Richter, and H. F. Sonnenschein, *Preferences Utility and Demand*, New York, Harcourt Brace, 1971).

Armington, P. S. (1969a), "A theory of demand for products distinguished by place of production," *International Monetary Fund Staff Papers*, Vol. 16, pp. 179–201.

(1969b), "The geographical pattern of trade and the effect of price change," *International Monetary Fund Staff Papers*, Vol. 16, pp. 159–78.

(1970), "Adjustment of trade balances: some experiments with a model of trade among many countries," *International Monetary Fund Staff Papers*, Vol. 17, pp. 488–526.

Arrow, K. J. (1951a), "Alternative approaches to the theory of choice in risk-taking situations," *Econometrica*, Vol. 19, pp. 404–37.

(1951b), *Social Choice and Individual Values*, New York: Wiley.

(1963), *Social Choice and Individual Values*, 2nd edition, New York: Wiley.

(1970a), "Exposition of the theory of choice under uncertainty," in K. J. Arrow, *Essays in the Theory of Risk-Bearing*, Amsterdam: North-Holland.

(1970b), "The theory of risk aversion," in K. J. Arrow, *Essays in the Theory of Risk-bearing*, Amsterdam: North-Holland.

(1973), "Higher education as a filter," *Journal of Public Economics*, Vol. 2, pp. 193–216.

(1977), "Extended sympathy and the possibility of social choice," *American Economic Review*, Vol. 67 (papers and proc.), pp. 219–25.

and F. H. Hahn (1971), *General Competitive Analysis*, San Francisco: Holden-Day.

Ashenfelter, O. (1977), "Unemployment as disequilibrium in a model of aggregate labour supply," *Econometrica*, Vol. 48, pp. 547–64.

and J. C. Ham (1979), "Education, unemployment and earnings," *Journal of Political Economy* Vol. 87, pp. S99–116.

Atkinson, A. B. (1970), "On the measurement of inequality," *Journal of Economic Theory*, Vol. 2, pp. 244–63.

(1975), *The Economics of Inequality*, Oxford: Clarendon Press.

Auspitz, R., and R. Lieben (1889), *Untersuchungen über die Theorie des Preises*, Leipzig: Duncker und Humbolt.

Azariadis, C. (1975), "Implicit contracts and unemployment equilibria," *Journal of Political Economy*, Vol. 83, pp. 1183–202.

Baily, M. N. (1974), "Wages and employment under uncertain demand," *Review of Economic Studies*, Vol. 41, pp. 37–50.

Bain, A. D. (1964), *The Growth of Television Ownership in the United Kingdom*, Cambridge: Cambridge University Press.

Ball, M. J. (1973), "Recent empirical work on the determinants of relative house prices," *Urban Studies*, Vol. 10, pp. 213–33.

and R. M. Kirwan (1977), "Urban housing demand: some evidence from cross-sectional data," *Applied Economics*, Vol. 9, pp. 343–66.

Barnett, V. D. (1973), *Comparative Statistical Inference*, London: Wiley.

Barnett, W. A. (1977), "Pollak and Wachter on the household production function approach," *Journal of Political Economy*, Vol. 85, pp. 1073–82.

(1979), "Theoretical foundations for the Rotterdam model," *Review of Economic Studies*, Vol. 46, pp. 109–30.

Barro, R., and Grossman, H. (1976), *Money, Employment and Inflation*, Cambridge: Cambridge University Press.

Barten, A. P. (1964), "Family composition, prices and expenditure patterns," in P. E. Hart, G. Mills, and J. K. Whitaker (eds.), *Econometric Analysis for National Economic Planning*, London: Butterworth.

(1966). *Theorie en empirie van een volledig stelsel van vraagvergelijkingen*, Doctoral dissertation, Rotterdam: University of Rotterdam.

(1967), "Evidence on the Slutsky conditions for demand equations," *Review of Economics and Statistics*, Vol. 49, pp. 77–84.

(1968), "Estimating demand equations," *Econometrica*, Vol. 36, pp. 213–51.

(1969), "Maximum likelihood estimation of a complete system of demand equations," *European Economic Review*, Vol. 1, pp. 7–73.

(1970), "Réflexions sur la construction d'un système empirique des fonctions de demande," *Cahiers du Séminaire D'Econometrie* No. 12, pp. 67–80.

(1974), "Complete systems of demand equations: some thoughts about aggregation and functional form," *Recherches Economiques de Louvain*, Vol. 40, pp. 3–20.

(1977), "The systems of consumer demand functions approach: a review," *Econometrica*, Vol. 45, pp. 23–51.

and E. Geyskens (1975), "The negativity condition in consumer demand," *Europear. Economic Review*, Vol. 6, pp. 227–60.

and S. J. Turnovsky, (1966), "Some aspects of the aggregation problem for composite demand equations," *International Economic Review*, Vol. 7, pp. 231–59.

Baumol, W. J. (1977), *Economic Theory and Operations Analysis*, 4th edition, London: Prentice-Hall.

and W. E. Oates (1974), *The Theory of Environmental Policy*, Englewood Cliffs, N.J.: Prentice-Hall.

Bean, C. (1978), "The determinants of consumers' expenditure in the U.K.," Government Economic Service, Working Paper, 4.

Becker, G. S. (1960), "An economic analysis of fertility," in *Demographic and Economic Change in Developed Countries*, NBER, Princeton: Princeton University Press.

(1962). "Irrational behaviour and economic theory," *Journal of Political Economy*, Vol. 70, pp. 1–13.

(1964), *Human Capital*, New York: Columbia University Press.

(1965), "A theory of the allocation of time," *Economic Journal*, Vol. 75, pp. 493–517.

(1971), *Economic Theory*, New York: Knopf.

(1974), "A theory of social interactions," *Journal of Political Economy*, Vol. 82, pp. 1063–94.

(1975), *Human Capital: a theoretical and empirical analysis with special relevance to education*, 2nd edition, New York: NBER.

(1976), *The Economic Approach to Human Behaviour*, University of Chicago Press.

and B. Chiswick (1966), "Education and the distribution of earnings," *American Economic Review*, Vol. 56 (papers and proc.), pp. 358–69.

Ben-Porath, Y. (1973), "Labor force participation rates and the supply of labor," *Journal of Political Economy*, Vol. 81, pp. 697–704.

Bergson, A. (1936), "Real income, expenditure proportionality, and Frisch's 'New methods of measuring marginal utility'," *Review of Economic Studies*, Vol. 4, pp. 33–52.

Berndt, E. R., M. N. Darrough, and W. E. Diewert (1977), "Flexible functional forms and expenditure distributions: an application to Canadian consumer demand functions," *International Economic Review*, Vol. 18, pp. 651–75.

Blackorby, C., and D. Donaldson (1978), "Measures of equality and their meaning in terms of social welfare," *Journal of Economic Theory*, Vol. 18, pp. 59–80.

D. Nissen, D. Primont, and R. Russell (1973), "Consistent intertemporal decision making," *Review of Economic Studies*, Vol. 40, pp. 239–48.

D. Primont and R. R. Russell (1978), *Duality, Separability and Functional Structure*, New York: American Elsevier.

and R. R. Russell (1978), "Indices and subindices of the cost of living and the standard of living," *International Economic Review*, Vol. 19, pp. 229–40.

Blaug, M. (1976), "Human capital theory: a slightly jaundiced survey," *Journal of Economic Literature*, Vol. 14, pp. 827–55.

Blinder, A. S. (1975), "Distribution effects and the aggregate consumption function," *Journal of Political Economy*, Vol. 83, pp. 447–76.

Bliss, C. J. (1975), *Capital Theory and the Distribution of Income*, Amsterdam: North-Holland.

Blokland, J. (1976), *Continuous Consumer Equivalence Scales*, Leiden: Stenfert Kroese.

Bonüs, H. (1973), "Quasi-Engel curves, diffusion, and the ownership of major consumer durables," *Journal of Political Economy*, Vol. 81, pp. 655–77.

Borch, K. (1969), "A note on uncertainty and indifference curves," *Review of Economic Studies*, Vol. 36, pp. 1–4.

Boskin, M. J. (1973), "The economics of labour supply" in G. Cain and H. Watts (1973), *Income Maintenance and Labour Supply*, Chicago: Markham.

Boyce, R., and D. Primont (1976), "An econometric test of the representative consumer hypothesis," Vancouver: University of British Columbia, Department of Economics. Discussion paper no. 76-31.

Branson, W. H. (1972a, 1979), *Macroeconomic Theory and Policy*, New York: Harper & Row. First edition: 1972; second edition: 1979.

(1972b), "The trade effects of the 1971 currency realignment," *Brookings Papers in Economic Activity*, Vol. 1, pp. 15–67.

Brems, H. (1956), "Long-run automobile demand," *Journal of Marketing*, Vol. 20, pp. 379–84.

Brittain, J. A. (1960), "Some neglected features of Britain's income levelling," *American Economic Review*, Vol. 50 (papers and proc.), pp. 593–603.

Brown, J. A. C. (1954), "The consumption of food in relation to household composition and income," *Econometrica*, Vol. 22, pp. 444–60.

and A. S. Deaton (1972), "Models of consumer behaviour: a survey," *Economic Journal*, Vol. 82, pp. 1145–236.

Brown, T. M. (1952), "Habit persistence and lags in consumer behaviour," *Econometrica*, Vol. 20, pp. 355–71.

Buiter, W. H. (1977), "'Crowding-out' and the effectiveness of fiscal policy," *Journal of Public Economics*, Vol. 7, pp. 309–28.

Burns, M. E. (1973), "A note on the concept and measure of consumer's surplus," *American Economic Review*, Vol. 53, pp. 335–44.

Burstein, M. L. (1961), "Measurement of the quality change in consumer durables," *Manchester School*, Vol. 29, pp. 267–79.

Buscheguenncce, S. S. (1925), "Sur une classe des hypersurfaces: à propos de l'index idéal de M. Irving Fisher," *Recueil Mathematique* (Moscow), Vol. 32, pp. 625–31.

Byron, R. P. (1970a), "A simple method for estimating demand systems under separable utility assumptions," *Review of Economic Studies*, Vol. 37, pp. 261–74.

(1970b), "The restricted Aitken estimation of sets of demand relations," *Econometrica*, Vol. 38, pp. 816–30.

Cagan, P. (1965), *The Effect of Pension Plans on Aggregate Saving*, Occasional Paper 95, New York: NBER.

(1966), "Measuring quality changes and the purchasing power of money: an exploratory study of automobiles," *National Banking Review*, Vol. 3, reprinted in Griliches (1971).

Cain, G. (1966), *Married Women in the Labor Force*, Chicago: University of Chicago Press.

(1976), "The challenge of segmented labor market theories to orthodox theory: a survey," *Journal of Economic Literature*, Vol. 14, pp. 1215–57.

and H. Watts (1973), *Income Maintenance and Labor Supply*, Chicago: Markham.

Caplovitz, D. (1967), *The poor pay more: consumer practices of low income families*, New York: Columbia University Press.

Carlevaro, F. (1976), "A generalization of the linear expenditure system," pp. 73–92 in L. Solari and J.-N. du Pasquier (eds.) *Private and Enlarged Consumption*, Amsterdam, North-Holland for Association Scièntifique Europeénne pour la Prevision Economique à Moyen et à Long Term (ASEPELT).

Cass, D., and J. E. Stiglitz (1970), "The structure of investor preferences and asset returns, and separability in portfolio allocation: a contribution to the pure theory of mutual funds," *Journal of Economic Theory*, Vol. 2, pp. 122–60.

Chenery, H. B. (1952), "Overcapacity and the acceleration principle," *Econometrica*, Vol. 20, pp. 1–28.

Chipman, J. S. (1974), "Homothetic preferences and aggregation," *Journal of Economic Theory*, Vol. 8, pp. 26–38.

L. Hurwicz, M. K. Richter, and H. F. Sonnenschein (1971), *Preferences, Utility and Demand*, New York: Harcourt Brace.

and J. C. Moore (1976), "The scope of consumers' surplus arguments," in A. M. Tang, F. M. Westfield, and J. A. Worley (eds.), *Evolution, Welfare and Time in Economics: Essays in Honor of Nicholas Georgescu-Roegen*, Lexington Books.

Chow, G. (1957), *Demand for Automobiles in the U.S.: a study in consumer durables*, Amsterdam: North-Holland.

(1960), "Statistical demand functions for automobiles and their use for forecasting," in A. C. Harberger (ed.), *The Demand for Durable Goods*, Chicago: University of Chicago Press.

Christensen, L. R., D. W. Jorgenson, and L. J. Lau (1975), "Transcendental logarithmic utility functions," *American Economic Review*, Vol. 65, pp. 367–83.

Clark, J. M. (1919), "Business acceleration and the law of demand: a technical factor in economic cycles," *Journal of Political Economy*, Vol. 25, pp. 217–35.

Clawson, M. (1959), *Methods of Measuring the Demand for and Value of Outdoor Recreation*, Reprint 10, Washington D.C.: Resources for the Future.

Clower, R. (1965), "The Keynesian counterrevolution: a theoretical appraisal," pp. 103–25 in F. H. Hahn, and F. P. R. Brechling (eds.), *The Theory of Interest Rates*, London: Macmillan for the International Economic Association.

Cochrane, J. L. (1970), *Macroeconomics Before Keynes*, Glenview, Ill.: Scott, Foresman.

Court, A. T. (1939), "Hedonic price indexes with automotive examples," in *The Dynamics of Automobile Demand*, New York: General Motors.

Cowell, F. A. (1977), *Measuring Inequality*, Oxford: Allan.

Cowling, K., and J. Cubbin (1971), "Price, quality and advertising competition," *Economica*, Vol. 38, pp. 378–94.

and J. Cubbin (1972), "Hedonic price indexes for U.K. cars," *Economic Journal*, Vol. 82, pp. 963–78.

Cragg, J. G. (1971), "Some statistical models for limited dependent variables with applications to the demand for durable goods," *Econometrica*, Vol. 39, pp. 829–44.

and R. S. Uhler (1970), "The demand for automobiles," *Canadian Journal of Economics*, Vol. 3, pp. 386–406.

Cramer, J. S. (1957), "A dynamic approach to the theory of consumer demand," *Review of Economic Studies*, Vol. 24, pp. 73–86.

(1962), *A Statistical Model of the Ownership of Major Consumer Durables*, Cambridge: Cambridge University Press.

(1969), *Empirical Econometrics*, Amsterdam: North-Holland.

Cubbin, J. (1975), "Quality change and pricing behaviour in the U.K. car industry 1956–1968," *Economica*, Vol. 42, pp. 43–58.

Dalton, H. (1920), "The measurement of inequality of incomes," *Economic Journal*, Vol. 30, pp. 361–84.

d'Aspremont, C., and L. Gevers (1977), "Equity and the informational basis of collective choice," *Review of Economic Studies*, Vol. 44, pp. 199–209.

David, P., and J. L. Scadding (1974), "Private saving: ultrarationality, aggregation, and 'Denison's Law,'" *Journal of Political Economy*, Vol. 82, pp. 225–49.

Davidson, J. E. H., D. F. Hendry et al. (1978), "Econometric modelling of the aggregate time-series relationship between consumers' expenditure and income in the United Kingdom," *Economic Journal*, Vol. 88, pp. 661–92.

Davies, H. D. (1974), "The consumer's choice among qualities of goods," London: Birkbeck College, *Discussion Paper in Economics*, 26.

Deaton, A. S. (1972a), "The estimation and testing of systems of demand equations," *European Economic Review*, Vol. 3, pp. 390–411.

(1972b), "Wealth effects on consumption in a modified life-cycle model," *Review of Economic Studies*, Vol. 39, pp. 443–53.

(1974a), "The analysis of consumer demand in the United Kingdom, 1900–1970," *Econometrica*, Vol. 42, pp. 341–67.

(1974b), "A reconsideration of the empirical implications of additive preferences," *Economic Journal*, Vol. 84, pp. 338–48.

(1975a), *Models and Projections of Demand in Post-war Britain*, London: Chapman and Hall.

(1975b), "The measurement of income and price elasticities," *European Economic Review*, Vol. 6, pp. 261–74.

(1975c), The structure of demand 1920–70, Vol. 6, Section 2, *The Fontana Economic History of Europe*, Collins: Fontana.

(1976), "Consumption," in T. S. Barker (ed.), *Economic Structure and Policy*, London: Chapman and Hall.

(1977), "Involuntary saving through unanticipated inflation," *American Economic Review*, Vol. 67, pp. 899–910.

(1978), "Specification and testing in applied demand analysis," *Economic Journal*, Vol. 88, pp. 524–36.

(1979), "The distance function and consumer behaviour with applications to index numbers and optimal taxation," *Review of Economic Studies*, Vol. 46 , pp. 391–405,

and J. Muellbauer (1980), "An almost ideal demand system," *American Economic Review*, Vol. 70, 312–36.

Debreu, G. (1951), "The coefficient of resource utilization," *Econometrica*, Vol. 19, pp. 273–92.

de Finetti, B. (1937), "La prévision: ses lois logiques, ses sources subjectives," *Annales de l'Institut Henri Poincaré*, Vol. 7, pp. 1–68.

De Groot, M. H. (1970). *Optimal Statistical Decisions*, New York: McGraw-Hill.

Deschamps, R., and L. Gevers (1978), "Leximin and utilitarian rules: a joint characterisation," *Journal of Economic Theory*, Vol. 17, pp. 143–63.

de Wolff, P. (1938), "The demand for passenger cars in the United States," *Econometrica*, Vol. 6, pp. 113–29.

Dhrymes, P. J. (1971), "Price and quality changes in consumer capital goods: an empirical study," in Griliches (1971).

Diewert, W. E. (1971), "An application of the Shephard duality theorem: a generalized Leontief production function," *Journal of Political Economy*, Vol. 79, pp. 481–507.

(1974a), "Applications of duality theory," Chapter 3 in M. D. Intriligator and D. A. Kendrick (eds.), *Frontiers of Quantitative Economics*, Vol. II, Amsterdam: North-Holland/American Elsevier.

(1974b), "Intertemporal consumer theory and the demand for durables," *Econometrica*, Vol. 42, pp. 497–516.

(1976a), "Exact and superlative index numbers," *Journal of Econometrics*, Vol. 4, pp. 115–45.

(1980a), "Symmetry conditions for market demand functions," *Review of Economic Studies*, Vol. 47, pp. 595–601.

(1981), "Duality approaches to microeconomic theory," in K. J. Arrow and M. D. Intriligator (eds.), *Handbook of Mathematical Economics*, Vol. 2, Amsterdam: North-Holland.

(1980b), "The economic theory of index numbers: a survey," in A. S. Deaton (ed.) *Essays in the Theory and Measurement of Consumer Behaviour*, Cambridge: Cambridge University Press.

Dixit, A. K. (1976), *Optimization in Economic Theory*, Oxford University Press.

   (1979), "Quality and quantity competition," *Review of Economic Studies*, Vol. 46, pp. 587–600.

Doeringer, P. B., and M. J. Piore (1971), *Internal Labor Markets and Manpower Analysis*, Lexington, Mass: Heath.

Dolde, W., and J. Tobin (1971), "Monetary and fiscal effects on consumption," in *Consumer Spending and Monetary Policy: The Linkages*, Boston: Federal Reserve Bank of Boston, Conference Series, No. 5.

Domencich, T. A., and D. McFadden (1975), *Urban Travel Demand: a behavioural analysis*, Amsterdam: North-Holland.

Dorfman, R., P. A. Samuelson, and R. Solow (1958), *Linear Programming and Economic Analysis*, New York: McGraw-Hill.

Douglas, P. H. (1934), *The Theory of Wages*, New York: Macmillan.

Drèze, J. H. (1972), "Econometrics and decision theory," *Econometrica*, Vol. 40, pp. 1–17.

   (1974), "Axiomatic theories of choice, cardinal utility and subjective probability: a review," pp. 3–23, in J. H. Drèze (ed.), *Allocation under Uncertainty: Equilibrium and Optimality*, New York: Macmillan.

Duesenberry, J. S. (1949), *Income, Saving, and the Theory of Consumer Behavior*, Cambridge, Mass.: Harvard University Press.

Dupuit, J. (1844), "De la mesure de l'utilité des travaux publics," *Annales des Ponts et Chauseés, Mémoires et documents relatifs à l'art des constructions et au service de l'ingénieur*, Vol. 8, pp. 332–75. Trans. in K. J. Arrow and T. Scitovsky (ed.), *Readings in Welfare Economics*, Homewood, Ill.: Irwin.

Easterlin, R. A., R. A. Pollak, and M. L. Wachter (1980), "Toward a more general economic model of fertility determination: endogenous preferences and natural fertility," in R. A. Easterlin (ed.), *Population and Economic Change in Developing Countries*, NBER.

Eisner, R., and R. H. Strotz (1963), "Determinants of business investment," in Commission on Money and Credit: *Impacts of Monetary Policy*, Englewood Cliffs, N.J.: Prentice-Hall.

Ekern, S., and R. Wilson (1974), "On the theory of the firm in an economy with incomplete markets," *Bell Journal of Economics*, Vol. 5, pp. 171–80.

Engel, E. (1895), "Die Lebenskosten Belgischer Arbeiter-Familien früher and jetzt," *International Statistical Institute Bulletin*, Vol. 9, pp. 1–74.

Evans, M. K. (1967), "The importance of wealth in the consumption function," *Journal of Political Economy*, Vol. 75, pp. 335–51.

   (1969), *Macroeconomic Activity, Theory, Forecasting and Control*, New York: Harper & Row.

Fama, E. F. (1976), "Multiperiod consumption–investment decisions: a correction," *American Economic Review*, Vol. 66, pp. 723–24.

Farrell, M. J. (1954), "The demand for motor cars in the United States," *Journal of the Royal Statistical Society*, Series A, Vol. 117, pp. 171–201.

   (1959), "The new theories of the consumption function," *Economic Journal*, Vol. 69, pp. 678–96.

   (1970), "The magnitude of rate of growth effects on aggregate savings," *Economic Journal*, Vol. 80, pp. 873–94.

Feldstein, M. S. (1969), "Mean-variance analysis in the theory of liquidity preference and portfolio selection," *Review of Economic Studies*, Vol. 36, pp. 5–12.

   (1974), "Social security, induced retirement, and aggregate capital accumulation," *Journal of Political Economy*, Vol. 82, pp. 905–26.

(1976a), "Social security and the distribution of wealth," *Journal of the American Statistical Association,* Vol. 71, pp. 800–7.

(1976b), "Social security and saving: the extended life cycle theory," *American Economic Review,* Vol. 66 (papers and proc.), pp. 77–86.

Ferber, R. (1973), "Consumer economics, a survey," *Journal of Economic Literature,* Vol. 11, pp. 1303–42.

Finney, D. J. (1947), *Probit Analysis,* Cambridge: Cambridge University Press.

Fisher, F. M., and K. Shell (1971), "Taste and quality change in the pure theory of the true cost of living index," in Griliches, (1971).

Fisher, I. (1907), *The Rate of Interest: Its Nature, Determination and Relation to Economic Phenomena,* New York: Macmillan.

(1922), *The Making of Index Numbers,* Boston and New York: Houghton Mifflin.

(1930), *The Theory of Interest,* New Haven, Conn.: Yale University Press, 1930.

Fleisher, B. M. (1970), *Labor Economics: Theory and Evidence,* Engelwood Cliffs, N.J.: Prentice-Hall.

Flemming, J. S. (1973), "The consumption function when capital markets are imperfect," *Oxford Economic Papers,* Vol. 25, pp. 160–72.

(1974), "Portfolio choice and liquidity preferences: a continuous time treatment," in H. G. Johnson and A. R. Nobay, *Essays in Monetary Economics,* Oxford: Oxford University Press.

(1978), "Aspects of optimal unemployment insurance: search, leisure and capital market imperfections," *Journal of Public Economics,* Vol. 10, pp. 413–25.

Forsyth, F. G. (1960), "The relationship between family size and family expenditure," *Journal of the Royal Statistical Scoiety,* (Series A), Vol. 123, pp. 367–97.

Friedman, M. (1957), *A Theory of the Consumption Function,* Princeton: Princeton University Press.

(1962), *Price Theory: A Provisional Text,* London: Cass.

and S. Kuznets (1954), *Income from Independent Professional Practice,* New York: NBER.

and L. J. Savage (1948), "The utility analysis of choices involving risk," *Journal of Political Economy,* Vol. 56, pp. 279–304.

Frisch, R. (1932), *New Methods of Measuring Marginal Utility,* Tübingen: Mohr.

(1936), "Annual survey of general economic theory: the problem of index numbers," *Econometrica,* Vol. 4, pp. 1–39.

(1959), "A complete scheme for computing all direct and gross demand elasticities in a model with many sectors," *Econometrica,* Vol. 27, pp. 177–96.

Fuss, M., and D. McFadden (eds.) (1978), *Production Economics: A Dual Approach to Theory and Applications,* Amsterdam: North-Holland.

Gaertner, W. (1974), "A dynamic model of interdependent consumer behaviour," *Zeitschrift für Nationalökonomie,* Vol. 34, pp. 327–44.

Geary, P. T., and M. Morishima (1973), "Demand and supply under separability," in M. Morishima (ed.), *Theory of Demand, Real and Monetary,* pp. 87–147, Oxford: Oxford University Press.

Ghez, G. R., and G. S. Becker (1975), *The Allocation of Time and Goods over the Life Cycle,* New York: NBER.

Gintis, H. (1974), "Welfare criteria with endogenous preferences: the economics of education," *International Economic Review,* Vol. 15, pp. 415–30.

Glahe, F. (1973), *Macroeconomics: Theory and Policy,* New York: Harcourt Brace.

Godley, W. A. H., and J. Shepherd (1964), "Long-term growth and short-term policy," *National Institute Economic Review,* No. 27, pp. 26–38.

Goldberger, A. S. (1972), "Structural equation methods in the social sciences," *Econometrica,* Vol. 40, pp. 979–1001.

(1974), "Unobservable variables in econometrics," pp. 193–213 in P. Zarembka (ed.), *Frontiers in Econometrics,* New York: Academic.

(1977), "Twin methods: a sceptical view," in P. A. Taubman (ed.), *Kinometrics,* Amsterdam: North-Holland.

(1978), "The genetic determination of income: comment," *American Economic Review,* Vol. 68, pp. 960–69.

and T. Gamaletsos (1970), "A cross-country comparison of consumer expenditure patterns," *European Economic Review,* Vol. 1, pp. 357–400.

Goldman, S. M., and H. Uzawa (1964), "A note on separability in demand analysis," *Econometrica,* Vol. 32, pp. 387–98.

Goodwin, R. M. (1951), "The nonlinear accelerator and the persistence of business cycles," *Econometrica,* Vol. 19, pp. 1–17.

Gordon, D. F. (1974), "A neoclassical theory of Keynesian unemployment," *Economic Inquiry,* Vol. 12, pp. 431–59.

Gordon, R. J. (1971), "The measurement bias in price indexes for capital goods," *Review of Income and Wealth,* Vol. 17, pp. 121–75.

Gorman, W. M. (1953), "Community preference fields," *Econometrica,* Vol. 21, pp. 63–80.

(1956), "A possible procedure for analysing quality differentials in the egg market," Ames: Iowa State College, mimeo. (Reprinted in *Review of Economic Studies,* Vol. 47, 1980, pp. 843–56.)

(1959), "Separable utility and aggregation," *Econometrica,* Vol. 27, pp. 469–81.

(1961), "On a class of preference fields," *Metroeconomica,* Vol. 13, pp. 53–6.

(1967), "Tastes, habits and choices," *International Economic Review,* Vol. 8, pp. 218–22.

(1968), "The structure of utility functions," *Review of Economic Studies,* Vol. 35, pp. 369–90.

(1970), "Quasi separable preferences, costs, and technologies," Chapel Hill: University of North Carolina. Mimeo.

(1971), Lecture notes, London School of Economics. Mimeo.

(1976), "Tricks with utility functions," in M. Artis and R. Nobay (eds.), *Essays in Economic Analysis,* Cambridge: Cambridge University Press.

(1980), "Some Engel curves," in A. S. Deaton (ed.), *Essays in Theory and Measurement of Consumer Behaviour,* Cambridge: Cambridge University Press.

Gould, J. P. (1968), "Adjustment costs in the theory of investment of the firm," *Review of Economic Studies,* Vol. 35, pp. 47–55.

Granger, C. W. J., and P. Newbold (1974), "Spurious regressions in econometrics," *Journal of Econometrics,* Vol. 2, pp. 111–20.

Green, H. A. J. (1961), "Direct additivity and consumers' behaviour," *Oxford Economic Papers,* Vol. 13, pp. 132–36.

(1964), *Aggregation in Economic Analysis,* Princeton: Princeton University Press.

(1976), *Consumer Theory,* 2nd edition, New York: Macmillan.

Greenberg, D. H., and M. Kosters (1973), "Income guarantees and the working poor: the effect of income maintenance programs on the hours of work of male family heads," in G. G. Cain and H. Watts, *Income Maintenance and Labour Supply,* Chicago: Markham.

Greenhalgh, C. (1980), "Participation and hours of work for married women in Great Britain," *Oxford Economic Papers,* Vol. 32, pp. 296–318.

paper No. 25.

Griliches, Z. (1961), "Hedonic price indexes for automobiles: an econometric analysis of quality change," in Griliches (1971).

(1971), Ed., *Price Indexes and Quality Change: Studies in New Methods of Measurement*, Cambridge, Mass.: Harvard University Press.

(1974), "Errors in variables and other unobservables," *Econometrica*, Vol. 42, pp. 971–98.

(1979), "Sibling models and data in economics: beginnings of a survey," *Journal of Political Economy*, Vol. 87, pp S37–64.

Gronau, R. (1973), "The effects of children on the housewife's value of time," *Journal of Political Economy*, Vol. 81, (Supplement) pp. S168–99.

(1974), "Wage comparisons–a selectivity bias," *Journal of Political Economy*, Vol. 82, pp. 1119–43.

Grossman, M. (1972), *The Demand for Health: A Theoretical and Empirical Investigation*, New York: NBER.

(1976), "The correlation between health and schooling," in Terleckyj (1976).

Grossman, S., and J. E. Stiglitz (1976), "Information and competitive price systems," *American Economic Review*, Vol. 66, pp. 246–53.

Groves, T., and J. Ledyard (1977), "Optimal allocation of public goods: a solution to the free-rider problem," *Econometrica*, Vol. 45, pp. 783–809.

Haavelmo, T. (1960), *A Study in the Theory of Investment*, Chicago: University of Chicago Press.

Haber, A., and R. P. Runyon (1973), *General Statistics*, Reading, Mass.: Addison-Wesley.

Hall, R. E. (1971), "The measurement of quality change from vintage price data," in Griliches (1971).

(1973a), "The specification of technology with several kinds of output," *Journal of Political Economy*, Vol. 81, pp. 878–92.

(1973b), "Wages, income and hours of work in the U.S. labor force," in G. Cain and H. Watts (eds.), *Income Maintenance and Labor Supply*, Chicago: Markham.

(1978), "Stochastic implications of the life cycle–permanent income hypothesis: theory and evidence," *Journal of Political Economy*, vol. 86, pp. 971–87.

Ham, J. C. (1977), "Rationing and the supply of labor: an econometric approach," working paper 103, *Industrial Relations Section, Princeton University*, November.

Hamburger, M. J. (1968), "Household demand for financial assets," *Econometrica*, Vol. 36, pp. 97–118.

Hammond, P. J. (1976a), "Equity, Arrow's conditions, and Rawls' difference principle," *Econometrica*, Vol. 44, pp. 793–804.

(1976b), "Endogenous tastes and stable long-run choice," *Journal of Economic Theory*, Vol. 13, pp. 329–40.

Hancock, K. (1960), "Unemployment and the economists in the 1920s," *Economica*, Vol. 27, pp. 305–21.

Hanoch, G. (1980), "Hours and weeks in the theory of labor supply," in J. P. Smith (ed.), *Female Labor Supply: Theory and Estimation*, Princeton: Princeton University Press.

(1977), "Risk aversion and consumer preferences," *Econometrica*, Vol. 45, pp. 413–26.

and M. Honig (1978), "The labour supply curve under income maintenance programs," *Journal of Public Economics*, Vol. 9, pp. 1–16.

Hansen, F. (1972), *Consumer Choice Behavior*, New York: Free Press.

Harberger, A. C. (ed.), (1960), *The Demand for Durable Goods*, Chicago: Chicago University Press.

(1971), "Three basic postulates for applied welfare economics: an interpretative essay," *Journal of Economic Literature*, Vol. 9, pp. 785–97.

Hart, O. D. (1975), "Some negative results on the existence of comparative statics results in portfolio theory," *Review of Economic Studies*, Vol. 42, pp. 615–21.

Hause, J. C. (1975), "The theory of welfare measurement," *Journal of Political Economy*, Vol. 83, pp. 1145–82.

Heckman, J. J. (1974), "Shadow prices, market wages and labor supply," *Econometrica*, Vol. 42, pp. 679–94.

(1978), "A partial survey of recent research on the labor supply of women," *American Economic Review*, Vol. 68 (papers and proc.), pp. 200–7.

(1979), "Sample selection bias as a specification error," *Econometrica*, Vol. 47, pp. 153–61.

and T. McCurdy (1980), "A life-cycle model of female labor supply," *Review of Economic Studies*, Vol. 47, pp. 47–74.

and R. Willis (1977), "A beta logistic model for analysis of sequential labor force participation by married women," *Journal of Political Economy*, Vol. 85, pp. 27–58.

Helliwell, J. (1974), "Aggregate investment equations: a survey of issues," in J. Helliwell (ed.), *Aggregate Investment*, Hammondsworth: Penguin Education, 1976.

Hemming, R. (1978), "State pensions and personal savings," *Scottish Journal of Political Economy*, Vol. 25, pp. 135–47.

Henderson, A. M. (1949–50a), "The cost of children," Parts I–III, *Population Studies*, Vol. 3, pp. 130–50, Vol. 4, pp. 267–98.

(1949–50b), "The cost of a family," *Review of Economic Studies*, Vol. 17, pp. 127–48.

Hendry, D. F. (1980), "Predictive failure and econometric modelling in macroeconomics: the transactions demand for money," in P. Ormerod (ed.), *Economic Modelling*, London: Heinemann Educational Books.

Hess, A. C. (1977), "A comparison of automobile demand equations," *Econometrica*, Vol. 45, pp. 683–702.

Hester, D. D., and J. Tobin (1967), *Risk Aversion and Portfolio Choice*, Cowles Foundation Monograph 19, New York: Wiley.

Hicks, J. R. (1936), *Value and Capital*, Oxford University Press.

(1946), *Value and Capital*, 2nd edition, Oxford: Oxford University Press.

(1956), *A Revision of Demand Theory*, Oxford: Oxford University Press.

and R. G. D. Allen (1934), "A reconsideration of the theory of value," *Economica*, Vol. 1, pp. 52–75, 196–219.

Hirsch, F. (1977), *Social Limits to Growth*, Henley-on-Thames: Routledge & Kegan Paul.

Hirshleifer, J. (1958), "On the theory of optimal investment decision," *Journal of Political Economy*, Vol. 66, pp. 329–52.

Hollister, R. G., and J. L. Palmer (1972), "The impact of inflation on the poor," in Boulding K. and M. Pfaff (eds.) *Redistribution to the Rich and the Poor*. Belmont, California: Wadsworth.

Hotelling, H. S. (1935), "Demand functions with limited budgets," *Econometrica*, Vol. 3, pp. 66–78.

(1938), "The general welfare in relation to the problems of taxation and of railway and utility rates," *Econometrica*, Vol. 6, pp. 269–72.

Houthakker, H. S. (1950), "Revealed preference and the utility function," *Economica*, Vol. 17, pp. 159–74.

(1952), "Compensated changes in quantities and qualities consumed," *Review of Economic Studies*, Vol. 19, pp. 155–64.

(1957), "An international comparison of household expenditure patterns commemorating the centenary of Engel's Law," *Econometrica,* Vol. 25, pp. 532–51.

(1960), "Additive preferences," *Econometrica*, Vol. 28, pp. 244–56.

and L. D. Taylor (1970), *Consumer Demand in the United States 1929–70, Analysis and*

Projections, Cambridge, Mass.: Harvard University Press., 2nd and enlarged edition.

Howard, D. H. (1978), "Personal saving behaviour and the rate of inflation," *Review of Economics and Statistics,* Vol. 60, pp. 547–54.

Hurd, M. (1976), "The welfare implications of the unemployment rate," Technical Report 218, Standford: Institute for Mathematical Studies in the Social Sciences.

Hurwicz, L., and H. Uzawa (1971), "On the integrability of demand functions," in Chipman et al. (eds.).

Ironmonger, D. S. (1972), *New Commodities and Consumer Behaviour,* Cambridge: Cambridge University Press.

Jackson, C. (1968), "Revised equivalence scales for estimating equivalent incomes or budget costs by family type," Washington, D.C. U.S. Department of Labor, *Bureau of Labor Statistics Bulletin,* pp. 1570–2.

Jencks, C. et al. (1972), *Inequality,* New York: Basic Books.

Jevons, W. S. (1871), *The Theory of Political Economy,* London: Macmillan.

Johnson, P. R., T. J. Grennes, and M. Thursby (1977), "Devaluation, foreign trade controls and domestic wheat prices," *American Journal of Agricultural Economics,* Vol. 59, pp. 619–27.

Joreskóg, K. G. (1973), "A general method for estimating a linear structural equation system," pp. 85–112, in A. S. Goldberger and O. D. Duncan (eds.), *Structural Equation Models in the Social Sciences,* New York and London: Seminar Press.

Jorgenson, D. W. (1967), "The theory of investment behavior," in R. Ferber (ed.), *Determinants of investment behavior,* New York: Columbia University Press.

Joshi, H. (1981), "Secondary workers in the employment cycle," *Economica,* Vol. 48, pp. 29–44.

Juster, F. T., and P. Wachtel (1972), "Anticipatory and objective models of durable goods demand," *American Economic Review,* Vol. 62, (papers and proc.) pp. 564–579.

Kalachek, F., W. Mellow, and F. Raines (1978), "The male labor supply function reconsidered," *Industrial and Labor Relations Review,* Vol. 31, pp. 356–67.

Kay, J., and M. A. King (1978), *The British Tax System,* Oxford: Oxford University Press.

Keynes, J. M. (1933), "Alfred Marshall," in *Essays in Biography,* New York: Macmillan.

(1936), *The General Theory of Employment, Interest and Money,* London: Macmillan.

King, A. T. (1976), "The demand for housing: integrating the roles of journey-to-work, neighborhood, quality, and prices," in Terleckyj (1976).

Klevmarken, A. (1977), "A note on new goods and quality changes in the true cost of living index in view of Lancaster's model of consumer behaviour," *Econometrica,* Vol. 45, pp. 163–73.

Knight, F. H. (1921), *Risk, Uncertainty and Profit,* New York: Houghton Mifflin.

Kolm, S.-C. (1969), "The optimal production of social justice," in J. Margolis and H. Guitton, *Public Economics,* New York: Macmillan.

(1976), "Unequal inequalities I and II," *Journal of Economic Theory,* Vol. 12, 13, pp. 416–42, 82–111.

Konüs, A. A. (1924), "The problem of the true index of the cost-of-living" (in Russian). *The Economic Bulletin of the Institute of Economic Conjuncture,* Moscow, No. 9–10, pp. 64–71. English translation: *Econometrica* (1939), Vol. 7, pp. 10–29.

(1939), "On the Theory of Means," *Acta Universitatis Asiae Mediae* (Tashkent), Series Va, Mathematica, Fasc. 24, pp. 3–10.

and S. S. Buscheguennce (1925), "On the problem of the purchasing power of money," *Voprosi Konyunktur,* II, pp. 151–172.

Kotowitz, Y., and F. Mathewson (1979), "Advertising, consumer information and product quality," *The Bell Journal of Economics*, Vol. 10, pp. 66–88.

Koyck, L. M. (1954), *Distributed Lags and Investment Analysis*, Amsterdam: North-Holland.

Kuznets, S. (1962), "Quantitative aspects of the economic growth of nations: VII: The share and structure of consumption," *Economic Development and Cultural Change*, Vol. 10, no. 2, part 2, pp. 1–92.

Laidler, D. (1974), *Introduction to Microeconomics*, Deddington: Allan.

Lancaster, K. J. (1966a), "A new approach to consumer theory," *Journal of Political Economy*, Vol. 74, pp. 132–57.

(1966b), "Change and innovation in the technology of consumption," *American Economic Review*, Vol. 56, pp. 14–23.

(1971), *Consumer Demand: A New Approach*, New York: Columbia University Press.

Lau, L. J. (1980), "Existence conditions for aggregate demand functions: the case of multiple indexes," *Econometrica*, Vol. 48, forthcoming.

W. T. Lin, and P. A. Yotopolous (1978), "The linear logarithmic expenditure system: an application to consumption–leisure choice," *Econometrica*, Vol. 46, pp. 843–68.

Layard, P. R. G., M. Barton, and A. Zabalza (1979), "Married women's participation and hours," *Economica*, Vol. 46.

Layard, P. R. G., and A. A. Walters (1978), *Microeconomic Theory*, New York: McGraw-Hill.

Leamer, E. E. (1978), *Specification Searches: Ad Hoc Inference with Nonexperimental Data*, New York: Wiley.

Leibenstein, H., (1950), "Bandwagon, snob and Veblen effects in the theory of consumers' demand," *Quarterly Journal of Economics*, Vol. 65, pp. 183–207.

(1974), "The economic theory of fertility decline," *Quarterly Journal of Economics*, Vol. 89, pp. 1–31.

Leland, H., (1973), "Capital assets markets, production and optimality: a synthesis," Technical Report No. 115, Stanford: Institute for Mathematical Studies in the Social Sciences.

(1979), "Quacks, lemons and licensing: a theory of minimum quality standards," *Journal of Political Economy*, Vol. 87, pp. 1328–46.

Leontief, W., (1936), "Composite commodities and the problem of index numbers," *Econometrica*, Vol. 4, pp. 39–59.

(1947), "Introduction to a theory of the internal structure of functional relationships", *Econometrica*, Vol. 15, pp. 361–73.

Leser, C. E. V., (1963), "Forms of Engel functions," *Econometrica*, Vol. 31, pp. 694–703.

Lewis, H. G., (1957), "Hours of work and hours of leisure," in *Proceedings of the Industrial Relations Research Association*, pp. 196–206. Reprinted in J. F. Burton, L. K. Benham, W. M. Vaughn, and R. J. Flanagan (eds.) *Readings in Labour Market Analysis*, New York: Holt, Rinehart and Winston.

Lillard, L. A. (1977), "Estimation of permanent and transitory response functions in panel data: a dynamic labor supply model," BLS working paper, mimeo.

Lippman, S., and J. J. McCall (1976), "The economics of job search: a survey," *Economic Inquiry*, Vol. 14, pp. 113–26.

Lipsey, R. G., and G. Rosenbluth (1971), "A contribution to the new theory of demand: a rehabilitation of the Giffen good," *Canadian Journal of Economics*, Vol. 4, pp. 131–63.

Little, I. M. D. (1957), *A Critique of Welfare Economics*, 2nd edition, Oxford: Oxford University Press.

Lluch, C., A. A. Powell, and R. A. Williams (1977), *Patterns in Household Demand and Saving,* Oxford: Oxford University Press.

Lucas, R. E. (1967), "Optimal investment policy and the flexible accelerator," *International Economic Review,* Vol. 8, pp. 78–85.

—— (1976), "Econometric policy revaluation: a critique," pp. 19–46, in K. Brunner and A. Meltzer (eds.), *The Phillips Curve and Labor Markets,* Carnegie Rochester Conference Series on Public Policy, New York: North-Holland.

—— and L. Rapping (1970), "Real wages, employment and inflation," in E. S. Phelps et al. *Microeconomic Foundations of Employment and Inflation Theory,* New York: Norton.

Lucas, R. E. B. (1975), "Hedonic price functions," *Economic Inquiry,* Vol. 13, pp. 157–78.

—— (1977), "Hedonic wage equations and psychic wages in the returns to schooling," *American Economic Review,* Vol. 67, pp. 549–58.

McCall, J. J. (1965), "The economics of information and optimal stopping rules," *Journal of Business,* Vol. 38, pp. 300–17.

—— (1970), "Economics of information and job search," *Quarterly Journal of Economics,* Vol. 84, pp. 113–26.

McClements, L. D. (1977), "Equivalence scales for children," *Journal of Public Economics,* Vol. 8, pp. 191–210.

—— (1978), *The Economics of Social Security,* London: Heinemann.

McKenzie, L. W. (1956–7), "Demand theory without a utility index," *Review of Economic Studies,* Vol. 24, pp. 185–89.

Malinvaud, E. (1972), *Lectures in Microeconomic Theory,* New York: American Elsevier.

—— (1977), *The Theory of Unemployment Reconsidered,* Oxford: Blackwell.

Malmquist, S. (1953), "Index numbers and indifference surfaces," *Tradajos de Estadistica,* Vol. 4, pp. 209–41.

Markowitz, H. M. (1959), *Portfolio Selection,* New York: Wiley.

Marshall, A. (1890), *Principles of Economics,* London: Macmillan.

Maskin, E. (1978), "A theorem on utilitarianism," *Review of Economic Studies,* Vol. 45, pp. 93–6.

Massy, W. F., D. B. Montgomery, and D. G. Morrison (1970), *Stochastic Models of Buying Behavior,* Boston: MIT Press.

Mayer, T. (1972), *Permanent Income, Wealth and Consumption,* Berkeley: University of California Press.

Merton, R. C. (1969), "Lifetime portfolio selection under uncertainty: the continuous time case," *Review of Economics and Statistics,* Vol. 57, pp. 247–57.

Michael, R. T., and G. S. Becker (1973), "On the new theory of consumer behaviour," *Swedish Journal of Economics,* Vol. 75, pp. 378–96.

Mincer, J. (1958), "Investment in human capital and personal income distribution," *Journal of Political Economy,* Vol. 66, pp. 281–302.

—— (1962), "Labor force participation of married women: a study of labor supply," in H. G. Lewis (ed.), *Aspects of Labor Economics,* Princeton: Princeton University Press.

—— (1970), "The distribution of labor incomes: a survey with special reference to the human capital approach," *Journal of Economic Literature,* Vol. 8, pp. 1–26.

—— (1974), *Schooling, Experience and Earnings,* New York: NBER.

—— (1976), "Progress in human capital analysis of the distribution of earnings," in A. B. Atkinson (ed.), *The Personal Distribution of Incomes,* London: Allen & Unwin, 1976.

Mishan, E. (1977), "The plain truth about consumer surplus," *Zeitschrift für Nationalökonomie,* Vol. 37, pp. 1–24.

Mizon, G. E. (1977), "Model selection procedures," in M. J. Artis and A. R. Nobay (eds.), *Studies in Current Economic Analysis,* Oxford: Blackwell.

and D. F. Hendry (1979), "An empirical application and Monte Carlo analysis of tests of dynamic specification," *Review of Economic Studies*, forthcoming.

Modigliani, F. (1970), "The life-cycle hypothesis and intercountry differences in the saving ratio," in W. Eltis, M. Scott, and J. Wolfe (eds.), *Induction, Growth and Trade; Essays in Honour of Sir Roy Harrod*, Oxford: Clarendon Press.

(1975), "The life cycle hypothesis of saving twenty years later," in M. Parkin and A. R. Nobay (eds.), *Contemporary Issues in Economics*, Manchester: Manchester University Press.

and R. Brumberg (1955a), "Utility analysis and the consumption function: an interpretation of cross-section data," in K. K. Kurihara (ed.), *Post Keynesian Economics*, London: George Allen & Unwin.

and R. Brumberg (1955b), "Utility analysis and aggregate consumption functions: an attempt at integration", mimeo.

Mood, A. M., F. A. Graybill, and D. C. Boes (1974), *Introduction to the Theory of Statistics*, New York: McGraw-Hill.

Mortenson, D. T. (1970a), (eds.), "A theory of wage and employment dynamics," in E. S. Phelps et al. (eds.), *Microeconomic Foundations of Employment and Inflation Theory*, New York: Norton.

(1970b), "Job search, the duration of unemployment, and the Phillips Curve," *American Economic Review*, Vol. 60, pp. 847–62.

Muellbauer, J. (1974a), "Recent UK experience of prices and inequality: an application of true cost of living and real income indices," *Economic Journal*, Vol. 84, pp. 32–55.

(1974b), "Household composition, Engel curves and welfare comparisons between households: a duality approach," *European Economic Review*, pp. 103–22.

(1974c), "Household production theory, quality, and the 'hedonic technique,'" *American Economic Review*, Vol. 64, pp. 977–94.

(1974d), "Inequality measures, prices and household composition," *Review of Economic Studies*, Vol. 41, pp. 493–504.

(1975a), "The cost of living and taste and quality changes," *Journal of Economic Theory*, Vol. 10, pp. 269–83.

(1975b), "Aggregation, income distribution and consumer demand," *Review of Economic Studies*, Vol. 62, pp. 525–43.

(1975c), "Price change, quality change and depreciation in the British second-hand car market," London: Birkbeck College. Mimeo.

(1976), "Community preferences and the representative consumer," *Econometrica*, Vol. 44, pp. 979–99.

(1977a), "The cost of living," in *Social Security Research*, Her Majesty's Stationary Office (HMSO): London.

(1977b), "Testing the Barten model of household composition effects and the cost of children," *Economic Journal*, Vol. 87, pp. 460–87.

(1978a), "Distributional aspects of price comparisons," in R. Stone and W. Peterson (eds.), *Econometric Contributions to Public Policy*, New York: Macmillan for IEA.

(1978b), "Generalized aggregation in neoclassical labour supply," London, Birkbeck College, Mimeo.

(1980), "The estimation of the Prais-Houthakker model of equivalence scales," *Econometrica*, Vol. 48, pp. 153–76.

(1981a), "Testing neoclassical models of the demand for durables," in A. S. Deaton (ed.), *Essays in the Theory and Measurement of Consumer Behaviour*, Cambridge: Cambridge University Press, forthcoming.

(1981b), "Linear aggregation in neoclassical labour supply," *Review of Economic Studies*, Vol. 48, pp. 21–36.

and R. Portes (1978), "Macroeconomic models with quantity rationing," *Economic Journal*, Vol. 88, pp. 788–821.

Neary, J. P., and K. W. S. Roberts (1980), "The theory of household behaviour under rationing," *European Economic Review*, Vol. 13, pp. 25–42.

Nelson, P. (1970), "Information and consumer behaviour," *Journal of Political Economy*, Vol. 78, pp. 311–29.

Nerlove, M. (1956), "Estimates of the elasticities of supply of selected agricultural commodities," *Journal of Farm Economics*, Vol., 38, pp. 496–509.

(1957), "A note on long run automobile demand," *Journal of Marketing*, Vol. 21, pp. 57–64.

(1958), *Distributed Lags and Demand Analysis*, Agriculture Handbook No. 141, Washington, D.C.: U.S. Department of Agriculture.

(1972), "On lags in economic behaviour," *Econometrica*, Vol. 40, pp. 221–52.

Neumann, J. von, and O. Morgenstern (1947), *Theory of Games and Economic Behavior*, Princeton: Princeton University Press.

Nicholson, J. L. (1942–3), "Rationing and index numbers," *Review of Economic Studies*, Vol. 10, pp. 68–74.

(1949), "Variations in working-class family expenditure," *Journal of the Royal Statistical Society*, (Series A) Vol. 112, pp. 359–411.

(1957), "The general form of the adding-up criterion", *Journal of the Royal Statistical Society*, (Series A) Vol. 120, pp. 84–5.

Nickell, S. J. (1979a), "The effect of unemployment and related benefits on the duration of unemployment," *Economic Journal*, Vol. 89, pp. 34–39.

(1979b), *The Investment Decision of Firms*, Cambridge: Cambridge University Press.

Niehans, J. (1971), "Money and barter in general equilibrium with transactions costs," *American Economic Review*, Vol. 61, pp. 773–83.

Ohta, M. (1975), "Production technologies of the US boiler and turbo generator industries and hedonic price indexes for their products: a cost function approach," *Journal of Political Economics*, Vol. 83, pp. 1–26.

and Z. Griliches (1976), "Automobile prices revisited: extensions of the hedonic hypothesis," in Terleckyj (1976).

Owen, J. D. (1969), *The Price of Leisure*, Rotterdam: Rotterdam University Press.

(1971), "The demand for leisure," *Journal of Political Economy*, Vol. 79, pp. 56–76.

Pareto, V. (1892), "La teoria dei prezzi dei Signori Auspitz e Lieben e le osservazioni del professore Walras," *Giornale degli Economisti*, Vol. 4, pp. 201–39.

Parkin, M. (1970), "Discount house portfolio and debt selection," *Review of Economic Studies*, Vol. 37, pp. 469–97.

Parks, R. W. (1971), "Maximum likelihood estimation of the linear expenditure system," *Journal of the American Statistical Association*, Vol. 66, pp. 900–3.

Parks, R. W., and A. P. Barten (1973), "A cross-country comparison of the effects of prices, income, and population composition on consumption patterns," *Economic Journal*, Vol. 83, pp. 834–52.

Paroush, J. (1965), "The order of acquisition of consumer durables," *Econometrica*, Vol. 33, pp. 225–35.

Pauly, M. V. (1968), "The economics of moral hazard," *American Economic Review*, Vol. 58, pp. 531–37.

Pearce, I. F. (1961), "An exact method of consumer demand analysis," *Econometrica*, Vol. 29, pp. 499–516. ·

(1964), *A Contribution to Demand Analysis*, Oxford: Oxford University Press.

Pesaran, M. H., and A. S. Deaton (1978), "Testing non-nested non-linear regression models," *Econometrica*, Vol. 46, pp. 677–94.

Peston, M. H. (1967), "Changing utility functions," in M. Shubik (ed.), *Essays in Honor of Oskar Morgenstern*, Princeton: Princeton University Press.

Phelps, E. S., et al. (1970), *Microeconomic Foundations of Employment and Inflation Theory*, New York: Norton.

Phlips, L. (1972), "A dynamic version of the linear expenditure model," *Review of Economics and Statistics*, Vol. 54, pp. 450–58.

(1974), *Applied Consumption Analysis*, Amsterdam and Oxford: North-Holland.

(1978), "The demand for leisure and money," *Econometrica*, Vol. 46, pp. 1025–43.

Piachaud, D. (1974), "Do the poor pay more?" London: Child Poverty Action Group *Poverty Research Series*, 3.

(1978), "Prices and the distribution of income," in *Royal Commission on the Distribution of Income and Wealth, Chairman: Lord Diamond*. Selected evidence for Report No. 6: Lower Incomes. HMSO, London 1978, pp. 441–57.

Pigou, A. C. (1910), "A method of determining the numerical value of elasticities of demand," *Economic Journal*, Vol. 20, pp. 636–40.

Pollak, R. A. (1969), "Conditional demand functions and consumption theory," *Quarterly Journal of Economics*, Vol. 83, pp. 70–8.

(1970), "Habit formation and dynamic demand functions," *Journal of Political Economy*, Vol. 78, pp. 60–78.

(1971a), "Additive utility functions and linear Engel curves," *Review of Economic Studies*, Vol. 38, pp. 401–13.

(1971b), "Conditional demand functions and the implications of separable utility," *Southern Economic Journal*, Vol. 37, pp. 423–33.

(1971c), "The theory of the cost-of-living index," Research Discussion paper No. 11, Office of Prices and Living Conditions, Washington, D.C.: U.S. Bureau of Labor Statistics.

(1975), "Subindexes in the cost-of-living index," *International Economic Review*, Vol. 16, pp. 135–50.

(1976a), "Habit formation and long-run utility functions," *Journal of Economic Theory*, Vol. 13, pp. 272–97.

(1976b), "Interdependent preferences," *American Economic Review*, Vol. 66, pp. 309–20.

(1977), "Price dependent preferences," *American Economic Review*, Vol. 67, pp. 64–75.

(1978), "Endogenous tastes in demand and welfare analysis," *American Economic Review*, Vol. 68 (papers and proc.), pp. 374–79.

and M. L. Wachter (1975), "The relevance of the household production function and its implications for the allocation of time," *Journal of Political Economy*, Vol. 83, pp. 255–77.

and T. J. Wales (1979), "Welfare comparisons and equivalence scales," *American Economic Review*, Vol. 69, (papers and proc.), pp. 216–21.

Powell, A. A. (1974), *Empirical Analytics of Demand Systems*, Lexington, Mass.: Heath.

Prais, S. J., and H. S. Houthakker (1955), *The Analysis of Family Budgets*, Cambridge: Cambridge University Press; 2nd edition, 1971.

Pratt, J. W. (1964), "Risk aversion in the small and the large," *Econometrica*, Vol. 32, pp. 122–36.

Primont, D. (1977), "Necessary and sufficient conditions for the aggregation of cost of living subindexes," Vancouver: University of British Columbia, Department of Economics. Paper 77-13. Mimeo.

Psacharopoulos, G., and R. Layard (1979), "Human capital and earnings: British evidence and a critique," *Review of Economic Studies,* Vol. 46, pp. 485–503.

Pyatt, G. (1964), *Priority Patterns and the Demand for Household Durable Goods,* Cambridge: Cambridge University Press.

Quandt, R. E. (1970), *The Demand for Travel,* Lexington, Mass.: Heath.

and W. J. Baumol (1966), "The demand for abstract transport modes: theory and measurement," *Journal of Regional Science,* Vol. 9, pp. 201–14.

Quigley, J. M. (1976), "Housing demand in the short run: an analysis of polytomous choice," *Explorations in Economic Research,* Vol. 3, pp. 76–102.

Raiffa, H. (1968), *Decision Analysis: introductory lectures on choices under uncertainty,* Reading, Mass.: Addison-Wesley.

and R. Schlaifer (1961), *Applied Statistical Decision Theory,* Boston: Harvard Business School.

Ramsey, F. P. (1928), "A mathematical theory of saving," *Economic Journal,* Vol. 38, pp. 543–59.

(1931), "Truth and probability," in *The Foundations of Mathematics and Other Logical Essays,* London: Paul, Trench, Trubner.

Rawls, J. (1971), *A Theory of Justice,* Cambridge, Mass.: Harvard University Press; and Oxford: Clarendon Press.

Rees, A. (1973), *The Economics of Work and Pay,* New York: Harper & Row.

Riley, J. G. (1979), "Testing the educational screening hypothesis," *Journal of Political Economy,* Vol. 87, pp. S227–52.

Roberts, K. W. S. (1979a), "Possibility theorems with interpersonally comparable welfare levels," *Review of Economic Studies,* forthcoming.

(1979b), "Interpersonal comparability and social choice theory," *Review of Economic Studies,* forthcoming.

Rosen, H. S. (1976), "Tax illusion and the labour supply of married women," *Review of Economics and Statistics,* Vol. 58, pp. 167–72.

Rosen, S. (1972), "Learning and experience in the labor market," *Journal of Human Resources,* Vol. 7, pp. 326–42.

(1974), "Human capital and the internal rate of return," *Proceedings of the Industrial Relations Research Association,* 26th Annual Meeting, pp. 243–50.

(1974b), "Hedonic prices and implicit markets: product differentiation in pure competition," *Journal of Political Economy,* Vol. 82, pp. 34–55.

(1977), "Human capital: a survey of empirical research" in Ehrenberg, R. (ed.), *Research in Labor Economics,* Vol. 1, Greenwich, Conn.: JAI Press.

and R. Willis (1979), "Education and self-selection" *Journal of Political Economy,* Vol. 87, pp. S7–36.

Rothbarth, E. (1941), "The measurement of change in real income under conditions of rationing," *Review of Economic Studies,* Vol. 8, pp. 100–7.

Rothschild, M. (1973), "Models of market organization with imperfect information: a survey," *Journal of Political Economy,* Vol. 69, pp. 213–25.

Roy, R. (1942), *De l'utilité, contribution à la théorie des choix,* Paris: Hermann.

Royal Commission on the Distribution of Income and Wealth (1978), *Report No. 6: Lower Incomes,* Command 7175, London: HMSO.

Russell, T. (1977), "Rate of growth effects on aggregate savings," *Review of Economic Studies,* Vol. 44, pp. 153–68.

Saito, M. (1977), "Household flow-of-funds equations," *Journal of Money Credit and Banking,* Vol. 9, pp. 1–20.

Samuelson, P. A. (1938), "A note on the pure theory of consumer behaviour," *Economica,* Vol. 5, pp. 61–71.

(1942), "Constancy of the marginal utility of income," in O. Lange, F. McIntyre, and T. O. Yntema (eds.), *Studies in Mathematical Economics and Econometrics,* Chicago: University of Chicago Press.

(1947), *Foundations of Economic Analysis,* Cambridge, Mass.: Harvard University Press.

(1950a), "Probability and the attempt to measure utility," *The Economic Review,* (Keizai Kenkyu), Vol. 1, pp. 167–173. Reprinted as Chapter 12 in J. E. Stiglitz (ed.) *The Collected Scientific Papers of Paul A. Samuelson,* Vol. 1, Cambridge, Mass.: M.I.T. Press.

(1950b), "The problem of integrability in utility theory," *Economica,* Vol. 17, pp. 355–85.

(1952a), "Probability, utility, and the independence axiom," *Econometrica,* Vol. 20, pp. 670–78.

(1952b), "The transfer problem and transport costs," *Economic Journal,* Vol. 62, pp. 278–304.

(1952c), "Utility, preference, and probability," Chapter 13, pp. 127–136 in J. E. Stiglitz (ed.), *The Collected Scientific Papers of Paul A. Samuelson,* Vol. 1., M.I.T. Press.

(1956), "Social indifference curves," *Quarterly Journal of Economics,* Vol. 70, pp. 1–22.

(1965), "Using full duality to show that simultaneously additive direct and indirect utilities implies unitary price elasticity of demand," *Econometrica,* Vol. 33, pp. 781–96.

(1966), "The fundamental singularity theorem for nonjoint production," *International Economic Review,* Vol. 7, pp. 34–41.

(1969), "Lifetime portfolio selection by dynamic stochastic programming," *Review of Economics and Statistics,* Vol. 51, pp. 239–46.

(1970), "The fundamental approximation theorem of portfolio analysis in terms of means, variances, and higher moments," *Review of Economic Studies,* Vol. 37, pp. 537–42.

(1972), "Maximum principles in analytical economics," *American Economic Review,* Vol. 62, pp. 249–62.

(1974), "Complementarity – An essay on the 40th Anniversary of the Hicks-Allen revolution in demand theory," *Journal of Economic Literature,* Vol. 12, pp. 1255–89.

(1977), "St. Petersburg paradoxes: defanged, dissected, and historically described," *Journal of Economic Literature,* Vol. 15, pp. 24–55.

and S. Swamy (1974), "Invariant economic index numbers and canonical duality: survey and synthesis," *American Economic Review,* Vol. 64, pp. 566–93.

Sandmo, A. (1970), "The effect of uncertainty on saving decisions," *Review of Economic Studies,* Vol. 37, pp. 353–60.

(1974), "Two-period models of consumption decisions under uncertainty: a survey," in J. H. Drèze (ed.), *Allocation under Uncertainty: Equilibrium and Optimality,* New York: Macmillan; pp. 24–35.

(1976), "Optimal taxation: an introduction to the literature," *Journal of Public Economics,* Vol. 6, pp. 37–54.

Sargent, T. J. (1977), "Observations on improper methods of simulating and teaching Friedman's time-series consumption model," *International Economic Review,* Vol. 18, pp. 445–62.

Sato, K. (1972), "Additive utility functions and double-log consumer demand functions," *Journal of Political Economy,* Vol. 80, pp. 102–24.

Savage, L. J. (1954), *The Foundations of Statistics,* New York: Wiley.

Schmalensee, R. (1978), "Entry deterrence in the ready-to-eat breakfast cereal industry," *Bell Journal of Economics,* Vol. 9, pp. 305–27.

Schultz, H. (1938), *The Theory and Measurement of Demand,* Chicago: Chicago University Press.

Schultz, T. P. (1969), "An economic model of family planning and fertility," *Journal of Political Economy,* Vol. 77, pp. 153–80.

Schultz, T. W. (1960), "Capital formation by education," *Journal of Political Economy,* Vol. 68, pp. 571–83.

(ed.) (1973), "New economic approaches to fertility," *Journal of Political Economy,* Vol. 81, supplement.

Schumpeter, J. (1954), *History of Economic Analysis,* New York and London: Oxford University Press.

Scitovsky, T. (1945), "Some consequences of the habit of judging quality by price," *Review of Economic Studies,* Vol. 12, pp. 100–5.

Seade, J. (1978), "Consumer's surplus and linearity of Engel curves," *Economic Journal,* Vol. 88, pp. 411–523.

Sen, A. K. (1967), "Isolation, assurance and the social rate of discount," *Quarterly Journal of Economics,* Vol. 81, pp. 112–24.

(1970), *Collective Choice and Social Welfare,* San Fransisco: Holden Day; and Edinburgh: Oliver and Boyd.

(1973a), "Behaviour and the concept of preference," *Economica,* Vol. 40, pp. 241–59.

(1973b), *On Economic Inequality,* Oxford: Clarendon Press; and New York: Norton.

(1977a), "Starvation and exchange entitlements: a general approach and its application to the Great Bengal Famine," *Cambridge Journal of Economics,* Vol. 1, pp. 33–60.

(1977b), "On weights and measures: informational constraints in social welfare analysis," *Econometrica,* Vol. 45, pp. 1539–72.

(1979), "The welfare basis of real income comparisons: a survey," *Journal of Economic Literature,* Vol. 17, pp. 1–45.

Shephard, R. (1953), *Cost and Production Functions,* Princeton: Princeton University Press.

Sheshinski, E. (1976), "Price, quality and quantity regulation in monopoly situations," *Economica,* Vol. 43, pp. 127–37.

Sibley, D. S. (1977), "The demand for labour in a dynamic model of the firm," *Journal of Economic Theory,* Vol. 15, pp. 252–65.

Silberberg, E. (1972), "Duality and the many consumer's surpluses," *American Economic Review,* Vol. 62, pp. 942–52.

Simmons, P. J. (1979), "A theorem on aggregation across consumers in neoclassical labour supply," *Review of Economic Studies,* Vol. 46, pp. 737–40.

Simon, H. A. (1955), "A behavioural model of rational choice," *Quarterly Journal of Economics,* Vol. 69, pp. 99–118.

(1978a), "On how to decide what to do," *Bell Journal of Economics,* Vol. 9, pp. 494–507.

(1978b), "Rationality as process and as production of thought," *American Economic Review,* Vol. 68 (papers and proc.), pp. 1–16.

Sims, C. A. (1979), "Macroeconomics and reality," *Econometrica,* Vol. 48.

Singh, B. (1972), "On the determination of economies of scale in household consumption," *International Economic Review,* Vol. 13, pp. 257–70.

and A. L. Nagar (1973), "Determination of consumer unit scales," *Econometrica,* Vol. 41, pp. 347–55.

Slutsky, E. (1915), "Sulia teoria del bilancio des consomatore," *Giornale degli Economisti,*

Vol. 51, pp. 1–26. English trans. in *Readings in Price Theory*, G. J. Stigler and K. E. Boulding (eds.), Chicago University Press, 1952.

Smith, R. P. (1974), "A note on car replacement," *Review of Economic Studies*, Vol. 41, pp. 567–70.

(1975), *Consumer Demand for Cars in the U.S.A.*, Cambridge: Cambridge University Press.

Solari, L., (1971), *Théorie des choix et fonctions de consommation semi-agrégées*, Geneva: Librarie Droz.

Sono, M. (1962), "The effect of price changes on the demand and supply of separable goods," *International Economic Review*, Vol. 2, pp. 239–71.

Spence, M. (1973), "Job market signalling," *Quarterly Journal of Economics*, Vol. 87, pp. 355–79.

(1974), *Market Signalling: Information Transfer in Hiring and Related Screening Processes*, Cambridge, Mass.: Harvard University Press.

(1975), "Monopoly, quality and regulation," *Bell Journal of Economics*, Vol. 6, pp. 417–29.

(1976), "Production selection, fixed costs, and monopolistic competition," *Review of Economic Studies*, Vol. 43, pp. 217–36.

Stigler, G. J. (1945), "The cost of subsistence," *Journal of Farm Economics*, Vol. 27, pp. 303–14.

(1950), "The development of utility theory," *Journal of Political Economy*, Vol. 58, pp. 307–27, 373–96.

(1954), "The early history of empirical studies of consumer behaviour," *Journal of Political Economy*, Vol. 62, pp. 95–113.

(1961), "The economics of information," *Journal of Political Economy*, Vol. 69, pp. 213–25.

and G. S. Becker (1977), "De gustibus non est disputandum," *American Economic Review*, Vol. 67, pp. 76–90.

Stiglitz, J. E. (1970), "A consumption-oriented theory of the demand for financial assets and the term structure of interest rates," *Review of Economic Studies*, Vol. 37, pp. 321–51.

(1975a), "Information and economic analysis," in M. Parkin, and A. R. Nobay, *Current Economic Problems*, Cambridge: Cambridge University Press.

(1975b), "The theory of screening, education and the distribution of income," *American Economic Review*, Vol. 65, pp. 283–300.

Stone, J. R. N. (1954a), *The Measurement of Consumers' Expenditure and Behaviour in the United Kingdom, 1920–1938*, Vol. I, Cambridge University Press.

(1954b), "Linear expenditure systems and demand analysis: an application to the pattern of British demand," *Economic Journal*, Vol. 64, pp. 511–27.

(1956), *Quantity and Price Indexes in National Accounts*, Paris, Organization for European Economic Cooperation.

(1966), "Spending and saving in relation to income and wealth," *L'Industria*, No. 4, pp. 1–29.

and G. Croft-Murray (1959), *Social Accounting and Economic Models*, London: Bowes and Bowes.

and D. A. Rowe (1957), "The market demand for durable goods," *Econometrica*, Vol. 25, pp. 423–43.

and D. A. Rowe (1958), "Dynamic demand functions: some econometric results," *Economic Journal*, Vol. 68, pp. 256–70.

Strasnick, S. L. (1975), *Preference priority and the maximization of social welfare*, Cambridge, Mass.: Harvard University doctoral dissertation.

References   435

Strotz, R. H. (1956), "Myopia and inconsistency in dynamic utility maximization," *Review of Economic Studies*, Vol. 23, pp. 165–80.

(1957), "The empirical implications of a utility tree," *Econometrica*, Vol. 25, pp. 269–80.

(1959), "The utility tree–a correction and further appraisal," *Econometrica*, Vol. 27, pp. 482–88.

Surrey, M. J. C. (1974), "Saving, growth, and the consumption function," *Bulletin of the Oxford Institute of Statistics*, Vol. 36, pp. 125–42.

Sydenstricker, E., and W. I. King (1921), "The measurement of the relative economic status of families," *Quarterly Publication of the American Statistical Association*, Vol. 17, pp. 842–57.

Taylor, L. D., and D. Weiserbs (1972), "On the Estimation of Dynamic Demand Functions," *Review of Economics and Statistics*, Vol. 54, pp. 459–65.

Terleckyj, N. (1976), *Household Production and Consumption*, New York: NBER.

Theil, H. (1951), *De invloed van de voorraden op het consumentengedrag*, Amsterdam: Poortpers.

(1952–3), "Qualities, prices and budget enquiries," *Review of Economic Studies*, Vol. 19, pp. 129–47.

(1954), *Linear Aggregation of Economic Relations*, Amsterdam: North-Holland.

(1965), "The information approach to demand analysis," *Econometrica*, Vol. 33, pp. 67–87.

(1967), *Economics and Information Theory*, Amsterdam: North-Holland.

(1975), (1976), *Theory and Measurement of Consumer Demand*, Vol, I, Vol. II. Amsterdam: North-Holland.

Threadgold, A. R. (1978) "Personal savings: the impact of life assurance and pension funds," Bank of England, Discussion Paper No. 1, London: Bank of England.

Tintner, G. (1938a), "The theoretical derivation of dynamic demand curves," *Econometrica*, Vol. 6, pp. 375–80.

(1938b), "The maximization of utility over time," *Econometrica*, Vol. 6, pp. 154–8.

Tipping, D. G. (1970), "Price changes and income distribution," *Applied Statistics*, Vol. 19, pp. 1–17.

Tobin, J. (1951), "Relative income, absolute income, and saving," in *Money, Trade and Economic Growth (Essays in Honour of John Henry Williams)*, New York: Macmillan.

(1952), "A survey of the theory of rationing," *Econometrica*, Vol. 20, pp. 512–53.

(1958a), "Estimation of relationships for limited dependent variables," *Econometrica*, Vol. 26, pp. 24–36.

(1958b), "Liquidity preference as behaviour towards risk," *Review of Economic Studies*, Vol. 25, pp. 65–86.

(1965), "The theory of portfolio selection," pp. 3–51 in F. H. Hahn and F. P. R. Brechling (eds.), *The Theory of Interest Rates*, New York: Macmillan for the IEA.

(1967), "Life-cycle saving and balanced growth," in *Ten Economic Studies in the Tradition of Irving Fisher*, New York: Wiley.

(1968), "The consumption function," in *International Encyclopedia of the Social Sciences*, Vol. III, pp. 358–68.

(1972), "Wealth, liquidity and the propensity to consume," in B. Strumpel, J. N. Morgan, and E. Zahn (eds.), *Human Behaviour in Economic Affairs (Essays in Honor of George S. Katona)*, Amsterdam: Elsevier.

(1973), "Comment," *Journal of Political Economy*, Vol. 8, pp. S275–S278.

and H. S. Houthakker (1951), "The effects of rationing on demand elasticities," *Review of Economic Studies*, Vol. 18, pp. 140–153.

Törnqvist, L. (1936), "The Bank of Finland's consumption price index," *Bank of Finland Monthly Bulletin,* Vol. 10, pp. 1–8.

Triplett, J. E. (1975), "The measurement of inflation: a survey of research on the accuracy of price indexes," in P. H. Earl (ed.), *Analysis of Inflation,* Lexington, Mass.: Lexington.

    (1976), "Consumer demand and characteristics of consumption goods," in Terleckyj (1976).

Ulph, A. M., and D. T. Ulph (1975), "Transactions costs in general equilibrium theory: a survey," *Economica,* Vol. 42, pp. 355–72.

Vartia, Y. O. (1983), *Relative Changes and Index Numbers,* Helsinki: Research Institute of the Finnish Economy.

    (1983), "Efficient methods of measuring welfare change and compensated income in terms of market demand functions," *Econometrica,* Vol. 51, pp. 79–98.

Ville, J. (1946), "Sur les conditions d'existence d'une ophélimité totale et d'un indice du niveau des prix," *Annales de l'Université de Lyon,* Vol. 9, pp. 32–9. Translated in *Review of Economic Studies,* Vol. 19, (1951–2) pp. 123–28.

Von Weizsäcker, C. C. (1971), "Notes on endogenous changes of tastes," *Journal of Economic Theory,* Vol. 3, pp. 345–72.

Wallis, K. F. (1974), "Seasonal adjustment and relations between variables," *Journal of the American Statistical Association,* Vol. 69, pp. 18–31.

Watts, H. W. and J. Tobin (1960), "Consumer expenditures and the capital account," in I. Friend and R. Jones (eds.), *Proceedings of the Conference on Consumption and Saving,* Vol. 2, Philadelphia: University of Pennsylvania.

Westin, R. B. (1975), "Empirical implications of infrequent purchase behaviour in a stock-adjustment model," *American Economic Review,* Vol. 65, pp. 384–96.

Williams, R. A. (1971), "Demand for consumer durables: stock adjustment models and alternative specifications of stock depletion," *Review of Economic Studies,* Vol. 39, pp. 281–95.

Williamson, J. G. (1977), "'Strategic' wage goods, prices and inequality," *American Economic Review,* Vol. 67, pp. 29–41.

Willig, R. (1976), "Consumer's surplus without apology," *American Economic Review,* Vol. 66, pp. 589–97.

Wold, H. (1943), "A synthesis of pure demand analysis, Parts I and II", *Skandinavisk Aktuarietidskrift,* Vol. 26, pp. 85–144, 220–72.

    (1944), "A synthesis of pure demand analysis, Part III," *Skandinavisk Aktuarietidskrift,* Vol. 27, pp. 69–120.

    (1953), *Demand Analysis,* assisted by L. Jureen, Uppsala: Almqvist, and Wiksells.

Woodside, A. G., J. N. Sheth, and P. D. Bennett (eds.) (1977), *Consumer and Individual Buying Behaviour,* New York: North-Holland.

Working, H. (1943), "Statistical laws of family expenditure," *Journal of the American Statistical Association,* Vol. 38, pp. 43–56.

Worswick, G. D. N. and D. G. Champernowne (1954–5), "A note on the adding-up criterion," *Review of Economic Studies,* Vol. 22, pp. 57–60.

Wu, De-Min (1965), "An empirical analysis of households' durable goods expenditure," *Econometrica,* Vol. 33, pp. 761–780.

Zabel, E. (1973), "Consumer choice, portfolio decisions and transactions costs," *Econometrica,* Vol. 41, pp. 321–36.

Zellner, A. (1971), *An Introduction to Bayesian Inference in Econometrics,* New York: Wiley.

LIST OF NOTATION

Frequently used concepts have a common notation throughout the book; hence, in this list, the notation is given for the first chapter in which it occurs. There are also a number of "floating" notations where symbols are used temporarily within a chapter; these may have different meanings in different chapters and are not given in this list.

Chapter 1

x	outlay, budget or total expenditure
q_i	quantity of the ith good; good 0 is leisure
p_i	price of the ith good
y_t	income in period t
ω	wage rate
μ	nonlabor income
T	the household's time endowment
$g_i(x, p)$	Marshallian or uncompensated demand function
w_i	budget share of good i
e_i	total expenditure elasticity of good i
e_{ij}	elasticity of Marshallian demand for ith good with respect to price of jth good
R^2	coefficient of determination
ι	vector of ones

Chapter 2

$\succeq$	the relation "at least as good as"
q^j	bundle j of goods
$\sim$	the relation of indifference
$A(q^1)$	the "at least as good as" q^1 set
$B(q^1)$	the "no better than" q^1 set
$v(q)$	utility function
λ	Lagrange multiplier
$h_i(u, p)$	Hicksian or compensated demand function
u	utility level
$\psi(x, p)$	indirect utility function
$c(u, p)$	cost function

s_{ij}	compensated cross price effect $\partial h_i(u, p)/\partial p_j$
S	matrix of $((s_{ij}))$ or Slutsky matrix
$d(u, q)$	distance function
$a_i(u, q)$	compensated inverse demand function
a_{ij}	derivative of the ith inverse demand function with respect to jth quantity
A	matrix of $((a_{ij}))$ or Antonelli matrix
r_i	normalized price p_i/x
s_{ij}^*	xs_{ij}
S^*	matrix of $((s_{ij}^*))$
$\nabla f(x)$	vector whose ith element is $\partial f(x)/\partial x_i$

Chapter 3

e_{ij}^*	compensated cross-price elasticity
P	an index of prices
Δ	first difference operator
d.w.	Durbin-Watson statistic
c_{ij}	$w_i e_{ij}^*$ or parameter on $d \log p_j$ in Rotterdam system
b_i	marginal propensity to spend in Rotterdam system
$a(p), b(p)$	functions of prices
z^h	the number of persons in household h

Chapter 4

X	$\mu + wT$, that is, full income including the value of the time endowment
τ	tax rate
ℓ	labor supply
r_t	interest rate
A_t	level of financial asset held at end of period t
y_t^*	real expected income in period t
r_t^*	real expected interest rate in period t
p_t^*	discounted expected price in period t
ρ_t	discount factor $1/(1 + r_t)(1 + r_{t-1}) \cdots (1 + r_2)$
ρ_t^*	real discount factor $1/(1 + r_t^*)(1 + r_{t-1}^*) \cdots (1 + r_2^*)$
W_1	lifetime wealth computed in period 1
L	length of time horizon
y^p	real permanent income
S_t	stock of durables at end of period t
δ	deterioration rate of durables
d_t	purchases of the durable good in period t
v_t	price of the durable good
v_t^*	user cost or rental equivalent price of the durable good

z	ration level of good 1
p^-	price vector excluding good 1
q^-	quantity vector excluding good 1
$c^*(u, p, z)$	rationed cost function
$h_i^*(u, p, z)$	rationed Hicksian or compensated demands
s_{ij}^*	rationed compensated cross-price effect
p_1^*	shadow price of (rationed) good 1
$\gamma(u, p^-, z)$	cost-minimizing expenditure on nonrationed goods

Chapter 5

q_G	vector of goods inside a group
$q_{\bar{G}}$	vector of goods outside a group
$c_G(u_G, p_G)$	group cost function
x_G	group expenditure
w_G	group budget share x_G/x
w_{iG}	intragroup budget share $p_i q_i / x_G$

Chapter 6

$\bar{q}_i$	mean purchases of good i
$\bar{x}$	mean total expenditure level
z^h	a household characteristic
$\bar{w}_i$	mean budget share of good i, that is, $p_i \bar{q}_i / \bar{x}$
H	number of households
$\log Z$	Theil's entropy measure of dispersion
κ_0	indicator of dispersion
x_0	representative budget level
δ^h	share of household h in aggregate total expenditure

Chapter 7

$P(p^1, p^0; q^R)$	price index using fixed basket q^R as weights
$P(p^1, p^0; u^R)$	cost-of-living index using indifference curve u^R as reference
$U(u^1, u^0; p^R)$	welfare or real consumption index with reference prices p^R
$Q(q^1 q^0; u^R)$	quantity index using reference indifference curve u^R
CV	compensating variation
EV	equivalent variation

Chapter 8

a^h	vector of characteristics of household h
m^h	equivalence scale
m_i	equivalence scale specific to good i

m_0	general or overall equivalence scale
$c(u, p, a)$	cost function conditional upon household characteristics a

Chapter 9

x_*^h	real household composition corrected budget
$V(x_*^1, x_*^2, \ldots, x_*^H)$	social welfare defined on x_*'s
E	index of equality
x_*^e	equally distributed equivalent real budget
I	index of inequality

Chapter 10

z_j	quantity of nonmarket good produced in the household
π_j	shadow cost associated with z_j
$C(p, \omega, z; k)$	minimum cost of producing vector z given market prices p, wage ω, and capital inputs k
b_{ji}	amount of nonmarket good j embodied in one unit of market good i
θ	quality index
b	vector of specification variables

Chapter 11

ω^*	shadow wage
u	unemployment proportion
s	length of time spent in schooling
$g(\tau - s)$	ratio of real earnings after $\tau - s$ years at work to initial real earnings
$\mathscr{L}$	likelihood
L	time horizon

Chapter 12

$E_t(W_1)$	point expectation at time t of lifetime wealth computed for time 1
Δ_4	four-period difference operator
Δ_1	one-period difference operator
δ_{t-s}	rate of time preference in intertemporally additive utility function

Chapter 13

R_t	replacement demand for a durable good

Chapter 14

π_j	probability of state j
E	expectation operator
ρ_A	absolute risk aversion
ρ_R	relative risk aversion
$m(t)$	moment generating function
m_n	minimum price of a good after n searches
$F(x)$	(cumulative) distribution function

SUBJECT INDEX